T-BIRD
45 YEARS OF THUNDER

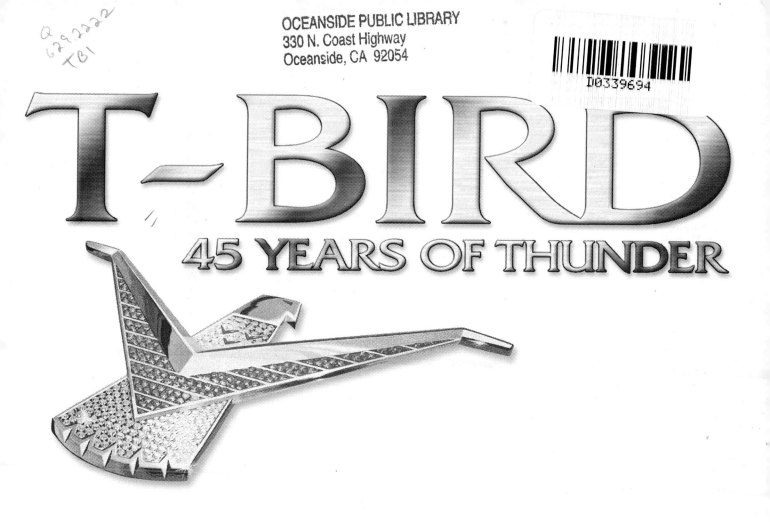

Edited by
John Gunnell & James T. Lenzke

© Copyright 2000

Published by

krause
publications

700 E. State Street • Iola, WI 54990-0001
Telephone: 715/445-2214

Please, call or write us for our free catalog of publications. To place an order or receive our
free catalog, call 800-258-0929. For editorial comment and further information, use our regular
business telephone at (715) 445-2214 or www.krause.com

Library of Congress Catalog Number: 95-76856
ISBN: 0-87341-581-7

Printed in the United States of America

22

Table of Contents

Dedication

This book is dedicated to Bill Coombe and Jerry Capizzi who were instrumental in bringing to light many previously unpublished facts about the history of Ford's fabulous T-Bird.

Credits & Acknowledgments

Photos Gil Baumgartner, Jerry Capizzi, Bill Coombe, Billy Cooper and Associates, Dick Dance, Ford Motor Company, Don Fymbo, James R. Goudie, Phil Hall, Wayne Huibregtse, & Dr. Richard L. Schatz.

Research Dean Batchelor, Gil Baumgartner, Martin Brugmans, Jerry Capizzi, Bill Coombe, Detroit Public Library Auto Collection, Chad Elmore, International Thunderbird Club, Ron Kowalke, Chuck Mill, James F. Petrik, Sandra L. Schatz, Dr. Richard L. Schatz, & Bob Welsch.

Thanks Bill Randel (Collector's Den), Alan H. Tast (Vintage Thunderbird Club International)

Cover Design Jon Stein   **Color Gallery Design** Tom Nelsen

Page Design Jeannie Altenburg, Cheryl Mueller, & Sally Olson

Introduction

T-Bird: 45 Years of Thunder, edited in year 2000 by James T. Lenzke, is the amended and extended second printing of 1995's *T-Bird: 40 Years of Thunder*, edited at that time by John Gunnell.

This book was originally conceived to observe Thunderbird's 40th anniversary, in 1995. Shortly after the project was started, it became apparent that previous titles that had focused on Thunderbird had left some stones unturned. Research that did not check out was encountered. Missing links in the chain of Thunderbird history were discovered. There were old questions to sort out and new facts to reveal.

Fortunately, a number of resourceful and knowledgable individuals made themselves available to aid John Gunnell in his efforts. Largely because of them, this book has a breadth and a depth considerably beyond what might otherwise have been possible.

Immense contributions of expertise and personal resources were made by collector-car literature dealer Bill Coombe, T-Bird collector and restorer Jerry Capizzi, race car expert Phil Hall, and Thunderbird enthusiast and writer James F. Petrik.

Bill Coombe and Rich (Dr. Richard L.) Schatz stepped forward again to lend their expertise to Jim Lenzke in amending and updating this second edition. In addition to his encouragement, Bill provided statistics, specifications, and illustrations relative to 1996 and 1997, Thunderbird's final two years of production—for the first time around. He also brought the literature checklists forward for those years and added to the information reported for 1957, 1962, and 1978. Rich and his family freely lent encouragement plus additional specifications and photographs. And Rich, as editor-in-chief of *Thunderbird Script*—the journal of the International Thunderbird Club—dug into its archives to unearth the writings of Martin Brugmans relating to the much misunderstood "Golde Top" model T-Bird of 1960.

So, with the help of these persons, and others, we are pleased to present a second edition that is even more comprehensive and informational than the first. We are particularly pleased to offer this volume coincident with Ford Motor Company's announcement that the legendary Thunderbird is to be reborn in 2001 as a 2002 model. Long may it fly!

James T. Lenzke
Iola, Wisconsin
May 26, 2000

1955 - 1957
"Early Birds"

1955
America's Newest Sports Car

Read almost any issue of *Motor Trend* magazine from early 1954, and you'll find its pages filled with stories like "Progress in Performance," "European Showcase," "How I Customized My Car", "14-Hour Sports Car" (Woodill Wildfire), "I Drove The Firebird" (featuring Mauri Rose behind the wheel of a GM gas turbine dream car), and "Sebring — How A 24-Hour Race Is Run." It was a time in which the interests of automotive enthusiasts were focused on V-8 engines, fuel-injection, imported sports cars, "Kalifornia Kustoms," sporty homemade and kit-type cars, "dream machines," and all types of auto racing. It was into this milieu, that the 1955 Ford Thunderbird came forth.

The Thunderbird or T-Bird was the perfect automobile for its era. It offered all the latest performance advances, including a special V-8 engine and Fordomatic (sometimes spelled Ford-O-Matic, even in contemporary magazine articles and factory literature) transmission. In its overall size and two-seat configuration, buyers found a pinch of European flavoring. It had features that were popular with customizers such as a hood scoop, dummy fender louvers and "frenched" headlights. It was a sporty car, if not a true sports car (people argued about how to classify it in 1954 and still do). Since it was previewed a year before it could be bought, it also seemed like a dream car brought to life. It was also rallied and raced with some degree of vigor. In short, the Thunderbird offered a bit of everything that interested the readers of automotive "wish-books" like *Motor Trend* in 1954.

If it was a trendsetter, the T-Bird was also a throwback. Thunderbird historian James F. Petrik linked Ford's creation of the 1955 two-seater to sporty, two-passenger cars made in America from ". . . before 1900 until the early '30s." Petrik suggested that early sports cars were popular with U.S. drivers until ". . . the Depression doomed such machines (as) impractical and frivolous." His view is supported by statistics in industry trade journals. They show that sales of both open cars (roadsters and tourings) and closed, two-passenger cars (coupes) declined in the decade leading to the outbreak of World War II. This trend, as reflected in the following table, coincided with the Great Depression and its aftermath.

Fairlane-style side moldings were seen on very late prototype T-Birds and turned up in several early advertisements, before vanishing. (Ford Motor Co. photo)

Body Style Trends 1932-1941 FORD

Model Year	Roadster & Touring	2-door Coupe	2-door Sedan	Other Closed-Body Models	Chassis Only
1932	4.7%	24.5%	30.6%	38.7%	1.5%
1933	1.5	21.3	32.8	43.6	0.8
1934	1.4	17.5	36.6	42.6	1.9
1935	0.7	15.9	38.4	42.9	2.1
1936	0.7	13.9	39.7	44.1	1.6
1937	0.5	15.3	38.4	44.2	1.6
1938	0.5	16.2	35.7	45.6	2.0
1939	0.3	17.7	36.7	43.9	1.4
1940	0.3	18.5	35.2	44.2	1.8
1941	0.2	19.1	37.8	41.9	1.0
Net Change in 10 Years	- 4.5%	-5.4%	+7.2%	+3.2%	+0.5%

No cars were made during World War II. Early postwar models were warmed-over 1942s rushed back into production to compensate for a five-year lack of availability. So, it wasn't until late 1948 that the ability to make cars began to catch up with demand. In 1949, modern automotive designs finally came forth from high-volume manufacturers. New models were lower, longer, wider, sleeker, and more powerful than ever before. The shortage of new vehicles, and the extended use of old ones caused by the war, had brought changes in the fickle tastes of buyers. They no longer wanted dark-colored, fat-fendered cars with mohair upholstered seats and "stick-shifted" gear boxes. Bright colors, envelope bodies, vinyl seats and automatic transmissions were in vogue.

While fighting in Europe, American soldiers had seen Italian, English, French, and German sports cars. They brought some home with them after the war. Interest in motor sports also boomed in this era. Most people did not have a television for home entertainment, so nighttime auto racing became a popular diversion. Parts for big race cars were very hard to find and expensive, due to postwar shortages. However, midget race cars were cheap to make and fun to see in action. In many cities, these small race cars competed at indoor arenas and ran all year long.

The 1955 glass-fibre hardtop could be easily removed from the T-Bird. It had solid "sail panels," which hindered the rear view of the driver. (Ford Motor Co. photo)

Ford brass insisted on roll-up windows to give the T-Bird an advantage over the Corvette in the comfort and convenience department. (Ford Motor Co. photo)

Also gaining in appeal were "jalopy racers" made from used, prewar parts. The sport of stock car racing eventually sprang from these cars. Late-model stock car racing started growing after 1950, as new cars (and parts) became more readily available. Other types of motorsports also became popular. With burgeoning interest in foreign-made cars, the evolution of sports car racing was a natural. By 1950, a wide range of imported cars, from Ferraris to Jaguars, were competing on the roads, tracks, and air-fields of America. Also gaining a following were the sports of drag racing and land speed racing. *Hot Rod* magazine—launched in 1948—was distributed at many drag racing strips. The first Speed Trials at Bonneville Salt Flats were held in 1950.

Given all of these influences, the introduction of the Thunderbird five years later was not surprising. In fact, the first photos of a prototype T-Bird appeared in the pages of *Motor Trend* even earlier. Page 34 of the magazine's April 1954 issue showed a two-seater that closely resembled the production model. The headlamp doors were not quite as peaked as those on the final car and the Thunderbird name script was missing from the upper rear fenders. The article said the prototype was made "entirely of clay (except for tires, some trim and glass)." It added that the production car would be made of metal, rather than fiberglass. Readers of *The New York Times* already had a hint of this, as the newspaper's April 3 issue had announced that Philadelphia's Budd Company was granted a contract to supply T-Bird bodies.

Above the center of the 1955 T-Bird's grille was a Ford crest above a crossed flags emblem. (Ford Motor Co. photo)

"Perhaps the outstanding feature of the new Ford Thunderbird is the clever wedding of sports car functionalism with American standards of comfort," wrote *Motor Trend's* Detroit editor Don MacDonald. "Rather than being the first in the field, much was gained by a period of watchful waiting, typical of shrewd L.D. Crusoe, Ford Motor Co. VP and general manager of Ford Division."

In reality, "watchful waiting" had little to do with the birth of the T-Bird. Ford had actually been scrambling to catch up with General Motors (GM), as well as with Kaiser-Frazer. At the GM Motorama, in January 1953, Chevrolet had revealed three versions of a fiberglass-bodied sports car called the Corvette. One was a roadster, one was a fastback called the Corvair, and one was a station wagon called the

Nomad. When Chevrolet announced that the roadster version would be built on a limited-production basis that year, Ford Motor Company (FoMoCo) executives quickly panicked. The Kaiser-Darrin 161 sports car, also fiberglass-bodied, was already on the drawing board and Donald Healey and Pinin Farina had been doing a low-production sports car for Nash since 1952. Although the Nash-Healey was not a big threat to Ford, the Corvette and the Kaiser-Darrin seemed more threatening.

By February 1953 a product letter was circulated within FoMoCo launching a crash program to build a two-seat sports car. From the beginning, the plan was to go "one up" on the competition by incorporating a steel body, a V-8 engine and features like roll-up windows. Don MacDonald said that the decision to use a metal body was "indicative of anticipated sales volume." His April 1954 article predicted (with some degree of exaggeration) that neck-snapping performance would be "guaranteed" by the T-Bird's 160-hp Interceptor engine and choice of standard or Fordomatic transmission. "Ford has stolen a jump on its competitors in the sports car field by specifying roll-up windows with power lifts optional," MacDonald suggested.

This seat spring supplier featured the T-Bird and the Corvette in its trade advertising.

An editorial in the same issue of *Motor Trend* reported that the magazine had conducted an unscientific survey that showed sports car owners wanted more weathertight tops and would pay $50 to $100 extra for roll-up windows. "Evidently the Ford Motor Company looked into this situation at some length, before deciding to come out with their version of a sports car," it noted. "When it is placed into production, one of the biggest advantages it will have over the Chevrolet Corvette and the Kaiser-Darrin 161 will be its roll-up windows (and, incidentally, its two-top combination)."

The T-Bird gave Ford salesmen this and many other selling features. Its styling was less radical than that of other American sports cars. Crusoe had insisted that it be based on a full-sized Ford for "family" identity and that major parts would be interchangeable with other 1955 Fords. Parts sharing cut development time, too. Historians have learned that designers skipped the time-consuming job of making mock-ups or models, going straight to the creation of full-sized drawings of the T-Bird's profile instead. The car's dimensions were based on those of the Corvette and the Jaguar XK-120. To save even more time, a used Ford sedan was obtained to serve as a designers' "mule." It was cut down with a torch and re-welded to fashion a small Ford with a 102-in. wheelbase. Ford's chief engineer, William Burnett, decided to go at the project this way. Those involved with it called the car the "Burnetti," after him. They thought this name had an Italian sports car ring to it.

In spite of getting the creative work done at a blistering rate of speed, it took until the fall of 1954 to finalize the production T-Bird for introduction as a 1955 model. The Corvette had been officially introduced on July 14, 1953, and the Kaiser-Darrin sports car bowed on Jan. 6, 1954. Interestingly, an exhibition of over 50 automobiles entitled "Sports Cars Unlimited," opened at the Henry Ford Museum, in Dearborn, Mich., on Jan. 8, 1954, just two days after the Kaiser-Darrin bowed.

Ford grew eager to show its new sports car off to the public. The Detroit Automobile Show was selected for this purpose. In its "What Happened In 1954" column, *Ward's 1955 Automotive Yearbook* notes: "Feb. 20 — *Thunderbird* sports car introduced." The car displayed was actually a Thunderbird mock-up. It was described as being "made of wood." When seen at the Detroit show, it had the word "Fairlane" spelled in chrome script above the grille. This could well have been the same prototype that *Motor Trend* pictured and described as a clay model, since such "clays" were built over a wooden framework. Thunderbird historian James Petrik believes this mock-up was covered with sheet plastic.

The 1955 T-Bird instrument panel had a modern, aircraft-inspired appearance. A two-spoke steering wheel was featured. (Ford Motor Co. photo)

Although the car-buying public got a few such peeks at the T-Bird early in 1954, it wasn't until October 22 that the production version was officially unveiled. Its introductory retail price was $2,695, less federal taxes and delivery and handling charges. This compared to $2,700 for a 1955 Corvette. (The Kaiser-Darrin was no longer offered in 1955.)

The first plan was to call the two-seater the Fairlane (after Henry Ford's estate in Michigan), but many other labels were considered. Lewis D. Crusoe was said to prefer the alternative "Savile," but he proposed a contest in which FoMoCo employees could suggest names. The winner was offered a prize of $250, but actually won a suit, which was worth $75-$100 according to James F. Petrik. Alden "Gib" Giberson, a stylist and native of the Southwest, suggested the Thunderbird designation. In Indian mythology, the Thunderbird helped humans by flapping its wings, bringing thunder, lightning and rain to alleviate a drought. On Feb. 15, 1954, the name was made official. The shortened form T-Bird may well have stemmed from Ford ads referring to the car's introductory date as "T-day."

The T-Bird still looks sharp and stylish today. (Old Cars photo)

The fact that the T-Bird arrived in late 1954 (as a 1955 model) was an additional factor behind its very respectable sales performance (16,155 T-Birds built in 1955 versus 700 Corvettes). In the three previous years, the automotive industry was beset with a variety of problems precipitated by the Korean War. In 1952, motor vehicle production was regulated by government edict, with the National Production Authority and Controlled Materials Plan suppressing output. In addition, there was a nationwide steel strike at midyear. Government controls ended in February 1953, leading to a third quarter rise in production. However, demand declined about the same time, perhaps indicating that the war had undercut buyer confidence. There were many close-out sales that season. Inventories of unsold units built up, spurring manufacturers to drastically reduce their output starting in May 1954. By fall, car dealer inventories were 62 percent lower than they were in April. As a result, model-year 1954 ended with the supply of cars getting short, although demand was rising again.

When 1955 models came out, car dealers were still cautious. They continued to offer heavy discounts, as they had during 1954. Even though demand was up and supplies were low, deals on new cars remained very attractive. This spurred a kind of buying and production frenzy early in the model-year. In fact, GM had to delay its introduction of a new line of trucks so that its production facilities could be better utilized for the manufacturing of cars. It was a buyer's market and would wind up a record year in production and sales. All of this was an advantage in selling the exciting new Thunderbird. However, such factors did not help the Corvette. Lackluster sales in the "off" years 1953 and 1954 had given Chevrolet's sports car the image of being a failure. Only a strong commitment by enthusiasts within Chevrolet's executive corps saved the "Vette" from extinction in 1957.

This ad pitched the T-Bird to professionals who were early risers. (Ford Motor Co.)

A turquoise Thunderbird and a yellow Corvette appeared on the front of the June 1954 issue of *Motor Trend* with a cover blurb promising performance figures for both. The article "New Fuel for an Old Duel" fanned a natural rivalry between the two-seaters. "Just like road-racing, it (the Chevy versus Ford battle) sparks competition-bred improvements which tend to make all cars a better breed," said Don MacDonald. "Nowhere is this more evidenced than in the recent revival of the *American-made* production sports car."

MacDonald traced the renaissance of sports car interest in the U.S. and the creation of the Corvette, Kaiser-Darrin, and T-Bird. As in earlier stories, he sounded somewhat pro-Thunderbird with statements like, "Thunderbird features which will not be changed are adequate bumpers, three-passenger seat, wind-up windows, and an all-metal body. Ford feels that these are essential qualifications for any American car." At the end of the well illustrated four-page story were charts comparing the T-Bird's *expected* performance with *actual* figures for the Corvette. They indicated that the Fordomatic T-Bird had a slight edge over the Corvette in off-the-line acceleration, with the Vette having a slight advantage at higher acceleration speeds. The T-Bird's top speed was shown as 112 mph, versus an average of 105.3 mph for the Vette. The publication of such figures prior to completion of the engineering package was total conjecture on MacDonald's part.

There's a touch of Thunderbird in every Ford . . . You can see it . . . You can *feel* it!

T-Birds were used as "image" cars to sell other Ford products. (Ford Motor Co.)

Evidence that the engineering of the Thunderbird was not locked in at mid-1954 is found in the preliminary specifications that Ford was publishing at the time. They included the following data, which is interesting to compare to the specifications chart at the end of this section.

ENGINE: Ohv V-8. Bore and stroke: 3-5/8 x 3-3/32 in. Stroke/bore ratio: 0.8534. Compression ratio: 7.5:1. Displacement: 256 cid. Advertised horsepower (bhp): 161 @ 4400 rpm. Horsepower per cubic inch: 0.63. Piston travel @ maximum horsepower: 2,273 feet per minute. Maximum torque: 238 lb.-ft. @ 2000 to 2800 rpm. Maximum bmep: 140.1 psi. DRIVE SYSTEM: Standard transmission is a three-speed synchromesh using helical gears. Ratios: (First) 2.78, (Second) 1.61, (Third) 1.0, (Reverse) 3.64. Optional was a planetary overdrive with standard gears and a 27 mph cut-in speed. Ratio: 0.7. Also optional was Fordomatic torque converter transmission with planetary gears. Ratios: (Drive) 1.48 and 1.00 x torque converter with a 2.1 maximum ratio @ stall, (Low) 2.44 x torque converter, (Reverse) 2.0 x torque converter. REAR AXLE RATIOS: Conventional: 3.90 standard, 4.10 optional. Overdrive: 4.10 standard, 3.90 and 3.31 optional. Fordomatic: 3.31 standard. DIMENSIONS: Wheelbase: 102 in. Tread: (front) 56 in.; (rear) 56 in. Wheelbase/tread ratio: 1.82. Overall width: 70.1 in. Overall length: 175.2 in. Overall height: 51.9 in. with top up. Steering ratio: 20:1. Curb weight: 2,837 lb. Horsepower-to-weight ratio: 17.7. Weight distribution: 50 percent front, 50 percent rear (loaded). Tire size: 6.70 x 15.

A two-page Ford advertisement in the September 1954 issue of *Motor Trend* announced, "Coming your way ... the new Ford Thunderbird." It showed pictures of the two-seater in convertible (top up and top down) and hardtop form. The ad copywriters keyed off general inquisitiveness about the T-Bird, listing a series of questions that might have been posed about horsepower, acceleration, cornering, ride, and availability. Stressing that they could not answer all questions yet, the ad men described the engine as a special edition of the "famous" short-stroke, overhead-valve Y-block V-8. They also hit on the ball-joint front suspension and low center of gravity, suggesting that the car held the corners "like a coat of paint." Also highlighted was the Astra-Dial control panel, telescoping steering wheel, roll-up windows, ample luggage space, extra-wide one-piece seat with foam rubber cushions, all-steel body, and availability of power-assisted steering, brakes and windows. The ad ended with the advice, "Keep in touch with your Ford Dealer —'T' Day's coming soon!"

Strangely, this first ad depicted the car in close to production format, although the headlight doors had non-stock chrome trim, and the front bumper guards were in line with the rear exhaust outlets (production models had them moved in a few inches, so as not to interfere with the fresh air intakes for the heater). This similarity to the production model was not seen in a color advertisement that appeared on the back cover of the same magazine's November issue. The latter showed essentially identical illustrations of the T-Bird wearing Fairlane-style body side moldings. This announcement was headlined "Enchantment unlimited ... the new Ford Thunderbird." It described the new model as "A distinguished kind of personal car that combines sports car styling and performance with passenger car convenience."

This may have been the only time that an all-new car depicted in an *early* ad looked closer to its production form than it did in a *later* ad. The last minute revisions did not escape the motoring press of the day. "For your personal use, the Thunderbird is officially on the market at the startling low price of $2,695, which includes hardtop and four-way power seat but not the folding top (an optional $70 extra) nor the attractive chrome moldings shown in some recent advertisements," said *Motor Trend's* "Spotlight on Detroit" column in December 1954. In the beginning, the Thunderbird came only with the soft convertible top, but this situation did not last very long. The "glass-fibre" (fiberglass) hardtop became *standard* equipment very early in the model run. Since the Thunderbird was the first 1955 car to be introduced, it became the first car to have tubeless tires as standard equipment. Tubeless tires had been available since 1949, but always as an aftermarket replacement item or optional equipment.

Thunderbird price changes came almost as suddenly as styling and equipment revisions. Gene Olson, of Portland, Oregon, sent a letter to *Motor Trend* in 1955 stating that the "startling low price" was "So startling that even the salesmen can't believe it." He advised that he had been quoted a price of $1,000 higher for a "stripped" Thunderbird and was told by the salesperson that the price published in the magazine was "a mistake." In February 1955, *Motor Trend* confirmed that $2,695 was the "first announced price." It added that the *current* price for the T-Bird Hardtop was $2,944. The Convertible sold for $3,019 at that point, and the "Combination" model (with both tops) was $3,234. These figures consisted of suggested retail price, federal taxes and delivery and handling charges. They did not include transportation from the factory, local taxes, options or dealer preparation. By April 1955, Ford's suggested retail price for the Hardtop model within the company's Boston sales zone was $3,278. The convertible top was a $75 option, making the soft-top $3,353. It was $290 extra for both tops or $3,568 for the Combination model. Like many cars that become popular overnight, the price of the T-Bird shot rapidly upwards.

A gleaming red T-Bird paces a Ford Crown Victoria, Mercury Montclair, and Lincoln Capri Convertible around the Dearborn Test Track. (Ford Motor Co.)

Standard under the hood of all T-Birds was a Y-block V-8 with a 3.75 x 3.30-in. bore and stroke. Based on the Mercury V-8, the production engine had 292 cid, which made it larger than indicated in early announcements. With an 8.1:1 compression ratio, the base version produced 193 bhp at 4400 rpm. It was used in cars with standard transmissions. Another version, used in Fordomatic-equipped T-Birds, had an 8.5:1 compression ratio and generated five additional horsepower at the same "revs."

The Thunderbird's standard transmission was a three-speed synchromesh using helical gears. Ratios were: (First) 2.32, (Second) 1.48, (Third) 1.00, and (Reverse) 2.82. Optional was a planetary overdrive with planetary gears and a 27 mph cut-in speed. It had a 0.7 ratio. Also optional was Fordomatic torque converter transmission with planetary gears. Its ratios were: (Drive) 1.48 and 1.00 x torque converter with a 2.1 maximum ratio @ stall, (Low) 2.44 x torque converter, (Reverse) 2.0 x torque converter. With the conventional transmission, a 3.90 rear axle was standard and a 4.10 axle was optional. The 4.10 axle was also standard in overdrive-equipped cars, with 3.90 and 3.31 axles optional. With Fordomatic transmission a 3.31 axle was standard.

There is still confusion as to whether the T-Bird was a "sports car." In December, *Motor Trend* pointed out that Ford preferred to call it a personal car. "The thinking behind this, as brought out in a discussion with W.R. Burnett, chief passenger car engineer for Ford, is that 'although the Thunderbird has the performance and attributes of most sports cars, management also felt that it should have a few more comforts to make it more appealing to a wider segment of the public,'" the magazine noted. James F. Petrik, the marque historian, references other sources to prove that FoMoCo was inconsistent in its presentation of the car's image.

"In the spring of '54, one began to see pictures and articles in the various magazines on Ford's new sports car," says Petrik in the *Standard Catalog of Ford 1903-1990*. "By the time the car was introduced, most of the car magazines were saying that Ford never called the car a sports car. Let us correct that right now. The first known showroom brochure, showing the car with a 1954 license plate, called the T-Bird a sports car. This folder had the wrong engine and tire size listed, incidentally. The Thunderbird advertisement in the Aug. 16, 1954 issue of *Sports Illustrated* also mentioned 'sports car.' Some Ford shop manuals, (printed) so late as to cover the 1957 Thunderbird, still called the car 'Ford Sports Car.'"

Looking very much like a scaled-down Ford, the Thunderbird was trim, though not sub-compact. The standard telescoping steering wheel allowed large T-Bird drivers to get comfortable, although many felt claustrophobic, inside, when the soft top was up. "With the top up you feel pretty closed in," *Motor Trend's* Walt Woron advised in December 1954. "Mostly because it's not like most of the new car 'glass bowls.'" The roomy trunk was 58.2 in. wide, 34.8 in. long, and 16.1 in. high. There was more seating and storage space in the T-Bird than typical 1955 sports cars offered.

The styling of the car was quite pleasing. The frenched headlamps gave it a forward-thrusting look at the front, while the crisp tail fins seemed to "flip-off" a little message to every slower car passed on the highway. They seemed to be saying, "I'm the latest and the greatest thing for the young and the young at heart." In its September 1955 issue, *Motor Trend* selected the Thunderbird as one of the six best-looking cars of 1955. "Over-all consistency of design. Width, height, length ratios show excellent proportion," noted the editors. "It's small Hardtop version has a very classic look." The low, square Ford-look emphasized the car's width, and the production version featured only minimal use of chrome. "Pretty well de-chromed and clean-looking," *Motor Trend* said. "First and fore-most a car for comfort and looks."

According to James F. Petrik, the gaudy chrome strips used on the pre-production cars were L.D. Crusoe's idea. "Some of his associates have said that this was one of his few mistakes," the historian notes. "The stylists did not want the chrome strips, so they were removed at the last moment" Only two cars are believed to have been built with the "Fairlane" trim moldings. A black one with wire wheel covers and a continental tire was made for L.D. Crusoe. This was also the *only* 1955 T-Bird with sun visors. *Motor Trend*

A Rayon convertible top was an extra-cost option for 1955 T-Birds and cost nearly $300 extra. (Ford Motor Co. photo)

Ford Motor Co. built a total of 16,155 first-year T-Birds in 1955, which was above its initial sales projection. (Courtesy Cappy Collection)

showed a picture of it in June 1955, noting it wouldn't be sold. In October, the same photo appeared again. "Glimpse of Thunderbird's new continental kit was unwittingly given by *MT* in June issue," read the caption. There was also a light green car built with the pre-production trim, but no sun visors.

This "big" little car also had a big list of standard equipment. It included the 292-cid V-8 with a four-barrel carburetor and built-in dual exhausts; three-speed manual transmission with all-helical gears and floor-mounted shift lever (gear ratios were 2.32:1 in low, 1.48:1 in second, 1.00:1 in high, and 2.82:1 in reverse); 6.70 x 15 four-ply tires; six-volt, 90-amp. battery; 40-amp. generator; automatic interior light; inside hood release; tachometer; Telechron (GE) electric clock with sweep second hand; power seat; left-hand outside rear view mirror; full-width seat with foam rubber padding; adjustable steering wheel; built-in arm rests; floor carpet; ash tray; dual horn; cigar lighter; horn ring; glove box lock; all-vinyl seat trim; Astra-Dial instrument panel; and 150-mph Astra-Dial speedometer. Some Thunderbirds shipped to Europe had metric speedometers that read from 0-240 km/hr, which was basically the same as 0-150 mph ("Perhaps one mile per hour off," says T-Bird historian James F. Petrik).

Like other Fords, the Thunderbird came with a wide selection of factory options. An eight-tube radio came with an antenna for $100. It was $85 for a MagicAire heater. For-domatic transmission cost $215 extra, while overdrive was only $110. It was $10 for a windshield washer, $35 for a set of wire wheelcovers, $92 for power steering, $40 for power brakes, $70 for power window lifts, $25 for tinted glass, and also $25 for an engine dress up kit with chrome parts. Buyers could add another $30 to get white side-wall tires installed.

At the beginning of the 1955 model-year, Ford projected that it would sell 10,000 Thunderbirds. This was a conservative estimate. Company dealers reportedly took 4,000 orders on Oct. 22, 1954, the first day it was available. This created an interesting situation. The Thunderbird turned out being the first and last 1955 Ford model in production.

According to the Classic Thunderbird Club International, the earliest production unit had serial number P5FH100005. This car was made on Sept. 9, 1954. It was referred to in the Oct. 4, 1954, issue of *Sports Illustrated*, which carried three pages of Thunderbird coverage entitled "America's newest Sports Car." The writer documented that the car was "not a pilot model Thunderbird, but the Number 1 production model."

In the summer of 1965, a Thunderbird owner named George Watts found the remains of serial number P5FH100005 sitting outside a small, Southern California body shop. It had only 78,000 miles on its odometer, but had deteriorated from obvious neglect and improper storage. The car's upholstery was bad, both tops were missing, and it had been repainted several times. Originally black, the car showed evidence of being refinished twice, once in white, and a second time in blue. The man who owned the car had an unsatisfied loan with a finance company. He also owed the body shop owner for some work he had commissioned. The bills on the car totaled $500. This situation helped Watts purchase the remains for a price he considered fair. After towing the T-Bird home, Watts checked the serial number. He found it was very low. He thought it was the fifth 1955 T-Bird made. A restoration was carried out while his research into the car's background continued. In February 1966, a letter from Ford Motor Company's General Counsel arrived at Watts' home. It revealed that he had the first production Thunderbird. Watts put 10,000 additional miles on the car, driving it until 1973. He then did a restoration and repainted P5FH100005 in its original Raven Black color.

Historian James F. Petrik, who has researched Thunderbird factory records, reports that a Thunderbird with serial number P5FH100004 has been discovered, but says the Classic Thunderbird Club International insists that P5FH100005 is considered the first production vehicle. Petrik adds that the first and last serial numbers for each year, which have often been published, "make no sense what-so-ever." He suggests that it was not uncommon for Ford to give two cars the same serial number. "I've found numerous contradictions in my copies of original factory invoices," Petrik explained.

The last T-Bird of the year (serial number P5FH260557) was the last FoMoCo car built before 1956 model changeovers began. According to James F. Petrik, the invoice for this car was typed Sept. 14, 1955 and it was reportedly constructed on Sept. 16, 1955. Due to the high demand, Ford had continued building the Thunderbird until the very end of the model-year.

The T-Bird helped make Ford's 1955 model run second best in company history, behind 1923, when Model Ts dominated sales. (Courtesy Cappy Collection)

T-Birds were so popular that they entered production before other 1955 Fords and were still being built when the 1956 Fords bowed. (Courtesy Cappy Collection)

Regardless of the first and last numbers, all T-Birds carried codes (similar to the numbers shown earlier) on their left-hand body pillars. They were also stamped at the top right-hand edge of the patent plates located on the dash panels, under the hoods. The first symbol "P" indicated the 292-cid engine. This was followed by a "5" indicating a 1955 model. The third symbol was an "F" to indicate assembly at the home factory in Dearborn, Mich., where all 1955 Thunderbirds were constructed. The fourth symbol "H" indicated the Thunderbird body style. The last six symbols indicated where the particular car fit into the sequence of numbers used on *all* Fords built at Dearborn. While sequential unit production numbers are listed as 100001 and up, the earliest known Ford in the 1955 build sequence is P5FH100005.

Ford patent plates also show other codes stamped in a horizontal band just below the center of the plate. These stampings indicate a body type code, color code, trim code, and production date code. The two-seat T-Birds' body type code was 40A. Colors offered on early 1955 T-Birds were Raven Black (code A), Torch Red (code R), and Thunderbird Blue (code T). Thunderbird Blue was actually a 1954 color called Skyhaze Green. In March 1955, Ford added Snowshoe White (code E), and Goldenrod Yellow (code V) to the offerings. Four color-coordinated all-vinyl interior trims were provided. These are shown on the chart below. The first number(s) in the production date code show the day of the month, followed by a letter indicating the month, two letters indicating the dealer code, and a group of numbers showing the scheduled item number.

Month codes used in 1955 began with "A" for January, and continued through "M" for December ("I" and "O" were not used to avoid confusion with the numbers "1" and "0"). A production code such as 15CSD155 breaks down as follows: 15 indicates 15th day of month C (March) and SD indicates the car was ordered by a Ford dealer in Boston, Massachusetts. The last three symbols 155 indicate the car was the 155th Ford (not all T-Birds) scheduled to be built on March 15, 1955.

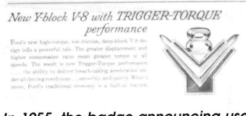

New Y-block V-8 with TRIGGER-TORQUE performance

In 1955, the badge announcing use of the Y-block engine clearly identified it as a V-8. (Ford Motor Co.)

1955 Thunderbird Interiors

Seat Type	Material	Black/ White	Red/ White	Black/ Yellow	Turquoise White
Bench Seat	All- Vinyl	XA	XB	XD	XC

For a 1955 American car, the Thunderbird offered excellent driving characteristics. Vision over the hood was exceptionally good, as the cowl stood just 37.2 in. above the surface of the road. Early ads described this measurement as "just over a yard high." The wraparound windshield created some distortion of vision at the corners. Inside, the operator was greeted with a modern-looking dashboard featuring a tachometer, "idiot lights" (to monitor oil pressure and electrical system output), and a clock with a sweep second hand that was great for rallying. A power seat was standard equipment. Power brakes were optional.

A firm ride made the first Thunderbird feel like a sports car. Still, it was somewhat prone to understeering and would break loose in a tight turn, before drifting around it like a competition racer. However, it hung in the corners well enough to take them at 10 to 15 mph faster than most contemporary, full-size American cars. Walt Woron's first spin in a Fordomatic T-Bird provided an 11 second 0 to 60 mph time. He estimated top speed to be over 120 mph. According to James F. Petrik, "He was wrong, and until the 1965 model with power front disc brakes, Thunderbirds all had — sorry to say — lousy brakes."

Ford's advertising highlighted the T-Bird's instant appeal. "Wherever the Ford Thunderbird has been exhibited, it has created a veritable sensation," said the copywriters. Besides selling quite well for a two-seater, the Thunderbird pulled many buyers of other models into Ford dealer showrooms. "There's a touch of Thunderbird in every Ford," said one advertisement. "The 1955 Ford shows it was cut from the same cloth as the heart-stealing Thunderbird." A similarity in appearance was noted, too. "Quite naturally, the styling of America's sauciest personal car is reflected in each of the four brilliant new series of Fords for '55," said one layout. Numerous announcements spoke of "Trigger-Torque" power being shared by Fords and Thunderbirds. Many mentioned the Ford's "Thunderbird-like ease of handling."

Racing "Pigeons"

When the T-Bird bowed as a 1955 model, it seemed to hold lots of potential as a race car. It was a small car with a relatively big and powerful V-8 engine. Sports car enthusiasts immediately took the new model racing, and stock car drivers weren't far behind them. But the small T-Bird did not really live up to this image, as far as racing on road or track.

While it would have some degree of success in drag racing and speed trials, the little two-seat Ford did not have the handling necessary to make it a winner in sports car rallying or stock car racing. Those who attempted to use the 1955 model in motorsports found it handled reasonably well up to 75-85 mph. At such speeds the fact that the steering and suspension systems came from a Ford "family" car began to reveal itself. "Steering is not tight enough for a sports car and too tight for a stock car," said *Speed Age*. "Suspension is the same."

In February 1955, Thunderbirds competed in the popular sports car venues at Sebring, Fla. and Willow Springs, Calif. In the 12-hour endurance race at Sebring a T-Bird finished 37th overall. It was, however, seventh in its particular class and ran for 138 laps. The car raced at Willow Springs picked up a pebble between the wheel rim and tubeless tire and the tire lost air. Within a few laps, this caused the car to spin out and quit the race.

The following month, a stock car driver named Herschel Buchanan raced a new T-Bird at a fairgrounds in Shreveport, Ala. His two-seater got off to a strong start in time trials at the Gulf States Championship race. He lapped the half-mile track in 31.67 seconds (about 57 mph). In a 15-lap preliminary contest, he outran "Wild Bill" Harrison to take the checkered flag with an 8:12.54 average.

"Buchanan and Harrison went at it like a pair of Kilkenny cats when the flag fell," noted *Speed Age*. Buchanan's roll-bar-equipped Thunderbird whipped the Topeka, Kansas driver's Olds 88, despite having steering problems in the heat.

Buchanan, who drove big cars in IMCA races, had a habit of riding high through the corners. With the loose steering, the T-Bird tapped the wall twice early in the main event, but held on to lead it through lap 54. Seven laps later, he got out in front again. That's where he was on lap 70 when his axle flange snapped. The 'Bird went flying through the air, flipping its (glass-fibre) top in the process. As *Speed Age* reported, "The T-Bird settled on its right rear fender, rebounded about 15 feet straight up, and made a complete flip to land on the roll bars." Buchanan's car did several more sideways rolls, before coming to a rest. He wound up in a hospital, alive but with serious injuries.

Later in 1955, a Thunderbird driven by Nick Cavaluzzi, of Long Island, N.Y. was entered in sports car races at the Weatherly and Sawyer Speedway in Virginia Beach, Va. This car finished third behind an Austin-Healey and an MGA in order.

An "Early 'Bird" in racing action at the Weatherly and Sawyer Speedway in Virginia Beach, Va. during 1955. (Old Cars photo)

There was no shortage of ideas on how to promote this exciting little car. In addition to advertising the T-Bird, Ford made efforts to get some cars into the hands of famous people. Actor Clark Gable was one personality who tooled around Hollywood in a black 1955 model. The T-Bird was so popular that it also inspired a miniature copy. Shown in the July 1955 issue of *Motor Trend*, this battery-driven plastic midget car was designed for kids. It had realistic proportions, including an overall length of 66 inches. The junior T-Bird was also 19 in. high and 30 in. wide. It weighed 140 lb. and could hit a speed of five mph. A child up to five feet tall could fit inside, with additional space for a companion. Manufactured by Power Car Co., of Mystic, Conn., this "wee-bird" sold for approximately $395. It was also featured in the August 1955 issue of *Road & Track*. Such promotions helped make the T-Bird very popular. Ford had considered 10,000 cars the break-even point for profitability. When 4,000 Thunderbirds were ordered the first day, it was clear the company was going to make money. By adding factory overtime and extending the normal model-year, T-Bird production was pushed to over 16,000 units.

Many sports car publications reflected an overall negative attitude towards the Thunderbird. "They were mean and insulting towards Ford's little newcomer," says James F. Petrik. "The popular saying among us T-Birders was that Henry (Ford) cried all the way to the bank, because the 'Bird was outselling all the cars the sports car publications were touting, when you put them all together."

Along with building the exciting new model and promoting it in exciting ways, Ford kept the interest in T-Birds rolling with rumors and revelations. As early as August 1955, "The Rumor Mill" column in *Motor Trend* predicted the introduction of a four-seat Thunderbird as a mid-1956 model. A second rumor hinted that the '56 T-Bird would come standard with a supercharger. "Possible," said the magazine. "More likely, however, that it will be optional equipment."

Supercharged or not, Thunderbirds were being raced before the year ended. They became fairly popular in the "A" Sports Cars class at drag races across the country. At the NHRA Regional Drags in Sioux City, Iowa, in the summer of 1955, Charlie Ward took Class A honors with a T-Bird that hit 81.32 mph in the quarter mile. That was the fifth fastest run of the event out of 15 winners in a wide assortment of classes. That summer, during a 100-degrees heat wave, John Hale topped the same class, in a T-Bird, during Columbus, Ohio's first organized drag event. His speed in the quarter was an even 80 mph. Other T-Birds drag raced at Lake City, Florida (Calvin Partin/ 80.86 mph), Memphis, Tennessee (Marshall Robillio/82.34 mph) and San Antonio (E.L. Kendrick/87.37 mph). The T-Birds got noticeably faster after firms such as Edelbrock Equipment Company began offering dual four-barrel and triple two-barrel carburetor intake manifolds and high-speed distributors designed specifically for Thunderbirds.

A Wisconsin enthusiast used his 1955 T-Bird to tow a midget race car. (James R. Goudie photo)

1955 Thunderbird Specifications

Wheelbase	102 in.	Standard Engine Type	90-degree OHV V-8 (man)
Curb Weight	2,837 lb.	Bore x stroke	3.75 x 3.30 in.
Overall Length	175.3 in.	Displacement	292 cid
Overall Width	70.2 in.	Compression Ratio	8.1:1
Overall Height	52.2 in.	Carburetor	Single 4-Barrel
Front Headroom (HT)	32.2 in.	Maximum BHP	193 @ 4400 rpm
Front Hip Room	58.8 in.	Maximum Torque	280 lb.-ft. @ 2500 rpm
Front Shoulder Room	53.3 in.	Optional Engine Type	90-degree OHV V-8 (auto)
Front Leg Room	45.4 in	Bore x stroke	3.75 x 3.30 in.
Top of Door Height	34.2 in.	Displacement	292 cid
Front Tread	56 in.	Compression Ratio	8.5:1
Rear Tread	56 in.	Carburetor	Single 4-Barrel

1955 Thunderbird Specifications

Standard Axle	3.73:1 hypoid	Maximum BHP	198 @ 4400 rpm
Tires	6.70 x 15 4-ply	Maximum Torque	286 lb.-ft. @ 2500 rpm
Brake Swept Area	175 sq. in.	HP per CID (man.)	0.66
Turning Diameter	36 ft.	HP per CID (auto)	0.68
Steering Ratio	20.0:1	HP per LB. (man.)	14.8
Steering Wheel	17 in. diam.	HP per LB. (auto)	14.5
Weight Distribution	50/50		

1955 Thunderbird Engineering

Chassis	X-frame
Front Suspension	Ball-joints; coil springs, tube shocks; stabilizer.
Rear Suspension	Composite axle; 5-leaf springs, double-acting shocks.
Steering	Symmetrical linkage type.
Steering wheel	Three-inch in-and-out adjustable
Front Brakes	11 in. diameter double-sealed
Brakes	11 in. diameter double-sealed

1955 Thunderbird Performance

Model	CID/HP	Performance
0-60 mph		
Two-seater	292/198	8.8 seconds
Two-seater	292/198	9.5 seconds
Two-seater	292/198	11 seconds
Two-seater	292/198	10.75 seconds
1/4-Mile		
Two-seater	292/198	16.9 seconds
Two-seater	292/198	17.1 seconds
Two-seater	292/198	17.75 seconds @ 83 mph
Top Speed		
Two-seater	292/198	120 mph

1956
Even Dreamier — Even Newer

The first T-Bird was a sellout. Every one built was bought and some buyers were still waiting to get one when the model-year ended. Ford advertised that the second T-Bird was "Even dreamier — even newer," but there was actually very little new about it. The big news at Ford was the $10,000 Lincoln Continental Mark II. It looked somewhat like a large T-Bird, and it stole the spotlight away from the little two-seater. The Continental Mark II was introduced on Oct. 21, 1955, more than a week before the Thunderbird bowed on November 2. This delay in the introduction of the T-Bird may have been related to problems associated with the addition of a continental tire to the rear of the car.

The Thunderbird remained a very appealing car, despite the fanfare Lincoln's new product drew. Ford announced that its target was to built 20,000 T-Birds in 1956. They were again used to attract attention to other Fords. In fact, T-Birds appeared in many FoMoCo ads featuring Mainline, Customline, and Fairlane models — especially sporty convertibles and hardtops. "Thunderbird styling, Thunderbird power," said an advertisement in *The Saturday Evening Post* showing the 1956 Fairlane Victoria Hardtop with a rocket ship-shaped front fender badge, which indicated use of the "Thunderbird Special" engine. "The pride you feel in the long, low Thunderbird lines of your '56 Ford ... the confidence you get from the new 202-hp Thunderbird Y-8 engine purring beneath the hood ," were also mentioned in this promotion.

Ford ultimately produced 15,631 copies of the 1956 T-Bird. This was below its target, but only 524 less than 1955, which was a record year for the entire auto industry. So the "Ford sports car" was still high on the car buyers' "hit parade," even though overall U.S. car sales slowed down.

Most exterior alterations to the T-Bird were not very obvious ones. The emblem on the front of the car, above the grille, was changed from crossed checkered racing flags to a stylized rendition of the American Indian thunderbird symbol. The headlight doors now had a rib under the hooded area. The badges behind the simulated louver trim on the front fenders were revised from V-8 insignias to Ford crests. This was a small, but logical change. The V-8 badge with the "8" inside the "V" had been shown prominently in many 1955 advertisements, but the engine was officially described as a "Y-block V-8." In 1956, ad copywriters called the motor a "Y-8," which had a distinctive Ford ring to it. This may explain why the V-8 badges disappeared.

The Lincoln Continental Mark II (center) was the big news at Ford in 1956, but the T-Bird helped promote it. (Ford Motor Co.)

Door-like air vents were added to the sides of the T-Bird's cowl to improve interior cooling. Also added for the same reason were wind-wings on the car's chrome windshield frame. The standard continental tire kit on the rear of the car was the most obvious update. "The Thunderbird's brand-new, rear spare-tire mounting folds back handily, as quick as a wink," advertisements boasted. "It adds greatly to your luggage space as it does to the overall beauty of the car."

The addition of the rear-mounted spare was inspired by the need to boost luggage space. Many aftermarket companies had made accessory continental tire kits available for 1955 T-Birds. There is even a factory photo showing a '55 with a continental kit with no front sidewall plate. The factory kit for 1956 wasn't a simple bolt-on item. Stylist William P. Boyer was a member of the Ford management team in charge of facelifting

Ford advertised that the 1956 T-Bird could give car buyers "A new lease on driving fun." (Ford Motor Co.)

A hardtop with rear quarter windows was mocked up, but not mass-produced. (Ford Motor Co. photo)

the 1956 T-Bird. In his book *Thunderbird an Odyssey in Automotive Design*, Boyer explains how rear deck clearance, bumper protection, and the 10-in. increase in overall length created design problems. One solution involved cradling the tire in a center section of bumper stock, wrapping the bumper ends around the body corners, and relocating the exhaust outlets. This meant a new rear bumper was needed to accommodate the rear-mounted spare. It had its built-in dual exhaust outlets at the outer corners.

The redo did not occur without unexpected problems. The clearance between the low point on the rear of most T-Birds and the ground was five inches. However, cars built before Nov. 14, 1955 had their continental spare tires raised for added clearance. Later, Ford dealers had to recall these cars to change the height of the continental kits by 1-3/8 in. Bill Boyer's book also reveals that the 1956 frame had to be modified for this feature. The original 1955 frame couldn't tolerate the "cantilever" effect of the heavy continental kit at the extreme rear of the vehicle.

The added trunk space afforded by the external spare was a practical advantage for many T-Bird buyers. It also improved the car's front-to-rear weight distribution. However, enthusiast magazines disliked the feature intensely. The Thunderbird had "good taste in everything but the incongruous spare wheel perched on the tailfeathers," *Hot Rod* moaned. "Even the original centuries-old Thunderbird of the Arizona Indian tribes had no such appendage to mar its appearance."

A new, vented gas cap was used on the center-fill gas tank's neck. The door that the gas filler hid behind was devoid of the checkered flag emblem used to dress it up in 1955. Slight modifications were made to the Thunderbird's taillights. Though still large and circular, the rear red lenses had a wider center protrusion with more elaborate

The 1956 glass-fibre hardtop was available with port windows to let more light into the interior and improve driving vision. (Henry Ford Museum photo)

chrome trim. The arch-shaped area above the round red lens was also restyled. In 1955 it had no reflector at the top of its chrome molding and was filled with either a ribbed metal plate or optional back-up lamp lens. In 1956, a small circular reflector was added to the chrome molding right at the top of the arch. Back-up lamps could again be ordered in place of the metal filler plate.

Offered again was the same glass-fibre hardtop used in 1955. A new version, with "port" windows in its side panels, was also available for 1956. The hardtop (with or without port windows) in matching body color was optional at no extra cost. Having the top finished in a contrasting color did cost extra, though. Some Ford dealers added the porthole windows to the standard-style hardtop when buyers found their T-Birds claustrophobic or complained about blind spots. A third type of top with rear quarter windows was designed for 1956. The so-called "five-window Hardtop" was never used on production cars.

In late 1956, still another T-Bird roof option was developed by a famous automotive designer. The late Gordon Buehrig is best known for his styling of classic Cords and Duesenbergs. He also invented the T-top that's in common use today. Buehrig's first roof with removable transparent sections appeared on a futuristic car called the Tasco Special which he developed in the late-1940s. This roof reflected the same idea as today's T-tops, but looked more like an airplane canopy than a T-roof. Buehrig's "flexible" roof for the two-seat Thunderbird was much closer to a true T-top. In fact, its introduction on the T-Bird may well have inspired the name used for this feature later on.

After doing numerous freelance design projects like the Tasco Special in the early postwar years, Buehrig went to work in the Ford design department. There, he was involved in the original Thunderbird project. A T-Bird he owned wore the prototype of his Flexible T-Bird top. The car's factory hardtop was cut, like a modern T-top, to accept two types of panels. One set of opaque panels was actually fashioned from the fiberglass sections cut out of the top. The second set of panels was made from clear Plexiglas.

Removable at the flick of a wrist, the panels were carefully sealed to make them leakproof. Both sets of panels could be carried behind the seat in a handy storage case. The fiberglass T-Bird hardtop could still be completely removed. Buehrig hoped to interest a company in manufacturing rights to his design. Interested parties were invited to contact him at 2200 Belmont Avenue, in Detroit, Mich., which was the address of his design firm. Some say that the flexible roof lived up to its name, since it tended to sag in the middle. This may be one reason why the product never reached the marketing phase, but it was certainly an advanced concept.

New trim patterns and a three-spoke steering wheel were among interior changes in 1956. (Old Cars photo)

23

In addition to the port window hardtop, the original version was carried over as a no-cost option in 1956. (Ford Motor Co. photo)

Whether it was driven hard-topped or topless, the 1956 T-Bird's interior door panels had new "stitching" embossments molded into the seams in the vinyl. The patterning on the seats, supplied by McInerney Spring & Wire Co., was also changed. In 1955, the vertically ribbed insert sections of the seats were separate from each other. The 1956 design brought the ribs across the center of the backrest. They ran nearly the full width of the seat back, and gave the visual impression that the seat had been widened. Six trim combinations were cataloged.

1956 Thunderbird Interiors

Seat Type	Material	Black/ White	Red/ White	Tan/ White	Green/ White	Brown/ White	Peacock/ White
Bench Seat	Vinyl	XA	XB	XD	XF	XG	XC

"Now you get the added protection of Ford's exclusive Lifeguard design," some 1956 Thunderbird ads trumpeted to promote a new package of car safety features. FoMoCo's "Lifeguard" interior package was truly ahead of its time. A three-spoke Lifeguard deep-dish steering wheel was standard equipment in the second T-Bird. It replaced the flat, two-spoke steering wheel used the previous year. The installation of the safer steering wheel required alterations to the signal lamp stalk, and the steering column adjusting collar. Also standard were Lifeguard door latches that were not supposed to open in a serious accident. Other Ford Lifeguard features, such as seat belts, a ribbed padded dash, and padded sun visors, were options for the T-Bird.

FoMoCo's Lifeguard safety program was largely a reaction to an announcement that a member of the Cornell University Medical College made about the auto industry on April 21, 1955. He had asserted that 1955 automobiles were no safer than those built between 1940 and 1949, and added that more motorists were likely to die in new cars. Ford reacted by launching months of research into auto safety. Auto accident statistics and data were gathered from safety research centers including the Cornell Medical College. As a result, Ford isolated injury-causing components of cars, and set up a test lab devoted to redesigning such components. On most 1956 models, Lifeguard safety design features were optional. As an extra-cost item, the safety features were a flop in the marketplace. Nevertheless, *Motor Trend* magazine did present Ford with its "1st annual *Motor Trend* Award," for making the most significant advancement on a U.S. production car. "Rising high in stature, above all other (advances), however, is the progress toward automotive safety made by the Ford Motor Co.," wrote editor Walt Woron and engineering editor John Booth. "This company, and each of its divisions, is not alone in its pursuit of those elusive qualities we'd like to see built into all cars. What this company has initiated is without a doubt the biggest step forward in 1956."

There were a few running production changes in 1956 T-Birds. With the spare tire out of the trunk, changes were made in the way that the luggage compartment was trimmed. A curtain made of material similar to the ribbed rubber trunk mat was added at first. Later, the rubber trim was replaced with trim made of a composition material called Burtex, and the curtain was no longer used. At mid model-year, a dual four-barrel carburetor "competition kit" was released for T-Birds with the manual transmission. Engines fitted with the kit, which was intended for serious racing, were rated at 260 hp.

Base engine for the 1956 Thunderbird with the standard three-speed manual transmission was the "M6" 292-cid "Thunderbird Y-8," which was also used in new Ford Fairlanes and station wagons. It generated 202 hp @ 4600 rpm in stick-shift T-Birds. Cars with overdrive or Fordomatic could be ordered with a new "P6" 312-cid "Thunderbird Special Y-8" with an 8.4:1 compression ratio and 215 hp @ 4600 rpm. For cars with Fordomatic only, the larger engine also came in a "power pack" version with a 9.1:1 compression ratio and 225 hp @ 4600 rpm. This version used the same P6 engine code. All of these power plants carried single four-barrel carburetors. Also new under the hood was a 12-volt electrical system.

Regarding the use of the smaller engine in stick-shift cars, *Motor Trend* surmised, "It would seem as if Ford is deliberately discouraging the racing of Thunderbirds, which may be just as well. In spite of various racing successes, they aren't designed for this purpose, as Ford has always pointed out." This theory went out the window at the middle of the model-year however, when Ford started advertising its racing accomplishments. Still later, the 260-hp competition kit with dual four-barrel carburetors was offered for stick-shift cars. These were considered better race cars, even though Fordomatic T-Birds *were* drag raced.

The company's early 1956 advertisements pushed the automatic transmission. "It is when you put the selector in drive position, and nudge the gas of the Fordomatic model that the Thunderbird will really take you by the heart," said one colorful layout depicting Peacock Blue, Sunset Coral, Fiesta Red, and Raven Black T-Birds in profile, rear, and front three-quarter views. "Beneath the hood is a new 225-hp Thunderbird Y-8 to revise your ideas of how a car should respond." Fordomatic was one of several types of automatic transmissions supplied by Borg-Warner Corp. A Borg-Warner advertisement of 1956 noted that it was "available in all new Ford models to give superb smoothness, dramatic acceleration, a real 'touch of the Thunderbird.'" A heavier-duty version of the transmission was also available in 1/2-ton Ford trucks.

An expanded range of colors was offered by all American car makers in 1956, and Fords and Thunderbirds were no exceptions. In fact, the first Thunderbird made that year (serial number P6FH 102661) was earmarked for L.D. Crusoe and left the assembly line with the body in primer. The car had white finish on the hardtop, and was planned to be painted a non-standard color. The year began with nine single colors and 17 two-tones being listed in early 1956 literature. By late in the model-year, this was reduced to seven singles and 13 two-tones. One single color called Thunderbird Gray was added at midyear, but Navajo Gray, Sunset Coral, and Goldenglow Yellow were dropped. Two-tone combinations were listed with the first hue (called Color A) sprayed on the body and the second hue (Color B) applied to the glass-fibre hardtop. Specific upholstery trims were available with each single or two-tone paint selection.

Wind wings on the windshield and cowl vents on each front fender were among changes in the 1956 model. (Cappy Collection)

Rising young Hollywood starlet Marilyn Monroe once owned this 1956 Sunset Coral T-Bird.

A rising young Hollywood starlet named Marilyn Monroe owned a Sunset Coral 1956 T-Bird with chromed headlight doors. It had a Brown and White interior, which was also new for 1956. Monroe damaged the upholstery with ashes from a cigarette. It was this fact that helped the car's owner Lew Robinson document its authenticity. In 1982, the Fresno, Calif. collector exhibited his rare 'Bird in the Veedol Starparade auto show in Berlin, Germany. With its unique history, it was quite a hit overseas.

The 1956 Thunderbird's available equipment list grew a bit longer. It included a full-flow oil filter, 4-Way Power seat, "Swift Sure" power brakes, "Master-Guide" power steering, Power-Lift windows, I-Rest tinted safety glass, Fordomatic, overdrive, white sidewall tires, a special vacuum and fuel pump unit, a heater, a radio, rear fender shields (the type of skirts with an edge molding and gravel shield, as used mostly from April 1955 on), full wheelcovers or simulated wire wheelcovers, an engine dress-up kit, "Auto-Wipe" windshield washers, and directional signals.

Dimensions of the 1956 model were virtually unchanged, except for overall length, which was up to 185.2 in. with the continental tire. For some unexplained reason the overall width measurement was increased almost an inch to 71.3 in. This may be because the new bumper was the widest point. Otherwise, even the height with design load measurement was unchanged, though some might have expected the weight of the continental tire to lower the riding height. The base T-Bird did tip the scales in the shipping department at 3,088 lb., making it 108 lb. heavier than year one. T-Birds continued to ride on 6.70 x 15 four-ply tubeless tires mounted on five-inch wide rims.

T-Birds again carried serial numbers on a plate attached to the left-hand body pillar. Instructions on how to de-code such numbers are listed in another section of this book. The earliest 1956 T-Bird, built on Oct. 17, 1955, for L.D. Crusoe, had number P6FH102661. The year's last T-Bird was built on Aug. 24, 1956. It had serial number P6FH 359516. As in 1955, the patent plate on each car was stamped to indicate a body type code, color code, trim code, and production date code. These codes are also explained elsewhere.

Motor Trend did its second annual Thunderbird versus Corvette comparison road test in June 1956. This time, the magazine was able to compare *production* versions of both sports cars. The magazine started off noting that GM had added "more fuel to an old duel" by adding a hardtop, roll-up windows and more power to the Corvette's equipment. "But don't get the idea that Ford has been lulled into a no-progress policy by their sales leadership with the Thunderbird," advised editor Walt Woron. "The No. 1 sales position is hard to come by and is jealously guarded."

Both cars were test-driven in convertible form. Even at that, the testers found the two American sports cars a bit hard to get in and out of. The T-Bird's seat was more comfortable, while the Corvette's was described as "snugger." Woron obviously felt the Thunderbird's dashboard layout was better thought out for the driver. The Corvette was a bit easier to see out of, with less windshield distortion and no obtrusive hood scoop.

Both cars had V-8s and automatic transmissions. The article wasn't specific about engine specifications, probably because photos showed that the Corvette had dual four-barrel carburetors. That would indicate use of the

All 1955 and 1956 Thunderbird were made at Ford's "home" plant in Dearborn, Mich. (Cappy Collection)

265-cid 225-hp "power pack" motor. The Thunderbird may have also had 225-hp (the rating for its power pack version of the 312-cid V-8), but with more cubes and a single four-barrel carburetor. In any case, it wasn't an apples-to-apples comparison. In addition, the magazine noted, "Thunderbird's engine, hampered with power equipment (power brakes, power steering, and a power seat), is no direct comparison." In fact, the only engine specifications given by the magazine were piston speed at maximum horsepower, and "maximum bmep," which mean nothing to most car enthusiasts.

In driving and handling, the cars had somewhat similar characteristics, with several distinctions. It was mentioned that both were larger than typical sports cars, being nearly as wide and just a few feet shorter than standard American sedans. The Corvette was stiffer and firmer, but the test T-Bird had power steering to go with its softer feel. Faster acceleration with the Corvette was vaguely described, but this was at least partly due to its multi-carb setup. Both cars ran cool and reliably. The T-Bird had a bit of brake fade and recovered quickly. As noted earlier, Thunderbird brakes were nothing to brag about until 1965. The Corvette had more sports car-like roadability. Both cars averaged just below 13 mpg for the 650-mile test circuit. Like the absence of engine and performance figures, the magazine's summary of the cars had a "politically correct" twinge to it. It described the Corvette as the better "sports car" and the T-Bird as the better "personal car."

The addition of a continental tire as standard equipment made the T-Bird a longer car with a roomier trunk. (Cappy Collection)

The 1956 T-Bird came from the factory with 6.70 x 15 four-ply tubeless tires. Whitewalls were optional. (Cappy Collection)

A different rear bumper configuration appeared in 1956 and the exhausts came out the side of the bumper. (Cappy Collection)

The 1956 T-Bird had an insignia above its grille with a stylized Thunderbird design. (John Gunnell photo)

Ward's Automotive Yearbook showed an introductory price of $2,842 for the Thunderbird, but most 1956 models were sold for about $300 more than that. The base price in June 1956 was $3,147.60. This included the suggested retail price at the main factory, federal tax, and delivery and handling (but not freight). Fordomatic was $215 extra. Other available options were: Overdrive ($146); power brakes ($34); power steering ($64); power windows ($70); power seat ($65); radio ($107); heater ($84); convertible top alone ($75); both tops ($290); and safety package ($22-$32). Check elsewhere in this book for a more complete listing of standard and optional equipment.

Hot Rod magazine did a "Rod Test" of the 1956 T-Bird in July, and expanded it to discuss Thunderbird modifications. According to editor Racer Brown, the car's popularity "was soon resolved into a matter of appearance." He believed that horsepower, performance, fuel economy, economics, and utilitarian value had little to do with the appeal of Ford's two-seater. "It was the bold American lines that captivated the majority (of buyers)," he opined. "Yet, these lines have been restrained by good taste."

The test vehicle had traveled 5,039 miles. It had Fordomatic, power steering, power brakes, a power seat, power window lifts, a deluxe radio and heater, the padded dash and visors, seat belts, and both tops. Brown found the car's general fit and finish good, but didn't like its soft seats. Controls and human engineering features were highly rated, except for the small glove box and the restricted rear view. The car did leak in the rain, however.

"Good roadability under most conditions," was discovered with the T-Bird, but the test driver felt that there was room for improvement, too. In turns, the car leaned too much for a sports-driving machine, and the suspension was rated too soft for spirited use. To stiffen and firm up the suspension, Racer Brown recommended the use of 1956 Ford passenger car springs in the front. The height of the coils would have to be reduced 5/16-inch for six-cylinder springs and 5/8-inch for V-8 springs. The hot rodder also suggested using the stabilizer bar from a 1955 Ford station wagon to improve the T-Bird's lateral stability. To beef up the rear suspension, the addition of extra spring leaves and Traction Master stabilizers was mentioned, along with doubling up the shock absorbers.

Under the hood was the 312.7-cid V-8 in its 225-hp "power pack" format. It was able to move the 3,088-lb. T-Bird from zero to 60 mph in an average 9.1 seconds, and from zero to 80 mph in an average 15.5 seconds by "shifting" the automatic transmission. Keeping the gear-shifter in drive range only, the comparable times were 9.8 seconds and 16.6 seconds. The test driver averaged 77 mph for the standing-start quarter-mile. "These figures certainly leave something to be desired from a car like the Bird," Racer Brown wrote. "To be sure, we have tested passenger cars capable of blowing the Bird right off the road at any speed."

The sluggish performance was traced to three factors: 1) Weight; 2) 3.31:1 rear axle ratio; and 3) Fordomatic. This led to a lengthy discussion of things that could be done, by hot rodders, to make the Thunderbird faster. Several interesting modification projects were written about in detail. One was Vic Edelbrock's 1955 T-Bird, which had a 340-cid Y-8 with a 1/8-inch over-bore and 1/4-inch larger than stock stroke, plus ported and polished

The 292-cid "Thunderbird V-8" engine generated 200 hp in stick-shift cars, as seen here, and 202 hp with Fordomatic transmission. (Courtesy Frank Hagerty)

heads, large valves, exhaust headers, and Iskenderian valve train improvements. With milled heads, a dual-coil ignition system and three two-barrel carburetors, it produced an honest 285 bhp, and pulled the car through the standing quarter at 103 mph with Fordomatic and 4.27:1 gearing.

Amazingly similar performance was delivered by another car pictured in the article. Built by Bob Kennedy, of Portland, Ore., this Thunderbird also featured a 1/8-inch over-bore, plus a McCulloch blower, an "Isky" cam, Spalding ignition system, and three two-barrel Holleys. It was equipped with Traction-Masters, and racing slicks, to give it a better "bite" coming off the line. In the quarter-mile, it turned a top speed of 102.27 mph.

Despite Ford's early attempts to discourage people from racing its products, some of the hottest U.S. production sports cars at the Daytona International Speed Trials/ NASCAR Speedweek, in February 1956, were Thunderbirds. One was Chuck Daigh's streamlined T-Bird with bullet-shaped headlight covers, no bumpers or windshield, smooth Moon Disc hubcaps, and a tonneau cover over its cockpit. (Not surprisingly, after Daigh's car appeared in enthusiast magazines, tonneau covers for T-Birds became a hot aftermarket item. They were offered by companies such as Robbins Auto Top, of Santa Monica, Calif., and De Ville Enterprises, of Los Angeles).

Daigh's slippery T-Bird hit an average top speed of 85.308 mph for the standing-start mile early in the trials, then averaged 92.142 mph three days later. It beat out a Corvette driven by Zora Arkus-Duntov. However, both vehicles were disqualified. The two car builders had misunderstood the rules and over-bored their engines. Both knew that a .030-inch overbore was allowed in NASCAR Grand National stock car racing, but did not realize that the speed trials had different rules.

Frank Hagerty showed this stark-looking T-Bird at Hershey '94. It had a 292-cid V-8, three-speed transmission, and "bottle cap" hubcaps. (John Gunnell photo)

Hel's Angel

What would you guess is the fastest speed ever achieved by a Thunderbird? Could it be the 134 mph that Andy Hotten and Suzanne La Fountain hit in the Daytona flying mile in 1956? How about Joe Weatherly's 144 mph 1959 T-Bird stock car racing rag-top? Both of those are very good guesses, but neither comes close to the correct answer of 241.786 mph. That's what Knot Farrington averaged in his streamlined 1956 "Hel's Angel" Thunderbird at the Bonneville Speed Trials in the fall of 1963.

A Louisiana mechanic who spent most of his time running a repair shop in New Orleans, Farrington was 37 years old in 1959. That's when he made his first trip to the famous salt flats near Wendover, Utah. Several Thunderbirds were running,, but none of them were doing particularly well. Then Farrington unveiled his latest spare-time creation.

His project car had started with a 1956 T-Bird which he "de-contented" to the point of tossing

A hot 456-cid Chrysler hemi with Hilborn fuel-injection system was stuffed into the car. The combination was good for 173.41 mph and third place in the sports car class at Bonneville its first year out in 1959.

away the x-braced frame. Aluminum was used to replace many interior body panels and to fashion a wind-cheating belly pan. The body, which looked fairly stock, was streamlined by removing most bolt-on items and smoothing things out as much as possible. A small plexiglas bubble on the driver's side replaced the stock windshield. The car wore number 230 AS (for Class A Sports racing) and had "Knot's Auto Service" lettered on the doors.

Knot Farrington's project car had started with a 1956 T-Bird. The body, which looked fairly stock, was streamlined by removing most bolt-on items and smoothing things out.

A hot-rodded 456-cid Chrysler hemi V-8 with a Hilborn fuel-injection system was stuffed into the car. Ed Iskendarian supplied the roller cam. A hotter spark was provided by a Hunt Scintilla ignition system. Suspension-wise, a 1934 Ford tube axle and leaf spring set up did the trick up front. At the rear was a hybrid axle made from 1948 Ford and Thunderbird guts with a Halibrand quick-change center.

The combination was good for 173.41 mph and third place in the sports car class. However, Farrington failed to nail down any records in 1959. He would return to try again.

Upon its return to the "Salt" in 1960, the most obvious change in the car was a "power blister" on the hood. It had a large air scoop on top of it. The two bolt-on items stood at least 12 in. high. Under them was a 429-cid Chrysler hemi with a GMC 6-71 Roots blower. The car also had new aluminum filler panels at the outboard ends of its cut-down T-Bird grille. Although it wore the same number on the body side, the car was

Upon its return to Bonneville in 1960, the most obvious change in the car was a power blister on the hood with a large air scoop on top of it. Underneath was a 429-cid Chrysler hemi with a GMC 6-71 Roots blower.

now dubbed "Hel's Angel" and it went as fast as that name implies. It set a new record in the Class A Sports Racing competition averaging 200.622 mph for a two-way run. It had hit 205.36 mph in qualifying trials.

Streamlining the car's body was Farrington's next goal. A body man named Floyd Pfeffer, of New Orleans, was engaged to turn the T-Bird into a super streamliner. Its design was patterned after a car that English automaker Donald Healey created for Bonneville runs. When completed, the T-Bird had a smooth, rounded front end, a faired-in rear deck headrest, a gun shell-shaped extended tail, and full-skirted rear fenders. The foot-high power blister/hood scoop combination was replaced with a smaller air scoop mounted on the cowl. The hood was totally smooth. The bubble windshield remained, as did the 429-cid Chrysler "Firepower" V-8. As indicated by the relocation of the hood scoop, the engine was set back into the cowl area. This improved the car's weight distribution characteristics. In addition, the radiator was mounted in tilted-back fashion to clear the low hood. The car was painted a rich maroon color. All non-painted body panels were polished to a mirror finish. The number 230 and the AS class designation were seen

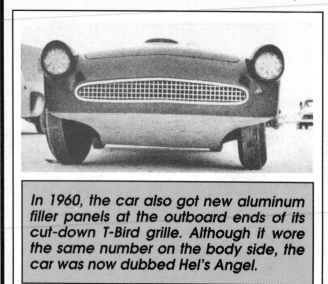

In 1960, the car also got new aluminum filler panels at the outboard ends of its cut-down T-Bird grille. Although it wore the same number on the body side, the car was now dubbed Hel's Angel.

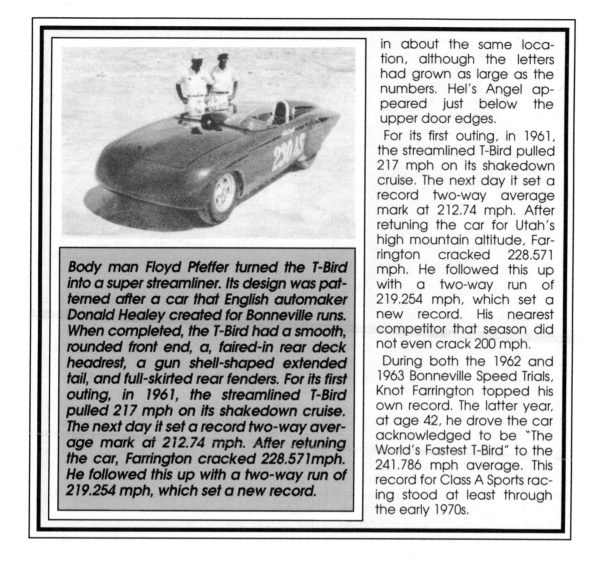

Body man Floyd Pfeffer turned the T-Bird into a super streamliner. Its design was patterned after a car that English automaker Donald Healey created for Bonneville runs. When completed, the T-Bird had a smooth, rounded front end, a, faired-in rear deck headrest, a gun shell-shaped extended tail, and full-skirted rear fenders. For its first outing, in 1961, the streamlined T-Bird pulled 217 mph on its shakedown cruise. The next day it set a record two-way average mark at 212.74 mph. After retuning the car, Farrington cracked 228.571mph. He followed this up with a two-way run of 219.254 mph, which set a new record.

in about the same location, although the letters had grown as large as the numbers. Hel's Angel appeared just below the upper door edges.

For its first outing, in 1961, the streamlined T-Bird pulled 217 mph on its shakedown cruise. The next day it set a record two-way average mark at 212.74 mph. After retuning the car for Utah's high mountain altitude, Farrington cracked 228.571 mph. He followed this up with a two-way run of 219.254 mph, which set a new record. His nearest competitor that season did not even crack 200 mph.

During both the 1962 and 1963 Bonneville Speed Trials, Knot Farrington topped his own record. The latter year, at age 42, he drove the car acknowledged to be "The World's Fastest T-Bird" to the 241.786 mph average. This record for Class A Sports racing stood at least through the early 1970s.

Since the misunderstanding was not intentional, Daigh was permitted to replace his T-Bird's over-size engine with a stock one. He worked for almost 48 hours straight making his power plant change. The result was a factory-spec 312-cid block fitted with the racing kit that Ford offered stock car racers. This kit consisted of a dual four-barrel intake manifold, and a pair of special Holley four-barrel carburetors, plus 10.0:1 high-compression heads with larger intake and exhaust ports, a limited advance distributor, a special cam and lifters, and tubular push rods, rocker arms and valve springs. At Daytona, Daigh wound up with an average of 88.779 mph performance for the standing mile. Another Thunderbird, driven by William Norkert, was second with an 87.869 mph two-way run. John Fitch came in third with a Corvette.

Daigh was unable to get his T-Bird ready in time for the flying mile runs, although his car was capable of over 130 mph. Another T-Bird built by Andy Hotten, of Dearborn Steel Tubing Co., had a faster official time. Both Hotten and Suzanne La Fountain drove the car. It ran 134 mph, for a third-place in the flying mile with Hotten behind the wheel. Bill Borkett's 1955 T-Bird was fourth with 133.087 mph, and Merritt Brown took his 1956 T-Bird to fifth place with a 122.491 mph performance. Other T-Birds were entered at Daytona by Bob Wallis and Jack Horsley. The latter, with its weird two-stage McCulloch blower, was also seen in the July issue of *Hot Rod*.

By this time, Chuck Daigh had equipped his car with a 4.56 rear end gear, Hi-Tork differential, eight shock absorbers, and a synchro gear box. It ran the quarter-mile at just over 100 mph. Another drag racer, Bill Williams, turned 105 mph in a supercharged "312" T-Bird with Fordomatic. The Thunderbird's racetrack potential was beginning to evolve more fully, at least in drag racing. "A well-modified Bird out there holds all the local drag strip records in the modified sports car class," noted Racer Brown. "Top time: 108 mph and there's more where that came from."

Despite its earlier stance against racing, FoMoCo produced a film entitled "Thunder Beach" that told the tale of the Daytona stock car races. Ford also wrote the results from Speedweek into a mid-1956 advertisement that promoted the Thunderbird as a "Mink coat for Father." Although they began by emphasizing the original image of a comfortable, deluxe-equipped, roomy car with roll-up windows and a glass-fiber hardtop, the copywriters boasted, "Talking of speed, have you heard how a Thunderbird dusted off all U.S. and foreign production sports cars in the acceleration tests at the Daytona Speed Trials? From a standing start it covered a mile in 40.5 seconds ... was pushing 150 mph when it took the flag. If you'd like to sample some of this sizzle, take a whirl in a Thunderbird with an over-square 225-hp Thunderbird Special V-8, floor-mounted three-speed transmission and 3.73:1 final drive."

By mid-1956, Corvettes were beginning to compete in international sports car races, but T-Birds stuck pretty much to the straight tracks. At the Rocky Mountain Regional drag races in Pueblo, Col., a 1955 Thunderbird piloted by William Burkhart of Phoenix, Ariz. took "A" Sports Car honors with a quarter-mile run of 15.15 seconds at 96.35 mph. There was also a Thunderbird at the Bonneville (Utah) Speed Trials in August 1956, but winner in the Closed Sports Car over 1500 cc. class was a fiberglass-bodied Sorrell coupe with an injected Chrysler hemi. The Larsen-Barnes team took it to 164 mph. Another dragging T-Bird was the 1955 Hardtop campaigned in "A" Sports class by Kirk White, of Glenside, Penn. With a McCulloch supercharged 292-cid V-8 blowing through triple two-barrel carbs, it turned 98.74 mph in the National Hot Rod Association's "1956 National Championship Drags" in Kansas City.

In December 1956, *Hot Rod* magazine printed an article called "300 Honest HP." It detailed a series of different steps taken to up the power output of a 312-cid Mercury V-8 (identical to the T-Bird power plant). After 17 separate modifications and dynometer tests, the engine was churning out 303 hp at 5350 rpm, and maximum torque of 360 lb.-ft. at 3500 rpm.

In September 1956, *Hot Rod* printed a story about how test pilot Bob Drew had Tom Ikkanda, of Los Angeles, install a 1955 Cadillac V-8 in his 1955 Thunderbird. To make the 330-hp engine fit in the car required a 1951 Oldsmobile Hydra-Matic transmission, which had a shorter output shaft. Several cross members and engine mountings had to be modified or manufactured, and the transmission tunnel in the T-Bird's floor pan was altered slightly. After a few other steps to tailor the steering, exhaust manifolds and linkages, the transplant was complete. No performance figures were given, but the added 132 hp must have packed quite a wallop in the sporty Ford.

Alberto Del Campo, of Mexico, didn't have a Thunderbird to modify, since duties on cars assembled outside his country boosted the price of a T-Bird in Mexico to $7,000. He did, however, have a 1949 Ford Fordor Sedan to modify into a two-seater. His custom was inspired by the T-Bird. He shortened the wheelbase to 102 in., moved the engine back 18 in., and chopped the drive shaft to fit. The stock springs were replaced with shortened Mercury coils, and Hudson shock absorbers were used on each wheel. The front fenders and hood were hammered out of sheet stock. Del Campo hand-cut the grille from a solid sheet of 1/8-inch steel, and had it chrome-plated. Sectioning and channeling the body lowered the car over a foot in height. The front firewall-windshield unit was joined with the rear window-turtle deck section. By cutting the front and rear doors in half and welding the slices together, new perfect-fitting doors were fashioned. Del Campo painted the car Arctic white.

Alberto Del Campo was not the only one who recognized the international appeal of Thunderbird styling. In August 1956, *Motor Trend* selected it as the year's "most beautiful sports-type car." The magazine said, "A neo-classic, blending a modern feeling with the crisp, sharp-edged look reminiscent of the '30s, the T-Bird has a huge number of admirers both here and in other countries. Tho it could do with less chrome and applied trim, these are more nearly a part of the overall design than in almost any other car. Here's another trend-setter, heralding smaller cars."

1956 Thunderbird Specifications

Wheelbase	102 in.	Engine No. 1 Type	90-degree OHV V-8
Curb Weight	3,550 lb.	Bore x stroke	3.75 x 3.30 in.
Overall Length	185.2 in.	Displacement	292 cid
Overall Width	71.in.	Compression Ratio	8.4:1
Overall Height	52.2 in.	Carburetor	Single 4-Barrel
Front Headroom (HT)	32.2 in.	Maximum BHP	202 @ 4600 rpm
Front Hip Room	58.8 in.	Maximum Torque	289 lb.-ft. @ 2600 rpm
Front Shoulder Room	53.3 in.	Engine No. 2 Type	90-degree OHV V-8

1956 Thunderbird Specifications

Front Leg Room	45.4 in	Bore x stroke	3.80 x 3.44 in.
Top of Door Height	34.2 in.	Displacement	312 cid
Front Tread	56 in.	Compression Ratio	8.4:1
Rear Tread	56 in.	Carburetor	Single 4-Barrel
Standard Axle (Man.)	3.73:1	Maximum BHP	215 @ 4600 rpm
Standard Axle (OD)	3.92:1	Maximum Torque	317 lb.-ft. @ 2600 rpm
Standard Axle (Auto.)	3.31:1	Engine No. 3 Type	90-degree OHV V-8
Tires	6.70 x 15	Bore x stroke	3.80 x 3.44 in.
Wheel Studs	5.5-in.	Displacement	312 cid
Wheel Stud Circle	4.5-in. diam.	Compression Ratio	9.0:1
Steering Ratio:	23.0:1	Carburetor	Single 4-Barrel
Turns lock-to-lock	3.4	Maximum BHP	225 @ 4600 rpm
Turning Diameter	36 ft.	Maximum Torque	324 lb.-ft. @ 2600 rpm
Weight Distribution	50/50	Engine No. 4 Type	90-degree OHV V-8
Brake Swept Area	175.5 sq. in.	Bore x stroke	3.80 x 3.44 in.
Electrical System	12-volt	Displacement	312 cid
HP/CID (Engine No. 1)	0.69	Compression Ratio	9.5:1
HP/CID (Engine No. 2)	0.69	Carburetor	Dual 4-Barrels
HP per LB. (man.)	14.8	Maximum BHP	260 @ NA
HP per LB. (auto)	14.5	Maximum Torque	NA

Notes: *Engine No. 1 is base Thunderbird V-8 with three-speed manual transmission only.*
Engine No. 2 is optional Thunderbird Special V-8 with overdrive or Fordomatic.
Engine No. 3 is optional Thunderbird Special V-8 with power pack with Fordomatic only.
Engine No. 4 is Thunderbird Special V-8 with dual four-barrel carburetors with all transmissions.
Other specifications based on standard engine, unless otherwise noted.

1956 Thunderbird Engineering

Chassis	X-frame
Front Suspension	Ball-joints; coil springs, tube shocks; and stabilizer.
Rear Suspension	Composite axle; 4-leaf springs, double-action shocks.
Steering	Parallel linkage type; three-inch in-and out adj.
Front Brakes	11 in. diameter double-sealed
Brakes	11 in. diameter double-sealed

1956 Thunderbird Performance

Model	CID/HP	Performance
0-60 mph		
Two-seater	312/215	11.5 seconds
Two-seater	312/215	11.5 seconds
Two-seater	312/225	9.3 seconds
Two-seater	312/225	10.2 seconds
1/4-Mile		
Two-seater	312/215	18.0 seconds at 76.5 mph
Two-seater	312/215	17.0 seconds
Two-seater	312/225	17.5 seconds
Top Speed		
Two-seater	312/215	119.4 mph
Two-seater	312/225	112.2 mph
Two-seater	312/225	113.9 mph
Two-seater	312/225	116.0 mph

Note: Some of these figures published in contemporary magazines do not seem to be totally accurate, as logic would suggest that cars with less powerful engines would be slower. However, there are always other factors, from maintenance to weather conditions, that affect acceleration and performance figures.

1957
Big Little Success

The 1957 T-Bird again came in three basic configurations soft top, Hardtop, and both tops, but all were based on the same Convertible body. (Old Cars photo).

Ford's Thunderbird had become an acknowledged success story. FoMoCo capitalized on the sporty model's appeal by making other 1957 Fords look like it. "The tremendous public acceptance of the Thunderbird was the big reason for Ford exploiting it via the 'kissin' cousin' route to help sell standard Ford passenger cars," said *Motor Life* magazine in December 1956." This automobile, universally and affectionately known as the 'T-Bird,' has achieved popularity that can't be measured by normal sales standards."

Ford Motor Company boasted that the T-Bird had outsold all other sports-type personal cars combined. According to *Popular Mechanic's 1957 Car Facts Book*, during 1956 it outsold its principal domestic competitor, the Chevrolet Corvette, by more than 10 to 1. Even though the Corvette had whipped the T-Bird in sports car racing, the T-Bird was the big winner on the boulevards of America. By the time its extended 1957 season came to a close, the three-year total of T-Bird production stood at 53,166 units. That compared to just 14,446 Corvettes built in five years.

Styling revisions were seen on both the front and rear of the 1957 model. The glass-fibre hardtop with port windows was standard. (Ford Motor Co. photo)

Also available in 1957, as a no-cost option, was the glass fibre top without port windows. (Ford Motor Co. photo)

There were big styling changes in the 1957 Thunderbird, but only minor mechanical alterations. New appearance features included a larger, stronger front bumper incorporating rectangular parking lamps. A larger front grille was said to improve engine cooling. The shape of the front wheel cutouts was modified, and chrome Thunderbird name scripts were added to the front fenders ahead of the louver decorations. Tail fins were added to the T-Bird. A body side feature line curved up and over the door handles, then swept to the rear atop the outward canted fins.

A higher deck lid had a reverse angle shape at its rear. The longer 1957 body provided more luggage space. After being externally mounted in 1956, the spare tire was moved back inside the six-inch longer trunk. This made getting into the trunk a lot easier. Ford said that it also helped enhance handling, due to improvements in weight distribution caused by the extra poundage at the rear. The spare tire sat at an upright angle in the trunk's tire well.

Numerous aftermarket continental kits were offered for the few buyers who felt they needed a continental spare tire. Eastern Auto Co., of Los Angeles, advertised one of these for $119.50. A chrome tire ring was $10 extra. Many other non-factory accessories were also available. The manufacturer of Traction-Masters suspension levelers used a cartoon T-Bird in its advertising. Camshaft wizard Ed Iskenderian showed a photo of a 1957 T-Bird at the top of one ad, with testimonials from drivers who raced them. De Ville Sports Car Accessories offered tonneau covers for T-Birds. The tan and black versions sold for $39.95, while the white cover was $5 extra. These had a zipper down the center, so the cockpit could be left uncovered.

A press release in the September 1957 issue of *Motor Trend* introduced two new "Thunderbird conversions." One was the Town Car kit, that allowed owners to carry their detachable hardtop on the rear deck, and move it over the driver's head in less than 15 seconds if it rained. Tie-down straps and standard toggle bolts were used to attach the top. In profile, this made the Thunderbird look like an old-fashioned town car. This kit was sold by Sanco, Inc. of Atlanta, Ga., as well as by Ford dealers, which made it "semi-factory" equipment. It originally cost $89.50. Also featured in the same release was the better known Thunderbird "rumble seat" marketed by Birdnest of Burbank, Calif. Made of pressed body steel, this accessory replaced the original

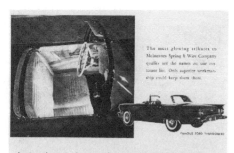

Springs for T-Birds and Vettes continued to come from McInernary Spring & Wire Co. (Old Cars photo)

A wider grille and more massive front end marked the 1957 T-Bird. Despite restyling, the basic car and wheelbase were unchanged. (Ford Museum photo)

trunk deck with a swiveling lid that had a naugahyde-upholstered seat and side panels on its inner surface. When swiveled to the "seat up" position, it could accommodate two adults or several kids on its in-the-trunk seat. The original price of the Birdnest was $239.

Ford engineer Jim Aldridge, a member of the Thunderbird development group, told *Motor Life* magazine that tests indicated the stock 1957 model had improved rear end stability. Writer Ken Fermoyle said there tended to be a bit less rear end steering effect during hard cornering. Karl Ludvigsen, writing in *Sports Cars Illustrated*, was less tactful. "The factory engineer was remarking on the superior handling of the '57 car," he lampooned. "We could hardly hear him above the anguished howling from the tires." However, even Ludvigsen noted that the "previously skitterish" rear end didn't act up at all.

It appears both magazines tested the same 1957 Thunderbird, since engine photos in the March 1956 issue of *Motor Life* and the January issue of *Sports Cars Illustrated* reveal the markings "EX-242-2-4" painted or chalked on the right-hand valve cover. *Motor Life* described it as a heavily-optioned car that had "covered lots of long hard miles." Ken Fermoyle said its performance was not up to his expectations. He criticized the slow steering, which required 4.5 turns lock-to-lock even with power assist. "In general, the Thunderbird still falls somewhere between a true sports car and a standard passenger car as far as overall handling and maneuverability are concerned," he noted.

Not all the experts felt the same way about the 1957 T-Bird's handling. Bob Veith, of *Speed Age*, compared it to the Corvette and Studebaker Hawk and found that it came out on top. "For handling and cornering, the Thunderbird gave its competitors a real run for their money," he wrote. "It felt to me the best-balanced of the three, with even weight distribution throughout to make cornering in tight turns a comparatively easy chore. High speed or low speed running, and even on slick pavement, it out-handled the others." Of course, at this time, neither the straight-axle Corvette or the Studebaker Hawk were the top-handling sports cars around.

Body side feature lines were totally different in 1957. New was a Thunderbird script in front of the simulated louvers. (Ford Motor Co. photo)

The 1957 model originally came in a choice of 10 colors. Five other paint choices were added or substituted during the year. (Cappy Collection)

The badge above the 1957 T-Bird's grille again showed a stylized American Indian thunderbird. (Cappy Collection)

The 1957 Thunderbird's longer, larger, finned rear fenders ended with large round tail-lamps in the rear, below the fins. As at the front, the rear bumper was enlarged and had more curves than in the past. Built-in exhaust outlets were featured at either side. The license plate was mounted in the center of the rear bumper. A badge on the center of the rear deck lid, shaped like a stylized Thunderbird, identified the model.

The new Thunderbird had a firmer ride than big sedans of its era. This was due mainly to its shorter wheelbase. However, it was plush, comfortable, and soft-riding in comparison to European sports cars. For 1957, the ride was improved through a lowered center of gravity, and the use of recalibrated shock absorbers. Five-leaf rear springs were reintroduced, after being dropped in favor of four-leaf springs in 1956.

Despite the fact that smaller wheels were employed in 1957, the front brakes were enlarged. At least one original source says the rear brakes stayed the same as in 1956, but they actually grew larger, too. In reality, there were slight differences in most brake lining dimensions in all three years that the two-passenger Thunderbirds were built. The front and rear wheel primary and secondary lining dimensions were as follows:

Brake Linings

Front Wheels		Rear Wheels	
Primary	**Secondary**	**Primary**	**Secondary**
(1955)			
10-19/32 x 1-3/4 x 3/16	11-29/32 x 2-1/4 x 15/64	11-29/32 x 1-3/4 x 3/16	11-29/32 x 1-3/4 x 3/16
(1956)			
10-19/32 x 1-3/4 x 3/16	11-29/32 x 2-1/4 x 3/16	10-19/32 x 1-3/4 x 3/16	11-29/32 x 1-3/4 x 3/16
(1957)			
11 x 2 x 3/16	11 x 2-1/2 x 1/4	11 x 1-3/4 x 7/32	11 x 2 x 7/32

Changes in the deck lid and rear quarter panels made the T-Bird about four inches longer and cut need for continental kit. (Cappy Collection)

Overall, the Thunderbird's effective brake lining area hopped from about 170 sq. in. to 176 sq. in. for 1957. *Sports Cars Illustrated* tested a car with non-power brakes and surmised "power boost would have been a worthwhile accessory." The standard brakes required high pedal pressure, although the larger linings seemed to help combat fade. *Speed Age* tested a car with power brakes. "Braking was rather severe on the Bird, on panic stops especially," said the magazine. "There was noticeable fade under constant use, but good recovery. Our power-brake panic stop was even, and we didn't do much fishtailing despite the wet pavement."

The smaller new 14-in. diameter safety rim wheels with 7.50 x 14 tires mounted were what brought the car closer to the ground. They were dressed up with handsome new louvered full-wheel disks. Front and rear treads were both identical and the same as in the past. Rear axles varied with the transmission, but all used lower gear ratios than in 1956. The Fordomatic rear axle ratio changed from 3.31:1 to 3.10:1. With stick shift, the ratio was switched from 3.73:1 to 3.56:1. Cars equipped with overdrive had 3.70:1 gearing, instead of last year's 3.92:1 This had a slight positive effect on top speed and fuel economy, although the use of smaller tires offset any gigantic gains in either category.

Despite a larger body, the 1957 Thunderbird's frame was virtually the same as before. However, the number four cross-member was changed to box section (instead of channel section) design. This provided added strength to support the extra bulk of the bigger body.

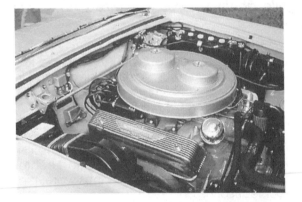

Stick-shift cars again came with 292-cid V-8, but most T-Birds had a 312-cid V-8 with either single or dual four-barrel carburetion. (Cappy Collection)

The Hardtop model was again really a convertible with a detachable fiberglass top. Ford literature still described it as a "glass-fibre standard hardtop." The standard top had port windows in 1957. Optional at no extra cost was the hardtop without port windows. Both were available in contrasting or matching colors. *Speed Age* noted that the solid top looked more attractive. "You can have your choice of a top with better side vision or one that restricts side vision, but looks nice," said the magazine. Buyers preferred better vision, though. Some 75 percent of all 1957s had the porthole tops, which had no trim badges. The plain tops featured round emblems with V-shaped Thunderbird insignias. Both hardtops used a revised clamping mechanism.

The Convertible model came with a folding fabric top. Modifications were made to the top mechanism to make it easier to operate. Two types of fabrics were offered. The rayon convertible top was available in three colors, while an optional vinyl top came only in one color. The neat setup then, as now, was to have two tops. In this case, the Convertible model was purchased with the hardtop as a separate option.

In October 1956, the Thunderbird was offered in 10 single colors. All 10 colors

Another option available in 1957 was the "F-bird." with this 312-cid supercharged V-8 good for 300 hp. (Old Cars photo)

were also offered on the fiberglass hardtops with specific body and interior color combinations. In the spring, Gunmetal Gray was changed to code H. Late in the production run, Sun Gold replaced Inca Gold, Torch Red replaced Flame Red, Seaspray Green replaced Willow Green, and Azure Blue replaced Starmist Blue.

Popularity of T-Birds continues today in Milwaukee, Wis., where members of a Thunderbird club exhibit during the annual new-car show. (Ron Kowalke photo)

Aftermarket suppliers continued to offer continental kits for the 1957 T-Bird, although the factory did not. (Old Cars photo)

Inside, the 1957 T-Bird had modest interior alterations. The dashboard was based on the one used in full-size 1957 Fords with a simulated engine-turned face panel added. The visor above the instrument panel no longer had a transparent "window." One complaint of many test drivers was that the tachometer was mounted low at the driver's left, where it was hard to see. Another slightly unpopular feature was the use of idiot lights to monitor oil pressure and battery.

The seats were redesigned. They had separate sections for the driver and passenger. New springs that gave better spine support, and much improved lateral support were employed. The seats were the same basic size and shape as in 1956, but the new springs were said to reduce driver fatigue. The door panels were also changed. An unpopular option was a "Dial-O-Matic" seat. Dash-mounted buttons permitted adjusting the seat to the driver's favorite position. When the ignition was turned off, it automatically moved to its rearmost position. When the ignition was turned on, the seat moved automatically to the pre-selected driving position. Many owners wound up disconnecting the electric controls for their Dial-O-Matic seats.

1957 Thunderbird Interiors

Seat Type	Material	Black/White	Blue/Blue	Green/Green	Red	White	Bronze
Bench Seat	All-Vinyl	XA	XL	XM	XH	XK	XJ

A new idea in radios was available in the Thunderbird. This was a speed-sensitive receiver. There was an electronic device built into the circuit between the radio volume control and the distributor. It automatically increased volume as the car speed got higher. As the engine speed increased, a capacitor wired in series with the distributor lead raised the volume. This maintained the listening level at a constant level at all times and kept the radio from blasting loudly when the car was idling at a traffic light.

A safety feature added to 1957 Thunderbird was a reflecting strip along the rear edge of the left door. When the door was opened at night, headlights from oncoming cars were reflected from the strip, warning drivers of another car's presence. The doors also had heavier hinges than those used in previous years.

Production of 1957 Thunderbirds began on Sept. 14, 1956 with car number D7FH100010. Ford continued building these cars after full-size Fords underwent the normal model changeover late in the summer of 1957. The company had set a production target of 20,000 units, but the '57s were popular and orders ran higher than expected. Model-year production eventually hit 21,380. The extended model run allowed Ford to "build out" the two-seat T-Bird and use up parts in inventory before switching to four-seat model production in 1958. The last 1957 model, reportedly owned by David Koto of Michigan, had serial number E7FH395813.

The "D" in the earlier serial number and the "E" in later one are engine codes. Two basic engines with three horsepower options were available when the year started. In addition, factory performance parts were made available to "hop up" one of these engines. Later, a supercharged V-8 was added to the mix. There was also a rare, extra-powerful NASCAR version of the supercharged

The "Birdnest" was an aftermarket conversion that Ford authorized for 1957 T-Birds. (Old Cars photo)

motor that was installed in a mere handful of cars. The standard T-Bird engine was the 292 cid V-8 and was available only with three-speed manual transmission. A floor-mounted gear selector was used in all early T-Birds. The optional "Thunderbird Special" engine was the 312 cid V-8 with a brand new "low-silhouette" Holley four-barrel carburetor specially-designed to fit under the T-Bird's low hood. The Thunderbird Special V-8 could be had with overdrive or Fordomatic transmissions. Next came the "Thunderbird Super" with two four-barrel Holley carburetors. This option had an "E" code and cars using the motor are known as "E-Birds." This engine was installed in the last 1957 model made. However, this was the last 312-cid engine on the options list. Later in the year, Ford tossed a supercharged V-8

When installed by owners, the Birdnest turned the trunk of the 1957 T-Bird into a rumble seat. (Old Cars photo)

into the mix. Known as option code "F," this single four-barrel V-8 had a VR-57 McCulloch/Paxton single-stage, variable-ratio centrifugal supercharger that boosted its output to 300 hp. A NASCAR version, intended strictly for racing, was good for 340 hp @ 5300 rpm. Only 208 supercharged "F-Birds" were built. Like the 270-, 285- and 300-hp engines, the 340-hp V-8 could be had with any transmission Ford offered for the T-Bird.

Most car magazines test drove early versions of the 1957 Thunderbird. The cars Ford loaned them for the tests seemed to have many convenience options like Fordomatic transmission, an adjustable steering wheel, a four-way power seat, and power windows. Usually the 245-hp Thunderbird Special engine was under the hood. *Motor Life's* Ken Fermoyle found this T-Bird's performance, "Frankly disappointing." He said he had trouble believing that the car needed 11.5 seconds to go from 0-60 mph. In May 1957, *Speed Age* did an "Expert Test" comparing the Corvette, T-Bird, and Studebaker Golden Hawk. Of the three, the T-Bird was slowest. However, it registered an 8.49-second 0-60 time and a top speed of 119.3 mph. "Any car that will accelerate from 0-60 in under nine seconds these days is fairly quick," said writer Bob Veith. "The take-off response up to 70 mph was neck-snapping all right, and the engine continued to deliver a good punch even on the high end."

The Birdnest turned the T-Bird into a four (or five) passenger car, It was featured in the company's customer magazine Ford Times. (Old Cars photo)

Battlebirds

In a situation not unlike the current Ford versus Chevy challenge unfolding on NASCAR superspeedways, racing buffs were treated to a "battle royal" in the spring of 1957, when Thunderbirds and Corvettes went head-to-head in straight-line racing and sports car competition.

It was a year in which Ford and Chevrolet were running neck-and-neck in show-room sales. Dearborn seemed to have a chance to unseat Flint as America's number one best-selling automaker. In addition, after four bad years, the Corvette was on the ropes and had an unsure future. Car magazines were filled with stories highlighting the T-Bird as a success and the Corvette as a failure. Needless to say, Ford was poised to pull out all the stops on the racing front.

This led to the creation of four special cars that came to be known as the "Battlebirds." They were prepared by Peter DePaolo Engineering, a Long Beach, Calif. firm named after its owner. As the late Dean Batchelor noted in the Jan./Feb. 1993 issue of *Vintage Motorsports*, this was the same Peter DePaolo who had raced at Indianapolis Motor Speedway, as well as on the classic board tracks way back in the 1920's.

According to Gil Baumgartner, authenticity chairman of the Classic Thunderbird Club International (CTCI, 1308 E. 29th St., Signal Hill, CA 90806) the Peter DePaolo team was selected by Ford Motor Company for an all out assault on the Daytona Beach Speed Week Trials in February 1957. During three years of intensive research, Baumgartner unraveled much of the true history of these cars. Most of this information is adapted from an article Baumgartner had published in the CTCI magazine in September/October 1994. It is based upon documented data, months of research, and actual restoration of the only remaining, highly-modified racing edition of the 1957 Thunderbird. A few details supplied by Dean Batchelor are also presented here.

This Battlebird has a VIN ending with 266 and has been restored. It was an all-out race car with major body and frame modifications. The car's engine was a 312-cid Thunderbird V-8 with extensive performance modifications. It has a Jaguar four-speed transmission and Halibrand quick-change rear end. (Jerry Capizzi photo)

Restorer Gil Baumgartner had to reproduce some components. The tonneau cover , plexiglas windscreen, and one headlight bezel had to be made. The fin behind the driver was crushed and repaired so that it would not fit on the deck lid. The rear portion had to be refabricated. (Jerry Capizzi photo)

Gil Baumgartner discovered that the first two Battlebirds were shipped to DePaolo Engineering on Dec. 18, 1956. They had consecutive vehicle indentification numbers ending with 265 and 266. Two other cars were shipped soon after, but their VINs were not consecutive with those of the first pair. All four were C-model Thunderbirds, and all were finished in Colonial White. Sheet metal aces Dwight "Whitey" Clayton and Dick Troutman used hand-formed aluminum hoods, doors, trunks, firewalls, and belly pans, plus faired-in headrests, to lighten and streamline the cars, but each Battlebird was different and had different degrees of modification ranging from mild to wild.

The car with the earliest number (VIN ending with 265) retained its stock appearance. It was built to compete in the stock sports car class at Daytona. Documentation has revealed that it received a specially-built 312-cid engine that was stroked to 348 cid, plus had a supercharger installed. Dean Batchelor recalled that this engine was reworked by Jim Travers and Frank Coon, before they formed Traco Engineering, but stressed that Peter DePaolo Engineering did the supercharger installation on it. The suspension and brakes were modified for better handling and stopping abilities. The body and interior remained stock looking.

The second car (VIN ending with 266) is the Thunderbird shown in the accompanying photos. It was turned into an all-out race car with major modifications done to the body by Clayton and Troutman. The car's engine was another 312-cid Thunderbird V-8, but with even more extensive modifications than the first car received. According to Dean Batchelor, Jaguar four-speed transmissions and Halibrand quick-change rear ends were used in the highly-modified Battlebirds, which Baumgartner's research verified. The chassis of "266" was also highly modified. When completed, the car competed in events for experimental and modified sports cars.

The third car (VIN ending with 333) looked exactly like "266," but had a highly modified 430-cid Lincoln V-8 installed. This engine was also prepped by Travers and Coon. According to Gil Baumgartner, both of these modified T-Birds passed the "point of no return" in changing from stock format. The frame cross member was removed and replaced with a tube. Some areas of the frame were boxed to compensate for the strength lost by removing the heavy cross member. The bodies were lightened by drilling large holes anywhere except on the exteriors. The outer skins of the doors, hoods, and deck lids were aluminum, as well as the vent doors, bezels, and splash pans behind the grilles. The firewalls were cut out and replaced with aluminum panels. Tonneau covers were formed from aluminum and small windscreens were made out of plexiglas. Streamlined headrests were added behind the driver compartments.

The fourth car was built to have a stock appearance and to race in the regular sports car class. It received the same treatment as "265," the other stock-appearing Thunderbird. It was fitted with a modified 312-cid Thunderbird V-8 and phase 1 supercharger. The suspension and brakes were also modified. The VIN of this car is not mentioned in Gil Baumgartner's research.

Dean Batchelor recalled that the Battlebirds arrived in Daytona Beach to run the speed trials on the beach course, plus an airport race at nearby New Smyrna Beach. Drivers Troy Ruttman, Danny Eames, Chuck Daigh (an employee of DePaolo Engineering), Marvin Panch, and Curtis Turner were selected to drive them in different events. They were first raced on February 9 in the two-way flying mile. A few days later they took a shot at the standing start mile. From there, the cars went to New Smyrna Beach. They were also scheduled to compete at the 12-Hours of Sebring in March, but the Automobile Manufacturer's Association's racing ban kicked in before that, and Ford pulled the plug on factory racing. The Battlebirds were then shipped back to California, with no side trip to Sebring.

The car depicted here wears the number 98, which it wore during its most famous performance on the road course at New Smyrna Beach. In that particular event, Marvin Panch qualified the T-Bird at 77.419 mph and drove it to a second place finish just seconds behind Carroll Shelby's 4.9 Ferrari. The qualifying mark had been set with an aluminum belly pan on the car, but it hurt engine cooling and was removed for the race. A basically stock Thunderbird was not supposed to be a close contender to a Ferrari.

The modified 312-cid Thunderbird V-8 under the hood is configured with the fuel-injection system as it was at the New Smyrna Beach Race in February 1957. (Jerry Capizzi photo)

In restoring this car, Baumgartner had to reproduce some components. The tonneau cover and plexiglas windscreen were missing, as well as one of the headlight bezels. They had to be fabricated. In addition, the fin behind the driver had been crushed and repaired in such a way that it would not fit on the deck lid. The rear portion had to be refabricated. As he worked, Baumgartner made a careful notes about some modifications originally made to the vehicle, plus items discovered during its restoration:

ENGINE: Modified 312-cid Thunderbird V-8. Currently configured with the fuel injection system as it was at the New Smyrna Beach Race in February 1957. The numbers seen in the engine compartment are the last three digits of the VIN. This number was stenciled or stamped numerous places throughout the vehicle -- frame, bellhousing, etc.

HILLBORN FUEL INJECTION: Also ran with the injectors pressurized using a phase 1 supercharger. This combination was used on the Daytona flying mile with unsatisfactory results. The compression was too high to be supercharged. This resulted in an engine failure. Although Chuck Daigh's one-way run was done in excess of 200 mph, this speed could not be duplicated on the way back and it did not go into the record books.

TRANSMISSION: Four-speed manual transmission from a Jaguar. The generator ran off the drive shaft.

REAR END: Halibrand quick-change type.

FUEL TANKS: The car had two fuel tanks. One was a larger than normal tank mounted under the rear of the car. The second tank was installed in the trunk. It fed into the lower tank and received by-passed fuel from the injectors.

REAR SPRINGS: The springs were lengthened and had seven leafs and adjustable shackles. The rear springs were adjustable for height, depending on race requirements.

SHOCK ABSORBERS: There are two shock absorbers per wheel, front and rear, for a total of eight on the Thunderbird.

BRAKES: The 2-1/2-in. wide brakes are air-cooled. The rear brakes have electric fans for additional cooling. The front brakes are ram-air-cooled.

FRONT COIL SPRINGS: Heavy-duty.

SWAY BAR: Heavy-duty and adjustable.

WHEELS: Halibrand quick-change magnesium knock-off wheels. Both 15- and 16-in. wheels were required. For high-speed runs in the sand, 15-in. wheels were used on the rear and 16-in. wheels were used on the front.

INTERIOR: The stock interior was removed. One lightweight seat was installed. The instrument panel was replaced with a small instrument cluster. An oil cooler tank was installed near the right side door.

"SPORTS CAR" RESULTS AT 8TH ANNUAL DAYTONA SPEED WEEKS — FEB. 1957

Two-Way Flying Mile "Sports Cars"

(Sports Class B - 305.10 to 488 cid)

1. Harold Mauck 1957 T-Bird, 138.755 mph. This was a full-bodied stock car with top installed. VIN ending with 265. Prepared by DePaolo Engineering.

2. Allen Adkins 1957 T-Bird, 135.313 mph. This was a full-bodied stock car with top installed. VIN unknown. Prepared by DePaolo Engineering.

3. Jean Howard 1957 T-Bird, 116.204 mph. This was a full-bodied stock car with top installed. VIN unknown. Private entry.

(Sports Class B - Modified)

1. Danny Eames 1957 T-Bird, 160.356 mph. This was a highly-modified Lincoln-powered car VIN ending with 333. Prepared by DePaolo Engineering.

2. Fred Lavell 1954 Corvette, 130.800 mph. This was a modified car with a Cadillac V-8.

3. Art Chrisman 1957 Mercury, 115.200 mph. Car prepared by Bill Stroppe.

Standing Mile Acceleration "Sports Cars"

(Sports Class B - Modified)

1. Danny Eames 1957 T-Bird, 97.33 mph. This was a highly-modified Lincoln-powered car VIN ending with 333. Prepared by DePaolo Engineering.

2. Fred Lavell 1954 Corvette. This was a modified car with a Cadillac V-8.

Standing Mile Acceleration "Experimental Cars"

1. Danny Eames 1957 T-Bird, 98.065 mph. This was a highly-modified Lincoln-powered car VIN ending with 333. Prepared by DePaolo Engineering.

2. Art Chrisman 1957 Mercury, 93.065 mph. Car prepared by Bill Stroppe.

3. Chuck Daigh 1957 T-Bird, 93.312. This was a highly-modified (312-cid) Ford-powered car VIN ending with 266. Prepared by DePaolo Engineering.

4. Ray Sidwell 1932 Ford, 91.162 mph.

5. Harold Mauck 1957 Ford Ranchero, 91.162 mph.

The stock interior was removed. One lightweight seat was installed. (Jerry Capizzi photo)

Gil Baumgartner has also traced what happened to the famous Battlebirds. It seems that the two stock-bodied cars were easy to return to the street by simply removing the performance equipment. The bodies and interiors had not been modified. When Ford pulled out of racing after the AMA ban was issued, one of the stock cars was given to Chuck Daigh. He owned the car until 1969. It was purchased by a Texas collector car dealer who owns it today. The whereabouts of the other stock-bodied car is not currently known.

The highly modified cars could not be returned to stock condition, due to their extensive modifications. They were purchased from Ford Motor Company by Andy Hotten of Dearborn Steel Tubing and one of his friends. Hotten recently told Gil Baumgartner that he purchased both cars ("266" and "333"), as well as the truck and trailer that Ford used to haul them to races.

These cars were raced successfully in the Midwest and several pictures of the Battlebirds in action have surfaced. Most show them leading Corvettes to the finish line. the "333" car (with the Lincoln engine) was destroyed. The "266" car (with the Ford engine) came into the possession of Parnelli Jones, who owned it for several years. Gerald Popejoy purchased this car in 1975 and took it to Dallas, Texas. It was displayed at the 1978 Classic Thunderbird Club International convention in Dallas, in unrestored condition. Mr. Popejoy moved to Springfield, Mo. and the car remained in storage until 1992. He then advertised it for sale in *Hemmings Motor News*. Robert "Bo" Cheadle then purchased the car and had it restored by Gil Baumgartner.

After restoration, the car was first shown at the CTCI's 1994 convention in Dearborn, Mich. It then appeared at the 21st Annual Pageant of the Thunderbird in Lakewood, Calif. At that time Chuck Daigh and Danny Eames, who drove it at Daytona in 1957, got to see the Battlebird. It was also displayed during the Monterey Historic Races at Laguna Seca Raceway in August 1994.

To summarize, one of the highly modified Battlebirds remains and one of the record-breaking stock-bodied cars survives in the Dallas area. The second stock-bodied car (which would have been built between December 15 and December 31, 1956) may still exist. In addition, at least one replica Battlebird exists. It can be traced to a regular-production T-Bird that was originally registered in Sacramento, Calif. It became the property of an insurance company which legally sold its remains to a body shop named Classic Productions in Sacramento. The frame and remains of this car were purchased from the restoration shop by its current owner. These components, coupled with parts from other Thunderbirds, were used to construct the replica. However, only one documented car exists that can be visually and historically verified as authentic.

The instrument panel was replaced with a small instrument cluster. (Jerry Capizzi photo)

Gil Baumgartner has most recently discovered documentation that stock car builders Holman and Moody owned both modified cars ("266" and "333") at one time. They later sold the Lincoln-powered car to a United Airlines pilot. Baumgartner stresses, however, that one of the stock-bodied Battlebirds (with VIN ending in 265) is the only car that can be traced through all of its owners. "Our research files on these cars are growing daily," he says.

Seen here in its current restored form is a 1957 Thunderbird which was highly modified to run during the eighth annual Daytona Speed Week events in 1957. (Gil Baumgartner photo)

As you can guess, the existence of a factory racing kit and a NASCAR version of the "F" engine encouraged some people to race 1957 Thunderbirds. For the 1957 Daytona Speed Weeks, Danny Eames took his modified T-Bird to an acceleration mark of 97.933 mph. He did the Flying Mile at 160.356 mph. There was also a factory-sponsored racing effort featuring 1957 models known as the "Battlebirds." One of these cars has been restored and is featured separately in this book.

1957 Thunderbird Specifications

Wheelbase	102 in.	Engine Code C	90-degree OHV V-8
Curb Weight	3,372 lb.	Bore x stroke	3.75 x 3.30 in.
Overall Length	181.4 in.	Displacement	292 cid
Overall Width	71.in.	Compression Ratio	9.1:1
Height (top of door)	33.6 in.	Carburetor	Single 2-Barrel
Height (top of hardtop)	51.6 in.	Maximum BHP	212 @ 4500 rpm
Height (top of soft top)	51.8 in.	Maximum Torque	297 lb.-ft. @ 2700 rpm
Front Headroom (HT)	33.1 in.	Engine Code D	90-degree OHV V-8
Front Headroom (Conv.)	33.6 in.	Bore x stroke	3.80 x 3.44 in.
Front Hip Room	58.8 in.	Displacement	312 cid
Front Shoulder Room	53.3 in.	Compression Ratio	9.7:1
Front Leg Room	44.9 in	Carburetor	Single 4-Barrel
Top of Door Height	34.2 in.	Maximum BHP	245 @ 4500 rpm
Front Tread	56 in.	Maximum Torque	332 lb.-ft. @ 2300 rpm
Rear Tread	56 in.	Engine Code E	90-degree OHV V-8
Standard Axle (Man.)	3.56:1	Bore x stroke	3.80 x 3.44 in.
Standard Axle (OD)	3.70:1	Displacement	312 cid
Standard Axle (Auto.)	3.10:1	Compression Ratio	9.7:1
Tires	7.50 x 14	Carburetor	Dual 4-Barrel
Wheel Studs	5.5-in.	Maximum BHP	270 @ 4500 rpm
Wheel Stud Circle	4.5-in. diam.	Maximum Torque	336 lb.-ft. @ 3400 rpm
Wheels	14-in Safety Contour	Engine Code E (Racing)	90-degree OHV V-8
Turns lock-to-lock	3.4	Bore x stroke	3.80 x 3.44 in
Turning Diameter	36 ft.	Displacement	312 cid
Steering wheel	17 in. Lifeguard	Compression Ratio	9.7:1
Steering Ratio:	23.0:1	Carburetor	Dual 4-Barrel
Steering Wheel Adj.	2 in.	Maximum BHP	285 hp @ 5200 rpm
Gas tank	20 gal.	Maximum Torque	343 lb.-ft. @ 3500 rpm
Weight Distribution	50/50	Engine Code F	90-degree OHV V-8
Brake Swept Area	176 sq. in.	Bore x stroke	3.80 x 3.44 in.
Brakes	11 in.	Displacement	312 cid

1957 Thunderbird Specifications

LB/HP (245 hp.)	13.76	Compression Ratio	8.5:1
HP/CID (245 hp)	.788	Carburetor	4-Bbl; Supercharged
		Maximum BHP	300 @ 4800 rpm
		Max. BHP (NASCAR)	340 @ 5300 rpm

Notes: C-code engine is base Thunderbird V-8 with three-speed manual transmission only. D-code engine is optional Thunderbird Special V-8 with overdrive or Fordomatic. E-Code engine is optional Thunderbird Super V-8 with dual four-barrel Holley carburetors. Both the regular and racing kit versions came with all T-Bird trans. F-code engine is Thunderbird Special Supercharged V-8 with all transmissions. A 340-hp NASCAR version of this engine was also available for racing. Both came with all T-Bird transmissions. Other specifications based on standard engine, unless otherwise noted.

1957 Thunderbird Engineering

Chassis	X-frame
Front Suspension	Ball-joints; coil springs, tube shocks; and stabilizer.
Rear Suspension	Composite axle; 5-leaf springs, double-action shocks.
Steering	Parallel linkage type; three-inch in-and-out adj.
Front Brakes	11 in. diameter double-sealed
Brakes	11 in. diameter double-sealed

1957 Thunderbird Performance

Model	CID/HP	Performance
0-60 mph		
Two-seater	312/270	9.50 seconds
Two-seater	312/245	8.49 seconds
Two-seater	312/245	12.7 seconds
Two-seater	312/225	11.5 seconds
Top Speed		
Two-seater	312/245	116 mph

1958 - 1960
"Square Birds"

1958
Car of the Year

The two-passenger Thunderbird was outselling all of its direct competitors, but it had not reached the sales level that Ford originally envisioned. The market for two-place sports cars, which experienced a boom in the early '50s, was no longer booming. It had expanded to about its maximum limit, and the market saturation point was reached earlier than anyone expected. In addition, the T-Bird, being a "sporty" car rather than a true sports car, could never satisfy some of the enthusiasts who were firmly entrenched in that niche. At the level where it had "maxed out," the two-passenger T-Bird was not generating adequate profits.

A sales boost would increase profits and Ford came to the realization that a four-place Thunderbird was the answer to boosting sales. At first, product planner Tom Case wanted to continue offering the two-passenger model (with a new power top), while adding a four-passenger model. This was almost guaranteed to bring a sales increase. Of course, there was no similar guarantee that profits would go up. Robert S. McNamara, the new general manager of Ford Division, deemed this very unlikely to happen and firmly ordered Case to drop the two-car idea.

According to T-Bird designer William P. Boyer, who wrote the book *Thunderbird An Odyssey in Automotive Design*, McNamara had convinced himself that the four-passenger car was a good concept. "He fought with the board of directors to get it," Boyer recalled. "And he won the fight." McNamara (who later became U.S. Secretary of Defense) had projected that the four-passenger car would realize higher profits. His estimates were borne out when the Thunderbird became one of only two U.S. cars to increase sales in 1958. "Despite a late introduction and the fact that 1958 was a miserable flop as a year for selling cars, the '58 T-Bird sold 37,000 units and dealers ended up at changeover time with orders backlogged for 800 cars," is how *Hot Rod* magazine put it in July 1959. In addition, 67,000 four-seat T-Birds were made in 1959, and 90,000 more during 1960.

The idea of a two-passenger Ford did not totally disappear, although it never got approval until many years later when the EXP was introduced. In 1961, there was some talk of revamping the original T-Bird body dies to make a two-passenger sports-personal car. In mid-1964, this car came on the market as the Mustang. However, instead of being a two-seater, it was a four-passenger car with front bucket seats and a small rear bench seat. There were also several two-passenger Mustang prototypes, starting with the first one. In addition, the Thunderbird Sports Roadster, introduced in 1962, was an attempt to give a four-passenger car the image of a two-passenger job.

Five groups of "hash marks" on door projectiles identify the 1958 T-Birds in profile view. The Hardtop came out first. (Ford Motor Co. photo)

The basic shape of the grille and the hood scoop looked familiar, but new-for-1958 were quad headlights and larger body proportions. (Old Cars photo)

The four-passenger Thunderbird entered production on Jan. 13, 1958. It was scheduled to be built in a brand new factory in Wixom, Mich. alongside the 1958 Lincoln and Continental Mark III. Since everything from the design of the engine to the assembly plant was new, the Thunderbird Hardtop came out months after the regular 1958 Fords. According to *The Standard Catalog of Ford 1903-1990*, dealer introductions of the new model took place on Feb. 13, 1958. It was one of the most totally changed cars in history. In addition to being much larger, it featured unit-body construction and many technical innovations. Only a two-door Hardtop was offered at first. A Convertible became available in June 1958. It was first listed in a revised sales catalog issued in May 1958. This model had the first power-operated cloth top offered on a T-Bird. However, it was not fully automatic in its operation.

With a 113-in. wheelbase, the 1958 T-Bird had a stance 11 in. longer than the 1957 model. It was two feet longer (205.4 in. overall) than the last of the two-passenger T-Birds. Overall width was 77 in. Amazingly, the overall height of this much enlarged Thunderbird was only fractions of an inch more than the two-passenger model. It stood a mere 52.5 in. from the ground. The weight of the car jumped by about 1,000 lb. The front tread was increased to 60 in., while the rear tread was only modestly larger at 57 in. Size 8.00 x 14 tires were specified.

The car had a square "Ford" look. In fact, these cars are now called "Square Birds." Many angular, sculptured feature lines characterized the hood scoop, the "almost-gull-wing" front

A sculptured body and "Safety-Twin" taillights bowed in 1958. (Ford Motor Co. photo)

fenders, the body side "projectiles," and the twin "jet-pod" rear end styling. There were dual headlamps up front. Chrome Thunderbird scripts adorned the front fender sides. On top of the fenders were chrome bombsight ornaments. The integral bumper-grille had a "lemon-sucker" appearance. Two bumper guards were mounted on the lower part of the grille frame opening. The grille insert was made from a piece of stamped sheet metal with round holes punched into it in diagonal rows. Five cast ornaments with groups of chrome hash marks decorated the projectiles on the lower body sides.

There's a lot of Thunderbird **GO** in the way a FORD moves

This fresh-looking car is America's only production steel-top convertible, the Ford Skyliner. The fresh-looking car beyond it is the all-new, exclusive 4-passenger Ford Thunderbird.

For one thing, you get the Thunderbird's own power plant. *That* means velvet with a capital V-8! Valves are cushioned by oil ... each engine is balanced running under its own power for smoothest performance.

It also means GO with a capital "GEE"! No engine in Ford's price range delivers so much getaway push at the rear wheels. Thunderbird engines are the newest, most advanced V-8's going. And they're the biggest power plants in Ford's field! *Ford gives you something special in savings, too.* New, versatile, ever-so-smooth Cruise-O-Matic Drive saves up to 15% on gas when teamed with the T-bird V-8.

But there's *more!* Amazing new Magic-Circle steering gives the true and easy sports-car-like handling of the Thunderbird to all Fords. And they *look* like the Thunderbird with their classically graceful, trend-setting lines. Ask your Ford Dealer for an Action Test!

58 FORD

First car ever to use the whole world as a test track

"There's a lot of Thunderbird in every Ford," said this 1958 T-Bird advertisement featuring the all-new four-passenger Hardtop on the left. (Ford Motor Co.)

Each of the rectangular "pods" at the rear of the car held two large, round taillights. They were surrounded by small painted grilles with inserts that had the same texture as the large grille in front. Back-up lights were optional. Fixtures attached them to the outboard taillamps. The license plate mounted between the taillamp pods. Small tail fins graced the top of the rear fenders. These started ahead of the door handles, on the sides of the car, and canted slightly outwards. The center area of the deck lid had a wide depression. It carried a chrome Thunderbird emblem in the center at the rear, directly above the license plate.

A formal-looking roof characterized the Hardtop model. It had a very long and low appearance. In fact, it was so low that the car actually had a "sunken living room" inside. On the outside, the sail panels were trimmed with small round Thunderbird medallions. Horizontally-ribbed bright metal strips decorated the bottom edges of both roof pillars. The standard full wheel disks had turbine-fins with large flat centers. This was also the first T-Bird to have vent windows. It was clear that the new Thunderbird had more in common with the Lincoln products built alongside it at Wixom, than it did with other Fords. Luxury was stressed far more in this design than it had been in 1955-1957.

Approval to make the 1958 Thunderbird Convertible was delayed. It wasn't until May 1957 that the final go-ahead was given. Consequently, the Convertible did not bow until the middle of 1958. June is usually given as the month it made its debut, but as late as October *Speed Age* magazine featured red and blue 1958 ragtops on its cover, even though the 1959 cars were coming on the market. The Convertible was designed somewhat along the lines of Ford's Skyliner Retractable. Its fabric top required a fraction of the storage space needed by Ford's Retractable

The Thunderbird front fender script was moved further forward in 1958. (Ford Motor Co. photo)

Hardtop, but it still provided the convenience of a top that disappeared completely into the trunk. With the top lowered, no fabric was exposed and the T-Bird had a smooth, unbroken trunk line.

The top was operated by two hydraulic cylinders which derived pressure from an electrically-operated rotor pump. To stack the top, the operator had to release the header clamps, unsnap the eight fasteners located in the quarter window area (above the side rails), and unlatch the luggage compartment door. After the latches were released by forward pressure on the cylinder of the luggage compartment door latch lock, the operator had to release the door safety catch, and raise the door by hand. After the door had been raised upright, the upper back finish panel had to be raised, and locked, by means of a release knob plunger. (The panel had to be raised, and locked in position, to avoid damage when the lid was lowered with the top stacked.) The top could then be lowered by means of a safety switch located in the luggage compartment. After the top was stacked, the luggage compartment door had to be lowered by hand, and latched by putting pressure on the door, near the latches. This procedure was reversed to raise the top.

Inside, the T-Bird was also totally redesigned. It was the first American car to come with bucket seats and a "panel console" as standard equipment. As mentioned above, to keep the overall height of the car as low as possible the passenger compartment was a deeper-than-usual well. The transmission/drive shaft tunnel was very high. The full-length console was placed on top of it to make it functional. Incorporated into the

The four-passenger Thunderbird Convertible bowed in the middle of 1958, a fact that held its production down. (Old Cars photo)

console were controls for the heater and air conditioner (if ordered), power window switches, a radio speaker, and front and rear ash trays. Only four people could be accommodated inside the car, and each had an almost separate "cubicle." The rear seat was a bench, but it was upholstered to give a bucket seat look. The dashboard had "twin pods" for driver and passenger. This enhanced the aeronautical feeling of the entire interior package. There was a deep-dish steering wheel, safety-padded instrument panel, and padded sun visors, plus a service-tray glove box door. Molded door and side panels were also new. Overall, the interior design was very attractive.

1958 Thunderbird Interiors

Seat Type All-Vinyl	Material	Blue/ White	Green/ White	Red White	Black/ White	Tan/ White
Bucket Seats	All-Vinyl	XE	XF	XG	XH	XL
Bucket Seats	All-Vinyl	XM				

Seat Type Cloth & Vinyl	Material	Blue/ Blue	Green/ Green	Black/ Black		
Bucket Seats	Cloth & Vinyl	XA	XB	XC		
Bucket Seats	Cloth & Vinyl	XK				

Convertible tops came in Black vinyl with gray headlining (code 1); Light Blue vinyl with blue headlining (code 4); Light Green vinyl green headlining (code 5); White vinyl with gray headlining (code 6); White vinyl with blue headlining (code 7); White vinyl with green headlining (code 8); and White vinyl with buff headlining (code 9).

Powering the 1958 Thunderbird was a new 352-cid "Interceptor" V-8. "Packing a 300-horsepower punch, this engine has many advanced design features that provide flashing sports car performance and response," said Ford's promotional copy. It could be had with three-speed manual, overdrive or automatic transmissions. Even the latter, called Cruise-O-Matic, was all-new. Optional power plants had been considered for the 1958 Thunderbird, since the long list of engines offered in 1957 had helped to sell cars. One plan was to use the 361-cid Edsel V-8 with a choice of four horsepower ratings. However, the total budget for styling, engineering and tooling work was only $50 million. After tooling costs absorbed 90 percent of the money, the plan was changed to one offering only one or two engines. Whether it was one or two, for 1958, no one seems to know for sure.

The March 1958 Thunderbird sales catalog, plus several magazine ads, all mention availability of a 430-cid 375-hp engine. This was a Lincoln V-8 used only with Cruise-O-Matic (Lincoln called it Turbo-Drive) transmission. *Motor Trend* tested a prototype Thunderbird with this engine and shaved about two seconds off normal 0-60 times. However, there is no confirmation that any 1958 production cars were actually built with this engine. This would hardly be impossible, though. As I found out when researching my book *55 Years of Mercury*, Ford installed some very limited-production performance engines to sell extra cars during the 1958 auto sales slump.

An angle-poised ball-joint front suspension, double-acting shock absorbers, and 11-in. duo servo brakes were chassis features of the 1958 model. It was the only Thunderbird to have a coil spring rear suspension prior to 1967. This happened because designers anticipated using the "Ford Aire" system, an early type of air suspension, in the T-Bird. When it proved unreliable in the Fords that bowed in the fall, the idea of using it for the T-Bird was dropped. Ford was stuck with the coil springs for 1958. However, the T-Bird went back to leaf springs in 1959.

T-Bird Convertible is on left in this 1958 Ford ad promoting Ford, Edsel and Lincoln ragtops. (Ford Motor Co.)

With its 113-in. wheelbase and 3,708-lb. shipping weight, the 1958 Thunderbird was only 511 lb. heavier than a V-8-powered Ford Custom Tudor. In addition, it lacked the Ford's ladder frame and rode a three inch shorter wheelbase. Gutted of its console and other goodies, the T-Bird held promise as a stock racing car. This wasn't lost on the NASCAR crowd. Some car builders wanted to start constructing competition versions of the four-seater right away. In fact, this may well have been envisioned by the Ford product planners who wrote the 430-cid V-8 into the sales catalog. As things turned out, the "Square-Bird" would go stock car racing, but not in 1958.

Motor Trend magazine picked the 1958 Thunderbird to win its "Car of the Year" award.

1958 Thunderbird Specifications

Wheelbase	113 in.	Standard Engine Type	90-degree OHV V-8
Curb Weight (Hardtop)	3,708 lb.	Bore x stroke	4.00 x 3.50 in.
Curb Weight (Conv.)	3,903 lb.	Displacement	352 cid
Overall Length	205.4 in.	Compression Ratio	10.2:1
Overall Width	77.0 in.	Carburetor	Single 4-Barrel
Overall Height (HT)	52.5 in.	Maximum BHP	300 @ 4400 rpm
Overall Height (Conv.)	53.1 in.	Maximum Torque	381 lb.-ft. @ 2800 rpm
Front Tread	60 in.	Exhaust System	Dual Exhausts
Front Tread	57 in.	Standard Axle (Auto.)	3.10:1
Tires	8.00 x 14 4-ply	Standard Axle (Man.)	3.70:1
Turning Diameter	39 ft.	Standard Axle (OD)	3.70:1
Steering Ratio:	25.0:1	Brake Swept Area	194 sq. in.

1958 Thunderbird Engineering

Chassis	Welded, integral body and frame.
Front Suspension	Ball-joints; coil springs, tube shocks; stabilizer.
Rear Suspension	Trailing arm type with coil springs, rubber-mounted pivots and double-action shocks.
Steering	Recirculating ball type gear.
Front Brakes	11 in. diameter double-sealed; ceramic linings.
Brakes	11 in. diameter double-sealed; ceramic linings.

1958 Thunderbird Performance

Model	CID/HP	Performance
0-60 mph		
Hardtop	352/300	12.9 seconds
1/4-Mile		
Hardtop	352/300	17.6 seconds

1959
Days of Thunder

On Oct. 17, 1958, Ford dealers across the country unveiled the company's 1959 models. Anyone anxiously awaiting the latest Thunderbird may have been disappointed on two counts. First, the T-Bird was not introduced until 10 days later. Second, it had very little in the way of changes from 1958. As *Motor Trend* said in its January 1958 preview of the car, "The Thunderbird's success in 1958 apparently convinced Ford there was no reason for radical changes in a basically sound, fast-selling product. '59 models show only refinements, styling touches." This viewpoint turned out to be on target, as Ford produced 57,195 Thunderbird Hardtops and 10,261 Convertibles during model-year 1959.

A new horizontal louver pattern in the Thunderbird's "air scoop" grille was among modest revisions seen for 1959. The same pattern was repeated in the recessed taillight

"America's Most Becoming Car!" *was the slogan used to promote the 1959 T-Bird as a stylish and fashionable automobile. (Ford Motor Co.)*

panels. Instead of hash marks on the body side projectile, the 1959 T-Bird had a chrome "arrow tip" at the front of the bulge. The chrome Thunderbird nameplates were moved from the front fender to the doors, where they decorated the projectiles. In addition, the round medallion seen on the rear window pillar of the 1958 Hardtop was replaced by a sculptured Thunderbird medallion.

Offered again was a pair of two-door, four-passenger models. The Convertible's top was power operated and folded down into the trunk. Then the rear deck panel hid it completely. All dimensional specifications were unchanged.

Specifications for the base 352-cid V-8 reflected a drop in compression, but some significant improvements to the ignition system. The "advertised" horsepower rating of the engine was unchanged, even though it had a lower compression ratio. According to *Hot Rod* magazine's technical editor Ray Brock, a dynamometer test of the 1958 engine at Edelbrock Equipment Co. had revealed it delivered "just a little better than 200 actual horsepower with no correction for temperature, barometric pressure or humidity." However, Edelbrock discovered that small changes in ignition advance gave the test engine about 225 hp. "Assuming that Ford's '59 ignitions have a better advance curve, the 352 engine should produce an honest 225 hp, which is ample for the average driver," Brock said. The 352-cid engine also switched to a new Holley model 9510 four-barrel carburetor.

This year the 430-cid Thunderbird Special V-8 was definitely available. This engine was sourced from Lincoln. It had the largest displacement in the industry at the time and came only with SelectShift Cruise-O-Matic transmission. "The Lincoln engine does not have a conventional combustion chamber in the head as does the 352 Ford engine," Ray Brock explained, to emphasize the motor's performance abilities. "Instead, the valves seat on a flat head surface and the chamber is formed between the tops of the pistons and the top of the block which is milled 10 degrees from perpendicular to the cylinder bore." Brock also noted that Bill Stroppe, who modified Lincolns for the Mexican Road Races in the early 1950s, had a triple carburetor setup for the 430-cid motor on the market. Dual exhausts were also standard with both Thunderbird power plants again. They also came with fuel filters and oil filters, which were optional on most other 1959 cars.

The projectile on the door of 1959 models had a chrome tip in place of "hash mark" louvers. The 1959 Convertible was available all year. (Ford Motor Co.)

Other technical revisions in T-Birds included a new radiator fan, a new auxiliary coolant tank, a relocated windshield washer system, and improved rear suspension. Ford also advertised features like the Angle-Poised ball-joint front suspension, four-foot wide doors, 20 cu. ft. of trunk space, Lifeguard design deep-center steering wheel (with a horn ring), and individually adjustable front seats.

The T-Bird's bucket seats had a kind of rounded and overstuffed look. Ford promoted them as "individually contoured seats with up to four inches of foam rubber in the cushions and backs." Buyers had a choice between deep-pleated all-vinyl upholstery or linen seat inserts with vinyl bolsters. The front passenger seat was of full-folding design to permit entry into the rear from the curb side of the car. The instruments and gauges had white faces, instead of black ones.

"America's most becoming car"
(and it's just right for you...in every way!)

Women buyers were targeted in this 1959 T-Bird advertisement. (Ford Motor Co.)

1959 Thunderbird All-Vinyl Interiors

Seat Type	Material	Blue/ Blue	Green/ White	Turq./ White	Black/ White	Red/ White
Bucket Seats	Vinyl	5X	6X	7X	8X	9X

1959 Thunderbird Cloth & Vinyl Interiors

Seat Type	Material	Blue/ Blue	Green/ Green	Turq./ Turq.	Black/ White
Bucket Seats	Cloth & Vinyl	1X	2X	3X	4X

1959 Thunderbird Leather Interiors

Seat Type	Material	Black	Tan	Turquoise	Red	Tan/ White
Bucket Seats	Leather	1Y	2Y	3Y	4Y	5Y

Legend: Turq. means Turquoise.

Ford continued using the sporty T-Bird to help sell its other cars. (Ford Motor Co.)

Convertible tops came in Black rayon with black headlining (code 1); Blue vinyl with blue headlining (code 4); Turquoise vinyl with turquoise headlining (code 5); White vinyl with black headlining (code 6); White vinyl with turquoise headlining (code 7); White vinyl with blue headlining (code 8); and White vinyl with buff headlining (code 9).

Ford listed the 1959 Hardtop for $3,696. The Convertible was $3,979. Both body styles came in 18 solid "Diamond Lustre" acrylic colors, only three of which were shared with other Fords. Many T-Bird colors were the same ones used on the Lincolns being manufactured in the same assembly plant, although the T-Bird colors usually had distinct names. There were 41 two-tone color combinations available for Hardtops. Several were combinations using the same colors in reverse. For instance, you could have the body in Brandywine Red with a Colonial White Top, or you could have a Colonial White Body with Brandywine Red top. Convertible tops came in seven colors, each with specific color headlining, and each used with specific body colors.

The T-Bird's unit-constructed body had the floor pan, frame, body side panels, front and rear fenders, roof panel, and cross braces all welded together into one durable unit of double-walled sculptured steel. The 1958-only coil spring rear suspension was replaced by a leaf spring setup. There were longitudinal springs on either side. *Motor Trend* referred to this as an "improved suspension" and said that it gave a more evenly balanced ride and slightly less lean in the corners.

Hot Rod magazine did a test of the 430-cid Thunderbird in its July 1959 issue. This started out with a rundown of all the changes between the two-seat and four-seat Thunderbirds. Ray Brock found that the car was not fast getting off the mark, requiring 3.9 seconds to reach 30 mph. "In the quarter-mile, slow takeoffs naturally keep the Bird

On the side of the 1959 Hardtop's roof, where a round emblem appeared in 1958, was a small, bird-shaped bright metal insignia. (Old Cars photo)

from setting any strip records," he wrote. "But once the car got to 75 mph, it seemed to take a new lease on life." The car averaged 14.4 mpg for a 600-mile test in a combination of heavy traffic, freeway driving and mountain climbing. However, in a cross-country economy test, another 430-equipped T-Bird registered 19.2 mpg. The magazine found the 352-cid and 430-cid T-Birds comparable for average driving. The bigger motor had better throttle response, but the difference was not as dramatic as might be expected. Overall the test was positive with the main complaint being a suggestion to move the driver's seat back from the dashboard.

The horizontal bars texture of the 1959 radiator grille was carried through to the taillight housings at the rear. (Old Cars photo)

While the addition of the larger V-8 did not seem to affect the average driver very much, it did have a big influence on the Thunderbird's role in professional motorsports. All of Ford's ladder-frame family-cars used a larger 118-in. wheelbase in 1959. This increased their weight by around 300 lb., making them less attractive for stock car racing. On the other hand, the unit-body Thunderbird gained only about 100 lb. This fact, combined with the release of the big engine, immediately enhanced its race car potential. Ford formed an association with Holman & Moody, a company that built stock cars, for the construction of several very hot 1959 T-Bird stockers.

The Holman & Moody T-Birds made their racing debut in Florida, in the inaugural stock car race at the new 2.5-mile International Speedway in Daytona Beach in February. "Conjecture at the beginning of the grueling 500-mile main event had

Standard engine in 1959 was a 352-cid V-8 with 300 hp. Available at extra-cost was a 430-cid Lincoln V-8 with 350 hp. (Old Cars photo)

favored two sets of cars, either Pontiac/T-Bird or T-Bird/Chevrolet as certain winners," said *Motor Trend* (May 1959). "Reasoning for this was compounded of three main factors: Performances in qualifying trials; ability of crew mechanics in preparing the cars; and last, but certainly not least, driver ability."

To *Motor Trend's* surprise, an Oldsmobile driven by Lee Petty won the race. T-Bird driver Johnny Beauchamp, of Harlan, Iowa was even more surprised. He had already been named the unofficial winner and had been greeted in victory lane by Scotie McCormick, who was "Miss Daytona Speedway" for the race. Three cars — Beauchamp's number 73 T-Bird on the inside, Petty's number 42 Olds in the middle, and Joe Weatherly's number 48 Chevrolet on the outside — had crossed the finish line "neck-and-neck." Weatherly was one lap down at the time, and Beauchamp and Petty were the leaders. When photos of the finish were reviewed by NASCAR officials, the camera showed that Petty had crossed the line first. His 1959 Olds, which had started in 15th position, won the 500-Mile Sweepstakes (as it was then known) in three hours and 41 minutes with an average speed of 135.521 mph. Beauchamp, who had started in 21st position, was credited with second place.

New Diamond-Lustre finishes in 18 single colors were offered in 1959. There were 41 two-tone options. (Cappy Collection)

Fabric tops for the 1959 T-Bird Convertible were available in seven different hues which were color-coordinated with the paint and trim options. (Cappy Collection)

Only 10,261 T-Bird Convertibles were built in 1959, but that was on top of 57,195 Hardtops, which together added up to an excellent year. (Cappy Collection)

T-Birds also held positions eight, nine, and 13. Those cars were driven by Tom Pristone of Chicago (196 laps), Tim Flock of Atlanta (195 laps), and Curtis Turner of Charlotte (189 laps). In addition, a 1959 Thunderbird piloted by Eduardo Dibos of Lima, Peru finished 44 laps and one driven by Fred Wilson, of Denver, left the race at 15 laps. An interesting thing about these statistics is that NASCAR considered Thunderbird a separate marque, instead of a Ford model. Therefore, the early T-Bird racing stats are not counted when NASCAR totals Ford wins over the years.

The program for the Daytona Speed Weeks events held Jan. 30-Feb. 14, 1960 was loaded with photos of 1959 T-Birds in racing action, or parked in the winner's circle. Several advertisements in the guide-book, such as the one for Grey-Rock brake linings, also featured the speedy Thunderbirds that competed in the inaugural event. In another ad, AMT model company suggested "Build your own Daytona Beach stock car racer ..." and offered a choice of 10 special AMT 3 in 1 Daytona Beach Race Car Kits for only $1.39 or $1.49 each. The 1960 Thunderbird model was one of the three higher-priced kits, along with the Buick and Corvette of the same year. Like the full-size racers, the model carried decals on its body for the hot 350-hp Thunderbird V-8.

1959 T-Bird Racing

NASCAR GRAND NATIONAL DIVISION Top 3 Car Point Standings for 1959 Season

Make of Car	Pts.	Entries	Avg.	1	2	3	4	5	6	7	8	9	10	Total
Chevrolet	1041	449	.273	14	19	14	22	22	19	28	22	20	21	201
Ford	490	270	.181	8	7	10	7	5	16	7	15	11	14	100
Thunderbird	342	86	.398	6	10	7	6	9	4	1	3	3	1	50

NASCAR CONVERTIBLE DIVISION Top 3 Car Point Standings for 1959 Season

Make of Car	Pts.	Entries	Avg.	1	2	3	4	5	6	7	8	9	10	Total
Chevrolet	666	286	.233	9	14	14	11	15	11	12	11	12	14	123
Ford	312	132	.236	5	6	3	6	5	7	9	7	7	5	60
Thunderbird	115	28	.411	5	2	2	2	2	-	-	1	1		15

NASCAR SHORT TRACK DIVISION Top 3 Car Point Standings for 1959 Season

Make of Car	Pts.	Entries	Avg.	1	2	3	4	5	6	7	8	9	10	Total
Ford	259	68	.381	7	6	8	2	2	3	3	4	2	2	39
Chevrolet	198	84	.236	1	4	1	5	6	4	7	3	5	6	42
Thunderbird	34	5	.680	2	-	1	-	-	1	-	-	1		5

1959 THUNDERBIRD RECORDS IN NASCAR

GRAND NATIONAL SWEEPSTAKES

Distance	Driver	Year of Car	Speed MPH	Date
275	Johnny Beauchamp	1959 T-Bird	136.160	2/22/59
400	Johnny Beauchamp	1959 T-Bird	135.75	2/22/59
475	Johnny Beauchamp	1959 T-Bird	135.34	2/22/59

CONVERTIBLE

Distance	Driver	Year of Car	Speed MPH	Date
5	Bob Burdick	1959 T-Bird	140.911	7/2/59

CONVERTIBLE SWEEPSTAKES

Distance	Driver	Year of Car	Speed MPH	Date
25	Joe Weatherly	1959 T-Bird	144.000	7/4/59
50	Joe Weatherly	1959 T-Bird	143.769	7/4/59
75	Joe Weatherly	1959 T-Bird	143.236	7/4/59
100	Joe Weatherly	1959 T-Bird	142.857	7/4/59
125	Joe Weatherly	1959 T-Bird	139.534	7/4/59
150	Joe Weatherly	1959 T-Bird	139.787	7/4/59
175	Joe Weatherly	1959 T-Bird	139.937	7/4/59
200	Joe Weatherly	1959 T-Bird	140.105	7/4/59
225	Joe Weatherly	1959 T-Bird	139.079	7/4/59
250	Joe Weatherly	1959 T-Bird	139.340	7/4/59

SEASON RECORDS

1-lap Convertible Qualifying: 140.911 mph. Set by Bob Burdick of Omaha, Nebraska driving a 1959 Thunderbird convertible on July 2, 1959.

1959 Ford Thunderbird
NASCAR Grand National Race Car

By Billy Cooper

At the request of Ford Motor Company, Holman & Moody, of Charlotte, N.C., built eight Thunderbirds for the late model stock car races at the new 2-1/2-mile Daytona International Speedway Feb. 20-22, 1959. Only one of these cars survives today. Completely restored, it is currently on display at Klassix Auto Museum in Daytona Beach, Fla. (904) 252-3800.

After completion by Holman & Moody, these cars were sold to the public. In race ready form, the cars went for $5,500. They were fitted with 430-cid Lincoln V-8s rated for 350 hp. Other modification included heavy-duty springs and shocks, heavy-duty spindles, special wheels, beefier brakes, a sheet metal firewall, a 22-gal. gas tank, and a complete roll cage. Otherwise, the T-Birds were essentially stock.

The surviving car wore number 64 at Daytona. It was purchased by "Fritz" Wilson, a rookie NASCAR driver who hailed from Denver, Col. In a 100-mile preliminary event held on Feb. 20, Wilson continuously pressed Bob Welborn for the lead from start to finish. He fell short by three feet, at the end, with Welborn's 1959 Chevrolet (car No. 49) winning. Both drivers finished all 40 laps. Wilson's qualifying speed of 140.449 mph was actually faster than Welborn's 140.121 mph. Wilson's No. 64 led on laps 8-12, 24-26 and 28.

Two days later, in the first Daytona 500, Wilson started third in No. 64. He completed 15 laps before burning a piston and dropping out. He was eventually awarded 56th position out of 59 starters. His Thunderbird was not credited with the lead in any full lap, although it's said he was in the lead at several times.

Wilson entered three more events between February and May 1959. He finished 14th in the Darlington Rebel 300 on May 9 and suffered mechanical failures in the two other races. Other pilots of the No. 64 Thunderbird included Cotton Owens (second place finisher in 1959 point standings who dubbed it the "Thunder-Chick"), Herb Shannon (one race), Larry Frank (two races), Jimmy Thompson (four races), and Doug Cox (five races). The last Grand National race for the car was on June 8, 1961 at Greenville, S.C. It ended with a crash on lap 27. The car ran a total of 25 Grand National events with two wins, five top-five finishes, 15 top-20 finishes and 12 DNFs.

A restored original photo of "Fritz" Wilson's No. 64 Thunderbird "zipper" car. Car was sponsored by Bill Tuthill's Museum of Speed on U.S. 1 in South Daytona, which was known as "Home of the Fabulous Bluebird" in 1959. Today it is exhibited at Klassix Auto Museum, in Daytona Beach. (All photos courtesy Billy Cooper)

Racing Record "Fritz" Wilson Thunderbird

1959

Track/Event	Start. Date	Finish Pos.	Car Pos.	No.	Driver	Owner	Reason Out
Daytona 100	2/20	15	02	64	Fritz Wilson	Fritz Wilson	Running
Daytona 500	2/22	03	56	64	Fritz Wilson	Fritz Wilson	Burned Piston
Atlanta, GA.	3/22	02	01	73	J. Beauchamp	Fritz Wilson	Running
Martinsville 250	5/03	22	28	14	Fritz Wilson	Fritz Wilson	Fuel Pump
Darlington 300	5/09	11	24	14	Fritz Wilson	Fritz Wilson	Running
Columbia 100	5/16	30	14	14	Fritz Wilson	Fritz Wilson	Engine
Daytona 250	7/04	21	08	6	C. Owens	W.H. Watson	Running
Weaverville 250	8/16	19	07	6	C. Owens	W.H. Watson	Running
Darlington 500	9/07	19	19	6	C. Owens	C. Owens	Running
Richmond 100	9/13	01	01	6	C. Owens	C. Owens	Running
Hillsboro 99	9/20	04	02	6	C. Owens	C. Owens	Running
Martinsville 250	9/27	10	33	6	C. Owens	C. Owens	Diff.
Weaverville 100	10/11	07	11	6	C. Owens	C. Owens	Running
Concord 150	10/25	02	28	6	C. Owens	C. Owens	R. Hose

Note: Cotton Owens finished second in 1959 point standings with 9,962 points and one win, 13 top-5 finishes, and 22 top-10 finishes.

1960

Track/Event	Start. Date	Finish Pos.	Car Pos.	No.	Driver	Owner	Reason Out
Atlanta 300	7/31	44	24	55	H. Shannon	Doug Cox	Running
Hillsboro 99	9/18	05	18	76	Larry Frank	Doug Cox	Heating
N. Wilkesboro	10/02	13	22	76	Larry Frank	Doug Cox	Diff.
Charlotte 400	10/16	26	33	76	J. Thompson	Doug Cox	Engine
Atlanta 500	10/30	21	17	55	J. Thompson	Doug Cox	Running
Jacksonville 100	11/20	07	17	55	J. Thompson	Doug Cox	Engine

1961

Track/Event	Start. Date	Finish Pos.	Car Pos.	No.	Driver	Owner	Reason Out
Greenville 100	4/01	21	12	30	Doug Cox	L. Hunter	Running
Columbia 100	4/20	21	17	30	Doug Cox	L. Hunter	Axle
Darlington 300	5/06	24	26	55	J. Thompson	Doug Cox	Wreck
Charlotte 600	5/28	51	54	51	Doug Cox	Doug Cox	Engine
Spartanburg 100	6/02	09	13	51	Doug Cox	Doug Cox	Engine
Greenville 100	6/08	13	21	51	Doug Cox	Doug Cox	Crash

Totals

Grand National Races Entered:	25
Wins	02
Top-five finishes	05
Top-20 finishes	15
Did Not Finish (DNF)	12

Before its restoration, the car sat in a back yard for nearly 20 years.

From late 1961 until late 1964, this car bounced around many "outlaw" tracks. It raced on numerous short tracks, both paved and dirt. It was then purchased from Lester Hunter by Carroll Twilley and used mainly for racing on the newly-paved 1/2-mile dirt track in Augusta, Ga. Marion Bell drove it in many events at Augusta and around the southeast. There are no available records of these races.

The car was retired from racing activity in late 1965. It sat, unused, until 1967. Then a local businessman built a 1/4-mile clay track in the small town of North, S.C. This was part of a reviving interest in local racing circles. Mr. Twilley let James Hall have the old T-Bird and he proceeded to build an engine, round up a few needed parts, and put some life back into the car. Marion Bell wheeled around the new tack behind the wheel of the car he had driven at Augusta. It finished fairly well considering that it ran on paved track tires and handled rather poorly because of this. When Bell became ill, Hall took over the driving for the races at the end of the season. He improved the car's handling and won the last two or three events. Then the track closed, after only one season, due to ecomonic problems.

The Thunderbird was parked again, until 1969, when racing fever revived interest in it. Donnie Johnson—who was anxious to drive—persuaded Hall to enter it in a race at Newberry, S.C. After that, it was run at Thunder Valley Speedway in Leesville, S.C. in a couple of events. Then the engine was over-revved and blew up. This led to the car's permanent retirement from motorsports. It sat in Hall's back yard for more than 20 years. In 1989, Billy Cooper & Associates of Barnwell, S.C. obtained the car in exchange for a complete restoration. It is now in like-new condition and on display at Klassix Auto Museum.

A billboard advertising Klassix Auto Museum shows the T-Bird.

The car occasionally makes public appearances at shows and races.

It's hard to believe it's the same car on display at the auto museum in Datona Beach.

A mannequin pit crew attends to the historic race car, which is the only one of the eight to survive.

THUNDERBIRDS IN 1959 NASCAR RACES

FIRST ANNUAL DAYTONA 500 MILE SWEEPSTAKES FEB. 1959

Position	Car Number	Driver	Car
2	73	Johnny Beauchamp, Harlan, Iowa	1959 T-Bird
8	59	Tom Pristone, Chicago, Ill.	1959 T-Bird
9	15	Tim Flock, Atlanta, Ga.	1959 T-Bird
13	41	Curtis Turner, Charlotte, N.C.	1959 T-Bird
48	37	Eduardo Dibos, Lima, Peru	1959 T-Bird
56	64	Fred Wilson, Denver, Colo.,	1959 T-Bird

100-MILE GRAND NATIONAL AT DAYTONA FEB. 1959

Position	Car Number	Driver	Car
2	64	Fred Wilson, Denver, Colo.,	1959 T-Bird
3	59	Tom Pristone, Chicago, Ill.	1959 T-Bird
5	37	Eduardo Dibos, Lima, Peru	1959 T-Bird
11	73	Johnny Beauchamp, Harlan, Iowa	1959 T-Bird
24	15	Tim Flock, Atlanta, Ga.	1959 T-Bird
29	41	Curtis Turner, Charlotte, N.C.	1959 T-Bird

25-MILE LATE-MODEL CONSOLATION FEB. 1959

Position	Car Number	Driver	Car
2	41	Curtis Turner, Charlotte, N.C.	1959 T-Bird
3	15	Tim Flock, Atlanta, Ga.	1959 T-Bird

1959 Thunderbird Specifications

Wheelbase	113 in.	Standard Engine Type	90-degree OHV V-8
Curb Weight (Hardtop)	3,971 lb.	Bore x stroke	4.00 x 3.50 in.
Curb Weight (Conv.)	4,061 lb.	Displacement	352 cid
Overall Length	205.4 in.	Compression Ratio	9.6:1
Overall Width	77.0 in.	Carburetor	Holley 4-Barrel #9510
Overall Height (HT)	52.5 in.	Maximum BHP	300 @ 4400 rpm
Overall Height (Conv.)	53.1 in.	Maximum Torque	381 lb.-ft. @ 2800 rpm
Front Tread	60 in.	Exhaust System	Dual Exhausts
Front Tread	57 in.	Optional Engine Type	90-degree OHV V-
Tires	8.00 x 14	Bore x stroke	4.30 x 3.70 in.
Turning Diameter	40 ft.	Displacement	430 cid
Steering Ratio:	25.0:1	Compression Ratio	10.0:1
Std. Axle (352/Auto.)	3.10:1	Carburetor	Holley 4-Barrel
Standard Axle (Man.)	3.70:1	Maximum BHP	350 @ 4400 rpm
Std. Axle (430/Auto.)	2.91:1	Maximum Torque	490 lb.-ft. @ 2800 rpm
Brake Swept Area	194 sq. in.	Ground Clearance	5.8 in.

1959 Thunderbird Engineering

Chassis	Welded, integral body and frame.
Front Suspension	Ball-joints; coil springs, tube shocks; stabilizer.
Rear Suspension	Outboard mounted rear leaf springs, tension-type shackles and wind-up control rubber bumpers over springs. Double acting shocks.
Steering	Recirculating ball type gear.
Front Brakes	11 in. diameter double-sealed; ceramic linings.
Brakes	11 in. diameter double-sealed; ceramic linings.

1959 Thunderbird Performance

Model	CID/HP	Performance
0-60 mph		
Hardtop	430/350	9 seconds
1/4-Mile		
Hardtop	430/350	17.0 seconds @ 86.57 mph

1960
A Last Backwards Look

It was the third year of the "Square-Bird" styling cycle and again only modest changes were made. There was a new grille with a large, horizontal main bar intersected by three vertical bars. Behind the bars was a grid pattern insert. Body side decorations returned to a hash mark motif. This year there was a trio of decorations, each consisting of three large vertical bars, on the rear fenders. They were positioned towards the rear, just ahead of new triple round taillight clusters. On Hardtops, the rear roof pillars had an elongated Thunderbird emblem in their center. There was also a winged badge on the trunk, just above the license plate. The lower body side projectiles no longer had chrome arrow tips. Instead they carried chrome Thunderbird scripts. An outside rear view mirror was now standard equipment. Several new exterior finishes were offered for the 1960 model. There were 19 single color choices and 28 two-tones in all.

The grille insert for 1960 T-Birds was of a square mesh design with three vertical bars and one horizontal bar added. (Cappy Collection)

Surrounding the taillights was the same mesh used in the grille. Continental kits were still available as a factory accessory. (Cappy Collection)

The new grille design gave the 1960 T-Birds a "toothy" appearance. These are the most popular of the "Squarebird" models. (Cappy Collection)

In a sense, the 1960 fit and finish changes were part of a cleanup effort. Some say they made the car look a little less glittery and a bit less cluttered. Personally, I like all three and really can't detect any difference in "flavor," although some of the paint colors are definitely more up to date. "Uncle" Tom McCahill, the famous automotive scribe, said that the Thunderbird made him picture a well-off "club woman" arriving at a fancy piano concert in a Duesenberg. "For many people, owning a new T-Bird is a last backwards look at their fleeting youth," he wrote. "And if they get a bounce out of it, I'm all for it."

Nineteen solid colors were offered in 1960 and 56 two-tones (28 color teams in reversible combos). Convertible tops came in three hues. (Cappy Collection)

Listing for $3,755, the 1960 Thunderbird Hardtop was a strong seller. It had 78,477 deliveries. The Convertible tickled the fancies of 11,860 additional buyers who were willing to spend $4,222 to own an open car. Speaking of open cars, a new option for the Hardtop was a roof that opened up. It had a manually-operated sliding sunroof. A large, circular chrome fixture inside the car locked the sliding panel in place. This was not the first American car to have a sunroof. GM had an optional "Sunshine Top" for higher-priced models in the early 1940s. However, the T-Bird's sunroof was a first for postwar U.S. production cars. It showed up in several clever Thunderbird advertisements, but only 2,536 buyers were motivated to order this model. It was listed as the "Golde Top" model in production figures obtained from Ford by Thunderbird expert Martin Brugmans (see "The Search for "Gold": Myth or Fact?" elsewhere in this book). Records extensively researched by automotive historian Jerry Heasley showed a total of 92,873 Thunderbirds built. This varies from the 92,843 shown in *Ward's 1961 Automotive Yearbook* by 30 units. Some sources list 80,938 Hardtops (which seems slightly off) and 11,860 Convertibles (which agrees with Heasley's extensive research).

Inside the 1960 Thunderbird were the same sort of dual-pod dash, front bucket seats, and panel console as before. There were several new upholstery options. One two-tone design had large squares stitched into the seat inserts and upper door panels. Another choice had lengthwise pleating on the seats, vertical pleats on the upper door panels, and monochromatic color schemes. The rear seats had built-in arm rests. Also new was a polarized day/night inside rear view mirror.

1960 Thunderbird All-Vinyl Interiors

Seat Type	Material	Med. Blue	Med. Green	White	Red	Black	Turquoise
Bucket Seats	Vinyl	52	53	54	55	56	57

1960 Thunderbird Cloth & Vinyl Interiors

Seat Type	Material	2-Tone Blue	2-Tone Green	2-Tone Beige	Black/ M. Gray	Med. Turq.	Turquoise
Bucket Seats	Cloth & Vinyl	72	73	74	75	76	77

1960 Thunderbird Leather Interiors

Seat Type	Material	2-Tone Blue	2-Tone Green	2-Tone Beige	Black/ M. Gray	Med. Turq.	Turquoise
Bucket Seats	Leather	82		84	85	86	87

Legend: Med. or M. mean Medium. Turq. means Turquoise.

The 1960 door projectile carried a Thunderbird script. Three groups of triple large "hash marks" decorated the rear fenders. (Ford Motor Co.)

Same color two tones use light shade of indicated color over medium shade of same color. Vinyl convertible tops came in Black (except with trims 52 and 72); White (with all trims); and Blue (with trims 52 and 72 only). All convertible tops had a black headlining.

Once again, there were two engines. Power choices started with the 352-cid Thunderbird Special V-8 rated at 300 hp. For less than $200, high-performance buffs could get the 350-hp Thunderbird 430 Special V-8 that they saw winning so many 1959 stock car races. A chrome dress-up kit was available to make the engine compartment shine. The smaller V-8 had a 20-qt. cooling system. The larger engine had a 23-qt. system. Ford cleverly advertised that this engine featured "Precision Fuel Induction." Actually, it had a conventional Holley four-barrel carburetor with what was called "precision fuel metering."

Ford also promoted that Cruise-O-Matic Drive was optional with either engine, although it was actually mandatory with the 430-cid Lincoln motor. You could not get the larger engine with any other transmission. The smaller engine also came with the three-speed manual gear box or three-speed manual with overdrive.

The bird-shaped badge above the center of the 1960 grille had straighter, almost horizontal, wings. It was repeated on the roof sail panels. (Old Cars photo)

71

The 1960 T-Birds were 77 in. wide, or just three inches narrower than a full-size Ford. They came with 8.00 x 14 size tires. (Cappy Collection)

As in 1959, the 430-powered T-Bird was capable of a nine second 0-60 runs. Handling was another matter. *Motor Trend* was rather critical of the car's road manners. The magazine described the car's steering as slow and imprecise. It found that the driving position compromised both visibility and control. "Nearly as costly as any standard luxury car, yet it has quality comparable only to a standard low-priced Ford," said the magazine. "Its styling is distinctive, but certainly not notable." Another criticism was against the poor fuel economy, which averaged only about 12 mpg. "There were many cars that would outperform the four seater," said the summary. "But, somehow the T-Bird has never been measured by these standards. It is a car apart, and like royalty, rarely required to count for ordinary deficiencies. These other qualities are, after all, quite commonplace. The Thunderbird is different, and that is all it ever has to be."

Strangely, another passage about the 1960 T-Bird, saying something totally different, was also printed in *Motor Trend* that year. "What it does have is originality, freshness, and newness of concept," noted the publication. "This is its secret. It has, *more than any other current domestic car*, the spirit and quality (author's emphasis) that made the classic roadsters and tourers of the 1930s such memorable favorites."

Not all that different were the Thunderbird stock cars that raced in 1960. Over half of the cars campaigned this season were 1959 models. At least some of these were cars built and prepped by racers John Holman and Ralph Moody. When the Automobile Manufacturer's Association forced its members out of racing in

A manual sun roof was added to 2,536 T-Birds in 1960. (Ford Motor Co.)

February 1957, Ford general manager Robert S. McNamara was happy to eliminate his competition budget. "The AMA ban supposedly was an agreement to end factory-sponsored racing and delete all high-performance hardware from parts catalogs," notes Alex Gabbard, the author of the HP Book's *Fast Fords*. "Horsepower ratings were not to be advertised, nor anything associated with speed and acceleration. McNamara went for it hook, line, and sinker."

T-BIRD RESULTS - DAYTONA LATE-MODEL POLE POSITION RACE #1 - JAN. 31, 1960
10 Laps/25 Miles

Final Position	Car Number	Driver	Car
7th	93	Banjo Matthews	1959 Thunderbird
9th	73	Bud Burdick	1960 Thunderbird
12th	30	Bob Kosiske	1959 Thunderbird
19th	79	Harold McCann	1959 Thunderbird

Time: 10 minutes .43 seconds
Average Speed: 149.892 mph
Other cars in top 10: 1960 Pontiacs placed first, second and fourth, a 1959 Pontiac placed third, a 1960 Chevrolet Impala was fifth. Two 1960 Plymouths came in sixth and eighth. A 1959 Chevrolet was 10th.

T-BIRD RESULTS - DAYTONA LATE-MODEL POLE POSITION RACE #2 - JAN. 31, 1960
10 Laps/25 Miles

Final Position	Car Number	Driver	Car
4th	93	Banjo Matthews	1959 Thunderbird
8th	73	Bud Burdick	1960 Thunderbird
16th	30	Bob Kosiske	1959 Thunderbird
17th	79	Harold McCann	1959 Thunderbird

Time: 10 minutes 7.43 seconds
Average Speed: 148.157 mph
Other cars in top 10: A 1960 Pontiac placed first. A 1959 Pontiac was second. Third and fifth spots went to 1960 Plymouths driven by Lee Petty and his rookie son Richard. In sixth and seventh were 1960 Chevrolet Impalas. A 1959 Chevrolet was ninth and a 1960 was 10th.

T-BIRD ENTRIES FOR NASCAR LATE-MODEL RACES - DAYTONA BEACH - 1960

Car No.	Driver	Home	Type of Car	Car Owner
30	Bob Kosiske	Omaha, Neb.	1959 Thunderbird	Joe Kosiske
36	Tommy Irwin	Purcellville, Va.	1960 Thunderbird	Tommy Irwin
61	Shorty Moore	Daytona Beach, Fla.	1959 Thunderbird	Dr. White
73	Bud Burdick	Omaha, Neb.	1960 Thunderbird	Roy Burdick
79	Harold McCann "Buzz"	St. Paul, Minn.	1959 Thunderbird	Robert Ranney
93	Banjo Mathews	Asheville, N.C.	1959 Thunderbird	Banjo Mathews

The company sold its cache of factory racing parts to Holman & Moody, who then continued building Ford racing cars. Their production included, among other things, six 1959 Thunderbirds with 430-cid/350-hp V-8s. The year-old cars passed into different hands in 1960. A few current models were also campaigned by private teams. Fords wound up with 15 national wins in 1960, but none were earned by Thunderbirds. Pontiacs had become dominant in stock car racing, with Chevys and Plymouths running close behind them.

Two new super-speedways, Charlotte and Atlanta, opened in 1960. Together with Daytona and Darlington, that brought the number of major races to four. It was the first year that stock car races were televised nationally. Ford's advertising and public relations people were aware of the opportunity for product exposure. When newly elected U.S. President John F. Kennedy picked Robert S. McNamara to serve as his Secretary of Defense, the door was opened for Ford's "Total Performance" program. This was launched, under Lee A. Iacocca — a real automotive enthusiast — in 1961.

Production of 1960 T-Birds ended earlier than usual, in July 1960. The model changeover was pushed up because a total revamp was coming in 1961. Almost as soon as production ended, two special cars were built. They had stainless steel bodies. Allegheny-Ludlum Steel Co., and Budd Body Co. teamed up to make these as a showcase for their product lines. A feature in this book tells more about them. They had to be built as the last 1959 production units, since fabricating the stainless steel bodies wrecked the dies.

Henry's Bright Idea

By Gene Makrancy with Carl H. Davis

Henry Ford was an innovator. In 1925, a Ford Model TT express truck was bodied in Monel metal for use by his airline. This lightweight metal was developed by the International Nickel Co. It was an early form of what became known as "rustless steel." This metal is called stainless steel today. Ford tested it in aircraft applications, but it proved impractical for automotive production use.

In 1928, when the Ford Model A made its debut, Henry Ford used rustless steel for many of its trim and accessory parts. About three years later, he made a decision to experiment with the use of rustless steel in manufacturing auto bodies.

An ad placed by Allegheny Steel Co. appeared in *TIME* magazine's Nov. 9, 1931 issue. Shown was a Model A Ford that looked normal, but wasn't. "Will next year's cars be like this?" the copy asked. "We just bought this special job with the body entirely of Allegheny Metal" (another name for stainless steel). It continued: "Our car will never need paint or polish. It will never grow dull because the body, from bumper to bumper, is Allegheny Metal. You've seen hundreds of Fords with bright parts of Allegheny Metal _ headlamps, radiator shell and trim. You've seen these parts stand years of abuse with never a sign of rust. Can you picture, then, a car entirely of Allegheny Metal?"

A Quick-Facts box in the right-hand lower portion of the ad layout gave the features of Allegheny Metal as follows: (1) Resists more corrosive agents than any other alloy; (2) Can be drawn, stamped, machined, spun, cast or forged; (3) Far stronger than mild steel; (4) Will take any finish from dull to mirror; (5) Is non-magnetic; (6) Resists denting and abrasion; (7) Is readily annealed; may be welded and soldered; (8) Is produced in practically all commercial forms; and (9) Immune to chemical reactions resulting from cooking and preparation or food...does not affect flavor, color or purity of any food.

According to FoMoCo expert Gene Makrancy, the stainless steel Model A show cars used production running gear and interiors. He adds, "They had wooden floor pans." Makrancy noted the cars were built with a lot of special hand-crafting and assembly work. Three were made. All were 1931 Tudor sedans outfitted with deluxe equipment. Apparently, all three carried single left-hand side mounted spares. They toured to cities across the country for exhibitions. One was displayed by Ford Motor Co., the second by Allegheny Steel Co. and the third by Universal Steel Co..

Allegheny-Ludlum Steel Corp. built several different stainless steel cars based on Fords and Lincolns. They included a 1960 T-Bird. (Allegheny-Ludlum Steel Corp.)

By 1935, Allegheny Metal Co. had become the Allegheny Ludlum Steel Corp. Stainless steel was just beginning to outgrow its adolescence. Company officials approached Ford again. This time the plan was to build six additional cars. According to a company brochure published in the 1960s, the reason for building the 1936 models was that "stainless engineers wanted to find out just how long a stainless steel car would last."

Production experts had discovered much about the properties of stainless steel since 1931. The addition of chromium to the metal made it stronger and springier than carbon steel.

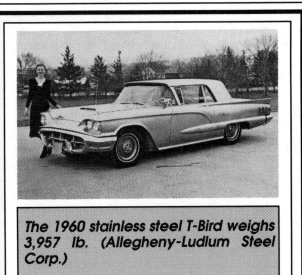

The 1960 stainless steel T-Bird weighs 3,957 lb. (Allegheny-Ludlum Steel Corp.)

However, the springiness became a problem in production. They knew that it didn't stamp like mild steel. This was finally solved through the re-working of dies and the creation of new processes. Welding presented another obstacle. Ian Kiltrie, an Allegheny Ludlum official who was close to the project, told Menno Duerksen of *Cars & Parts* magazine, "The welding equipment had to be set up to special settings to handle the stainless steel. It took a bit of experimenting." A lot of hand-work and special assembly operations were necessary to build the six 1936 Ford Tudor sedans from stainless steel.

Apparently the making of all six vehicles also took longer than expected. They seem to have been made at different times. While some reports said that all of the cars left the assembly line on the same day, it is a fact that the serial numbers stamped on two of the 1936 models are 2,474 numbers apart. The "spread" between these numbers suggests that the two Fords were widely separated in the overall production sequence.

The stainless steel 1936s shared several distinctions from the stainless steel Model As. While the earlier cars had wooden floorboards, the newer ones had normal carbon steel floor pans, which later rusted and had to be replaced. Both the Model As and the 1936 Fords used production type running gear and interiors. However, in the late 1960s, one of the 1936s was fitted with a non-authentic red leather interior. People who have seen this car might mistakenly believe that this was the original upholstery.

A photo of three stainless steel cars taken in 1967. (Allegheny-Ludlum Steel Corp.)

The 1936s were not identical in specifications to standard production type Fords. According to a Michigan certificate of registration for one of the cars, it weighed 3,100 lb. That compares to 2,786 lb. for a stock model. The stainless steel cars also had the following equipment: Temperature gauge, oil gauge, ash tray, side view mirror, hot water heater, chrome wheel discs, dual windshield wipers, and locking gas caps.

Two Cleveland newspaper clippings of October 1956 and October 1962 have additional information on the histories of the stainless steel 1936s and tell many facts. One of the 1936s, along with one of the Model As, was melted down to promote a World War II scrap metal drive. The other cars remained in the possession of Allegheny Ludlum until after the war. At least some of them had traveled over 200,000 miles by this time. One report said that two of them were painted.

In 1946, the five cars remaining in the fleet were sold for $200 each. One eventually came into the possession of an Allegheny Ludlum painter named Gerald Richards. He reconditioned it and traveled extensively, adding another 50,000 miles of use. Later, he all but abandoned the car, allowing it to be used as a play area for his kids and their friends.

Another car was sold to a man in Cleveland, Ohio. He resold it to a used car dealer in Williamsport, Pa.. It was seen, about a year later, in Harrisburg, Pa. Then it dropped out of sight.

Dr. Jerome Vlk, a Chicago dentist who pioneered the use of stainless steel for straightening teeth, purchased a third car at the original disposal sale in 1946. He had it restored and used it as his daily transportation for many years. It is still in the possession of his widow and is now the only example known to positively remain in private hands.

A fourth car was sold to a Philadelphian who also had an interest in stainless steel. When he moved from the city, he took the car with him and it dropped out of sight.

The fifth car, which was kept at Allegheny Ludlum's Detroit sales office for years, was sold to F.D. Crawford of Thompson Products Co., in Cleveland. It was put into his Thompson Products Museum, which later became the Frederick D. Crawford Auto & Aviation Museum. The car is still located there today.

In 1955, Allegheny Ludlum's president, F.J. Hanley, decided to find and repurchase one of the cars. By the fall of 1956 it was under renovation. The 1956 newspaper article said, "It was badly in need of repairs and replacement of working parts," but noted that the stainless steel exterior was "in excellent condition and only needed to be cleaned."

Hanley told the press that his company's renewed desire to own one of the cars was based on a desire for public awareness. "We reach a technical audience with much of our research data and literature," he noted. "We hope to show an even greater audience the value of stainless steel with this car."

The car was the same one owned by Gerald Richards. It had first been used by employees at Allegheny Ludlum's New York sales office. Then, a company salesman bought it. He had the car only a short while, before trading it in on a newer model. Richards then obtained it, used it, and allowed it to deteriorate before selling it back to his employer.

Another of the cars was repurchased by Allegheny Ludlum later. It is not quite clear whether this is the car the company had traced to Williamsport in 1956 or the one that dropped out of sight after leaving Philadelphia. In any case, a 1976 article about the stainless steel Fords in *Cars & Parts* indicated that this car was found in a private museum in Cleveland (not the Thompson Products Museum). The owner of this museum then sold it back to the steel-maker. It is now kept at the company's Detroit sales office.

Two stainless steel T-Birds were the last ones built in 1960. They had to be made last in the run, as the hard metal ruined the dies. (Allegheny-Ludlum Steel Corp.)

The special T-Birds (in center) had bodies made of Type 302 stainless steel and trim made of Type 430 stainless steel with a mirror finish. (Allegheny-Ludlum Steel Corp.)

Rumors have placed the fifth car that survived World War II in California, Alabama and other states, usually in the South. However, extensive searching has failed to turn it up.

The 1936 stainless steel Ford that is stored at Allegheny Ludlum's Brackenridge, Pa. factory today has traveled over 466,600 miles and has had at least four different engines. It was restored by the Greater Pittsburgh Region of the Early Ford V-8 Club of America. It has body number 7006TS27466 and serial number 183330716. There are approximately 107,000 miles on the odometer. Another car is still kept at the company's Detroit sales office. It has an earlier serial number, 18-3327242.

It was not until Monday, July 11, 1960, that another batch of stainless steel Fords rolled off an assembly line. These were built at the company's Wixom, Mich. factory. They were 1960 Thunderbirds. The Budd Co., manufacturer of regular T-Bird bodies, was also experienced in the fabrication of stainless steel. Budd accepted a special assignment to fashion two special cars out of this material. Parts for both cars were produced at the tail end of the 1960 T-Bird production run. This timing was based on the fact that stainless steel fabrication work is hard on conventional auto body dies because of the metal's extra strength. To prevent ruining the dies too early in the year, it was decided to stamp out the stainless steel T-Birds just prior to 1961 model changeover.

Both bodies were made on regular production dies from stainless steel taken from a regular run. Budd then returned them to Ford for completion. The stainless steel T-Birds were powered by 300 horsepower V-8 engines. The frames and suspension parts were regular production items. Carbon steel, painted white, was used for the inner hoods, trunks and door frames. The inner wheel housings and some floor panel parts were made of galvanized steel. It was considered too difficult to stamp these parts from stainless.

After being extensively publicized and utilized for promotional purposes, the T-Birds were retained by Allegheny Ludlum Steel Corp. Both of them survive today. One is kept at the company's Brackenridge factory. The other resides at the firm's Detroit sales office. Articles stating that the second T-Bird was buried in a time capsule are false. This is one of several myths about the stainless steel Fords.

Modern methods of constructing car roofs, in use by the 1960s, had caused problems when the two T-Birds were made. The difficulties in roof fabrication led to the use of a different body style for the next group of stainless steel Ford products. This occurred when it was decided to make stainless steel Lincoln Continentals in 1966. Both Allegheny Ludlum and Ford agreed that Hardtop styling was out. They decided to build stainless steel four-door Convertibles.

Three such cars were made at a reported cost of $30,000 each. Two of them were primarily 1966 models made for Allegheny Ludlum. While they were being hand-assembled in the shop area of the Wixom plant. Ford's Lincoln-Mercury Div. decided to build a third car for its own promotional use. This last four-door ragtop was equipped mostly with 1967 style trim.

This is another unusual fact about the stainless steel Lincolns. It came about because the cars were again assembled late in the production run. The first two Convertibles were trimmed like 1966 models, but titled as 1967s. The third was updated to 1967 trim, but still had a 1966 style Continental star ahead of the front wheel opening. All three received dark blue, pleated leather interiors and black convertible tops.

Following their stint as promotional items, the Lincolns were put into storage. The Lincoln-Mercury Division neglected its car. It deteriorated and was ultimately damaged. Allegheny Ludlum later bought this vehicle, in wrecked condition, and had it repaired. Today, all three Lincolns are in excellent shape with a future as bright as their body panels.

Actually, all of the stainless steel cars that survive today at Allegheny-Ludlum are in good condition. They are sometimes displayed at old car shows. The star-shaped emblems on the doors reflect the firm's obvious pride in these historic Ford products.

After 1967, the use of stainless steel in automobiles began to decline. Now, it's usage is climbing again. Will there be other stainless steel cars in the future? Can you imagine cars like the 1995 Thunderbird 40th anniversary model, the Lincoln Mark VIII or the new Mustang Cobra R rendered in stainless steel? Perhaps someone at Ford or Allegheny Ludlum is thinking along the same lines.

1960 Thunderbird Specifications

Wheelbase	113 in.	Standard Engine Type	90-degree OHV V-8
Curb Weight (Hardtop)	3,955 lb.	Bore x stroke	4.00 x 3.50 in.
Curb Weight (Conv.)	4,222 lb.	Displacement	352 cid
Overall Length	205.32 in.	Compression Ratio	9.6:1
Overall Width	77.0 in.	Carburetor	Holley 4-Barrel
Overall Height (HT)	52.5 in.	Maximum BHP	300 @ 4600 rpm
Overall Height (Conv.)	53.1 in.	Maximum Torque	381 lb.-ft. @ 2800 rpm
Front Tread	60 in.	Exhaust System	Dual Exhausts
Front Tread	57 in.	Optional Engine Type	90-degree OHV V-
Tires	8.00 x 14	Bore x stroke	4.30 x 3.70 in.
Turning Diameter	40 ft.	Displacement	430 cid
Steering Ratio:	25.0:1	Compression Ratio	10.0:1
Std. Axle (352/Auto.)	3.10:1	Carburetor	Holley 4-Barrel
Standard Axle (Man.)	3.70:1	Maximum BHP	350 @ 4400 rpm
Std. Axle (430/Auto.)	2.91:1	Maximum Torque	490 lb.-ft. @ 2800 rpm
Brake Swept Area	194 sq. in.	Ground Clearance	5.8 in.

1960 Thunderbird Engineering

Chassis	Welded, integral body and frame.
Front Suspension	Ball-joints; coil springs, tube shocks; stabilizer.
Rear Suspension	Outboard mounted rear leaf springs, tension-type shackles and wind-up control rubber bumpers over springs. Double-acting shocks.
Steering	Recirculating ball type gear.
Front Brakes	11 in. diameter double-sealed; ceramic linings.
Brakes	11 in. diameter double-sealed; ceramic linings.

No Rust Restoration

Adapted from a Gene Makrancy story

On July 11, 1960 a stainless steel Thunderbird came off Ford Motor Co.'s Wixom, Mich. assembly line. Two of these cars were made as part of a series of "factory" specialty cars that had started back in the days of the 1928-1931 Model Ford. All of the stainless steel Ford products were built to showcase the features and benefits of this metal. Ford Motor Co., Budd Body Co., and Allegheny-Ludlum Steel Co. were jointly behind these unique promotional vehicles.

The Thunderbird's body was made of Type 302 stainless steel. It had trim made of Type 430 stainless steel. The body cost between $25,000 and $30,000 to create. It required more than 1,000 dies to make the 300-plus stainless steel Thunderbird parts used on the car.

Ford scheduled production of the stainless steel cars for July, since that was when manufacturing of "Square-Birds" was slated to end. The assembly lines were halting earlier in the year than they normally do, because the next model changeover would bring the "projectile" style 1961 T-Bird to America. Since this required the conversion of a lot of manufacturing equipment, more time than normal was needed to change the factory over to production of the '61s. Stamping out parts for the stainless steel cars could damage the dies, so they had to be the last 1960 T-Birds made.

When assembly work was finally completed, the cars rolled out. Ford felt that the stainless steel bodies looked too shiny. They would have to be buffed out to dull them to a satin finish. This operation cost approximately $5,000.

One of the stainless steel Fords has been in the possession of Allegheny-Ludlum Steel Corp. It is stored in the company's Brackenridge, Pa. factory. This car has the Ford serial number 0471Y190331. As of the early 1980s, it had only 130,000 original miles showing on its odometer.

Although the car's stainless steel body does not rust, by 1982 time had taken its toll on the vehicle. Some restoration work was in order. Carl Davis, a member of the Vintage Thunderbird Club of America who lives in Baltimore, Md., took on the task.

Davis had once before had this car. That was around 1964, when it was only a few years old. He knew that someone had painted it under the hood. Davis pulled the engine out and restored the engine bay. He also cleaned and detailed the V-8, and had it worked on while it was out of the vehicle. Carl also wanted to put a leather Thunderbird interior in the car. The steel company did not approve of this idea.

The shiny T-bird was trailered from the steel factory to Davis' back yard. The hood was removed and the V-8 engine was extracted. With the engine out, the underhood area was detailed. Mike Dutch rebuilt the 352-cid V-8. It was the first time (at 130,000 miles) that this had been done. Davis removed the doors from the car to work on them while smoothening dings in the metal. Benches from a picnic table were used to support the doors while they were refinished.

When the car was restored, it was returned to the steel factory and placed in the care of Bill McCoy, who keeps it under proper security. Apparently, both Bill and his employer were happy with how Carl Davis restored the car. A few years later, they had him do work on the stainless steel 1966-1/2 Lincoln Continental. We'll save that story in case we do a Lincoln book.

The sun roof was a $212 option in 1960. Hardtops with it also had a chrome rail on the front edge of their roofs, to deflect air over the opening. (Ford Motor Co.)

1960 Thunderbird Performance

Model	CID/HP	Performance
0-60 mph		
Hardtop	430/350	9 seconds
1/4-Mile		
Hardtop	430/350	17.0 seconds @ 86.57 mph

1961 - 1963
"Bullet Birds"

1961
Space Shot

The third all-new Thunderbird in seven years showcased many changes. It had a brand new body and interior. Appearance-wise, the car was a sensational departure from the "Square Bird" look of 1958-1960. Instead of corners and angles, this car had smooth, curving lines. Virtually nothing was the same as in the past. The drastic alterations went far beneath the car's surface, too. The sporty Ford boasted not only a new chassis, but a larger, more powerful engine. "To many Thunderbird owners, the greatly restyled 1961 model will look like a bird from another nest," said *Science and Mechanics* magazine in its December 1960 issue.

Ford stylists were surely inspired by events of the era when they created this racy-looking car-of-the-future. The advent of commercial jet aircraft in the late-1950s, the "space shots" of 1959, and the launching of the Echo I communications satellite in 1960 set the stage for the new T-Bird's futuristic image. "Because this is an age of aerodynamics, high speeds and rockets, we must keep in tune with the times," said George Walker, Ford's vice president in charge of styling. He told *Science and Mechanics'* Bill Callahan that the company had squeezed extra years out of the previous design. "It was time for a change," was how Walker put it. "Why not move forward?"

The downward curved hood of the T-Bird seemed to be moving forward while the car was standing still. It was really dramatic-looking in its day. Two headlamps appeared on either side of the front end. They were nicely integrated into the upper edge of the grille. Gone were the "eyebrows" that shielded the 1958-1960 headlights. A swept-under grille blended smoothly in with the rest of the torpedo-shaped car. "Bullet Bird," the nickname given this T-Bird today, projects the impression of their smooth, aerodynamic, high-impact appearance. Some collectors also call them "Rocket 'Birds."

The 1961 T-Bird was all-new. It was longer, lower, wider, and heavier than any earlier edition and launched the marque's "golden years." (Cappy Collection)

One expansive piece of metal formed the 1961 T-Bird grille surround and front bumper. (Ford Motor Co. photo)

Side trim consisted of a front fender tip Thunderbird script and four, stacked horizontal blades at the extreme rear end of the car. (Ford Motor Co. photo)

"Our first impression of the T-Bird for '61, upon seeing it at FoMoCo's Dearborn, Mich. test track early in September, was that it had plenty of eye appeal." said Mel Jocolow and Joe Petrovec in a 1961 *Cars* magazine review. "Although 1/2-in. (actually 3/10ths in.) shorter than the '60 model, this car gives the impression of being longer, and its uncluttered body, emphasizing unbroken expanses of contoured sheet metal rather than chrome gee-gaws, exhudes a sleekness that its more square predecessor did not." There were no traces of the heavily sculptured side panels seen on the "Square Birds."

George Walker said that sculpturing was dropped from the T-Bird because it added nothing to aerodynamic design. In one sense, this is incorrect. Sculptured metal is stronger than flat metal, so it did contribute something to the Square Bird's structural integrity, if not its aesthetics. "They are very strong cars until they start rusting," says *Old Cars* research editor Ken Buttolph. "Then, they turn into rust buckets." Walker was right, though, when he noted that sculpturing hurt a car's aerodynamics. Surely, the new-for-1961 body was more at home in a wind tunnel than any previous 'Bird.

The author of this book was 14 years old when the '61 T-Birds arrived. A high school freshman in New York, I had dreams of becoming an industrial designer. The Thunderbird seemed like a "dream car" brought to life. Its shape resembled that of many of the cars I saw in the renderings hanging in the industrial design gallery at Brooklyn Technical High School. Come to think of it, even the cars that I constantly scribbled in the margins of my loose-leaf book pages had that same kind of pointy, rocket ship front end.

The 1961 T-Bird V-8 had 390 cid and 300 hp. (Cappy Collection)

Despite the degree of departure from earlier designs, the new Thunderbird did have some traits that were traditionally associated with the marque. It was long-looking, and extremely low-slung for a large car. It again had a sloped nose and a hood scoop. The roof was fairly flat. Rear roof pillars had a "formal" T-Bird-like appearance. Although much of the interior design reflected obvious updating, the Thunderbird remained a four-place automobile with bucket seats and a center console. Short, outward-canted rear fins, a T-Bird trademark dating back to 1957, were continued this year. Round tail-light lenses had adorned the marque since its beginning in 1954. In fact, Ford returned to single lenses in 1961, which is what had been used in 1955-1957.

Unit construction remained a T-Bird benefit. The frame and body components were welded into an integral unit, rather than bolted together. Ford actually made the car of two unitized sections with a rigid, box sectioned joint at the cowl area. For the first time ever, the T-Bird hood was hinged at the rear. It was also wider than the 1960 hood, while the fenders were narrower. They were designed for bolt-on attachment to make major body repairs simpler. Gone entirely was the "dog leg" wraparound windshield that was all the rage in the mid-'50s. The new, thin-pillared "straight line" windshield was much easier to peer through without distortion. The exteriors of 1961 Thunderbirds could be finished in any of 19 different "Diamond Lustre" colors, and 30 two-tones (including seven reversible combinations) were offered for Hardtops.

Cars magazine pointed up something interesting about American car interiors when it described the '61 T-Bird's "Luxury Lounge" passenger accommodations. "Although the exterior greenhouse length has been increased by 10 in. this year, interior passenger dimensions remain about the same as in '60s, or equal roughly to those of a Volkswagen," the writer pointed out. "Utilization of some of these extra inches for increased passenger room would have been in order."

Though tight-fitting, the T-Bird was not tight with comfort and convenience equipment. Standard interior features included: Manually adjustable individual front seats, Lifeguard cushioned instrument panel and sun visors, double-grip door locks, "Safety-Swivel" day/night type inside rear view mirror, deep-center steering wheel with horn ring, electric clock, automatic dome lamp (Hardtop), courtesy-map light, glove box and ash tray light, cigarette lighter, and coat hooks.

Ford once planned to give the 1961 T-Bird front-wheel-drive. (Cappy Collection)

Though radically different looking, the 1961 styling did retain a family identity with its hood scoop, skirted fenders, and bird-shaped emblems. (Cappy Collection)

The sportiness of past T-Birds was enhanced with an extra dose of luxury in the new 1961 interior offering 16 different upholstery combinations in six colors. There were six standard all-vinyl trims offered in all colors. Combinations of vinyl and bedford cord cloth totaled five. They were offered in all colors but Red. Seat inserts and bolsters were also available in five shades of genuine leather. The optional leather trim was not offered in Green. Convertible tops came in white, black or blue and were color-keyed to the interiors. The center console was 25 percent smaller. This helped passengers who found it necessary to climb from one side of the car to the other. It also provided more leg room for all people riding inside the car. One new idea used on the T-Bird was gluing the rear view mirror directly to the windshield.

1961 Thunderbird Interiors

Seat Type	Material	Blue	Green	Beige	Red	Black	Tur-quoise
Bucket Seats	Vinyl	52	53	54	55	56	57
Bucket Seats	Cloth & Vinyl	72	73	74		76	77
Bucket Seats	Leather	82		84	85	86	87

Convertible tops came in Black vinyl (code 1); White vinyl (code 2); and Blue vinyl (code 4). All convertible tops had a black headlining.

The Convertible featured a fully-automatic top-retracting mechanism operated by the turn of a switch on the inside of the left-hand door. The lifting mechanism and pump assembly were relocated to the quarter panels, instead of behind the seat. To raise the top, the trunk lid opened to the rear. Then, powerful motors lifted the top, extending it nearly straight up until it lowered over the passenger compartment. This isolated the top top-riser mechanism from the passengers, and made operation of the top quieter. It was also something to watch the system do its job. A drawback of the design was a noticeable lack of storage space in the trunk, when the top was folded and stored there.

Additional standard equipment included a 390-cid "Thunderbird Special" premium fuel V-8 with an automatic choke, dual exhausts, and full-flow oil filtration. The engine package came with aluminized mufflers, a "Super-Filter" air cleaner, and an "Anti-Fume" positive crankcase ventilation system. Free-turning overhead aluminized valves were used in conjunction with hydraulic lifters to eliminate the need for periodic

Another T-Bird styling tradition continued at the rear of the 1961 model was the use of large, round taillights. (Ford Motor Co.)

valve adjustments. The cross-flow cooling system featured a 180-degrees thermostat. Also on the list were Cruise-O-Matic drive, power steering, power brakes, a trunk light, dual horns, turn signals, back-up lamps, and full wheel covers. Popular options included a Swing-Away steering wheel, SelectAire Conditioner, power seat, power windows, push-button radio, and MagicAire ventilation system.

Cars magazine tested a pre-production Convertible and a full-bore test of the 1961 T-Bird's performance wasn't possible with the prototype. "Those figures registered indicated to our satisfaction that this 300-bhp T-Bird will hold its own with the hottest Detroit machinery, excepting the Corvette," said the editors. "We were assured by Ingram Taylor, quality analysis technician and former Ford test driver, that a `61 `Bird in good tune should attain a maximum speed in excess of 130 mph."

A "Swing-Away" steering wheel was a new 1961 option. (Ford Motor Co. photo)

Motor Trend made a "Special Report" on the 1961 T-Bird in its December 1960 issue, picturing the car with a 1957 two-seat model. Associate editor John Lawlor had praise for everything from the Swing-Away steering wheel to the new springs and wider tread width. He found that riders were well-insulated from road shocks and vibrations. The car cornered with less lean than previous T-Birds and had improved brakes. Lawlor was unable to get any hard performance figures, as he too was driving a pre-production car at Ford's Dearborn test track. "On the basis of the prototype, though, I believe the `61 model shows a new level of sophistication in its engineering," he wrote. "Without diminishing the particular appeal of the old two-seater nor the trailblazing of the previous four-seater, the latest Thunderbird looks to me like the best one yet." In February 1961, Motor Trend followed up its initial review with a road test article entitled "Thunderbird: A Real Change ... For the Better." The title said it all, as the report praised just about everything except luggage accommodations in the Convertible.

The all-new 1961 Thunderbird was not competitive in stock car racing. However, some of the 1959 and 1960 models continued to race. Many of the cars were battle-worn and fell into the hands of lesser known drivers with smaller budgets. Lenny Page did a good job racking up his number 3 Thunderbird in the 1961 Charlotte 400 race. The car spun out and slammed head-first into the guard rail. It then did a "180" and tail-boned into the guard rail again. Next, Page's T-Bird was hit by car number 35, a 1960 Pontiac Ventura. This inflicted more damage than the guard rail. The driver was injured in the accident, which was captured in a film sequence seen in the Feb. 1961 edition of Motor Life. The magazine advised that Page did recover from head injuries and neck lacerations that he endured during his wild ride.

A Thunderbird Convertible was picked to be "Official Pace Car" at Indianapolis Motor Speedway for the annual Memorial Day classic. (IMSC Photo Dept.)

1961 Thunderbird Hardtop Specifications

Wheelbase	113 in.	Engine Type	90-degree OHV V-8
Curb Weight	4,048 lb.	Compression Ratio	9.6:1
Front Seat Headroom	37.7 in.	Maximum BHP	300 @ 4600 rpm
Rear Seat Headroom	37.61 in.	Taxable HP	52.50
Front Seat Leg Room	45.4 in.	Maximum Torque	427 lb.-ft. @ 2800 rpm
Rear Seat Leg Room	38.9 in.	Displacement	390 cid
Overall Length	205 in.	Bore x Stroke	4.05 x 3.78 in.
Overall Height	52.5 in.	Gas Tank Capacity	20 gallons.
Overall Width	75.9 in.	Cooling Capacity	19.5 quarts
Front Shoulder Room	58.1 in.	Standard Axle	2.91:1 (3.10:1 optional)
Rear Shoulder Room	57.8 in.	Tires	8.00 x 14
Front Tread	61 in.	Effective Brake Area	233.75 sq. in.
Rear Tread	60 in.	Turning Diameter	40.2 ft.

1961 Thunderbird Convertible Specifications

Wheelbase	113 in.	Engine Type	90-degree OHV V-8
Curb Weight	4,222 lb.	Compression Ratio	9.6:1
Front Seat Headroom	39.4 in.	Maximum BHP	300 @ 4600 rpm
Rear Seat Headroom	38.2 in.	Taxable HP	52.50
Front Seat Leg Room	45.4 in.	Maximum Torque	427 lb.-ft. @ 2800 rpm
Rear Seat Leg Room	38.9 in.	Displacement	390 cid
Overall Length	205 in.	Bore x Stroke	4.05 x 3.78 in.
Overall Height	53.3 in.	Gas Tank Capacity	20 gallons.
Overall Width	75.9 in.	Cooling Capacity	19.5 quarts
Front Shoulder Room	58.1 in.	Standard Axle	2.91:1 (3.10:1 optional)
Rear Shoulder Room	57.8 in.	Tires	8.00 x 14
Front Tread	61 in.	Effective Brake Area	233.75 sq. in.
Rear Tread	60 in.	Turning Diameter	40.2 ft.

1961 Thunderbird Engineering

Front Suspension	Independent SLA ball-joint with coil springs
Rear Suspension	Hotchkiss
Steering	20.31: 1 power steering, 4.5 turns lock-to-lock
Front Brakes	11.03 x 3.00-in. drums
Rear Brakes	11.03 x 2.50-in. drums
Weight Distribution	66 percent front/44 percent rear
Fuel economy	13-21 mpg
Driving Range	260-420 miles

Wider seats and more sound-proofing were two new features found inside 1961 Thunderbirds. The Convertible interior is shown. (Ford Motor Co.)

1961 Thunderbird Performance

Model	CID/HP	Perform.
0-60 mph		
Convertible	390/300	8.5 seconds
Convertible	390/300	10.5
1/4-Mile		
Convertible	390/300	18.6 sec. at 76 mph
Top Speed		
Convertible	390/300	130 mph (estimated)

1962
Poppin' Pupils in Peoria

The 1962 Thunderbird had a new grille and taillights. Also new were two new models. One was called the Landau. It had a custom interior and a fabric covered top with S-curved landau bars on the side. The other new model was called the Sports Roadster. It had a cover over the rear seats and wire wheels, but lacked the fender skirts that other models came with. Of the two, the Sports Roadster was a much more exciting car. As "Uncle" Tom McCahill put it, "Ford has fielded a Convertible T-Bird, called a Sports Roadster, with some real wild innovations that are bound to have eyes popping in Peoria."

Before we get to the innovations, let's cover the basics. In trendy, early-'60s "Kalifornia' Kustom" influenced style, the '62 had a reworked grille with four rows of shiny chrome "drawer pulls" between thin horizontal bars. Replacing the four moldings stacked on the rear fender of the '61 model were horizontal "hyphens" of ribbed chrome. Late in the spring, some cars were built with a horizontal chrome accessory stripe on their body sides. The trademark large round taillights also had more chrome to dress them up. Sports Roadsters and Landaus had other special trim items, which are covered below in discussions of the specific models.

Prices went up $151 each on the carryover models. That seems modest now, but may not have been in 1962. Actually, it's hard to say how the hike was perceived. From 1958-1960 increases of about $60 per year were average, but the all-new '61 T-Bird jumped more than $400 in price. A $150 hike in 1962 would have seemed steep to the buyer trading in a 1959 model. However, for those who bought a new 'Bird annually, it was less than the rise they'd seen the year before. It's also worth noting that the Convertible cracked the $4,000 barrier for the first time in 1960, while the Hardtop did the same in 1961. For 1962, the $5,000 barrier fell to the Convertible Sports Roadster. That must have shook up the folks in Peoria, too. The wholesale and retail prices for the four T-Bird

Minor detail changes were seen on the 1962 T-Bird Hardtop. (Old Cars photo)

models looked like this:

Model No.	Body Style	Dealer Cost	(EOH) Fed. Excise Tax	Cost w/ EOH	Suggested Retail Factory Price
83	Hardtop	$3,041.28	$321.00	$3,362.28	$4,321.00
87	Hardtop Landau.	$3,096.72	$326.00	$3,422.72	$4,398.00
85	Convertible	$3,375.46	$354.00	$3,729.46	$4,788.00
89	Sports Roadster (Conv.)	$3,841.58	$399.00	$4,240.58	$5,439.00

A long list of standard equipment accounted for the T-Birds' hefty price tags. According to *Car Fax 1962*, they came with built-in dual exhausts; fuel filter; oil filter; 390 cid four-barrel V-8; padded instrument panel; padded sun visors; electric clock with sweep second hand; courtesy lights; turn signals; a deep-center steering wheel; dual horns and horn rings; individually adjustable front seats; a day-night tilt type mirror; double-grip door locks; full wheel covers; built-in armrests; floor carpet; full-width foam rubber

The four stacked blades of chrome at the extreme rear fender were replaced, in 1962, by three "dashes" of ribbed bright metal. (Ford Motor Co. photo)

seats; all-vinyl upholstery; ashtray; cigar lighter; air cleaner; automatic transmission; power brakes; power steering; electric windshield wipers; undercoating; parking brake, glove box, ashtray, luggage, back-up, and compartment lights; a heater and defroster; a movable steering column (new to the standard equipment list); a console between the front seats; and five black 8.00 x 14 tires. The Convertible Sports Roadster also included the molded tonneau cover with padded headrests, chrome wire wheels, and an instrument panel mounted passenger assist bar.

To appreciate the Thunderbird's stature at the time, you have to realize that in the 1961-'62 period, base-trim-level models from Ford and Chevrolet were just beginning to include things like turn signals, dual sun visors, and oil filters as standard. The equipment list for most cars was two or three lines long. In contrast, the 1962 T-Bird came with nearly as many regular features as a fairly well-equipped 2000 model might have today (one big difference being that air conditioning is much more common now). The T-Bird was also known for its extreme quietness at a time when noisy cars were commonplace. Some 45 lb. of sound-deadening materials, including aluminum insulation, fiber or mastic felt, undercoating, and fiberglass were applied to the hood, wheel well housing, dash, instrument panel, passenger and trunk floors, roof panels, package tray, and quarter panels.

There were a few additional revisions to the '62 Thunderbird. A hand-operated parking brake, slight upholstery changes, and redesigned gauge indicators were among them. On the underbody, the zinc-coated stock that the unitized body was stamped out of had enhanced rust-proofing. This included a bath in a zinc-rich coating and three coats of primer. On top of this, two finish coats of "never wax" enamel were applied. Also, the aluminized muffler was improved and stainless steel parts were used in some critical places in the exhaust system, such as the resonators.

The T-Bird engine featured revised manifolding. There were 15 improvements to the carburetor alone, plus a disposable fuel filter designed to function for 30,000 miles. Oil filter life was also extended to 4,000-6,000 mile intervals by eliminating a crossover valve. At this time, most motorists used engine coolant that required changing semi-annually. Thunderbird buyers received permanent antifreeze that gave protection to minus 35-degrees and had to be changed only every two years or 30,000 miles. They also got better brakes. A larger master cylinder was said to increase braking efficiency while reducing pedal pressure. For better durability and fade resistance, new brake lining materials were used. Nevertheless, the T-Bird was still three years away from getting the disc brakes that marque enthusiasts knew it needed.

On the exterior, 18 single colors were available for the Hardtop. Twelve of the single colors were exclusive to Thunderbirds. One color, Diamond Blue, was added during the model-year. Including Diamond Blue, there were 21 two-tones. Nineteen interior options were available on the four Thunderbird models in seven basic color "suites." Seats came in seven all-vinyl selections, five vinyl and bedford cloth combinations, and seven all-leather options.

1962 Thunderbird Interiors

Seat Type	Material	Silver Blue	Black	Chest Tan	Pearl Beige	Tur- quoise	Blue	Red
Bucket Seats	Vinyl	50	56	59	54	57	52	55
Bucket Seats	Cloth & Vinyl	70	76		74	77	72	
Bucket Seats	Leather	80	86	89	84	87	82	85

Convertible tops came in Black vinyl (code 1); White vinyl (code 2); and Blue vinyl (code 4). All convertible tops had a black headlining.

There were 18 monotone finishes available for the 1962 T-Bird Hardtop, plus 24 two-tone combinations. (Ford Motor Co. photo)

The 1962 Thunderbird seats were low and soft. Heater controls and a glove compartment were incorporated into the center console between the seats. The Swing-Away steering wheel moved 10 in. to make getting in and out of the car easier, but it functioned only when the gear selector was in Park. *Car and Driver* (August 1962) mentioned "wide-opening doors and generous interior dimensions" on both models. However, the magazine said that the front seat went too far back for passengers in the rear (cramping their knee room), but not back far enough for a driver to straighten his arms.

A quick look at the 1962 body codes shows that the four 1962 models had only two different model numbers. This means that the differences between cars of similar body style are in the area of body trim, rather than structure. Had there been just a minor difference in the shape of the windshield or roof line, Ford would have used a different code number to separate the cars. Both body styles had the same "projectile" front end and twin jet tube rear design brought out in 1961. The Hardtop's roof was again slightly on the formal-looking side. The Convertible had a flip-up deck and "accordion" top mechanism that Tom McCahill joked about in the May 1962 issue of *Mechanix Illustrated*.

"The first time I lowered the top, I thought the car was about to eat itself," said McCahill. "Deck flips open, panels unfold, the top shoots up, all to the accompaniment of a whining noise similar to launching a guided missile. The sight of this operation is enough to cause a coronary in a slightly inebriated 3rd Avenue playboy. The total operation makes Buck Rogers look like a rail-splitting partner of Abe Lincoln's and the end result, though successful in concealing the top, leaves less trunk room than you'll find in a Volkswagen."

A formal Hardtop with a vinyl top and carriage-roof S-bars was called the Landau. It looked like a T-Bird in a top hat. (Ford Motor Co. photo)

Fabric tops for the 1962 T-Bird Convertible were offered in three colors. This one has factory-optional body belt moldings. (Old Cars photo)

The Convertible was the basis for the Sports Roadster. A large, fiberglass tonneau cover converted it into a "two-place" car. The convertible top had to be down to install the tonneau, but the cover could be added or removed in less than three minutes. Tom McCahill liked the idea of an instant two-place conversion and exclaimed, "This fiberglass gizmo dresses up the 'Bird like a top hat in an Easter Parade." Back in 1955 (The balding McCahill's dating system was, "when I had three more hairs on my noggin.") the scribe had set a record driving a T-Bird at Daytona's speed trials. He loved the two-seaters. But, Uncle Tom just as fluently addressed the question of what to do with the cover far away from home. "It could work into a problem slightly larger than the one in the Congo," he warned, referring to a huge political hot spot of the era.

The Motor Sport, a British magazine, noted that the tonneau cover was "made of rather thinnish glass fiber laminate." It raised the question of whether the thin cover would make a drumming noise. However, the tonneau was very well designed. The headrest section was horseshoe-shaped to fit over the Thunderbird's bucket seats. A quick-release catch secured it to the transmission tunnel between the rear seats. The tonneau actually slid under the deck lid to secure it at the rear. It was possible to raise or lower the convertible top with the tonneau in place. The seat back recessed into the headrest for a smooth, aerodynamic fit. A gap between the bottom edge of the tonneau and the rear seat was provided. This allowed small items to slide under the cover and onto the seat cushion for storage. Access to this "cubby hole" was provided by simply folding the front seat forward.

To some the Sports Roadster looks like a toy streamlined racing car with two figurines in the front seat. Tim Howley, writing in *Collectible Automobile*, said it gave the impression of a big attack aircraft with pilot and co-pilot sitting in front of the headrests. *Car Life* magazine compared the long surface between the headrest and the rear of the car to the deck of the aircraft carrier USS Enterprise. "As a prestige car in the true Midwest culture school, this little item should be hard to beat," chimed McCahill. "It won't get a second glance from the Ferrari and E-Jag buffs, but it will singe a lot of wheat in Nebraska."

Sports Roadster equipment also included real Kelsey-Hayes wire wheels with knock-off hub caps, a front passenger grab handle (a horizontal bar bridging the space under the visored section of the padded dash on the right-hand side of the instrument panel), a special insignia under the Thunderbird front fender script, and the deletion of fender skirts. Tom McCahill said, "The Roadster is the only Thunderbird that comes with wire wheels and simulated knock-off hubs. However, *Car Fax 1962* lists them as a regular T-Bird option with a $262.90 dealer cost and $372.30 factory suggested retail price. Ford expert Tim Howley agrees that this was the case. It is possible that other T-Birds sold with wire wheels used center caps in place of the knock-off hubs. The fender skirts were deleted on Sports Roadsters because of clearance problems with the knock-off hubs—although restorers have found ways to get around this. Open fenders also look more sports car-like and facilitate brake cooling. The wire wheels did not work well with tubeless tires and required the use of inner tubes.

Another new 1962 T-Bird was the Sports Roadster. Its removable fiberglass tonneau turned the four-place ragtop into a two-seat car. (Ford Motor Co. photo)

The "forgotten" new model of the year was the Landau or Landau Hardtop. It came with a black or white vinyl top covering. The covering was designed to look like a leather-padded carriage top. To further this impression the roof was decorated in a classic manner. "The Landau has, as might be expected, 'landau irons' in vestigial, attractive form, on the sides of its rear roof panels," reported *The Motor Sport*. "It's a very pleasing combination, with genuine leather upholstery optional on order." The number of Landaus built was not recorded separately, but the model did push the overall sales performance of the Thunderbird Hardtop upwards by 7,000 units.

The T-Bird's road performance was largely unchanged from 1961. The standard 390-cid, 300-hp Thunderbird V-8 made the car fast enough for the typical T-Bird buyer, but no muscle car. McCahill reported averaging 9.7 seconds for 0-60 mph with his 4,530-lb. Sports Roadster. According to *Motor Trend* (Sept. 1962), a 4,842 lb. Sports Roadster they tested took 11.2 seconds to accomplish the same thing. *Car and Driver* managed 11.3 seconds with a 4,400-lb. Convertible. It's very possible that the tonneau cover's aerodynamic properties made McCahill's Sports Roadster faster, but the closeness of the other figures suggests they are more accurate. The big engine started smoothly and ran silently most of the time. *Car and Driver* said, "It was almost undetectable." *Car and Driver's* Convertible recorded a top speed of 110 mph, while McCahill said that his Sports Roadster's high point was six miles per hour faster than that. (Old Tom probably didn't adjust for speedometer error.) *Motor Trend* mentioned "an honest 107 mph on our Weston electric speedometer." The exact figure isn't important though. The car's go-power was fast enough to impress one's neighbors or the whole gang at the country club, and that's what really mattered.

Real wire wheels were standard on Sports Roadsters. (Old Cars photo)

An optional engine was available in 1962. Supplies were limited. " I am told that under pressure of a thumbscrew and with the possible aid of your congressman, you might be able to order a 'Bird with a hotter engine, "joked Tom McCahill. This motor was a version of the 390 with three progressively-linked Holley two-barrel carburetors, a 10.5:1 compression ratio, and a distinctive cast aluminum Thunderbird air cleaner. Known as the M-code power plant, it generated 340 hp and 430 lb.-ft. of torque at 3200 rpm. *Car Fax* shows that the motor had a $171 dealer cost and added $242.10 to retail price. It was truly hard to get, with a reported total of just 120-M-code

Sports Roadsters being put together. An "M" Roadster could move from 0-60 in approximately 8.5 seconds and hit a top speed of 125 mph.

Although the T-Bird was sports car fast, if not muscle car fast, it came nowhere near handling or braking like a sports car. The steering was slow and vague and unsuitable for directing the car over twisting roads. The softly-sprung T-Bird bottomed out when pushed hard. Professional driving techniques were needed to race it through sharp corners, due to understeering combined with the slow-to-react steering gear. Body roll was also excessive. "These are conditions most owners will never encounter," *Car and Driver* said. *Motor Trend* rated the car higher, but printed a photo caption critical of understeer and body roll. Braking problems were blamed on the linings, rather than the rest of the system. The brakes functioned fine under all conditions, but the linings heated up quickly and caused severe fade when the car was driven hard. All of the car magazines dwelled on brake fade and the fact that once they faded, they took a long time to cool off and come back.

If Thunderbirds had troubles stopping, they must have spilled over to the sales department, since there was no stopping the steady increase in demand for '62s. From their introduction on October 12, 1961, the cars sold well. The combination of good looks, advanced styling, many creature comforts, luxury appointments, and reliable performance was a winner in the early 1960s. "Ford's plush style setter

The large tonneau came off easily, but storing it was hard. (Ford Motor Co. photo)

Seats folded into the tonneau to create "Slipstream Headrests." (Ford Motor Co.)

has its share of faults and shortcomings," said *Motor Trend*'s technical editor Jim Wright. "But, it's still the classic example of a prestige car." In addition, other than the limited-production Chrysler 300 letter car, the Thunderbird had the personal-luxury niche to itself. There was no Buick Riviera to contend with in 1962, and the new Pontiac Grand Prix had not yet developed the distinctive styling that would make it a big hit in 1963. On the other hand, Thunderbird's two added models helped fill out the niche and boosted production by 5,000 units. According to marque historian James F. Petrik's extensive research, the Wixom factory cranked out a combined total of 69,554 Hardtops and Landaus, plus 7,030 Convertibles and 1,427 Sports Roadsters.

1962 Thunderbird Hardtop Specifications

Wheelbase	113 in.	Engine Type	90-degree OHV V-8
Curb Weight	4,292 lb.	Bore x Stroke	4.05 x 3.78 in.
Front Seat Headroom	34.3 in.	Displacement	390 cid
Rear Seat Headroom	33.1 in.	Compression Ratio	9.6:1
Front Seat Leg Room	44.9 in.	Carburetor	4-Barrel
Rear Seat Leg Room	37.3 in.	Maximum BHP	300 @ 4600 rpm
Overall Length	205 in.	Maximum Torque	427 lb.-ft. @ 2800 rpm
Overall Height	52.5 in.	Exhaust System	Dual Exhausts
Overall Width	76 in.	Engine Type	90-degree OHV V-8
R. Axle Road Clearance	5.3 in.	Bore x Stroke	4.05 x 3.78 in.
Body Road Clearance	7.2 in.	Displacement	390 cid
Front Tread	61 in.	Compression Ratio	10.5:1
Rear Tread	60 in.	Carburetor	Triple 2-Barrels
Gas Tank Capacity	20 gal.	Maximum BHP	340 @ 5000 rpm

1962 Thunderbird Hardtop Specifications

Cooling System Capacity	20.5 qt.	Maximum Torque	430 lb.-ft. @ 3200 rpm
Steering Ratio	20.7:1	Standard Axle	3.00:1
Turning Diameter	40.2 ft	Optional Axle	3.00:1 Equa-Lok
Effective Brake Area	234 sq. in.	Tires	8.00 x 14

1962 Thunderbird Engineering

Front Suspension	Independent wishbone type with coil springs
Rear Suspension	Live axle attached to semi-elliptic leaf springs
Steering	Integral-type power-steering, 4.5 turns lock-to-lock
Brakes	11-in. drums with 432 sq. in. swept area
Weight Distribution	66 percent front/44 percent rear
Fuel economy	11-20 mpg
Driving Range	220-400 miles

1962 Thunderbird Performance

Model	CID/HP	Performance
0-60 mph		
Sports Roadster	390/300	12.4 seconds
Sports Roadster	390/300	9.7 seconds
Convertible	390/300	11.3 seconds
Sports Roadster	390/340	8.5 seconds
1/4-Mile		
Sports Roadster	390/300	19.2 seconds at 78 mph
Sports Roadster	390/300	18.7 seconds
Convertible	390/300	18.6 seconds at 76 mph
Top Speed		
Sports Roadster	390/300	114-116 mph
Convertible	390/300	110 mph (estimated)
Sports Roadster	390/340	125 mph

1963
The Party's Over

A sculptured body side feature line was added in 1963 and the slanting bright metal "hash marks" were moved to the center of the door. (Ford Motor Co. photo)

Price tags for the 1963 T-Bird Landau Hardtop started at $4,548. Vinyl tops came in white, blue, brown and black. (Cappy Collection)

The 1963 Landau had new simulated wood-grain interior trim, plus a walnut-colored steering wheel. (Cappy Collection)

Most of the styling of the 1961 and 1962 T-Birds was retained in the 1963 model. A sculptured body side feature line was added, along with a modestly revised grille, restyled taillights and new side trim and wheel covers. Inside, buyers found metal-clad brake and accelerator pedals. An AM/FM radio was a new option. As an accessory, a tachometer was made available, too. Models offered were the same as the previous year. This was the first model to use hydraulic windshield wipers run by the power steering pump. Other technical changes included making the brakes more fade-resistant, and adding nearly 100 more pounds of sound-deadening materials. Suspension and exhaust improvements, lifetime chassis lubrication, and an alternator in place of a generator were other updates. Dimensions were basically the same as in the two previous years.

Thunderbird window stickers rose about $125 per model from 1962. The Hardtop listed for $4,495, the Landau was $4,548, the Convertible was $4,912, and the Sports Roadster was $5,563. These prices included basically the same standard

The 390 cid V-8 was again used in 1963. (Cappy Collection)

equipment as in 1962, plus an FM radio, which was new to the list this year. The Sports Roadster and Landau had additional standard features, some of which were slightly changed from their initial appearance in 1962. For example, the 1963 Landau had simulated walnut trim and a walnut-colored steering wheel replaced last season's color-keyed steering wheel. In midyear, a special Limited Edition Landau was released.

The grille insert for 1963 had mostly thin vertical bars that gave it an "electric shaver" look. It now incorporated a concealed hood latch, eliminating the old cable-operated release. The chrome Thunderbird script was moved to the rear fender. The front fender had a horizontal crease line that started just behind the grille, passed over the front wheel opening, and continued past the middle of the door. There it slanted downwards for a few

inches, and faded into the door. Just below the crease line, near the center of the door, were three groupings of forward-slanting chrome hash marks with five strips to each group. *Motor Trend* (October 1962) said these were supposed to remind one of turbine waste gates. New deep-dish wheel covers also followed the turbine motif. The Thunderbird this year was available in 20 single colors, and 23 two-tone combinations. As in 1962, convertible tops were offered in black, white, and blue, all with a black lining.

A selection of lush interiors came in a choice of 17 colors. There weren't any big changes to the inside of the basic models, although the inner door panels had new white and red courtesy lights for added safety when passengers were entering or exiting the car. Individual bucket seats, a console, recessed

A total of 14,139 Thunderbird Landau Hardtops were built in 1963. Standard tires were 8.00 x 14 tubeless whitewalls. (Cappy Collection)

instrumentation, and the optional Swing-Away steering wheel made the T-Bird luxurious and sporty inside. This year, Ford claimed that it was using 140 lb. of sound insulation materials in the Thunderbird. This included aluminum foil, thick fiber, mastic felt, and spray-on underbody deadener. Soundproofing, which was already considered excellent, was beefed up in many areas. The hood, wheel houses, instrument panel, dashboard, passenger and luggage compartment floors, roof panel and rails, package tray, and rear quarter panels all got more attention.

The 1963 T-Bird Convertible listed for $4,912 and a total of 5,913 were built, excluding Sports Roadsters. (Old Cars photo)

The license on this Cappy Collection T-Bird tells that it's rare. Only a handful of 1963 Sports Roadsters were made with the M-code V-8. (John Gunnell photo)

The Cappy Collection's M-code Sports Roadster. The "M" indicated the 390-cid/340-hp V-8 with three two-barrel carburetors. (John Gunnell photo)

1963 Thunderbird Interiors

Seat Type	Material	Silver Blue	White	Black	Chest nut	Rose Beige	Pearl Beige	Tur- quoise
Bucket Seats	Vinyl	50	53	56	59	51	54	57
Bucket Seats	Cloth & Vinyl			76			74	77
Bucket Seats	Leather		83*	86			84	

Seat Type	Material	Blue	Red	Gold
Bucket Seats	Vinyl	52	55	58
Bucket Seats	Cloth & Vinyl	72		
Bucket Seats	Leather	82	85	

* Code 83 white leather upholstery exclusive to 1963-1/2 Limited Edition Thunderbird Landau introduced in Monaco. This package also included Corinthian White exterior finish and Rose Beige roof of deeply grained vinyl. Interior had White and Rose Beige accents and White leather seat upholstery.

For 1963, the Sports Roadster got less attention from product planners, as well as from buyers. It had few changes and production dropped considerably. The "Roadster" could be had in eight colors. It again included the headrest style tonneau cover, bolt-on wire wheels with simulated knock-off hubs, Swing-Away steering wheel, and a passenger assist handle. It remained skirtless, and the special front fender insignia was used again. This insignia was affixed in the same front fender location, even though the Thunderbird "signature" had moved to the rear fender. Some publicity photos, including one that ran in *Motor Trend*, showed the Sports Roadster without the little T-Bird emblem.

Sports Roadsters were $5,563 in 1963. Just 455 were made. (Ford Motor Co.)

The 1963 Landau had more changes than the Sports Roadster, perhaps because it was perceived as the new Buick Riviera's direct competitor. Ford already knew that open T-Birds really didn't fit this market niche all that well. Although overall T-Bird business had been on an upswing (until this year) Convertible sales were gradually dropping. Buick and Pontiac did not even bother to offer ragtop versions of their Riviera and Grand Prix personal-luxury cars. Ford knew that the Thunderbird Hardtop needed the lion's share of attention, if it was going to do battle with these new GM challengers. Four vinyl top colors (black, white, brown, and blue) could now be had on the Landau. In addition, the simulated walnut trim and steering wheel were part of the package.

On Feb. 7, 1963, a special Limited-Edition Thunderbird Landau made its debut in the Principality of Monaco. Princess Grace of Monaco was given the number one car. This car was then dubbed the "Princess Grace" model by Ford salesmen. Only 2,000 were built and all were painted white. They had White leather upholstery, and a white steering wheel. The interior trim was accented with simulated rosewood, instead of walnut. The vinyl top was in a maroon color called Rose Beige. On the dashboard of each car was a special gold-toned nameplate with the car's special serial number 1 to 2,000. The price of $4,748 included special wheel covers with simulated knock-off hubs.

Base engine for the T-Bird was the same 390-cid 300-hp V-8. The optional "six-barrel" version stayed available until December 1962. A single exhaust system was now used with the 300-hp engine. This was supposedly a quieter and longer lasting system featuring 2.0-in. diameter laminated tubing (double pipes, one inside the other). It was used in conjunction with an asbestos-wrapped, aluminized steel muffler. A 1.78-in. diameter tailpipe was employed. With the optional 340-hp engine, dual exhausts were again used. The "six-barrel" again cost $242.10 extra. Both used an alternator instead of a generator. This was an Autolite model with a 2.25:1 drive ratio and maximum 40-amp. charge rate. A heavy-duty alternator was optional.

In January 1963, the Special Limited Edition Landau was introduced in Monaco. This one is parked outside the Monte Carlo Opera. (Ford Motor Co.)

Hooked to the 390 was a three-element Cruise-O-Matic automatic transmission with the old-fashioned Park/Reverse/Neutral/Drive-1/Drive-2/Low quadrant layout. This had a 2.10:1 stall ratio and 5.04:1 ratio at breakaway. The gears were: (first) 2.40:1; (second) 1.47:1; (third) 1.0:1; and (reverse) 2.00:1. It had a maximum upshift speed of 70 mph and a maximum kick-down speed of 65 mph. This ran into a 3.00:1 ratio conventional rear axle, or an optional limited-slip version with the same ratio. Again, no optional axle ratios were offered for the T-Bird.

1963 Ford T-Bird Landau

Coil springs with a ride rate of 105 lb.-in. were used in the front suspension, along with an 0.660-in. stabilizer or anti-roll bar. The 1963 T-Bird front suspension was lubricated for the "life of the car," which Ford estimated as 100,000 miles or seven years. Of course, a lot of collectors today would disagree with that statement. Lifetime seals and lubricants with better aging properties made this possible. Road noise and vibrations were also reduced through use of a newly developed rubber compression-type shock mount for the steering box, plus a flexible coupling between the gear assembly and the steering shaft. The link-type power steering system had a 20.3:1 overall ratio and required 3.6 turns lock-to-lock. Manual steering was not available. The leaf-type rear springs were 2.5 in. wide and 60 in. long. They also had a ride rate of 105 lb.-in. Telescoping 1/19-in. piston diameter shocks were mounted on the T-Bird suspension. Brake shoes were of duo-servo design. Drum diameter times width was 11.00 x 3.00 in. up front and 11.00 x 2.50 in. at the rear.

This 1963 ragtop paced USAC stock car races in Milwaukee. (Phil Hall photo)

One Thunderbird factory "dream car" was built this year for display at auto shows. It was called the Italien and had to be one of the sleekest T-Bird styling exercises ever built. When viewed from the side it looked like a fastback, but it actually had a notchback roof line like the original 1965 Mustang 2+2. This car had wire wheels, unique taillight trim, and special trim on the front fenders and doors.

The 1963 Thunderbird is considered by many to be the best-looking of the three-year group, primarily because of its new grille. Unfortunately, the party was over. With new competitors in the market-place, the '63s sold the worst of the bunch. Hardtop deliveries tumbled to just 42,806 units. The total output of regular Landaus was recorded separately this year and came to 12,139. That did not include the 2,000 "Princess Grace" Limited-Edition Landaus. The regular Convertible saw production of 5,913 units. Only 455 Sports Roadsters were built, including a mere 37 with the optional M-code engine. Overall, nearly 15,000 fewer Thunderbirds were built.

1963 Thunderbird Hardtop Specifications

Wheelbase	113.2 in.	Standard Engine Type	90-degree OHV V-8
Curb Weight	4,195 lb.	Compression Ratio	9.6:1
Frontal Area	22.5 sq. ft.	Carburetor	Single four-barrel
Box Vol.	476 cu. ft.	Maximum BHP	300 @ 4600 rpm
Front Overhang	38.3 in.	Taxable HP	52.50
Front Approach Angle	20.6 degrees	Maximum Torque	427 lb.-ft. @ 2800 rpm
Rear Overhang	53.6 in.	Engine Weight (Approx)	660 lb. (both V-8s)
Rear Departure Angle	12.7 degrees	Optional Engine	90-degree OHV V-8

1963 Thunderbird Hardtop Specifications

Front Hip Room	2 x 21.5 in.	Compression Ratio	10.5:1
Rear Hip Room	52.3 in.	Carburetors	Triple two-barrels
Front Seat Headroom	34.3 in.	Maximum BHP	340 @ 4600
Rear Seat Headroom	33.1 in.	Taxable HP	52.50
Front Seat Legroom	44.9 in.	Maximum Torque	430 lb.-ft. @ 3200 rpm
Rear Seat Legroom	37.3 in.	Displacement	390 cid (both V-8s)
Overall Length	205 in.	Bore x Stroke	4.05 x 3.78 in. (both V-8s)
Overall Height	52.5 in.	Gas Tank Capacity	20 gallons.
Overall Width	76.5 in.	Cooling System Capacity	20.5 quarts
R. Axle Road Clearance	5.6 in.	Standard Axle	3.00:1 hypoid (no-options)
Body Road Clearance	7.2 in.	Tires	8.00 x 14
Front Tread	61 in.	Effective Brake Area	234 sq. in.
Rear Tread	60 in.	Turning Diameter	40.2 ft.

Note: In 1963 only, the 300-hp engine had single exhausts.

1963 Thunderbird Engineering

Front Suspension	Independent wishbone type with coil springs
Rear Suspension	Live axle attached to semi-elliptic leaf springs
Steering	Link-type; power-assist, 3.6 turns lock-to-lock
Brakes	11-in. drums with 381 sq. in. swept area
Weight Distribution	56 percent front/44 percent rear
Fuel economy	11-20 mpg
Driving Range	220-400 miles

1964 - 1966
"Flair Birds"

1964
All You Need is a Flight Plan

The 1964 Thunderbird had completely new styling that put it in a "flight pattern" with other sports personal cars like the Buick Riviera, the Chrysler 300-K, and the Pontiac Grand Prix. In the end, it flew right past them, outselling all by wide margins. A longer hood and shorter roof line were seen. The hood line was also raised so that it blended in with the front fenders. There were "mirror-image" upper and lower feature lines at the belt line and lower body sides. At the time, the newness of the T-Bird design was stressed by car magazines. However, something about the general look of the car, with its air vent grille, "eyebrow" headlights, sculpturing, and rectangular taillamp housings, reminds me of the 1958-1960 models. In both cases, the cars also look extremely low to the ground. Overall heights ranged from 52.5 in. for the 1964 Hardtop to 53.3 for the Convertible, which were very close to the "Square Bird" specifications.

Car Life was one of the magazines that bought the "all-new" concept. An article in the October 1963 issue noted that there were more changes between the '63 and '64 models than first met the eye. "While the basic under-structure — unit-body inner and floor pan sections — probably do remain much the same as the '63s (and the '61s-62s, too), virtually all of the outer sheet metal stampings are new and different," said the magazine. Dimensions were virtually unchanged though. The wheelbase remained 113.2 in. and overall length was 205.4 in., making the '64 just a hair's breadth longer. Height was unchanged, width jumped just over a half inch, front and rear overhangs changed slightly, front hip room was the same, and the rear hip room was two-inches narrower (due mainly to a seat redesign). Tread widths were still 61 in. up front and 60 in. towards the rear. Significant technical change was just about non-existent.

The rear of the 1964 T-Bird featured rectangular taillights set within a massive bumper. The Hardtop was base-priced at $4,486. (Ford Motor Co. photo)

There was a touch of the 1958-1960 "Squarebirds" in the redesigned 1964 model. The Landau Hardtop had prices beginning at $4,589. (Ford Motor Co.)

If the T-Bird's size and engineering had changed little, despite its new "flight suit," the essential nature of the machine seemed to be changed even less. "What it is is a heavy, luxurious, prestige four-seater that gives its owner a soft, smooth ride and every imaginable creature comfort," *Motor Trend* suggested in its February 1964 road test. "Granted, it's not everyone's cup of tea, but for 'Bird lovers, it's the 'only way to fly.'" Magazines aimed at 1960s sports car buffs always seemed to be a bit more critical of the Thunderbird's two-and-one-half ton, gadget-heavy, Boulevard-friendly character. *Car and Driver*, in August 1964, complained, "The Thunderbird is 205.5 in. of steel and chrome with one purpose: gratification of the ego."

While they looked perhaps a tad slimmer, the '64 T-Birds outweighed the '63s by more than 300 lb. Frontal area was a tenth of a square foot less, but box volume of the car actually went up by six cubic feet. If the T-Bird was slightly larger, it was also slightly cost-lier. Base prices went up about $40 for closed cars, and $50 for open cars. The Hardtop and the Landau returned at prices of $4,486 and $4,589, respectively. Only one Con-vertible was marketed with a list price of $4,953. The Convertible again had an all-vinyl, wrinkle-resistant top that retracted under the power-operated deck lid. It was automat-ically stacked in the trunk, eliminating the need for an outside boot to store the top. It also eliminated most trunk storage space and brought a lot of criticism. Options could be purchased to turn a Convertible into a car like the Sports Roadster. Ford dealers sold wire wheels for $415, and a new headrest Sports Tonneau cover was priced at $269. You could not get a passenger grab bar, though, or any special front fender badges. The term Sports Roadster was no longer in official use by Ford, so offering Sports Road-ster model badges would have made no sense.

A "Chinese pagoda" shape characterized the Thunderbird's front grille opening. Tex-tured horizontal bars made up the 1964 grille insert. Thunderbird was spelled out along the lip of the hood in widely-spaced chrome letters. Amber-colored rectangular park-ing lamps were recessed into the bumper directly under the headlamps. The dual headlamps sat side by side under the sculptured eyebrows. A dual directional light indi-cator system was standard. There were little indicator lamps on the front fender tops for the driver to visualize when turning. Side sculpturing created a kind of flat "Parker pen" shaped indentation on the upper body sides. Thunderbird styling trademarks included a scooped hood (with the scoop also growing larger), chrome Thunderbird script nameplates (now placed behind the front wheel openings), and a formal-style roof . On regular Hardtops the wide sail panels were decorated with T-Bird emblems. Full wheel covers of a new design were standard, of course. The rear of the car was shaped like an electric razor that had no blades. The large, rectangular taillights sported bright frames and a Thunderbird symbol in the middle. Many writers suggested they were the industry's largest taillights because Ford had planned to make them flash sequentially. The company had this technology ready to go, but some state laws prohibited sequential lamps in 1964. Between the taillights was a white center piece bearing the Thunderbird name.

There were 20 single paint colors at the start of the 1964 model year. Prairie Bronze and Sunlight Yellow were added at midyear. The fiberglass Sports Tonneau cover came in eight colors. A couple of welcome additions to the Thunderbird's standard equipment list were full instrumentation, an automatic parking brake release, and a Silent-Flow fresh air circulation system. An optional Safety-Convenience panel had toggle switches for safety flashers and automatic door locks, plus lights to indicate low fuel, door ajar, and safety flasher operation.

A restyled "Flight-Deck" instrument panel was one of the 1964 T-Bird's big selling features. The complete interior sported an aircraft look. The instruments were mounted in separate pods and illuminated by soft green lighting. New, thin-shell bucket seats with headrests were featured up front. They were usually rated more comfortable than the previous design. A highly touted option was a front passenger seat with a fully-reclining back rest. The bucket seats were mounted on pedestals, which increased rear passenger leg room. The seats and interior came in 18 optional colors and trims including genuine leather.

1964 Thunderbird Interiors

Seat Type	Material	Rose	White	Black	Tan	Gray	Beige	Aqua
Bucket Seats	Vinyl	50	53	56	59	51	54	57
Bucket Seats	Cloth & Vinyl			76		71	74	
Bucket Seats	Leather		83	86	89			

Seat Type	Material	Blue	Red	Green
Bucket Seats	Vinyl	52	55	58
Bucket Seats	Cloth & Vinyl	72		
Bucket Seats	Leather	82	85	

Convertible top colors were Black (code 1); White (code 2); and Blue (code 4).
Sports Tonneau colors were Raven Black 1 (code A); Wimbledon White 17 (code M); Rangoon Red 12 (code J); Silver Mink 5 (code E); Brittany Blue 19 (code Q); Patrician Green 23 (code U); Prarie Bronze 9 (code G); and Somoan Coral 15 (code L).
Landau roof colors were Black (code A); White (code B); Brown (code C); and Blue (code D).

At $4,853, the 1964 Thunderbird Convertible was a great bargain. Only 9,198 of these cars were built. (Ford Motor Co.)

No longer offered as a "model" in 1964 was a Sports Roadster. However, Ford dealers offered a factory-optional Sports Roadster kit. (Ford Motor Co. photo)

Wider doors and a difference in the roof line made getting in and out of the T-Bird noticeably easier. New crank-type vent windows aided ventilation. The "Silent-Flo" fresh air circulation system let air into the car through vents at the base of the windshield. It then exited through a grille vent just below the rear window. A new asymmetric full-length console was offset to the driver's side, where it blended into the instrument panel. Between the front seats, the console rose up to double as a center foam-padded arm rest. It also separated the all-new wraparound Lounge style rear seats, which had a fold-down center arm rest.

The fiberglass tonneau for 1964 Convertibles cost $269. (Ford Motor Co. photo)

Safety and convenience were stressed in the new interior. A two-spoke steering wheel made the controls and gauges easier to see. It incorporated a padded hub. The dashboard and sun visors were also padded. The speedometer was of drum design with progressive illumination. A red indicator light grew in size as speed increased. This was promoted as a safer design. It was "trick," but actually harder to read. All control levers, buttons, and wheels for operating the heater, air conditioner, cruise control, radio, air vents, and power windows were clustered around the console. However, the gear shift lever was on the steering column for greater safety. There were stronger new "bear hug" door latches to hold the larger doors shut. Flood type reading lamps, mounted in the rear roof pillars behind the seats, enhanced both safety and convenience. New inertia reels were provided to retract the outboard front seat belts and make them easier to store and use.

The Landau model still wore a padded vinyl top and had landau bars attached to the roof sail panels. Although they had the traditional style S-shape with chrome finish, the landau irons now carried a new horizontal oval badge at their center. The Landau Hardtop's vinyl top came in four different colors: Black, White, Brown, and Blue. Simulated walnut graining on the instrument panel and interior door sills returned, but Rosewood trim was no longer offered. The vinyl top now had corner creases that gave it a crisper appearance.

The engine was again the 390 cid/300 hp. It had a higher 10.8:1 compression ratio, although the horsepower and torque ratings were unchanged from 1963. The only changes in the engine that stand out on spec sheets are microscopically smaller intake and exhaust valve diameters, a reduction in exhaust pipe diameter from 2.5 in. to 2.0 in., a corresponding reduction in tailpipe diameter from 2.0 in. to 1.75 in., and some ignition timing revisions. There were no changes in valve lengths, valve timing, or carburetion. Another improvement was that the main bearing thrust surface was increased 1/4 in. in diameter for increased durability and ruggedness. A transistorized ignition system was a new option. Ford said it could increase ignition points and spark plug life to 48,000 miles. Part of the fuel system was a new 22-gallon gas tank. One of its biggest advantages was that its new location provided a deep, wide well and more space in the luggage compartment. Ford offered larger V-8 engines in 1964, but none were available as a regular production option in the Thunderbird.

Continuing its quest of the "lifetime" car, Ford promoted 24,000-mile wheel bearing lubrication intervals, 100,000-mile chassis lubes, and 6,000-mile oil changes for T-Birds this year. The smooth-shifting Cruise-O-Matic transmission had no specifications changes. Also unchanged were the front and rear suspensions. There was a new integral power steering system, but the ratio, turns lock-to-lock, and turning circle specifications stayed the same. The self-adjusting brakes with flared drums were the same sizes front and rear. There was a switch to 15-in. wheels and 8.15 x 15 low-profile tires were standard. These were said to have a special tread and composition developed specifically for T-Birds. In a T-Bird road test, *Motor Trend* reported that fast, hard driving on twisting mountain roads had caused excessive front tire wear. It said that the car's weight, front suspension geometry, and body lean caused tire scuffing in fast corners. Of course, the problem was that such magazines drove the car harder than 90 percent of Thunderbird buyers intended to. Convertibles with the optional wire wheels had to use 8.00 x 14 tires.

A 'Bird's-eye view of utter luxury for four in 1964. (Ford Motor Co.)

The 1964 T-Bird "Flight Deck" instrument panel looked smart. (Ford Motor Co.)

Another change in 1964 was the availability of a long list of rear axle options. Standard again was the 3.00:1 axle. However, buyers could substitute 3.25:1, 3.50:1, 3.89:1, and 4.11:1. In addition limited-slip axles were offered.

Despite all its big changes in looks and small technical enhancements, the Thunderbird continued to leave the folks who tested cars for "buff" books largely unimpressed. *Motor Trend* reported that the car wallowed in corners and plowed sideways when taking corners at high speeds. The magazine said that the brakes halted the car in a shorter than average distance during a panic stop from 30 mph. However, in braking from 60 mph, they heated up and faded badly, taking much longer than average to stop the vehicle. "Shockingly flabby front end and awesome quantities of understeer," exclaimed *Car and Driver* about the 'Bird. The magazine said the brakes were "grabby" and that handling was "reminiscent of prewar Packards."

Critics aside, this was a very good year for Thunderbird. Along with the rest of Ford Motor Company's Total Performance Products, the Thunderbird shared *Motor Trend* magazine's "Car of the Year" award for "the best possible use of high-performance testing in bringing to the motoring public a product that lives up to the claims of the maker: Total Performance." Thunderbird sales and production missed the all-time record, set in 1960, by just 378 cars (the 1960 total was 92,843). The factory in Wixom, Mich. produced 60,552 Hardtops, 22,715 Landaus, and 9,198 Convertibles.

A Thunderbird show car called the "Golden Palomino" made its way around the circuit this year. It was a Landau with roof sections that flipped-up. The car had both genuine wire wheels and fender skirts. While touring the country it was put on display at many Ford dealerships nationwide.

Don Fymbo of Denver, CO has one of only 52 units produced by the Great Dale Company between 1961 and '66. Utilizing the front end and frames of production passenger vehicles, the company hand-assembled one RV per month. While many body styles were incorporated, Fymbo's unit is the only one built on the 1964 Ford Thunderbird.

Equipped with a sink, a stove, a furnace, a fold-down table, a three-way refrigerator and three-way lights, it will sleep four people. The Ford 390 four-barrel with dual exhaust and passing gear, combined with factory air, cruises at 65 mph--at a respectable 16 mpg. In superb condition and with only 40,000 original miles on it, this piece of RV history has a lot of travel left in its future.

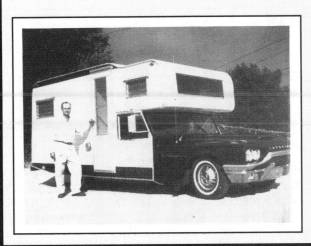

1964 Thunderbird Hardtop Specifications

Wheelbase	113.2 in.	Standard Engine Type	90-degree OHV V-8
Curb Weight	4,740 lb.	Bore	4.05 in.
Frontal Area	22.4 sq. ft.	Stroke	3.78 in.
Box Vol.	482 cu. ft.	Displacement	390 cid
Front Overhang	37.7 in.	Carburetor	Single 4-Barrel C3AF
Front Approach Angle	19.5 degrees	Compression Ratio	10.8:1
Rear Overhang	54.5 in.	Maximum BHP	300 @ 4600 rpm
Rear Departure Angle	12.9 degrees	Taxable HP	52.50
Front Hip Room	2 x 21.5 in.	Maximum Torque	427 lb.-ft. @ 2800 rpm
Rear Hip Room	49.9 in.	Engine Weight	660 lb.. (approx.)
Overall Length	205.4 in.	Block Length	21.6 in.
Overall Height	52.5 in.	Gas Tank Capacity	22 gallons.
Overall Width	77.1 in.	Cooling System Capacity	20.5 quarts
R. Axle Road Clearance	5.56 in.	Standard Axle	3.00:1 hypoid
Body Road Clearance	9.0 in.	Standard Tires	8.15 x 15
Front Tread	61 in.	Optional Tires	8.00 x 14 (w/ wire wheels)
Rear Tread	60 in.	Effective Brake Area	238 sq. in.
Turning Diameter	40.2 ft.		

1964 Thunderbird Engineering

Front Suspension	Independent wishbone type with coil springs
Rear Suspension	Live axle attached to semi-elliptic leaf springs
Steering	Integral; power-assist, 3.6 turns lock-to-lock
Brakes	11-in. drums with 381 sq. in. swept area
Weight Distribution	56 percent front/44 percent rear
Average Fuel Economy	11.1 mpg (ranged from 8.3 mpg - 14.5 mpg)
Driving Range	183-319 miles

1964 Thunderbird Performance

Model	CID/HP	Performance
0-60 mph		
Hardtop	390/300	11.2 seconds
Convertible	390/300	10.0 seconds
1/4-Mile		
Hardtop	390/300	18 seconds at 76 mph
Convertible	390/300	16.8 seconds
Convertible	390/300	17.7 seconds at 81.5 mph
Top Speed		
Hardtop	390/300	105
Convertible	390/300	110 mph (estimated)

1965
"Braking" Tradition

The 1965 Thunderbirds had no drastic appearance changes. They were virtually identical to the 1964s in appearance. Thunderbird lettering no longer appeared on the edge of the hood. It was replaced with a stylized T-Bird emblem. Wide-spaced vertical moldings added to the former horizontal bars grille. The script plate with the model name moved from the front fender to the rear fender. There were dummy air vents (Ford called them "simulated waste gates") on both sides of the vehicle, just behind the front wheel openings. New emblems also adorned the roof sail panels. They had a stylized Thunderbird partly encircled by a chrome ring. The center section of the rear bumper gained a Thunderbird crest replacing the name spelled out across it and the broad tail-lights were divided into six square segments by short vertical chrome moldings.

The wheelbase, overall length, height, width, front tread, rear tread, and all other dimensions were the same as the year before. In fact, not even the prices of the three models changed. The Hardtop was still $4,486, the Landau was $4,589, and the Convertible was $4,953. It almost seemed like the Thunderbird was trying to rival the Volkswagen for the least year-to-year changes in an automobile. However, some small details did differ. The doors could now be locked without using a key, and the keys went into the door locks with either edge up. Also, a "fasten seat belt" light now went off when the driver's belt was pulled out and latched. In 1964, the light had stayed lit.

For 1965 the Thunderbird adopted sequential taillights. (Ford Motor Co. photo)

Standard features were about the same, except for the significant additions of front wheel disc brakes and sequential taillights. FoMoCo did not install any super-high-output engines (like its brutal 427-cid V-8s) in T-Birds, although they were used in some other 1965 Fords. The 390-cid 300-hp V-8 was standard again. There were no options. While the engine was virtually the same as 1964 and earlier 390s on the inside, there were several external difference. The oil filler tube disappeared from in front of the manifold. There was a breather cap and filler tube on the driver's side valve cover instead. Also, two engine mount bosses were added on each side of the block casting, due to the use of a new engine mounting system.

The T-Bird continued to come with many more "goodies" than most 1965 cars included. However, there were at least 25 factory options, plus additional dealer accessories. Even rear fender skirts were $32.70 extra. A vacuum-operated trunk release ($12.90) was a new accessory. A couple of options disappeared. The headrest-style Sports Tonneau cover was dropped. However, the '64 Sports Tonneau fit the '65 Convertible and, for buyers who demanded one, a cover could often be obtained from some Ford dealer's parts inventory.

Except for minor detail changes, the 1965 T-Bird Hardtop looked like the 1964 model. Disc brakes were now available. (Ford Motor Co.)

In 1965 Thunderbird side scripts moved from front to rear fenders. Front fenders also got "waste gate" trim. The Landau Hardtop returned. (Ford Motor Co.)

White sidewall tires were available for the Thunderbird at $44 over the price of the standard 8.15 x 15 blackwalls. Red band tires, another new option, were also $44 extra. Only 15-in. tires were offered in 1965. Fourteen-inch tires had been used, in 1964, on cars with the optional wire wheels. However, the new disc brakes did not work with wire wheels, so the wire wheel option was dropped in 1965. Deluxe wheel covers were $16. For anyone interested in what might have been, the October 1964 issue of *Motor Trend* had a story about designing wheel covers. It showed six prototype designs envisioned for 1965 Thunderbirds. None of the six mock-ups made the assembly line, although the T-Bird did have new wheel covers. They were very handsome, indeed, with fine radial rib textures and spun satin finish.

Models available again were the Hardtop, Landau and Convertible. A Limited-Edition Special Landau was released in March 1965. It featured Emberglow exterior finish with matching interior carpet and color-coordinated seat trim. Historian James F. Petrik notes that at least one Limited-Edition Special Landau had White paint on its exterior. Special wheel discs with Emberglow trim dressed up the wheels. The vinyl roof, steering wheel, and vinyl upholstery were done in a special color called Parchment. A plate was affixed to the console of all 4,500 examples built with the owner's name and "Limited Edition" engraved on it. This model had a $4638.60 window sticker. For $50 over the price of the base Landau Hardtop, it was quite a bargain.

Twenty single colors were offered for the outside of 1965 models at first. Eleven were T-Bird exclusives. Later, Emberglow Metallic (code V) was added as an exclusive color for the Limited-Edition Landau model. Twenty-four two-tone paint combinations greatly expanded the buyer's choices. Vinyl top and convertible top colors were the same as in 1964. Inside, the T-Bird had an instrument panel inspired by aircraft design motifs. *Car Life* quipped that driving a T-Bird for the first time at night could "remind its driver of the main drag of Las Vegas, if all the lights are blinking in front of him." At the rear, the sequential tail-lights were a real attention getter. They operated through an arrangement of multiple taillight bulbs that flashed, in order, from the inner side of the broad red lens to its outer edge.

Car Life found the T-Bird's thin-shell bucket seats "an aid to the continual ease of riding" and strongly recommended the optional reclining passenger seat with pull-up headrest. "The seats provide a fine compromise between wrap-around support and lounge chair squirm room," reported *Car Life*. "Once tried, the 'Bird's accommodations actually invite long (and normally dreary) drives, rather than discouraging them." However,

Instead of letters, a T-Bird insignia flew between the '65 taillights. (Ford Motor Co.)

the magazine gave low marks to the rear passenger compartment. Though admitting the wrap-around rear seats *could* be comfortable, the testers found it impossible to *get* comfortable due to the intruding full-length center console. The magazine comically described some contortions its staff members went through to ride in the rear compartment for long periods of time. There were 35 interior options early in the model-year, and 37 after the Limited Edition Landau arrived.

The '65 convertible tops continued to come in several colors. (Old Cars photo)

1965 Thunderbird Interiors

Seat Type	Material	Black	Blue	Silver Mink	Palo-mino	White	Beige	Red
Bucket Seats	Vinyl	26	22	21	29	20	24	25
Headrest Bucket Seats	Vinyl	56	52	51	59	50	54	55
Bucket Seats	Cloth & Vinyl	16	12	11	19			
Headrest Bucket Seats	Cloth & Vinyl	46	42	41	49			
Bucket Seats	Leather	36	32		39			35
Headrest Bucket Seats	Leather	66	62		69			65

Seat Type	Material	Aqua	Gold	White Pearl	Burgundy
Bucket Seats	Vinyl	27	28		
Headrest Bucket Seats	Vinyl	57			
Bucket Seats	Cloth & Vinyl				
Headrest Bucket Seats	Cloth & Vinyl				
Bucket Seats	Leather			30	33
Headrest Bucket Seats	Leather			60	63

The new Kelsey-Hayes vented disc brakes featured 4-piston calipers and brought a vast improvement in T-Bird braking performance. "Deceleration rates and stopping distances are nothing short of phenomenal for a 5,000-lb. car," said *Car Life*. The disc brake system was the same one used in the Lincoln Continental, except that the T-Bird did not have a front wheel pressure-limiting valve. A proportioning valve was used in the system to balance pressure to the lightly loaded rear wheels. The disc brake pads were advertised to last 30,000 miles.

The 1965 T-Bird Convertible had a $4,851 list price. Only 6,846 of these cars left the assembly line, making survivors rare today. (Ford Motor Co.)

111

The 1965 Thunderbird Special Landau featured sportier-looking two-tone color schemes. It also had special color-coordinated wheel covers. (Ford Motor Co.)

The Private World of Thunderbird

A PRODUCT OF *Ford* MOTOR COMPANY

Inside, the 1965 Thunderbird Special Landau highlighted the "private world of Thunderbird" with exclusive trim and burled walnut accents. (Ford Motor Co.)

Used again in the Thunderbird was the 390-cid V-8 with 300 hp. It had a new carburetor and possibly a running change in compression ratio. *Car Life's* road test, published in November 1964, said 10.8:1. However, the magazine's annual multi-page chart of car specifications in April 1965 said 10.1:1. While the magazine's test car had a small problem — some harshness occurring at speeds around 85 mph — the T-Bird still got a good review. With countless gadgets and accessories running, *Car Life* reported, "So quiet and effortless was the running that the red ribbon type speedometer all too often crept past the 80 mph mark." As usual, the T-Bird was assessed as being "hard-pressed to exhibit much control with less than ideal road surfaces." But the magazine said that the car had to be admired for inspiring "dozens of lesser imitations which, by their very imitation, prove the 'Bird a better beast."

Although 1965 was a strong year for car sales in general, production of 1965 Thunderbirds declined from the previous season. The figures according to body style were: Hardtop 42,652, Landau 20,974, Special Landau 4,500, and Convertible 6,846. The grand total was 74,972 cars.

1965 Thunderbird Hardtop Specifications

Wheelbase	113.2 in.	Standard Engine Type	90-degree OHV V-8
Curb Weight	4,693 lb.	Bore	4.05 in.
Frontal Area	22.5 sq. ft.	Stroke	3.78 in.
Box Vol.	482.5 cu. ft.	Displacement	390 cid
Front Overhang	37.7 in.	Carburetor	Single 4-Barrel C5AF
Front Approach Angle	19.5 degrees	Compression Ratio	10.8:1 (*)
Rear Overhang	54.5 in.	Maximum BHP	300 @ 4600 rpm
Rear Departure Angle	12.9 degrees	Taxable HP	52.50
Front Hip Room	59.7 in.	Maximum Torque	427 lb.-ft. @ 2800 rpm
Rear Hip Room	49.9 in.	Engine Weight	660 lb. (approx.)
Overall Length	205.4 in.	Block Length	21.6 in.
Overall Height	52.5 in.	Gas Tank Capacity	22 gallons.
Overall Width	77.1 in.	Cooling System Capacity	20.5 quarts
R. Axle Road Clearance	5.5 in.	Standard Axle	3.00:1 hypoid
Body Road Clearance	9.0 in.	Tires	8.15 x 15
Front Tread	61 in.	Brake Lining Gross Area	133 sq. in.
Rear Tread	60 in.	Turning Diameter	40.2 ft.

*Reported as 10.8:1in 11/64 and 10.1:1 in 4/65.

1965 Thunderbird Engineering

Front Suspension	Independent wishbone type with coil springs
Rear Suspension	Live axle attached to semi-elliptic leaf springs
Steering	Integral; power-assist, 3.6 turns lock-to-lock
Front Brakes	11.87-in. K-H ventilated 4-piston caliper disc
Rear Brakes	11.1 x 2.50-in. drums with 412 sq. in. of swept area
Weight Distribution	56 percent front/44 percent rear
Average Fuel Economy	13-16 mpg
Driving Range	286-352 miles

1965 Thunderbird Performance

Model	CID/HP	Performance
0-60 mph		
Landau	390/300	10.3 seconds
1/4-Mile		
Landau	390/300	17.5 seconds at 79 mph
Top Speed		
Landau	390/300	115
Hardtop	390/300	117 mph (calculated)

Dealers sold "roadster" tonneaus in '65, though option was gone. (Old Cars photo)

1966
Aladdin on "Autopilot"

Although using the previous body, the 1966 T-Bird looked quite new with its back-slanting grille carrying a big T-Bird emblem in the center. (Old Cars photo)

The '66 had a full-width taillight with back-up light in center. (Ford Motor Co. photo)

An early prototype of the 1966 Thunderbird featured clear plastic headlight covers. *Motor Trend* magazine ran a sketch of this design and predicted the next Thunderbird would have it. This was incorrect, although the headlights did get a new bright metal face plate around them and the rest of the front end was changed quite a bit. It had a more aggressive-looking wedge shape. The hood grew longer, and the scoop on top of it was flatter and more sharply pointed. The front lip of the hood had no decorative trim and use of a heavy chrome grille surround was eliminated. An "ice cube tray" grille carried a big stylized T-Bird ornament right in its center. There was a much slimmer "nerf-bar" style bumper with a body-color splash pan showing below it. The parking lamps were mounted in the splash pan.

In profile, the T-Bird Hardtop and Convertible bodies looked much the same. Ford removed the simulated "waste gates" from the front fenders, but the "Thunderbird" name script remained on the extreme rear of the body sides. Thin chrome moldings highlighted the front and rear wheel openings. "Ford tried to do away with fender skirts," explains James F. Petrik, the marque historian. "That was a mistake, as the car did not look right without fender skirts." Fender skirts were an option, however. When they were ordered, the rear wheel arch moldings were eliminated and the fender skirts had chrome moldings along the bottom. This was the last year for fender skirts, as well as for front ventipanes.

A glittery, but attractive full-width rear end treatment was part of the 1966 package. The back-up light lens was right in the middle of the sequential taillamp lenses. The lenses once again had a series of side by side square segments, although the individual squares were no longer trimmed with chrome moldings. The regular full wheel covers were again restyled. New pentastar wheel covers with a "mag" wheel look and color-coordinated sections that matched the body color were used on some new models.

For the second year in a row, the T-Bird Convertible dropped in price. It listed for $4,845. Nevertheless, its production fell to 5,049 cars. (Ford Motor Co. photo)

The 1966 Thunderbird model count was increased to four with the additions of a Town Hardtop and a Town Landau. These shared a new roof line that was luxuriously stylish, if not very practical. The roof had wider sail panels, and no rear quarter windows. As a result, vision from inside the car was reduced. Both the regular Hardtop and Town Hardtop had Thunderbird insignias on the roof sail panels, while the Town Landau carried S-shaped landau irons in the same location. There was no landau -trimmed version of the regular Hardtop and this would also be the last year (so far) for a factory-issued T-Bird Convertible.

This view of the 1966 T-Bird Convertible interior provides a good look at the contoured rear seats. (Ford Motor Co. photo)

Thunderbirds had the same wheelbase, overall length, front and rear tread, and tire size as in 1965. Overall width was microscopically larger since the new bumper was wider and, being the widest point on the car, was where the measurement was taken. The 390-cid engine was up-rated to 315 hp at 4600 rpm. For the first time in years an engine option was offered. This was a 428-cid V-8 that produced 345 hp at 4600 rpm. It was $64 extra. Another new option, priced at $128, was a stereo tape player that was built into the AM radio. It provided up to 80 minutes of music per cartridge. Four speakers were included with this sound system. The Safety-Convenience Control Panel was optional for the Hardtop and Convertible and standard with the Town Hardtop and Town Landau models. On the latter pair it was incorporated into an overhead roof console.

"The flying-carpet-on-autopilot" is how *Car Life* (June 1966) referred to the Thunderbird that it tested. "Aladdin himself would be astounded at the things this Ford-built 'jinni' can do — and without all that tiresome rubbing of lamps." The writers, of course, were referring to the car's "bells and whistles," which they had the opportunity to try out during a cruise from Los Angeles to Las Vegas. Their "magic carpet" was described as a Town Landau carrying "Aquamarine Blue lower body paint, a pebbled White vinyl-covered top with aluminized plastic landau bars at the windowless rear quarter panel, special tires with both red and white striping, Beige leather-like vinyl upholstery, interior trim of chromium and walnut, loop pile nylon carpeting in a matching blue-green shade and a Beige molded fiberglass headliner." It was loaded with the 428-cid V-8, air conditioning, California emission controls, vacuum door locks, a door warning light, a low-fuel warning lamp, emergency flashers, power seats, speed control, and a special steering wheel for the speed control. Naturally, this was all in addition to such standard features as Cruise-O-Matic transmission, power steering, power front disc brakes, AM radio, bonded mirror, heater, hydraulic wipers, and Swing-Away steering wheel.

Car Life, in its test, had nothing but praise for the Thunderbird. This included advice that the car with power front discs drew quickly to a halt, in a straight line, hardly screeching the tires. The steering was assessed as "a definite surprise when compared to mushy, imprecise, and slow-turning assisted systems." The magazine liked the car's "steering only" (with speed control on) operation, plus its Swing-Away steering wheel, electric seat, power windows and air conditioning system. It did, however, note the shortage of rear seat leg room and some wind rumble at speeds above 60 mph. With the big engine the car could do 0-30 mph in 3.1 seconds, 0-50 in 6.8 seconds, and 0-100 in 29 seconds. Moving from 30-70 mph in passing gear took 9.3 seconds.

A rare 1966 T-Bird is the 428-V-8-powered Convertible. (Cappy Collection)

An egg-crate pattern gave the new-for-1966 grille a very aggressive look in tune with the "muscle car" mentality of its era. (Cappy Collection)

Ford dealers continued to add Sports Roadster tonneaus for buyers who wanted the option, although the factory no longer made this item. (Cappy Collection)

Thunderbirds came in 20 Super Diamond Lustre single-color enamels, eight of which were exclusively offered on T-Birds. For Hardtops and Town Hardtops, 34 two-tone paint combinations were available. Interior options included 10 basic all-vinyl trims, three cloth and vinyl trims, and four leather upholstery options. When two-tones and different seat options were tossed into the mix, there were 21 color schemes and 51 separate trim codes. A variety of "appointments" (carpets, console coverings, dash pads, and other interior items), were available with specific interiors. Convertible top colors were the same: Black, White, and Blue. The vinyl tops were offered in Black, White, Sage Gold, and Parchment.

1966 Thunderbird Interiors

Seat Type	Material	Black	Blue	Dark Blue	Palo-mino	Parch-ment	Silver Mink	Bur-gundy
Bucket Seats	Vinyl	26	22		49		21	23
Headrest Bucket Seats	Vinyl	56	52		69		51	53
Bucket Seats	Cloth & Vinyl	16	12	42		1D		
Headrest Bucket Seats	Cloth & Vinyl	46				4D		
Bucket Seats	Leather	66		62				

Seat Type	Material	Ember glow	Red	Aqua	Ivy Gold	Blue/ Parch	Ember/ Parch	Black/ Parch
Bucket Seats	Vinyl	24	25	27	28	B2	B4	B6
Headrest Bucket Seats	Vinyl	54	55	57	58		K4	K6
Bucket Seats	Leather		65			L2	L4	L6

Seat Type	Material	Turq/ Parch	Gold/ Parch	Palo/ Parch	Burg/ Parch	Blue/ White	Burg/ White	Turq/ White
Bucket Seats	Vinyl	B7	B8	B9	B3	G2	G3	G7
Headrest Bucket Seats	Vinyl	K7	K8	K9	K3	P2	P3	P7
Bucket Seats	Leather	L7	L8	L9	L3			

Seat Type	Material	Gold/ White	Palo/ White	SMink/ White	Ember/ White	Black/ White
Bucket Seats	Vinyl	G8	G9	G1	G4	G6
Headrest Bucket Seats	Vinyl	P8	P9	P1	P4	P6

Legend: Palo means Palomino; Burg means Burgundy; Turq means Turquoise; Ember means Emberglow; Smink means Silver Mink.

Prices for carryover models actually *decreased* this year. The Hardtop listed for $4,395 and the Convertible was $4,845. The Town Hardtop and Town Landau were also reasonably priced at $4,452 and $4,552, respectively. Despite the decrease in factory retail prices, most T-Bird sold for a bunch more. *Motor Trend's* test car, the Town Landau with the 390 V-8, went for $6,010.12. *Car Life's* "loaner," equipped with the 428 V-8, was $6,153 out the door. Even at that, production took another dip and a total of 69,176 Thunderbirds were built. That included 13,389 Hardtops, 5,049 Convertibles, 15,633 Town Hardtops, and 35,105 Town Landaus. Did we say the Town Landau wasn't a practical car? In just one season it had become the best-selling Thunderbird accounting for more than 50 percent of all deliveries.

1966 Thunderbird Town Landau Specifications

Wheelbase	13.0 in.	Standard Engine Type	90-degree OHV V-8
Curb Weight	4,840 lb.	Bore	4.05 in.
Frontal Area	22.5 cu. ft.	Stroke	3.78 in.
Box Vol.	482.5 cu. ft.	Displacement	390 cid
Front Overhang	37.7 in.	Carburetor	Single 4-Barrel C6SF
Front Approach Angle	19.5 degrees	Compression Ratio	10.5:1
Rear Overhang	54.5 in.	Maximum BHP	315 @ 4600 rpm
Rear Departure Angle	12.9 degrees	Taxable HP	52.50
Front Hip Room	59.7 in.	Maximum Torque	427 lb.-ft. @ 2800 rpm
Rear Hip Room	49.9 in.	Engine Weight	660 (approx.)
Overall Length	205.4 in.	Block Length	21.6 in.
Overall Height	52.5 in.	Optional Engine Type	90-degree OHV V-8
Overall Width	77.3 in.	Bore	4.13 in.
Front Hip Room	2 x 21.5 in.	Stroke	3.98 in.
Front Shoulder Room	57 in.	Displacement	428 cid
Front Headroom	37.4 in.	Carburetor	Single 4-Barrel C6SF
Rear Hip Room	49.9 in.	Compression Ratio	10.5:1
Rear Shoulder Room	54 in.	Maximum BHP	345 @ 4600 rpm
Rear Leg Room	33.2 in.	Taxable HP	54.6
Rear Headroom	37.6 in	Maximum Torque	462 lb.-ft. at 2800 rpm
R. Axle Road Clearance	6.4 in.	Engine Weight	680 lb. (approx.)
Body Road Clearance	9.0 in.	Block Length	21.6 in.
Front Tread	61 in.	Transmission	Cruise-O-Matic
Rear Tread	60 in.	Brake Lining Gross Area	133 sq. in.
Gas Tank Capacity	22 gallons	Brake Lining Swept Area	408 in.
Cooling System Capacity	20.5 quarts	Axle (390 V-8)	3.00 (std.); 3.25 (opt.)
Tires	8.15 x 15	Axle (428 V-8)	2.80 (std); 3.00/3.50 (opt)
Turning Diameter	42.6 ft		

The third, but not last, 1966 T-Bird model was the Landau Hardtop. In standard trim, its prices started at $4,552. (Ford Motor Co. photo)

1966 Thunderbird Engineering

Front Suspension	Coil springs with ball joints
Rear Suspension	Live axle attached to semi-elliptic leaf springs
Steering	Integral; power-assist, 3.6 turns lock-to-lock
Front Brakes	11.87-in. K-H ventilated 4-piston caliper disc
Rear Brakes	11.09 x 2.50-in. drums with 412 sq. in. of swept area
Weight Distribution	(428 V-8) 53.9 % front /46.1 % rear
Average Fuel Economy	(390 V-8) 13-16 mpg; (428 V-8) 12-14 mph
Driving Range	(390 V-8) 286-352 miles; (428 V-8) 264-308 miles

1967 - 1969
"Glamor Birds"

1967
"Va-Va-Voom" Sedan

For 1967, the Thunderbird was redesigned from the ground up. With a perimeter frame, semi-unit body, and all-coil spring suspension, the new model was quieter than ever. Two big surprises were reflected in the roster of Thunderbird body styles. No longer available was the Convertible. In its place was a sedan model with center-opening doors. It was called the four-door Landau. "Heretofore, a buyer of Ford products had no place to go between the Mercury Park Lane and the Lincoln Continental," said the company's sales instruction book, in an effort to explain the role of the new model. "Now he has Thunderbird."

The '67 front end was dominated by new full-width grille. (Old Cars photo)

The sporty four-door seemed to be Ford's answer to the Jaguar Mark II and the Maserati Quatrroporte. However, many T-Bird buffs were left unimpressed. "In the Autumn of 1966, a dyed-in-the-wool Thunderbird enthusiast had good reason to feel disappointment," wrote marque historian James F. Petrik in *Old Cars*. "His or her favorite automobile, introduced 12 years earlier as a convertible, would no longer be able to have its top folded and, as an even greater shock, the Thunderbird would be available as a four-door Landau."

At least one buff magazine had a *no-big-deal* reaction to the four-door model. "The idea of adding two more doors to the T-Bird is being treated like the invention of the cotton gin by Ford, but the change is hardly worth the hoopla," *Car and Driver* opined. "The result is a sharply styled, slightly smaller Galaxie with all the trimmings." Nevertheless, it's interesting to note that the four-door received excellent public exposure. It quickly appeared in the October 1966, September 1966 and February 1967 issues of *Car Life*, the November 1966 issue of *Motor Trend*, and the October 1967 issue of *Motorcade*, a British magazine.

A two-door Landau Hardtop was also part of the 1967 model lineup. It had a base price of $4.704 and was the year's most popular T-Bird. (Ford Motor Co. photo)

The four-door was one of three models offered in 1967. It was the most expensive Thunderbird with a suggested list price of $4,858. The others were a two-door Hardtop and two-door Landau. They listed for $4,636 and $4,737, respectively.

All set to set trends...Thunderbird Luxury in 2-doors

...Thunderbird Luxury in 4-doors

Advertisement showing 1967 two-door Hardtop and four-door Landau announced the year's big news. The Convertible was quietly dropped. (Ford Motor Co.)

Ford used the long hood, short deck styling motif popularized by the Mustang to give all the new Thunderbirds a muscular appearance. A long front overhang seemed to emphasize the impression that there was something powerful lurking under the hood. *Car Life* (October 1966) described the new design as "a low, thrusting shape nestled around four big wheels" and added that "the frankly gaping snout is followed by an acre of hood." The full-radiused wheel openings did, indeed, make the wheels look very large, although tire size was one of the car's few unchanged specifications. Since skirted rear fenders did not go with the "open-wheel" look, fender skirts were not offered.

Up front, the new T-Birds were dominated by a full-width oval bumper-grille featuring a lattice work insert and "Hide-Away" headlights. In the center of the grille was a large Thunderbird-shaped trim piece. The headlights disappeared on panels that rotated. As the lenses flipped to the inside of the grille, a panel flipped out to become part of it. One-piece curved door glass eliminated the use of vent windows. Two-door Hardtops had rear quarter windows that slid horizontally to retract. Both Landau models had roofs with wide "C" pillars, which gave them a close-coupled appearance. The cars had a "Coke bottle" shape in profile and wall-to-wall sequential taillights at the rear.

An unusual feature of the new four-door Landau was its "suicide" style rear doors. These center-opening (rear-hinged) doors were a throwback to the 1930s. They earned their nickname by creating life-threatening situations when unlatched while a vehicle is moving. The wind created by movement of the vehicle would swing such a door open with force great enough to pull the person who opened it right from the vehicle. (I once had a rear suicide door on my 1936 Pontiac shake open while driving at about 20 mph. Since the door opened by itself, no one was holding onto it and yanked from the vehicle. However, the wind nearly ripped the door off its hinges, which would have made my Pontiac a three-door!)

In 1967, the only cars available with center-opening doors were the Thunderbird four-door Landau and the Lincoln-Continental four-door Sedan and Convertible. Like the two-door Landau, this new model had a vinyl top and S-shaped landau irons with center medallions. Due to the wideness of the rear roof pillars, a section of each sail panel underneath the decorative landau bar was designed to swing open with the door. This provided sufficient room for passengers to enter or leave the rear compartment without slamming into the roof pillar.

Inside the T-Bird had new front and rear seats, a restyled console, new door panels, and a different dash treatment. While retaining the basic "Flight Deck" theme of recent years, the new look was somewhat smoother and cleaner. "We were pleased to see that Ford has finally cooled it with the airplane-pilot syndrome that has turned previous Thunderbirds into bogus jet-liners," said *Car and Driver*. "The Twenty-First Century instruments are gone, replaced by a set of four straightforward — if mildly illegible — dials across the dash. The optional warning lights are still in their old hangout on the molding under the roof but they are more subdued." The Thunderbird's Swing-Away steering wheel turned into a Tilt-Away type. In addition to swinging aside, it tilted to make it easy to enter or leave the car.

Other standard T-Bird features included power front disc/rear drum brakes, power steering, and an automatic parking brake release. Although Ford had promoted safety features much earlier than any American car maker, the 1967 Thunderbird took driver and passenger safety to new levels. In addition to a padded, shock-absorbing steering wheel, padded dashboard, and backup braking system, Ford provided front seat shoulder harnesses that stowed above the doors with Velcro fasteners, plus recessed sun visors, and pliable rubber door grab handles and front fender trim pieces. Unfortunately, the low roof and high belt line created smaller windows, which affected driver vision from inside the vehicle.

The first-ever T-Bird four-door was the second most popular model for 1967. Note the front-opening "suicide" doors in the rear. (Ford Motor Co. photo)

Car of the Gods

By Dr. Richard L. Schatz

Five very special Thunderbirds were created in 1967 for the Abercrombie & Fitch company to display at its upscale sporting goods stores in different cities. These Apollo Thunderbirds were loaded with luxury features and cost $15,000 each. They were built by Andy Hotten's Dearborn Steel Tubing Co. of Dearborn, Mich.., and delivered through Ford dealerships. Only five of the cars were made. They were sent to Abercrombie & Fitch outlets in Miami and Palm Beach, New York City, Chicago, and San Francisco. However, the car shipped to the West Coast was destroyed while in transit.

Converting the cars was a first-class operation. Dearborn Steel Tubing Co. was associated with much of Ford's specialty car work. Andy Hotten had raced Thunderbirds at Daytona in 1956. Among his other notable commissions was creation of factory light-weight Ford race cars in the 1960s. The Fairlane-based "Thunderbolts" that left his shop dominated professional drag racing for a while. Ford sent Hotten the five option-loaded 1967 Thunderbird two-door Hardtops (later converted into Landaus) to be customized for Abercrombie & Fitch.

Each car was finished in a special Metallic Apollo Blue color. A Metallic Blue vinyl top was installed, along with an electric sun roof with a Metallic Blue vinyl covering. Each Thunderbird Apollo was fitted with quartz iodine driving lights, unique gold-colored landau bars, special exterior side marker lights, chromed door jambs, and special blue-chromed wheel covers. A gold-toned Thunderbird insignia appeared on the radiator grilles.

Inside, the cars had Philco televisions and dial-operated radio telephones. They were equipped with a special reclining passenger seat that had a power headrest and footrest. There were fold-away conference tables built into the front seat backs, special adjustable rear compartment reading lamps, and a special fiberglass center console. The interior was trimmed in Blue leather, with special blue cut-pile carpeting. Each car also had a Rover automatic ice detector.

At least two of the 1967 Thunderbird Apollos survive today. One is owned by J. Thomas Hart, Jr. of Connecticut. According to an article in *The Thunderbird Script*, this car has traveled only 1,666 original miles, and is in like-new, original condition. This car — serial number 7Y81Q122573 — was the car sold in Miami. It was sold through Earle Wallace Ford of Delray Beach, Fla. An area businessman purchased it for his wife. He gave it to her on the condition that no one, except she could drive it. This included restaurant valets. The car was used very little over the next 25 years. It was kept in a garage, but driven around the block each month as part of a periodic maintenance program. It was sold to the current owner in April of 1992.

Matthews Ford, of West Palm Beach, Fla. delivered a second Thunderbird Apollo destined for the Palm Beach store. This car had serial number 7Y81Q122570. It was purchased on Jan. 4, 1967 by the wife of a part owner of the store. In 1970, it was resold to a Pennsylvania man who still owns it. Until recently, this vehicle was used as a daily driver. It has been driven around 80,000 miles. The car was refinished in gray and partly restored a while ago. However, it needs additional work to be like new. It was offered for sale not too long ago, but its current status is uncertain at the time of publishing this book.

(Adopted from a story in *Thunderbird Script*, published by the International Thunderbird Club, 8 Stag Trail, Fairfield, NJ 07004 and updated by owner. Used with permission.)

The 1967 Thunderbird Apollo was a very special limited-production model with many custom features and a high price tag. (James Hart, Jr. photo)

Super Diamond Lustre enamel finish was offered in 20 single tones for 1967 T-Birds. Thirty-five two-tone combinations were offered for the Hardtop. Color-keyed trim selections included seven with cloth and vinyl, seven with all vinyl upholstery, and one with leather and vinyl trim. A minor criticism made about the T-Bird interior involved the lack of roomy storage compartments in the new console. Vinyl tops came in four colors.

1967 Thunderbird Interiors

Seat Type	Material	Black	Blue	Red	Saddle	Ivy Gold	Aqua	Parch- ment
Bucket Seats	Vinyl	2A	2B	2D	2F	2G	2K	2U
Bucket Seats	Cloth & Vinyl	8A	8B	8D	8G	8K	8U	
Bucket Seats	Leather	HA						

Seat Type	Material	Silver
Bucket Seats	Vinyl	
Bucket Seats	Cloth & Vinyl	8L

Underneath, the '67s were the first T-Birds in 10 years to not have unitized body construction. In addition to readopting separate body-and-frame construction, the T-Bird series was changed into a car-line that included two different sized cars. The front and rear sections of the perimeter frames were identical, and also matched those found under full-size 1967 Fords. However, different-sized straight frame side-rails were used to give two-door models a 115-in. stance, and four-door models a two-inch longer wheelbase. Computer-tuned mounting pads carried the Thunderbird's semi-unit body on the frame, allowing it to "float" on the mountings. The front and rear coil spring suspensions were basically out-of-the-box Ford assemblies. The front suspension had a drag strut-braced lower A-arm. A four-link design was used at the rear. Improved front disc brakes were again standard equipment.

Despite extensive styling and chassis changes, Ford left the T-Bird's power train pretty much alone for 1967. The 390-cid 315-hp V-8 was again standard. For less than $100 extra, buyers could opt for the 428-cid engine with 345 hp. Both came only with a new three-speed SelectShift Cruise-O-Matic transmission. Although the Thunderbird had its gear selector on the steering column, the shift pattern was similar to the manual shifting setup used on the high-performance Fairlane GTA model. A 3.0:1 ratio rear axle was standard. With the base engine, the Thunderbird was a fairly good performer. With the optional 428-cid engine, it was even more fun to drive. "While no dragster, the (428) test car's accelerative ability was at least adequate for all present-day driving needs," noted *Car Life.*" Zero to 60 mph acceleration in 10 seconds will take care of the exigencies of on-ramp maneuvering, while sprinting to 82 mph within a quarter-mile's space certainly implies more briskness than most drivers will ever require or employ."

In proper Thunderbird tradition, the '67s were described as a quiet riding cars on the highway. The new bodies were extremely rigid, due to the use of stamped-in stiffeners in the floor pan, heavy sheet metal cross members, and a full-length drive shaft tunnel. A 14-point body mounting system contributed to the reduction of noise and vibration inside the cars. All body mounts were of bridge-type design and all were located ahead of or behind the passenger compartment. *Motor Trend* guessed that the new T-Bird's body integrity would be close to that of unit-body cars, while its body-and-frame design would make it cheaper to repair in case of a collision.

The 1967 T-Bird two-door Hardtop was the year's least popular model, despite the fact that it appeared in many ads. Only 15,567 were built. (Ford Motor Co.)

Car and Driver published a comparison test between the Thunderbird four-door and Cadillac Eldorado coupe in November 1966, incorrectly referring to the Ford product as the fourth edition (it was actually the fifth) of "America's first mass-class, va-va-voom, fantasy-sports 'personal' car." The magazine noted that the T-Bird had started the market niche in which the Eldorado was the latest contender. It also pointed out that Ford had experimented with a front-wheel-drive T-Bird in the late-1950s and that some developments from that project were covered by patents that GM purchased rights to for the Eldorado and Toronado. Ford had abandoned the effort in 1960 due to the layout's high unsprung weight and costliness. The T-Bird continued to get high marks for its improved braking ability (with discs), but driveability and handling continued to suffer due to the size and weight of the car.

Despite being unpopular with T-Bird traditionalists, the four-door Landau was a success in the marketplace. In its first season, the car had a 24,967-unit production run. That was more than the combined total of 1964-1966 Thunderbird Convertibles. In addition, Ford made 15,567 two-door Hardtops and 37,422 two-door Landaus. Model-year assemblies of 77,956 cars made 1967 the fourth best sales year in Thunderbird history.

The four-door Landau interior was sporty and luxurious. It was offered with bucket seats and center console. Door panels had wood accents. (Ford Motor Co.)

1967 Thunderbird Two-Door Landau Specifications

Wheelbase	115.0 in.	Standard Engine Type	90-degree OHV V-8
Curb Weight	4,256 lb.	Bore	4.05 in.
Frontal Area	22.8 sq. ft.	Stroke	3.78 in.
Box Vol.	505.1 cu. ft.	Displacement	390 cid
Front Hip Room	2 x 22.5 in.	Carburetor	Single 4-Barrel C7AF-AD
Rear Hip Room	54.3 in	Compression Ratio	10.5:1
Overall Length	206.9 in.	Maximum BHP	315 @ 4600 rpm
Overall Width	77.3 in.	Maximum Torque	427 lb.-ft. @ 2800 rpm
Overall Height	54.6 in.	Engine Weight	660 lb.. (approx.)
Front Tread	62 in.	Block Length	21.6 in.
Rear Tread	62 in.	Optional Engine Type	90-degree OHV V-8
Effective Head Room	38.4 in.	Bore	4.13 in.
Tires	8.15 x 15	Stroke	3.98 in.
Effective Brake Area	398 sq. in.	Displacement	428 cid
Turning Diameter	43.1 ft.	Carburetor	Single 4-Barrel C7AF-AD
Gas Tank Capacity	22 gallons	Compression Ratio	10.5:1
Cooling System			
Capacity	20.5 quarts (390)	Maximum BHP	345 @ 4600 rpm
Standard Axle	3.00:1 hypoid	Maximum Torque	462 lb.-ft. @ 2800 rpm

1967 Thunderbird Four-Door Landau Specifications

Wheelbase	117.0 in.	Standard Engine Type	90-degree OHV V-8
Curb Weight	4,348 lb.	Bore	4.05 in.
Frontal Area	22.8 sq. ft.	Stroke	3.78 in.
Box Vol.	505.1 cu. ft.	Displacement	390 cid
Front Hip Room	2 x 22.5 in.	Carburetor	Single 4-Barrel C7AF-AD
Rear Hip Room	54.3 in	Compression Ratio	10.5:1
Overall Length	209.4 in.	Maximum BHP	315 @ 4600 rpm
Overall Width	77.3 in.	Maximum Torque	427 lb.-ft. @ 2800 rpm
Overall Height	53.8 in.	Engine Weight	660 lb.. (approx.)
Front Tread	62 in.	Block Length	21.6 in.
Rear Tread	62 in.	Optional Engine Type	90-degree OHV V-8
Effective Head Room	38.4 in.	Bore	4.13 in.
Tires	8.15 x 15	Stroke	3.98 in.
Effective Brake Area	398 sq. in.	Displacement	428 cid
Turning Diameter	43.1 ft.	Carburetor	Single 4-Barrel C7AF AD
Gas Tank Capacity	22 gallons	Compression Ratio	10.5:1
Cooling System			
Capacity	20.5 quarts (428)	Maximum BHP	345 @ 4600 rpm
Standard Axle	3.00:1 hypoid	Maximum Torque	462 lb.-ft. @ 2800 rpm

The 1967 T-Bird four-door Landau was actually a sedan body style with fixed center post. Vinyl top and S-shaped landau irons were featured. (Ford Motor Co.).

1967 Thunderbird Engineering

Front Suspension	Independent SLA w/ ball joints and coil springs
Rear Suspension	Four-link type with coil springs
Steering	Recirculating ball; power-assist, 3.68 turns lock-to-lock
Front Brakes	11.87 x 1.125 in. power front disc
Brakes	11.03-in. X 2.25 in. drums with 398 sq. in. swept area

1967 Thunderbird Performance

Model	CID/HP	Performance
0-60 mph		
Four-door Landau	390/315	12 seconds
Four-door Landau	428/345	9.8 seconds
1/4-Mile		
Four-door Landau	390/315	17.8 seconds @ 78 mph
Four-door Landau	428/345	16.4 seconds @ 82 mph
Top Speed		
Four-door Landau	390/315	111 mph esfimated
Four-door Landau	428/345	120 mph
Two-door Hardtop	390/315	118 mph

1968
Unique in All the World

The 1968 Thunderbird was advertised as "Unique in All the World." In the personal-luxury car market, the T-Bird stood out from the pack, but there was not a great deal of change from 1967. The full-width grille still consisted of a latticework of vertical and horizontal elements. Now they had were wider spaced and the rectangular openings that they formed were larger. Gone from the center of the grille was the large T-Bird emblem. Instead, the grille sides of the rotating headlight doors had smaller T-Bird emblems at their centers. There was a narrower new two-piece bumper. The lower part of the bumper was painted body color. It had large slots below it, on either side, to provide increased air flow. The parking lamps were embedded in these slots.

Three models were offered again at the start of the 1968 model-year. The entry-level model was the two-door Hardtop priced at $4,716. The two-door Landau was in the middle with a $4,845 price tag. On top of the list was the four-door Landau with a $4,924 window sticker. Late in the fall of 1967, a new Thunderbird four-door Town Sedan was promoted in several car magazines. Its roof was painted, instead of vinyl-clad. Wider S-shaped Landau bars decorated the sail panels of this Sedan. However, little is heard about whether it was actually sold as a separate model. Its production is not recorded separately in Ford's totals.

The 1968 two-door Hardtop was again the least popular T-Bird model, proving that vinyl tops really were in vogue then. Only 9,977 were made. (Ford Motor Co.)

Thunder for sale:
2 doors or 4.

Top: 1968 Thunderbird 2-door Hardtop.   Bottom: 1968 Thunderbird 4-door Landau.

Ford's 1968 ad advised that two- and four-door T-Birds could be had in four-, five-, or six-passenger seating configurations. (Ford Motor Co.)

Federally-mandated side marker lamps were located on the sides of the front fenders. The rear fenders had red reflectors that served a similar purpose. Much thinner rocker panel moldings were used. Other standard safety features required under new government regulations included an energy-absorbing steering column (the Tilt-Away steering wheel became optional equipment), hazard flasher lights, recessed instruments, windshield washers, and several items — such as a padded dashboard and sun visors — which had long been standard on Thunderbirds. Shoulder belts, which were previously a $23.38 option, were added to the standard equipment list effective Jan. 1, 1968.

Ford advertised 20 single Diamond Lustre enamel colors for the 1968 models. Thirty-four two-tone combinations were offered for the Hardtop and the Town Hardtop. Carryover colors were Raven Black, Beige Mist, Diamond Green, Wimbeldon White, Diamond Blue, Pewter Mist, Brittany Blue, Candyapple Red, Tahoe Turquoise, and Pebble Beige. So half of the tones offered in 1968 were brand new. This being a presidential election year, one new color was named Presidential Blue. Literature listed each exterior color and the interior trims it could be ordered with, depending upon the type of seat and upholstery material.

T-Bird interiors remained tasteful and luxurious. A total of 17 interior trim combinations were available. The color-keyed selections included three cloth and vinyl , 10 all-vinyl, and four genuine leather and vinyl combinations. There were four colors for vinyl roofs.

1968 Thunderbird Interiors

Seat Type Standard	Material	Black	Blue	Red	Saddle	Ivy Gold	Aqua	Nugget Gold
Bucket Seats	Vinyl	2A	2B	2D	2F	2G	2K	2Y
Bench Seat	Vinyl	4A	4B		4F			4Y
Bucket Seats	Leather	8A			8F			
Luxury								
Bench Seats (*)	Cloth & Vinyl	3A	3B	3D		3G	3K	3Y
Bucket Bench (+)	Cloth & Vinyl	1A	1B	1D		1G	1K	1Y

Seat Type Standard	Material	Parchment
Bucket Seats	Vinyl	2U
Bench Seat	Vinyl	4U

Legend: (*) Two-door Hardtop and Landau only. (+) Four-door Sedan and Landau only.

A new interior layout increased passenger capacity from four to six. Ford's three-passenger Flight Bench front seat was now standard. Front Flight Bucket seats and a center console cost extra. Also available, as an option, was a console-mounted gear selector lever. The T-Bird also featured new squeeze-type inside door handles. Rear seat leg room was increased due to a lower floor tunnel, which was made possible by a new type of universal joint.

The 1968 model specifications showed a slight decrease in wheelbase (from 115 in. to 114.70 in.). In addition, ground clearance dropped from 5.50 in. to 5.40 in. Overall height decreased from 52.80 in. to 52.60 in. Front-to-rear weight distribution also changed slightly from 54.1/45.9 percent in 1967 to 55.3/44.7 percent in 1968. Gas tank capacity jumped from 22 gallons to 24 gallons.

At the start of the model-year the base engine for the T-Bird was again the 390-cid 315-hp V-8. A new IMCO exhaust emission control system was used on all 1968 T-Bird power plants. It incorporated a different carburetor with a preheated air feature and ignition modifications designed to provide more complete fuel combustion. Specifications published in the English magazine *Motorcade* indicated that early-year 1968 Thunderbirds with the standard engine were slightly faster than a 1967 model with the same size engine. However, we do not have 0-60 mph or quarter-mile times. A new option was a 429-cid "Thunderjet" thin-wall V-8 rated at 360 hp. Based on Ford's lightweight 289-cid V-8, this "big-block" version provided more horsepower with lower emissions. Effective Jan. 1, 1968, the 429 became standard equipment in Thunderbirds and the 390 was discontinued.

Side maker lights were integrated into the 1968 restyling to conform with government safety regulations. (Ford Motor Co.)

Other technical changes for 1968 included new "floating" caliper front disc/rear drum brakes. Carried over was the Thunderbird's basic body-frame construction with coil springs all around. Independent suspension was continued up front, while a solid axle housing was again found at the rear.

The 1968 two-door Landau remained the most popular T-Bird, but only by the narrowest of margins, as nearly as many four-door Landaus sold. (Ford Motor Co.)

There were no major changes in the ride and handling traits of the 1968 Thunderbird. *Motor Trend* (November 1967) described it as "the ideal car for pleasant journeying." The following month, the magazine published an article titled "How the 429 really performs." In it, editor Steve Kelly drove a 429-powered 1968 Thunderbird two-door Landau at the Ford Motor Co. test track in Dearborn, Mich. The car had only 500 miles on its odometer. A 2.80:1 final drive ratio allowed it to cruise at 27.6 mph per 1000 rpm, keeping engine speed down and gas mileage up. With two people on board, 150 lb. of test equipment, and a full tank of gas, the car moved from 0-60 mph in 9.5 seconds and covered the quarter-mile in 17.4 seconds at 84 mph.

"The times were very good, but below those of a 428-cid V-8-powered 'Bird tested in the August '67 MT," said Kelly. "The 428 car, though, had nearly 5,000 miles of careful break-in, and from what we learned of the new engine from behind the wheel and from the engineering department, we can safely predict that the 429 will reveal itself a better performer than the earlier 428. In our judgment, not only is the 429 V-8 a breakthrough in low emission design power plants, it is an amazingly good performer with reserve power and reliability."

A historical milestone was marked this year when Thunderbirds were produced in two different factories. Of the total 64,931 cars built, only 51,429 were manufactured at Wixom, Mich. An additional 13,502 units left a Ford assembly plant in Los Angeles, Calif. This was a good year for T-Bird sales, but not a great one. The two factories recorded the

Effective Jan. 1, 1968 a 429-cid 360-hp V-8 became standard in T-Birds like this four-door Landau, and the 390-cid V-8 was dropped. (Ford Motor Co.)

assembly of 5,420 two-door Hardtops with bucket seats, 4,557 two-door Hardtops with bench seats, 19,105 two-door Landaus with bucket seats, 13,924 two-door Landaus with bench seats, 4,674 four-door Landaus with bucket seats, and 17,251 four-door Landaus with bench seats. There is no separate breakout for the production of four-door Town Sedans.

Another significant event in the history of Ford Motor Co. occurred this year in the hiring of "Bunkie" Knudsen, a veteran General Motors executive, as FoMoCo's new president. He came to Dearborn on Feb. 6, 1968. This was too late to influence product changes scheduled for 1969, but — even though his tenure at Ford turned out to be very brief — Knudsen would have a role in planning the fifth-generation T-Birds that bowed in 1970, and survived only two model-years.

New standard bench seat (left) gave room for three up front. Flight bucket seats (right) were available in various trims, including leather and vinyl. (Ford Motor Co.)

1968 Thunderbird Two-Door Landau Specifications

Wheelbase	114.70 in.	Standard Engine Type	90-degree OHV V-8
Curb Weight	4,372 lb.	Bore	4.05 in.
Frontal Area	22.8 sq. ft.	Stroke	3.78 in.
Box Vol.	505.1 cu. ft.	Displacement	390 cid
Front Hip Room	2 x 22.5 in.	Carburetor	Single 4-Barrel C8AF-B
Rear Hip Room	54.3 in	Compression Ratio	10.5:1
Overall Length	206.9 in.	Maximum BHP	315 @ 4600 rpm
Overall Width	77.3 in.	Maximum Torque	427 lb.-ft. @ 2800 rpm
Overall Height	52.60 in.	Engine Weight	660 lb.. (approx.)
Front Tread	62 in.	Block Length	21.6 in.
Rear Tread	62 in.	Optional Engine Type	90-degree OHV V-8
Effective headroom	38.1 in.	Bore	4.36 in.
Tires	8.15 x 15	Stroke	3.59 in.
Effective Brake Area	373 sq. in.	Displacement	429 cid
Turning Diameter	45.9 ft.	Carburetor	Single 4-bbl. Motorcraft
Gas Tank Capacity	24 gallons	Compression Ratio	10.5:1
Cooling System			
Capacity	20.5 quarts	Maximum BHP	360 @ 4600 rpm
Standard Axle	3.00:1 hypoid	Maximum Torque	480 lb.-ft. @ 2800 rpm

1968 Thunderbird Four-Door Landau Specifications

Wheelbase	117.2 in.	Standard Engine Type	90-degree OHV V-8
Curb Weight	4,458 lb.	Bore	4.05 in.
Frontal Area	22.8 sq. ft.	Stroke	3.78 in.
Box Vol.	505.1 cu. ft.	Displacement	390 cid
Front Hip Room	2 x 22.5 in.	Carburetor	Single 4-Barrel C8AF-B
Rear Hip Room	54.3 in.	Compression Ratio	10.5:1
Overall Length	209.4 in.	Maximum BHP	315 @ 4600 rpm
Overall Width	77.3 in.	Maximum Torque	427 lb.-ft. @ 2800 rpm
Overall Height	52.60 in.	Engine Weight	660 lb. (approx.)
Front Tread	62 in.	Block Length	21.6 in.
Rear Tread	62 in.	Optional Engine Type	90-degree OHV V-8
Effective headroom	38.1 in.	Bore	4.36 in.
Tires	8.15 x 15	Stroke	3.59 in.
Effective Brake Area	373 sq. in.	Displacement	429 cid

1968 Thunderbird Four-Door Landau Specifications

Turning Diameter	45.9 ft.	Carburetor	Single 4-bbl. Motorcraft
Gas Tank Capacity	24 gallons	Compression Ratio	10.5:1
Cooling System Capacity	20.5 quarts	Maximum BHP	360 @ 4600 rpm
Standard Axle	3.00:1 hypoid	Maximum Torque	480 lb.-ft. @ 2800 rpm

1968 Thunderbird Engineering

Front Suspension	Independent SLA w/ ball joints and coil springs
Rear Suspension	Four-link type with coil springs
Steering	Recirculating ball; power-assist, 3.68 turns lock-to-lock
Front Brakes	11.80 x 1.125 in. power front disc
Brakes	11.03 in. X 2.25 in. drums with 373 sq. in. swept area

1968 Thunderbird Performance

Model	CID/HP	Performance
0-60 mph		
Two-door Landau	429/360	9.5 seconds
1/4-Mile		
Two-door Landau	429/360	17.4 seconds at 84 mph
Top Speed		
Two-door Landau	390/315	118 mph

1969
Class Act

Another year was added to the fifth-generation T-Bird styling cycle in 1969. Ford's new president, "Bunkie" Knudsen, arrived too late to influence these cars with his GM-thinking. In fact, with all the goings on at the top of the corporate ladder, Ford product planners moved very conservatively. The Thunderbird was basically unchanged in any significant way. Naturally, the front and rear end treatments were modestly updated. The two-door Landau model also received a new roof treatment with wider "C" pillars. This gave it a more stately look. T-Bird buyers seemed to like such formal roof lines. However, this design had a down-side, as it obstructed driver vision to the rear of the car.

The 1969 T-Bird continued to use the same body with minor styling detail changes and some variations in color and appointments. (Ford Motor Co. photo)

The Thunderbird name returned to the panel between the rectangular taillights. The two-door Landau was the most popular '69 model. (Ford Motor Co.)

A new die-cast radiator grille identified the 1969 T-Bird. It had a full-width horizontal center bar and three widely-spaced vertical bars. They crossed to form eight slim rectangular segments. Each segment had a horizontally textured background, and the outer grille segments (actually the headlamp doors) had additional segmentation. There was a large Thunderbird emblem in the center of the grille as there had been in 1967. The front bumper was like the 1968 style bumper, but had indentations cut into the air slots for housing the rectangular parking lamps.

At the rear of the car, the full-width Thunderbird taillights were gone. Instead, on each side of the car, one large red rectangular lens carried the T-Bird emblem in its center. Sequentially flashing taillight bulbs were used again, however. The center rear panel section, which had the Thunderbird name lettered across it, was no longer illuminated. New front fender side marker lamps had a simpler design. Also, the red reflectors on the rear fenders were much smaller.

Three body styles were offered again. The two-door Hardtop and the two-door Landau remained at prices under $5,000 (they were $4,807 and $4,947, respectively), but the 1969 four-door Sedan cracked that barrier by $26. This model had the highest price ever asked for a T-Bird. At the time, you could have purchased two or three, pretty good two-seat 'Birds with that much money and had some change left over to buy gas.

Like all 1969 Ford products, the Thunderbirds came with FoMoCo's package of "Lifeguard Design Safety Features." This was the promotional name tag for some two dozen items in a safety equipment package. Most were required by recently enacted federal law. They ranged from outside rear view mirrors to "safety" coat hooks. Another new safety feature found on all Ford front seats was a headrest.

Thunderbirds came in 20 different Super Diamond Lustre acrylic enamel exterior colors. Upholstery was offered in nylon cloth and vinyl, all-vinyl, or leather and vinyl combinations. Twenty-five color-keyed upholstery selections were shown in the Ford fabric and upholstery guide. There were standard vinyl bench and bucket seat options, Brougham bucket and bench options, and a Brougham leather option for bucket seat interiors only. A center console was included when bucket seats were ordered. Consoles swept upwards in the front, to integrate with the dash. They included two extra storage boxes to supplement the regular glove box in the dashboard. Bucket seats with standard vinyl trim were not provided in four-door Landaus, but you could get bucket seats with fancier trims in that model. Reclining seats were optional and available on all seats at extra cost. Specific seat trims were available in up to six color choices. Vinyl tops came in Black, White, Dark Blue and Ivy Gold. Interiors included a recessed, five-pod gauge cluster with full instrumentation as standard equipment.

The 1969 grille had fewer and wider segments. A power-operated sun roof was once again offered for the Thunderbird. (Ford Motor Co. photo)

1969 Thunderbird Interiors

Seat Type	Material	Black	Blue	Red	Ivy & Gold	White	Nugget Gold
Standard							
Bench Seat	Vinyl	4A	4B	4D		4W	4Y
Bucket Seats (*)	Vinyl	2A	2B	2D	2G	2W	2Y
Brougham							
Bench Seats	Cloth & Vinyl	8A				8W	
Bucket Bench	Cloth & Vinyl	1A	1B	1D			1Y
Bucket Seats	Leather	3A	3B	3D	3G		3Y

Also standard in Thunderbirds was a 429-cid 360-hp V-8. SelectShift automatic was the only transmission. The big engine featured dual exhausts as regular equipment, but regular gas was a no-no. Premium gasoline was required. Ford's biggest automatic transmission had a P-R-N-D-2-1 shift pattern which provided a choice of manual-style or fully-automatic gear selection. In addition, other standard equipment included a power ventilation system, ventless door windows, reversible keys, an AM radio, a lockable lighted glove box, a MagicAire heater-defroster, a map light, and an alligator-grain vinyl roof (on Landau models). The options list was extensive and even included a rear lamp monitor that showed, in the rear view mirror, if your taillights were functioning. Several new options were introduced this year. One was a wire-in-glass type rear window defroster, and the other was a push-button sliding electric sun roof.

Constructed entirely of metal, the sun roof (last offered in 1960) was power-operated. *Motor Trend* (February 1969) said, "The roof itself is a solid, well-built unit that seals tightly into place when closed." Also noted were a lack of turbulence with the roof open, and the fact that the car stayed warm when the roof was rolled back on chilly, but sunny days. A crank was provided to operate the roof in case of electrical failure. The option was priced at $453.30.

Technical improvements for 1969 were mainly refinements, and most mechanical systems were carried over without change. All Thunderbirds came equipped with an Autolite "Sta-Ful" battery, Autolite "Power-Tip" spark plugs, Autolite shock absorbers, and an Autolite 6,000-mile oil filter. Ford promoted "Twice-A-Year Maintenance" based on the fact that recommended oil change intervals were 6,000 miles or six months. Coolant replacement was called for at 24 months, and major chassis lubrication was sup-

A rear view of the 1969 T-Bird four-door Landau. (Ford Motor Co. photo)

posed to be good for 36,000 miles. "The '69 Thunderbird needs so little service it's just good sense to see that it gets the best—at your Ford dealer's," said the sales catalog.

There were some important suspension modifications on 1969 two-door models and all T-Birds were lowered one-half inch. The coupes got what amounted to a heavy-duty suspension package. It included stiffer springs with a ride rate of 135 lb.-in. up front and 123 lb.-in. in the rear, larger shock absorbers, and a fatter 0.812-in. diameter anti-roll bar. While this gave a ride that was still on the traditional "T-Bird-soft" side, it was firmer than in the past. "Ride and handling characteristics are vastly improved in the two-door models due to suspension modifications," *Motor Trend* reported. "The change in suspension has reduced roll and gives a flatter, smoother ride when cornering."

On a bottom line basis, the 1969 T-Bird was designed to do battle with personal-luxury cars like the Buick Riviera, front-drive Cadillac Eldorado and Oldsmobile Toronado, Dodge Charger, and Pontiac Grand Prix, which had all arrived in the market since 1962. And considering that the T-Bird was the "old buzzard" of the bunch, the competition had actually strengthened it. "Ford hasn't just 'added on' the '69 'Bird, but has made definite and worthwhile improvements right down the line—in ride, handling, comfort, and convenience," *Motor Trend* pointed out. "It has that elusive, diffident air known as class."

1969 Thunderbird 2-door Landau.

THUNDERBIRD Ⓕ𝑜𝑟𝑑

The 1969 Thunderbird was advertised as being for "the open road and the open sky." The 429-cid "Thunderjet V-8 remained standard. (Ford Motor Co.)

While the 1969 T-Bird was the "class of its class," it was still basically a 1967 model, and its aging did have a negative effect on sales in a new-product-driven marketplace. In fact, Thunderbird model-year production dropped to its lowest point since 1958. It included 1,983 four-door Landaus with bucket seats, 13,712 four-door Landaus with bench seats, 2,361 two-door Hardtops with bucket seats, 3,552 two-door Hardtops with bench seats, 12,425 two-door Landaus with bucket seats, and 15,239 two-door Landaus with bench seats. Production was split between the Wixom, Mich. plant (40,571), and the Los Angeles, Calif. plant (8,701). Even this output — 49,272 total units — outpaced the production of front-wheel-drive Eldorados (27,100) and Toronados (28,500) and came within striking distance of the 52,700 Rivieras built. However, both the less expensive Charger (69,000) and the all-new Pontiac Grand Prix (112,500) found many more buyers, some of which were taken away from Ford. Change was needed and on its way.

Unfortunately, the changes coming in the T-Bird would not last very long for two reasons. First, they had virtually no effect on the car's popularity. Sales climbed microscopically in 1970, then plummeted again in 1971. Second, they were changes that "Bunkie" Knudsen brought in, and he was gone even before they hit the market. In August 1969, the former GM executive was fired after a personality conflict with FoMoCo Chairman Henry Ford II erupted in Dearborn. Some observers blamed the firing on the fact that Knudsen wanted to involve Ford in motorsports and HFII did not want to go that route. Others said that Knudsen's management concepts went against the Ford family's concept of centralized control of the company. Whatever the reason, Knudsen's departure was probably good for the Thunderbird, since he seemed incapable of understanding what made the car sell.

Now selling for just shy of $5,000, the 1969 T-Bird four-door Landau saw its production total slip to just 15,650 units. (Ford Motor Co. photo)

1969 Thunderbird Two-Door Landau Specifications

Wheelbase	114.7 in.	Standard Engine Type	429 cid 90-degree ohv V-8
Curb Weight	4,360 lb.	Bore x Stroke	4.36 x 3.59 in.
Front Hip Room	23 x 2 (bucket seats)	Carburetor	Single 4-Barrel
Rear Hip Room	53.5 in	Compression Ratio	10.0:1
Overall Length	206.9 in.	Maximum BHP	360 @ 4600 rpm
Overall Width	77.3 in.	Maximum Torque	480 lb.-ft. @ 2800 rpm
Overall Height	52.3 in.	Tires	8.45/8.55 x 15
Front Tread	62 in.	Brake Swept Area	373.2 sq. in.
Rear Tread	62 in.	Turning Diameter	43.4 ft.
Front Head Room	37.1 in.	Gas Tank Capacity	24 gallons
Rear Head Room	36.7 in.	Cooling System Capacity	20.5 quarts
Door Opening Width	40.5 in.	Standard Axle	3.00:1 hypoid

1969 Thunderbird Four-Door Landau Specifications

Wheelbase	117.0 in.	Standard Engine Type	429 cid 90-degree ohv V-8
Curb Weight	4,460 lb.	Bore x Stroke	4.36 x 3.59 in.
Front Hip Room	23 x 2 (bucket seats)	Carburetor	Single 4-Barrel
Rear Hip Room	53.5 in	Compression Ratio	10.0:1
Overall Length	209.9 in.	Maximum BHP	360 @ 4600 rpm
Overall Width	77.3 in.	Maximum Torque	480 lb.-ft. @ 2800 rpm
Overall Height	52.3 in.	Tires	8.45/8.55 x 15
Front Tread	62 in.	Brake Swept Area	373.2 sq. in.
Rear Tread	62 in.	Turning Diameter	43.4 ft.
Front Head Room	37.1 in.	Gas Tank Capacity	24 gallons
Rear Head Room	36.7 in.	Cooling System Capacity	20.5 quarts
Door Opening Width	40.5 in.	Standard Axle	3.00:1 hypoid

1970-1971
"Bunkie's Birds"

FOR 1970:
A
NEW FLIGHT
OF BIRDS

Soaring into the '70's far ahead of the rest . . . 1970 Thunderbird. With dramatic new front end styling, shaped to slice the wind. Longer, lower and wider for '70. Yet, still uniquely Thunderbird. With its impressive list of standard luxury features you'd pay extra for in other cars. Options other cars don't even offer. And standards of quality most others only aspire to. Choose from three distinctive models. The New Flight of Birds is ready for take-off.

Above: Pan Am's Boeing 747 Jet and the 1970 Thunderbird 2-Door Landau with Special Brougham interior.

THUNDERBIRD ●Ford●

1970
Bunkie's Birds

"Bunkie" Knudsen was gone from Ford Motor Co., but his sixth-generation Thunderbirds bowed in the fall of 1969 as 1970 models. They were not a big hit in the marketplace and lasted just two model-years. One might guess that as a low-production item they could grow more collectible as they age. Only the future will tell if the cars grow in value. Though not a radical departure from previous models, they are different because Knudsen viewed the T-Bird as a Pontiac Grand Prix. Consequently, he tried to make the Ford look more like the long-nose Pontiac with its "ship's prow" hood and classical radiator grille. All front end sheet metal was revised.

The 1970 Thunderbird models were also one inch closer to the ground than in 1969. They were about six inches longer, too. The wheelbase of two-door models remained at 115 in. and four-door Landaus had the 117-in. wheelbase. Treads front and rear were 62 in. The new radiator grille stuck way out and came to a point. Unfortunately, its protruding center section proved to be very delicate and prone to damage. This caused insurance companies to charge higher premiums on Thunderbirds. The headlights were no longer hidden, but the radio antenna and the windshield wipers were tucked out of sight. Full-width taillights returned. They had a new inverted "U" appearance, but retained sequentially flashing turn signals.

The length and lowness of the T-Bird was accented by a single horizontal feature line along the mid-section of the body. The four-door Landau seemed to have the same body shell it had since 1967. However, the two-door models continued to confuse people with an endless array of side window and roof treatments.

Three models were offered again. In standard format, the two-door Hardtop had a $4,916 window sticker. The two-door Landau was sticker-priced at $5,104, while the four-door Landau listed for $5,182.

Brilliant and rich Super Diamond Lustre enamels came in up to 31 colors on all models. There were 24 single colors. All interior trim selections were keyed to the exterior colors. A full-width "Flight Bench" front seat was again standard, with high-back bucket seats and a console available for $78. A split bench seat was an option on four-door models. The standard trim was all-vinyl. Optional Brougham interior trims came in nylon cloth-and-vinyl or leather-and-vinyl. The "Special Brougham" option featured hopsack-and-vinyl upholstery. There were seven colors available for different interiors. Vinyl tops came in at least four colors. Revised instrument panel registers gave the T-Bird's standard ventilation system and optional SelectAire air conditioning system improved ventilation and directional control.

In 1970, two-door T-Birds had a 114.7-in. wheelbase, while four-door Landaus rode on a 117-in. stance. (Ford Motor Co. photo)

New at the rear of 1970 models was an "inverted-U" shaped full-width taillight design. (Ford Motor Co. photo)

1970 T-Bird Interior Trim Options & Codes (U.S. & Canada)

Type of Seat	Material	Bl	B	R	I	T	W	N	G
Standard									
2d HT/Bench	Vinyl	4A	4B		4G		4W		
2d HT/Bucket	Vinyl	2A	2B		2G		2W		
2d Lan/Bench	Vinyl	4A	4B		4G		4W		
2d Lan/Bucket	Vinyl	2A	2B		2G		2W		
4d Lan/Bench	Vinyl	4A	4B		4G		4W		
2d HT/Buckert	Leather	8A		8D					8F
2d Lan/Bucket	Leather	8A		8D					8F
4d Lan/Split-Bench	Leather	6A		6D		6Z			
Standard With Brougham Option									
2d Lan/Bucket	Fabric/Vinyl	1A	1B	1D	1G				1F
2d HT/Bucket	Fabric/Vinyl	1A	1B	1D	1G				1F
Special Brougham Option									
2d HT/Bench	Brougham	3A	3B	3D	3G			3Y	3F
2d Lan/Bench	Brougham	3A	3B	3D	3G			3Y	3F
4d Lan/Split-Bench	Brougham	5A	5B	5D	5G	5Z		5Y	

Legend: (Top line): Bl means Black; B means Blue; R means Red; I mean Ivory; T means Tobacco; W means White; N means Nugget Gold; G means Ginger. (Chart): 2d means two-door; 4d means four-door; HT means Hardtop; Lan means Landau.

Most luxury equipment was still included in T-Birds at standard prices. A long list of extras was available, too. This year the steering wheel was a tilt type only. Ford's "better idea"—the Swing-Away steering wheel—was gone. Color-keyed wheel covers added to the rich look of Thunderbirds with the Brougham package. A power-operated sun roof remained a costly option. For $194, the T-Bird buyer could also add a "Sure-Track" braking control system to ensure swift, straight-line stops under all road conditions. Motive power was still the 429-cid engine with 360 hp at 4600 rpm. It had a 10.5:1 compression ratio and a big four-barrel carburetor with an automatic choke. Dual exhausts were standard and premium fuel was required to operate this beast. It was coupled to a SelectShift Cruise-O-Matic transmission.

Additional standard features included ventless side glass, reversible keys, "keyless" locking, power steering, electric clock, MagicAire heater and defroster, lockable lighted glove box, map light with automatic time delay, Cayman Grain vinyl roof (Landau models), power front disc brakes, lined and lighted luggage compartment, full wheel covers, articulated accelerator pedal, pedal trim appliqués, hidden radio antenna, front and rear ash trays, back-up lights, cigarette lighter, coat hooks, courtesy lights, carpeting, all-vinyl headliner, day/night rear view mirror, bright Thunderbird emblems on "C" pillars, bright "S" bar with teak-toned insert (on four-door Landau), bright window frames, and bright seat side shields. Size 215-R15 radial-ply tires became standard equipment.

The Thunderbird's strong frame and body design consisted of a front end assembly, rear end assembly, and four torque box assemblies connected by formed center rails (which were longer on the four-door models). The frame featured rugged ladder-type construction with five reinforced cross-members. Node-point body mounting at 14 computer-designed positions resulted in superior noise and vibration suppression characteristics. Up front, the suspension used drag-struts and ball joints, plus a rubber-bushed stabilizer bar. The rear suspension was again by a three-link coil spring system with a long and short mounting-link arrangement. A lateral track bar centered the axle. All of the links, as well as the track bar, had rubber bushings.

Integral-design power steering featured an overall ratio of 21.9:1. The tilt steering wheel was optional at extra cost. Two-door models required 42.7 ft. to turn around and the four-doors had a 43.4-ft. turning circle. The self-adjusting brakes used floating caliper discs in front and drum-shoe brakes at the rear. The drums were cross-ribbed and flared. Swept area was 217.3 sq. in. up front and 155.9 sq. in. in the rear. True-Center wheels on precision-machined hubs carried the radial ply tires.

Motor Trend did a comparison road test pitting the T-Bird against the Chevrolet Monte Carlo and Pontiac Grand Prix. It was published in November 1969. "The '70 'Bird is practically an entirely new car, even without what should be called a major change" suggested writer Bill Sanders with a bit of wordsmithing. He was talking about its lower height and new body-hugging roof line. "The first thing that comes to mind when looking at the two-door in profile is the beautiful custom work of the late '40s and early '50s," chimed Sanders. "The '70 'Bird is reminiscent of some of those early creations and looks like it has been chopped and channeled."

Mentioned in the article was the T-Bird's adoption of the Lincoln Mark III's sound insulation package to reduce noise inside the car, the fact that the seats had additional comfort padding, and the use of an in-the-windshield wire-type radio antenna. Despite its larger size and heavier weight, the 1970 model performed almost exactly the same as the 1969 edition. "Unlike the Monte Carlo or Grand Prix, the 'Bird is not specifically a performance-oriented car, but is more at home with the luxury aspects," said Sanders. "For instance, acceleration may not be as rapid, but it is fluid smooth with no quick shifting movements." With its new suspension and radial tires, the car was a better handler than previous Thunderbirds. It had very little understeer and driver control was described as "uncanny." All in all, the car was summarized as combining a custom luxury feeling with outstanding ride and handling abilities.

To be totally fair, the first "Bunkie 'Bird" actually wound up with a 0.7 percent share of the total new-car market, which was an improvement from 1969's 0.6 percent. The four-door Landau bucket seat model grew more popular for the year and 5,005 were made. The counterpart model with bench seats reached another 3,396 buyers. The two-door Hardtop saw just 5,116 assemblies of which only 1,925 had bucket seats. The top seller was the two-door Landau with 36,847 assemblies and 16,953 of them came

The 1970 T-Bird Special Brougham option group included grille lamps, color-keyed wheel covers, and high-back bucket seats. (Ford Motor Co. photo)

Seen here on the 1970 T-Bird four-door Landau is the year's new longer and lower hood and three-section extruded aluminum grille (Ford Motor Co.)

with bucket seats. Of the total production of 50,364 cars for the 1970 model year, 30,830 were manufactured at the Wixom, Mich. plant and 19,534 were made at the Ford Assembly Plant in Los Angeles, Calif. As we suggested at the start of this section, the 1970 models have several attractions that could make them collectible. They had relatively low production, lots of luxury features, rather unique T-Bird styling, and they were highly-rated automobiles.

1970 Thunderbird Two-Door Landau Specifications

Wheelbase	115 in.	Standard Engine Type	429 cid 90-degree ohv V-8
Curb Weight	4,430 lb.	Bore x Stroke	4.36 x 3.59 in.
Overall Length	212.5 in.	Carburetor	Single 4-Barrel
Overall Width	77.4 in.	Compression Ratio	10.0:1
Overall Height	51.4 in.	Maximum BHP	360 @ 4600 rpm
Front Tread	62 in.	Maximum Torque	480 lb.-ft. @ 2800 rpm
Rear Tread	62 in.	Transmission	SelectShift Cruise-O-Matic
Tires	215R-15	Standard Rear Axle	2.80:1

1970 Thunderbird Four-Door Landau Specifications

Wheelbase	117 in.	Standard Engine Type	429 cid 90-degree ohv V-8
Curb Weight	4,464 lb.	Bore x Stroke	4.36 x 3.59 in.
Overall Length	215 in.	Carburetor	Single 4-Barrel
Overall Width	78 in.	Compression Ratio	10.0:1
Overall Height	53.6 in.	Maximum BHP	360 @ 4600 rpm
Front Tread	62 in.	Maximum Torque	480 lb.-ft. @ 2800 rpm
Rear Tread	62 in.	Transmission	SelectShift Cruise-O-Matic
Tires	215R-15	Standard Rear Axle	2.80:1

1970 Thunderbird Engineering

Front Suspension	Independent coil springs
Rear Suspension	Trailing link coil springs
Steering	Integral; power-assist, 3.6 turns lock-to-lock
Front Brakes	Power front disc
Brakes	Power drums

1970 Thunderbird Performance

Model	CID/HP	Performance
0-60 mph		
Two-door Landau	429/360	9.0 seconds
1/4-Mile		
Two-door Landau	429/360	16.9 seconds @ 84.6 mph
Top Speed		
Two-door Landau	429/360	125 mph

1971
Drive in Confidence

The '71 T-Bird grille had wider blades on every third rung. (Ford Motor Co. photo)

The 1971 Thunderbird was essentially a 1970 model with only slight trim revisions. The grille had slightly wider bright metal blades at every third rung, giving it a horizontally segmented look. There were also nine vertical bars in the new frontal design. Front side marker lamps with a one-piece lens were introduced. In addition, the front bumper had more massive wraparound edges. A few bits of chrome were revised. *Motor Trend* suggested this was done "To enable salesmen to distinguish the difference in models." Some new exterior appearance options were color-keyed wheel covers, body side moldings with color-keyed protective vinyl inserts, and wheel opening moldings. These all came as part of the $170.13 Brougham interior option.

The same three Thunderbird models were offered again in 1971 and prices climbed around $330 for each of them. The manufacturer's suggested retail prices were $5,295 for the Thunderbird two-door Hardtop, $5,438 for the two-door Landau, and $5,516 for the four-door Landau. By the way, this was the final curtain call for the Sedan. Its sales had declined steadily over five years: (1967) 24,967; (1968) 21,925; (1969) 15,650; (1970) 8,401; and (1971) 6,553. Initially, it had seemed like a good idea to replace the Convertible with the four-door. However, in five short years, its production was in the same "territory" that the 1965-1966 Convertibles were. Twenty-four exterior color options were offered for 1971 Thunderbirds sold in the U.S. and Canada. Four of these—Burgundy Fire, Blue Fire, Green Fire, and Walnut Fire—were optional at extra cost. Five colors were available for vinyl tops.

Some notable standard features on 1971 Thunderbirds were the 429-cid, 360-hp V-8, Selectshift Cruise-O-Matic transmission, AM radio, power steering, electric clock, cornering lights, power front disc brakes, power ventilation, 100 percent nylon carpeting, full instrumentation, fuel evaporative and emission control system, locking steering column, outside left-hand remote-control mirror, Uni-Lock safety harness, Cayman Grain vinyl roof (Landau models), full-width taillights with sequential turn signals, hydraulic windshield wipers with electric windshield washers, MagicAire heater and defroster, glove box, map and luggage compartment courtesy lights, Flight Bench seat with bright side shields, front

New front side-marker lights with a one-piece lens were used on 1971 T-Birds, including this two-door Hardtop. (Ford Motor Co. photo)

and rear seat center arm rests, and belted sidewall tires. H78 x 15 belted bias-ply tires were standard. Michelin 215R15 steel-belted radials were standard with the Special Brougham option. In 1971, the T-Bird was the only U.S. car offered with radial tires as an option. The Michelin radials could be easily spotted by their very narrow band of white on the sidewalls. The H78 x 15s looked different, as they had two narrow bands of white.

On the inside, this was the only year that the four-door Landau model was not available with optional front bucket seats. A front bench seat was also standard in two-door models, but bucket seats were optional. Front seating options included standard vinyl bench seats (all models), vinyl bucket seats (optional in two-door models), Brougham bench seat (optional in two-door models), Brougham split bench seat (optional in four-door models), Brougham leather bucket seats (optional in two-door models),

Brougham leather bench seat (optional in four-door models), and Special Brougham bucket seats (optional in two-door models). With eight different colors available, this represented a total of 31 different variations for cars sold in both the U.S. and Canada.

Full-width, down-turned, U-shaped taillights continued in 1971. (Ford Motor Co.)

1971 T-Bird Interior Trim Options & Codes (U.S. & Canada)

Type of Seat	Material	B	DB	DR	MG	DG	W	GG	DT
Standard									
2d HT/bench	Vinyl	4A	4B			4R	4W		
2d HT/bucket	Vinyl	2A	2B			2R	2W		
2d Landau/bench	Vinyl	4A	4B			4R	4W		
2d Landau/bucket	Vinyl	2A	2B			2R	2W		
4d Landau/bench	Vinyl	4A	4B			4R	4W		
Brougham									
2d HT/bench	Fabric/Vinyl	CA	CB	CD	CF	CR		CY	
2d HT/bucket	Fabric/Vinyl	AA	AB	AD	AF	AR			
2d HT/buckert	Leather	8A	.	8D	8F				
2d Landau/bench	Fabric/Vinyl	CA	CB	CD	CF	CR		CY	
2d Landau/bucket	Fabric/Vinyl	AA	AB	AD	AF	AR			
2d Landau/bucket	Leather	8A		8D	8F				
4d Landau/Comfort	Fabric/Vinyl	EA	EB	ED		ER		EY	EZ
4d Landau/Comfort	Leather	FA		FD					FZ

Legend: (Top line): B means Black; DB means Dark Blue; DR means Dark Red; MG means Medium Ginger; DG means Dark Green; W means White; GG means Gray Gold; DT means Dark Tobacco. (Chart): 2d means two-door; 4d means four-door; HT means Hardtop; Comfort means Comfort Lounge seat.

In December 1970, *Motor Trend* published an article by Jim Brokaw entitled "Almost a Limousine." It was a comparison road test featuring 1971 versions of the "boattail" Riviera, the front-drive Olds Toronado, and the Brougham-optioned Thunderbird two-door Landau. It was the first of a series of annual articles that compared various cars, but almost always included the T-Bird. The 1971 model tested had a list price of $6,649.71, which compared to $6,667.72 for the Buick and $6,457.15 for the Oldsmobile. "These cars are expensive," said the writer. "If you have to check your budget to see whether you can handle the payments, you can't afford one."

The five-page story pointed out that the Thunderbird's four-coil suspension differed from that of the other two cars in how the lateral and longitudinal restraints were handled with drag-strut bars up front and three control arms and one track bar at the rear. The T-Bird's system was rated the firmest, but it also exhibited much less roll control than the "Riv" and the "Toro." Brokaw concluded, "The 'Bird requires a bit of attention going into a corner at high speed, but produces no surprises after the initial turn is passed."

Of the three cars, the T-Bird was fastest in the quarter-mile acceleration test and the quickest to stop from 30 mph (27 ft.) and 60 mph (129 ft.). However, a chart published at the end of the story apparently had a typographical error and recorded the stopping distance from 60 mph as *second* best at 145 ft. The figures given in the text are more consistent and believable. A slight steering correction was necessary to keep the Thunderbird (and the Olds) tracking straight during the higher-speed stop. The Riviera needed more steering effort to keep from losing control.

Overall length of the 1971 T-Bird Hardtop was 215 in. It had H78 x 15 fiberglass-belted tires as standard equipment. (Ford Motor Co, photo)

After a very slight upwards blip in 1970, model-year production of 1971 Thunderbirds tapered off again. The two-door Landau was the big loser and nearly 16,500 fewer examples were made for a total of just 20,356 units. Of those, 8,133 had bucket seats. The two-door Hardtop gained over 4,000 orders, and came in with a total of 9,146 assemblies, including 2,992 bucket seat cars. Four-door Landau production was 6,553 units versus 8,401 the previous year. Exactly 4,238 of the four-doors had the split bench seat in front. Of the total 36,055 Thunderbirds built in the 1971 model year, 29,733 were manufactured at the Wixom, Mich. assembly plant. An additional 6,322 cars were produced in Ford's Los Angeles assembly plant. Part of the reason for the year's poor showing may have been that sales of the "Bunkie" Knudsen-designed 1971 models were the responsibility of Lee A. Iacocca, who had a totally different concept of what a Thunderbird should be. Iacocca would soon give the car a new personality and turn the sales trend around.

1971 Thunderbird Two-Door Landau Specifications

Wheelbase	114.7 in.	Standard Engine Type	429 cid 90-degree ohv V-8
Curb Weight	4,430 lb.	Bore x Stroke	4.36 x 3.59 in.
Overall Length	212.5 in.	Carburetor	Single 4-Barrel
Overall Width	77.4 in.	Compression Ratio	10.0:1
Overall Height	51.4 in.	Maximum BHP	360 @ 4600 rpm
Front Tread	62 in.	Maximum Torque	480 lb.-ft. @ 2800 rpm
Rear Tread	62 in.	Transmission	SelectShift Cruise-O-Matic
Tires	H78 x 15	Standard Rear Axle	3.00:1

1971 Thunderbird Four-Door Landau Specifications

Wheelbase	117.2 in.	Standard Engine Type	429 cid 90-degree ohv V-8
Curb Weight	4,464 lb.	Bore x Stroke	4.36 x 3.59 in.
Overall Length	215 in.	Carburetor	Single 4-Barrel
Overall Width	78 in.	Compression Ratio	10.0:1
Overall Height	53.6 in.	Maximum BHP	360 @ 4600 rpm
Front Tread	62 in.	Maximum Torque	480 lb.-ft. @ 2800 rpm
Rear Tread	62 in.	Transmission	SelectShift Cruise-O-Matic
Tires	H78 x 15	Standard Rear Axle	3.00:1

1971 Thunderbird Engineering

Front Suspension	Independent coil springs
Rear Suspension	Trailing link coil springs
Steering	Integral; power-assist, 3.6 turns lock-to-lock
Front Brakes	Power disc
Rear Brakes	Power drum

1955 Thunderbird owned by Jack &
Maxine Smittle, Westerville, Ohio.

1957 Thunderbird (white) and 1955 Thunderbird (black) owned by John McGrane, Nutley, New Jersey.

1956 Thunderbird owned by SuEllyn & Brian
McCabe, Santa Rosa Beach, Florida.

1957 Thunderbird owned by Larry Tucker, Old Saybrook, Connecticut.

1957 Thunderbird
owned by John W. &
Susan L. Larson,
Fort Collins, Colorado.

1957 Thunderbird owned by Allen & Donna Brown, Santa Rosa, California.

1958 Thunderbird convertible formerly owned by Don Bryce, Lynnwood, Washington.

1959 Thunderbird hardtop owned by Donald Forman, Colchester, Vermont.

1959 Thunderbird hardtop owned by John S. Palumbo, La Grange, Illinois.

1955

1957

1959

1960

Cappy Collection cars/John Gunnell photos

1961

1962

1963

1966

Cappy Collection cars/John Gunnell photos

1960 Thunderbird hardtop
(with factory sunroof)
owned by Roger & Judy Gill,
Chicago Heights, Illinois.

1960 Thunderbird convertible owned by John C. Flory, Topeka, Kansas.

1961 Thunderbird hardtop owned by Kenneth & Alice Crosbie, Elk River, Minnesota.

1961 Thunderbird Indy Pace Car convertible owned by Michael P. Sercer, Brownsburg, Indiana.

THUNDERBIRD
OFFICIAL PACE CAR

GOLDEN ANNIVERSARY
"500 MILE RACE"
INDIANAPOLIS MOTOR SPEEDWAY
MAY 30, 1961

INDIANAPOLIS MOTOR SPEEDWAY

GOLDEN ANNIVERSARY
"500 MILE RACE"

THUNDERBIRD
OFFICIAL PACE CAR

1962 Thunderbird Sports Roadster owned by John Rosman, Middle Island, New York.

1962 Thunderbird Sports Roadster owned by Paul & Charlotte Nichols, Dearborn, Michigan.

1963 Thunderbird Landau hardtop owned by Charles Kurtz, Sussex, Wisconsin.

1963 Thunderbird convertible (*Old Cars* photo).

965 Thunderbird Special Landau hardtop (one of just 4,500 built) owned by
Don Baudhuim, Corfu, New York.

1965 Thunderbird hardtop
owned by William M. Dilick,
Kittanning, Pennsylvania.

1966 Thunderbird convertible
owned by Charles & Lois Poole,
Hampstead, Maryland.

1967 Thunderbird four-door Landau
Sedan owned by Ken Leaman,
Fairfield, New Jersey.

1968 Thunderbird two-door Landau
owned by Don & Norma Seymour,
Farmington, New Hampshire.

1970 Thunderbird two-door Landau owned by Rico Ghilardi, Millbrae, California.

1972 Thunderbird two-door Landau. This is the one-millionth Thunderbird built. It is owned by R.D. Peterson, Cedar Rapids, Iowa.

Closeup of one of the landau bar medallions on R.D. Peterson's Thunderbird proclaiming "1955-1972 Millionth Thunderbird." In addition to its custom gold paint and white vinyl roof, another medallion appears inside on the dashboard.

1976 Thunderbird two-door hardtop owned by Eliott Weiner, Babylon, New York.

1978 Thunderbird coupe (with sports décor option) owned by Doug Bakkene, Worthington, Minnesota.

1985 30th Anniversary Limited-Edition Thunderbird coupe owned by James Finney, Bowie, Maryland.

1986 Thunderbird coupe owned by Lane & Terri Kasen, Grayslake, Illinois.

1990 Thunderbird
Super Coupe owned
by Dr. Jeff Gasser,
Coleman, Wisconsin.

1995 Thunderbird 40th
Anniversary Edition
coupe owned by
Norman Mummert,
Hanover, Pennsylvania.

1997 Thunderbird LX coupe
owned by Ronald Cotugno,
West Hempstead, New York.

**Throughout their 45-year history, Thunderbirds have even been the subject of art.
Shown here are two renderings of the 1955 model by automobilia artist Wayne Huffaker, of Katy, Texas.**

1972 - 1976
"Big Birds"

1972
Big 'Bird

Thunderbirds were completely restyled for 1972. They were the biggest Thunderbirds Ford had ever offered. Lee Iacocca was responsible for the creation of these cars and his philosophy was "the bigger the better." He based the new T-Birds on the new Lincoln Continental Mark IV. The two cars shared the same chassis and sheet metal with only minor changes inside and out. As a result, the Thunderbird gave up all hopes of truly being sporty. It was converted into an out and out luxury car.

For the first time since 1957, the T-Bird came in just a single model. It was a two-door Hardtop with a long, long hood and

Rear view of 1972 T-Bird Hardtop shows new taillight design. (Ford Motor Co.)

a short rear deck. Perched on a 120.4-in. wheelbase, the body stretched 216 in. bumper-to-bumper. Width was up to 79.3 in., but height remained remarkably low at 52.1 in. Track widths front and rear were 63 in. and 62.8 in., respectively. The T-Bird's grille was given a neo-classic look. It featured horizontal bars above and below the massive front bumper. The horizontal bars texture was also used in the large rectangles housing the dual headlamps. There was a Thunderbird emblem on the car's nose. Notches in the leading edges of the front fenders held the parking lamps, which doubled as side marker lamps. Separate side marker and signal lamps for the front fender sides were optional.

The Thunderbird's large, thick doors had guard beams built into them to protect occupants in side impact collisions. A low semi-fastback roof bridged the extremely wide "C" pillars. A single wall-to-wall taillight lens used once again. It contributed to a very

Ford described the 1972 T-Bird as the "third generation" model. It had a bold, horizontal grille texture and quad headlights in large rectangles. (Ford Motor Co.)

massive rear end appearance. There were 10 taillamp bulbs that lit up the car like a light-bar. Thunderbirds in both the U.S. and Canada came in 24 different colors, eight of which were optional Glamour Paint choices. The Glamour colors — Burgundy Fire, Blue Fire, Green Fire, Lime Fire, Walnut Fire, Cinnamon Fire, Copper Fire, and Gold Fire — were particularly brilliant. They came in a package that included color-coordinated wheel covers and moldings, hood and body side pin striping, and tooled-silver S-shaped landau bars on cars with vinyl tops.

With absolutely no options the T-Bird had a 4,503-lb. curb weight. This was a format that few cars came in. As historian James F. Petrik said, "The standard 1972 T-Bird had no vinyl roof or landau bars, although you never see one like this." Ford's suggested base retail price was $5,293. This price again included SelectShift Cruise-O-Matic, power steering, power front disc brakes, automatic brake release, electric clock, carpeting, power ventilation, MagicAire heater and defroster, and more. For 1972, even the Michelin steel-belted radial tires (with black sidewalls) were standard, along with a split bench seat, a remote-control driver's side mirror, and a fully lined and lighted trunk. The options list remained long, too. In fact, with some of the typical equipment that most buyers ordered in 1972, the majority of T-Birds were actually retailed for $6,500-$7,000.

Lamont cloth-and-vinyl trim was featured on the standard split bench seat and came in Black, Dark Blue, Green, and Tobacco colors. Leather-and-vinyl choices in Black, White, Dark Red, Ginger, Dark Blue, Dark Green, and Tobacco were available at extra cost. Front bucket seats upholstered in hopsack cloth-and-vinyl were also optional. These came in Black, Dark Red, Dark Blue, Dark Green and Ginger. All in all, a total of 17 color-keyed interior options were available. A front seat center arm rest was standard equipment. There was also a new dashboard. "The instrument panel was legible and well laid out, but not as 'Buck Rogers' as those of earlier models, due to the leveling effect of safety regulations," said *Road Test* magazine when it test-drove the Thunderbird in April 1972. Full instrumentation was abandoned in favor of warning lights. With the six-inch longer wheelbase, the rear compartment had more leg room.

Full-width taillights were used on 1972 T-Birds, like this Landau Hardtop, and all bulbs could be lit to serve as running lights when needed. (Ford Motor Co. photo)

1972 Thunderbird Interiors

Seat Type	Material	Black	Dark Blue	Dark Red	Medium Ginger	Dark Green	White	Dark Tobacco
Lo-Back Split Bench	Fabric & Vinyl	HA	HB	HD		HR		HZ
High-Back Buckets	Fabric & Vinyl	GA	GB	GD	GF (+)	GR		
Lo-Back Split Bench	Leather		KA	KB	KD	KF (+)	KR	+KZ

Legend: (*) White with color-keyed components; (+) With tobacco components

Ford had originally planned to use a 400-cid two-barrel V-8 as the standard 1972 Thunderbird power plant. Sales catalog no. 5303 dated 8/71 lists this smaller engine as standard equipment and the 429-cid four-barrel V-8 as an option. In real life, however, the base engine was a new version of the 429-4V and Lincoln's big 460-cid four-barrel V-8 was optional. The 429-4V was de-tuned to operate on unleaded gas and its output was expressed as a net horsepower rating. (From this point on, all engine ratings in this book use the net horsepower system.) The new "lead-free friendly" compression ratio was 8.5:1. Although it was not widely advertised, the 429-4V had a rating of 212 net hp at 4400 rpm. It developed 327 lb.-ft. of torque at 2600 rpm. The optional 460-4V came with a net horsepower rating of 224 hp at 4400 rpm. It generated more torque (342 lb.-ft. at 2800 rpm) than the standard engine. "Evidently, the 400-2V engine's performance was not what they hoped it would be," said *Road Test* magazine. "The 460-4V can be expected to give slightly better acceleration, but decreased gas mileage."

Body and frame construction was reintroduced in the new model. S-shaped front frame rails provided energy absorption on impact. The T-Bird body was mounted at computer-designated points for noise and vibration suppression characteristics. For its time, the mounting system worked very nicely. "In the new 'Bird you can turn off the radio and enjoy the silence; we don't see how Ford or anyone else can significantly improve upon it," said *Road Test*. "It seemed that everything we drove after giving up the 'Bird was a bit uncouth and noisy."

As in the past, testers found Ford emphasizing a good ride, but de-emphasizing handling in the T-Bird. Initial steering response was slightly improved, but the four-turns-lock-to-lock system was still slow and unpredictable, especially considering the longer new wheelbase. The overly soft suspension led to some ground-scraping and bent up underpinnings. On the plus side, a new rear stabilizer bar tended to improve roll stiffness. The Thunderbird's brakes had now been accepted as perhaps the best system in the sports-personal car market segment. Ford's optional "Sure Track" antilock braking system made them work even better. A heavier-duty 9.38-in. rear axle ring gear was used with this system, as ABS tended to create some rear axle chattering that could wreck the standard 9-in. ring gear.

As might be expected, the 1972 Thunderbird was no economy car. The 429-4V normally averaged about 9.0 to 9.1 mpg. *Road Test* magazine averaged 10.6 mpg for its entire trial, but had a low figure of 8.2 mpg during acceleration testing. *Motor Trend* (December 1971) averaged 11.67 mpg, also with the 429-4V. The 460-4V engine was good for 10-10.6 mpg on average. When the '72 models were about 10 years old, the editors of *Consumer Guide* said that the Thunderbird was "A possible collector's item one day, but awful mileage means you'll spend more time looking at it than driving it."

Motor Trend's December article was an unusual three-way comparison between the Buick Riviera, the Thunderbird, and the Jaguar XJ6. The buff book made the point that America's personal luxury cars had grown as large as its four-door sedans, thereby justifying — in its "editorial mind" at least — stacking the pair of destroyer-sized domestics against one of Britain's hottest "sports saloon" models (saloon meaning four-door sedan in the King's English.). The conclusion arrived at through this methodology was nearly as unique as the underlying concept. "You can bet your bottom dollar that the next generation of both Thunderbird and Riviera will be smaller and will handle better," predicted writer Jim Brokaw."...take a peek at tomorrow and promote a ride in an XJ6." While obviously favoring the Jaguar, Brokaw gave the T-Bird high marks for its handling improvements, braking, steel-belted tires and absence of what FoMoCo called "NVH" (noise, vibration, harshness). He also liked its optional sliding sun roof and lack of quality control problems.

The new Thunderbird was well-received by the car buying public and production soared back up to 57,814 cars. Of these, 22,229 were assembled in Los Angeles and 35,585 were assembled in Wixom, Mich. A significant historical milestone was marked during the year when the one millionth Thunderbird ever built was assembled. It was specially finished with Anniversary Gold paint and wore a White vinyl-clad landau roof. The wheel covers had color-coordinated gold accents. Up front was a gold-finished radiator grille. Commemorative "Millionth Thunderbird" emblems were found on the right-hand side of the instrument panel, and in the center

With powerful V-8s, '72 T-Birds had no trouble pulling trailers. (Ford Motor Co.)

of the S-shaped landau bars on either side of the roof. The car was presented to a member of the Classic Thunderbird Club International to use for one year. The following year it was purchased by George Watts, the collector who owns the earliest production Thunderbird known to have been built.

1972 Thunderbird Two-Door Hardtop Specifications

Wheelbase	120.4 in.	Standard Engine Type	90-degree ohv V-8
Curb Weight	4,503 lb.	Bore	4.36 in.
Overall Length	216.0 in.	Stroke	3.59 in.
Overall Width	79.3 in.	Displacement	429 cid
Overall Height	51.3 in.	Carburetor	Single 4-Barrel
Front Tread	63 in.	Compression Ratio	8.5:1
Rear Tread	62.8 in.	Maximum BHP	212 @ 4400 rpm
Trunk Volume	13.9 cu. ft.	Maximum Torque	327 lb.-ft. @ 2600 rpm
Tires	215R-15 SBR	Optional Engine Type	90-degree ohv V-8
Turning Diameter	43 ft.	Bore	4.36 in.
Total Brake Swept Area	387.9 sq. in.	Stroke	3.85 in.
Ground Clearance	5.4 in.	Displacement	460 cid
Fuel Tank Capacity	22.5 gal.	Carburetor	Single 4-Barrel
Coolant Capacity	18.8 qt.	Compression Ratio	8.5:1
Transmission	3-speed auto.	Maximum BHP	224 @ 4400 rpm
Rear Axle	2.75:1	Maximum Torque	342 lb.-ft. @ 2600 rpm

1972 Thunderbird Engineering

Front Suspension	Independent drag-strut, ball-joint type w/ coil springs
Rear Suspension	Four-link rubber-cushioned w/integral stabilizer bar
Steering	Integral; power-assist, 21.7:1 overall ratio
Front Brakes	Power disc with 232 sq. in. swept area
Brakes	Power drum with 155.9 sq. in. swept area

1972 Thunderbird Performance

Model	CID/HP	Performance
0-60 mph		
Two-door Hardtop	429/212 (net)	11.2 seconds
1/4-Mile		
Two-door Hardtop	429/212 (net)	17.4 seconds @ 81.2 mph
Top Speed		
Two-door Hardtop	429/212 (net)	120 mph

1973
For Your Driving Pleasure

The 1973 Thunderbird continued to share the basic body of the Lincoln Mark IV. It had just a few minor alterations. There was an eggcrate grille in place of the horizontal-bars grille of 1972, plus a stand-up hood ornament. These changes made the car look richer, but many marque enthusiasts prefer the sportier image of the previous edition. The 1973 grille no longer showed below the bumper, which was of a more massive type designed to withstand five mile per hour impacts. Developed by Ford to absorb collision damage, the Twin I-Beam bumper had a shelf-like appearance and added nearly three inches to the car's length. Vertical guards near the center of the bumper were standard equipment. The Thunderbird name was spelled out on the car's nose, where a winged T-Bird emblem had "flown" before. Twin headlamps on either side of the grille were mounted in separate square bezels. New notched-into-the-fender parking lights had a "three-story" appearance. They could be seen from the front, as well as the side.

In profile, the 1973 Thunderbirds had wider body side moldings with color-keyed protective vinyl inserts. Opera windows were optional for the roof sail panels early in the year. They helped eliminate a blind spot caused by the massive "C" pillars. In June 1973 opera windows became standard equipment, along with a half-dozen other items. The windows were basically of a low, rectangular shape, but the trailing edge was slanted to match the rear roof line. Landau bars were no longer offered for roof decoration. Full wheel covers were standard and followed the same general design theme as the 1972 covers, although they had some detail changes.

The rear of the T-Bird again had wall-to-wall taillights and a winged Thunderbird emblem was in the center of the lens. The huge lens had more of a wedge shape than an inverted U-shape. Ford's sales catalog described the T-Bird's trunk as being "vacation-size." It offered 13.9 cu. ft. of total luggage capacity. The bumper was massive in size and wrapped around the rear body corners. Two large vertical guards flanked a huge license plate "frame" in the center. As at the front, the energy absorbing rear bumper system met newly required 1973 Federal Safety Standards.

Once again, the list of standard equipment was long. Ford broke it up into categories including Comfort and Convenience, Smooth Quiet Ride, Safe Driving, Performance and Handling, Appearance, and Economy and Durability. A few items from the list that have not been specifically mentioned up to this point were wood-tone accents to dress up interiors, bright moldings on the rear hood edge and door belts and drip rails, a 61-amp. alternator, and a spare tire lock. Designed to help foil vandals, a new item was a fixed mast radio antenna made of strong stainless steel with a screw-on attaching device. The June sales catalog (5402 Rev. 6/73) that added opera windows as standard equipment also added six more items. They were: SelectAire Conditioner, tinted glass, power side windows, an automatic seat back release that unlatched the seat when you opened the door (to simplify entering the car with bulky packages), power steering, and a vinyl roof.

Exteriors could be finished in any of 15 standard colors, or eight Glamour paint options. The Glamour paints contained a higher amount of metallic particles for greater reflectivity and iridescence. Cayman Grain vinyl tops were available in Black, White, Dark Blue, Dark Green, Dark Brown, Beige, Gold, and Light Blue. Odense Grain vinyl tops (available on cars having the Exterior Decor Group option) came in Copper, White, Blue, Green, and Brown. Individually adjustable, deep-cushioned spilt bench front seats with fold-down arm rests were standard in all Thunderbirds. Also featured was cut-pile carpeting on the floor, lower seat backs, and lower door panels. Cloth-and-vinyl interior trims were standard for the split bench seat. Optional all-vinyl trim was available in all seven colors. Optional leather-and-vinyl trim for the split bench seat was offered. Optional bucket seats came only in cloth-and-vinyl.

The 1973 T-Bird Landau Hardtop had only detail changes from its 1972 counterpart. (Ford Motor Co. photo)

New options available for this 1973 T-Bird Hardtop included the opera windows and Exterior Decor Group depicted here. (Ford Motor Co. photo)

The 1973 Exterior Decor Group included a padded vinyl top and wide body belt moldings with color-coordinated vinyl inserts. (Ford Motor Co. photo)

1973 Thunderbird Interior Trim Codes (US & Canada)

Seat Type	Material	Black	Dark Blue	Medium Ginger	Dark Green	Light Gold	Dark Tobacco	White
Lo-Back Split Bench	Fabric & Vinyl	HA	HB	HF	HR	HY	HZ	
High-Back Buckets	Fabric & Vinyl	GA	GB	GF	GR			
Lo-Back Split Bench	Leather	KA			KR		KZ	*
Lo-Back Split Bench	Vinyl	JA	JB	JF	JR	JY	JZ	*

Legend: (*) White with color-keyed components

The 1973 Thunderbirds had an improved impact-absorbing laminated safety glass windshield. Other product improvements included suspension system refinements, increased front and rear headroom, and whitewall steel-belted radial tires as standard equipment. An inside hood release and spare tire lock were also new. The 429-cid four-barrel V-8 was standard. Like all 1973 Ford engines, it was designed to operate on regular gasoline with an octane rating of at least 91 (Research Method) with the engine adjusted to factory specifications. The 460-cid four-barrel V-8 was optional. Sales catalogs said nothing about horsepower or torque ratings.

This year the manufacturer's suggested retail price for the Thunderbird, at the start of the year, was $5,577. However, the car used by *Motor Trend* in a four-car comparison (June 1973) listed for $8,105. This car was tested against the Pontiac Grand Prix, Buick

Riviera, and Oldsmobile Toronado. It was the most expensive of the quartet. Although it used the optional 460-4V engine, it had the lowest horsepower rating. Nevertheless, it was second fastest from 0-60 mph. It also had the second fastest terminal speed in the quarter-mile, but the third lowest elapsed time. Writer Jim Brokaw found the T-Bird's handling good, but sensitive to tire inflation. He joked about its cigarette lighter having more stages than a Saturn V rocket and said, "If you threw it out the window in Belfast, you'd clear the streets in three seconds." Brokaw especially noted the 460-cid V-8 was a good low-end torquer that could easily burn rubber. He actually rated it second highest in performance, next to the 455-cid 250 hp Grand Prix. Criticisms were directed at a too small ashtray and glove box and excessive wind noise for a Ford product. He also gave the T-Bird his top rating in the "prestige" department.

New-for-1973 were crash bumper and a hood ornament. (Ford Motor Co. photo)

Model-year production for 1973 totaled 87,269 cars, which was nearly 30,000 units higher than the previous year. This was quite an impressive endorsement of the Lincoln-like "Big 'Bird" and represented a 0.2 percent increase in overall market share. All of the cars were manufactured in two assembly plants. The Los Angeles plant contributed 40,593 units, while the Wixom, Mich. plant accounted for 46,676 assemblies.

Ford published separate Thunderbird literature for dealers in Canada, although all of the 1973 models were built in the United States. Under a free trade agreement that went into effect around 1970 cars could be shipped across the border, in either direction, duty-free. This allowed automakers to avoid sourcing cars from both countries to avoid tariffs and helped them make more efficient use of their production facilities. There are no dramatic differences in the wording of the U.S. and Canadian sales catalogs, although at least three small differences appear in Canadian literature. First, the phrase "1973 Federal Motor Vehicle Standards" is changed to "1973 Canadian Motor Vehicle Standards." Second, instead of mentioning specific mileage intervals for service operations Canadian catalogs say "details are contained in the Owner's Manual." Third, instead of listing a "22.5-gal." fuel tank, the Canadian literature says "18.7 gal."

Base-priced at $5.577 models, the two-door Hardtop was the sole model offered in the 1973 T-Bird lineup. Over 87,000 were made. (Ford Motor Co. photo)

1973 Thunderbird Two-Door Hardtop Specifications

Wheelbase	120.4 in.	Standard Engine Type	90-degree ohv V-8
Curb Weight	4,742 lb.	Bore	4.36 in.
Overall Length	218.9 in.	Stroke	3.59 in.
Overall Width	79.7 in.	Displacement	429 cid

1973 Thunderbird Two-Door Hardtop Specifications

Overall Height	53.1 in.	Carburetor	Single 4-Barrel
Front Tread	63 in.	Compression Ratio	8.5:1
Rear Tread	63.1 in.	Maximum BHP	208 @ 4400 rpm
Trunk Volume	13.9 cu. ft.	Maximum Torque	327 lb.-ft. @ 2800 rpm
Tires	230-15 X SBR	Optional Engine Type	90-degree ohv V-8
Turning Diameter	43 ft.	Bore	4.36 in.
Total Brake Swept Area	405.2 sq. in.	Stroke	3.85 in.
Ground Clearance	5.4 in.	Displacement	460 cid
Fuel Tank Capacity	22.5 gal.	Carburetor	Single 4-Barrel
Coolant Capacity	18.8 qt.	Compression Ratio	8.5:1
Transmission	3-speed auto.	Maximum BHP	219 @ 4400 rpm
Rear Axle	2.75:1	Maximum Torque	338 lb.-ft. @ 2800 rpm

1973 Thunderbird Engineering

Front Suspension	Coil springs, stabilizer, shocks, axial strut
Rear Suspension	Coil spring, shocks. and stabilizer
Steering	Integral; power-assist, 21.73:1 overall ratio
Front Brakes	Power disc with 232 sq. in. swept area
Brakes	Power drum with 155.9 sq. in. swept area

1973 Thunderbird Performance

Model 0-60 mph	CID/HP	Performance
Two-door Hardtop	446/208 (net)	9.0 seconds
1/4-Mile		
Two-door Hardtop	429/208 (net)	17.4 seconds @ 85 mph
Top Speed		
Two-door Hardtop	429/212 (net)	120 mph

1974
"Big Brother" 'Birds

To most people, the 1974 Thunderbird looked like the 1973 Thunderbird, but Ford said it was designed to be the finest Thunderbird ever. It was, claimed the year's sales brochure "A magnificent expression of personal car luxury, which has long been a hallmark of Thunderbird."

This informative piece of factory literature, entitled *Thunderbird: An engineering achievement*, talked about the engineers, designers and assembly line workers who built the car, and their desire to achieve a higher standard of quality. It suggested that this was reflected in the fit of T-Bird parts, the look of the paint, an exceptionally smooth and quiet ride, and painstaking attention to detail.

In most details, the 1974 model was changed very little from 1973. With Ford's annual struggle to meet Federal safety and emissions standards and get the cars certified for sale, there was little time or money left to redesign grille inserts and door handles. However, there were a number of refinements in the car. The bumpers and bumper guards were slightly altered, and there was a new rear appearance with the addition of an impact-absorbing bumper and redesigned full-width taillights. Overall length of the car grew one-half-foot to 22.8 in. Better performance was promised, as the 460-cid four-barrel V-8 became standard equipment. It had a new solid state ignition system, and a 220-hp rating. The T-Bird also gained 500 pounds since 1973. Four additional gallons of regular, unleaded gasoline in the fuel tank contributed to its higher curb weight. New luxury options included an electrically-heated quick-defrost windshield and rear window, plus a transparent moon roof.

1974 THUNDERBIRD BURGUNDY SPECIAL EDITION

Most of the luxuries in Thunderbird come *standard:* things like air conditioning. The vinyl roof. Steel-belted radial ply tires. And it doesn't require premium gas. Now, for a little more, you can have this very limited Special Edition. The Burgundy Luxury Group is sumptuous, from its discreet gold stripes and distinctive wire wheel covers, to its deep Victoria Velour seating surfaces (or choose red leather and vinyl). Here's the car to remember. Better still, to own. Thunderbird 1974. *In the world of personal luxury cars, it's the unique value.*

This is your year. Make a little Thunder of your own.

THUNDERBIRD

FORD DIVISION *Ford* 1974 Thunderbird with optional Burgundy Luxury Group, moonroof, convenience, protection and bumper groups, power antenna, cornering lamps and speed control.

The 1974 T-Bird Hardtop came with a new Burgundy Special Edition trim package that made it a luxury car. (Ford Motor Co.)

170

The basic Thunderbird body was largely unaltered. Only one model (two-door Hard-top Coupe) was offered again. It listed for a whopping $7,221. Since the start of the model-year 1973, the T-Bird's list price had jumped some $1,700. At this time, many automakers were hiking prices several times a year, often enlarging their equipment lists at the same time. Sometimes the price increases offset the costs of Federally required safety or anti-pollution equipment. In other cases, they were a way to increase revenues without actually selling more cars. There was at least one midyear 1973 price hike when more standard equipment was added to the Thunderbird. These features were carried over as part of the 1974 "base" model.

Standard appearance features of Thunderbirds listed in the sales catalog printed in July 1973 included opera windows, Odense vinyl roofs in nine colors (Brown, Copper, Medium Green, Tan, Black, Medium Silver Blue, Gold, White, and Dark Blue), simulated woodtone accents, deluxe seat belts, full wheel covers, unique Thunderbird identification features including a hood ornament, moldings on hood edge/door belts/drip rails/wheel openings, and vinyl insert body side moldings. A revision made in a new catalog printed in January 1974 changed the term "simulated woodtone" to "woodtone" for some inexplicable reason.

Initially, twenty-one exterior colors were offered on '74 T-Birds and eight were optional Glamour Colors. In January 1974, the Autumn Fire Glamour Paint color was deleted from the revised sales catalog. At the same time, a pair of Special Edition Thunderbirds was added to the offerings. The Burgundy Luxury Group option included all basic T-Bird equipment, plus dual body side and hood stripes, special body side moldings, and simulated wire wheel covers. An exclusive Dark Red Odense grain vinyl top was also featured. White and Gold Special Edition Thunderbirds came with color-coordinated wide body side moldings, color-keyed wheel covers, body side accent stripes, hood and deck lid accent stripes, and an exclusive Gold Levant grain vinyl top. Both special Thunderbirds also offered Glamour colors and luggage compartment trim as standard equipment.

All of the Comfort and Convenience features found on mid-1973 Thunderbirds were standard again in 1974 including the adjustable split bench front seat with fold-down center arm rest. Lustrous Aurora cloth-and-vinyl trim was standard and came in six of the total eight interior colors offered. Leather-with-vinyl trim was optional and came in all eight colors, as did the new "Super Soft" vinyl options. Picardy Velour cloth trim, also a new option, was offered in three colors.

1974 Thunderbird Interior Trim Codes (US & Canada)

Seat Type	Material	Black	Blue	Green	Red	Gold	Tan	Saddle	White
Split Bench	Fabric & Vinyl	HA	HB	HR	HD		HU	HZ	
RPO Split Bench	Velour & Vinyl		FB			FY	FU		
RPO Split Bench	Vinyl	JA	JB	JR	JD		JU	JZ	JW
RPO Split Bench	Leather & Vinyl	KA	KB	KR	KD	KY	KU	KZ	KW

Legend: (RPO) Regular Production Option

Front outboard retractable lap/shoulder belts with the infamous starter interlock system were one of the 1974 T-Bird's least popular "features." This system was required by a new standard established by the National Highway Traffic Safety Administration (NHTSA). It caused such a violent public reaction that it was canceled by the U.S. Congress at the end of the year. Ford initially told customers "you buckle up to start the engine" which made people feel like "Big Brother" was watching over them. The description of the system was revised in the January sales catalog to say "it encourages you to buckle up before starting the engine."

The ignition interlock prevented the engine from starting if belts for occupied front seats were not buckled in the proper sequence. A warning buzzer (after January a warning light and buzzer) reminded outboard passengers to buckle up. Additionally, a logic circuit prevented the engine from starting if any outboard passenger attempted to "beat the system" by extending the harness before sitting or buckling belts together behind him or her. *Ward's Automotive Yearbook 1975* scored slow-thinking "Washington 'experts'" who in late 1974 killed the starter interlock and cast new doubt on the catalytic converter — long after both multi-million dollar devices had begun being installed in cars."

Although the 1974 Thunderbird averaged only 11.6 mpg on a 73-mile loop of city, suburban, freeway, and hilly roads driving conducted by *Motor Trend* magazine (March 1974), Ford literature included a list of "Economy and Durability" features. Self-adjusting brakes, the two-year coolant-antifreeze, a long-life Motorcraft Sta-Ful battery, the corrosion-resistant aluminized muffler, zinc-coatings on underbody parts, and the fact that the 460 operated on regular fuel were highlighted as economy features. In the durability department, Ford promoted its 36,000-mile major chassis lubrication, 6,000-mile oil changes, and 12,000-mile (after the first time) oil filter changes.

The 460-4V engine retained its 8.0:1 compression ratio to permit operation on 91 octane regular fuel. The new Solid State ignition system was standard and made starting the car easier than ever (as long as you locked your seat belts first.) The system eliminated ignition parts like points, cam, and condenser with highly reliable, low-maintenance electric components. The results were a stronger spark , reduced maintenance, more dependable cold weather starting, lower emissions, and the virtual elimination of misfiring.

This year's Jim Brokaw road test in *Motor Trend* continued the practice of comparing the T-Bird to other American personal-luxury cars. It featured eight vehicles — the most ever — of which three were new models. The Thunderbird had already face off against the Riviera, Toronado, Grand Prix, and Monte Carlo in previous competitions. Now it was also being stacked up against the AMC Matador "Oleg Cassini" model, the Mercury Cougar, and the Ford Torino Elite. With an $8,607 price tag and 5,270-lb. weight as tested, the Thunderbird was the most expensive and heaviest car in the group. It had the most cubic inches, but only the sixth highest net horsepower rating. Though tied for second in torque, the T-Bird's fuel economy was on the very bottom. The other cars averaged 13.3-16.2 mpg over the same test loop.

Jim Brokaw actually said very little about the Thunderbird in his report, except for mentioning that its typical strong low-end torque was absent, that it was unusually thirsty for fuel, and that it was probably the quietest car of the bunch. He concluded that all eight models shared the same basic features, and a high level of execution. "It's really a matter of product loyalty and styling tastes," he felt about picking one over the other. Overall, he favored Ford's mid-size product — the Torino Elite — as the best choice for car buyers in 1974. Ironically, even the Elite would look like an inefficient gas guzzling barge after the Arab oil embargo caused a severe energy shortage in the U.S. from January-March 1974. The embargo signaled that it was time for American cars to go through a "change of life," and this change would ultimately have a drastic and very positive effect on the Thunderbird's long-term popularity.

Unfortunately, the 1974 Thunderbird was substantially less popular — or at least less successful in sales — than the previous edition. It lost about 30,000 customers and two-tenths of a point of market share. A grand total of 58,443 of these cars were produced. The Ford plant in Los Angeles built 20,500 of them, while the Wixom, Mich. factory manufactured 37,943. No Thunderbirds were built in Canada, although a separate Canadian sales catalog was issued in August 1973. It was the same as the July 1973 U.S. catalog, except for one difference that some collectors might be interested in ... cars sold in Canada (although made in the U.S.) were *not* required to have the seat belt/starter interlock system.

1974 Thunderbird Two-Door Hardtop Specifications

Wheelbase	120.4 in.	Standard Engine Type	90-degree ohv V-8
Curb Weight	5,068	Bore	4.36 in.
Overall Length	224.8 in.	Stroke	3.85 in.
Overall Width	79.7 in.	Displacement	460 cid
Overall Height	53.0 in.	Carburetor	Single 4-Barrel
Front Tread	63 in.	Compression Ratio	8.0:1
Rear Tread	63.1 in.	Maximum BHP	220 @ 4000 rpm
Trunk Volume	13.4 cu. ft.	Maximum Torque	355 lb.-ft. @ 2600 rpm
Fuel Capacity	26.5 gal.	Rear Axle Ratio	3.00:1

1974 Thunderbird Engineering

Front Suspension	Coil springs, stabilizer, shocks, axial strut
Rear Suspension	Coil spring, shocks. and stabilizer
Steering	Integral; power-assist
Front Brakes	Power disc
Brakes	Power drum

1975
Lookin' Good

The Thunderbird turned 20 in 1975 and all T-Birds marketed that year were considered 20th Anniversary models. This remained Ford's top-of-the-line personal luxury car. In fact, there was more richness and elegance than ever before when the line was introduced on Sept. 27, 1974 . Still more was added during the model-year. Silver Luxury and Copper Luxury trim options with special half-vinyl tops, crushed velour or leather seats, deluxe trunk appointments, deluxe wheel covers, and more joined last year's Gold and White Luxury Group option. In April 1975, a Jade Luxury Group was added. It included three distinct variations of the use of Jade-Green colored paint and trim, along with other upscale enhancements.

The Anniversary Thunderbirds rode the same wheelbase, but grew even longer overall. From front bumper to rear bumper the huge two-door Hardtops stretched 225.6 in. This year their weight increased only modestly, however, and 5,101 lb. was the official specification. Physical appearance was virtually unchanged, except that the front bumper guards were spaced further apart.

Featured once more was separate body and frame construction. The strong, durable frame came with closed box-section members and five cross-members. Self-adjusting rear brakes, a long-life battery, an aluminized muffler, and zinc-coated chassis parts were standard. All Thunderbirds were endowed with an impressive list of standard luxury features, including SelectAire Conditioner, automatic transmission, power steering, power front disc brakes, and more. Options available to personalize the cars included a power-operated glass moon roof, electric windshield and rear window defrosters, and AM/FM stereo radio with tape player.

Twenty exterior colors were offered for Thunderbirds in both the U.S. and Canada. There were initially 11 standard color selections, plus nine optional color choices. This did not include the midyear additions. The standard Odense grain vinyl roof came in 11 colors: Black, White, Blue, Silver Blue, Green, Brown, Tan, Gold, Red, Copper, and Silver. A half-vinyl roof was standard with Copper, Silver, and Jade Luxury groups. The standard interior featured Aurora cloth-and-vinyl trim in four colors. Picton velour cloth-and-vinyl trim was optional in five colors. The optional Super Soft vinyl interior came in seven colors. Leather seats with vinyl trim were offered in nine color choices. In addition, Jade Thunderbirds offered White leather seating surface (code P5) or Jade Media Velour upholstery (code NR), both with Jade vinyl trim, and attractive color-keyed components.

1975 Thunderbird Upholstery Color & Trim Choices

Interior Color	Standard Aurora Cloth & Vinyl	Picton Velour Cloth & Vinyl	Super-soft Vinyl Trim	Leather Seating & Vinyl Trim
Black	X		X	X
White			X	X
Medium Green	X	X	X	X
Medium Blue	X	X	X	X
Saddle/Tan *			X	X
Saddle	X	X	X	X
Dark Red		X	X	X
Copper **		X		X
Silver				X
Jade		X		

Legend: (*) is Tan seating and door panel inserts with Saddle components; (**) is velour is Media Cloth

1975 Thunderbird Interior Trim Codes (US & Canada)

Seat Type	Material	Black	Blue	Dark Red	Green	Tan Saddle	Saddle	White	Jade
Split Bench	Fabric & Vinyl	HA	HB		HG		HZ		
RPO Split Bench	Velour & Vinyl		FB	FD	FG				
RPO Split Bench	Vinyl		JA	JB	JD	JG	JU		JW
RPO Split Bench	Leather & Vinyl	KA	KB	KD	KG	KU	KZ	KZ	P5
RPO Split Bench	Media & Leather								NR

Legend: Jade Thunderbird trim P5 includes white leather seating surfaces

Seat Type	Material	White/Red	White/Black	White/Green	White/Copper	White/Saddle	Red	Copper	Silver
RPO Split Bench	Picton & Leather						FD		
RPO Split Bench	Velour & Leather						KC		KP
RPO Split Bench	Media & Leather							MC	
RPO Split Bench	Vinyl		JN	JW	J5	J6	J9		
RPO Split Bench	Leather & Vinyl	KN	KW	K5	K6	K9		KC	

Legend: (RPO) Regular Production Option

Though still available in only one basic body style, the 1975 T-Bird offered a lengthy list of interior and exterior options. (Ford Motor Co.)

"How do you make the 20th Anniversary Thunderbird even more distinctive?" asked Ford in its midyear 1975 sales catalog (no. 5637 4/75). "You create a new and beautiful Thunderbird Jade Luxury Group option." This stand-out car featured new colors, new textures, and new fabrics in three exterior and two interior decor combinations. The All-Jade version had numerous exterior distinctions like a Normande grain padded vinyl half-top, color-keyed vinyl-clad rear window moldings, color-keyed roof moldings, a silver Thunderbird opera window insignia, color-keyed wide body side moldings, Jade Starfire glamour finish, dual hood and body side stripes, and wire wheel covers.

In addition to the all-green model, the Jade Thunderbird came in two equally distinctive alternate trim combinations. One featured Polar White exterior finish smartly topped with a Jade half-vinyl roof. Another offered Jade Starfire glamour finish with a white half-vinyl top. Both of these cars came with wide body side moldings color-keyed to the roof, the silver Thunderbird insignia on their opera windows, rear window and roof moldings, color-keyed dual hood and body side paint stripes and wire wheel covers.

The T-Bird still featured a 460-cid four-barrel V-8. No horsepower rating was listed in sales literature and different sources show different numbers. According to *Ward's Automotive Yearbook 1975* the specification was 194 nhp at 3800 rpm. Other sources say 216 hp, 218 hp, and 220 hp. In reality, the early net horsepower ratings used in the industry were relative to vehicle weight, so the fully-loaded T-Bird could, theoretically, have less horsepower than the base model. Therefore, all of the ratings we discovered could be correct. The biggest technical innovation of 1975 was an optional four-wheel disc brake system powered by Ford's new Hydro-Boost hydraulic brake booster. It included the Sure Trac rear brake anti-skid package. In addition, the anti-freeze was now advertised to last three years, instead of two.

Again this year, all Thunderbirds were manufactured in plants located in the U.S. However, not all of the cars were produced for the U.S. market and those that were not may have had minor differences. For instance, the sales literature issued by Ford of Canada did not include a paragraph that appeared in U.S. catalogs saying that T-Birds were designed to operate on unleaded gas. Also, the American literature specified mileage intervals for oil changes and major chassis lubrication, while Canadian catalogs eliminated such references. Sales and production saw another decline and the Thunderbird's share of market dropped, too. Only 24,455 cars were made at Wixom, Mich. The Los Angeles factory added 18,230 more units. That made the model-year production 42,685, or some 15,800 less than the previous year.

1975 Thunderbird Two-Door Hardtop Specifications

Wheelbase	120.4 in.	Standard Engine Type	90-degree ohv V-8
Curb Weight	5,101	Bore	4.362 in.
Overall Length	225.8 in.	Stroke	3.85 in.
Overall Width	79.7 in.	Displacement	460 cid
Overall Height	53.0 in.	Carburetor	Single 4-Barrel
Front Tread	62.9 in.	Compression Ratio	8.0:1
Rear Tread	62.8 in.	Maximum BHP	194 @ 3800 rpm
Trunk Volume	13.4 cu. ft.	Maximum Torque	355 lb.-ft. @ 2600 rpm
Fuel Capacity	26.5 gal.	Rear Axle Ratio	3.00:1

1975 Thunderbird Engineering

Front Suspension	Coil springs, stabilizer, shocks, axial strut
Rear Suspension	Coil spring, shocks. and stabilizer
Steering	Integral; power-assist
Front Brakes	Power disc
Brakes	Power drum

1976
The Metternich of Autodom

The 1976 Thunderbird was another of the "Big Birds" that were first introduced in 1972 and related to the Lincoln Continental Mark IV. Ford described it as "Possibly the best luxury car buy in the world today." Since it listed for over $3,000 less than the Mark IV, there was some validity to the claim. However, several European competitors like the BMW 2002, Audi, and Alfa-Romeo Alfetta Sports Sedan could be had for less than the price of a Thunderbird.

No drastic product changes were made for the last year of this series. From a business standpoint, none were really needed. Third in sales out of the 11 cars in the Ford stable, the T-Bird was some $2,100 pricier than the fanciest LTD Landau. It was a big money maker for Dearborn.

Only one basic model was marketed in the Thunderbird line. It was a two-door Hardtop with the same wheelbase as before. Front head room and leg room were substantial. It had a cavernous trunk. In base form, the $7,790 T-Bird scaled-in at 4,808 lb. That did not include the weight of a full load of unleaded gasoline in its huge fuel tank. The standard equipment list for this luxury-level car was quite long. Most new-for-1976 features were optional. They included a power lumbar seat, AM/FM radio with search function, a quadrosonic AM/FM stereo and 8-track tape player, an engine block heater, a Kasman cloth interior and an automatic headlamp dimmer.

Seventeen exterior colors were offered. Seven used optional Starfire finishes. A vinyl roof was standard in Black (code A), Blue (code B), Red (code D), Dark Jade (code R), Silver (code P), Brown (code T), White (code W) and Gold (code Y) Odense grain or Creme Normande grain. Dual body side and hood paint stripes were optional at extra cost with standard exterior colors, but included with optional Starfire colors. They came in Black, Blue, Silver, Green, Brown, White, Red, Gold, Yellow and Tan, with specific applications color-keyed to the vinyl roof, exterior color, and interior trim. Four styles of wheel covers were available: Base, Deluxe (not available with Luxury groups), simulated wire (included with Bordeaux and Lipstick Red Luxury groups), and deep-dish aluminum wheels (included with the Creme-and-Gold package). Buyers of cars with the Creme and Gold Luxury group could swap the aluminum wheels for the simulated wire wheels and receive a credit.

"Fine tailoring and uncommon comfort are customary inside Thunderbird," boasted Ford in a 1976 sales catalog. Silky Aurora nylon cloth and vinyl trim was standard on the deep-cushioned split-bench seats front and rear. The interior included assist straps, burled walnut wood-tone appliqués, and plush cut-pile carpeting to enhance the feeling of luxury. Kasman cloth trim, which had the look and feel of cashmere, was optional in four colors. T-Bird customers could also pick from super-soft vinyl trims in 11 single and two-tone combinations or more than a dozen optional trims featuring genuine leather seating surfaces.

An ad for the 1976 Creme and Gold T-Bird with leather trim. (Ford Motor Co.)

The new-for-1976 Creme and Gold Luxury Group featured two-tone Glamour paint and a Gold padded half-vinyl top. (Ford Motor Co. photo)

1976 Thunderbird Interiors

Seat Type	Material	Black	Blue	Red	Jade	Saddle	Gold	Tan
Standard								
Bucket Seats	Cloth & Vinyl	HA	HB		HR	HZ		
Decor Group								
Bucket Seats	Cloth & Vinyl		FB	FD	FR			FU
Split-Bench	All-Vinyl	JA	JB	JD	JR	JZ		
Split Bench	Leather	KA	KB	KD	KR		KY	KU

1976 Thunderbird Interiors

Seat Type	Material	Black	Blue	Red	Jade	Saddle	Gold	Tan
Luxury Group								
Bucket Seats	Velour & Vinyl			QD			QY	
Split-Bench	Leather			RD			RY	

Seat Type	Material	W. & Green	W. & Copper	W. & Saddle	Red & W.
Decor Group					
Split-Bench	All-Vinyl	J5	J8	J9	JN
Split Bench	Leather	K5	K8	K9	KN

Legend: W. & means White and another color.

Also new for 1976 were four special T-Bird option packages. The Lipstick Red and White Luxury group, as listed in the 1976 Color & Trim book, had a Lipstick Red Normande grain half-vinyl roof with Lipstick Red exterior finish. Also featured in this package were color-keyed body side, border, and back window moldings, and color-keyed paint and tape stripes. White with Lipstick Red accents were available in both vinyl or vinyl and leather interiors. If the buyer wanted the optional Silver moon roof, a color-keyed full vinyl roof was required.

A "feature car" for 1976 was the Thunderbird with a Lipstick Red Luxury group that included the same Lipstick Red exterior color, but came with a Bright Red Odense grain vinyl half-top, color-keyed border and wide body moldings, dual body and hood paint stripes, wire wheel covers, White leather seating surfaces or White super-soft vinyl upholstery, Red and White door trim panels, color-keyed interior components, 24-oz. cut-pile carpeting, and color-keyed luggage compartment trim.

The Bordeaux luxury package included Bordeaux Starfire exterior finish, a Dark Red or Silver Odense grain vinyl half-top, color-keyed border and wide body side moldings, dual body and hood paint stripes, wire wheel covers, rich Red leather or plush Red velour Media cloth (code QD) seating appointments, color-keyed interior components, 24-oz. cut-pile carpeting, and color-keyed luggage compartment trim

The Creme and Gold luxury group was an ultra-luxurious option. It included Gold Starfire glamour paint on the body sides, Creme paint on the hood, deck, and front half of the roof, unique double tape stripes along the upper fender edges, a fully-padded Gold Odense grain half-vinyl roof, color-keyed border moldings, wide Creme body side moldings, Gold Thunderbird emblems in the opera windows, and deep-dish aluminum wheels. Interior touches included Creme and Gold leather seating or plush Gold velour Media cloth trim, a gold instrument panel appliqué, color-keyed 24-oz. cut-pile carpeting, and a luggage compartment dress-up package.

During late June and early July of 1976, the country was in a fever pitch with the Bicentennial Celebration theme. It was from this celebration that a "Commemorative" model Thunderbird evolved. Only 32 of these cars were made. These cars had many special features and a sticker price of nearly $10,000.

A brighter 1976 option was the Lipstick (red) Luxury Group. It cost between $337 and $546, depending upon options it was teamed with. (Ford Motor Co. photo)

A total of 52,935 T-Birds were made in 1976. (Old Cars photo)

Motor Trend's Tony Swan wrote a "Farewell to the Big Bird Thunderbird" in February 1976. He related the car to an earlier, pre-oil-embargo product planning era, and suggested that it had sloppy handling, lazy performance, so-so economy, and flashy styling. "The Metternich of autodom," he called it. "A Rubenesque leather-padded salon on wheels for middle-class Sybarites and damn the expense."

Swan did not miss the T-Bird's strong points, and clearly noted that judging it by traditional road-testing criteria was like "judging the edibility of a duck by his performance in the 100-yard dash." The writer said that his deepest affection for the Thunderbird surfaced while stuck in rush hour traffic jams or dashing across Interstate highways through Nebraska. In such stressful or boring situations, its many accessories and convenience items could be used to block out motoring unpleasantries. He described the T-Bird as "a car for people who like to ride, not drive." It was the best-insulated, and quietest car built by Ford at the time. The silence experienced in the interior helped to isolate the driver from his or her surroundings.

A rundown of the T-Bird's luxury touches followed: Power-operated seat with lumbar support, steering wheel-mounted cruise control buttons, a "first-rate" AM/FM radio with quadrosonic tape player, and so on. Two cars were actually tested by the *Motor Trend* staff. One had a moon roof, and a power antenna. The other did not have these extras, but did have some electrical problems with its "door ajar" light, and its automatic headlamp dimmer. Also coming in for criticism were the "out of step" floor-mounted manual headlamp dimmer switch, and an automatic temperature control system that constantly blew air in the driver's face.

The 1976 Thunderbird was found to have a cushiony ride. Its power steering lacked good road feel. This caused the car to wander a lot, especially on twisting roads. The floaty ride, which was typical of many luxury class offerings of the time, was accompanied by roly-poly handling. Both conditions contributed to premature tire wear. In addition, the front-heavy T-Bird tended to under-steer and plow when it was pushed. Swan compared parking it to docking a houseboat. Other experts found the car's performance "pretty good" however. And surprisingly, its recall history, and repair record, were not all that bad. In fact, overall reliability of the 1976 model was rated "better than average" by *Consumer Guide*.

Under the Thunderbird's hood was the huge 7.5-liter V-8 with a four-barrel carburetor. Amazingly, the testers were able to chirp the tires with this engine, and Cruise-O-Matic transmission. The option-loaded T-Bird, with a curb weight of 5,200 lb. was far from an economy car. However, due to an increasing emphasis on gas mileage, Ford changed rear axle ratios. One *Motor Trend* test car had a 3.00:1 axle. It registered 13 mpg. At a steady 55 mph using cruise control, the 1976 T-Bird was capable of 15 mpg. In earlier years, this same engine had a tested economy range of 10 to 10.6 mpg. A 1974 *Motor Trend* test car had unofficially logged 11.69 mpg over a 73-mile test loop . Swan explained that Ford had improved the fuel economy of the 1976 model by advancing the timing to a point where climbing hills caused pinging. "Its an extremely irritating deficiency in a car marketed as quality goods and could conceivably lead to valve trouble." he warned.

Swan suggested that the T-Bird had a "Las Vegas" look which BMW owners sneered at, but owners of lesser Fords envied. Of course, there were more of the latter. This may explain why 52,935 Thunderbirds were built in model-year 1976. Along with strong sales, the T-Bird pulled down a good price. Swan put the car's base cost at $8,230, which probably included taxes, and destination charges. His more modestly equipped test car, with its tape player, and power vent windows (which were standard the previous year) had an $11,149 window sticker. The second car, which also had four-wheel disc brakes, and a moon roof, was just over $12,000.

The conclusion reached in *Motor Trend* was "Big Birds rank high in the lists of all-time opulent glamour boats and they're habit-forming in the extreme. They'll be missed." Other writers have agreed with this viewpoint. In his *Illustrated Thunderbird Buyer's Guide*, Ford expert Paul G. McLaughlin writes, "The 1976 Thunderbirds were fine cars in their own right, but the time had come for them to take on a new image; an image more in tune with the needs of late-1970s society. The Thunderbirds that would follow were smaller, more agile, lighter, and more performance-oriented. They'll never be more luxurious, though, because as far as luxury goes in a Thunderbird package, the epitome was reached in 1976."

Euro-deck Look used on 32 Rare 'Birds

By James F. Petrik

During late June and early July 1976, America was celebrating its bicentennial at a fever pitch. It seemed like every business had thought up a special gimmick to tie into the United States' 200th birthday party. It was a great opportunity for car manufacturers to introduce special models. Into this carnival atmosphere came the 1976 Thunderbird "Commemorative" model.

You say you never heard of this car? That is a natural reaction. In fact, people throughout most of the country had no knowledge of this offering when it was new. There are at least four good reasons for this. First, the Commemorative model was a special-edition car. Second, it had only limited distribution in the Charleston, West Virginia and Cincinnati-Dayton, Ohio regions. Third, a mere 32 Commemorative model Thunderbirds were ever sold (29 in West Virginia and three in Ohio). Fourth, there was a total lack of publicity, with no showroom folders and no magazine advertisements. In fact, Ford Motor Company's Dearborn Photographic Department never even heard of this model, so they never photographed one. With no publicity photos, none of the automotive magazines ever had any kind of article about this car, not even a tongue-in-cheek publicity release.

Before any misunderstandings develop, two qualifying statements are in order. The first is that the Commemorative model had nothing to do with the nation's bicentennial. The timing of the car's release was just pure coincidence. The second is that the car was designed to commemorate the loss of an old friend in the large and opulent Thunderbird, whose demise was imminent.

This motivation for doing a Commemorative model was the guiding spirit that inspired Ford's Cincinnati District Sales Office to develop the car for local sales. The factory cooperated and the car was strictly a local matter. This accounts for the lack of photos from the Photographic Department in Dearborn.

The regular 1976 Thunderbird (based on the Mark IV Continental) was available in many colors and was as luxurious a vehicle as one could ever want. However, to get even fancier (read that as "more expensive"), one could order a car with the Luxury Group option. These options were started about January of 1974. For the 1976 model year, there were three of these Luxury Group packages: Creme-and-Gold, Bordeaux (Maroon), and Lipstick (Bright Red with White interior). These cars had special exterior paint colors, as well as special color-coordinated interiors.

Just what was the Commemorative model? What did it look like? How can you recognize one? "Triple Black" best describes these cars. Black leather and vinyl interiors, black vinyl half-roofs, and special Silver Metallic paint was the manner in which these cars were finished. The special paint alone added $209 to the price of the car, and one owner wrote in his owner's manual that the paint code number was MX823-967. He further noted that if paint was needed, it was necessary to contact a certain gentleman at Ford's Industrial and Chemical Division (actually it is Plastics, Paint, and Vinyl Division) in Mt. Clemens, Mich. A subsequent check on this matter netted the information that the paint later became available from any paint supplier mixing Ditzler paints. The Ditzler code was 33263.

The second item making the Commemorative model non-standard was the electrically-operated moon roof (dark gray glass) in conjunction with a vinyl half roof. Anyone familiar with Thunderbirds of this era knows that one "must" have a full-vinly roof in order to get a moon roof (glass) or a sun roof (steel). This car ignored those rules.

The main appearance item, however, was the "fifth wheel" false spare tire mounting that rested horizontally on the trunk lid, which was similar to that used on the 1960 Chrysler Imperial.

Some of these cars were equipped with the standard narrow-band white wall tires, while others had the special wide-band white walls. All were steel-belted radial tires, of course. Most, if not all, of these cars also had chrome rocker panel moldings.

These 32 cars were produced in late May of 1976 at the Wixom, Mich. assembly plant. The serial numbers indicate that these cars were made in three groups. The first group of 11 cars had serial numbers 6Y87A-132367 through 6Y87A-132377 inclusive. The second group of 15 had serial numbers 6Y87A-132729 through 6Y87A-132743 inclusive. The third group of six cars had serial numbers 6Y87A-132807 through 6Y87A-132812 inclusive.

At least one car left the Wixom factory with a "bottom line" sticker price of $9,595. As an interesting trade secret, the dealer's invoice price was $7,497.45. This included special paint; vinyl half-roof; body side and hood paint stripes; leather interior trim; steel-belted radial whitewall tires, convenience group package; front cornering lamps; tilt steering wheel; six-way power driver's seat, electric rear window defroster, AM/FM stereo radio; protection group; tinted glass; simulated wire wheel covers; and wide vinyl body side moldings.

After leaving the Wixom assembly plant, the cars went to American Sunroof Corp. (ASC) of Wixom, Mich. for the addition of the moon roof, and the deck-top spare tire mounting (called a "European Rear Deck" by the supplier). This operation added $1,300 to the price, and there was also a transportation charge of $112.55 added on. This brought the "bad news" on the window sticker to $11,007.05.

One day in early July of 1978, these cars managed to have their moment of glory. The cars formed an eye-filling parade (complete with police escort) from Stouffer's Inn (where a 1977 Ford new products review was held for area Ford dealers) through downtown Cincinnati and out to River Downs Racetrack, where all the dealers enjoyed a day at the horse races. After this outing, the cars were delivered to their respective dealers.

Anyone touring southwest Ohio is advised to keep the camera on "ready," as one of these cars just might show up at any time.

Perhaps other Sales Districts sponsored special projects similar to this one. The author would be most interested in hearing about any.

(Reprinted from *The Best of Old Cars* Vol. 5. Thanks for the original story went to Robert E. Jones, a sales manager with Ford's Cincinnati Sales District, the late Ray Hass of Cincinnati, Ohio, and Lois C. Eminger, Dearborn, Mich. for their cooperation and information.)

While researching the 1976 models, I ran across an interesting "for sale" advertisement that Nikolas Rogers of Colorado Springs, placed in *Motor Trend* in May 1980. It read: "1976 Thunderbird. Last of the Classics. Creme and Gold trim interior, matching leather upholstery. Every available option, yet excellent mpg. Truly magnificent. Asking $5,000." This car sold for over $12,000 when it was new, but in just four years it had lost well over *half* its value. There simply was no market for big, V-8-powered luxury cars in the early 1980s. In fact, a 1981 "blue book" listed the price range for 1976 T-Birds as $1,900-$2,300.

1976 Thunderbird Two-Door Hardtop Specifications

Wheelbase	120.4 in.	Standard Engine Type	90-degree ohv V-8
Curb Weight	4,808 lb.	Bore	4.362 in.
Overall Length	225.7 in.	Stroke	3.85 in.
Overall Width	79.7 in.	Displacement	460 cid (7.5-liter)
Overall Height	52.8 in.	Carburetor	Single 4-Barrel
Front Head Room	36.9 in.	Compression Ratio	8.0:1
Front Leg Room	42.2 in.	Maximum BHP	202 @ 3800 rpm
Rear Head Room	36.5 in.	Maximum Torque	355 lb.-ft. @ 2600 rpm
Rear Leg Room	36.4 in.	Rear Axle Ratio	3.00:1
Front Tread	63 in.	Tires	JR78 x 15
Rear Tread	63.1 in.	Fuel Capacity	26.5 gal.
Trunk Volume	13.9 cu. ft.	MPG	15.5

1976 Thunderbird Engineering

Front Suspension	Coil springs, stabilizer, shocks, axial strut
Rear Suspension	Coil spring, shocks. and stabilizer
Steering	Integral; power-assist
Front Brakes	Power disc
Brakes	Power drum

1977 - 1979
"Birds of a Feather"

1977
The Ultimate in Luxury

The all-new 1977 Thunderbird was a contemporary luxury car with a shorter 114-in. wheelbase. Its overall length was cut 10 in. It tipped the scales at 3,907 lb. compared to 4,808 lb. for the 1976 model. Height, width, and front and rear treads did not change drastically, but it was clearly a mid-size— rather than full-size — automobile. Nevertheless, it offered the same six-passenger accommodations as before. All new sheet metal and sharp styling attempted to conceal the fact that the shrunken T-Bird was essentially a Ford LTD II.

There was less standard equipment than earlier T-Birds offered, but buyers didn't seem to care. They loved the smaller size, the lower weight, the smaller engine, and the fact that the whole package was more modern-looking and fuel efficient. The car's profile was pleasantly different. A chrome wrap-over roof molding, and small opera windows with beveled-glass, decorated the "B" pillars. These pillars separated the front door windows from large coach windows at the far rear end of the "greenhouse." Buyers also appreciated the price, which was about $2,700 lower than the year before. Demand for T-Birds soared and Ford scrambled to keep up with a six-fold increase in production.

Distinctive T-Bird features included concealed headlights (hidden behind large flip-up doors), and functional front fender louvers. The chrome-plated cross-hatch grille had a bright surround molding. Its styling was patterned after the previous design theme, but the new grille had horizontal bars that were a more dominant part of the design. The grille's lower edge was designed to swing rearward under impact, to avoid damage from slow-speed collisions. The parking and signal light lenses were again notched into the front fender tips. At the rear of the car were tall, full-width taillights, and a sculptured deck lid. A Thunderbird nameplate dressed up the deck section that extended down between the taillights.

A smaller engine was installed in T-Birds this year. This 302-cid (5.0-liter) V-8 had a DuraSpark ignition system. In the California market, a cleaner-burning 351-cid V-8 was substituted. Both the 351- and 400-cid V-8s were optional in federal (non-California) cars. To improve handling, the 1977 Thunderbird had higher-rate springs, a larger front stabilizer bar, and a standard rear stabilizer bar. Standard goodies included SelectShift Cruise-O-Matic drive, power steering, power front disc and rear drum brakes, moldings on the wrap-over roof, rocker panel moldings, and moldings on the wheel openings, body belt and rear edge of the hood. Steel-belted radial tires were mounted. An engine coolant recovery system was added.

All-new sheet metal and a sharp down-sizing to a 114-in. wheelbase attempted to conceal the 1977 T-Bird's LTD heritage. (Ford Motor Co. photo)

In 1977, T-Bird prices dropped dramatically to just over $5,000 for the basic 'bird. This sent production skyrocketing to 318,140 cars. (Ford Motor Co. photo)

The Thunderbird interior featured bench seats with Wilshire cloth and vinyl upholstery. There was a new five-pod instrument cluster with European-type graphics. Instruments included an 85-mph speedometer, a trip odometer, a 0-6000-rpms tachometer, an amp gauge, a fuel gauge, a temperature gauge, an oil pressure gauge and a clock. Warning lights were provided as directional signal and high-beam indicators, and to indicate when the hand-brake was on, the door was ajar, the seat belts were in use, and the rear defogger was being used. A simulated engine-turned trim or simulated burled wood-grain accents were used on the dashboard. The stitching pattern on the standard bench seat was brand new. A split-bench seat or bucket seats were optional. Also available was a front center console with twin storage bins. The interior included an electric clock and an AM radio as standard equipment.

1977 Thunderbird Interiors

Seat Type	Material	Blue	Red	Jade	Dove Gray	Chamois	Saddle	W. & Blue
Standard								
Bench Seat	Cloth & Vinyl	AB	AD	AR	AS	AT	AZ	
Bench Seat	All-vinyl	BB	BD	BR	BS	BT	BZ	
Bucket Seats	Cloth & Vinyl	HB	HD	HR	HS	HT	HZ	
Bucket Seats	All-vinyl	CB	CD	CR	CS	CT	CZ	CQ
Decor Group								
Bucket Seats	Cloth & Vinyl	JB	JD	JR	JS	JT	JZ	
Bucket Seats	All-vinyl	GB	GD	GR	GS	GT	GZ	GQ
Split-Bench	Cloth & Vinyl	DB	DD	DR	DS	DT	DZ	
Split-Bench	All-Vinyl	EB	ED	ER	ES	ET	EZ	
Split-Bench	Leather/vinyl	FB	FD	FR	FS	FT	FZ	FQ
Interior Luxury Group								
Split-Bench	Velour	RB	RD	RR	RS	RT	RZ	
Split-Bench	US Leather -vinyl	SB	SD	SR	SS	ST	SZ	
Town Landau & Luxury Interior								
Split-Bench	Velour Cloth	RB	RD	RR	RS	RT	RZ	
Split-Bench	US Leather-vinyl	SB		SR	SS	ST	SZ	SQ

Seat Type	Material	W. & Red	W. & Jade	W. & Cham.	W. & Saddle	Saddle & W.	W. & Lipstick	
Standard								
Bucket Seats	All-vinyl		CN	C5	C2	C9	C3	
Decor Group								
Bucket Seats	All-vinyl			G5	G2	G9	G3	
Split-Bench	All-Vinyl		EN	E5	E2	E9	E3	EL
Split-Bench	Leather/vinyl	FN	F5	F2	F9	F3	FL	
Town Landau & Luxury Interior								
Split-Bench	US Leather-vinyl	SN	S5	S2	S9		SL	

Legend: W. & means White. Cham. means Chamois. US Leather-vinyl means Ultra-Soft leather and vinyl.

Major new Thunderbird options included an illuminated entry system, a day and night quartz clock, a leather-wrapped sports steering wheel, a front seat center console, turbine-style cast-aluminum wheels, an automatic-temperature air conditioning system, and front and rear vinyl roofs. An optional exterior decor package could be ordered to accent the T-Bird's roof. Also optional was an interior decor group option. It contained Ardmore and Kasman knit cloth upholstery choices, fold-down center arm rests, a reclining passenger seat, a visor vanity mirror, and color-keyed seat belts.

At the base-model level, the 1977 Thunderbird two-door Hardtop listed for $5,063. Two personalized versions of the T-Bird were also offered. Both were announced in the *1977 Car Facts Bulletin* headlined "New Sales Opportunities for 1977-1/2." It promoted four midyear additions to Ford's car-line: A pair of LTD options (Landau and Brougham Feature Packages), a T-Bird option (Silver/Lipstick Feature Package), and an all-new T-Bird model (Town Landau). "Ford is introducing three special feature cars and an entirely new Thunderbird model. These vehicles provide unique decor features which are specifically designed to enhance their personal appeal," the automaker advised its dealers. "The addition of these four vehicles to your model line-up will provide customers with the opportunity to select from even more distinctive levels of styling within each of these car-lines."

The "special feature" Thunderbird was the 1977-1/2 Silver/Lipstick feature package. This was basically a paint and vinyl trim option. A flyer showed the base vehicle price of $5,063, and prices for three separate options (vinyl roof at $132, interior decor group at $299, and all-vinyl trim at $22). They added up to $5,516. However, the same flyer also noted that a vinyl roof was not required, so you could get a Silver or Lipstick decor car with an all-steel roof for as little as $5,384. It's doubtful that many (if any) were ordered without a vinyl roof, which was a popular feature. The decor package's actual content included a Silver Metallic exterior color or Lipstick Red exterior color. Both were usually combined with a vinyl roof in a choice of the matching or contrasting color. This added up to six combinations, since buyers could get either color of paint without a vinyl top or with a choice of a Silver or Lipstick Red vinyl top. You also got a Dove Grey all-vinyl interior with a choice of a split bench seat or bucket seats up front. This interior featured Lipstick Red accent straps and welts, Dove Grey door and quarter trim with Lipstick Red carpets, moldings, and components, plus Dove Grey trim above the belt line. This package could be teamed with all other T-Bird regular production options except leather seat trims and Tu-tone paint treatments.

Also available for $7,990 was the Town Landau. This was considered a separate model. It was said to offer "an entirely new level of personal luxury and distinction in the classic Thunderbird tradition." On the exterior, it featured a special die-cast Town Landau hood ornament with color-coordinated acrylic insert; stripes on the hood, grille opening panels, headlight doors, and deck lid; accent paint on the fender louvers; dual upper body side paint stripes; turbine spoke cast-aluminum wheels with accent paint; silk-screened Town Landau signatures on the opera windows; a color-keyed roof cross-over molding (when the optional vinyl roof was ordered); a brushed aluminum roof wrap-over appliqué; front cornering lamps; wide color-keyed body side moldings; white sidewall tires; a deluxe bumper group; and tinted glass. The Thunderbird Town Landau was available in many distinctive color combinations, including an exclusive Pastel Beige color that was compatible with the T-Bird's Red, Chamois, and Saddle colored upholstery. In addition, the 400-cid two-barrel V-8 was a part of the Town Landau package.

The Town Landau model seen here had prices beginning at $7,990. It included an aluminum roof wrapover appliqué. (Ford Motor Co. photo)

The Town Landau also had a fully-loaded interior package with high-gloss wood-tone door and instrument panel appliqués, a special Town Landau instrument panel plaque, luxury door trim panels with velour inserts, 18-oz. luxury carpeting, luggage compartment trim, a special sound insulation package, a luxury steering wheel, a day/date clock, an illuminated visor/vanity mirror, courtesy lamps in the quarter trim panels, an automatic seat back release, color-keyed deluxe seat belts, a convenience group, a light group, power windows, a power driver's seat, an AM/FM stereo radio with search function, a power lock group, and a tilt steering wheel. A split bench seat with a reclining passenger seat and luxurious velour cloth upholstery was standard. Ultra-soft leather upholstery was optional. After purchasing a Thunderbird Town Landau, buyers were sent a 24-karat-gold-finished nameplate. It had a T-Bird insignia and the words "specially made for" on it. The owner's name was then engraved at the bottom.

"New Ford Thunderbird: The Best in 15 Years," announced the cover of the April 1977 issue of *Road Test* magazine. The article inside the publication hit the nail on the head when it explained that Ford had made the right decision by taking the T-Bird "off the hill of the custom built homes" and rolling it down the road "where it can punch it out with all the Monte Carlos, Grand Prixs, Cordobas, and Cougars." The magazine was loaned a Sport version of the T-Bird with a 400-cid V-8 that averaged 17 mpg. While summing up the T-Bird's appearance as "practically every styling cliché known to civilized Western man," the magazine stressed how much T-Bird buyers were getting for the car's now-more-affordable price tag. It said that the car was "qualitatively no different" than a Ford or a Mercury Cougar. "But in a market where you sell quantity, this new T-Bird is a lot of car," the testers concluded. "You can roll that thing into your driveway and the whole neighborhood can tell it says Thunderbird."

Another way to spot the 1977 T-Bird Town Landau is by the stylized Thunderbird silk-screened on the opera windows. (Ford Motor Co. photo)

On a scale of 0-100, Road Test rated acceleration at 79 points. The brakes were scored 89 points. Handling warranted 73 points. Interior noise levels (92 points) and tire reserve (100 points) were the highest-rated categories. Fuel economy got 30 points. Overall, the 1977 Thunderbird earned 76 points. This was only two to three points under the three best cars that had been tested, which were the Volkswagen Super Scirocco, the Saab EMS, and the Porsche Turbo Carrera. From a contemporary buyer's standpoint, these cars were a vast improvement over the "Big 'Birds" of the past few years in terms of maneuverability and economy. The cars had no major mechanical problems, but the bodies of the 1977 models proved very prone to rust. The 1978 and 1979 editions had improved rust protection. Cars of 1977 vintage with tilt steering were also the subject of a recall, since some had been built with Ford truck tilt steering parts. This caused some of the cars to start with the gear selector in neutral.

While these Thunderbirds lack the degree of distinction from other Ford products that earlier T-Birds reflected, they were tremendously well received by the car-buying public and T-Bird production saw a more than six-fold increase. The Los Angeles assembly plant put together more 'Birds than it had in the last three years combined — a total of 82,256. This was over twice as many T-Birds as had ever been made there in a single year. Production at the Wixom, Mich. factory saw a huge *drop*. In fact, it was *zero*. However, 235,884 Thunderbirds were manufactured at a new factory in Chicago, Ill. The grand total of 318,144 Thunderbirds was more than 60,000 higher than Ford had built in the first six years of the Thunderbird's history combined. Of these, 295,779 were made for the U.S. market and the rest were shipped to Canada and other countries.

1977 Thunderbird Two-Door Hardtop Specifications

Wheelbase	114.0 in.	Standard Engine (Type)	90-degree ohv V-8
Curb Weight	3,907 lb.	Bore x Stroke	4 x 3 in.
Overall Length	215.5 in.	Displacement:	302 cid (5.0 L)
Overall Width	78.5 in.	Carburetor:	2-Barrel
Overall Height	53.0 in.	Compression Ratio	8.4:1
Front Headroom	37.3 in.	HP @ RPM	130-137 @ 3400-3600
Front Leg Room	42.1 in.	Torque	248 lb.-ft @ 1600
Rear Headroom	36.2 in	Optional Engine (Type)	90-degree ohv V-8
Rear Leg Room	32.6 in.	Bore x Stroke	4 x 3.5 in.
Front Tread	63.2 in.	Displacement	351 cid (5.8 L)
Rear Tread	63.1 in.	Carburetor	4-Barrel
Transmission	3-speed auto.	Compression Ratio	8.3:1
Wheels	15 x 6.5 in.	HP @ RPM	149-161 @ 3200-3600
Tires	H78 x 15	Torque	275-285 lb-ft @ 1600-1800
Trunk Capacity	15.6 cu. ft.	Optional Engine (Type)	90-degree ohv V-8
Brakes Swept	372.3 sq. in.	Bore x Stroke	4 x 4 in.
Brakes Swept/1000 lb.	82.5 sq. in.	Displacement	400 cid (6.6 L)
Steering Ratio	21.9:1	Carburetor	2-Barrel
Turn Circle	43.1 ft.	Compression Ratio	8.0:1
Fuel Tank Capacity	21gal.	HP @ RPM	173 @ 3800
Rear Axle	2.50:1	Torque	326 lb-ft @ 1600
Weight Distribution	57/43	Power-to-Weight Ratio	26.1 (400 cid)

1977 Thunderbird Engineering

Front Suspension	Independent, upper and lower control arms, coil springs, tubular shocks, anti-roll bar
Rear Suspension	Live axle, four-link control arms, coil springs, tubular shocks, anti-roll bar
Steering	Recirculating ball; power-assist
Front Brakes	Power vented disc
Brakes	Power drum

1977 Thunderbird Performance

Model	CID/HP	Performance
0-60 mph		
Hardtop	402/173	10.3 seconds
1/4-Mile		
Hardtop	402/173	17.7 seconds @ 78.6
Top Speed		
Hardtop	402/173	110 mph

1978
Diamond Jubilee

The styling of Ford's Thunderbird personal-luxury coupe was similar to that of the downsized 1977 model. However, marque experts can generally identify 1978 models by the T-Bird emblems that Ford added to the headlight doors. Six new body colors, four added vinyl roof colors, bold striped cloth bucket seat trim, and a new Russet interior option were offered. Technical improvements included a more efficient torque converter, a new lighter weight battery, revisions to the engine air induction system, and a new lighter weight power steering pump with quick-disconnect hydraulic fittings. A T-Roof Convertible option was a midyear innovation. However, the biggest news of the year was the limited-edition Diamond Jubilee Edition Thunderbird created to commemorate Ford's 75th year of making cars.

This year the Thunderbird Hardtop listed for $5,411. It came with all standard FoMoCo safety, anti-theft and convenience equipment, and a 302-cid two-barrel V-8 with DuraSpark ignition system (a 351-cid 149-hp two-barrel V-8 was standard in California). Select-Shift automatic transmission was also included, along with power steering, power front disc/rear drum brakes, concealed headlights, opera windows, full wheel covers, and other Thunderbird goodies. Dimensions and specifications were virtually unchanged from the previous model. New options included a power radio antenna, and a 40-channel CB radio. A slightly hotter "modified" version of the 351-cid V-8 with a four-barrel carburetor, plus the 400-cid (actually 402 cid) two-barrel V-8 remained available at extra cost. The base engine provided about 15.1 mpg on average. The 351 used as standard equipment in California cars averaged around 14.1 mpg. The more powerful version of the 351-cid V-8 was good for about 13.6 mpg overall. The larger 400-cid engine averaged around 12.8 mpg. Obviously, none of the T-Birds were economy cars.

T-Bird interiors came with deep-cushioned bench seats as standard equipment. They had knit cloth and vinyl trims. Heavy carpeting, full-length door arm rests, and burled walnut wood tone accents gave even the base model a rich look inside. Optional bucket seats came in all-vinyl or cloth and vinyl. An interior decor package with special door panels was a separate option. A front split-bench seat was included with the Town Landau model and the interior luxury group option. It came with either standard velour cloth trim or optional Ultra-Soft leather and vinyl trim. Both included interior decor type door trim panels. The Diamond Jubilee Edition T-Bird featured an interior done in one of two exclusive colors of luxury cloth with a split bench style front seat.

A 302-cid V-8 was the standard engine for the 1978 T-Bird, but 351- and 400-cid versions were optional. (Ford Motor Co. photo)

What Ford called a "T-Roof Convertible" was added to the T-Bird model lineup in the spring of 1978. Tempered glass panels fit into trunk. (Ford Motor Co. photo)

1978 Thunderbird Interiors

Seat Type	Material	Blue	Blue	Russet	Jade	Dove Gray	Chamois	W. & Saddle
Standard								
Bench Seat	Cloth & Vinyl	AB	AE	AR	AS	AT	AZ	
Bench Seat	All-vinyl		BB	BE	BR	BS	BT	BZ
Bucket Seats	Cloth & Vinyl	HB	HE	HR	HS	HT	HZ	
Bucket Seats	All-vinyl	CB	CE	CR	CS	CT	CZ	CQ
Decor Group								
Bucket Seats	Cloth & Vinyl	JB	JE	JR	JS	JT	JZ	
Bucket Seats	All-vinyl	GB	GE	GR	GS	GT	GZ	GQ
Town Landau & Luxury Interior								
Split-Bench	Velour Cloth	RB	RE	RR	RS	RT	RZ	
Split-Bench	US Leather-vinyl	SB	SE	SR	SS	ST	SZ	
Diamond Jubilee Edition								
Split-Bench	Luxury Cloth	TB				TT		

Seat Type	Material	W. & Russet	W. & Jade	W. & Cham.	W. & Saddle
Standard					
Bench Seat	Cloth & Vinyl			A2	
Bucket Seats	All-vinyl	C7	C5	C2	C9
Decor Group					
Bucket Seats	All-vinyl	G7	G5	G2	G9
Town Landau & Luxury Interior					
Split-Bench	US Leather-vinyl	S7	S5	S2	S9

Legend: W. & means White and the color below. Cham. means Chamois. US Leather-vinyl means Ultra-Soft leather and vinyl.

New this year was a sports decor option that added a bold grille with blacked-out vertical bars, unique imitation deck lid straps, paint stripes, twin remote sport mirrors, spoke-style road wheels, HR70 x 15 raised white letter tires, polycoated Chamois color paint, and a tan vinyl roof with color-keyed rear window moldings. This was $396 extra on cars that had the convenience group option and $446 on all other models.

The Thunderbird Town Landau, which bowed as a 1977-1/2 model, returned in 1978. This was again merchandised as a separate model with a manufacturer's suggested retail price of $8,420. Its roof line displayed a brushed aluminum wrapover applique. Color-coordinated roof cross-over moldings were included when an optional vinyl roof was added. Also included were pinstriping, silk-screened scripts on the opera windows, a color-keyed jewel-like hood ornament, cast-aluminum wheels with accent paint, wide vinyl insert body side moldings with partial wheel lip moldings, front cornering lamps, and an interior luxury group. Town Landaus came in 14 body colors. Standard fittings also included radial whitewall tires, accent stripes, a lighted visor vanity mirror, and dual sport mirrors.

Crushed velour upholstery and a split-bench seat with fold-down center arm rest were part of the Town Landau interior package. Six velour trim colors were available, along with options featuring leather seating surfaces. Burled walnut wood-tone appliques dressed up the instrument panel. Also found inside this luxury model were a SelectAire Conditioner, a six-way power driver's seat, power windows, power door locks, an AM/FM stereo search radio, a day and date clock, and a trip odometer.

Billed as "the most exclusive Thunderbird you can buy," the $10,106 Diamond Jubilee anniversary model included several items never before offered on a Thunderbird. It had an exclusive monochromatic exterior done in Diamond Blue Metallic or Ember Metallic paint. A matching thickly padded vinyl roof was part of the package. There was also a color-keyed grille texture, a unique quarter window treatment, accent striping, a jewel-like hood ornament, cast aluminum wheels, and special body side moldings. A Diamond Jubilee Edition signature was seen on the opera windows. There was also a hand-painted "DJ" monogram on the door which carried the owner's initials. Also featured were color-keyed bumper guard rub strips, dual sport mirrors, turbine-style aluminum wheels, and whitewall tires.

By Valentine's Day in 1978, Ford announced that it had sold 100,000 of the year's T-Birds and that six percent were Diamond Jubilee Editions. (Ford Motor Co. photo)

Inside the Diamond Jubilee Edition was a split-bench seat with manual passenger recliner, and unique Biscuit cloth upholstery. Diamond Blue models had blue luxury cloth upholstery. Diamond Ember models had chamois-colored cloth seats. Other ingredients were a hand-stitched leather-covered instrument panel pad (above a tachometer and gauge set), a leather-covered steering wheel, twin illuminated visor vanity mirrors, seat belt warning chimes, a Super Sound package with AM/FM stereo search radio and power antenna, and other luxury items. Finishing off the interior were ebony wood-tone appliques and a 22-karat gold-finished owner's nameplate.

After a great 1977, the popularity of the down-sized Thunderbird grew even more in Ford Motor Co.'s anniversary year. A grand total of 352,752 T-Birds were manufactured in factories in the U.S. This represents the largest number of Thunderbirds ever built in a single year so far. The bulk of these cars, 260,792 units, were manufactured at the Chicago plant, which built only Thunderbirds. The Los Angeles assembly plant accounted for 91,959 additional builds. Some collectors say the production totals included just under 19,000 Diamond Jubilee Editions.

Diamond Jubilee Edition T-Bird was issued in 1978 to commemorate Ford's 75th anniversary. It included all the "goodies." (Ford Motor Co. photo)

Unique, imitation deck lid straps and spoke-style wheels were popular features of the 1978 Sports Decor Group. (Ford Motor Co. photo)

An estimated 20,000 of the T-Birds made in the U.S. were destined for the export market, and were shipped to Canada and other countries. These offered almost the same equipment, color schemes, and trim as the cars made for the U.S. market. However, they were not necessarily 100 percent identical. For example the "California" version of the 351-cid two-barrel V-8 was not offered in cars marketed in Canada. Also the Canadian version of the Diamond Jubilee Edition did not include a power antenna. In Canadian literature the gas tank capacity was expressed in Imperial gallons (17.3), the trunk space was expressed in liters (402), and other measurements were given in millimeters. Interestingly, service mileage intervals used in the U.S. did not apply to Canadian cars, but the cars sold in Canada were backed by a no-extra-charge Duraguard system that offered 36-month protection against sheet metal rust-through. There was no such program offered in the U.S.

During calendar-year 1978, a total of 144 additional Thunderbirds were actually put together in a factory in Canada. As far as we can tell, these were the first cars bearing the Thunderbird name to be manufactured in Canada. They were early 1979 models, however, and not 1978 models.

It was, however, the 1978 Thunderbird that brought the marque back into NASCAR racing. Drivers Bobby Allison, Dick Brooks, and Jody Ridley found the new down-sized T-Bird well-suited to Grand National competition with the proper modifications. It had been 18 years—since 1960—from the T-Bird's last appearance in a stock car race. And 1978 would be only the beginning of the T-Bird's latter day motorsports history. Allison's number 15 T-Bird, built by Bud Moore, took the checkered flag in events like the NAPA 400 at Riverside, Calif. That particular event was conducted in 103-degree weather, and Allison's car held up until his clutch linkage broke. However, he managed to keep the T-Bird going and came home 32.9 seconds in front of Darrell Waltrip.

1978 Thunderbird Two-Door Hardtop Specifications

Wheelbase	114.0 in.	Standard Engine (Type)	90-degree ohv V-8
Curb Weight	4,082 lb.	Bore x Stroke	4 x 3 in.
Overall Length	215.5 in.	Displacement:	302 cid (5.0 L)
Overall Width	78.5 in.	Carburetor:	2-Barrel
Overall Height	53.0 in.	Compression Ratio	8.4:1
Front Headroom	37.3 in.	HP @ RPM	134 @ 3400
Front Leg Room	42.1 in.	Torque	248 lb.-ft. @ 1600
Rear Headroom	36.2 in	Optional Engine (Type)	90-degree ohv V-8
Rear Leg Room	32.6 in.	Bore x Stroke	4 x 3.5 in.
Front Tread	63.2 in.	Displacement	351 cid (5.8 L)
Rear Tread	63.1 in.	Carburetor	4-Barrel
Transmission	3-speed auto.	Compression Ratio	8.3:1
Wheels	15 x 6.5 in.	HP @ RPM	152 @ 3600
Tires	H70 x 15	Torque	278 lb.-ft. @ 1800
Trunk Capacity	15.6 cu. ft.	Optional Engine (Type)	90-degree ohv V-8

1978 Thunderbird Two-Door Hardtop Specifications

Brakes Swept	372.3 sq. in.	Bore x Stroke	4 x 4 in.
Brakes Swept/1000 lb.	82.5 sq. in.	Displacement	400 cid (6.6 L)
Steering Ratio	21.9:1	Carburetor	2-Barrel
Turn Circle	45.1 ft.	Compression Ratio	8.0:1
Fuel Tank Capacity	21 gal.	HP @ RPM	166 @ 3800
Rear Axle	2.50:1	Torque	319 lb.-ft. @ 1800
Weight Distribution	57/43	Power-to-Weight Ratio	26.1 (400 cid)

1978 Thunderbird Engineering

Front Suspension	Independent, upper and lower control arms, coil springs, tubular shocks, anti-roll bar
Rear Suspension	Live axle, four-link control arms, coil springs, tubular shocks, anti-roll bar
Steering	Recirculating ball; power-assist
Front Brakes	Power vented disc
Brakes	Power drum

1979
For the Discerning Collector

The name of this section comes from a special brochure for the 1979 Thunderbird Heritage Edition, but it seems to fit many of the year's models. A bolder, heavier-looking grille greeted T-Bird customers in 1979. It had a neo-classic look with a heavy chrome shell around it. Three thin horizontal moldings criss-crossed three vertical bars to form large rectangular openings arranged in a four across by four high pattern. The headlights were again hidden. The headlight doors were double-framed with chrome moldings and had large chrome Thunderbird insignias at their centers. There was a script nameplate on the left one. A massive, angular front bumper carried heavy, low bumper guards. A new spoiler went below the front bumper. Clear fender-notched parking lamp lenses with adjoining amber-colored marker lenses each held three horizontal divider strips.

Each front fender sported a set of six simulated vertical louvers just behind the front wheel opening. Horizontal cornering lamps that mounted low on the fenders, just ahead of the wheel opening, were optional or included as part of decor packages. A forward-slanting wrap-over roof was getting to be a T-Bird trademark. The wrap-over

A much bolder, heavier-looking box-texture grille greeted 1979 T-Bird buyers. The Sports Decor Group returned at $459-$518. (Ford Motor Co. photo)

section showed narrow, slanting opera windows. At the rear of most models were large, swept-back side windows. However, the upscale Heritage Edition Thunderbird had a unique solid quarter panel appearance instead of rear quarter windows. Chrome Heritage scripts decorated the solid panels.

Separate large, rectangular-shaped two-piece taillights characterized the rear of 1979 Thunderbirds. These replaced the former full-width units. They looked like rectangles within rectangles. A winged T-Bird emblem was in the center. A single back-up light stood between the taillights. It was centered over the new rear bumper guards, which were standard equipment.

Ford merchandised three Thunderbird models for 1979. The base Thunderbird Hardtop had a suggested retail price of $5,877 and weighed in at 3,893 lb. The Town Landau sold for $8,866 and tipped the scales at 4,284 lb. Since the company's 75th anniversary year had ended, the Diamond Jubilee model disappeared. However, the new Heritage Edition was designed to take its place. "Heritage is the most exclusive new Thunderbird you can own," said the advertising copy. "And one which may become a collector's item in the future. Providing the classic styling and spirit which have made the name 'Thunderbird' a legend, it is also built with distinctive custom touches."

There were 12 conventional exterior colors, plus five Metallic Glow glamour colors. Twenty-four two-tone combinations were listed, not including special Town Landau combinations. The Valino grain vinyl tops found on most models came in 12 colors. Standard inside T-Birds was a comfort-contoured Flight Bench front seat with Rossano cloth seating surfaces and vinyl trim. A large, fold-down arm rest hid in the center of the seat back. There were six solid interior colors and five Tu-Tone combinations with White as the base color. Specific color choices were offered in various materials: Vinyl, vinyl and cloth, standard cloth, luxury cloth, or ultra-soft leather. Eight body colors, five vinyl roof colors, and four interior colors were all-new for 1979. Bucket seats in vinyl or cloth and vinyl were an extra-cost item. Optional split-bench seats came with these same materials, plus regular cloth, luxury cloth or ultra-soft leather. On the floor was 10-oz. cut-pile carpeting color-keyed to match the upholstery. The door panels had full-length arm rests.

1979 Thunderbird Solid Interior Trim Codes (U.S. & Canada)

Seat Type	Material	Dove Grey	Dark Red	Blue	Jade	Cha- mois	Cor- dovan
T-Bird							
Flight Bench	Cloth & Vinyl	KS	KD	KB	KR	KT	KF
Flight Bench	All-Vinyl	LS	LD	LB	LR	LT	LF
Bucket	Cloth & Vinyl	HS	HD	HB	HR	HT	HF
Bucket	All-Vinyl	CS	CD	CB	CR	CT	CF
T-Bird Interior Decor							
Split-Bench	Cloth & Vinyl	DS	DD	DB	DR	DT	DF
Split-Split Bench	All-Vinyl	ES	ED	EB	ER	ET	EF
Bucket	Cloth & Vinyl	JS	JD	JB	JR	JT	JF
Bucket	All-Vinyl	GS	GD	GB	GR	GT	GF

1979 Thunderbird Solid Interior Trim Codes (U.S. & Canada)

Seat Type	Material	Dove Grey	Dark Red	Blue	Jade	Cha- mois	Cor- dovan
Interior Luxury & Town Landau							
Split-Bench	Cloth	RS	RD	RB	RR	RT	RF
Split-Bench	U-Soft Leather	SS	SD	SB	SR	ST	SF
Heritage Edition							
Split-Bench	Luxury Cloth		TD	TB			
Split Bench	U-Soft Leather		UD	UB			

1979 Thunderbird Tu-Tone Interior Trim Codes (U.S. & Canada)

Seat Type	Material	White/ Red	White/ Blue	White/ Jade	White/ Cham.	White/ Cordovan
T-Bird						
Bucket	All-Vinyl	CN	CQ	C5	C2	C6
T-Bird Interior Decor						
Split-Split Bench	All-Vinyl	EN	EQ	E5	E2	E6
Bucket	All-Vinyl	GN	GQ	G5	G2	G6
Interior Luxury & Town Landau						
Split-Bench	U-Soft Leather	SN	SQ	S5	S2	S6

Legend: U-Soft Leather means Ultra-Soft Leather

Replacing the Diamond Jubilee in 1979 was a new T-Bird Heritage Edition model with monochromatic paint and many standard extras. (Ford Motor Co. photo)

On the technical front, Thunderbirds had a new electronic voltage regulator. The carburetor on the standard 302-cid V-8 was also a refined two-barrel design. Door and ignition locks were modified for better theft protection. Corrosion protection was also becoming a factor in the U.S. market. "Ford takes steps to see that your new Thunderbird is engineered and built to quality standards," noted one 1979 sales brochure. "And in order to keep your Thunderbird looking new, we incorporate the use of pre-coated steels, such as galvanized steel and chromium/zinc-rich primer coated steels, vinyl sealers, aluminized wax in critical areas, and enamels as a finishing coat." In Canada, the no-extra-cost Duraguard system, offering 36-month, unlimited-distance warranted protection, was in effect again early in model-year 1979. However, later in the year, the Duraguard system was still promoted, but the mileage limits were removed from Canadian sales literature.

Returning as a Thunderbird option package was the Sports decor group. It included a Chamois vinyl roof with color-keyed backlight moldings; Chamois dual accent paint stripes; Chamois hood/GOP and fender louver paint stripes, Chamois deck lid straps, styled road wheels with Chamois paint accents, dual sport mirrors, and blacked-out vertical grille bars. It was available on cars with Black, Polar White, Midnight Blue Metallic, Dark Cordovan Metallic, Burnt Orange Glow, Dark Jade Metallic, or Pastel Chamois exterior finish. Chamois-colored interior trims were available with all exterior body colors. Chamois and White trims were offered with Polar White or Dark Cordovan Metallic exteriors. Chamois or Cordovan trims came in cars with Dark Cordovan Metallic exteriors. Also available were Chamois or Jade upholstery trims in cars with Dark Jade Metallic bodies. The deck lid straps gave these cars a hint of the classic image embodied in the sporty Stutz and Bentley touring coupes of the 1930s.

The Thunderbird Town Landau included a Town Landau instrument appliqué, a 22-karat gold-finished owner's nameplate, AM/FM stereo search radio, tilt steering wheel, Select-Aire conditioner, tinted glass, interior luxury package, 6-way power driver's seat, seat belt warning chimes, power side windows, luxury sound insulation, brushed aluminum wrap-over roof appliqué, opera windows with Town Landau insignia, color-coordinated translucent hood ornament insert, cast aluminum wheels with accent paint, accent striping, wide color-insert vinyl moldings, dual remote-control mirrors, front cornering lamps, bumper rub strips, 15-in. steel-belted radial whitewalls, and an extended range fuel tank. The Town Landau was offered in Black, Polar White, Dark Red, Midnight Blue Metallic, Dark Jade Metallic, Pastel Chamois, and Dark Cordovan Metallic conventional paints, plus Burnt Orange, Chamois and Red Glow colors. Specific interior trims were color-coordinated with each different exterior color. The Town Landau's split-bench seat could be had with cloth or Ultra-Soft leather upholstery.

A posh new Heritage Edition Thunderbird replaced the Diamond Jubilee model. It was identified by Heritage scripts on its large, blank roof C-pillars. The Heritage Edition had no rear side windows. Two monochromatic color schemes were available for this luxury car. One was Maroon and the other Light Medium Blue. A matching Lugano grain formal-style padded vinyl roof was featured. The split-bench seats had unique biscuit design all-cloth upholstery and a T-Bird insignia on the upper seat back bolsters. There were assist straps on the front seat backs and doors. Elegant 36-oz. cut-pile carpeting lined the floors. The interior door panels had molded-in arm rests and extra padding. Ebony wood-tone accents dressed-up the interior and steering wheel. Also standard was a Sports instrumentation package, dual illuminated visor-vanity mirrors, bright pedal trim, 18-oz. trunk carpeting, a molded deck lid liner, a leather-wrapped steering wheel, fingertip speed control, convenience and light groups, an illuminated entry system, a color-keyed grille and bumper guards and rub strips, color-accented cast-aluminum wheels, tri-band body side tape stripes, door plaques with the owner's initials, a power antenna, and rocker panel moldings. Luxury cloth or Ultra-Soft leather were the only interior options and came only in Dark Red or Blue.

As might be expected after three years, the down-sized Thunderbird was no longer the newest thing to hit the market. It did not benefit from a sales campaign such as the Diamond Jubilee promotion that helped push many extra 1978 models into showrooms. In addition, the second Arab oil embargo occurred this year, reviving American car buyers' fears of larger, V-8-powered cars. As a result of these three factors, and others, the sales and production of T-Birds began to taper off. However, the T-Bird was still five times more popular than it had been five years earlier. A total of 284,141 cars were made in the U.S. factories during the 1979 model-year. Specifically, 208,248 were built in Chicago and 75,893 were made in Los Angeles. In addition, though many U.S.-built T-Birds were sent to Canada, there were also 1,752 units built north of the border in the 1979 calendar-year.

Bobby Allison continued to race a Thunderbird for the Bud Moore NASCAR team during 1979. He encountered his share of disappointments such as finishing 16th in the Busch Nashville 420, after starting in second place. In the World 600, at Charlotte Motor Speedway, he crossed the line in 22nd position, after spending 38 minutes on an engine change. Allison did manage to claim second spot at the Southern 500 in Bristol, Tenn., coming in between the Monte Carlos of Dale Earnhardt and Darrell Waltrip. Allison would get a milestone win in a T-Bird a few years later, but not this season.

A historical milestone of sorts was marked in 1979. This was the firing of Lee Iacocca by Henry Ford II. Iacocca departed Dearborn at the beginning of the model-year, in October 1978. A month later, he was working for Chrysler Corp. in nearby Highland Park. As things turned out, the "father" of the Ford Mustang would go on to save the number three automaker from doom. Both the creation of the Mustang and the salvation of Chrysler are accomplishments that Mr. Iacocca deserves tremendous credit for. However, let's not overlook the fact that nearly a million of his 1977-1979 Thunderbirds were sold. Taking a nameplate that was selling 60,000 copies a year up to 300,000 copies a year represented a great automotive marketing achievement.

1979 Thunderbird Two-Door Hardtop Specifications

Wheelbase	114.0 in.	Standard Engine (Type)	90-degree ohv V-8
Curb Weight	4,028 lb.	Bore x Stroke	4 x 3 in.
Overall Length	217.7 in.	Displacement:	302 cid (5.0 L)
Overall Width	78.5 in.	Carburetor:	2-Barrel
Overall Height	52.8 in.	Compression Ratio	8.4:1
Front Head Room	37.3 in.	HP @ RPM	134 @ 3400
Front Leg Room	42.1 in.	Torque	248 lb.-ft @ 1600
Rear Head Room	36.2 in	Optional Engine (Type)	90-degree ohv V-8
Rear Leg Room	32.6 in.	Bore x Stroke	4 x 3.5 in.
Front Tread	63.2 in.	Displacement	351 cid (5.8 L)
Rear Tread	63.1 in.	Carburetor	4-Barrel
Transmission	3-speed auto.	Compression Ratio	8.3:1
Wheels	15 x 6.5 in.	HP @ RPM	152 @ 3600
Tires	215-R15 SBR	Torque	278 lb.-ft. @ 1800
Trunk Capacity	15.6 cu. ft.	California Engine (Type)	90-degree ohv V-8
Brakes Swept	372.3 sq. in.	Bore x Stroke	4 x 4 in.
Brakes Swept/1000 lb.	82.5 sq. in.	Displacement	351 cid (5.8 L)
Steering Ratio	21.9:1	Carburetor	4-Barrel
Turn Circle	43.1 ft.	Compression Ratio	8.3:1
Fuel Tank Capacity	21gal.	HP @ RPM	152 @ 3600
Rear Axle	2.50:1	Torque	278 lb.-ft. @ 1800
Weight Distribution	57/43		

1980 - 1982
"Silver Birds"

1980
Silver 'Bird

To celebrate its 25th year in the Ford lineup, Thunderbird got a new size and a new standard engine. This year's car rode a 108.4-in. wheelbase and stretched 200.4 in. end-to-end. It was 17 in. shorter and 700 lb. lighter than its immediate predecessor. This 'Bird was created by stretching the Ford Fairmont/Mercury Zephyr platform and was identical to the new 1980 Mercury Cougar XR-7. It carried a standard 255-cid V-8. This engine, which was better known as the 4.2-liter, carried the same stroke as the 302-cid (5.0-liter) V-8. However, it had a smaller diameter bore. The 5.0-liter V-8 was optional.

For the first time in 15 years, the Thunderbird featured unitized body construction. Jack Telnack, who later gained fame for his Taurus, was the head designer of the new T-Bird. William P. Boyer, who had helped create the original two-seat T-Birds, was also assigned to the project. Arthur I. Querfield, another member of the original T-Bird design team, was also involved in doing the 25th edition 'Birds. They were considered four-passenger models, instead of a six-passenger cars. The base Hardtop came with a manufacturer's list price of $6,432 and a curb weight of just 3,262 lb. The Town Landau returned with a $10,036 window sticker and some 240 lb. of additional equipment. For the marque's silver anniversary, there was an appropriate model. The Thunderbird Silver Anniversary Hardtop sold for $11,679 and weighed 3,225 lb.

Traditional T-Bird styling trademarks such as hidden headlights and wrap-over roof styling were blended into the T-Bird's new appearance. The body also featured strong sculpturing along the main body side feature lines, single opera windows to the rear of the wrap-over roof band, and solid-panel roof pillars like the previous Heritage Edition. The grille was again neo-classic in shape, but had a new eggcrate pattern insert. Some of the grille texture showed below the bumper. Soft, color-keyed urethene-clad bumpers were used up front and in the rear. Bumper guards were optional. The large rectangular headlight covers were integral with the huge signal/parking lights that wrapped around the body corners to double as side marker lights.

Ford very wisely used many T-Bird hallmarks to give this all-new generation of cars a strong identity that loyal buyers would recognize. At the rear of the body, wraparound wall-to-wall taillights returned. The general shape was like an upside-down telephone receiver. At each end, the red lens had a white back-up light lens in its center and these carried a stylized winged T-Bird logo. The entire unit followed the forward slant of the rear deck lid and the lenses wrapped around the rear body corners to function as side markers. Above the right-hand lens was Thunderbird lettering.

1980 T-Birds offered three vinyl top treatments with eight different Valino grain coverings or pigskin grain coverings in Caramel color only. (Ford Motor Co.)

There were 10 conventional exterior colors and five extra-cost Glow colors offered in 1980. This included Anniversary Silver Glow, which was available for only one special model. Standard Valino grain vinyl tops came in eight different colors. Pigskin grain vinyl roofs came only in Caramel color. Full vinyl tops, half vinyl tops, and luxury half vinyl tops were offered. A total of 63 interior choices were offered, with Silver Anniversary options included.

1980 Thunderbird Solid Interior Trim Codes (US & Canada)

Seat Type	Material	Dove Grey	Red	Blue	Caramel	Bittersweet
T-Bird						
Flight Bench	Cloth & Vinyl	AS	AD	AB	AT	
Flight Bench	All-Vinyl	BS	BD	BB	BT	
Bucket	All-Vinyl	DS	DD	DB	DT	
T-Bird Interior Decor						
Split-Bench	Cloth & Vinyl	ES	ED	EB	ET	EC
Split-Split Bench	SSVinyl	FS	FD	FB	FT	FC
Bucket	All-Vinyl	GS	GD	GB	GT	GC
Recaro Buckets	Cloth & Vinyl	NS(a)	ND		NT	NC
Interior Luxury & T. Landau						
Split-Bench	Cloth	JS	JD	JB	JT	JC
Split-Bench	U-Soft Leather	KS	KD	KB	KT	KC
Recaro Buckets	Cloth & Vinyl	PS (a)	PD		PT	PC
Silver Anniversary						
Split-Bench	Cloth	LS				
Split Bench	U-Soft Leather	MS				

1980 Thunderbird Tu-Tone Interior Trim Codes (US & Canada)

Seat Type	Material	White/Red	White/Blue	White/Caramel	White/Bittersweet
T-Bird					
Bucket	All-Vinyl	DN	DQ	D2	D7
T-Bird Interior Decor					
Split-Split Bench	SS Vinyl	FN	FQ	F2	F7
Bucket	All-Vinyl	GN	GQ	G2	G7
Interior Luxury & Town Landau					
Split-Bench	U-Soft Leather	KN	KQ	K2	K7

Legend: (a) Black cloth inserts with Dove Gray facings on door panels and carpets; SS Vinyl means Super-Soft Vinyl; U-Soft Leather means Ultra-Soft Leather

A modified McPherson strut front suspension was used, with four-bar-link coil springs at the rear. Along with the 700-lb. weight loss came higher axle ratios, both contributing to better fuel economy. Power-assisted, variable-ratio rack and pinion steering was another technological advance. A new four-speed overdrive automatic transmission was available with the optional 5.0-liter V-8.

Base and Town Landau models were available early in the year. The Town Landau included 31 standard options early in the year, but this was reduced to 30 at midyear, when wood-tone instrument panel appliqués were deleted from the list. A complete equipment list is included at the rear of this book, but the Landau's basic distinctions were its padded rear half-vinyl roof with wrap-over band and coach lamps, a luxury interior with a split-bench seat, cast-aluminum wheels, and an engraved owner's nameplate. Naturally, all the interior and exterior appointments were color-keyed for a *designer* look.

Ford dealers introduced the Silver Anniversary Thunderbird in the spring. "The new model commemorates a quarter-century of innovative automobiles bearing the Thunderbird nameplate," announced Philip E. Benton, Jr., Ford Motor Company vice president and Ford Division general manager. "The Silver Anniversary Thunderbird is the most fully equipped production Thunderbird in our history, and combines tradition and innovation with a sleek new profile in a contemporary space-and-fuel-efficient design in keeping with today's motoring demands."

A standard 5.0-liter V-8 and automatic overdrive transmission gave the Silver Anniversary T-Bird a 45 percent improvement in highway fuel economy compared to a 1979 Thunderbird with the same engine and conventional automatic transmission. It received a 29 mpg EPA highway rating. Its city driving rating — 17 mpg — also reflected a 21 percent gain. Benton noted that the 1980 Thunderbird's combined ratings represented the greatest fuel-economy improvement of any current Ford Division products.

The Silver Anniversary model had its own distinctive roof treatment. Mr. & Mrs. Lionel Bestul have owned this example since it was new.

Additional standard appointments in the Silver Anniversary Thunderbird included an electronic instrument cluster, diagnostic warning lights, a keyless entry system, TR-type tires, cast-aluminum wheels, a garage door opener, fingertip speed control, air conditioning, an auto lamp on-off delay system, and electronic AM/FM stereo search radio. The car's Silver Glow exterior was highlighted by black accents, a special padded rear-half vinyl roof, a high-gloss roof wrap-over molding, and distinctive horizontal coach lamps with Silver Anniversary scripts.

In addition to the featured Anniversary Silver paint color, Black, Light Gray, Red Glow, and Midnight Blue Metallic solid exterior finishes could be substituted. There was also a special two-tone combination mating Black with Anniversary Silver. In each case, the color of the roof wrap-over bands, vinyl tops, body side accent stripes, body side moldings, and bumper rub strips were coordinated with the exterior color selected.

Inside the Silver Anniversary model was a thickly cushioned split-bench front seat upholstered in velvet-like knit-velour and color-keyed 36-oz. carpets. There were burled rosewood wood-tone instrument panel appliqués, a special leather-wrapped steering wheel, and dual illuminated visor-vanity mirrors. The car owner was also sent a bright rhodium nameplate with his or her name engraved on it.

Fuel efficiency of the second down-sized T-Bird was better than previous models with the 4.2 typically delivering 17-20 mpg and the 5.0 good for 16-19 mpg. However, the T-Bird did not guzzle less gas than some other cars in its class. Likewise, it was not as agile as some competitors. The unit-body also made the car slightly noisier. Ford wrestled with claims that its automatic transmission slipped gears and settled out of court. It also recalled some 1980 models that were built with too-small Mustang brakes. Brakes, electrical problems, and body integrity were other shortcomings of the new car. Also entering repair shops more often than normal were cars with 5.0-liter V-8s using variable-venturi carburetors.

Motor Trend put two 1980 T-Birds on the cover of its September 1979 isue. One was a monotone Red Glow car with no vinyl roof, white stripe tires, and spoke-style wheel covers. The second was a Chamois and Bittersweet Glow two-toned version with a Luxury half-

From the rear, the 1980 Silver Anniversary model had a " big window " look. (Lionel Bestul)

vinyl roof, and simulated wire wheel covers. "All-New ... Split Personality: Performance, Luxury," read the cover blurb. Peter Frey's article about the new car was a positive review sub-titled, "A living legend rises from the ashes of obesity to reclaim its heritage." The article gave specifications for the 1980 model, but no performance numbers.

In its third "Country Wide Test" in June 1980, *Motor Trend* tried out a Thunderbird with the 5.0-liter V-8, four-speed overdrive transmission, luxury exterior group, Recaro bucket seats, electronic instrumentation, and Bittersweet Glow Metallic finish. This car was driven on both coasts and made two cross-country trips in the course of four months. Nearly 15,000 miles were driven during the evaluation. Various editors took stints behind the wheel. "Down-sizing has unquestionably improved the breed," said associate editor Bob Nagy. "The fact that, in not many more years, no one will produce a car like this makes me sad," Washington editor Ted Orme noted. However, executive editor Jim McGraw felt differently. "We'd rather spend $11,000 buying an original Thunderbird restoration," he headlined his report that criticized the car's exterior and interior designs. (Unfortunately, two seat Thunderbirds were selling for $15,000-$18,000 at the time, so McGraw would have had a hard time getting one on his budget). Associate editor Peter Frey said the T-Bird made him smile and engineering editor Chuck Nerpel — who had road tested a '55 model for *Motor Trend* — said, "It has better handling than any T-Bird of the past."

Though popular with most magazine editors, the 1980 T-Bird had the misfortune of bowing at a time when Americans were rethinking what they needed and wanted in automobiles. It's true that the automobile industry, as well as the national economy, was in a slump at this time. However, even in a weakened market, the Thunderbird's slice of the smaller pie was shrinking. The nameplate owned 3.09 percent of the total market in 1979, but only 2.31 percent in 1980. This figure would also continue falling to 1.30 percent in 1981 and 0.88 percent in 1982. Total production for model-year 1980 came to 156,803 units. Of these, 93,634 were built in Chicago and 63,169 were manufactured at a plant in Lorain, Ohio. The Los Angeles factory no longer built T-Birds and this was also the last year for assemblies of this model at Chicago. No cars were made in Canada. However, 18,702 of the U.S.-built cars were made for the export market and many of these were shipped to our neighbor to the north.

By looking at optional equipment installations, it was easy to tell the type of transition the T-Bird had gone through in its 25 years. What had started out as a fancy two-seat sporty car had become an ostentatious luxury coupe. Of the 138,101 T-Birds built for the domestic market in model-year 1980, vinyl tops were added to 81.4 percent, adjustable steering columns were found on 49.3 percent, 100 percent had automatic transmission, and 96.1 percent had V-8 engines (an inline six was installed in a small number of cars late in the model run). On the opposite side of the coin, a mere 4.1 percent of the cars were equipped with bucket seats, only 16.2 percent had styled wheels, and just 6.2 percent had sun roofs.

In racing, there were big questions about the future of Grand National stock car racing at this time. The new down-sized cars coming out of Detroit were too small for the Grand National wheelbase and size specifications. Nevertheless, the October 1979 issue of *Motor Trend* featured a sketch of Bobby Allison's proposed 1980 Thunderbird stock car, saying in the caption that it was unclear if the new model would be approved by NASCAR. A few of these cars did eventually race, but without the much-needed factory backing.

1980 Thunderbird Two-Door Hardtop Specifications

Wheelbase	108.4 in.	Standard Engine (Type)	90-degree ohv V-8
Curb Weight	3,281 lb.	Bore x Stroke	3.68 x 3.00 in.
Overall Length	200.4 in.	Displacement:	255 cid (4.2 L)
Overall Width	74.1 in.	Carburetor:	2-Barrel
Overall Height	53.0 in.	Compression Ratio	8.8:1
Front Head Room	37.1 in.	HP @ RPM	115 @ 3800
Front Leg Room	41.6 in.	Torque	194 lb.-ft @ 2200
Rear Head Room	36.3 in.	Optional Engine (Type)	90-degree ohv V-8
Rear Leg Room	36.5 in.	Bore x Stroke	4.00 x 3.00 in.
Front Tread	58.1 in.	Displacement	302 cid (5.0 L)
Rear Tread	57.2 in.	Carburetor	2-Barrel
Ground Clearance	6.0 in.	Compression Ratio	8.4:1
Trunk Space	17.7 cu. ft.	HP @ RPM	131 @ 3600
Tires	P/185/75R14	Torque	231 lb-ft @ 1600
Fuel Tank Capacity	17.5 gal.	Transmission	3-speed auto.

1980 Thunderbird Two-Door Hardtop Specifications

Crankcase Capacity	4 qts.	Power to Weight Ratio	24.9 lb./h
Cooling System	13.4 qts.	Turns Lock-to-Lock	3.4
Rear Axle	2.79:1	Turning Circle	40.1 ft.

1980 Thunderbird Engineering

Front Suspension	Modified McPherson strut
Rear Suspension	Four-link-bar with coil springs
Steering	Variable-ratio power rack and pinion
Front Brakes	10-in. power-assisted discs
Brakes	9-in. power-assisted drums

1980 Thunderbird Performance

Model	CID/HP	Performance
0-60 mph		
Hardtop	302/131	11.10 seconds
Hardtop	302/131	11.10 seconds
1/4-Mile		
Hardtop	302/131	18.01 seconds @ 75.70 mph

1981
Sensible Six

Appearance-wise the 1981 Thunderbird was like the 1980 model, except that the grille texture no longer showed through below the bumper. The license plate sat in a recessed opening low on the bumper. At the rear, huge full-width taillights again had T-Bird emblems on each side. The deck lid protruded halfway between each taillight half. New options included a Carriage Roof that made a car look like a Convertible, a Traction-Lok axle, pivoting front vent windows, a convex remote-control left-hand rear view mirror, and self-sealing puncture-resistant tires.

The six-cylinder engine that was a delete-option in a small number of late-1980 T-Birds became the base engine for the 1981 series, a fact which shocked many marque enthusiasts. To make matters worse, it wasn't a special high-performance V-6, but a standard 200-cid Ford inline six-banger. This 3.3-liter engine was attached to the conventional SelectShift automatic transmission. The 4.2-liter and 5.0-liter V-8s were both extra-cost items.

In six-cylinder form the base Hardtop listed for $7,551 and weighed 3,167 lb. This model had more standard equipment and upgraded trimmings. Some of the ingredients had formerly been part of the exterior luxury group package. New standard features included halogen headlights, vinyl insert body side moldings with partial wheel lip moldings, a remote-control left-hand rear view mirror, and continuous-loop deluxe color-keyed seat belts with a comfort regulator feature, and pleasant reminder chimes. A Flight Bench front seat was standard with a choice of all-vinyl or cloth and vinyl upholstery.

For $8,689 buyers could purchase a six-cylinder Town Landau. This 3,267-lb. car had standard equipment including a tilt steering wheel, diagnostic warning lights, AM/FM stereo, interval wipers, light group, dual remote-control mirrors, wire wheel covers, whitewall tires, wide door belt moldings, cornering lamps, a padded rear half vinyl roof with coach lamps, and "Town Landau" fender scripts. The Valino grain vinyl roofs came in half and luxury half styles with a choice of seven colors. The Town Landau interior offered a standard split-bench seat with dual recliners and knit-cloth fabric upholstery. Super-soft vinyl was optional, as were all-vinyl bucket seats. Town Landau fans got a Recaro bucket seat option, too. Town Landaus came in seven colors: Black, White, Midnight Blue, Fawn, Medium Red, Bittersweet, and Silver with color-coordinated roof wrap-over moldings and specific color (Black or Silver) accent tape on the opera windows.

The 1981 Thunderbird Town Landau featured a padded half vinyl roof with a color-coordinated wrapover band and luxury wheel covers. (Ford Motor Co.)

The top T-Bird was the Heritage Hardtop. This $11,355 car weighed-in at 3,303 lb. That included the 4.2-liter V-8. Also standard were the auto lamp system, power locks and windows, automatic parking brake release, and many other goodies including a padded rear half vinyl roof with brushed aluminum wrap-over band and coach lamps, a "Frenched" backlight, distinctive "arrowheads" at the forward end of the body stripes, a unique hood ornament with a "cut-glass" look, Heritage fender scripts, and wire wheel covers. Inside a split-bench seat with velour cloth trim was standard. Ultra-soft leather upholstery was an option, as were Recaro bucket seats with cloth and vinyl trim.

As in 1980, there were 10 standard exterior colors. The number of optional Metallic Glow colors was reduced to four. In addition to the vinyl roof styles and colors previously mentioned, shoppers could order a Diamond grain carriage roof treatment in Midnight Blue, Fawn or White. Nine body striping colors were available. In all, counting colors, seat styles, and materials, there were 63 interior options.

1981 Thunderbird Solid Interior Trim Codes (U.S. & Canada)

Seat Type	Material	Med. Fawn	Dark Red	MW Blue	Dove Grey	Vaquero
T-Bird						
Flight Bench	Cloth & Vinyl	AL	AD	AB	AS	
Flight Bench	All-Vinyl	BL	BD	BB	BS	
Bucket	All-Vinyl	DL	DD	DB	DS	

1981 Thunderbird Solid Interior Trim Codes (U.S. & Canada)

Seat Type	Material	Med. Fawn	Dark Red	MW Blue	Dove Grey	Vaquero
Interior Decor & Town Landau						
Split-Bench	Cloth & Vinyl	EL	ED	EB	ES	EZ
Split-Bench	SS Vinyl	FL	FD	FB	FS	FZ
Bucket	All-Vinyl	GL	GD	GB	GS	GZ
Recaro Buckets	Cloth & Vinyl		ND	NB	NS	NZ
Interior Luxury & Heritage						
Split-Bench	Cloth	JL	JD	JB	TS	TZ
Split Bench	U-Soft Leather	KL	KD	KB	KS	KZ
Recaro Buckets	Cloth & Vinyl		PD	PB	PS	PZ

1981 Thunderbird Tu-Tone Interior Trim Codes (U.S. & Canada)

Seat Type	Material	White/ M. Fawn	White/ D. Red	White/ MWB	White/ Vaquero
T-Bird					
Split-Bench	All-Vinyl	B3	BN	BQ	
Bucket	All-Vinyl	D3	DN	DQ	

1981 Thunderbird Tu-Tone Interior Trim Codes (U.S. & Canada)

T-Bird Interior Decor & Town Landau

Split-Split Bench	SS Vinyl	F3	FN	FQ	F9
Bucket	All-Vinyl	G3	GN	GQ	G9

Interior Luxury & Town Landau

Split-Bench	U-Soft Leather	K3	KN	KQ	K9

Legend: Med. is medium; D. Red is Dark Red; MWB or MW Blue is Medium Wedgewood Blue; SS Vinyl is Super-soft vinyl; U-Soft Leather means Ultra-Soft Leather

As we have already indicated in the 1980 section, the T-Bird's share of market continued to decline in 1981. Only 86,693 cars were manufactured and all of them were built at the assembly plant in Lorain, Ohio. Of these, 76,979 were U.S.-market cars and the others were made for the export markets. The T-Bird remained a very popular car in Canada, for example. This year the number of cars with luxury features like vinyl roofs (84.2 percent), adjustable steering columns (66.8 percent), and reclining seats (73.3 percent) went up across the board. Meanwhile, sporty options like bucket seats (3.4 percent) and sun roofs (5.3 percent) continued to lose favor with those who were still purchasing T-Birds. However, it is interesting to note that even the traditional upscale T-Bird buyers were interested in economy, as reflected by the fact that only 83.6 percent had V-8s. That meant that 16.4 percent of those purchasing 1981 models opted for the inline six.

Neil Bonnett drove the Wood Brother's 1981 Thunderbird during the year's NASCAR Winston Cup stock car racing series. Without factory help, there were very few 'Birds of this vintage on the circuit.

1981 Thunderbird Two-Door Hardtop Specifications

Wheelbase	108.4 in.	Standard Engine	Inline Six one-barrel
Curb Weight	3,167 lb.	Bore x Stroke	3.68 x 3.13 in.
Overall Length	200.4 in.	Displacement	200 cid (3.3 liters)
Overall Width	74.1 in.	Compression Ratio	8.6:1
Overall Height	53.0 in.	HP @ RPM	88 @ 3800
Front Headroom	37.1 in.	Torque	154 lb.-ft. @ 1400
Front Leg Room	41.6 in.	Optional Engine (Type)	Inline ohv V-8
Rear Headroom	36.3 in.	Bore x Stroke	3.68 x 3.00 in.
Rear Leg Room	36.5 in.	Displacement:	255 cid (4.2 L)
Front Tread	58.2 in.	Carburetor:	2-Barrel
Rear Tread	57.0 in.	Compression Ratio	8.8:1
Trunk Space	17.7 cu. ft.	HP @ RPM	115 @ 3800
Tires	P/185/75R14	Torque	194 lb.-ft @ 2200
Fuel Tank Capacity	18.0 gal.	Optional Engine (Type)	90-degree ohv V-8
Rear axle	2.79:1	Bore x Stroke	4.00 x 3.00 in.
Turns lock-to-lock	3.4	Displacement	302 cid (5.0 L)
Turning Circle	40.1 ft.	Carburetor	2-Barrel
Transmission	3-speed auto.	Compression Ratio	8.4:1
Power to weight ratio	24.9 lb./h	HP @ RPM	131 @ 3600
Ground Clearance	6.0 in.	Torque	231 lb.-ft. @ 1600

1981 Thunderbird Engineering

Front Suspension	Modified McPherson strut
Rear Suspension	Four-link-bar with coil springs
Steering	Variable-ratio power rack and pinion
Front Brakes	10-in. power-assisted discs
Brakes	9-in. power-assisted drums

1981 Thunderbird Performance

Model	CID/HP	Performance
0-60 mph		
Hardtop	302/131	11.10 seconds
1/4-Mile		
Hardtop	302/131	18.01 seconds @ 75.70 mph

1982
Future Collectible

The appearance of the 1982 Thunderbird was similar to the 1981 model, with the same front and rear end styling. The cross-hatched grille had an 8 x 6 pattern of wide holes. Lettered into the grille header was the Thunderbird name. A wide see-through hood ornament held a T-Bird insignia. That insignia also highlighted the roof sail panels and the taillight lenses. Three models were again offered: Base Thunderbird Hardtop ($8,492); Town Landau ($9,703); and Heritage ($12,742). Dimensions of the cars were virtually unaltered and curb weights saw a slight decrease of just a few pounds.

There were 11 standard exterior colors, plus three Metallic Glow colors. Convertible-like carriage roofs were optional in three colors. Base and luxury rear half vinyl roofs both came in eight different colors. There were nine color-coordinated body striping colors. Buyers could also select from 86 specific interior colors, materials, and seat design combinations offering 46 distinct option codes. Ford Motor Co. created elaborate charts to let buyers know which tops, interiors, and stripes were available with which exterior body colors. The company's designers must have kept very busy working out all the details.

1982 Thunderbird Solid Interior Trim Codes (U.S. & Canada)

Seat Type	Material	MN Blue	Dark Red	Med. Fawn	Van-lilla	Vaqueroe
T-Bird						
Flight Bench	Cloth & Vinyl	AB	AD	AL		AZ
Flight Bench	All-Vinyl	BB	BD	BL		BZ
Bucket	All-Vinyl	CB	CD	CL		CZ
Split-Bench	Cloth & Vinyl	EB	ED	EL	EV	EZ
Split-Split Bench	All-Vinyl	FB	FD	FL	FV	FZ
T-Bird Interior Decor & Town Landau						
Split-Bench	Cloth & Vinyl	EB	ED	EL	EV	EZ
Split-Split Bench	All-Vinyl	FB	FD	FL	FV	FZ
Split-Bench	Luxury Cloth	JB	JD	JL	JV	JZ
Split-Split Bench	U-Soft Leather	KB	KD	KL	KV	KZ
Bucket	All-Vinyl	CB	CD	CL		CZ
Recaro Bucket	Cloth & Vinyl	NB	ND			NZ
Interior Luxury & Heritage						
Split-Bench	Luxury Cloth	JB	JD	JL	JV	JZ
Split-Bench	U-Soft Leather	KB	KD	KL	KV	KZ
Recaro Bucket	Cloth & Vinyl	NB	ND			NZ

1982 Thunderbird Tu-Tone Interior Trim Codes (U.S. & Canada)

Seat Type	Material	Opal/ D. Red	Opal/ M. Blue	Opal/ M. Fawn	Opal/ Pewter	Opal/ Vaquero
T-Bird						
Flight Bench	All-Vinyl	BN	BQ	B3	B6	B9
Bucket	All-Vinyl	CN	CQ	C3	C6	C9
Split-Split Bench	All-Vinyl	FN	FQ	F5	F6	F9
T-Bird Interior Decor & Town Landau						
Split-Split Bench	SS-Vinyl	FN	FQ	F3	F6	F9
Split-Split Bench	Luxury Cloth				J6	
Split-Split Bench	U-Soft Leather				K6	
Bucket	All-Vinyl	CN	CQ	C3	C6	C9
Interior Luxury & Heritage						
Split-Split Bench	Luxury Cloth				J6	
Split-Bench	U-Soft Leather				K6	

Legend: MN blue is Midnight Blue; Med. is Medium; U-Soft Leather is Ultra-Soft leather; D. is Dark Red; M. is Medium; SS-Vinyl is Super-Soft Vinyl.

Technical changes in 1982 models started with engines. The 3.3-liter inline six was the base power plant in the base 'Bird and Town Landau. A 3.8-liter V-6 was now standard equipment in the Heritage. In fact, it was the only engine offered for that upscale model. Buyers could get the V-6 as an option in the base 'Bird and Town Landau. These two cars, but not the Heritage Hardtop, could also have the 4.2-liter V-8 installed under the hood at extra cost. SelectShift automatic was standard in the base T-Bird and Town Landau, while automatic overdrive transmission was standard in the Heritage edition. The three-speed SelectShift transmission used this year had noticeable improvements for smoother, more efficient operation, but the four-speed automatic overdrive gave much better fuel economy. It was optional in the base 'Bird and the Town Landau. The gas tank was also enlarged to 21-gal. capacity.

A new optional Tripminder computer showed not only time and speed, but figured and displayed elapsed time, distance traveled, fuel used, average speed, and current or average mpg. Also, the new luxury vinyl roof treatment was standard on the Town Landau. The Carriage Roof was not available on the Town Landau teamed with the flip-up sun roof, keyless entry system, or wide door belt molding packages. The base type rear half vinyl roof was standard with the exterior decor group, but not available on Town Landau or Heritage models. When used on the base 'Bird, wide door belt moldings were required, too. The luxury vinyl half roof was standard on Town Landau and Heritage models according to some factory literature, and "not available" according to other printed matter.

In 1982, Ford recommended an engine oil change every 7,500 miles; a spark plug change every 30,000 miles; air filter replacement every 30,000 miles; and engine coolant replacements at 52,500 miles or every three years. Even cars that were serviced properly seemed to run into big fuel system problems, and minor suspension problems. Also needing a little more than normal repairs was the air conditioning system. However, *Consumer Report's* overall trouble index rated the T-Bird a "good" car, although it was slightly costlier than average to fix when repairs were required.

Consumer Reports also found the seats extremely comfortable, the car quiet and smooth riding, the comfort control system excellent, the power adequate, and the brakes impressive.

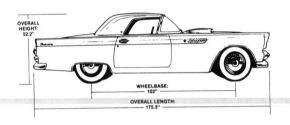

1982 FORD EXP

First T-Bird was in promotional piece for Ford's new two-seat EXP model. (Ford Motor Co.)

Handling was sluggish and washer/wiper controls were inconvenient. With the 3.8-liter V-6, the car used 675 gallons of fuel in 15,000 miles. It averaged 16 mpg in the city and 29 mpg on the highway. "These rear-wheel-drive Ford products are our models of choice in the domestic specialty coupe field," said the magazine. "Primarily because of their relatively good overall repair records." In addition, a bumper crash test produced no damage, so the T-Bird was safe to drive, too.

Thunderbird production, which had been declining every year, reached another low point in 1982. Only 45,142 cars were manufactured in the Lorain, Ohio assembly plant. None were made elsewhere. Only 61.4 percent of the year's T-Birds had V-8s. Other rare options were bucket seats (used on 1.6 percent of the cars) and sun roofs (used on 7.3 percent). Although this was not a good year for T-Bird sales, it may turn out to be a good vintage for collectors to look for. The 1982 models are generally reliable cars, they are relatively rare, and current prices for them are quite affordable.

Dale Earnhardt — a NASCAR driver better known as "Mr. Chevrolet — piloted a 1982 Thunderbird this year. He drove the Bud Moore car to victory in events like the Rebel 500 at Darlington, which was his first checkered flag since winning the 1980 Winston Cup Championship. Bill Elliott, who would play a bigger role in racing the next generation of 'Birds against Earnhardt's Monte Carlo, also raced a 1982 Thunderbird. He spent most of his time, this year, chasing other cars across the finish line, such as in the Winston 500 at Talladega, where he placed 26th in his Melling Tool Co. sponsored car.

1983 - 1986
"Aero Birds"

1983
Aero 'Bird

The all-new 10th-generation Thunderbird had a slick aero look. "Conceived for today with an eye on tomorrow" is the way the factory catalog described it. It was exciting, as well as more fuel efficient. "High Tech" was a buzz word in the auto industry at this time and the new Thunderbird seemed quite advanced. It offered all of the latest technology in a smooth, sexy, good-looking automobile.

Although down-sized again, the T-Bird wasn't as small as it seemed at first. It was three inches shorter and narrower than the 1982 model, with a 2.8 in. shorter wheelbase. However, the front compartment was actually larger in terms of both head room and leg room. Two inches less leg room made the rear compartment tighter-fitting and cargo volume dropped from 17.7 cu. ft. to 14.6 cu. ft. The changes had the most affect on owners who drove T-Birds as their family cars. This car was aimed at the "youth movement" and some traditional T-Bird buyers had a negative reaction to the "Dearborn jelly bean." In fact, Ford discovered that customers over 40 years old preferred the 1982 model. Nevertheless, the Aero 'Bird would ultimately become such a big success that it nearly tripled the popularity of Thunderbirds.

Much curvier than before, the new T-Birds looked very radical in 1983. Exposed quad rectangular halogen headlamps flanked a small, bright, neo-classic eggcrate grille with an 8 x 6 pattern. A T-Bird insignia was stamped on the header bar. The grille and headlamp surrounds sloped backwards, as did the cornering lamps (which doubled as side markers) at each rounded front body corner. The center of the hood had a tapering bulge. A curved, urethane-clad front bumper held slit-like rectangular parking lights. The windshield slanted back at a rakish angle. It was really a very slippery-looking car. The body was the product of extensive wind tunnel testing and had a low 0.35 coefficient of drag.

Trim on the T-Bird was minimal. Wide, color-keyed moldings were optional on the base model and standard on others. The designers continued the bumper line around the smooth, curving body sides. The sculpturing of the previous model was gone. Full-width wraparound taillights met the recessed rear license plate housing in a sloping back panel. T-Bird insignias and back-up lights were in the center of each taillight lens.

The all-new 1983 Thunderbird was wrapped in a dramatic new envelope that had a .35 coefficient of drag. (Ford Motor Co.)

206

"Before we made it beautiful, we made it right," boasted Ford advertisements for the radically different 1983 T-Bird.

Three distinct models were merchandised. The base Thunderbird Coupe was $9,197 and weighed 2,905 lb. Strangely, the old Heritage name was carried over for this one year on the new style. It had a $12,228 base sticker price and weighed 3,027 lb. There was also a Turbo Coupe with a high-tech 2.3-liter (140 cid) turbocharged four-cylinder MPEFI engine. A Garrett AIResearch T-03 turbocharger helped it produce 145-hp at 5000 rpm. It promised an estimated 172 lb.-ft. of torque at 3800 rpm and 10-second 0-60 mph performance, teamed with 21-26 mpg average fuel economy. The Turbo Coupe listed for $11,790.

A unique front fascia with an air dam and Marchal fog lamps gave the Turbo Coupe instant recognition. It wore unique 14-in. aluminum wheels and P205/70HR14 performance tires. Bumper rub strip extensions, wide body side moldings, and striping on the body side and deck lid were also included. Turbo Coupes were offered in Black, Pastel Charcoal, Bright Red, Desert Tan, Silver Metallic Clearcoat, Dark Charcoal Metallic Clearcoat, and Medium Red Metallic Clearcoat. The clearcoat paint colors were optional. A special Turbo Coupe paint scheme featured Dark Charcoal accents around the entire lower body perimeter. It was available with all Turbo Coupe colors except Black, Light Desert Tan, and Dark Charcoal Clearcoat Metallic. A five-speed manual transmission, special handling suspension, and Traction-Lok axle were included. Inside were special Lear-Siegler articulated bucket seats with back rest and bolster adjustments, a leather-clad floor shifter, fishnet map pockets on the door panels, and a few other goodies, plus some exclusive options. The Turbo was the darling of the automotive press at the time.

Other 1983 Thunderbirds came in a choice of 13 exterior finishes. Five were extra-cost Metallic Clearcoat colors. Base interiors featured individually reclining bucket seats with knit cloth and vinyl trim, plus a padded console with a flocked and illuminated interior and a removable trash bin. The standard all-vinyl door trim panels had assist straps and storage bins. The fancier Heritage model had the interior luxury group, a wood-grained steering wheel, and clock and sound system upgrades.

Sporting the optional Exterior Accent group is a 1983 T-Bird depicted in a rear three-quarter view that shows off its sleek new lines. (Ford Motor Co.)

1983 Thunderbird Solid Interior Trim Codes (U.S. & Canada)

Seat Type	Material	Char-coal	Med. Red	Acad. Blue	Wal-nut	Desert Tan
Base T-Bird						
40/40 Buckets	Cloth & Vinyl	AA	AD	AB	AE	AH
40/40 Buckets	SS-Vinyl	CA	CD	CB	CE	CH
Base/Interior Luxury Group						
Articulated Buckets	Cloth & Vinyl	BA	BD			BH
Articulated Buckets	U Soft Leather	FA	FD			FH
Interior Luxury Group/Heritage						
40/40 Buckets	Velour Cloth	DA	DD	DB	DE	DH
40/40 Buckets	U Soft Leather	EA	ED	EB	EE	EH

1983 Thunderbird Tu-Tone Interior Trim Codes (U.S. & Canada)

Seat Type	Material	Char	Opal/ Red	Opal/ Blue	Opal/ Tan
T-Bird					
40/40 Buckets	S-Soft Vinyl	CW	CN	CQ	C3

Legend: Med. is Medium; Acad. Blue is Academy Blue; U Soft Leather is Ultra-Soft leather; SS-Vinyl is Super-Soft Vinyl, Char is Charcoal.

Technically, the basic 1983 Thunderbird retained a modified McPherson strut front suspension with gas-filled struts. At the rear once again was a four-bar-link suspension with gas-filled shock absorbers. Steering was again of rack and pinion type with power-assist. The base and Heritage models used a variable-ratio system, while the Turbo Coupe featured increased power steering effort and a 15.1:1 non-variable ratio.

Seven cars competed for *Motor Trend* magazine's "Car of the Year Award" in 1983, and the new Thunderbird was among them. Each of the cars was rated in eight categories, including styling and design, comfort and convenience, ride and drive, quality control, instrumented performance, fuel economy, handling, and value. The Thunderbird V-6

Heritage offered velour cloth-trimmed individually reclining bucket seats.

SuperSoft vinyl individual seats were standard in base T-Birds. (Ford Motor Co.)

Individual seats also came with cloth and vinyl trim. (Ford Motor Co.)

placed third overall, but came in first in handling, and second in the appearance, quality and value categories. The car did 0-60 in 13.07 seconds and the quarter-mile in 19.04 seconds at 72.90 mph. Unbelievably, the award was given to the Renault-AMC Alliance. The Buick Skyhawk T-Type was second. In the long run, this was not one of the better "Car of the Year" choices, although the Alliance was, back then, the right car at the right time. Over the long haul, however, the better quality of the T-Bird gives it greater potential as a collector's item.

Motor Trend made up for its slight by featuring the Thunderbird Turbo Coupe in its June 1983 issue. "Three decades later, the T-Bird finally becomes what it started out to be," crowed writer Ron Grable, who loved both the form and functioning of the Turbo Coupe. His test car with air, AM/FM cassette, and tinted glass listed at $12,709. It had the five-speed manual gear box (the sole Turbo option) and the 3.45:1 rear axle. With a curb weight of 2,982 lb. it did 0-60 in 8.56 seconds. The standing quarter-mile took 16.45 seconds at 81 mph. Top speed was 142 mph. Grable concluded the Turbo needed some handling and interior refinements. "It is also an excellent base from which to build," he stated, somewhat prophetically, at the end of his report.

It didn't take long for race car builders to realize the competition potential of the powerful, great-handling, wind-cheating Aero 'Birds. In stock car racing, Dale Earnhardt, Buddy Baker, and Bill Elliott were among the drivers who got new T-Birds to campaign during the 1983 season. The cars did handle well and got plenty of factory support, but some developmental problems and bad racing luck worked against them. By summer, *Motor Trend* was referring to the cars as "a group of promising but still teething T-Birds." At midyear, NASCAR made some rules changes, outlawing certain valve train modifications that worked to the advantage of cars with Chevrolet V-8s. Then the tides started to turn. Driving the Wood Brother's T-Bird, Buddy Baker took first place in Daytona's Firecracker 400. A week later, Dale Earnhardt was victorious at Nashville in the 'Bird that Bud Moore built for him. Earnhardt also took his T-Bird to a checkered flag at Talladega two races later. The final race of the season was the Winston Western 500 (km) at Riverside, Calif. It was in this event that driver Bill Elliott collected his first Winston Cup win with the Melling Ford T-Bird.

In 1982, the T-Bird held a .88 percent share of total U.S. car production. In 1983, this leaped to 2.14 percent, as total model-year production zoomed to 121,999 units. Of these, 76,005 were made at Lorain, Ohio and 45,994 were built in Atlanta, Ga. Although all T-Birds were built in the U.S., the number made for sale here was 113,676. That left 8,323 for the Canadian and export markets. Of the U.S.-market cars, 57.8 percent had V-6s, 31.9 percent had V-8s, and 10.3 percent were Turbo Coupes. Automatic transmissions were used in 89.7 percent of domestic units, and 2.2 percent had the flip-up sun roof option.

Standard for 1983 was a lockable glove box with flocked storage bin. (Old Cars)

Auto Lamp on/off delay was standard with Heritage Edition. (Old Cars)

Automatic overdrive transmission was standard, except on Turbo Coupe. (Old Cars.)

Optional V-8 had 5.0 liters and electronic fuel injection. (Old Cars)

1983 Thunderbird Coupe Hardtop Specifications

Wheelbase	104.0 in.	Standard (except Turbo)	90-degrees V-6
Curb Weight	3,169 lb.	Bore x Stroke	3.80 x 3.40 in.
Overall Length	197.6 in.	Displacement	232 cid (3.8 L)
Overall Width	71.1 in.	Carburetor	2-Barrel
Overall Height	53.2 in.	Compression Ratio	8.65:1
Front Head Room	37.7 in.	HP @ RPM	114 @ 4000
Front Leg Room	42.0 in.	Torque	175 lb.-ft @ 2200
Front Shoulder Room	55.2 in.	Optional	90-degree V-8
Rear Head Room	36.7 in.	Bore x Stroke	4.00 x 3.00 in.
Rear Leg Room	34.3 in.	Displacement	302 cid
Front Tread	58.1 in.	Injection	EFI
Rear Tread	58.5 in.	Compression Ratio	8.4:1
Trunk Space	14.6 cu. ft.	HP @ RPM	130 @ 3200
Tires	P195/75R14	Torque	240 lb.-ft. @ 2000 RPM
Fuel Tank Capacity	18 gallons	Standard (Turbo Coupe)	Inline, OHC Four
Turn Circle	38.6 ft..	Bore x Stroke	3.78 x 3.13 in.
Turns Lock-to-Lock	2.5	Displacement	140 cid (2.3 L)
Steering Ratio	15.0-13.0:1	Injection	EFI
Brakes Swept/1000 lb.	275.6 sq. in	Compression Ratio	8.0:1
Rear Axle (5S manual)	3.45:1	HP @ RPM	145 @ 4600
Rear Axle (3S auto)	2.47:1	Torque	172 lb.-ft. @ 3800
Rear Axle (4S auto)	3.08:1	Weight Distribution	56/44 % front/rear
		Power to Weight Ratio	20.56 lb./hp

The T-Bird (lower left) and its cousin the Cougar (lower right) were the headliners of the 1983 Ford product lineup seen here. (Ford Motor Co.)

1983 Thunderbird Engineering

Front Suspension	Modified McPherson strut
Rear Suspension	Four-bar-link
Steering	Variable-ratio, power, rack and pinion
Front Brakes	Power vented disc
Brakes	Power drum

1983 Thunderbird Performance

Model	CID/HP	Performance
0-60 mph		
Base Coupe	232/114	13.07 seconds
Turbo Coupe	140/145	8.56 seconds
Turbo Coupe	140/145	10
1/4-Mile		
Base Coupe	232/114	19.04 seconds @ 72.90 mph
Turbo Coupe	140/190	16.45 seconds @ 81 mph

1984
Thirty Somethin'

New-for-1984 Thunderbird features included electronic controls (including fuel-injection) for all engines, an automatic transmission for Turbo Coupes, and Elan and FILA models. There were few visual changes in the base T-Bird, but all models now had bumper rub strip extensions as standard equipment. A slightly curved 8 x 6-hole cross-hatched grille texture characterized the front end. A wide Thunderbird insignia was seen on the grille header bar. Staggered, exposed and recessed quad headlamps flanked the grille, two per side. Set into the bumper were new parking lights of clear, rather than amber, plastic. Small amber wraparound marker light lenses were used at each front body corner. Thunderbird

The Turbo Coupe was a fuel-injected, turbocharged car with sophisticated performance, unique styling accents, and special tires. (Ford Motor Co.)

insignias dressed up the roof sail panels. Wraparound wall-to-wall taillamps again lit the rear of the T-Bird. The T-Bird insignias on the taillight lenses had a new molded appearance.

The model line up was revised this year. The former Heritage took the new Elan name. It listed for $12,661 and weighed 2,956 lb. By comparison, the base T-Bird was $9,633 and 3,097 lb. The 3.8-liter V-6 was standard in both models. New this year was an electronic fuel injection system for this engine. The extra-cost 5.0-liter V-8 pushed the T-Bird's price to $10,253 and added 207 lb. Price and weight for the V-8-powered Elan were $13,281 and 3,163 lb.

The new FILA model was developed in conjunction with FILA Sports, Inc., an Italian manufacturer of apparel for active leisure sports such as skiing and tennis. It listed for $14,471 with the V-6 and $14,854 with the V-8. Weights were 3,061 lb. and 3,268 lb., respectively. The FILA model had exclusive Pastel Charcoal paint with a Dark Charcoal Metallic lower accent treatment and unique red and blue tape stripes to emulate the graphics of the company's logo. Bright trim was minimal. Instead of chrome, the grille and wheels had distinctive body-color finish. Charcoal windshield and backlight moldings were also featured. Inside, the FILA edition had Charcoal trim components. Its articulated bucket seats were done in Oxford White leather with perforated leather inserts or in Oxford Gray luxury cloth with perforated cloth inserts.

Interior Luxury group came in Elan and Turbo Coupe models. (Ford Motor Co.)

Base 'Bird had 40/40 individual seats in vinyl or cloth-and-vinyl. (Ford Motor Co.)

Turbo Coupes added Charcoal greenhouse moldings and a new viscous clutch fan, as well as a starter/clutch interlock system and oil temperature warning switch. The Turbo Coupe retained the 140-cid (2.3-liter) turbocharged four, but now came with automatic transmission, as well as the five-speed manual gear box. This year the Turbo Coupe was merchandised heavily in both the U.S. and Canada. Starting on March 16, 1984 three Special Value Packages with a $1,128 discount were available. Each package included the same 11 basic extras, which priced out at $1,623 separately before the discount. Package 161V ($495 net) included only the basic contents. Package 162V ($1,285 net) added seven options worth about $800 additional. Package 163V ($2,051 net) added six more items worth about another $800. Collectors are likely to find many well-loaded 1984 Turbo Coupes today because of this promotion.

The 1984 T-Bird models were the base Thunderbird (top photo), the Turbo Coupe (bottom photo), the Elan, and the FILA (next page). (Ford Motor Co.)

Only eight exterior paint colors were offered in 1984, and five were optional Clearcoat Metallic colors. Four paint stripe colors were offered, but each was used only with specific body colors. A special Turbo Coupe paint treatment was available once again with all colors except Black and Dark Charcoal Metallic. These colors could not be teamed with the special two-tone scheme, since it used Dark Charcoal Metallic as a contrasting accent color below the body side moldings and bumper rub strips. Interiors came in seven colors. Eight different types of seats and seat trims were listed, but not all seat/trim options. A total of 32 variations could be ordered.

1984 Thunderbird Solid Interior Trim Codes (U.S. & Canada)

Seat Type	Material	Char-coal	Oxford Gray	Can Red	Aca Blue	Desert Tan	Wheat	Oxford White
Base T-Bird								
40/40 Buckets	Cloth & Vinyl	AA	AJ	AD	AB	AH	AR	
40/40 Buckets	SS-Vinyl		CA	CJ	CD	CB	CH	CR
Base/Interior Luxury Group/Turbo Coupe								
Articulated Buckets	Cloth & Vinyl	BA		BD		BH		
Articulated Buckets	U Soft Leather	FA		FD		FH		

1984 Thunderbird Solid Interior Trim Codes (U.S. & Canada)

Interior Luxury Group/Elan

40/40 Buckets	Velour Cloth	DA	DJ	DD	DB	DH	DR
40/40 Buckets	U Soft Leather	EA	EJ	ED	EB	EH	ER

FILA

Articulated Buckets	Cloth			MJ			
Articulated Buckets	Leather						GW

Legend: First letter denotes seat type; second letter denotes color. Can Red means Canyon Red. Aca Blue means Academy Blue. SS-Vinyl means Super-Soft Vinyl. U Soft Leather means Ultra Soft Leather.

The 1984 T-Bird models the Elan (top photo), and the FILA (bottom photo). (Ford Motor Co.)

Notable standard engineering features included power front disc/rear drum brakes, modified McPherson strut front suspension with gas-filled struts, four-bar-link rear suspension with gas shocks (Special Handling package with quadra-shocks standard on Turbo Coupe), DuraSpark ignition, electronic voltage regulator, dual fluidic windshield washer system, and maintenance-free battery. The Turbo Coupe also came with a tachometer with boost and overboost lights, Traction-Lok rear axle, and (also on FILA coupe) HR-rated Goodyear performance tires. All models had power-assisted rack and pinion steering with a 15.1:1 ratio and on all models, except the Turbo Coupe, variable-ratio steering was standard. The Turbo Coupe used a non-variable ratio to increase power steering effort for better high-speed control.

Turbo Coupes offered Ultrasoft leather interior option in 1984. (Ford Motor Co.)

214

Motor Trend (April 1984) tested the Turbo Coupe, describing it as a "show and go that you can afford to keep on the road." The car traveled from 0-60 mph in 8.98 seconds and ran the quarter-mile in 16.73 seconds at 80.9 mph. Writer Jim Hall focused on its economy of operation. In 13,257.3 miles of long-term use, the Silver T-Bird cost $987.65 (7.4 cents per mile) to operate. The total included $55.45 in maintenance costs and $932.20 worth of gas. Surging upon acceleration and pinging on climbing steep hills were two problems. After 1,000 miles of use, the surging went away. The pinging was minimized by use of unleaded premium fuel. An air conditioning compressor was also replaced under the factory warranty. There were additional problems with the car's cruise control system and the synchronizer on the transmission's second gear made a crunching noise. However, the T-Bird was summarized as a "good looking performance car that won't cost the driver an arm and a leg during the first year of ownership."

The base 1984 T-Bird is shown here with optional Exterior Accent group and black sidewall tires. (Ford Motor Co.)

In an interesting comparison report, *Motor Trend's* long-term Turbo test car was later (July 1984 issue) compared to a Turbo-Bird modified by Creative Car Products (CCP) of Hawthorne, Calif. The CCP Thunderbird featured a front air dam, side skirts, rear valance panel, rear spoiler, and a Turbo Auto intercooler atop its engine. Additional upgrades included chrome-silicon coil springs front and rear, larger anti-roll bars, and Koni adjustable shocks, plus special Hayashi wheels and Goodyear tires. The magazine described the car's overall look as "reminiscent of the NASCAR Grand National cars." At Sears Point Raceway, the CCP Thunderbird took 9.11 seconds to do 0-60, and covered the quarter-mile in 16.86 seconds at 80.4 mph. Although it was slower-accelerating than the stock Turbo because of its "stickier" tires, the sleek CCP 'Bird performed better in braking and handling tests.

This example of the 1984 FILA Coupe has optional pivoting front vent windows. (Ford Motor Co.)

In addition to street-performance modifications, the new-generation Aero 'Birds were also gaining the attention of the race car set. In stock car racing, Ford's Special Vehicle Operations (SVO) parts pipeline was funneling hardware to race car builders that made the T-Birds even more competitive in 1984. Bill Elliott took his Coors Melling T-Bird to the first back-to-back victories in the 1984 NASCAR Winston Cup Series in October, putting him third in the overall point standings with two races to go. Other stock car drivers racing T-Birds this year included Benny Parsons in the number 55 Copenhagen car, Ricky Rudd in the Wrangler T-Bird, Dick Brooks in the Chameleon Sunglasses T-Bird, Kyle Petty's 7-Eleven car, Kenny Schrader in the Sunny King/Honda Bird, and Buddy Baker in the Valvoline T-Bird. In sports car racing, John Bauer campaigned his number 77 T-Bird. The blue and white car, with Ford/Motorcraft sponsorship, dominated GTO competition. At Pikes Peak, Leonard Vahsholtz and Larry Overholser raced T-Birds up the mountain with mixed success. They were competitive in the event, but wound up in second and fourth place, respectively. Finally, in drag racing, Chief Auto Parts announced its principal sponsorship of Bob Glidden's Pro Stock Thunderbird.

40/40 seats with Interior Luxury trim were standard in 1984 Elan. (Ford Motor Co.)

The 30th anniversary of the T-Bird's introduction was celebrated in the fall of 1984, and by the end of the year, there would be more to celebrate as model-year production in the U.S. leaped to 170,551, a gain of nearly 50,000 over 1983. Of these, 136,301 units were manufactured at Lorain, Ohio and an additional 34,250 were built at Ford's Atlanta, Ga. assembly plant. Most of these cars — 162,024 to be exact — were intended for sale in the U.S. The rest were for other markets, such as Canada. Of the U.S. market cars, 93,813 had the V-6, 53,467 had fuel-injected V-8s, and 14,744 were Turbo Coupes. A full 93.3 percent of the cars sold here were automatics, but only 8.7 percent of them had an optional sun roof.

1984 Thunderbird Coupe Specifications

Wheelbase	104.0 in.	Standard (except Turbo)	90-degrees V-6
Curb Weight	3,091 lb.	Bore x Stroke	3.80 x 3.40 in.
Overall Length	197.6 in.	Displacement:	232 cid (3.8 L)
Overall Width	71.1 in.	Injection	EFI
Overall Height	53.2 in.	Compression Ratio	8.65:1
Front Head Room	37.7 in.	HP @ RPM	120 @ 3600
Front Leg Room	42.0 in.	Torque	205 lb.-ft. @ 1600
Front Shoulder Room	55.2 in.	Optional	90-degree V-8
Rear Head Room	36.7 in.	Bore x Stroke	4.00 x 3.00 in.
Rear Leg Room	34.3 in.	Displacement	302 cid
Front Tread	58.1 in.	Injection	EFI
Rear Tread	58.5 in.	Compression Ratio	8.4:1
Trunk Space	14.6 cu. ft.	HP @ RPM	140 @ 3200
Tires	P195/75R14 WSW	Torque	250 @ 1600
Fuel Tank Capacity	21 gallons	Standard (Turbo Coupe)	Inline, OHC Four
Turn Circle	38.6 ft..	Bore x Stroke	3.78 x 3.13 in.
Turns Lock-to-Lock	2.5	Displacement	140 cid (2.3 L)
Steering Ratio	15.0-13.0:1	Carburetor	EFI
Brakes Swept/1000 lb.	275.1 sq. in.	Compression Ratio	8.0:1
Rear Axle (5S manual)	3.45:1	HP @ RPM	142 @ 5000
Rear Axle (3S auto)	2.47:1.	Torque	172 lb.-ft. @ 3800
Rear Axle (4S auto)	3.08:1		

1985
Happy Anniversary

Ford celebrated the 30th Anniversary of the Thunderbird in 1985, and issued a special limited-edition commemorative model with unique exterior and interior trim. Regular T-Birds got a new color-keyed grille, and full-width taillights with inboard back-up lights. There was also a new Thunderbird emblem, which appeared on the taillight lenses, the "C"pillars, and the grille header bar. Model availability included the base Coupe, the Elan Coupe, and the FILA Coupe with prices (for V-6 versions) of $10,249, $11,916, and $14,974, respectively. Optional V-8 engines were offered in all three for around $650 extra. The Turbo Coupe was the only four-cylinder model. It listed for $13,365 and offered no engine options. For 1985, the Turbo Coupe was "dechromed" to give it a more purposeful look. It also got larger tires on aluminum wheels.

Ford offered 14 colors for the exterior of T-Birds. Seven were standard colors and seven were Clearcoat Metallics. Seven color-coordinated paint stripe colors were used. The Turbo Coupe first came in three standard colors and five clearcoats, all with a Dark Charcoal lower accent treatment. However a 1985-1/2 running change offered three of the same exterior colors (Bright Canyon Red, Oxford White, or Medium Regatta Blue Clearcoat Metallic) in a Monotone treatment without Dark Charcoal lower accenting. The FILA model again offered a Pastel Charcoal exterior with Dark Charcoal lower accent treatment. However, the Red and Blue tape stripes of 1984 were changed to Red Orange and Dark Blue. Three other Monotone color options were added: Black, Bright Canyon Red, and Medium Charcoal Metallic Clearcoat. All three also came with the same FILA tape stripes. The most collectible car of the year was the 30th Anniversary Limited-Edition Thunderbird. It came exclusively with Medium Regatta Blue Metallic exterior finish highlighted with Silver Metallic graduated paint stripes.

Interior changes included a new instrument panel with a digital speedometer and analog gauges. Also revised were the door trim panels. The front center console was shortened and a third seat belt was added in the rear. Both of these changes in the rear compartment permitted five-passenger seating. A total of 33 interior trim options were listed in 1985. They included a special Regatta Blue luxury cloth split-bench seat interior for the 30th Anniversary Thunderbird.

1985 Thunderbird Solid Interior Trim Codes (U.S. & Canada)

Seat Type	Material	Char-coal	Oxford Gray	Can Red	Rega Blue	Sand Beige	Oxford White
Base T-Bird							
Split-Bench	All-Cloth	HA		HD	HB	HY	
Split Bench	SS-Vinyl	JA		JD	JB	JY	
Individual	All-Cloth	AA		AD	AB	AY	
Individual	SS-Vinyl	CA		CD	CB	CY	
Base/Elan/Turbo							
Articulated Buckets	All-Cloth	BA		BD		BY	
Articulated Buckets	Leather	FA		FD		FY	
Elan							
Split-Bench	Luxury Cloth	KA	KJ	KD	KB	KY	
Split-Bench	Leather	LA		LD		LY	
FILA							
Articulated Buckets	Cloth Surfaces		MJ				
Articulated Buckets	Leather						GW
30th Anniversary Limited Edition							
Split-Bench	Luxury Cloth				SB		

Legend: First letter denotes seat type; second letter denotes color. Can Red means Canyon Red. Rega Blue means Regatta Blue. SS-Vinyl means Super-Soft Vinyl. U Leather means leather seating surfaces.

Thunderwords.

...dent Conspicuous Consummate Contemporary Controlled Daring Dashing Dauntless Deb
...rous Definitive Dexterous Direct Disciplined Distinguished Dramatic Dulcet Dynamic Edu
...tive Efficacious Effulgent Elegant Elite Elysian Eminent Energetic Enlightened Enriching Enterta
...eric Es... Exhilarating Exceptional Exhilarating Expeditious Expre...ive Extraord
...onable Fas...ious ... Fulger
...tional Ga... G...and
...nious Honest Idyllic Illuminative Illustrious Immaculate Impassioned Impeccable Impe
...essive Incisive Incredible Indefatigable Individual Indomitable Ineluctable Ingenious Inim
...vative Inspiring Instinctive Intense Intrepid Inviting Inventive Irresistible Jaunty Joie de vivre
...tic Knock-out Landmark Lasting Laudatory Laureate Legendary Lithesome Lively Logical L
...able Luminous Maneuverable Manifest Mannerly Marvelous Masterly Matchless Memorable Mer
...torious Natty Natural Nimble Noble Nonpareil Notable Oeuvre Optimum Oracular Orderly Or
...tanding Panache Paragon Passionate Peerless Performance Personal Persuasive Picturesque Pi
...ing Poetic Poised Portent Practical Praiseworthy Precise Premium Prestigious Pristine Prodi
...cient Progressive Propitious Provocative Pure Purposeful Quadrashock Qualified Quality Q
...ntessential Quixotic Radiant Radical Rapid Rational Reactive Recherche Redoubtable Refined Ref
...iant Resplendent Responsive Rev... ...lient Sanguine Satisfying Scintillating S
...ctive Sensational Sensuo... ...us Sleek Solid Sovereign S
...ted Splendid Spo... ...stematic Tailored Tal
...ful Taut Timele... Turbocharged Un
...dulterated Un... ...mmon Unconven
...erstated Une... ...rmating Unmista
...mpeachable... ...ation Unpreter
...aralleled U... ...bane Utile Ut
...valed Unus... ...nturous Ver...
...Volupt... ...nty Visionar
...ntutional Win...
...es Wonderful W
...ed Xenophile Xi
...ating Yardstick Yo
...Zealous

Thunderbird

This interesting advertisement pictured the 1985 T-Bird against a background of positive "Thunderwords" used to describe the car. (Ford Motor Co.)

The Turbo Coupe received a modified 2.3-liter four-cylinder engine with electronic boost control and higher flow-rate fuel injectors to increase power. The improvements were the result of research and development done for the Merkur XR4Ti, built by Ford of Germany, which used the same engine. There was also a new five-speed manual transmission with new gear ratios, plus an automatic. "The automatic transmission is hardly new," said one Ford ad. "But when it's mated with the turbocharged engine in the Thunderbird Turbo Coupe, it's news." The transmission was designed to handle the Turbo Coupe's high-revving capabilities. When the driver accelerated quickly, it stayed in low gear right through the power curve, not shifting until higher performance could be gained by going to a higher gear.

In racing, the Thunderbirds were flying high this season, with Ricky Rudd's Bud Moore-built Motorcraft Thunderbird making him one of the most promising newcomers in NASCAR events. The T-Birds were so dominant that Chevy buff Junior Johnson convinced Winston Cup officials that he should be able to lower his Monte Carlos to the same roof height specs applied to T-Birds (50 in. instead of 51 in.). At midyear, NASCAR established a new uniform minimum roof height dimension of 50 in. It didn't matter. Bill Elliott's Coors-sponsored T-Bird continued to "rule" NASCAR and set a record qualifying speed in its next outing. That was the Winston 500 at Talladega Superspeedway, a race in which Thunderbirds finished 1-2-3. Elliott took the checkered flag with a mind-blowing average speed of 186.288 mph. He also won the Daytona 500, the Transouth 500 at Darlington, the Budweiser 500 at Dover, Del., the Pocono Summer 500, the Champion Spark Plug 500 at Michigan International, and the Southern 500 at Darlington. His victory in the latter event made Elliott the winner of the new Winston Million series, which earned him a check for $1 million from R.J. Reynolds.

Ultimately, Darrell Waltrip would come from behind to take the 1985 points championship, which created a bit of controversy over the way the scoring was handled. Elliott, though, had become the first driver to ever win 11 Winston Cup superspeedway races in a single season. It was still a great year for Bill's pocketbook and the T-Bird's long performance history. Cale Yarborough (Hardees Ranier T-Bird), Kyle Petty (Woods Brothers T-Bird), and Bobby Allison were other T-Bird pilots in NASCAR. In drag racing, Rickie Smith's Motorcraft Thunderbird broke the 180 mph and eight second barriers in Pro Stock competition. This car was a star on both the NHRA and IHRA circuits in 1985. In a third venue, Darin Brassfield had success with his Brooks Racing T-Bird in the IMSA Camel GT Series.

Ford built 131,215 T-Birds in Lorain, Ohio this year, plus 20,637 in Atlanta for a total of 151,852. This was a slight decrease from 1984 and represented a smaller (1.94 percent) share of total domestic car production. The U.S. market absorbed 144,426 of these units, of which 52 percent were V-6s, 34.3 percent were V-8s, and 13.7 percent were Turbos. Only 8 percent of these cars had five-speeds and 7.6 percent had sun roofs.

1985 Thunderbird Coupe Specifications

Wheelbase	104.0 in.	Standard (except Turbo)	90-degrees V-6
Curb Weight	3,069 lb.	Bore x Stroke	3.80 x 3.40 in.
Overall Length	197.6 in.	Displacement:	232 cid (3.8 L)
Overall Width	71.1 in.	Injection	EFI
Overall Height	53.2 in.	Compression Ratio	8.7:1
Front Head Room	37.7 in.	HP @ RPM	120 @ 3600
Front Leg Room	42.0 in.	Torque	175 lb.-ft @ 2200
Front Shoulder Room	55.2 in.	Optional	90-degrees V-8
Rear Head Room	36.7 in.	Bore x Stroke	4.00 x 3.00 in.
Rear Leg Room	34.3 in.	Displacement	302 cid (5.L)
Front Tread	58.1 in.	Injection	EFI
Rear Tread	58.5 in.	Compression Ratio	8.4:1
Trunk Space	14.6 cu. ft.	HP @ RPM	140 @ 3200
Tires	P195/75R14 WSW	Torque	250 lb.-ft. at 1600
Rear Axle (5S manual)	3.45:1	Standard (Turbo Coupe)	Inline, OHC Four
Rear Axle (3S auto)	2.47:1	Bore x Stroke	3.78 x 3.13 in.
Rear Axle (4S auto)	3.08:1	Displacement	140 cid (2.3 L)
Fuel Tank Capacity	21 gallons	Injection	EFI
Turn Circle	38.6 ft..	Compression Ratio	8.0:1
Turns Lock-to-Lock	2.5	HP @ RPM	155 @ 4600
Steering Ratio	15.0-13.0:1	Torque	190 lb.-ft. @ 2800
Brakes Swept/1000 lb.	275.6 sq. in	Weight Distribution	56/44 % front/rear
		Power to Weight Ratio	20.56 lb./hp

1985 Thunderbird Engineering

Front Suspension	Modified McPherson strut
Rear Suspension	Live axle; Four-bar-link; quad shocks on Turbo
Steering	Power-assisted rack and pinion with 15.1:1 ratio
Front Brakes	Power disc
Brakes	Power drum

1986
Win and Sell

A two-page advertisement in the February 1986 issue of *Motor Trend* featured a race driver with wavy red hair leaning against his Red and White No. 9 stock car in a red Nomex driving suit. "Bill Elliott's two million dollar Thunderbird; Racing into the Future," said the headline. Copy pointed out that Elliott had won his money by victories in a record 11 Winston Cup superspeedway races. It explained how car and driver had rewritten the record books with the fastest qualifying lap at Daytona (205.114 mph), the fastest qualifying lap at Talladega (209.398 mph), and the fastest average speed (186.288 mph at Talladega) ever recorded for any 500-mile race, including the Indy 500. While this ad gave no hint at what would transpire during the 1986 racing season—which Chevrolets dominated—it did help to sell many extra 1986 Thunderbirds. By the end of the year, Ford's sporty personal-luxury car had a 2.09 percent share of the American automobile industry's total domestic production.

Styled road wheels were one of three options for this base 1986 T-Bird. Buyers could also get alloy wheels or locking wire-style wheel covers. (Ford Motor Co.)

T-Bird styling for 1986 was very similar to 1985, except for the addition of a high-mounted stop lamp. Most changes this year were in equipment applications and technical features. A revised electronic climate control system was among them. Also, an electronically-tuned AM/FM stereo was standard equipment in the base model. The Thunderbird's hood now featured counter-balanced springs to hold it open, in place of the inconvenient prop rods.

The 1986 T-Bird Elan interior featured upgraded trim. (Ford Motor Co.)

Larger 215/70R14 tires replaced the previously standard 205/70R14s. A collapsible spare tire with an on-board compressor to inflate it was another innovation. The compressor plugged into the cigarette lighter and operated on 12 volts. Added to the options list was a power-operated moon roof. A specially-designed Tot-Guard child seat was another extra available from authorized Ford dealers. For buyers, a big change this year was the switch to a three-year unlimited mileage warranty on major power train components.

This year the base T-Bird Coupe had an $11,452 window sticker. It gained just a few pounds from 1985 and tipped the scales at 2,923 lb. The Elan returned with a $12,554 sticker. It was 54 lb. heavier. The

FILA edition was dropped for 1986. It had not generated much interest among buyers. Performance buffs still had the Turbo Coupe to quench their thirst for the exotic. It was $14,143 and weighed 3,016 lb. Five conventional finishes and eight extra-cost Clearcoat paints were offered for base and Elan models. Five of these colors were available in two-tone combinations. There were nine striping colors used in specific color-keyed applications. The Turbo Coupe came in three regular colors and five Clearcoat Metallic colors. Four of these (including Black) were available in combination with Dark Charcoal lower body accent treatments. Five interior colors were listed for the base Coupe and Elan. A sixth color, called Raven, could be had only in Elan models with articulated seats. Articulated sports seats were available only on the Elan and Turbo Coupe. Turbos came with only three interior colors. A wood-tone instrument panel applique was also added to the 1986 interior.

1986 Thunderbird Solid Interior Trim Codes (U.S. & Canada)

Seat Type	Material	Med. Gray	Can. Red	Rega. Blue	Sand Beige	Taupe	Raven
Base T-Bird							
Split-Bench	All-Cloth	HG	HD	HB	HY	HE	
Split Bench	SS-Vinyl	JG	JD	JB	JY	JE	
Individual	All-Cloth	AG	AD	AB	AY	AE	
Elan							
Split-Bench	All-Cloth	KG	KD	KB	KY	KE	
Split-Bench	Leather	LG	LD		LY	LE	
Turbo/Elan							
Articulated Buckets	All-Cloth		BD		BY		BH
Articulated Buckets	Leather		FD		FY		FH

Legend: First letter denotes seat type; second letter denotes color. Med means Medium; Can Red means Canyon Red; Rega Blue means Regatta Blue; SS-Vinyl means Super-Soft Vinyl. Leather means leather seating surfaces.

Turbo Coupe features included 2.3-liter turbo engine, close-ratio five-speed gearbox, special Goodyear tires, and articulated sport seats. (Ford Motor Co.)

Standard power train on the 1986 Thunderbird was a 3.8-liter fuel-injected V-6 engine hooked to a three-speed SelectShift automatic transmission. New hydraulic engine mounts made the car smoother-running. The 5.0-liter V-8 was optional. It now featured sequential fuel-injection, roller tappets, low-tension piston rings, fast-burn combustion chambers and hydraulic engine mounts. A four-speed automatic overdrive transmission was standard with the V-8, as well as a new upgraded rear axle. The Turbo Coupe model featured a standard 2.3-liter turbocharged engine and five-speed manual transmission.

In June 1986, *Motor Trend* tested a Turbo and announced, "There is almost nothing to dislike about the Ford Thunderbird Turbo Coupe." Writer Daniel Charles Ross averaged 18.23 mpg with the car during the 2,493 miles he drove it. His test T-Bird had the three-speed automatic transmission, which came with a slightly less powerful engine. It developed 145 hp at 4400 rpm and 180 lb.-ft. of torque at 3000 rpm. "The car looks like it was designed by someone with an engineering degree from MIT and an art degree from the Sorbonne," Ross wrote. He managed 0-60 mph in 9.29 seconds and estimated that times in the eight second range would be possible with 91 octane gas or premium unleaded fuel. Turbo lag, usually in stop-and-go traffic, was the only problem experienced with the car.

NASCAR enacted a number of rules changes affecting the racing T-Birds in 1986. One changed the allowable dimensions for rear spoilers to increase down force. This helped the narrow T-Bird stick better in the corners. Front air dams and larger carburetors were also allowed. Bill Elliott had his frustrations this season, but he managed to take the checkered flag (and $240,000 in prize money) in the Winston 500 at Atlanta International Raceway. T-Birds continued to win stock car races, as well as other events, but the Thunderbird dominance of 1985 was not apparent this season. Nevertheless, Ford did a great job promoting its 1985 wins and managed to translate those victories into new-car sales.

Thunderbird output for model-year 1986 increased to 163,965 units. This year all T-Bird production was quartered at Lorain, Ohio, as the Atlanta factory was changed over to Taurus/Sable production. Of the Ohio-built T-Birds, 156,461 were made for sale in the U.S. This total included 67.8 percent with V-6s, 19.2 percent with V-8s and 13 percent with turbocharged four-cylinder engines. Also, 8.3 percent had five-speed transmissions. The exported cars included 2,002 T-Birds sold in Mexico during calendar-year 1986.

1986 Thunderbird Coupe Specifications

Wheelbase	104.0 in.	Standard (except Turbo)	90-degrees V-6
Curb Weight	3,089 lb.	Bore x Stroke	3.80 x 3.40 in.
Overall Length	197.6 in.	Displacement:	232 cid (3.8 L)
Overall Width	71.1 in.	Injection	EFI
Overall Height	53.2 in.	Compression Ratio	8.7:1
Front Head Room	37.7 in.	HP @ RPM	120 @ 3600
Front Leg Room	42.0 in.	Torque	205 lb.-ft. @ 1600
Front Shoulder Room	55.2 in.	Optional	90-degrees V-8
Rear Head Room	36.7 in.	Bore x Stroke	4.00 x 3.00 in.
Rear Leg Room	34.3 in.	Displacement	302 cid (5.L)
Front Tread	58.1 in.	Injection	EFI
Rear Tread	58.5 in.	Compression Ratio	8.9:1
Trunk Space	14.6 cu. ft.	HP @ RPM	150 @ 3400
Tires	P215/70R14 WSW	Torque	270 lb.-ft. @ 2000
Rear Axle (5S manual)	3.45:1	Standard (Turbo Coupe)	Inline, OHC Four
Rear Axle (3S auto)	2.47:1	Bore x Stroke	3.78 x 3.13 in.
Rear Axle (4S auto)	3.08:1	Displacement	140 cid (2.3 L)
Fuel Tank Capacity	22.1 gallons	Carburetor	EFI
Turn Circle	38.6 ft..	Compression Ratio	8.0:1
Turns Lock-to-Lock	2.5	HP @ RPM	155 @ 4600 (145 w/auto.)
Steering Ratio	15.0-13.0:1	Torque	190 lb.-ft. @ 2800
Brakes Swept/1000 lb.	75.6 sq. in	Weight Distribution	56/44 % front/rear
Fuel Economy	19-26 mpg	Power to Weight Ratio	20.56 lb./hp

1986 Thunderbird Engineering

Front Suspension	Modified McPherson strut
Rear Suspension	Live axle; Four-bar-link; quad shocks on Turbo
Steering	Power-assisted rack and pinion with 15.1:1 ratio
Front Brakes	Power disc
Brakes	Power drum

1986 Thunderbird Performance

Model	CID/HP	Performance
0-60 mph		
Turbo Coupe	140/145	9.29 seconds

1987 - 1988
"Bubble Birds"

1987
Car of the Year Again

Even though the Thunderbird's profile didn't undergo a dramatic alteration this year, evolutionary styling changes were very apparent. The front and rear ends were totally new, along with the hood, roof, rear deck lid, doors and quarter panels. All models also sported flush aero-style headlights and notched-in full-width taillights that wrapped around the body corners to function as side marker lights. Flush-fitting side window glass was another part of the effort to enhance aerodynamics. Antilock brakes and automatic ride control were also made standard equipment for all 1987 models.

Four separate models were merchandised again. Standard power train on the 1987 Thunderbird Coupe and LX was a 3.8-liter fuel-injected V-6 engine with a new four-speed automatic overdrive transmission. The base Coupe listed for $12,972 in V-6 format and weighed in at 3,133 lb. For those buyers wanting a fancier T-Bird, there was the LX. Also featuring the V-6, it had a $15,383 window sticker and 3,176 lb. curb weight. A seqentially-injected 5.0-liter V-8 with a four-speed overdrive automatic transmission was optional in either of these models, but standard in a new $15,079 Sport model. Base Sports had a 3,346-lb. weight. The heaviest T-Bird, in both price and weight, was the Turbo Coupe. Ford added an air-to-air intercooler to its 2.3-liter turbocharged four-cylinder engine. It had a list price of $16,805 and weighed 3,380 lb.

Four standard exterior colors and a record nine Clearcoat paint colors were offered for non-Turbo models. All of the extra-cost options were Clearcoat Metallics this year. Seven colors were available with optional two-tone treatments. There were 11 paint stripe colors, and specific stripes were used with specific exterior/interior color combinations. For example, you could get a Black stripe on a Light Gray car with a Medium Gray interior, but not with a Scarlet Red interior, in which case a Medium Red stripe was used. Raven interiors were also limited to LX models with articulated seats. Turbo Coupes came in two conventional colors and six Clearcoat Metallic colors. Only four interior colors were offered for Turbos, compared to six for other models. Two-tone paint treatments were not available for Turbos.

For 1987, new 16 x 7-in. aluminum wheels were offered exclusively on Turbo Coupes. Taillight design was modified. (Ford Motor Co.)

Seat Type	Material	Med. Gray	Scar. Red	Shad. Blue	Sand Beige	Taupe	Raven
T-Bird Standard							
Split-Bench	All-Cloth	HG	HD	HB	HY	HE	
Split Bench	SS-Vinyl	JG	JD	JB	JY	JE	
Individual	All-Cloth	AG	AD	AB	AY	AE	
Thunderbird Sport							
Individual	All-Cloth	AG	AD	AB	AY	AE	
Thunderbird LX							
Split-Bench	Luxury Cloth	KG	KD	KB	KY	KE	
Split-Bench	Leather	LG	LD	LB	LY	LE	
Thunderbird Turbo/Thunderbird LX							
Articulated Buckets	All-Cloth		BD	BB	BY		BH
Articulated Buckets	Leather		FD	FB	FY		FH

Legend: First letter denotes seat type; second letter denotes color. Med. means Medium; Scar. Red means Scarlet Red; Shad. Blue means Shadow Blue; SS-Vinyl means Super-Soft Vinyl. Leather means leather seating surfaces.

An aggressive "holes-in-the-hood look" announced the arrival of the 1987 T-Bird Turbo Coupe, Motor Tend magazine's "Car of the Year." (Ford Motor Co.)

The new Turbo Coupe featured a grilleless front end and functional hood scoops. There was a large T-Bird emblem on the car's nose. Its engine upgrades reflected research and development done by Ford's SVO (Special Vehicle Operations) branch. It had a new IHI turbocharger designed to optimize low-end and mid-range response and to minimize turbo lag. Also featured were new higher-flow manifolds and a dual exhaust system. The improvements boosted engine output to 190 hp.

A "Preview Test" by Gary Witzenberg in the October 1986 issue of *Motor Trend* put the 1987 Turbo Coupe through its paces. Witzenberg did some brief measured tests at Ford's proving grounds in Romeo, Mich. and put 0-60 performance at 8.4 seconds. The car did the standing quarter-mile in 16.13 seconds and 81.8 mph. It also exhibited improved handling and braking, as well as an outstanding "high-performance" premium sound system. "We've liked Ford's Thunderbird—especially the sleek-looking, smart-handling Turbo Coupe—since its '83 reincarnation," said Witzenberg in his summary. "We like it even better for 1987, and we'll likely go on liking it for some time to come. Think of it as the average man's 635CSi and you won't be far wrong." *Motor Trend* gave the 1987 Thunderbird Turbo Coupe its "Car of the Year" award.

A new-for-1987 model was the T-Bird LX which featured accent stripes, and styled road wheels as standard equipment. (Ford Motor Co.)

Road & Track (August 1987) also wrung out the Turbo and came up with a number of criticisms. It found the new styling "fussy," the dashboard too high, and noted "there is simply not enough torque below 3000 rpm to climb the tall gearing." Also scored were the location of the windshield wiper stalk, engine vibrations, a stiff throttle spring, turbo lag, and sluggish steering. In addition, Ford's automatic ride control system got mixed reviews. However, the handling and braking abilities of the T-Bird were highly praised, and the writer said it had an "attractive shape." In summary, the magazine liked the handsome body design, the ABS brakes, and the advantage of a large dealer network. What it liked least was a thirst for fuel, an "unrefined" power plant, and what it called "untidy handling under some conditions."

In racing, Bill Elliott and Kyle Petty were two of the leading drivers of Thunderbird stock cars. In fact, Ford's ads were still making hay over the records Elliott established during 1985. Davey Allison, driver of the number 28 Havoline T-Bird, was 1987 "Rookie of the Year" and the first driver to ever win more than one Winston Cup event in his first season on the circuit. Over in the drag racing fraternity, Ford had the winningest driver in the history of NHRA competition. Bob Glidden's bright red 1987 Pro Stock Thunderbird helped him become the only seven-time NHRA World Champion.

Unfortunately, not everyone liked the '87 Thunderbirds as much as *Motor Trend*, although production totals clearly suggest that the "Car of the Year" honors helped Ford sell more Turbo models that year. Overall output dropped to 128,135 T-Birds and a 1.74 percent share of industry in model-year 1987. The Lorain, Ohio factory accounted for all 128,135 units. Of these, 122,059 were made for sale in the U.S. This total included 59.2 percent with a V-6 and 22.2 percent with a V-8. However, Turbo Coupe output climbed to an all-time high of 23,833 cars or 18.6 percent of all domestic-market T-Birds. Accordingly, a record high 12 percent had five-speed transmissions this season.

1987 Thunderbird Coupe Specifications

Wheelbase	104.2 in.	Standard (except Turbo)	90-degrees V-6
Curb Weight	3,133 lb.	Bore x Stroke	3.80 x 3.40 in.
Overall Length	202.1 in.	Displacement:	232 cid (3.8 L)
Overall Width	71.1 in.	Injection	EFI
Overall Height	53.4 in.	Compression Ratio	8.7:1
Front Head Room	37.7 in.	HP @ RPM	120 @ 3600
Front Leg Room	42.0 in.	Torque	175 lb.-ft. @ 2200
Front Shoulder Room	55.2 in.	Optional	90-degrees V-8
Rear Head Room	36.7 in.	Bore x Stroke	4.00 x 3.00 in.
Rear Leg Room	34.3 in.	Displacement	302 cid (5.L)
Front Tread	58.1 in.	Injection	EFI
Rear Tread	58.5 in.	Compression Ratio	8.9:1

1987 Thunderbird Coupe Specifications

Trunk Space	14.1 cu. ft.	HP @ RPM	150 @ 3200
Tires	P195/75R14 WSW	Torque	270 lb.-ft. @ 2000
Rear Axle (5S manual)	3.45:1	Standard (Turbo Coupe)	Inline, OHC-4 Intercooled
Rear Axle (3S auto)	2.47:1.	Bore x Stroke	3.78 x 3.12 in.
Rear Axle (4S auto)	3.08:1	Displacement	140 cid (2.3 L)
Fuel Tank Capacity	18.2 gallons	Carburetor	EFI
Turn Circle	38.6 ft..	Compression Ratio	8.0:1
Turns Lock-to-Lock	2.4	HP @ RPM	190 @ 4600
Steering Ratio	15.0-13.0:1	Torque	240 lb.-ft. @ 3400 rpm
Brakes Swept/1000 lb.	275.6 sq. in	Weight Distribution	53/47 % front/rear
(Turbo)	150 hp (auto. trans.)	Power to Weight Ratio	20.56 lb./hp

1987 Thunderbird Engineering

Front Suspension	Modified McPherson strut
Rear Suspension	Live axle; Four-bar-link; quad shocks on Turbo
Steering	Power-assisted rack and pinion with 15.1:1 ratio
Front Brakes	Power disc
Brakes	Power

1987 Thunderbird Performance

Model	CID/HP	Performance
0-60 mph		
Turbo Coupe	140/190	8.40 seconds
Turbo Coupe	140/190	8.5 seconds
1/4-Mile		
Turbo Coupe	140/190	16.13 seconds @ 81.8 mph
Turbo Coupe	140/190	16.3 seconds @ 84.5 mph

1988
Roadburner

The 1988 Thunderbird was available in base Coupe, LX, Sport and Turbo Coupe models. Prices started at $13,599 for the standard V-6 Coupe. It had a 3,215-lb. shipping weight. The LX was fancier. It had a higher price ($15,885) and weight (3,259 lb.) reflecting its additional equipment. Both of these models could have a V-8 installed at extra cost. The V-8 was standard in the Sport model, which logged in at $16,030 and 3,450 lb. Sport models switched from a standard electronic instrument cluster to analog gauges and came with articulated sport seats. As before, the Turbo Coupe carried a turbocharged 2.3-liter four. Its window sticker said it was the most expensive T-Bird with a $17,250 manufacturer's suggested retail price. It was not the heaviest, though, and weighed 3,415 lb., slightly less than the Sport model. Also standard on the Turbo Coupe was a five-speed gear box, anti-lock brakes, electronic ride control, and 16-in. tires.

Five conventional exterior colors were offered for base and LX models in 1988. Available at extra cost were nine Clearcoat Metallics. Of the 14 total colors offered, five could be had in two-tone combinations. Body striping was color-coordinated to both the exterior and interior colors. Eight different stripe colors were used, but only in specific applications. There were five monotone interiors. Sport models could not be had in two of the 14 exterior hues and offered only four interior shades. Turbo Coupes offered only two conventional colors and five Clearcoat Metallics. None of the exterior colors were exclusive to this model, but a Raven colored interior was. However, Medium Gray and Cinnabar interiors could not be ordered for the Turbo.

1988 Thunderbird Solid Interior Trim Codes (U.S. & Canada)

Seat Type	Material	Med. Gray	Scar. Red	Shad. Blue	Lt. Sandalwood	Cinnabar	Raven
T-Bird Standard							
Split-Bench	All-Cloth	HG	HD	HB	HP	HK	
Thunderbird LX							
Split-Bench	Luxury Cloth	KG	KD	KB	KP	KK	
Split-Bench	Leather	LG	LD	LB	LP	LK	
Thunderbird Sport							
Articulated	All-Cloth	BG	BD	BB	BP		
Articulated	Leather	FG	FD	FB	FP		
Thunderbird Turbo							
Articulated Buckets	All-Cloth		BD	BB	BP		BH
Articulated Buckets	Leather		FD	FB	FP		FH

Legend: First letter denotes seat type; second letter denotes color. Med means Medium; Scar Red means Scarlet Red; Shad Blue means Shadow Blue; Lt. means Light; SS-Vinyl means Super-Soft Vinyl. Leather means leather seating surfaces.

Multi-point fuel injection replaced the former single-point system in the Thunderbird's base V-6 engine this year. This boosted horsepower by 20. Inside that engine was a new balance shaft to produce smoother-running operation. Dual exhausts were now standard with the 5.0-liter V-8, which was standard on the Sport model and optional on the base and LX models.

Volume 39 Number 12 of *Motor Trend* magazine was out in December 1987. Instead of being labeled as the "December" issue, it was simply called a "Special Issue." It was 100 percent about Fords from cover to cover — from the lead story to road tests and features, to a "Retrospect" on the 1955 Thunderbird. Even regular departments, such as "Motorsport," were entirely devoted to Ford information. Included in the issue was a road test of the Thunderbird Turbo Coupe. As might be expected, the article written by Don Fuller carried a Ford-friendly title, "Thunderbird Turbo Coupe: Redefining the American high-tech performance car."

In his story, Fuller described the Turbo Coupe as "the dream of every enthusiast who has waited for all the positive elements of the modern age to be wrapped up in one American roadburner." One of the highlights of the article was a fabulous, two-page 3/4-front view phantom illustration of the 1988 Turbo Coupe drawn by David Kimble. Though possibly not the most objective appraisal of this outstanding car, this review was part of a package that every Ford fan should beg, borrow or steal a copy of. The magazine is loaded with lavish color photography of all types of Fords, plus beautiful ads and the "Retrospect" featuring the '55 'Bird is a real collector's item. Ford's factory racing efforts were also covered.

The 1988 T-Birds sported all-new sheet metal and sleek aero-style headlights. Standard, Sport, LX and Turbo Coupe models were offered. (Ford Motor Co.)

In August 1988, NASCAR Winston Cup drivers got a preview of the 1989 Thunderbird they would be racing the next year. The all-new design was of great interest to (from left) Mark Martin, Benny Parsons, Brett Bodine and Bill Elliott, who would all be driving new T-Birds. (Phil Hall Collection)

In NASCAR racing Bill Elliott won the 1988 Winston Cup with his Coors/Melling T-Bird. However, his most exciting experience of the year probably came two days after he took the checkered flag at the 1988 Atlanta Journal 500 race. That's when he went to Dobbin Air Force Base, in Marietta, Ga., to film a recruiting commercial for the U.S. Air Force. Like many race car drivers, Elliott is a pilot and has an interest in flying. He was offered the opportunity to take an "orientation" flight in an F-16 fighter aircraft. During this flight, the F-16 was attempting a maneuver and struck a Georgia National Guard F-15 Eagle. The pilot bailed out of the damaged Eagle, while USAF Major Wayne F. Conroy was able to get the F-16, with Elliott aboard, back safely. "I think I'll go home and have a nervous breakdown," Elliott cracked, after being asked to compare the crash to driving a race car.

Although Elliott took the cup, Chevrolet was able to walk off with the Manufacturer's Championship again in 1988. However, the margin of winning was a slim two (2) points. Other 1988 Ford drivers included Davey Allison of Hueytown, Ala., Kyle Petty of High Point, N.C., Ralph Jones of Upton, Ky., Derrike Cope of Charlotte, N.C., Benny Parsons of Ellerbe, N.C., Brett Bodine of Chemung, N.Y., Phil Barkdoll of Phoenix, Ariz., Mark Martin of Batesville, Ark., and Alan Kulwicki of Concord, N.C. Kulwicki won his first Winston Cup race during 1988. Another name associated with Ford was that of IHRA driver Floyd Cheek. His drag-racing T-Bird was champion in the 8.90-second class.

Ford was getting a lot of credit for its both its racing performance, as well as for its product improvements, in 1988. This, combined with efforts like the special issue of *Motor Trend*, plus good reviews in other magazines, helped to push Thunderbird production upwards by some 20,000 units. A grand total of 147,243 cars were manufactured at the Lorain, Ohio factory for the model year. This was a strong 2.11 percent of total industry output. Of this grand total, 139,411 cars were made for the domestic market. Out of these, 25.3 percent were Turbo Coupes, 46.3 percent had V-6s, and 28.4 percent featured V-8 power. Five-speed transmissions were used in 15.4 percent of the domestic-market cars, and 12.9 percent had sun roofs.

1988 Thunderbird Coupe Specifications

Wheelbase	104.2 in.	Standard (except Turbo)	90-degrees V-6
Curb Weight	3,215 lb.	Bore x Stroke	3.80 x 3.40 in.
Overall Length	202.1 in.	Displacement:	232 cid (3.8 L)
Overall Width	71.1 in.	Injection	EFI
Overall Height	53.4 in.	Compression Ratio	9.0:1
Front Head Room	37.7 in.	HP @ RPM	140 @ 3800

1988 Thunderbird Coupe Specifications

Front Leg Room	42.0 in.	Torque	215 lb.-ft. @ 2400
Front Shoulder Room	5.2 in.	Optional	90-degrees V-8
Rear Head Room	36.7 in.	Bore x Stroke	4.00 x 3.00 in.
Rear Leg Room	34.3 in.	Displacement	302 cid (5.L)
Front Tread	58.1 in.	Injection	EFI
Rear Tread	58.5 in.	Compression Ratio	8.9:1
Trunk Space	14.6 cu. ft.	HP @ RPM	155 @ 3400
Tires	P195/75R14 WSW	Torque	265 lb.-ft. @ 2200
Rear Axle (5S manual)	3.45:1	Standard (Turbo Coupe)	Inline, OHC-4, Intercooled
Rear Axle (3S auto)	2.47:1.	Bore x Stroke	3.78 x 3.13 in.
Rear Axle (4S auto)	3.08:1	Displacement	140 cid (2.3 L)
Fuel Tank Capacity	21 gallons	Carburetor	EFI
Turn Circle	38.6 ft.	Compression Ratio	8.0:1
Turns lock-to-lock	2.5	HP @ RPM	190 @ 4600 (Man.)
Steering Ratio	15.0-13.0:1	Torque	240 lb.-ft. @ 3400 (Man.)
Brakes Swept/1000 lb.	275.6 sq. in	Weight Distribution	56/44 % front/rear
		Power to Weight Ratio	20.56 lb./hp

1988 Thunderbird Engineering

Front Suspension	Modified McPherson strut
Rear Suspension	Live axle; Four-bar-link; quad shocks on Turbo
Steering	Power-assisted rack and pinion with 15.1:1 ratio
Front Brakes	Power disc
Brakes	Power drum

1988 Thunderbird Performance

Model	CID/HP	Performance
0-60 mph		
Turbo Coupe	140/190	8.59 seconds
1/4-Mile		
Turbo Coupe	140/190	16.48 seconds @ 85.1 mph
Top Speed		
Turbo Coupe	140/190	143 mph

1989 - 1997
"Super Birds"

1989
Closer to the Stratosphere

Although anticipated to be a front-wheel-drive car, the 1989 Thunderbird was a completely redesigned rear-drive model with a longer wheelbase and lower profile. It was one of the year's most outstanding new vehicles and took "Car of the Year" honors from *Motor Trend* magazine. Ford Chairman Donald Petersen received lots of credit for turning the T-Bird into a world-class "image" car for his company. Over $1 billion was spent to develop a new body, chassis, suspension, engine and interior package. The car was 3.4 in. shorter from bumper-to-bumper and 7/10ths of an inch wider and lower. It had a nine-inch longer wheelbase. The last change provided more space in the rear compartment and contributed to its improved ride quality.

The 1989 Super Coupe included narrow body side moldings, lower body side cladding, and cast aluminum wheels. (Ford Motor Co.)

The car's "grille-less" front end appearance emphasized its lowness and width. It made the car look much leaner. Below the integrated front bumper on most models were horizontal "louvers" and a long center air slot. The new flush-fitting headlights were of low-profile, composite design. They ended with parking lamps that swept around the body corners to function as side marker lights. The hood dipped down between the headlights and carried a T-Bird emblem on its center. A unique trapezoid-shaped greenhouse featured increased glass area for improved vision. It had extremely thin rear roof pillars to minimize blind spots. At the rear were full-width taillights with the T-Bird insignia on each side. The hot new Super Coupe (replacing the Turbo Coupe) featured a completely different frontal treatment with a large horizontal air intake punched into the bumper below each headlight. Between the air slots the letters SC (for Super Coupe) were embossed in the bumper. It also had a front spoiler, narrow body side skirting, and a lower rear valance that incorporated a race-car-like under-body air extractor.

There were four Thunderbird "factory" models. The standard Coupe had prices starting at $14,612 and weighed 3,542 lb. It was about $1,000 costlier and 300 lb. heavier than the comparable 1988 model. Next came the dressier LX version with a $16,817 window sticker and a dozen more pounds. Both of these models featured a 3.8-liter V-6 engine teamed with a four-speed automatic transmission. The Super Coupe listed for $19,823 and tipped the scales at 3,701 lb. It came standard with a supercharged 3.8-liter V-6 rated for 215 hp. This engine was coupled to a standard five-speed manual gear box. A four-speed automatic transmission was extra. C & C Inc. (formerly Cars & Concepts) was working on a glass-roofed T-Bird at its factory in Brighton, Mich. A bird's eye view of the car was seen in the March 13, 1989 edition of *Autoweek*. However, the T-Bird never really became a popular basis for conversions, including this one or aftermarket custom convertibles.

The standard Thunderbird Coupe came fairly loaded with equipment including air conditioning, power steering, brakes and windows, and an electronic AM/FM search radio with digital clock. It also wore wide body side moldings and full wheel covers. The LX added fancier trims, electronic instrumentation, power locks, a cassette player, and styled road wheel covers. In addition to its engine, the Super Coupe had narrow side moldings, lower body cladding, 16-in. cast aluminum wheels, fat performance tires, and front fog lights. It was the model that stole the spotlight in many of the buff magazines.

The Thunderbird also sported a new interior with reclining bucket seats, a floor-length console, a floor shift, and new motorized front seat belts with active lap belts. Three-point belts were added in the rear compartment. Upholstery with cloth seating surfaces and vinyl trim was standard on the reclining bucket seats in standard models. The base interior also featured vinyl door trim panels with storage bins and courtesy lights. The LX included luxury cloth seat trim, luxury door trim, illuminated visor mirrors, an instrument panel storage compartment, a leather-wrapped steering wheel, and a six-way power driver's seat. The articulated seats used in the Super Coupe had power lumbar and seat back bolster adjustments. It also came with performance instrumentation and a Sport soft-feel steering wheel.

Color and trim options varied between the Super Coupe and the less expensive models. The others offered a total of 11 exterior finishes and seven were Metallic Clearcoats. They came with four different color interiors, although the offerings were color-keyed to specific exterior hues. For instance, the Shadow Blue interior could not be ordered in cars with Black, Bright Red, Currant Red, Deep Titanium, or Twilight Blue paint on the outside. As had been the case previously with the Turbo Coupe, the new performance model came in fewer colors. Three regular finishes and two Metallic Clearcoats were available for the Super Coupe, which also used only three of the interior color options.

1989 Thunderbird Solid Interior Trim Codes (U.S.)

Seat Type	Material	Titan-ium	Currant Red	Shadow Blue	Lt. San-dalwood
Standard					
Buckets	Cloth Surface	CB	CF	CB	CP
LX					
Bucket Seats	Cloth Surface	DA	DF	DB	DP
Bucket Seats	Leather Surface	FA	FF	FB	FP
Super Coupe					
Articulated Buckets	Cloth Surface	EA	EF	EB	
Articulated Buckets	Leather Surface	GA	GF	GB	

Legend: Lt. mean Light

All models had some engineering improvements to go with their great new looks. The 3.8-liter V-6 received friction-reducing roller tappets, light-weight magnesium rocker covers, and an aluminum hub crankshaft damper. Sequential operation of the multi-port EFI system enhanced the precision of the fuel delivery system. Also featured was a "distributorless" ignition system with electronic engine controls. To achieve exceptionally smooth operation, Ford employed hydraulic engine mounts and isolation in the third cross member. The Super Coupe engine used a custom-made Roots-type positive displacement supercharger for its power boost. The engine crankshaft drove the 90-cid supercharger via a poly V-belt running at 2.6 times crankshaft speed. This produced a maximum boost of 12 psi at 4000 rpm. Twin three-lobe helical rotors helped the blower do its work more smoothly and quietly. It also had an engine oil cooler and an intercooler to lower intake air temperature.

By January 1989, Ford had 20,000 orders for the new Super Coupe, which had been appearing on the cover of (and inside) enthusiast magazines since the middle of the previous summer. The company also seemed to have a problem. "Early production SCs have a tendency to leave main bearing remains in the crankcase after extended hard use," one dealer told *Autoweek* (Jan. 16, 1989). But other dealers and Ford officials denied the rumor. The magazine went on to quote *Automotive News* concerning reports of porous crankshafts and the possibility of switching to forged cranks. However, the story added that Ford "insiders" had mentioned a different reason for engine failures—that the main bearing cap bolts used on some cars were found to have off-center heads, causing some engines to "spill their guts" after just 100-400 miles of use.

And there's never been a Thunderbird

The challenge was to create a new car worthy of wearing the Thunderbird wings. The result is the most aerodynamic Thunderbird ever. And a car with performance to match its looks.

A responsive 3.8 litre V-6 engine with sequential electronic fuel-injection is standard. So is an independent rear suspension. And there's even the option of four-wheel-disc anti-lock brakes.

Inside, Thunderbird achieves a new level of comfort and convenience with increased room for five adults and a long list of standard features, including air conditioning, power windows and an electronic AM/FM stereo.

Many new design and engineering features were included in the changed 1989 was standard under the lower profile hood. A new option was four-wheel-disc

like this.

It all adds up to an automobile that's impressive even by Thunderbird standards. The 1989 Ford Thunderbird.

Transferable 6-Year/60,000-Mile Powertrain Warranty.

Covers you and future owners, with no transfer cost, on major powertrain components for 6 years/60,000 miles. Restrictions and deductible apply. Ask to see this limited warranty at your Ford Dealer.

New Ford Thunderbird

Have you driven a Ford...lately?

T-Bird models, which had a slippery new front end. A responsive 3-8-liter V-6 anti-lock brakes. (Ford Motor Co.)

The Super Coupe's introduction was delayed. The real problem indeed turned out to be durability problems with production versions of the original Duracast crankshaft. Duracast metal — actually a kind of cast iron — had tested fine in pre-production prototype engines. However, Ford found out later that the manufacturer had custom-selected the cranks used in the prototypes. The metal in production versions, which were manufactured for an engine that had been considerably upgraded, did turn out to be too porous to stand up in severe use. And Ford did decide to use a forged crankshaft. This change in plan was accomplished in near-record time and the supercharged V-6 entered production on January 30, 1989 at a FoMoCo plant in Essex, Ontario, Canada. Ford then announced that it would build 300 engines daily (up from a planned 200-per-day schedule) and ship 600 by the end of February.

Ford actually tested some of the earliest production supercharged engines by installing 15 of them in fleet vehicles and police cars. The cop cars were 1988 Thunderbird LXs. Three belonged to the police department in Dearborn, Mich., where Ford has its headquarters. This allowed the automaker to monitor the engine's performance in a cold environment. Seven more were installed in Arizona Highway Patrol cars for the opposite reason. A Dallas, Texas courier service also got five engines. *AutoWeek* magazine got to try out two of the Dearborn Police Department cars and did a report in its Feb. 20, 1989 issue. Myron Stokes' side bar story revealed that two cars had also been given to a testing service in Flint, Mich., and three were assigned to Ford's Arizona Proving Grounds.

The sheet metal, interior, and engine changes were accompanied by improvements that affected the Thunderbird's ride and handling. Chief among them was four-wheel independent suspension. On standard and LX models, a long-spindle short and long arm (SLA) setup was used in front, along with variable-rate coil springs, double-acting gas-pressurized shocks, and a .27-mm diameter stabilizer bar. At the rear there was also an SLA setup with toe control link, plus variable-rate springs, gas shocks and a .25-mm diameter stabilizer. The Super Coupe added Automatic Ride Control to the front and rear suspensions, plus beefier stabilizer bars at both ends. Power rack-and-pinion steering with a 14.1:1 ratio on center was standard. It was speed-sensitive on the LX and Super Coupe.

Motor Trend gave the Super Coupe preliminary coverage in its October 1988 issue. The report, by Daniel Charles Ross, called it "a remarkable step forward for a car that was already impressively potent." His early opinion was backed up with a comparison test in the magazine's February 1989 issue. On the cover was a dramatic "X-ray" photo of the Super Coupe that showed the engine through the hood. "Super Charged, Super Styled, Super Coupe!" said one cover blurb. Another announced, "The Winner! '89 Car of the Year." In tough competition against Dodge's Spirit ES, Mercury's Cougar XR-7 (the T-Bird's sister car), and Plymouth's Acclaim LX, the T-Bird placed at or near the top in most categories except comfort and convenience, and fuel economy. "In 1987, when we named the Thunderbird Turbo Coupe our Car of the Year, we called it the highest-flying Thunderbird ever produced," said the Golden Caliber givers. "Little did we realize as we penned those words that Ford was, at the same moment, preparing a new supercharged vehicle that would take the Thunderbird name closer to the stratosphere." Except for minor concerns over gear spacing, the T-Bird was found to look, go, handle, and stop better than its competition. In fact, the nearest car to it was the Cougar XR-7, a virtual twin.

A spy report, by *Car and Driver's* Rich Ceppos (July 1988), hinted that the Super Coupe would do 0-60 mph in the low-seven-second bracket and hit 145 mph at top end. Actually, the mid-sevens was more accurate for the acceleration figure, but the guess at maximum speed was dead on. Ceppos also reported a co-worker's experience with a pre-production base T-Bird. The magazine's technical director Csaba Csere liked the car's "killer good looks" and its handsome and modern interior. "It seems somewhat roomier than before," Csere said. However, the base model did lack sufficiently comfortable seats with lumbar support and — though smooth and responsive in performance — its ride over blemishes in the pavement was rated worse than the 1988 model's.

In August 1988, prior to the Champion Spark Plug 400 at Michigan International Speedway, the Ford drivers who ran in NASCAR got their first look at the competition version of the 1989 Thunderbird. They were aptly impressed with the aerodynamic shape of this so-called "Super Coupe" stock car. Brett Bodine told *Autoweek* (Aug. 29, 1988) that he liked the front end and side treatments, and its production car identity. "They've done a great job making it look like the stock passenger car," said Bodine, who added that Buick's Winston Cup cars looked like "big snowplows."

The new T-Bird race cars came out of the gate running strong, though not ahead of the entire pack. Davey Allison put his Robert Yates/Havoline T-Bird across the finish line second at Daytona. "The car worked well, handled well and the motor ran well," Allison bragged. Terry Labonte's Jr. Johnson/Bud 'Bird placed third at Daytona. Alan Kulwicki's Zerex Ford placed second in the Goodwrench 500 at Rockingham and Allison did likewise at the TransSouth 500 at Darlington. In the First Union 500 at North Wilkesboro, Kulwicki was number two again, while Mark Martin's Stroh's/ Rousch Racing 'Bird was third, and Labonte was fifth.

By July, Elliott was starting to come on, with a win in the AC Spark Plug 500 at Pocono moving him into fourth position in the point standings. Then Terry Labonte took the checkered in the Diehard 500 at Talladega. "The '89 Ford Thunderbird Super Coupes,

Super Coupe's front fascia had "SC" embossment and fog lights. (Ford Motor Co.)

introduced in February at Daytona International Speedway are on a roll, winning the last five Winston Cup races and propelling Ford into the lead over six-time defending champion Chevrolet in the Manufacturer's Championship standings," wrote *Autoweek* (Aug. 7, 1989), noting that it was the longest winning streak for Ford in 20 years. In fact, from the start of the 30-race Winston Cup series in 1972, through 1989, Chevy had won 15 championships versus three for Ford. Chevys had also taken 227 wins in that period, compared to 82 for Fords. Bill Elliott was responsible for 31 of the 82 victories!

Late summer and early fall brought Ford a few more seconds at Watkins Glen, Dover Downs and North Wilkesboro, and a couple of firsts at Rockingham and Phoenix. The AC Delco 500 at Rockingham was Mark Martin's first victory in his 113 Winston Cup starts since 1987. By placing third at the Checker Auto Works 500 in Phoenix, (where Fords finished 1-2-3) Martin slipped into second rank in the Winston Cup points championship. He couldn't hold it though. Pontiac driver Rusty Wallace stole the cup from Chevy pilot Dale Earnhardt. Martin took third in the standings and two other Ford drivers were in the top 10.

For 1989, Martin had one win, placed second five times, and also took six thirds, one fourth, and one fifth. He wound up with 4,053 total points on the season. Elliott was sixth in Winston Cup rankings with three firsts (Michigan, Pocono and Phoenix), one third, three fourth place finishes and a single fifth. He earned 3,774 points. Terry Labonte was 10th with 3,569 points. He had wins at spring Pocono and Talladega, plus two second place finishes, one third, one fourth, and three fifths.

T-Birds also saw some action in other types of racing. In NHRA Funny Car competition Tom Heney's T-Bird racked up 7,774 points to earn him an eighth place national ranking. At Pike's Peak, Leonard Vasholtz pushed his Thunderbird up the 12.42-mile, 156-turn course in 12:23:31. That was enough the make him a big winner in the Stock Cars class. Also, in October 1988, a specially-prepared 1989 Thunderbird circled Alabama International Motor Speedway with Lyn St. James at the wheel. "The new Ford Thunderbird," said an advertisement. "Even before it was introduced, it set 21 new records." Among the marks established by the businesswoman/author/race driver was a new National Women's 10-Mile Closed Course Speed Record of 212.57 mph.

With the Super Coupe's production delay, and some other lateness, business tapered off this year. Ford stopped production of 1989 models at Lorain, Ohio on July 28, after it had built 114,868 T-Birds. That represented 1.61 percent of all cars made in the United States, also a drop from 1988. Only 107,996 cars were made for the domestic marketplace. Of these, 88.7 percent had the standard fuel-injected V-6 and 11.3 percent or 12,204 cars were Super Coupes. (The total number of Super Coupes built for domestic and export markets was 12,962). Only seven percent of the U.S.-markert cars had five-speed gear boxes, so most Super Coupe buyers opted for the extra-cost automatic. Fifteen percent of the domestic T-Birds also had the optional sun roof.

1989 Thunderbird Coupe Specifications

Wheelbase	113.0 in.	Standard (except SC)	90-degrees V-6
Curb Weight	3,542 lb.	Bore x Stroke	3.80 x 3.40 in.
Overall Length	198.7 in.	Displacement:	232 cid (3.8 L)
Overall Width	72.7 in.	Injection	SEFI
Overall Height	52.7 in.	Compression Ratio	9.0:1
Front Tread	61.6 in.	HP @ RPM	140 @ 3800
Rear Tread	60.2 in.	Torque	215 lb.-ft. @ 2400
Trunk Space	14.7 cu. ft.	Standard Super Coupe	90-degrees V-6
Tires	P205/70R15 BSW	Bore x Stroke	3.80 x 3.40 in.
Turns Lock-to-Lock	2.5	Displacement:	232 cid (3.8 L)
Steering Ratio	14.1:1	Injection	SEFI (Supercharged)
Fuel Tank Capacity	19 gallons	Compression Ratio	8.2:1
Power to Weight Ratio	20.56 lb./hp	HP @ RPM	210 @ 4000
Turn Circle	38.6 ft.	Torque	315 lb.-ft. @ 2600

1989 Thunderbird Engineering

Front Suspension	Independent, upper and lower control arms, coil springs, tubular shocks, anti-roll bar
Rear Suspension	Live axle, four-link control arms, coil springs, adjustable tubular shocks, anti-roll bar
Steering	Power rack-and-pinion; speed-sensitive on LX and Super Coupe
Front Brakes	Power vented disc
Brakes	Power drum

1989 Thunderbird Performance

Model	CID/HP	Performance
0-60 mph		
Super Coupe	232/210	7.5 seconds
Super Coupe	232/210	7.84 seconds
1/4-Mile		
Super Coupe	232/210	15.3 seconds @ 88 mph
Super Coupe	232/210	16.24 seconds @ 88.7 mph
Top Speed		
Super Coupe	232/210	145 mph

1990
Take the Road by Storm

"Take the road by storm in a Thunderbird for 1990," said the captivating copy in the year's sales catalog. "The latest generation of the T-Bird, so dynamic in style and performance, has been refined by the driving spirit that has made Ford a recognized leader in automotive design." Following its striking 1989 redesign and selection as *Motor Trend's* "Car of the Year," Ford's hot, rear-drive personal coupe changed little. The clean, smooth lines of a car virtually shaped in a wind tunnel again characterized three different models.

The base V-6 Thunderbird Coupe listed for $15,076. It weighed 3,267 lb. Standard equipment included a 3.8-liter sequential port fuel-injected V-6, four-speed automatic overdrive transmission, four-wheel independent suspension with gas-pressurized shocks, and air conditioning. The fancier LX model had a $17,310 price tag and tipped the scales at 3,311 lb. It included electronic instrumentation, electronic speed-sensitive power steering, a trip computer, speed control, and an AM/FM stereo with cassette.

Available exclusively with a supercharged and intercooled V-6 was the Super Coupe. The Roots-type positive displacement supercharger raised its horsepower rating to 210. The boost at lower compressor rpm was delivered over a broad engine-rpm range. A base price of $20,394 applied to this 3,467-lb. car. It had a standard five-speed manual gear box, automatic ride control suspension, variable-ratio speed-sensitive steering, and four-wheel ABS brakes. Two new option groups were seen for 1990 models. The Power Equipment and Luxury Groups were included in the content of expensive option packages, rather than merchandised separately.

This was the Thunderbird's 35th anniversary year. To celebrate the occasion, an optional 35th Anniversary commemorative package was made available for the Super Coupe during the year. A limited-edition of 5,000 copies was announced by Ford at the end of October 1989. The anniversary models used the same supercharged 3.8-liter V-6 as the standard Super Coupe. They made their debut in January 1990. The anniversary editions were done up in a unique Black and Titanium two-tone paint scheme. They had blue accent stripes, black road wheels, and commemorative fender badges. A special interior trim featured suede and leather bucket seats, a split fold-down rear seat, and commemorative badges on the interior door panels. Also standard was an anti-lock brake system, a handling package with automatic ride control, and a Traction-Lok axle. The 35th Anniversary package (option no. 563) carried a dealer cost of $1,584. Its factory-suggested retail price added $1,863 to the regular cost of a Super Coupe.

Two new exterior colors were offered for 1990 T-Birds, Alabaster and Sandalwood Frost Clearcoat Metallic. In all, there were 11 colors for the base Coupe and the LX, and eight used were Clearcoats. The Super Coupe came in the same five colors as last season, three of which were extra-cost Clearcoat Metallic finishes. Interiors were color-coordinated with the exterior finishes. On base Coupes and LXs, a total of four colors was offered: Crystal Blue, Currant Red, Black, and Light Sandalwood. You could not "mix-and-match" all the options. For example, you could not order a Black interior with an Albaster exterior. Also, the Light Sandalwood interior color was not available for the Super Coupe. There were 18 different interior trim codes.

1990 Thunderbird Solid Interior Trim Codes (U.S. & Canada)

Seat Type	Material	Cry. Blue	Cur. Red	Black	Lt. Sandalwood
Standard					
Buckets	Cloth & Vinyl	QB	QF	QJ	QP
LX					
Bucket Seats	Luxury Cloth	RB	RF	RJ	RP
Bucket Seats	Leather	SB	SF	SJ	SP
Super Coupe					
Articulated Buckets	Cloth	TB	TF	TJ	
Articulated Buckets	Leather	UB	UF	UJ	

Legend: Cry. Blue means Crystal Blue; Cur. Red means Currant Red; Lt. means Light; Leather means leather seating surfaces.

The 1990 T-Bird LX came with bright window moldings and dual electric remote-control mirrors, but cast aluminum wheels were extra. (Ford Motor Co.)

Other than color and trim revisions, there were only modest changes in 1990 T-Birds like this Super Coupe. (Ford Motor Co.)

A special 35th Anniversary model was added to the 1990 T-Bird lineup. It was a Super Coupe with special interior and exterior trim. (Ford Motor Co.)

Ford made a lot of noise about its equipment list in 1990. "Your 1990 Thunderbird comes equipped with a high level of standard equipment," read the sales literature. "If you would like to personalize your Thunderbird even more, you may do so by choosing individual options or selecting an Extra Value Package. These packages are combinations of popular options which, when purchased as a group, provide a significant savings over the price of the same options if purchased separately. They are a desirable way to add value and save money."

As an example of the savings, the standard 151C Preferred Equipment Package included an electronic AM/FM cassette radio with clock, a rear window defroster, a 6-way power driver's seat, cast aluminum wheels, and the Luxury Option Group. Individually, these options were worth $1,446, but the package price was $796. Among some options receiving strong selling efforts were an anti-theft system, a power sun roof, all-season tires, a Ford JBL sound system, a compact disc player, a keyless entry system, and a light package.

Motor Trend magazine road tested the Super Coupe again in its September 1990 issue. The car moved from 0-60 mph in 7.4 seconds and covered the quarter-mile in 15.8 seconds at 90.8 mph. During lateral acceleration the car pulled .82g. It took 136 ft. to come to a complete halt from 60 mph. Its average EPA city mileage rating was 17 mpg.

In racing, it was a good year for Thunderbirds, with five Fords in NASCAR's top 10 Winston Cup standings. Dale Earnhardt's nine victories gave Chevrolet its eighth manufacturer's title in a row. However, the T-Birds were really nipping at the heels of his No. 3 Lumina. Earnhardt had only a 26-point margin over Mark Martin's Folgers Coffee Ford. Martin took checkered flags at Richmond, Michigan, and North Wilkesboro. Bill Elliott's

Coor's Ford was third, although his only win was at Dover. Geoff Bodine's Budweiser 'Bird was fourth. It had two victories at Martinsville and one at Pocono. Morgan Shepard's Motorcraft Ford was sixth, although he came in first only at Atlanta in the fall. The other Ford was Alan Kulwicki's Zerex Ford in eighth place, including a win at Rockingham.

All 1990 Thunderbirds were again built at the Lorain, Ohio assembly plant. There were 113,957 made in all, including 90,247 Coupes, 20,339 Super Coupes, and 3,371 of the 35th Anniversary Edition Thunderbird. The domestic market absorbed 107,996 cars, a decrease of 40,000 units from 1989. Of these, a higher percentage (21 percent) were Super Coupes. In addition, 5.8 percent came with five-speed manual gear boxes and 19.16 percent had an optional sun roof.

Celebrating Thunderbird!
Thunderbird Model-Year Sales Since Birth

Year	Sales
1955	14,771
1956	14,912
1957	17,011
1958	35,698
1959	67,090
1960	80,376
1961	82,087
1962	74,871
1963	63,801
1964	92,510
1965	68,663
1966	68,435

1955 – MODEL THUNDERBIRD

1990 – MODEL THUNDERBIRD

Year	Sales
1967	71,815
1968	60,748
1969	48,464
1970	47,441
1971	34,944
1972	56,421
1973	82,276
1974	54,112
1975	36,397
1976	46,713
1977	300,066
1978	319,328

Year	Sales
1979	219,465
1980	164,795
1981	80,942
1982	47,903
1983	99,176
1984	156,583
1985	169,770
1986	144,577
1987	126,767
1988	127,356
1989	118,107

Total Model Year
Sales 1955 – 1989   3,294,391

1990 Thunderbird Coupe Specifications

Wheelbase	113.0 in.	Standard Engine (Type)	90-degree ohv V-6
Curb Weight	3,267 lb.	Bore x Stroke	3.80 x 3.40 in.
Overall Length	198.7 in.	Displacement:	232 cid (3.8 L)
Overall Width	72.7 in.	Injection	SEFI
Overall Height	52.7 in.	Compression Ratio	9.0:1
Trunk Capacity	14.7 cu. ft.	HP @ RPM	140 @ 3800
Fuel Tank Capacity	19-gal.	Torque	215 lb.-ft. @ 2400
Seating capacity	Five (5)	Optional Engine (Type)	90-degree ohv V-6
Fuel Economy	17-24 mpg	Bore x Stroke	3.80 x 3.40 in.
Front Tread	61.6 in.	Displacement	232 cid (3.8 L)
Rear Tread	60.2 in.	Induction	SEFI (Supercharged)
Transmission	4-speed auto.	Compression Ratio	8.3:1
Wheels	16 in.	HP @ RPM	210 @ 4000
Tires	P225/60VR16	Torque	315 lb.-ft. @ 2600

1990 Thunderbird Engineering

Front Suspension	Independent, upper and lower control arms, coil springs, tubular shocks, anti-roll bar
Rear Suspension	Live axle, four-link control arms, coil springs, adjustable tubular shocks, anti-roll bar
Steering	Power rack-and-pinion; speed-sensitive on LX
Front Brakes	Power vented disc
Brakes	Power drum

1990 Thunderbird Performance

Model	CID/HP	Performance
0-60 mph		
Super Coupe	232/210	7.4 seconds
1/4-Mile		
Super Coupe	232/210	15.8 seconds @ 90.8 mph

1991
Trends & Traditions

T-Bird enthusiasts helped bring the V-8 engine back in 1991. They asked their Ford dealers for the type of engine that was traditional in their favorite car. The company finally took the 5.0-liter Mustang motor and stuffed it into the T-Bird's smaller engine bay. This was not as simple as it sounds though. It had originally been anticipated that Ford's modular V-8 could be used below the lower T-Bird hood that appeared in 1989. However, the new engine was still three years away when buyers started really pressing Ford for a V-8.

The automaker first tried to create an optional hood with a "power bulge." This appeared in an *Autoweek* spy photo as early as May 1, 1989. It didn't look at all bad. The bulge in the hood allowed clearance for the engine, but the magazine noted that designer Jack Telnack didn't like it. According to *Autoweek*, Telnack felt the lower nose "makes the whole car." He apparently "flattened" the idea of putting a bulge on the hood.

Ford ultimately redesigned the 5.0-liter engine's intake manifold and other parts to fit the lower-profile hood. Making the engine fit required some hefty modifications. Its length was shortened by 2-1/2 in. Its height was also lowered by redesigning the intake manifold. The changes reduced the horsepower rating from 225 in the Mustang to 200 in the Thunderbird. But, the V-8 was installed in nearly 21 percent of all 1991 T-Birds and took nearly equal shares away from the other motors. Useage of the base V-6 dropped from 85.3 percent in 1990 to 74.2 percent in 1991, while the supercharged V-6's popularity dropped from 14.7 percent in 1990 to 4.8 percent in 1991.

The new Thunderbirds were released on Sept. 17, 1990. Three models were offered again. Very few revisions were made to 1991 models outside, inside, or underneath. In fact, the biggest change was the reinstatement of the V-8 engine. It was optional in the standard and LX models. The standard Thunderbird also received some interior upgrades. Leather seat facings and cloth and vinyl door panel inserts were added on the LX model. The Super Coupe's seats had a T-Bird insignia embroidered into them.

The standard model had a base price of $15,318. The V-8 cost $1,080 extra. Major standard Thunderbird features included daytime running lights, a rear window defroster, a 72-amp. battery and 65-amp. alternator, wide body side protection moldings, deluxe wheel covers, manual air conditioning, tinted glass, power steering, power windows, interval wipers, and all-season radial tires. The interior had a full-length console with floor-mounted shifter, vinyl door trim with storage bins, cloth bucket seats with recliners, analog gauges, and an electronic AM/FM stereo search radio with digital clock.

The LX listed for $17,734, or $1,080 additional with a V-8. If you placed an option-less LX next to a standard Coupe without extras, you might notice the LX's bright window moldings, dual electric remote control mirrors, and styled road wheel covers. However, the two models remained very similar on the outside. The interiors were different, however. As standard equipment, the LX provided luxury level door trim and carpeting, an illuminated entry system with convenience lights, an upper storage compartment for the instrument panel, illuminated visor mirrors, luxury cloth bucket seats with recliners, a front seat center arm rest, a leather-wrapped luxury steering wheel, a power lock group, speed control, tilt steering, and speed-sensitive power steering.

The top-of-the-line Super Coupe was the high-performance model. It carried a $20,390 window sticker. Under the hood again was the supercharged V-6 with 210 hp. This engine combined exceptional performance with an EPA fuel economy rating of 17 mpg (city)/24 mpg (highway). Its features list added or substituted fog lamps, narrow body side moldings, lower body side cladding, 16-in. cast aluminum wheels with P225/60R16 performance tires, luxury door trim and carpeting, articulated sport seats, a soft-feel steering wheel, a heavy-duty alternator, the automatic ride control suspension, and performance instrumentation.

The standard Thunderbird Coupe came with cloth bucket seats with recliners, and vinyl door trim panels with storage bins. It had dome, luggage compartment, ashtray, and driver's footwell lights. Analog instrumentation was standard, as was a full-length console with floor-mounted shift. The LX interior added luxury cloth/leather/vinyl bucket seats with recliners and 6-way power for the driver. It also had luxury-level door trim and carpeting, a leather-wrapped steering wheel and a tachometer. Articulated sport seats were added in the Super Coupe, along with a sport soft-feel steering wheel. Standard and LX models came in 11 exterior colors, and eight of these were new. Five were Clearcoat finishes, and four of those were metallic. Three of the non-Clearcoat colors were also metallics. Five of the same colors were offered for Super Coupes, including two of the new ones. Except for Oxford White, all Super Coupe paints were Clearcoats and two of those were metallics. Five interior colors (four for Super Coupes) were available.

1991 Thunderbird Interior Trim Codes (U.S. & Canada)

Seat Type	Material	Titan-ium	Crys. Blue	Cur. Red	Mocha	Black
Standard						
Buckets	Cloth	WA	WB	WF	WH	WJ
LX						
Bucket Seats	Luxury Cloth	5A	5B	5F	5H	5J
Bucket Seats	Leather	4A	4B	4F	4H	4J
Super Coupe						
Articulated Buckets	Cloth	3A	3B	3F		3J
Articulated Buckets	Leather	UA	UB	UF		UJ

Legend: Crys. Blue means Crystal Blue; Cur. Red means Currant Red; Luxury Cloth interior includes leather and vinyl components.

Road & Track road tested the 1991 Thunderbird LX Coupe and published the results in its April 1991 issue. The car, as tested, priced out at $23,181. It was equipped with the four-speed automatic transmission. In the acceleration category, the car did 0-60 mph in 9.0 seconds. The quarter-mile took 16.7 seconds. The car's top speed was 140 mph. Braking performance was also good, with 255 ft. required to stop the car from 80 mph. It averaged 60.3 mph through the slalom.

For 1991, the T-Bird line offered Standard, LX and Super Coupe models with numerous features, options and Preferred Equipment packages.

Thunderbirds also turned in impressive performances in various types of racing events during 1991. Hot-driving NASCAR competitors running Fords included Davey Allison, Mark Martin and Sterling Marlin. Ford was a close second to Chevrolet in the battle for the Manufacturer's Cup. Also, for the first time since 1988, Ford managed a super-speedweay triumph in ARCA stock car racing when Greg Trammell put his Melling-Elliott T-Bird across the finish line first in the March 16 race at Atlanta Motor Speedway. He averaged a blistering 131.532 mph to set an event record. Bobby Bowsher placed third in his Don Thompson Excavating Thunderbird. In NHRA drag racing, Bob Glidden's Pro Stock Thunderbird struggled to a fifth place finish.

Automobile sales were "in the cellar" in 1991. In fact, I bought my first-ever new-car that year and got such a good bargain that I bought a new pickup truck later that fall. Ford workers in Lorain, Ohio cranked out a total of 82,973 Thunderbirds for the model-year. This included 7,267 Super Coupes (slightly more than one-third of the 1990 total), and 75,706 other models. Thunderbird sales were following the national trend, but the T-Bird's share of total industry production was also dropping. It stood at just 1.43 percent, versus 2.11 percent three years earlier. This meant that the T-Bird was losing customers at a greater rate than automakers as a group.

1991 Thunderbird Coupe Specifications

Wheelbase	113.0 in.	Standard Engine (Type)	90-degree ohv V-6
Curb Weight	3,267 lb.	Bore x Stroke	3.80 x 3.40 in.
Overall Length	198.7 in.	Displacement:	232 cid (3.8 L)
Overall Width	72.7 in.	Injection	SEFI
Overall Height	52.7 in.	Compression Ratio	9.0:1
Trunk Capacity	14.7 cu. ft.	HP @ RPM	140 @ 3800
Fuel Tank Capacity	18-gal.	Torque	215 lb.-ft. @ 2400
Seating Capacity	Five (5)	Optional Engine (Type)	90-degree ohv V-6
Fuel Economy	17-24 mpg	Bore x Stroke	3.80 x 3.40 in.
Front Tread	61.6 in.	Displacement	232 cid (3.8 L)
Rear Tread	60.2 in.	Induction	SEFI (Supercharged)
Transmission	4-speed auto.	Compression Ratio	8.3:1
Wheels	16 in.	HP @ RPM	210 @ 4000
Tires	P215/70R15	Torque	315 lb.-ft. @ 2600
Fuel Economy (EPA)		Optional Engine (Type)	90-degree ohv V-8
City (V-6)	19 mpg	Bore x Stroke	4.00 x 3.00 in.
Highway (V-6)	27 mpg	Displacement	302 cid (5.0 L)
City (SC)	17 mpg	Injection	SEFI
Highway (SC)	24 mpg	Compression Ration	8.9:1
City (V-8)	15 mpg	HP @ RPM	200 @ 4000
Highway (V-8)	23 mpg	Torque	275 lb.-ft. @ 3000

1991 Thunderbird Engineering

Front Suspension	Independent, upper and lower control arms, coil springs, tubular shocks, anti-roll bar
Rear Suspension	Live axle, four-link control arms, coil springs, adjustable tubular shocks, anti-roll bar
Steering	Power rack-and-pinion; speed-sensitive on LX
Front Brakes	Power vented disc
Brakes	Power drum

1992
Grand Touring

Minor changes were seen on 1992 Thunderbirds. The LX and Sport models now had the same aggressive front fascia used on the Super Coupe, without the "SC" initials embossed in the bumper. The standard Thunderbird Coupe was base-priced at $16,345 and had a 3,550-lb. curb weight. The Sport Coupe was $18,611, the LX $18,783, and the Super Coupe $22,046.

By this time, the T-Bird was becoming a unique vehicle, due to its retention of a rear-drive platform. It also retained its fully independent suspension with A-arms in front and H-arms at the rear. Power-assisted rack-and-pinion steering and four-wheel disc brakes remained standard, as well. Ford stuck to its three engine options, with the 140-hp V-6 and 200-hp V-8 available in the base and LX models, and the V-8 standard in the Sport model. The Super Coupe had exclusive use of the supercharged 210-hp V-6, which was the only engine it came with. The 1992 Sport Coupe also featured cast aluminum wheels, a leather-wrapped steering wheel, and analog-type performance instrumentation.

Eleven exterior colors were offered on standard, Sport, and LX models. Four of them—Cayman Green Clearcoat Metallic, Dark Plum Clearcoat Metallic, Opal Grey, and Silver—were brand new for 1992. The Super Coupe came only in five colors. There were five different color interiors for all but the Super Coupe, which offered four choices. Only one exterior color—Oxford White—was available with all interior colors. The others could be ordered only with specific color-keyed interior selections. There was a total of 54 possibilities in all.

1992 Thunderbird Interior Trim Codes (U.S. & Canada)

Seat Type	Material	Titan- ium	Crys. Blue	Cur. Red	Mocha	Black
Standard & Sport						
Buckets	Cloth	WA	WB	WF	WH	WJ
LX						
Bucket Seats	Luxury Cloth	5A	5B	5F	5H	5J
Bucket Seats	Leather	4A	4B	4F	4H	4J
Super Coupe						
Articulated Buckets	Cloth	3A	3B	3F		3J
Articulated Buckets	Leather Surfaces	PA	PB	PF		PJ

Legend: Crys. Blue means Crystal Blue; Cur. Red means Currant Red; Luxury Cloth interior includes leather and vinyl components.

"For some of us who love cars, the most intriguing models are not racing cars or sports cars, but big coupes. Grand Touring Cars. Cars with powerful engines, good road manners, style, and grace," said *Road & Track's Complete '92 Car Buying Guide.* "A gentleman's car like the Jensen Interceptor III, Facel-Vega HK 500. Aston Martin DB4. If there is a modern successor to these machines, it is the Ford Thunderbird."

Consumer Reports annual auto issue was a bit rougher on the 1992 T-Bird, commenting that "reliability has been slipping." Brakes were a problem with the V-6 model. The Supercharged V-6 had big problems with brakes and automatic transmission, and smaller problems with the electrical system and manual gear box. Insufficient data on the revived V-8s kept their reliability a secret, but the earlier V-8s had experienced above average electrical system and steering and suspension repair rates. Overall owner satisfaction appeared to be right in the middle between the most reliable and least reliable cars.

In racing, the 1992 Thunderbirds proved more reliable. They came out of the gate strong in 1992 NASCAR Winston Cup racing, earning consecutive wins in the first nine races. Between the Charlotte race in the fall of 1991, and the spring 1992 Winston Cup event at the same track, Ford drivers netted 14 checkered flags. Still, the season wound up being another cliff-hanger. Back-to-back Geoff Bodine victories finally clinched the Winston Cup Manufacturer's Championship for Ford. Bodine's number 15 Bud Moore/Motorcraft T-Bird race car crossed the line first at Martinsville and North Wilkesboro, taking both events on Mondays after Sunday rain-outs. It was the first time in nine years that the blue oval cars wrestled the Manufacturer's Cup away from Chevrolet. The *coup de grace* came at season's end, when Bill Elliott put his T-Bird across the line first in the Hooters 500 at Atlanta Motor Speedway in Ford's 400th NASCAR victory, and Ford pilot Alan Kulwicki captured the Winston Cup Championship with his Hooters T-Bird. That gave Kulwicki, Elliott and Davey Allison the top three places in the point standings. In all, the Fords had 16 wins on the season, led the most laps, took a dominating 57 top-five finishes, and ran in the top 10 places 142 times!

Another flock of 'Bird jockeys — led by title-winner Bobby Bowsher — performed nearly as well in 1992 ARCA competition. A win by another Ford in the last race of the season settled the title bout between Bowsher, and Chrysler LeBaron driver Bob Keselowski. This came in the Motorcraft 500K race at Atlanta, which Loy Allen, Jr. won with his Robert Yates-built number 2 Hooters T-Bird.

Ford drivers struggled in NHRA drag racing, with Bob Glidden's Pro Stock T-Bird placing only third at the Keystone Nationals and second at Topeka. Glidden managed to pull out a late-season win at Dallas and finished fifth in the point standings again. In IHRA competition, Glen May's "Cranberry Connection" Thunderbird did become the first "door-slammer" car to break the 220-mph barrier.

A grand total of 77,789 Thunderbirds were built in Lorain, Ohio this year for worldwide distribution. This broke down as 4,614 Super Coupes and 73,175 other T-Birds and represented 1.38 percent of all cars made in U.S. factories. It also included 73,892 cars made for sale here. Of these, 77.3 percent had the standard V-6; 5.7 percent had the supercharged V-6; and 17 percent had V-8s. No 1992 T-Birds used manual transmissions. Four-speed overdrive automatics were put in 98.3 percent of the domestic cars, and 1.7 percent used the three-speed SelectShift automatic. Sun roofs were added to 12.2 percent of those cars

Ford reintroduced a V-8-powered T-Bird for 1992. This necessitated changes in the length and height of the power plant to fit under the low hood. (Ford Motor Co.)

1992 Thunderbird Specifications

Wheelbase	113.0 in.	Standard Engine (Type)	90-degree ohv V-6
Curb Weight	3,267 lb.	Bore x Stroke	3.80 x 3.40 in.
Overall Length	198.7 in.	Displacement:	232 cid (3.8 L)
Overall Width	72.7 in.	Injection	SEFI
Overall Height	52.7 in.	Compression Ratio	9.0:1
Front Leg Room	41.5 in.	HP @ RPM	140 @ 3800
Fuel Tank Capacity	18-gal.	Torque	215 lb.-ft. @ 2400
Seating Capacity	Five (5)	Optional Engine (Type)	90-degree ohv V-6
Fuel Economy	17-24 mpg	Bore x Stroke	3.80 x 3.40 in.
Front Tread	61.6 in.	Displacement	232 cid (3.8 L)
Rear Tread	62.2 in.	Induction	SEFI (Supercharged)
Transmission	4-speed auto.	Compression Ratio	8.3:1
Wheels	15 in.	HP @ RPM	210 @ 4000
Tires	P215/70R15	Torque	315 lb.-ft. @ 2600
Turn Circle	37.5 ft.	Optional Engine	90-degree ohv V-8
City (base V-6)	20 mpg	Bore x Stroke	4.00 x 3.00 in.
Highway (baseV-6)	27 mpg	Displacement	302 cid (5.0 L)

Warranties

		Injection	SEFI
Bumper-to-bumper	3 yrs./36,000 mi.	Comp. Ratio	8.9:1
Power train	3 yrs./36,000 mi.	HP @ RPM	200 @ 4000
Rust-Through	6 yrs./100,000 mi.	Torque	275 lb.-ft. @ 3000
Trunk Capacity	14.7 cu. ft.	Weight distribution	57 %/43 %

1992 Thunderbird Engineering

Front Suspension	Independent, upper and lower control arms, coil springs, tubular shocks, anti-roll bar
Rear Suspension	Live axle, four-link control arms, coil springs, adjustable tubular shocks, anti-roll bar
Steering	Power rack-and-pinion; speed-sensitive on LX
Front Brakes	Power vented disc
Brakes	Power drum

1993
Head of the Class

Although somewhat different-looking than the original, the Aero 'Bird was now entering its second decade. It had risen to the head of its class by outlasting competitive rear-drive luxo-coupes like the Cutlass Supreme, Monte Carlo, and Cordoba. In fact, the T-Bird was virtually in a class of its own. Ford decided to streamline its niche by reshuffling models and "value pricing" the LX model. The standard Thunderbird Coupe and the Sport Coupe disappeared from the Thunderbird model lineup. The LX was available with a new $15,797 list price, which was considerably lower than the $18,783 window sticker of a year earlier. The Super Coupe price was also cut, but only by $16. It now had a window sticker of $22,030.

Major standard features of the LX included the 3.8-liter 140-hp V-6 with sequential multi-port electronic fuel-injection; automatic overdrive transmission; luxury level upholstery, door trim and carpets; bucket seats and console; analog instrumentation; body-color side protection moldings; and 15 x 6-in. stamped steel wheels with styled road wheel covers and P205/70R15 black sidewall tires. The 5.0-liter EFI V-8 with automatic overdrive transmission was optional.

Added or substituted on the Super Coupe were the 210-hp supercharged and intercooled version of the V-6 (with boost gauge); standard five-speed manual transmission; automatic ride control; handling suspension; Traction-Lok axle; four-wheel ABS disc brakes, all-cloth articulated sport seats; a lighting package; a Sport soft-feel steering wheel; narrow black side moldings; lower body side cladding; a unique rear fascia; and 16 x 7-in. wheels with P225/60ZR black sidewall performance tires.

Ten exterior finishes were offered for early-1993 LXs. One used conventional Oxford White paint, eight used Clearcoat Metallic paints, and the 10th had non-metallic Black Clearcoat. Only five colors were available for Super Coupes early in the year, including an exclusive non-metallic Crimson Clearcoat which could become a rare color in the future. During the year, several color changes were made. A Bright Red non-metallic Clearcoat color was added for both models. Also, the Midnight Opal Clearcoat Metallic offered for early LXs was replaced with Opal Gray Clearcoat Metallic. In addition, the non-metallic Crimson Clearcoat, offered only on early Super Coupes, was dropped in favor of the new Bright Red. Four interior colors were featured for early LXs, while Super Coupe buyers had a choice of just three. In late-production, a new Titanium interior replaced Opal Grey, and a color called Currant Red replaced Ruby Red. Also available was a limited-edition Opal Grey and White interior for a special feature car offered in early production.

Colors and Trims (1993 Early Production)

EXTERIOR COLORS	INTERIOR TRIM COLORS				
Thunderbird LX	Opal Grey	Crystal Blue	Ruby Red	Mocha	Black
Oxford White (C)	X	X	X	X	X
Cayman Green (CM)	X			X	X
Mocha Frost (CM)				X	X
Electric Red (CM)	X		X	X	X
Dark Plum (CM)	X			X	X
Crystal Blue Frost (CM)	X	X			X
Twilight Blue (CM)	X	X			X
Black (NC)	X	X	X	X	X
Midnight Opal (CM)	X		X		X
Silver (CM)	X	X	X		X
Super Coupe					
Oxford White (C)	X	X	X		X
Crimson (NC)	X		X		X
Black (NC)	X	X	X		X
Twilight Blue (CM)	X	X			X
Silver (CM)	X	X	X		X

Legend: C means conventional paint; CM means Clearcoat metallic; NC means non-metallic Clearcoat.

Colors and Trims (1993 Late Production)

EXTERIOR COLORS	INTERIOR TRIM COLORS				
Thunderbird LX	Titanium	Crystal Blue	Currant Red	Mocha	Black
Oxford White (C)	X	X	X	X	X
Cayman Green (CM)				X	X
Mocha Frost (CM)				X	X
Electric Red (CM)	X		X	X	X
Bright Red (NC)	X			X	X
Dark Plum (CM)	X			X	X
Crystal Blue Frost (CM)	X	X			X
Twilight Blue (CM)	X	X			X
Black (NC)	X	X	X	X	X
Opal Grey (CM)	X		X		X
Silver (CM)	X	X	X		X
Super Coupe					
Oxford White (C)	X	X	X		X
Bright Red (NC)	X				X
Twilight Blue (CM)	X	X			X
Black (NC)	X	X	X		X
Silver (CM)	X	X	X		X

Legend: C means conventional paint; CM means Clearcoat metallic, NC means non-metallic Clearcoat.

1993 Thunderbird Interior Trim Codes (Early Production)

Seat Type	Material	Opal Grey	Crys. Blue	Mocha	Black	Ruby Red	Opal Grey & White (*)
LX							
Bucket Seats	Luxury Cloth	56	5B	5H	5J	5R	
Bucket Seats	Leather	46		4H	4J		4X
Super Coupe							
Articulated Buckets	Cloth	36	3B		3J	3R	
Articulated Buckets	Leather	P6			PJ		PX

Legend: Luxury Cloth interior includes leather and vinyl components; Crys. Blue means Crystal Blue.

The 1993 stock car racing season caused frustration for Thunderbird fans, as Ford lost the battle for the Manufacturer's Cup after winning seven of the final 12 Winston Cup events. That put the blue oval racers one point behind Chevrolet in the title race. Drivers piloting T-Birds this season included Bill Elliott, Mark Martin, and Ernie Irvan. Driving the Texaco/Robert Yates car, Irvan won his fourth race as a Ford driver when he took the checkered flag at Martinsville on September 26.

A sad note for Ford motorsports was the death of Ford driver Alan Kulwicki in an April 1 small-plane crash near Bristol Speedway. Geoff Bodine later purchased Kulwicki's T-Bird to drive for the Bud Moore/Motorcraft team in 1994.

Towards the end of 1993, Bill Stroppe — the builder of many Ford and Lincoln race cars from the early 1950s on — launched a new Winston Cup effort with three Thunderbirds and Parnelli Jones' son as one driver. Venable Racing also entered NASCAR Winston West competition with a pair of T-Birds. Bob Glidden continued campaigning a 429-powered T-Bird Pro Stocker in NHRA drag racing, while finishing work on a new Pro Stock Mustang. In addition, "Animal" Jim Feuer, made news with a new Pro Mod car called the "Wunderbird," which didn't last long. Late in the 1993 season, the Wunderbird disintegrated after smashing into a guardrail at Maryland International Raceway.

As usual, efforts like the Ford motorsports program kept interest in the new Thunderbirds at a peak. In addition, the fact that the base price of the LX model was substantially reduced helped Thunderbird sales soar upwards. Production reached its highest level since 1988. For the model-year, combined output of LX and Super Coupe models was 122,415 units.

1993 Thunderbird Specifications

Wheelbase	113.0 in.	Standard Engine (Type)	90-degree ohv V-6
Curb Weight	3,267 lb.	Bore x Stroke	3.80 x 3.40 in.
Overall Length	198.7 in.	Displacement:	232 cid (3.8 L)
Overall Width	72.7 in.	Injection	SEFI
Overall Height	52.5 in.	Compression Ratio	9.0:1
Front Tread	61.6 in.	HP @ RPM	140 @ 3800
Rear Tread	60.2 in.	Torque	215 lb.-ft. @ 2400
Front Head Room	38.1 in.	Optional Engine (Type)	90-degree ohv V-6
Rear Head Room	37.5 in.	Bore x Stroke	3.80 x 3.40 in.
Front Leg Room	42.5 in.	Displacement	232 cid (3.8 L)
Rear Leg Room	35.8 in.	Induction	SEFI (Supercharged)
Front Shoulder Room	59 in.	Compression Ratio	8.3:1
Rear Shoulder Room	58.9 in..	HP @ RPM	210 @ 4400
Trunk Volume	15.1 cu. ft.	Torque	315 lb.-ft. @ 2500
Fuel Tank	18 gal.	Optional Engine	90-degree ohv V-8
Tires (LX)	P205/70R15 BSW	Displacement	302 cid (5.0 L)
Tires (SC)	P225/60ZR16 BSW	Injection	SEFI
Weight Distribution	57/43 front/rear	HP @ RPM	200 @ 4000
Turn Circle	39 ft.	Torque	275 lb.-ft. @ 3000

1993 Thunderbird Engineering

Front Suspension	Long spindle SLA type, variable-rate coil springs, tubular gas shocks, stabilizer bar
Rear Suspension	Independent, H-arm design with toe control link variable-rate coil springs, gas shocks, stabilizer bar
Steering	Power rack-and-pinion
Brakes	Power front disc/rear drum on LX; Power four-wheel disc with ABS on Super Coupe

1994
The Evolution Continues

In the 40th year since its introduction, the Thunderbird remained a large, well-equipped, rear-wheel-drive luxury coupe with a relatively affordable price. Window stickers did inch up slightly from 1993. The base model was tagged $16,830, and the Super Coupe listed for $22,240. The first significant styling changes in five years were seen, along with some interior upgrades, and changes in the engine department.

Both models had a more rounded front end and rear end. More pronounced air intake slots characterized the front. A T-Bird badge "flew" in the slot between the new Aero-design halogen In the 40th year since its introduction the Thunderbird remained a large, well-equipped, rear-headlamps, which blended more smoothly into the front feature line. Air for engine cooling was now taken from under the bumper, rather than through a conventional grille. Integrated flush bumpers enhanced the streamlined appearance. An all-new hood was shorter, and the front fenders curved into the hood line to provide even more aerodynamic contours. The doors merged into the roof line and the drip rails were fully concealed. New aero-designed rear view mirrors completed the sleek-looking body package. Ford said that fine-tuning the body surface directed air flow in such a way to create more down-force and improve handling. However, it should be noted that Consumer Reports, while reporting that the '94 Thunderbird exhibited good ride qualities, scored its handling "fairly clumsy."

The totally restyled "organic" interior featured an aircraft-inspired look with twin "pods" for driver and front passenger. Analog gauges were standard equipment. The console swept up into the instrument panel and its curved feature line continued smoothly through to the door panel. A large glove box and dual cup holders in the console were new. Easy-twist round knobs controlled many driving functions. Back-lit instrument panel switches, dual air bags, and a CPC-free manual air conditioning system were also standard equipment. A new option was an Electronic Traction Assist system that linked to the 4-wheel anti-lock brakes.

Exteriors on LX models came with 11 finish options, and eight were new. Nine were Clearcoat Metallics, one was a featured non-metallic Clearcoat, and one used a regular type paint. The Super Coupe offered seven color options. Three were Clearcoat Metallics, one used conventional paint, and two were non-metallic Clearcoats. Crimson, one of the non-metallics, was exclusive for the Super Coupe. Five different color interiors came in the LX. Super Coupe buyers had a choice of four interior colors.

1994 Colors and Trims

EXTERIOR COLORS	INTERIOR TRIM COLORS				
Thunderbird LX	Opal Grey	Evergreen	Mocha	Portofino Blue	Ruby Red
Champagne (CM)	X	X	X		
Electric Red (CM)	X		X		X
Lt. Evergreen Frost (CM)	X	X	X		
Indigo (CM)	X			X	
Midnight Blue (CM)	X		X	X	
Deep Emerald Green (CM)	X	X	X		
Teal (CM)	X		X		
Black (NC)	X	X	X	X	X
Vibrant White (C)	X	X	X	X	X
Opal Frost (CM)	X	X	X	X	X
White Opalescent (NC)	X	X	X	X	X
Super Coupe					
Midnight Blue (C)	X		X	X	
Teal (CM)	X		X	X	X
Black (NC)	X		X	X	X
Vibrant White (C)	X		X	X	X
Crimson (NC)	X		X		X
Opal Frost (CM)	X		X	X	X
White Opalescent (NC)	X		X	X	X

Legend: C means conventional paint; CM means Clearcoat metallic; NC means non-metallic Clearcoat; Lt. means light

250

Minor electronic improvements were made to the base V-6 used in LXs, but the "headline news" was Ford's new 4.6-liter Modular V-8 becoming an option. This single overhead cam engine developed 205 hp. It came attached to an electronically-controlled four-speed automatic transmission that provided "seamless" part-throttle shifts, and positive full-throttle gear-shifting. "I believe the 4.6-liter Modular-powered Thunderbird can hold its own against such highly regarded coupes as the $39,000 Lexus SC 300 — at about half the price," wrote Ron Sessions in *Road & Track's Road Test Annual*. In addition to being more refined than the previous 5.0-liter push rod engine, the new V-8 was also cleaner-burning, and more fuel efficient. It increased gas mileage by one to two miles per gallon.

The 1994 Super Coupe also had a couple of engine refinements. A new Eaton supercharger with low-drag Teflon-coated rotors was used. In addition to being quieter, it upped output by 10 percent to 230 hp. Torque also increased by five percent. Also new were an improved camshaft, a cam-over-cable throttle linkage, and heftier pistons, rods, and cylinder heads to complement the harder-working motor. A five-speed manual gear box remained standard fare, but the electronic four-speed automatic overdrive transmission was optional.

Motor Trend magazine gave its "Driving Impression" of the 1994 Thunderbird LX Coupe in its December 1993 issue. "As the middle child in the Thunderbird lineup, the LX with optional 4.6-liter power suffers from a slight personality crisis," said writer Don Sherman. "It lacks the power-to-weight ratio to fly with the eagles, and its ride and steering calibrations are too firm for the unadulterated luxury set. Of course, it's possible that creative fence straddling is Ford's secret survival strategy for the Thunderbird." Later, in February 1994, *Motor Trend* road tested the V-8-optioned LX. It moved from 0-60 mph in 8.5 seconds, and did the quarter-mile in 16.4 seconds at 87.6 mph. It braked from 60-0 mph in 139 feet.

Apparently, Ford's "secret" strategy worked well, and led to more than just mere survival. Although production totals were not available at the time this book went to the printer, Ford's 12-month sales total for calendar-year 1994 included 130,713 Thunderbirds. This represented a nice increase over the 122,415 cars sold in calendar-year 1993.

In stock car racing, Thunderbirds had a super year in 1993, led by Rusty Wallace in his No. 2 Miller Genuine Draft Ford. Wallace took 10 first place finishes. Geoff Bodine (three wins) and Mark Martin and Jimmy Spencer (two wins each) also put in strong performances all year long. Bill Elliott and Ricky Rudd both had a win apiece, while Brett Bodine, Morgan Shepard, Rick Mast, and Lake Speed contributed valuable Winston Cup points. In 31 contests, Fords sat on the pole 25 times and won 20 checkered flags. They also established 17 new track records. However, it became a clear case of winning the battles and losing the war, as Chevy pilot Dale Earnhardt nailed his seventh Winston Cup points championship with his consistent high-place finishes. One thing that hurt the blue oval effort was Ernie Irvan's wreck of his Texaco T-Bird. The car was a hot contender, with three victories during the first half of '94, but the wreck put Irvan out for the season and longer. Ford did capture NASCAR's Manufacturer's Cup for the second year running.

1994 Thunderbird Specifications

Wheelbase	113.0 in.	Standard Engine (Type)	90-degree 12 ohv V-6
Curb Weight	3,570 lb.	Bore x Stroke	3.80 x 3.40 in.
Overall Length	200.3 in.	Displacement	232 cid (3.8 L)
Overall Width	72.7 in.	Injection	SEFI
Overall Height	52.5 in.	Compression Ratio	9.0:1
Front Tread	61.6 in.	HP @ RPM	140 @ 3800
Rear Tread	60.2 in.	Torque	215 lb.-ft. @ 2400
Front Head Room	38.1 in.	Optional Engine (Type)	90-degree 12 ohv V-6
Rear Head Room	37.5 in.	Bore x Stroke	3.80 x 3.40 in.
Front Leg Room	42.5 in.	Displacement	232 cid (3.8 L)
Rear Leg Room	35.8 in.	Induction	SEFI (Supercharged)
Front Shoulder Room	59 in.	Compression Ratio	8.3:1
Rear Shoulder Room	58.9 in.	HP @ RPM	230 @ 4400
Trunk Volume	15.1 cu. ft.	Torque	330 lb.-ft. @ 2500
Fuel Tank	18 gal.	Optional Engine	90-degree 16 ohv V-8
Tires (LX)	P205/70R15 BSW	Displacement	281 cid (4.6 L)
Tires (SC)	P225/60ZR16 BSW	Injection	SEFI
Weight Distribution	57/43 front/rear	HP @ RPM	205 @ 4500
Turn Circle	39 ft.	Torque	265 lb.-ft. @ 3200

1994 Thunderbird Engineering

Front Suspension	Long spindle SLA type, variable-rate coil springs, tubular gas shocks, stabilizer bar
Rear Suspension	Independent, H-arm design with toe control link variable-rate coil springs, gas shocks, stabilizer bar
Steering	Power rack-and-pinion
Brakes	Power front disc/rear drum on LX; Power four-wheel disc with ABS on Super Coupe

1995
Not Since Hitchcock

After capturing its second NASCAR Manufacturer's Cup in a row, Ford entered 1995 with a dramatic television ad promoting its latest stock cars as the most ominous thing to come from "bird-dom" since Alfred Hitchcock's classic thriller film "The Birds." It was a fitting throwback to the era in which the first Thunderbird was created, and a reminder to many of the marque's continuing vitality on its 40th birthday. As the '95 Ford sales catalog asks, "How many cars on the road today can you identify at a glance, whose badges elicit instant recognition and admiration? There certainly aren't many, but one should readily come to mind. It's the familiar Thunderbird wide wingspan."

In 1994, the T-Bird got its first significant changes since 1989 with new interiors and a freshened up exterior. This 1995 T-Bird LX was little-changed. (Ford Motor Co.)

The 1995 T-Bird SC sported integral front fog lamps, lower body cladding, and a unique rear fascia. (Ford Motor Co.)

The 1995 T-Bird LX instrument panel featured analog performance instrumentation. Driver and front passenger air bags were standard. (Ford Motor Co.)

The sales catalog also notes that the Thunderbird has undergone changes in its 40-year history. "Changes in size. Changes in shape. Evolution." But, it accurately points out that the current model may be the closest in spirit to the original Thunderbird concept (at least when the original had its fiberglass hardtop attached). "Its identity as a distinctive personal coupe is as evident today as it was when it came on the scene for the first time," says the brochure. "Its performance side, represented by the exhilarating Super Coupe with its high-tech componentry, is more exciting than ever."

The 1995 Thunderbird itself has few changes from the 1994 model. Offered again, are the LX and Super Coupe models. Both have slightly more shoulder room front and rear and modest weight changes. The LX continues to utilize the 3.8-liter 140-hp V-6 as the standard power plant, with the Modular V-8 as an option. The Super Coupe again comes with a 230-hp supercharged version of the V-6, plus a standard five-speed manual transmission and anti-lock braking system. Dual air bags are standard in both models and a Traction Control system is optional with both. The LX is base-priced at $17,225, and the Super Coupe is $22,735.

Speed-sensitive power steering that reduces the amount of power assist as speed increases has become an option for the LX with a V-6 engine. Conventional power steering is standard on that model. Variable-assist steering is standard in LXs with the optional V-8, and in Super Coupes. Also, Ford no longer locates its compact disc (CD) changer in the Thunderbird's trunk. Instead, an in-dash CD player is optional. An anti-theft alarm is also on the T-Bird's options list.

Although it is early in the year, both the 1995 sales picture and stock-car racing picture seem gloomy. Thunderbird sales for January and February 1995 total 15,140 cars, compared to 25,107 for the same period a year earlier. In addition, early racing results at Daytona, Rockingham, and Richmond suggest that the new-for-1995 Chevy Monte Carlo race cars will pose a serious threat to the T-Birds in NASCAR Winston Cup competition. Will a hot-selling "40th Anniversary" edition T-Bird race to the rescue in the sales battle? Will the blue oval stock cars start flocking to the finish line? Don't be amazed if such things happen. After all, through 40 years of thunder, the T-Bird has proven itself an amazing American automobile.

Luxury cloth bucket seats were standard in the 1995. (Ford Motor Co.)

1995 Thunderbird Specifications

Wheelbase	113.0 in.	Standard Engine (Type)	90-degree 12 ohv V-6
Curb Weight	3,536 lb.	Bore x Stroke	3.80 x 3.40 in.
Overall Length	200.3 in.	Displacement:	232 cid (3.8 L)
Overall Width	72.7 in.	Injection	SEFI
Overall Height	52.5 in.	Compression Ratio	9.0:1
Front Tread	61.6 in.	HP @ RPM	140 @ 3800
Rear Tread	60.2 in..	Torque	215 lb.-ft. @ 2400
Front Head Room	38.1 in.	Optional Engine (Type)	90-degree 12 ohv V-6
Rear Head Room	37.5 in.	Bore x Stroke	3.80 x 3.40 in.
Front Leg Room	42.5 in.	Displacement	232 cid (3.8 L)
Rear Leg Room	35.8 in.	Induction	SEFI (Supercharged)
Front Shoulder Room	59.1 in.	Compression Ratio	8.3:1
Rear Shoulder Room	58.9 in..	HP @ RPM	230 @ 4400
Trunk Volume	15.1 cu. ft.	Torque	330 lb.-ft. @ 2500
Fuel Tank	18 gal.	Optional Engine	90-degree 16 ohv V-8
Tires (LX)	P205/70R15 BSW	Displacement	281 cid (4.6 L)
Tires (SC)	P225/60ZR16 BSW	Injection	SEFI
Weight Distribution	57/43 front/rear	HP @ RPM	205 @ 4500
Turn Circle	39 ft.	Torque	265 lb.-ft. @ 3200

1995 Thunderbird Engineering

Front Suspension	Long spindle SLA type, variable-rate coil springs, tubular gas shocks, stabilizer bar
Rear Suspension	Independent, H-arm design with toe control link variable-rate coil springs, gas shocks, stabilizer bar
Steering	Power rack-and-pinion
Brakes	Power front disc/rear drum on LX; Power four-wheel disc with ABS on Super Coupe

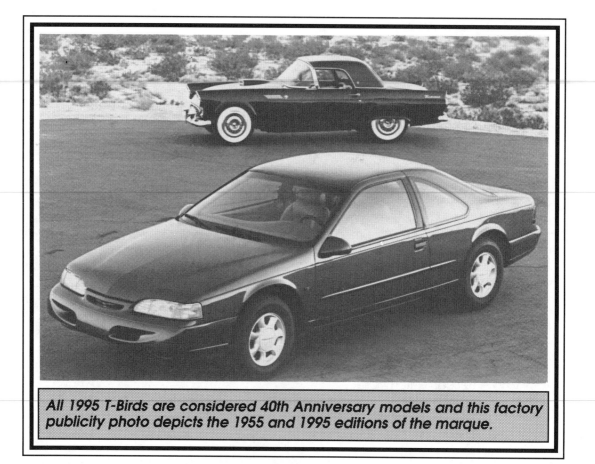

All 1995 T-Birds are considered 40th Anniversary models and this factory publicity photo depicts the 1955 and 1995 editions of the marque.

1996
Winding Down

With the discontinuation of the Super Coupe for 1996, Thunderbird was reduced to a one-model series, the LX Coupe. Just four years earlier, for 1992, the lineup had consisted of four distinct models—base Coupe, Sport Coupe, LX Coupe, and Super Coupe. But even with four separate offerings for that year, total sales had come in at a disappointing 73,892. For 1993 the series was dropped to two models, LX and Super Coupe, and sales recovered rather impressively to 129,712. Continuing for 1994 with two models, sales dipped slightly to 120,320 and again, for two-model 1995, to 114,823. With this latest move to just one model, it didn't take a rocket scientist to see the writing on the wall. Ford product planners were taking at hard look at the continuing viability of the venerable T-Bird in a changing and highly competitive marketplace. Their concerns were justified when sales for 1996 tallied up to just 85,029.

The obvious was not lost on the editors of Automobile Magazine who had the following to say about the 1996 offering: "The Thunderbird has received a mild face-lift for the 1996 model year; it seems to get a nip here and a tuck there about once every two years. This is, we suppose, the sign of an aging automobile. Nevertheless, this is one of Ford's best chassis thanks to some thoughtful and careful tuning. The Thunderbird handles well when you really lean on it, although the power steering feels overassisted, making it difficult to dive neatly into a fast bend. The real problem with the Thunderbird, though, has always been that it's not sure what it wants to be, a sports car or a luxury coupe. After all, it's a big car, stretching 16.7 feet, a full sixteen inches more than the four-door Ford Contour, so it feels out of place on a tight twist of road. Inside, everything looks okay, but you feel cramped and crowded, and you can forget about using the rear seats. On the other hand, we appreciate the rear-wheel-drive layout, and both of the engines are quite good. The standard engine is a 145-bhp, 3.8-liter V-6, which is fine for most people, but we favor the optional 205-bhp, SOHC 4.6-liter V-8. Neither engine, however, can be mated to a five-speed manual gearbox. In the end, the Thunderbird may be a good value, but it lacks the liveliness of the Ford Probe GT or the Ford Taurus SHO."

For 1996 the LX model received a mild restyling in the hood, grille, headlight, and bumper cover areas. Wide body cladding and now door handles were color-keyed to match the exterior paint for what Ford called "a sporty, monochromatic look." The stan-

A mild face-lift for 1996 included a center-mounted T-Bird ornament on a honeycomb grille, new hood and front bumper facing, complex-reflector clear-lens head- and signal lights, wider body cladding, and door handles color-keyed to the exterior paint. (Ford Motor Co.)

dard 3.8-liter V-6 was upgraded and was now rated at 145 hp. At a list price of $17,485, also standard were dual front air bags, manual air conditioning, full-length console with floor-mounted shift lever, full analog instrumentation, luxury cloth seats with front buckets, and an AM/FM stereo cassette sound system with four speakers. The revised 4.6-liter SOHC V-8 was part of an option package that cost $835 and also included speed-sensitive power steering, battery upgrade, six-way power driver's seat, power windows, illuminated entry system, and leather-wrapped steering wheel. Optional at no cost was a package consisting of rear window defroster, P215/70R15 tires, and cast aluminum wheels. An antitheft system and traction control returned as optional equipment after not being offered the year previous. The four-speed automatic overdrive transmission was standard.

1996 Thunderbird Specifications

Wheelbase	113.0 in.	Weight Distribution	57/43 front/rear
Curb Weight	3,561 lb.	Turn Circle	39 ft.
Overall Length	200.3 in.	Standard Engine (Type)	90-degree 12 ohv V6
Overall Width	72.7 in.	Bore x Stroke	3.80 x 3.40 in.
Overall Height	52.5 in	Displacement:	232 cid (3.8 L)
Front Tread	61.6 in.	Injection	SEFI
Rear Tread	60.2 in.	Compression Ratio	9.0:1
Front Head Room	38.1 in.	HP @ RPM	145 @ 4000
Rear Head Room	37.5 in.	Torque	N/A
Front Leg Room	42.5 in.	Optional Engine	90-degree SOHC V-8
Rear Leg Room	35.8 in.	Bore & Stroke	3.60 x 3.60
Front Shoulder Room	59.1 in.	Displacement	281 cid (4.6 L)
Rear Shoulder Room	58.9 in.	Injection	SEFI
Trunk Volume	15.1 cu. ft.	HP @ RPM	205 @ 4500
Fuel Tank	18 gal.	Torque	265 lb.-ft. @ 3200
Tires	P205/70R15 BSW		

1996 Thunderbird Engineering

Front Suspension	Long spindle SLA type, variable-rate coil springs, tubular gas shocks, stabilizer bar
Rear Suspension	Independent, H-arm design with toe control link variable-rate coil springs, gas shocks, stabilizer bar
Steering	Power rack-and-pinion
Brakes	Power front disc/rear drum

For 1996, rear-view identification was enhanced by the stylized Thunderbird emblem displayed on each taillight. (Ford Motor Co.)

1997
End of an Era

In its final appearance after 43 years of continuous production, Thunderbird entered the marketplace for 1997 once again as a one-model series, the LX Coupe. T-Bird sales had been sliding steadily downward for the preceding four years with 1996 totals off fully 34.4 percent from those of 1993. It was becoming abundantly obvious to industry insiders and the automotive press that the fate of Thunderbird was hanging by a thread. *Car and Driver* magazine, in its October 1996 "Charting the Changes" feature, pointed out that, "Last year a major styling makeover didn't cure the T-Bird's slipping sales, but Ford is leaving the big two-door alone for 1997."

The editors of *Automobile Magazine* once again offered their sage insights into the situation saying, "The Thunderbird has at times been an important car to Ford, first as a glamour car that the wealthy and famous arrived in and middle-class strivers aspired to. Later recast as a popularly priced car with a measure of style, the T-Bird's importance came from sheer sales volumes, which reached 1.3 million during the '70s. But now, it seems this famous nameplate is on Ford's back burner. The current T-Bird has been around since 1989. It gets a new grille and front bumper every couple of years and periodic interior updates. For 1997 there's a new gauge cluster, newly standard four-wheel-disc brakes, and minor tweaks to improve the shift quality of the automatic transmission. The supercharged Thunderbird SC is gone (Ed. note: The last appearance of the Super Coupe was for 1995), but a fine engine is available in the 205-bhp, 4.6-liter V-8. It's worth the extra money over the standard 145-bhp, 3.8-liter V-6. The problem with the Thunderbird is that it's going through one of its periodic identity crises. Though it has an impressive overhead-cam V-8 and rear-wheel drive, it's too big and heavy to be a sporty car. The rear-wheel drive ends up being a negative for people who live in snowy climates. The coupe body is swoopy enough to make the back seat useless, but it isn't especially good looking." *Automobile Magazine* then offered this bit of prophecy and advice, "The new T-Bird will arrive early in the next decade; it's time Ford gave it a new flight plan."

Ford Motor Co., on the other hand, understandably tried to put a more positive spin on things calling T-Bird, "The leader of the midsize specialty market . . . ." and pointing out that it, ". . . also offers new options, like a power sliding moonroof and fresh exterior and interior colors."

In a press release dated Sept. 4, 1996, Ford Public Affairs summed up the new, 1997 Thunderbird thusly, "Aggressive and sporty, Ford Thunderbird is recognized as the classic American sport coupe. True to its 42-year heritage, Thunderbird is an affordable rear-wheel-drive sport coupe built for those who love to drive.

While praised by the automotive press for its excellent engine offerings (particularly the 4.6-liter SOHC V-8), Thunderbird drew criticism for being ". . . too big and heavy to be a sporty car." (Ford Motor Co.)

257

For those looking for extra performance, Thunderbird offers the only V-8 in its segment and a Sport package that includes 16-inch wheels and an upgraded suspension.

The standard 3.8-liter V-6 produces 145 horsepower at 4000 rpm and 215 lb-ft of torque at 2750 rpm. The optional 4.6-liter V-8 develops 205 hp at 4250 rpm and 280 lb-ft of torque at 3000 rpm." The press release also mentioned that, "Thunderbird's standard 4R70W four-speed electronically-controlled automatic overdrive transmission is upgraded for better quality and corrosion protection."

Addressing the matter of changes and new features Ford went on to say, "A new instrument cluster prominently arranges key functions in three separate displays, and a new console provides easy-access dual cup holders, a larger ashtray, and a coin holder. In addition to the new Sport package, other options geared to Thunderbird's free-sprited buyers include a power sliding moonroof with a one-touch open feature and 15-inch, seven-spoke chrome aluminum wheels. A decklid spoiler with integrated stoplight became available in late 1996. Three new exterior color selections include: Light Prairie Tan, Light Denim Blue, and Arctic Green. Prairie Tan is also a new interior color."

The list price of $17,885 was up very slightly from 1996 and still represented excellent value with standard features like the 145-hp V-6, dual front air bags, manual air conditioning,

In its final year of production, 1997, the external appearance of the Thunderbird LX Coupe remained virtually unchanged from that of 1996. (Ford Motor Co.)

Of the 1997 version, Ford Public Affairs enthusiastically declared "Aggressive and sporty, Ford Thunderbird is recognized as the classic American sport coupe." Few outside of Ford's inner circle knew that this would be its final appearance. (Ford Motor Co.)

power four-wheel-disc brakes (improved over 1996's front disc/rear drum setup), full analog instrumentation, luxury cloth seats with front buckets, cruise control, power windows, tilt steering wheel, dual remote-controlled electric color-keyed exterior mirrors, power door locks, and a four-speaker AM/FM stereo cassette sound system. The 4.6-liter SOHC V-8 was again part of an option package—this time priced at $840—that also included speed-sensitive power steering, battery upgrade, six-way power driver's seat, illuminated entry system, and leather-wrapped steering wheel. Optional at no cost was a package consisting of rear window defroster, P215/70RX5 tires, and cast aluminum wheels. An antitheft system and traction control returned as optional equipment. Also offered were leather-faced seats, chrome-plated wheels, Power-operated moonroof, and rear decklid spoiler. Drivers of a more adventurous bent could opt for the Sport package, which consisted of 16-inch, nine-spoke aluminum wheels wearing P225/60R16 touring tires, a larger rear stabilizer bar, larger front disc brake rotors, revised spring rates, revised front lower arm bushings, revised shock absorber valving, and the rear decklid spoiler with integral stop lamp. The four-speed automatic overdrive transmission was standard.

When the 1997 model year ended, sales had totalled just 73,814 units, the lowest level in six years. So, perhaps inevitably, the plug was finally pulled on one of the best-known American automobile nameplates in history. *Car and Driver* magazine, commenting in its "Charting the Changes for '98" section (October 1997), delivered a rather abrupt and unceremonious obituary when it pronounced, "The Aerostar, the Aspire, the Probe, and the Thunderbird are dead."

1997 Thunderbird Specifications

Wheelbase	113.0 in.	Weight Distribution	57/43 front/rear
Curb Weight	3,561 lb.	Turn Circle	39 ft.
Overall Length	200.3 in.	Standard Engine (Type)	90-degree 12 ohv V-6
Overall Width	72.7 in.	Bore x Stroke	3.80 x 3.40 in.
Overall Height	52.5 in	Displacement	232 cid (3.8 L)
Front Tread	61.6 in.	Injection	SEFI
Rear Tread	60.2 in.	Compression Ratio	9.0:1
Front Head Room	38.1 in.	HP @ RPM	145 @ 4000
Rear Head Room	37.5 in.	Torque	215 lb.-ft. @ 2750
Front Leg Room	42.5 in.	Optional Engine	90-degree SOHC V-8
Rear Leg Room	35.8 in.	Bore & Stroke	3.60 x 3.60
Front Shoulder Room	59.1 in.	Displacement	281 cid (4.6 L)
Rear Shoulder Room	58.9 in.	Injection	SEFI
Trunk Volume	15.1 cu. ft.	HP @ RPM	205 @ 4500
Fuel Tank	18 gal.	Torque	280 lb.-ft. @ 3000
Tires			P205/70R15 BSW

1997 Thunderbird Engineering

Front Suspension	Long spindle SLA type, variable-rate coil springs, tubular gas shocks, stabilizer bar
Rear Suspension	Independent, H-arm design with toe control link variable-rate coil springs, gas shocks, stabilizer bar
Steering	Power rack-and-pinion
Brakes	Power front/rear disc

THE 1997 LIMITED EDITION THUNDERBIRD

(Shown in Laser Red Tinted Clearcoat with Silver molding insert)

Since the first Thunderbird rolled off the line in 1954, this brand has had an avid following. Car enthusiasts are always looking for ways to distinguish their vehicles from other Thunderbirds. That is why we are introducing the clean yet tasteful 1997 Limited Edition Thunderbird.

SIMPLE HASSLE FREE ORDERING

- Just add Option Code 31B D9H
- Arrives to your dealership complete.
- 7 years parts availability.

WARRANTY

- The Limited Edition package is fully backed by a one year/12K warranty.

QUALITY COMPANY

- Promotional Trim Conversions, Inc. is one of the first companies worldwide to receive QS9000 certification.
- "Limited Edition" package has been approved and is monitored by Ford Motor Company.

In what may have been a last-ditch effort to revive sagging sales, Ford Motor Co. offered its dealers the opportunity to specify Option Code 31B D9H when ordering new, 1997 T-Birds. The option package added distinctive cosmetic elements to the basic Thunderbird in an attempt to lure more buyers.

PACKAGE CONTENTS & ORDERING INFORMATION

- Two cloisonné "Limited Edition" fender medallions.
- Color keyed, high pile embroidered floormats in Medium Graphite or Light Prairie Tan.
- Colored rub strip molding insert in red or silver with "Limited Edition" nomenclature.
- *Do not order with factory floor mats.*
- Availability on all exterior colors and pep packages.
- *Only available on Thunderbirds with Medium Graphite or Light Prairie Tan interiors.*
- **Option Code 31B D9H.**

PRICED FOR PROFIT

- **45% mark-up.**
- WSD $165.00
- MSRP $239.00*

  * You will be invoiced separately for the Limited Edition package by Promotional Trim Conversions, Inc. An addendum window label will list the suggested retail price.

MOLDING INSERT COLOR CHART

Exterior Color	Code	Medium Graphite	Light Prairie Tan
Light Prairie Tan	BA	N/A	R
Arctic Green	D6	S	R
Laser Red	E9	S	S
Moonlight Blue	KM	S	N/A
Pacific Green	PS	S	R
Alpine Green	SR	S	R
Silver Frost	TS	R	N/A
Black	UA	S	R
White Opalescent	WR	S	R
Vibrant White	WT	S	R
Light Denim Blue	K1	S	N/A

S = Silver   R = Resilient Red

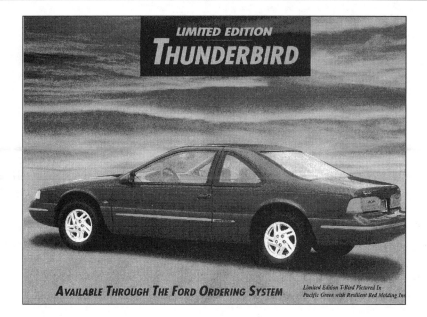

LIMITED EDITION THUNDERBIRD

AVAILABLE THROUGH THE FORD ORDERING SYSTEM

Limited Edition T-Bird Pictured In Pacific Green with Resilient Red Molding Insert

Days of Thunder
Motorsport
NASCAR
Thunderbirds

Coors/Motorcraft Ford Thunderbird

Havoline Star Ford Thunderbird

Crisco/Motorcraft Ford Thunderbird

Citgo Ford Thunderbird

Zerex/Amoco Ford Thunderbird

Bull's Eye Barbecue Sauce Ford Thunderbird

Stroh Light Ford Thunderbird

Seven of the NASCAR Thunderbirds that raced in 1988. Davey Allison drove the number 28 Havoline T-Bird. Kyle Petty drove the number 21 Citgo T-Bird. Benny Parsons drove the number 90 Bull's Eye BBQ 'Bird. Bill Elliott was the driver of the Coors T-Bird, number 9 Car number 15, sponsored by Crisco, was driven by Buddy Baker. Alan Kulwicki piloted the number 7 Zerex-sponsored car. Strohs sponsored Mark Martin in car number 6. (Phil Hall Collection)

Sticking out from behind 1953 'Vette you can see a T-Bird fender. The unauthorized drag race took place just outside Pinecastle Air Force Base, in Orlando, Fla. in 1955. (Werner Schleissing photo)

Johnny Beauchamp's No. 73 T-Bird nearest camera was named winner of first Daytona 500. Joe Weatherly's No. 48 Chevy was a lap down. Lee Petty's No. 42 Olds, in center, was the actual winner.

Before pictures of photo finish were reviewed, Scottie McCormick — Miss Daytona Speedway — greeted T-Bird driver Johnny Beauchamp in the winner's circle. (Gray-Rock Archives)

Tom Pistone drove the No. 59 Thunderbird in the first Daytona 500 in 1959. He was running with the leaders prior to this pit stop. He eventually finished eighth. (Gray-Rock Archives)

Neil Houston wheels a battered ex-Holman & Moody Thunderbird in a 1962 USAC stock car race at Milwaukee, Wis. The car, owned by Grover Farbin, was updated from a 1959 to a 1960 model to meet the three model-year rule in effect at the time. (Phil Hall Collection)

The April 1, 1979 Southeastern 500 at Bristol, Tenn. Dale Earnhardt's No. 2 Monte Carlo won, Bobby Allison's No. 15 T-Bird was second and Darrell Waltrip's No. 88 Chevy was third (Phil Hall Collection)

Cale Yarbrough shocked the NASCAR troops when he switched from GM to Ford for the 1985 season. Eventually, many other top drivers would do the same. (Phil Hall Collection)

Not all Thunderbirds were raced in NASCAR. The Thrush Turbo 500 T-Bird was active in drag racing during 1983. It was sponsored by the Thrush Mufflers Co. (Old Cars photo)

The Hardee's No. 28 T-Bird made an appearance at the Chicago Historic Races at Road America, in Elkhart Lake, Wis., in 1992. (Ron Kowalke photo)

Bud Moore's crew pushes the Bobby Allison 1979 Thunderbird to the starting line for the July 14, 1979 Busch Nashville 420 at Nashville (Tenn.) International Raceway. Allison started second and finished 16th in the event. (Phil Hall Collection)

The Aero 'Bird was car of choice for the 7-Eleven/Brooks Racing team in IMSA Camel GTO road racing in 1985. David Brassfield's car had a tube frame, fiberglass body and 351-cid V-8. (Phil Hall Collection)

Mark Martin and Jack Roush jelled as a 1989 team. Mark got his first Winston Cup win and six poles, tying him with Alan Kulwicki for the most poles. Here Mark tests the Strohs Light T-Bird. (Phil Hall Collection)

It took Ford awhile, but a V-6 program evolved for NASCAR Busch Grand National events. Here Morgan Shepherd warms up in the Texas Pete entry prior to the 1991 Goody's 300 at Daytona. (Phil Hall Collection)

Upon switching to the Junior Johnson Coors T-Bird for 1992, Bill Elliott got off to a fast start. He won four races in a row after the Daytona 500, but didn't win again until the season finale. (Phil Hall Collection)

Alan Kulwicki, in car No. 7, battled Bill Elliott's number 11 T-Bird, plus all the other Winston Cup drivers on the circuit, to take the 1992 championship. The pair of Thunderbird drivers ended up first and second in points, with Kulwicki taking the title by the slimmest of margins ... only 10 points. (Phil Hall Collection)

In Search of "Gold": Myth or Fact?

(**Ed. note:** The following material is reprinted from *Thunderbird Script*, the journal of the International Thunderbird Club (ITC), with the permission of its editor, Dr. Richard L. Schatz, of Sugarloaf, Pa.)
Lately, on the Internet, a lot of questions have again surfaced concerning a "Gold Top" Thunderbird. This car was to have been a rare production number with a vinyl half-roof and a sliding roof panel. Jim Cassidy, chairman of the very successful 6th Annual ITC convention, claims to have seen one years ago so described. Mark Conforzi, guest speaker from Ford Motor Company at our awards banquet, told Jim that there was an experimental unit with a landau-type leatherette top made in the early '60s.

Given the above information to perhaps carry some weight, I think we can be sure that numbers of these, if any, were in fact *not* produced. There have, however, been some stories of owners who, on their own, installed vinyl tops and other paraphernalia on their sunroofs or other hardtop birds. So what really was this "Golde" top designation? Read now, in the reprint article from our premiere issue of the *Script* (January 1994), what concours guru Martin Brugmans has to say on the subject.

Dr. Richard L. Schatz

This title may lead you to think that I have finally flipped out and am heading for the Klondike to strike it rich. Well, rest assured this hasn't happened yet, although some days I may get close to it, especially during these winter months.

For years now, when traveling around the country and attending regional and national meets, at some point in conversation (talking T-Birds, of course) the subject of the 1960 square bird "Gold Top" comes up. Some of you may have had the same experience. Has anyone ever seen one? No! Nobody that I know or have ever talked to. Have any of you reading this ever seen one? I would like to hear from you if you have.

The story of the Gold Top seems to be that they are very rare, a limited production. Apparently, as some tell the story, the hardtop unit had a vinyl-covered roof such as the later Landau, a sort of golden-brown color. The production numbers of these units varied from story or magazine articles to be from 500 to 2500, or so. This is not so rare that somebody shouldn't know of one somewhere. Needless to say, this rare Thunderbird was becoming more intriguing (to me) as time went by. Towards the end of 1992, I happened to purchase Consumers Guide Publications' *New Complete Book of Collectible Cars 1930-90* by the authors and editors of same. Once again, and in print in a resource book for all to read and carry on the phantom Gold Top story is reference to this rare Thunderbird. One thing this book gave was the production number of 2536 units. This is the exact same number as the very desirable 1960 sunroof. But the sunroofs were included in the production numbers of the 1960 hardtop.

Toward the end of the year, I made a visit to Ford Motor Company of Canada Ltd. to pick up some literature on production numbers from Sandy in the archives. As soon as I saw the model year 1960 and the description of body type, it all came to light. Listed here in plain view were two-door hardtops, convertibles, and the two-door Golde Top (2536 units built). There was no listing of a sunroof, but the Golde Top production number was the same. This can no longer be coincidence. The Gold Top (now Golde) and sunroof are the same car. It must then be assumed that Ford, in 1960, used a different name in reference to the "sunroof" as we know it today. Perhaps it was named after one of the design engineers or someone in the executive (branch) at Ford. Sandy and I tried to find out through internal channels, but could not then discover the origin of the name.

It is also curious to note that under "body type", on paper Ford referred to this model as a 63B. On the actual sunroofs, all data plates show the body type as 63A, the same as the regular hardtops. Not until 1962 would 63B be used to identify the Landau models. However, in 1960 and 1962, models were already in the design and prototype stages.

Since these late developments in my search for Gold (Golde), I had occasion to talk with Gary Kerr, one of the founding members of the Southern Ontario Thunderbird Club (he used to come to some of our events). Gary told me that in conversations with Larry Seyfarth in the early 1980s (Larry was president of the Vintage Thunderbird Club of America back then and also worked for FoMoCo), the sunroof came up in conversation and Larry made mention of a company called Golde that was involved in the sunroof project.

A lot of questions we had earlier were now starting to make sense.

As we know today, all 1955-1960 Thunderbird bodies were built by the Budd Company and assembled at the Wixom, Mich. assembly plant. It would seem that a German company by the name of Golde must have supplied the technology and mechanical parts for the sunroof option offered only for one year, 1960. There is also a reference to this made In a technical article "Ford Buyers Guide" (October 1992) by Willam Wonder, who is currently the 1961-1963 Technical Advisor for ITC's *Thunderbird Script*.

So, In closing, let me conclude that all findings seem to indicate the "Gold Top" and sunroof are one in the same. The production numbers also back this up. The use of 63B to indicate a body type may have led to the confusion of a vinyl roof as in the 1962 Landaus. The term "Golde Top" was Ford's way of identifying the new, open-top model that we today refer to simply as "sunroof."

It is hoped that this is the end of my search for Gold. If however, someone out there can prove me wrong, I would be happy to hear from you. In the meantime, I'll refer to all of you with 1960 sunroofs as owners of a rare and desirable Golde Top, unique in all the world.

Martin Brugmans

(**Ed. note:** Martin Brugmans currently serves as the official Concours Chair for the International Thunderbird Club and resides in Oakville, Ontario, Canada.

Model Year 1960 - Production Figures

On the Internet Thunderbird list, there are a lot of questions posed to me concerning the Thunderbird "Gold Top" edition or option. I must say that I never saw a reference to a "Golde Edition." The production of 377 with the 430-cid V-8 engine option and the balance of 2,159 with the standard 352-cid engine, for a total of 2,536 seems correct. Ford did differentiate body types of the three models, but only on paper, not on the actual vehicle data plates. From the Automotive Assembly Division, General Office, production numbers for 1960 Thunderbirds are listed as follows:

Vehicle Line	Model	Design	Body Type	Number Produced
Thunderbird	63A	2 Door	Hardtop	78,447
Thunderbird	76A	2 Door	Convertible	11,860
Thunderbird	63B*	2 Door	Golde Top	2,536
Total Thunderbird				92,843

The above information came from the Ford archives.

*Note: The model number 63B designated the 1960 2 door Golde Top on Ford Motor Company paperwork, but was never used on the 1960 Thunderbird Data Plate. The 63B was not used again on 'Birds until the "Vinyl Top Landaus" came on the scene for 1962. If someone had seen the reference "63B" on a 1960 model as above, it may have led to confusion and the assumption that there was a 1960 with a gold-colored vinyl top out there somewhere. One has never been found yet, unless an aftermarket addition.

Martin Brugmans

This photo clearly shows the airfoil at the leading edge of the roof on the 1960 Thunderbird two-door Golde Top (sunroof) owned by Robert Horan, a member of the International Thunderbird Club from Hazlet, New Jersey. Its purpose is to minimize drafts to the interior when the sunroof is in the open position.

The Golde-design movable sunroof panel of Robert Horan's 1960 Thunderbird drops downward before retracting into the rear portion of the vehicle's roof.

Addendum:

As a follow-up to the Golde Top article, Sandy Notarianni—an historian at Ford Motor Company of Canada Ltd. and the "Sandy" referred to in Martin Brugmans' article—made a further discovery. She found that George H. Dammann and James K. Wagner, in their book *The Cars of Lincoln Mercury*, captioned one photo for 1968 in part, "The electrically-powered sunroof pictured on this particular Mark III was a custom creation, made and installed by American Sunroof Corporation, of Southgate, Mich., a licensee for the German Golde design."

So, the final nail is driven down, and we can lay this Golde Top to rest—the story, that is, not those beautiful sunroofs!

Dr. Richard L. Schatz

The 1960 Thunderbird two-door Golde Top (sunroof) owned by Roger and Judy Gill, of Chicago Heights, Illinois.

A New Beginning?

The Ford Thunderbird was quietly and unceremoniously phased out of production at the end of the 1997 model year. First introduced in 1954 as a 1955 model, the T-Bird underwent many transformations over its 43-year production run reflecting the changing tastes of the car-buying public as well as economic and environmental concerns. But the plug was ultimately pulled during that final year. A subsequent press release from Ford recounted in detail the changing fortunes of the Thunderbird during its history and concluded by saying, "But as the 20th century grew to a close, customer's tastes again shifted away from Thunderbird, as they had in the late 1950s. Continuing sales declines led Ford to announce the 1997 model would be the last—for a time." At the same time, Jac Nasser, then president of Ford's automotive operations, let there be no mistake when he declared that although the old platform was going away, the Thunderbird nameplate would see a bright future in a very familiar form.

Nasser's comments had left the door open for an eventual return of Thunderbird to the marketplace, but just what was meant by "in a very familiar form"? Chrysler Corp. had won overwhelming acceptance of its retro-style concept vehicles beginning in the late 1980s. Parting from convention, Chrysler actually began bringing some of these concepts to the marketplace thereby enjoying immense corporate image enhancement. Dodge's Viper emerged for 1992, Plymouth's Prowler entered production in March of 1997, and most recently the Chrysler PT Cruiser hit the streets as a 2001 model. And, as if these weren't enough, Volkswagen's "New Beetle" retromobile was a runaway, unqualified success right out of the gate. The market impact of these offerings was not lost on Ford.

Could a retro T-Bird be what Ford had in mind? Determined Dearborn watchers of the automotive press wasted no time in raising their periscopes and zeroing in on just such a possibility. On the cover of its June 1998 issue, *Car and Driver* magazine featured an artist's conception of what it called "Ford's Retro Thunderbird." The article inside cited Chrysler's successes with its own approach to the retro look and suggested that Ford would jump on the same bandwagon ". . . though probably to a less startling degree . . . ." It continued, "Our sources say it won't be an exact replica of the 1955-'57 T-Bird, but that's where the new car's styling inspiration comes from." *Car and Driver* even had some insights into the proposed vehicle's platform engineering saying, "The new Thunderbird has been designed from the ground up as a convertible, and it's definitely not a chopped-up hardtop or a stretched Mustang. Our spies tell us it's built on the same platform that the new Lincoln LS8 and Jaguar X200 sedans will share." Discussing the likely use of underpinnings like rack-and-pinion steering, independent suspension, and four-wheel-disc brakes, the magazine speculated that the new car would have a definitely sporting nature. Commenting on what would be under the hood, *C and D* said, "The engine will likely be a 4.0-liter V-8, also destined for the new mid-size X200. It's derived from the 290-hp V-8 that powers current Jaguars, but it will make less power . . . ."

Car and Driver followed up on this in the "Charting the Changes for '99" feature of its October 1998 issue saying, "And of cars that disappear, what's the word? **Thunderbird:** A retro-roadster based on the new Lincoln LS platform will pick up the T-Bird moniker in 2000."

In its own October 1998 issue, *Motor Trend* magazine, in a piece entitled "New Ford T-Bird Ready To Fly, First Look", announced, "Along with resurrecting the two-seat/rear-drive configuration of the classic '55-'57 models, the troops in Dearborn plan to infuse this modern rendition with a good bit of the visual impact of those first T-Birds, as well." *MT* also cited the recent retro success stories from Chrysler and Volkswagen, but went one step further in pointing out a Ford/Volkswagen connection. "J Mays, recently appointed vice president of design at Ford Motor Company, did express some minor concern to us about whether this new/old T-Bird may be pushing the envelope too far—despite his perspective that 'retro appears to be very commercial, although you wouldn't want to do it on everything.'

An automotive legend was reborn when the Ford Thunderbird made its return as an all-new concept car on Jan. 3, 1999 at the North American International Auto show in Detroit. (Ford Motor Co.)

"Mays well knows the viability of re-invigorating classic sheet metal themes. In his former life (pre-Ford) as chief designer at Volkswagen of America's think tank in Simi Valley, California, he was largely responsible for the Concept 1, which eventually became the New Beetle."

Motor Trend, like *Car And Driver*, called for performance-oriented chassis and suspension features such as light-weight alloys, traction control, and 17-inch aluminum wheels, but predicted, ". . . it'll be geared to a luxury-with-sportiness ride character that targets the current two-seat offerings from BMW and Mercedes rather than the new Vette." *MT* also speculated as to what the drivetrain of the new 'Bird might consist of, but admitted, "At press time, there was still talk as to whether a 3.0-liter/210-horsepower Duratec V-6 would be offered in a mild version of the car with either a Getrag five-speed manual gearbox or a five-speed automatic. More likely, there will be a single drivetrain: the 3.9-liter/260-horse multivalve V-8 coupled with a five-speed automatic."

Finally, after much speculation in the automotive press and elsewhere, the pent-up curiosity of millions as to what the new Thunderbird might look like was satisfied. On Jan. 3, 1999, Jac Nasser, the new CEO of Ford, unveiled a new two-seat Thunderbird concept car at the 1999 North American International Auto Show in Detroit. A Ford press release at the time described the vehicle, in part, by saying, "The sunmist-yellow roadster includes key styling cues from its classic 1955-1957 forebears" and called the concept car ". . . a design exercise intended to revitalize excitement in the car market and gauge consumer reaction."

Press kits distributed at the Detroit show by Ford's Media Information Center contained a release that trumpeted "Ford Thunderbird Concept: American Icon is Back." It went into more detail as to Ford's rationale and the philosophy behind the new concept's design saying, "An automotive legend is reborn as the Ford Thunderbird makes its return as an all-new concept car at the North American International Auto Show.

Since its introduction in October 1954, the Thunderbird has been an American cultural icon—with trademark design cues that set it apart from the crowd of sports cars available at the time. Today, the all-new Thunderbird concept draws on that rich heritage and introduces a modern interpretation of an automotive legend.

'The Ford Thunderbird has an emotional hold on the American public that spans decades and generations,' says Jac Nasser, Ford president and chief executive officer. 'This timeless classic is an important part of Ford Motor Company's heritage and, indeed, this country's automotive history.

'The new concept car is an indication of where we're headed with the Thunderbird when it goes back into production for the new millennium,' Nasser continues, 'It's also just one example of the exciting and dynamic new cars we plan to introduce in the future.'

The new concept features elements from Thunderbirds of 1955-57 and 1961-62, simplified into contemporary forms. The cues include porthole windows, aluminum-finished chevrons, hood scoop, round headlamps, taillamps, and fog lamps, and the trademark Thunderbird badge.

The Thunderbird concept's stance is designed to be relaxed and confident—achieved through a negative-wedge design in which the front of the vehicle appears to be set slightly higher than the rear. The 18-inch, eight-spoke aluminum wheels and 245R50/18 tires help give the car an equally sporting stance. (Ford Motor Co.)

'The design of the Thunderbird concept reflects the attitude of a simpler time,' explains J Mays, Ford vice president of Design. 'The unbridled optimism and the confident attitude of the 1950s comes through in an absolutely modern design.'

The Thunderbird concept's stance is designed to be relaxed and confident—achieved through a negative-wedge design in which the front of the vehicle appears to be set slightly higher than the rear. The 18-inch, eight-spoke aluminum wheels and P245R50-18 tires help give the car an equally sporting stance.

A circular theme runs through the vehicle, starting with the round headlamps and fog lamps and extending to the taillamps. The removable hard top with its porthole windows has the signature cue from the original Thunderbird.

'This is an aspirational design,' Mays says. 'Simple shapes combined with timeless materials and textures convey a relaxed, confident look and a feel that is the true essence of the original Thunderbird.'

The oval grille opening remains true to the original with an aluminum-finished eggcrate design. Two large fog lamps are set into the front bumper along with a secondary grille opening below them.

A circular theme runs throughout the new Thunderbird concept, starting with the round headlamps and fog lamps and extending to the taillamps. The removable hardtop with its round porthole windows takes its signature cue from the original Thunderbird. (Ford Motor Co.)

The scoop is integrated into the hood design rather than serving merely as a prominent addition.

The wraparound windshield is set at a 64-degree angle and surrounded by a wide band of chrome, as are the porthole windows. The signature windows are also functional, allowing additional light to enter the vehicle and providing better rearward visibility when the top is on.

Chrome slash marks on the front quarter panels are cut into the sheet metal. they are a modern interpretation of the chevrons that were prominent on the original car.

The concept also features cues from 1961-62 Thunderbirds, which were more equally proportioned than their predecessors. Thus, doors are set to the center rather than to the rear, and a crisp line runs from the headlamp straight back to the taillamp, hinting at one of the car's legendary fins.

The car's interior continues the design theme by combining modern materials and finishes with the flair of two-tone interiors of the past. Two black leather-wrapped bucket seats are stitched with a washboard-like pattern.

The interior door panels are covered in black leather with yellow leather inserts and brushed aluminum accents. The instrument panel sports white gauges with turquoise pointers. The upper instrument panel, steering wheel, and floor-mounted shifter are covered in yellow leather, matching the car's sun-mist yellow exterior.

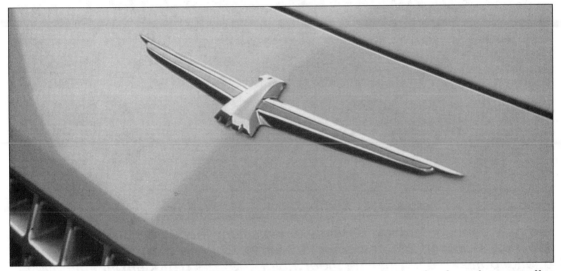

The aluminum-finished Thunderbird badge features a turquoise insert across the wings and is prominently placed on the vehicle's nose, rear, and across the front seat backs. (Ford Motor Co.)

A black leather-wrapped tonneau cover is visible when the hard top is removed.

The aluminum-finished Thunderbird badge features a turquoise insert across the wings and is prominently placed on the vehicle's nose, rear, and across the front seat backs. The aluminum-finished Thunderbird script stretches across both rear quarter panels.

The Thunderbird name has a rich automotive heritage, but originates from Arizona and New Mexico. According to legend, Thunderbird ruled the sky and was a divine helper of man. The great wings—invisible to mortal man—created the winds and the thunder and provided rains in the desert, where fate had brought the Native Americans.

The name is fitting for a car that has become an American legend. Thunderbird's appeal extended far beyond its roots in Dearborn. In 1961, the car caught the eye of the newly elected President of the United States, John F. Kennedy. Kennedy demonstrated his passion for the Ford Thunderbird by including 50 of them in his inaugural procession.

This is only one example of the Thunderbird's role as an American icon. Thunderbird represented the carefree and youthful attitude of the 1950s and 1960s. The Beach Boys' "Fun, Fun, Fun" heralded, in a song, aspects of the American car culture, as did the street cruising scenes of Thunderbird in the film "American Graffiti."

So, the new T-Bird was at last reality, at least in prototype form. But how was it received by the public? The March 1999 issue of *Car and Driver* contained a review of the January North American International Auto Show. It had this to say about the debut of the

Thunderbird concept car, "The long-awaited Thunderbird concept tended to polarize show goers. Some called it 'a shapeless blob', some viewed it as 'simply stunning.' Reportedly, the concept was well under way before Ford hired design chief J Mays, who promptly began tweaking it in earnest. The result: Mays, who used to design cars for Volkswagen and made the New Beetle a thoughtfully inspired version of the original, has done exactly that with the 1955-'57 Thunderbird. Word has it that the production Thunderbird will be extremely close in appearance to the concept car. Expect it in 2000 as a 2001 model. Based on the Lincoln LS rear-wheel-drive platform, the Thunderbird will use that car's 3.9-liter V-8 and offer manual and automatic transmissions. The removable hardtop will be made of an as-yet-undecided material, but removing it will be a two-person job, as making it power-retractable would raise the price. The element most likely to change would be the 18-inch, eight-spoke aluminum wheels and the 245/50R-18 tires. Expect a first-year production run of about 32,000 and a price near $35,000. Whereas the colors will be similar to the soft pastels of the early 'Birds, they are not identical to them, as the pale-yellow car shown here confirms. Performance will be invigorating, but more akin to that of a Mercedes SLK than a Chevrolet Corvette."

The new concept features design elements from Thunderbirds of 1955-'57 and 1961-'62, simplified into contemporary forms. Chrome slash marks on the front quarter panels are cut into the sheet metal. They are a modern interpretation of the chevrons that were prominent on the original car. (Ford Motor Co.)

Car and Driver and *Motor Trend* were not the only enthusiast magazines predicting a new Thunderbird in 2000. *Automobile Magazine's* "Leinert Report" dated Feb. 24, 1999 said, "Ford insiders predict the all-new Thunderbird, which is slated to debut in spring 2000, will be sold out before the first vehicle ever reaches the showroom—even at a projected retail price of more than $32,000. The company is planning an annual production run of about 20,000 units at its Lincoln plant in Wixom, Michigan. The new Thunderbird will share its underpinnings with the Lincoln LS sedans."

Automobile Magazine scooped them all, however, when it actually drove a new T-Bird prototype as reported by European Bureau Chief Georg Kacher in a June 1999 article entitled "Bird on the Wing: First encounter with the 2001 Thunderbird." Kacher was able to do a hands-on examination of the Thunderbird in Switzerland. Obviously enthused, of the bright red roadster he said, "It looks gorgeous, absolutely gorgeous. On the road, in real-time motion backed up by live engine noise, the 2001 Ford Thunderbird is an even more impressive machine than the one we admired on the auto show circuit. The stance is spot-on. The proportions are 99.5 percent perfect. The highlights are exactly where they should be. There's no doubt that this car is drop-dead beautiful. Best of all, the design exercise is very close to the real thing that will go into production next year." He went on to describe the interior and exterior of the prototype in detail, which others had done before, but things really got interesting when he became the first automotive journalist to report to us how the car sounds. He said, "The engine of the handmade bright red prototype fires at the third turn of the key. Even at idle speed, the 270-bhp-or-so 4.0-liter V-8—which uses four valves per cylinder and double overhead camshafts,

The car's interior continues the design theme by combining modern materials and finishes with the flair of two-tone interiors of the past. Two black leather-wrapped bucket seats are stitched with a washboard-like pattern. (Ford Motor Co.)

just like the upcoming Lincoln LS and the brand-new Jaguar S-type—sounds like the mechanical equivalent of Darth Vader. Blip the throttle, and the rumble turns into an angry roar. Put the foot down one more inch, and that roar becomes a pure, mean, and barely legal thunder. " Kacher went on to discuss technical aspects of the vehicle's platform and its shared relationship to upcoming models of Lincoln, Jaguar, and Mustang. Summing up, he left no doubt in the reader's mind as to where he stood on the new T-Bird, saying, "Even at this early stage, the reborn Thunderbird is a car that stirs the emotions and truly has character—vital traits if you want to sell cars in an increasingly competitive market. Its self-confident personality reflects Ford's newfound optimism, and its style defines an automotive spirit that is both traditional and contemporary. More important, the way it moves is, just like the noises it makes, positively addictive. We can't wait to point the trademark bulging fenders and proud air-intake scoop at a set of challenging roads. Only then will we be able to tell you whether the new $35,000 Thunderbird really marks the reincarnation of the relatively affordable classic grand tourer. From our brief drive in the prototype, the omens look remarkably good."

While public reaction to the Thunderbird concept may have been somewhat mixed, the automotive press seemed generally optimistic that Ford would have no trouble selling the anticipated relatively small first-year production run.

So, what is the status of the new Thunderbird at the time of this writing in May of 2000? We had hoped that the release of this book would coincide with the entry into production of the new Thunderbird. Obviously, since its introduction in January 1999, and through all the ballyhoo that followed, the automotive press had expected it to be on the streets by now. Instead, the car returned to the auto show circuit for 2000 and Ford became considerably more reticent on the imminence of its production. An inquiry as to the current status of the Thunderbird was sent to the Ford Media Information Center on March 22, 2000. The following response was received from Miles Chase Johnson, Technical Information Specialist, "The Ford Thunderbird that is currently on the show circuit is a concept vehicle that is being used to gauge public reaction. When Thunderbird does go into production, it could be built at Wixom assembly along with the LS. A production date has not been announced yet. The Thunderbird will be out sometime in the new millennium. This (is) all the information I can provide you at this time."

A subsequent request for updated information sent May 9, 2000 went unanswered, but at long last, on May 22, 2000, Ford's much-anticipated and long-awaited plans for the new T-Bird were revealed. In a release entitled "Thunderbird: The American Dream Car Returns; Cross-country Tour Rekindles the Excitement" Ford's Media Information Center made the following announcement:

"The legendary Ford Thunderbird returns, as Ford confirms it will begin building the 2002-model production car beginning next year.

Meanwhile, this summer, Americans in major cities across the country have a chance to win one of three 1950s-era classic Thunderbirds as part of a special tour designed to build on the excitement of the car that has become a national icon.

Beginning Memorial Day weekend on May 27, three mid-1950s-era white, two-seat roadsters will begin a tour driving through the streets of 144 cities and towns as part of Ford's "American Dream Car Tour." The tour kicks off in Southern California, South Florida, and the greater New York area. It continues through Aug. 20.

People spotting one of the classic white cars sporting the American Dream Car Tour logo can enter a sweepstakes and could win one of the three vintage cars. Launched in 1955, few of these classic Thunderbird cars remain, and some are valued as high as $60,000 by classic car buffs."

The release went on with specific sweepstakes registration instructions and then continued, "Dealers are not yet taking orders for the new 2002 Thunderbird. However, the American Dream Car Tour is the first step in Ford's marketing efforts for the new car. Other efforts will follow, including the debut of a special limited-editon model at this year's Pebble Beach Concours d'Elegance in August. The new 2002 Thunderbird will closely resemble the concept introduced last year at auto shows across the country.

The car is designed as a modern interpretation of the 1955 original, featuring many design cues from the past, including the signature "porthole" windows and removable hardtop."

A New Beginning? At last, it was on the way.

Scale Model

The Maisto 1/18-scale Thunderbird concept model has the appearance of the real thing.

One of the highest tributes that can be accorded a motor vehicle is that it be mimicked in the form of a scale model. This is unusual enough for a production vehicle that has distinguished itself through popularity due to design, dependability, or sheer numbers produced. It is truly unusual, however, for a car that hasn't even gone into regular production yet.

But such is the case with the highly-detailed model of the 1999 Thunderbird concept pictured on these pages. The 1/18th-scale rendition is made in Thailand by Maisto and only the keenest observer, upon examining these photos, would determine that it is not the genuine article.

With hardtop removed, the model displays a leather-wrapped tonneau cover, just like the full-scale version.

With engine exposed, the hinged hood supports are a clue that this is a model rather than the actual vehicle.

Prior to the introduction of the 1999 Thunderbird concept at Detroit's North American International Auto Show on Jan. 3, 1999, and in the ensuing months of publicity surrounding that car, the automotive press was virtually unanimous in referring to its styling as "retro." In that context, any discussions of the new T-Bird's design usually referred to the recent successes of both Chrysler and Volkswagen with their respective approaches to retro styling. The official stance of Ford Motor Company, however, was *not* to refer to the new T-Bird's styling as retro. This may have been an attempt to avoid a "copycat" image for Ford as a relative newcomer to the retro design scene. In a Ford Media Information Center release issued at the time of the T-Bird concept's public introduction, Ford media flacks attempted to put a different spin on the new car's styling, saying, "When college students buy bell bottoms from a secondhand store, that's retro. When car designers put whitewall tires and fins on a vehicle, that's retro, too. But the new Ford Thunderbird concept vehicle is a modern interpretation of a classic American icon--a phenomenon that Ford calls "modern heritage."

'Styling heritage comes from the soul of a great automotive nameplate,' says J Mays, Ford's vice president of Design. 'There are only a few select nameplates that have earned their way into the hearts of the motoring public by establishing a true heritage. Thunderbird is certainly one of them.'

The doors open and the interior appears authentic, but the thickness and position of the door hinges hint that this actually a model.

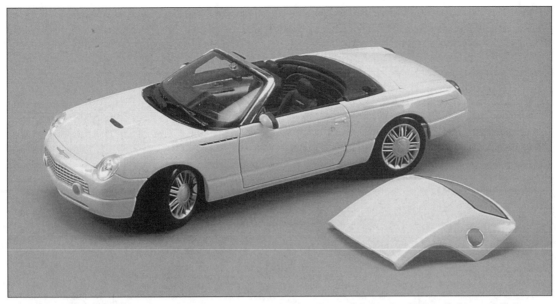

The model's "heritage" porthole hardtop is removable, just like the real thing.

Just as the rounded cowl, headlamps, and leaper on the new Jaguar S-type strike a chord with 1960s-era Mark II enthusiasts and the three-element taillamps and side scoops of the 1999 Mustang light a fire under those with a passion for pony cars, the styling elements of the Thunderbird concept have meaning beyond the sheet metal.

With the Thunderbird concept, Ford designers had a wealth of styling cues to call upon. The project direction was to recreate the enthusiasm of the original by building a two-seat roadster with Thunderbird elements—but in a distinctly modern interpretation. The original Thunderbird, introduced in 1954 as a 1955 model, was a two-seat sporty car with a long cowl set off by elegant round headlamps, an egg-crate grille, and a wrap-around, aircraft-style windshield. A hood scoop and row of chrome-like vents in the fenders hinted at the car's V-8 power, while a simple streamlined accent line ran from the vents to the taillamps. In 1956, the famous porthole window was added to Thunderbird's optional removable hardtop.

Economic realities of later years saw a shift for the Thunderbird from a two-seat car to a full-size coupe. But, despite 43 years of design and size changes, the unique styling of the original two-seater has come to symbolize an era of American history.

The egg-crate grille, rounded headlamps, and Thunderbird nose badge echo the original two-seat T-Birds.

'The 1955 through 1957 Thunderbirds are as symbolic of the times as carhops, bobby socks, and 45-rpm records,' says Mays. 'Today's Thunderbird concept salutes the original, but also symbolizes turn-of-the-millennium automotive styling.'

From the machined aluminum egg-crate grille and hood scoop to the leather-wrapped instrument panel and porthole window, any enthusiast will spot the touches of heritage. But the same enthusiasts should never doubt that the Thunderbird concept is a car pointing toward the future, Mays says.

'It's not retro,' says Mays. 'While the Thunderbird concept is loaded with heritage cues, it is a decidedly modern machine. This hints at the direction we plan to take when we bring back the production car early in the next century.' "

From every angle the scale and proportions of the model are faithful to the genuine concept car.

FORD THUNDERBIRD '59

The car <u>everyone</u> would love to own!

STANDARD AND OPTIONAL EQUIPMENT

This section details the standard and factory optional equipment for Thunderbirds from 1955-1995. The style of listing standard equipment on price sheets or in sales catalogs changed many times over the 40 years the Thunderbird has been produced. Our list reflects such changes in style and should be considered a *guide* to the equipment Thunderbirds came with from the factory.

The options information gives original prices charged for the extra-cost equipment in *most* years. These are *retail* prices, unless otherwise noted in the text. Some options are merchandised in *packages*. We have not detailed the contents of every package for every model-year. Cross-referencing may help determine the contents of similar packages offered in different years.

Availability of equipment and options, as well as prices, was always subject to change. This may cause slight differences between our prices and your car's original window sticker or invoice. However, the prices listed below should be in the "ballpark" for each year.

In these listings, "Thunderbird" indicates the base model. The abbreviations used to describe certain features are standard abbreviations explained elsewhere in the book.

We welcome any contributions that can improve the information we have gathered. Please send additions or corrections to: Automotive Books Dept., Krause Publications, 700 E. State St, Iola, WI 54990.

1955

1955 Thunderbird Standard Equipment: 292-cid Y-block V-8 engine; 6-volt electrical system; 40-amp generator; 90 amp-hr battery; three-speed manual transmission; Hotchkiss drive; ball-joint front suspension; 5-leaf spring rear suspension, five 6.70 x 15 tubeless tires; Black and pleated White, Red and pleated White, or Thunderbird Blue and pleated White vinyl upholstery; Astra-Dial control panel with illuminated control knobs; parcel compartment with locking-type push-button latch; 4-way illuminated starter-ignition switch; panel courtesy light with integral switch and automatic door switches; rear view mirror on windshield upper molding; dual horns; half-circle steering wheel horn ring; and (as a running addition) glass-fibre hardtop.

1955 Thunderbird Options: Full-flow oil filter. Oil bath air cleaner. 4-way power seat. Swift-Sure power brakes ($40). Master-Guide power steering.($92). Power-Lift windows ($70). I-Rest tinted safety glass ($25). Fordomatic Drive ($215). Overdrive ($110). White sidewall tires ($30). Tachometer. Electric clock. Cigarette lighter. Convertible fabric top ($75). Special fuel and vacuum pump unit. MagicAire Heater ($85). Radio ($100). Rear fender shields. Full wheel covers. Simulated wire wheels. Engine dress-up kit ($25) Windshield washers ($10). Both tops ($290 until glass-fibre hardtop became standard equipment).

1956

1956 Thunderbird Standard Equipment: 292-cid Y-block V-8 engine; automatic choke; 12-volt electrical system; dual exhausts; three-speed manual transmission; Hotchkiss drive; ball-joint front suspension; 5-leaf spring rear suspension, five 6.70 x 15 tubeless tires; White and Red, White and Black, White and Peacock, White and Brown, or White and Green all-vinyl interiors with harmonizing looped-rayon carpeting; 17-in. diameter deep-center Lifeguard steering wheel with 2-in. adjustment; Lifeguard double-grip door latches; Lifeguard rear view mirror; Astra-Dial control panel with illuminated control knobs; parcel compartment with locking-type push-button latch; 4-way illuminated starter-ignition switch; panel courtesy light with integral switch and automatic door switches; dual horns; half-circle steering wheel horn ring; and glass-fibre hardtop.

1956 Thunderbird Options: Full-flow oil filter. 4-way power seat ($65). Swift Sure power brakes ($34). Master-Guide power steering ($64). Power-Lift windows ($70). I-Rest tinted safety glass. Fordomatic Drive ($215). Overdrive ($146). White sidewall tires. Fuel and vacuum pump unit. MagicAire Heater ($84). Radio ($107). Rear fender shields. Full wheel covers. Simulated wire wheel covers. Engine dress-up kit. Auto-Wipe windshield washers. Turn signals. Lifeguard seat belts (Match 1956). Lifeguard padded sun visors and Lifeguard instrument panel padding starting in March 1956 ($22-$32). Thunderbird 312-cid four-barrel V-8. Thunderbird 312-cid dual four-barrel V-8. Convertible fabric top alone ($75). Both tops ($290). Tonneau cover.

1957

1957 Thunderbird Standard Equipment: 292-cid Y-block V-8 engine; automatic choke; Super-Filter air cleaner with reusable paper element (effective Feb. 1957); 12-volt electrical system; dual exhausts; three-speed manual transmission; Hotchkiss drive; ball-joint front suspension; 5-leaf spring rear suspension, five 7.50 x 14 tubeless tires; Safety-Contoured 14-in. wheel rims; pleated Colonial White and Raven Black, Starmist Blue and Dresden Blue, Willow Green and Cumberland Green all-vinyl Tu-Tone interiors or Flame Red, Bronze, or Colonial White all-vinyl monochromatic interiors with harmonizing looped-rayon carpeting; standard glass-fibre hardtop with port windows or optional glass-fibre hardtop without port windows (in contrasting or matching colors); Lifeguard cushioned sun visors and Lifeguard instrument panel padding; deep-center Lifeguard steering wheel; Lifeguard double-grip door latches; Lifeguard rear view mirror; parcel compartment with locking-type push-button latch; 4-way illuminated starter-ignition switch; panel courtesy light with integral switch and automatic door switches; dual horns; and half-circle steering wheel horn ring.

1957 Thunderbird Options: Dial-O-Matic 4-way power seat. Swift Sure power brakes. Master-Guide power steering. Power-Lift windows. I-Rest tinted safety glass. Fordomatic Drive. Overdrive. White sidewall tires. Special fuel and vacuum pump unit for positive-action windshield wipers. MagicAire Heater. Volumatic radio. Deluxe antenna. Rear fender shields. Back-up lights. Locking gas cap. Hooded mirror. Auto-Home electric shaver. Turbine wheel covers. Simulated wire wheel covers. Engine dress-up kit. Aquamatic windshield wipers/washers. Thunderbird 312-cid four-barrel V-8. Thunderbird 312-cid Super V-8. Convertible fabric top. Tonneau cover. Seat belts. Full-flow oil filter (left off some early literature). Super Filter air cleaner (changed to standard equipment effective Feb. 1957).

1958

1958 Thunderbird Standard Equipment: *(Dec. 1957 for Hardtop only)* 300-hp 352-cid Thunderbird Special V-8; four-barrel carburetor; dual exhausts; full-flow oil filtration; automatic choke; three-speed manual transmission; Lifeguard padded instrument panel; cushioned sun visors; cigarette lighter; horn ring; dual horns; automatic dome light; turn signals. *(Jan. 1958 for Hardtop only)* 300-hp 352-cid Thunderbird Special V-8; four-barrel carburetor; dual exhausts; full-flow oil filtration; automatic choke; three-speed manual transmission; Lifeguard padded instrument panel; cushioned sun visors; double-grip door locks; safety-swivel inside rear view mirror; deep-center steering wheel with horn ring; manually-adjustable driver's seat; automatic dome light; cigarette lighter; coat hooks in rear compartment; dual horns; turn signals. *(May 1958 for Hardtop and Convertible)* 300-hp 352-cid Thunderbird Special V-8; four-barrel carburetor; dual exhausts; full-flow oil filtration; automatic choke; Cruise-O-Matic drive; Lifeguard padded instrument panel; cushioned sun visors; double-grip door locks; safety-swivel rear view mirror; deep-center steering wheel; manually-adjustable front seats; electric clock; automatic dome light in Hardtop and courtesy light in Convertible; cigarette lighter; gunsight front fender ornaments; dual horns; and turn signals.

1958 Thunderbird Options: Manually adjustable front passenger seat (Manually-adjustable front seats became standard in May 1958). Power brakes ($37). Overdrive transmission ($108). Power windows ($101). 4-way power driver's seat ($64). Tube-type radio ($77). Signal-seeking radio ($99). Five 8.00 x 14 whitewall tires in place of black sidewall ($36). I-Rest Tinted glass ($20). Windshield washers-wipers ($12). Back-up lights ($10). Power steering ($69). MagicAire heater ($95). SelectAire conditioner (N/A). Leather interior ($106). Radio antennas. Seat belts. Positive windshield wipers. Electric clock (became standard after May 1958). Outside mirrors. Rear fender shields. Fashion-Ray wheel covers. Locking gas cap (first offered in Jan. 1958). Gunsight front fender ornaments (became standard in May 1958). Cruise-O-Matic transmission (Sale literature says "optional, installed in production" after May 1958).

1959

1959 Thunderbird Standard Equipment: Built-in arm rests; floor carpets; individually-adjusted seats with deep-foam rubber seat cushions; full folding front passenger seat; optional choice of deep-pleated all-vinyl interior or linen seat inserts with vinyl bolsters; padded dash and sun visors; front and rear ash trays; cigarette lighter; electric clock; courtesy lights; dual exhausts; fuel filter; deep-center steering wheel; turn signals; dual horns with horn ring; spare tire; and bumper jack.

1959 Thunderbird Options: Cruise-O-Matic ($242). Overdrive ($145). Radio ($105). Signal seeker radio ($92.60 *). Rear seat speaker ($13.50 *). Power brakes ($43). Fresh air heater and defroster ($83). Driver's side power seat ($86). Select Air Conditioner ($446). 350-hp engine ($177). Genuine leather interior ($106). Rear fender shields ($27). Two seat belts ($26). White sidewall tires ($36). Full wheel disks ($17). Back up lights ($36). Tinted glass ($38). Power windows ($102). Windshield washers ($14). Left-hand OSRV mirror ($5) Tu-Tone paint ($26). Two-speed electric wipers ($7.10 *). Pair of regular floor mats ($3.50 *). Pair of contoured floor mats ($7.95 *). Equa-Lock differential ($32.15 *). Heavy-duty 70-amp battery ($8). Door-mounted side view mirror ($5.95 *). Fender-mounted side view mirror ($8.95 *). Visor-vanity mirror ($1.95 *). Factory undercoating ($15 *). Tu-Tone paint ($22 *). Clear plastic seat covers ($29.95 *). Antifreeze ($6.95 *). Tissue dispenser ($6.75 *) Note: (*) indicates dealer wholesale price; retail prices for these items are unknown.

1960

1960 Thunderbird Standard Equipment: Built-in dual exhausts; fuel filter; oil filter; 352-cid four-barrel V-8 engine; padded instrument panel and sun visors; electric clock with sweep second hand; courtesy lights; turn signals; deep-center steering wheel; dual horns and horn rings; individually-adjustable front seats; day-night tilt type mirror; double-grip door locks; wheel covers; built-in arm rests; floor carpets; full-width foam rubber seat, all-vinyl upholstery; ash tray; cigar lighter; air cleaner; and five black 8.00 x 14 tubeless tires.

1960 Thunderbird Options: Cruise-O-Matic drive ($242). Overdrive ($144.50). Central console radio and antenna ($112.80). MagicAire heater and defroster ($82.90). Air conditioner ($465.80). Tinted glass ($37.90). 8.00 x 14 rayon whitewall tires ($35.70 extra). 8.00 x 14 nylon white sidewall tires ($63.50 extra). 8.50 x 14 white sidewall tires (N/A). 350-hp V-8 engine ($177). Master Guide power steering ($75.30). Power windows ($102.10). Swift Sure power brakes ($43.20). Four-way power driver's seat ($92.10). Left- or right-hand OSRV mirror ($5.10). Back-up lights ($9.50). Windshield washers ($13.70). Rear fender shields — skirts ($26.60). Leather interior ($106.20). Heavy-duty 70-amp battery in Hardtop ($7.60). Tu-Tone paint ($25.80). Underseal ($14.10). Sliding sun roof ($212.40). Two seat belts ($22.80). Two-speed electric windshield wipers (N/A). Pair of regular floor mats (N/A). Pair of contoured floor mats (N/A). Equa-Lock differential (N/A). Fender-mounted side view mirror (N/A). Visor-vanity mirror (N/A). Clear plastic seat covers (N/A). Antifreeze (N/A). Tissue dispenser (N/A). Full wheel covers (N/A).

1961

1961 Thunderbird Standard Equipment: Built-in dual exhausts; fuel filter; oil filter; 390-cid four-barrel V-8 engine; padded instrument panel and sun visors; electric clock with sweep second hand; courtesy lights; turn signals; deep-center steering wheel; dual horn and horn rings; individually-adjustable front seats; day-night tilt type mirror; double-grip door locks; wheel covers; built-in arm rests; floor carpets; full-width foam rubber seat, all-vinyl upholstery; ash tray; cigar lighter; air cleaner; and five black 8.00 x 14 tubeless tires; Cruise-O-Matic transmission; power brakes; power steering; electric windshield wipers; undercoating; parking brake light; glove box light; ash tray light; luggage compartment light; and positive crankcase ventilation system on California cars only.

1961 Thunderbird Options: Radio and antenna ($112.80). Fresh air heater ($82.90). SelectAire conditioner ($462.80). Tinted glass ($43). 8.00 x 14 rayon whitewall tires ($42.10 extra). 8.00 x 14 nylon white sidewall tires ($70.40 extra). Power windows ($106.20). Four-way power driver's seat ($92.10). Left- or right-hand OSRV mirror ($5.10). Windshield washers ($13.70). Rear fender shields — skirts ($26.60). Front seat belts ($22.80). Leather interior ($106.20). Heavy-duty 70-amp battery ($7.60). Tu-Tone paint ($25.80). Equa-Lock differential axle ($38.60). Movable steering column ($25.10).

1962

1962 Thunderbird Standard Equipment: Built-in dual exhausts; fuel filter; oil filter; 390-cid four-barrel V-8; padded instrument panel; padded sun visors; electric clock with sweep second hand; courtesy lights; turn signals; a deep-center steering wheel; dual horns and horn rings; individually adjustable front seats; day-night tilt type mirror; double-grip door locks; full wheel covers; built-in arm rests; floor carpet; full-width foam rubber seats; all-vinyl upholstery; ash tray; cigar lighter; air cleaner; automatic transmission; power brakes; power steering; electric windshield wipers; undercoating; parking brake, glove box, ash tray, luggage, back-up, and compartment lights; heater and defroster; movable steering column; console between the front seats; and five black 8.00 x 14 tires. The Convertible Sports Roadster also included the molded tonneau cover with padded headrests, chrome wire wheels, and an instrument panel mounted passenger assist bar.

1962 Thunderbird Options: Radio and antenna ($112.80). Rear seat radio speaker with reverb ($15.50). Thunderbird 390-cid V-8 with triple two-barrel carburetors ($242.10). SelectAire conditioner ($415.10). Tinted glass ($43). 8.00 x 14 rayon whitewalls ($42.10). 8.00 x 14 nylon whitewalls ($70.40). Power windows ($106.20). One 4-way power front seat ($92.10). Outside rear view mirror ($5.10). Windshield washers ($13.70). Rear fender shields ($26.60). Front seat belts ($22.80). Leather seat ($106.20). Heavy-duty 70-amp battery ($.7.60). Tu-Tone paint ($25.80). Chrome wire wheels ($372.30). Automatic speed control ($80.50). Deluxe wheel covers with simulated knock-off hubs ($15.60). Automatic vacuum door locks ($34.10). Note: Leather seats included leather seat inserts and bolsters.

1963

1963 Thunderbird Standard Equipment: Built-in dual exhausts; fuel filter; oil filter; 390-cid four-barrel V-8; padded instrument panel; padded sun visors; electric clock with sweep second hand; courtesy lights; turn signals; deep-center steering wheel; dual horns and horn rings; individually adjustable front seats; day-night tilt type mirror; double-grip door locks; full wheel covers; built-in arm rests; floor carpet; full-width foam rubber seats; all-vinyl upholstery; ash tray; cigar lighter; air cleaner; automatic transmission; power brakes; power steering; electric windshield wipers; undercoating; parking brake, glove box, ash tray, luggage, back-up, and compartment lights; heater and defroster; movable steering column; console between front seats; AM radio and antenna; remote-control left-hand outside rear view mirror; and five black 8.00 x 14 tubeless tires. The Convertible Sports Roadster also included the molded tonneau cover with padded headrests, and chrome wire wheels.

1963 Thunderbird Options: Rear speakers in Hardtop and Landau ($15.60). AM/FM push-button radio and antenna ($83.70). Thunderbird 390-cid 340-hp 6V V-8 ($242.10). SelectAire Air Conditioner, except with 6V engine ($415.10). Banded tinted glass ($43). Five 8.00 x 14 rayon whitewalls ($42.10). Five 8.00 x 14 nylon whitewalls ($70.40). Power windows ($106.20). One 4-way power front seat ($92.10). Power door locks ($34.10). Windshield washers ($13.70). Rear fender shields, except with wire wheels ($26.60). Front seat belts ($16.80). Leather seat ($106.20). Heavy-duty 70-amp battery ($.7.60). Tu-Tone paint ($25.80). Chrome wire wheels ($372.30). Speed control system ($80.50). Deluxe wheel covers with simulated knock-off hubs ($15.60). Note: Leather seats included leather seat inserts and bolsters.

1964

1964 Thunderbird Standard Equipment: 300-hp 390-cid four-barrel V-8; Cruise-O-Matic transmission; power steering; power brakes; movable steering column; padded instrument panel; padded sun visors; hydraulic windshield wipers; electric clock; push-button radio and antenna; heater; automatic parking brake release; turn signals; seat belts with retractors; wheel covers; undercoating; back-up lights; glove box light; ash tray light; courtesy light; map light; luggage compartment light; remote-control mirror; windshield wipers-washers; and alternator.

1964 Thunderbird Options: 4-way power driver's seat ($92.10). 4-way power driver and passenger seats ($184.10) Power windows ($106.20). Air conditioner ($415.10). Am/FM push-button radio with antenna ($83.70). Rear seat speaker ($15.50). 8.15 x 15 white sidewall tires ($42.10 additional). Tonneau cover ($269). Chrome wire wheels and 8.00 x 14 white sidewall tires ($415.20). Deluxe wheel covers ($15.60) Leather seat trim ($106.20). Reclining seat and headrest ($38.60). Heavy-duty battery ($7.60). Rear fender shields ($26.60). Tinted with banded windshield glass ($43). Transistorized ignition system ($51.50). Safety Convenience Control Panel, includes vacuum door locks, door ajar warning light, low fuel warning light, simultaneous flashing parking and taillights ($45.10). Speed control system ($63.40).

1965

1965 Thunderbird Standard Equipment: Built-in dual exhausts; fuel filter; oil filter; 390-cid 300-hp four-barrel V-8; windshield washers; front seat belts; padded instrument panel; padded sun visors; electric clock with sweep second hand; courtesy lights; turn signals; deep-center steering wheel; dual horns and horn rings; individually adjustable front seats; day-night tilt type mirror; double-grip door locks; full wheel covers; built-in arm rests; floor carpet; full-width foam rubber seats; all-vinyl upholstery; ash tray; cigar lighter; air cleaner; automatic transmission; power brakes; power steering; hydraulic windshield wipers; undercoating; parking brake, map, glove box, ash tray, luggage, back-up, and compartment lights; heater and defroster; movable steering column; AM radio and antenna; remote-control left-hand outside rear view mirror; five black 8.15 x 15 tubeless tires; and alternator.

1965 Thunderbird Options: SelectAire air conditioner ($424.90). Heavy-duty 70-amp battery ($7.60). California type closed emission system ($5.30). Automatic deck lid release, except Convertible ($12.90). Limited-slip differential ($47.70). Extra-cooling package ($7.90). Rear fender shields — skirts ($32.70). Tinted glass with banded windshield ($43). Leather seat bolsters and inserts ($106.20). Tu-tone paint ($25.80). Retracting power antenna ($29.60). 4-way power driver's seat ($92.10). 4-way power driver and passenger seats ($184.10). Power windows and power vent windows ($159.40). Power windows ($106.20). AM/FM push-button radio and antenna ($83.70). Safety Convenience Control Panel includes vacuum door locks, door ajar light, low fuel light, and safety flashers ($58). Reclining passenger seat with headrest ($45.10). Rear seat speaker ($16.90). Studiosonic rear seat speaker ($54.10). Speed control system ($63.40). Heavy-duty suspension with front and rear heavy-duty springs and shock absorbers ($28.60). Five rayon 8.15 x 15 whitewall tires ($43.90 additional). Transistorized ignition system ($76). Deluxe wheel covers with simulated knock-off hubs ($15.60).

1966

1966 Thunderbird Standard Equipment: Built-in dual exhausts; fuel filter; oil filter; 390-cid 300-hp four-barrel V-8; windshield washers; front seat belts; padded instrument panel; padded sun visors; electric clock with sweep second hand; courtesy lights; turn signals; deep-center steering wheel; dual horns and horn rings; individually adjustable front seats; day-night tilt type mirror; double-grip door locks; full wheel covers; built-in arm rests; floor carpet; full-width foam rubber seats; all-vinyl upholstery; ash tray; cigar lighter; air cleaner; automatic transmission; power brakes; power steering; hydraulic windshield wipers; undercoating; parking brake, map, glove box, ash tray, luggage, back-up, and compartment lights; heater and defroster; movable steering column; AM radio and antenna; remote-control left-hand outside rear view mirror; five black 8.15 x 15 tubeless tires; and alternator.

1966 Thunderbird Options: 428-cid 345-hp V-8.. 6-way power driver's seat. 6-way power driver and passenger seats. Power windows. Retracting power antenna. Heavy-duty battery. Limited-slip differential. Transistorized ignition system. Highway-Pilot speed control. Safety Convenience Control includes vacuum door locks, door ajar light, low fuel light, and safety flashers. Tinted glass. SelectAire conditioner. AM/FM radio with antenna. Remote deck lid release. Reclining passenger seat. AM radio and Stereosonic 8-track tape player. rear fender shields — skirts. License plate frames. Leather seat trim. Tu-Tone paint. White sidewall tires. Deluxe wheel covers with simulated knock-off hubs.

1967

1967 Thunderbird Standard Equipment: Comfort Stream ventilation system; retractable headlamp doors; built-in dual exhausts; windshield washers; front and rear seat belts with front retractors and warning light; emergency flashers; automatic brake release; padded instrument panel; padded sun visors; padded windshield pillars; electric clock; courtesy lights; sequential turn signals; adjustable front seats; day-night tilt-type mirror; wheel covers; SelectShift Cruise-O-Matic drive; power front disc/rear drum brakes; power steering; hydraulic windshield wipers; undercoating; parking brake light; map light; glove box light; ash tray light; luggage compartment light; back-up lights; heater and defroster; movable steering column; AM push-button radio and antenna; remote-control left-hand OSRV mirror; five 8.15 x 15 tubeless tires; 315-hp V-8 engine; alternator; and all standard FoMoCo safety features.

1967 Thunderbird Options: Body side accent stripe ($13.90). SelectAire air conditioner ($421.49). 80-amp heavy-duty battery ($7.44). Limited-slip differential ($46.69). California type emissions control system with EECS only ($5.19). Exhaust emission control system, California type ($49.45). 345-hp V-8 with Cruise-O-Matic transmission, extra charge over base V-8 ($90.68). Extra heavy-duty cooling package, standard with air conditioning ($7.73). Tinted glass with banded windshield ($47.49). Tu-Tone paint, Hardtops only ($25.25). Retracting power antenna ($28.97). Power deck lid release ($12.63). 6-way power driver's seat ($97.32). Power windows ($103.95). Two-door Protection group ($25.28). Four-door Protection group ($29.17). Note: Protection Groups include front and rear color-keyed floor mats, license plate frames, and door edge guards. AM/FM Multiplex stereo radio with speakers ($163.17). AM manual Stereosonic tape system ($128.49). AM/FM radio with dual rear speakers ($89.94). Convenience Control Panel, includes speed-actuated power door locks, door ajar light, low-fuel light, and emergency flashers ($77.73 for two-door models; $101.10 for four-door models). Reclining passenger seat with headrests ($57.08). Shoulder harness ($27.27). Dual rear speaker for AM radio only ($33.07). Fingertip speed control, including specific steering wheel ($129.55). Heavy-duty suspension includes front and rear heavy springs and shocks ($27.99). 8.15 x 15 four-ply tires, whitewall with red band ($51.98). 8.15 x 15 four-ply tires, whitewall ($43.12). Split leather trim interior with unique seat trim style and wood-grain accents ($201.06). Deluxe wheel covers ($19.48). Styled steel wheels ($35.70).

1968

1968 Thunderbird Standard Equipment: All standard FoMoCo safety features; Comfort Stream ventilation system; retractable headlamp doors; 315-hp four-barrel V-8; SelectShift Cruise-O-Matic drive; power front disc/rear drum brakes; power steering; full-width front seat; heater and defroster; electric clock; courtesy lights; front running lights; wheel covers; glove box light; map light; ignition light; ash tray light; luggage compartment lights; remote-control left-hand OSRV mirror; push-button AM radio with antenna; and dual-stream windshield wipers. Landau models have vinyl roof. Two-door models have 8.15 x 15 four-ply-rated black sidewall tires. Four-door model has 8.45 x 15 four-ply-rated black sidewall tires.

1968 Thunderbird Options: Body side accent stripe ($13.90). SelectAire air conditioner ($427.07). SelectAire conditioner with automatic climate control ($499.22). High-ratio axle, standard with 390-cid engine ($6.53). Heavy-duty battery, standard with 429-cid engine ($7.44). Two-door Brougham interior trim with bucket seats ($129.54). Four-door Brougham interior trim with bench seats ($161.98). Brougham leather interior for models with Black or Saddle colored bucket seats ($194.31). Note: Brougham interior trim includes unique seat trim style, wood-grain appointments, door courtesy lights, cut-pile carpets, unique door trim panels, door pull handles, and rear seat center arm rest. Deluxe front or rear shoulder belts ($15.59). Deluxe front and rear shoulder belts ($18.22). Passenger side reclining seat ($41.49). Tilt-Away steering wheel ($66.14). Heavy-duty suspension with front and rear heavy springs and shocks ($27.99). Deluxe wheel covers ($57.08) Styled steel wheels ($35.70). Extra charge for non-standard tires on two-door models without air conditioning: 8.15 x 15 4-ply whitewalls ($43.12). 8.15 x 15 4-ply red band whitewalls ($51.98). 8.45 x 15 4-ply black sidewalls ($18.07). 8.45 x 15 4-ply whitewalls ($61.26). 8.45 x 15 4-ply red band whitewalls ($70). 8.45 x 15 (215 R15) radial-ply whitewalls ($117.64). Extra charge for non-standard tires on two-door models with air conditioning and all four-door models: 8.45 x 15 4-ply whitewalls ($43.19). 8.45 x 15 4-ply red band whitewalls ($52.04). 8.45 x 15 (215 R15) radial-ply whitewalls ($101.30).

1969

1969 Thunderbird Standard Equipment: All standard FoMoCo safety features plus 429-cid 360-hp four-barrel V-8; SelectShift Cruise-O-Matic transmission; power steering; power front disc/rear drum brakes; retractable headlight doors; 8.55 x 15 black sidewall tires; electric clock; courtesy lights; Flight Bench seat with arm rest; adjustable head restraints; wheel covers; power vent system; AM push-button radio; front and rear running lights; remote-control OSRV mirror; light package. Landau models have vinyl roof.

1969 Thunderbird Options: SelectAire air conditioner ($427.07). SelectAire conditioner with automatic climate control ($499.22). Electric sun roof in Landau model ($453.30). Sure Track anti-lock braking system ($194.31). Flight Bucket seats and console ($64.77). Reclining front passenger seat ($41.49). 6-Way power seat ($98.89) Power window lifts ($109.22). Power trunk lid release ($14.85). Power retracting antenna ($28.97). Rear window defogger ($22.23). Electric defroster ($84.25).

Tinted windows ($47.49). Highway-Pilot speed control, requires Tilt-Away steering wheel ($97.21). Tilt-Away steering wheel ($66.14). Four-door convenience group ($101.10). Two-door convenience group ($77.73). AM/FM stereo with speakers ($150.29). Stereo sonic AM radio with tape player ($128.49). Dual rear speakers, standard with stereo sonic or stereo ($33.07). Limited-slip differential axle ($46.69) Four-note horn ($15.59). Brougham cloth and vinyl interior trim with bucket seats ($129.54). Brougham cloth and vinyl interior trim with bench seats ($161.59). Brougham vinyl and leather interior for models with Black or Saddle colored bucket seats ($194.31). Note: Brougham interior trim includes unique seat trim style, wood-grain appointments, door courtesy lights, cut-pile carpets, unique door trim panels, door pull handles, and rear seat center arm rest. Deluxe seat belts with warning light ($15.59). Rear lamp monitor ($25.91). High-level rear window brake lamp, supplemental, four-door Landaus only ($33.70). Two-door Protection group ($25.28). Four-door protection group ($29.17). Heavy-duty suspension ($27.99). Simulated styled steel wheel covers ($57.08). Extra charge for non-standard tires: 8.55 x 15 whitewalls ($42.88). 8.55 x 15 red band whitewalls ($52.04). Size 215-B15 A (6.55 x 15) steel-belted radial whitewall tires ($101.30).

1970

1970 Thunderbird Standard Equipment: All standard FoMoCo safety features plus 429-cid 360-hp four-barrel V-8; SelectShift Cruise-O-Matic transmission; power steering; power front disc/rear drum brakes; sequential turn signals; courtesy and side marker lights; remote-control OSRV mirror; electric clock; trunk light; 215-R15 radial-ply black sidewall tires. Landau models have vinyl roof.

1970 Thunderbird Options: SelectAire air conditioner ($427). SelectAire conditioner with automatic climate control ($499). Traction-Lok differential ($47). Sure Track anti-lock braking system ($194). Rear window defogger ($26). Evaporative emissions control system, all California registered cars only ($37). Tinted windows ($48). Convenience group with seat belt and headlights on lights, fuel flasher, door ajar light, vacuum power door locks, headlights on buzzer, and automatic seat back latch on two-door models ($101). Electric rear window defroster, requires clock and with high-level brake light ($84). Heater and defroster delete, in Hawaii only ($17 credit). Color-keyed vinyl insert body side moldings, includes wheel lip molding ($26). Color-keyed dual racing mirrors ($26). Glamour paint ($130). Power deck lid release ($14). Power 6-way full-width bench seat ($99). Power 6-way driver's bucket seat ($99). Power 6-way driver and passenger seats ($198). Power side windows ($110). Protection group with color-keyed floor mats, license plate frames, and door edge guards (two-door $26; four-door $30). AM/FM radio with two front speakers ($150). Dual rear seat speakers, standard with stereo radio and tape system ($33). Stereosonic tape system ($150). High-back bucket seats and console, except four-door Landau ($78). Manual reclining passenger bench seat ($41). Split-Bench seat in four-door Landau ($78). Fiera Special Brougham option, includes high-back bucket seats and console, cloth and vinyl trim, rear seat center arm rest, body side protection moldings, courtesy lights, color-keyed wheel covers, rim-blow deluxe steering wheel, cut-pile carpeting, 85-amp. battery, door pull handles, and grille lamps with color-keyed stone shield and deflectors ($304). Fingertip speed control ($97). Tilt steering wheel ($52). Power-operated sun roof ($453). Heavy-duty suspension ($28). High-level taillamps ($34). Trailer towing package ($50). Cloth and vinyl Brougham interior including unique seat and door trim, wood-grain appointments, rim-blow deluxe steering wheel, door courtesy lights, cut-pile carpets, and rear seat center arm rest, with bench or split-bench seats ($162). Brougham vinyl and leather interior including unique seat and door trim, wood-grain appointments, rim-blow deluxe steering wheel, door courtesy lights, cut-pile carpets, and rear seat center arm rest, with high-back bucket or split-bench seats ($227). All-vinyl seats ($19). Deluxe wheel covers ($52). Simulated magnesium wheel covers ($36). 215 R15 radial-ply whitewalls, except standard with two-doors having Special Brougham option ($30).

1971

1971 Thunderbird Standard Equipment: All standard FoMoCo safety, anti-theft, convenience items, and emissions control equipment; sequential rear turn signals; remote-control left-hand OSRV mirror; electric clock; front cornering lights; AM radio; power ventilation; automatic parking brake release; carpeting; five-pod instrument panel cluster; fuel evaporative emission control system; hydraulic wipers with electric washers; courtesy lights; MagicAire heater and defroster; Flight Bench seats with bright seat shields; front seat center arm rest; pleated all-vinyl interior fabric; Cruise-O-Matic transmission; power steering; power front disc brakes; 429-cid 360-hp four-barrel V-8 engine; and H78-15 black sidewall belted tires. Landau models also have vinyl roof.

1971 Thunderbird Options: SelectAire conditioner ($448). Automatic temperature control with 55-amp alternator and electric rear window defroster ($519). Traction-Lok differential ($49). Sure Track brake control system ($194). Electric rear window defroster, includes interior light located in the heater control ($84). Complete tinted glass ($52). Glamour paint ($130). Body side protection moldings, includes wheel lip moldings, but standard with Brougham package and exterior appearance group ($34). Power antenna ($31). 6-way power full-width seat or 6-way power driver's high-back bucket seat ($104). 6-way power driver and passenger high-back bucket seats ($207). Power side windows ($133). Power trunk lid release ($14). AM/FM stereo radio including dual front and rear seat speakers ($150). Vinyl roof, except standard on Landau models ($141). High-back bucket seats and center console for two-door Thunderbirds, except standard with Brougham option ($78). Manual reclining passenger seat, except standard with Turnpike group ($41). Dual rear seat speakers, standard with AM/FM stereo radio or tape system ($33). Fingertip speed control including rim-blow deluxe three-spoke steering wheel (standard with Turnpike group, otherwise ($97). Tilt steering wheel ($52). Stereophonic tape system with AM radio only ($150). Power-operated sun roof, requires vinyl roof on Hardtop ($518). Heavy-duty suspension with heavy front and rear springs and shocks, front stabilizer bar ($28). Deluxe wheel covers, not available with Brougham package ($52). Exterior appearance group ($78). Convenience check group including seat belt light, fuel flasher and door ajar light, vacuum power door locks, front lights-on warning light and buzzer, and automatic seat back release, for two-doors only ($101). Turnpike convenience group includes fingertip speed control, manual reclining passenger seat, and Michelin steel-belted radial-ply whitewall tires with 40,000-mile tread life guarantee on Thunderbirds with Brougham option ($196). Turnpike convenience group includes fingertip speed control, manual reclining passenger seat, and Michelin steel-belted radial-ply whitewall tires with 40,000-mile tread life guarantee on Thunderbirds without Brougham option ($227). Exterior appearance group includes color-keyed stone shields and grille finish panels, body side moldings with color-keyed vinyl inserts, color-keyed wheel covers, and wheel lip moldings ($61 only with specific selected exterior colors and not available teamed with special wheel covers, Brougham option, or special paint colors). Protection group includes color-keyed floor mats, license plate frames, and door edge guards for two-doors ($26), for four-doors ($30).

1972

1972 Thunderbird Standard Equipment: All regulation safety, anti-theft, convenience items, and emissions control equipment; Cruise-O-Matic transmission; power steering; power front disc/rear drum brakes; automatic parking brake release; electric clock; split-bench front seat (individually adjustable); front seat center arm rest; seat belt reminder system; cut-pile carpeting; left OSRV remote-control mirror; protective body side moldings with vinyl inserts; all courtesy lights and trunk light; 400-cid two-barrel V-8; and Michelin steel-belted 215 R15 radial-ply black sidewall tires.

1972 Thunderbird Options: SelectAire conditioner ($436.52). Automatic temperature control with 61-amp alternator and electric rear window defroster ($505.68). Traction-Lok differential ($47.71 without optional axle ratio, $60.33 with optional axle ratio). Deluxe seat belts with warning light ($35.94). Bumper guards front and rear, except standard with protection group ($36.97). Electric rear window defroster, includes 65-amp alternator and panel light ($81.91). 460-cid four-barrel V-8, air conditioning required ($75.97). California emissions system ($15.14). Complete tinted glass ($50.74). Rocker panel moldings ($25.37). Color Glow paint ($37.99). Dual accent body side stripes ($12.62). Power antenna ($30.17). Door lock group, includes remote deck lid release ($59.45). 6-way power driver's seat ($101.34). 6-way power driver and passenger seats ($201.67). Power side windows ($129.60). Power trunk lid release ($13.63). AM/FM stereo radio including dual front and rear seat speakers ($146.14). Vinyl roof ($137.43). Note: Vinyl roof includes "S" landau bars with wood-grain inserts (or tooled silver landau bar inserts when Glamour paint is ordered) on Thunderbirds. Manual reclining passenger seat, except standard with Turnpike group ($40). High-back bucket seats and console ($75.97). Spare tire cover ($86.32). Dual rear seat speakers, standard with AM/FM stereo radio or tape system ($32.18). Fingertip speed control including rim-blow deluxe three-spoke steering wheel (standard with Turnpike group, otherwise $103.14). Deluxe three-spoke rim-blow steering wheel ($37.99). Tilt steering wheel ($50.74). Stereosonic tape system with AM radio only ($146.14). Power-operated sun roof, requires vinyl roof on Hardtop ($504.80). Heavy-duty suspension with heavy front and rear springs and shocks, front stabilizer bar ($27.26). Leather trim for split-bench seats ($63.65). Deluxe wheel covers, except not available with Glamour Paint option ($87.07). Intermittent windshield wipers, requires recessed windshield wipers ($25.37). Convenience group includes low fuel and door ajar light and buzzer, dual overhead map lights, engine compartment light ($43.79). Glamour Paint option, includes color-keyed wheel covers, dual body side and hood paint stripes, tooled silver landau bar inserts without vinyl roof ($161.79). Protection group includes color-keyed floor mats, license plate frames, and door edge guards ($25.37). Heavy-duty trailer towing package, includes heavy-duty suspension, extra-cooling package, wiring harness, high-ratio axle, and trailer towing decal ($45.82). Turnpike convenience group includes fingertip speed control, manual reclining passenger seat, and trip odometer ($132.51). Michelin 215 15R steel-belted radial-ply single band whitewall tires with 40,000-mile tread life guarantee (Michelin black sidewalls were standard and the whitewalls were $31.17 extra).

1973

1973 Thunderbird Standard Equipment: All regulation safety, anti-theft, convenience items, and emissions control equipment; 429-cid four-barrel regular fuel V-8; SelectShift Cruise-O-Matic transmission with uniform transmission shift quadrant; power steering; power front disc/rear drum brakes; front bumper guards; body side moldings with protective vinyl inserts; bright window reveal moldings; remote-control left-hand OSRV mirror; full wheel covers; individually adjustable split-bench seats; Aurora cloth seat trim with vinyl facings; cut-pile carpeting; wood-tone interior dress up accents; deluxe arm rests; interior courtesy lights; steel-belted radial tires; power front disc/rear drum brakes; power ventilation system; 80-amp battery; inside the car hood release, constant-ratio power steering; AM radio; MagicAire heater and defroster; electric clock; full wheel covers; spare tire lock; back-up lights; side marker lights; unique Thunderbird identification and ornamentation; hood ornament; bright moldings at rear of hood, door belts, drip rails and wheel lips; 61-amp alternator maintains battery charge even at low engine speeds; automatic parking brake release; aluminized muffler with stainless steel components; self-adjusting brakes; and choice of 23 exterior colors. Added to standard equipment list on June 11, 1973 were opera windows; power windows; tinted glass; vinyl roof; and automatic seat back release.
1973 Thunder Options: 6-way power seat ($201). Power windows ($130). Fingertip speed control ($103). Tilt steering wheel ($51). Automatic temperature control air conditioning ($505). AM/FM stereo radio ($146). Electric rear window defogger ($36). Power-operated sun roof ($505). Vinyl roof ($137). Turnpike convenience group ($132). A complete list of options for this model-year was unavailable at time of publication. The options availability and prices for 1973 Thunderbirds were similar to 1974 data.

1974

1974 Thunderbird Standard Equipment: All regulation safety, anti-theft, convenience items, and emissions control equipment; power steering; ignition and map lights; Cruise-O-Matic transmission; 460-cid V-8 engine; power front disc/rear drum brakes; AM radio; electric clock; split-bench front seat; vinyl roof; opera windows; full front seat with arm rests; cut-pile carpeting; remote-control left-hand OSRV mirror; protective body side moldings with vinyl inserts; all courtesy lights; all door light switches; ash tray and trunk lights; LR78/15 steel-belted radial white sidewall tires; full wheel covers; SelectAire conditioner; tinted glass; front bumper guards; and full coil spring suspension.
1974 Thunderbird Options: Automatic temperature control air conditioner ($74). Traction-Lok differential ($50). Sure Track brake control system ($197). Deluxe bumper group including front and rear bumper guards with rubber inserts and full-width rub strips ($51). Electric rear window defroster, including panel indicator light and 70-amp alternator ($85). California emissions testing ($21). Dual exhaust system, including sound package ($53). Dual body side and hood stripes ($18). Fire Metallic paint ($131). Starfire Metallic paint ($172). Dual body side accent stripes ($18). Power antenna ($31). Power door locks group including remote trunk release ($62). 6-way power full-width seat ($210). 6-way power split-bench seat ($105). Power Moon roof ($798). Power mini -vent windows ($70). AM/FM stereo radio ($152). AM/FM stereo radio with tape player ($311). Dual rear seat speakers (standard with stereo radio or tape system, otherwise $33). Manual reclining passenger seat, standard with Turnpike convenience group ($42). High-back bucket seats with central console ($120). Fingertip speed control, including rim-blow steering wheel and standard with Turnpike convenience group ($103). Rim-blow steering wheel alone ($40). Tilt steering wheel ($53). Power-operated sun roof ($525). Heavy-duty suspension includes heavy front and rear springs and shocks ($28). Trailer equalizing hitch, requires trailer towing package ($90). Super-soft vinyl seat trim ($35). Luggage compartment trim ($57). Picardy velour cloth trim ($64). Leather seat trim ($105). Deluxe wheel covers ($64). Color-keyed wheel covers ($20). Simulated wire wheel covers ($85). Rear window quick defrost ($315). Convenience group, including interval windshield wipers and right-hand remote-control OSRV mirror ($53). Turnpike convenience group, including visor-vanity mirror, interval windshield wipers, right- and left-hand remote-control mirrors, speed control, manual reclining passenger seat, and trip odometer ($138). Convenience light group, including illuminated visor mirror, headlights-on light and buzzer, low fuel warning light, door opening warning light, overhead map light, and engine compartment light ($130). Exterior decor group, including partial wheel lip moldings, front cornering lights, and wide lower body side moldings with padded grain-tone vinyl inserts ($141). Protection group with door edge guards, license plate frames, spare tire lock and cover, and front and rear floor mats with carpet inserts (with exterior decor group $68, without exterior decor group $75). Class III trailer towing package with heavy-duty handling suspension, heavy-duty alternator, wiring harness, extra-cooling package, coolant recovery system, heavy-duty frame, and trailer towing decal ($48, but not offered for cars registered in California). Theft-Foil alarm system with alarm and decals ($79). LR78 steel-belted radial-ply whitewall tires ($33 extra). Burgundy luxury group, including Burgundy Victorian velour or Red leather seats and door trim, deluxe luggage compartment trim, gold insert Thunderbird opera window ornaments, Burgundy Fire Metallic paint, simulated wire wheel covers, gold paint stripes, and Dark Red Odense grain vinyl roof ($411).

1975

1975 Anniversary Thunderbird Standard Equipment: All regulation safety, anti-theft, convenience items, and emissions control equipment; body and frame construction with closed box-section members and five cross-members; power steering; ignition and map lights; Cruise-O-Matic transmission; 460-cid V-8 engine; self-adjusting power front disc/rear drum brakes; three-year coolant and antifreeze; long-life Motorcraft Sta-Ful battery; corrosion-resistant aluminized muffler; zinc-coated underbody parts; AM radio; electric clock; split-bench front seat; vinyl roof; opera windows; full front seat with arm rests; standard cloth and vinyl seat trim; cut-pile carpeting; remote-control left-hand OSRV mirror; protective body side moldings with vinyl inserts; all courtesy lights; all door light switches; ash tray and trunk lights; LR78/15 steel-belted radial white sidewall tires; full wheel covers; SelectAire conditioner; tinted glass; front bumper guards; and full coil spring suspension. Copper Starfire or White exterior; Copper padded vinyl half roof with color-coordinated wrap-over moldings; color-keyed vinyl insert body side moldings; Gold-toned T-Bird insignia
1975 Anniversary Thunderbird Copper Luxury Group Standard Equipment substitutes or adds: Copper Starfire or Polar White exterior finish; Copper Odense grain padded vinyl half roof with color-coordinated wrap-over moldings; color-keyed vinyl insert body side moldings; Gold-toned T-Bird insignia on opera windows; color-accented cast-aluminum wheels; color-keyed pin stripes on hood and body belt; Copper velour cloth or Copper leather interior trim; Copper dash, door panel, and headliner accents; Copper floor carpeting; Copper colored trunk compartment trim.
1975 Anniversary Thunderbird Silver Luxury Group Standard Equipment substitutes or adds: Silver Starfire exterior finish; Silver Odense grain padded vinyl half roof with color-coordinated wrap-over moldings; color-keyed vinyl insert body side moldings; silver silk-screened T-Bird insignia on opera windows; choice of Red velour, Red leather, or Silver leather deluxe interior trim; and color-coordinated trunk compartment trim.
1975 Anniversary Thunderbird Jade Luxury Group Standard Equipment substitutes or adds: Choice of Polar White exterior body finish with Jade Green half vinyl roof, or Jade Starfire Glamour paint exterior body finish with Jade Green half vinyl roof; or Jade Starfire Glamour paint exterior body finish with White half vinyl roof, plus wide body side molding color-keyed to roof, opera window Thunderbird insignia, rear window and roof moldings also color-keyed, dual hood and body side paint stripes, wire wheel covers, and rich White leather seating (code P5) with Jade vinyl trim and components, or deep-cushioned seats tailored in plush Jade Green Media velour cloth trim (Code NR) with Jade vinyl trim and color-keyed components.

287

1975 Thunderbird Options: 4-wheel disc brakes. Sure-Track braking system. Traction-Lok differential. Front cornering lamps. Dual exhaust system. Fingertip speed control. Heavy-duty suspension. Class III towing package. Low-vacuum warning light. Optional axle ratios. AM/FM stereo radio. AM/FM stereo radio with 8-track tape player. SelectAire conditioner. Electric rear window defroster. Power-operate moon roof. Power-operated sun roof. Power antenna. 6-way power driver's seat. 6-way power passenger's seat. Power mini-vent window. Reclining passenger seat. Space-Saver spare tire. Tilt steering wheel. Super-soft vinyl seat trim. Rear window Quick-defroster. Windshield Quick-defroster. Convenience group. Light group. Power lock group. Protection group.'Turnpike convenience group. Wide body side moldings. Anti-theft system. Deep-dish cast-aluminum wheels. Starfire paint. Dual body and hood pin striping. Leather seat surfaces. Pictor velour cloth seat trim. Deluxe wheel covers. Simulated wire wheel covers. Radial-ply tires with wide-band white sidewalls. Note: Prices for 1975 Thunderbird options were not available at time of publication, but similar to 1974 prices.

1976

1976 Thunderbird Standard Equipment: 1977 Thunderbird Standard Equipment: All standard FoMoCo safety, anti-theft, convenience items, and emissions control equipment; 460-cid four-barrel V-8 with solid state ignition; SelectShift Cruise-O-Matic transmission; power steering; power front disc/rear drum brakes; manual SelectAire Conditioner; automatic parking brake release; AM radio with dual front door-mounted speakers; power windows; 61-0amp alternator; burled wood-tone interior appliqués; inside hood release; power ventilation; door courtesy lights; under-panel courtesy lights; glove box light; front ash tray light; individually-adjusted front split-bench seat with dual fold-down center arm rests; Aurora cloth and vinyl upholstery (Saddle, Blue, Jade or Black); electric clock; 24-oz. cut-pile carpeting; color-keyed deluxe seat belts; Thunderbird sound package; Odense grain full vinyl roof; (Black, Blue, White, Dark Jade, Silver, Gold, Brown or Dark Red); Normande grain vinyl top in Creme; opera windows with Thunderbird insignia; remote-control left-hand OSRV mirror; stand-up hood ornament; bright moldings at hood rear, door belts, drip rails; vinyl insert body side moldings; wheel lip moldings; deluxe bumper group (guards and rub strips with white inserts); gas-saving steel-belted radial-ply whitewall tires; and full wheel covers.

1976 Thunderbird Options: Bordeaux luxury group ($624-$700). Creme and Gold luxury group ($717-$793). Lipstick luxury group ($337-$546). Turnpike group ($180). Convenience group ($84). Protection group ($79-$87). Light group ($164). Power lock group ($86). Security lock group ($18). Automatic temperature control air conditioning ($488). Anti-theft alarm system ($84). Electric rear defroster ($99). Electric windshield/rear window defroster ($355). Fingertip speed control ($120). Tinted glass ($29- $66). Power mini-vent windows ($79). Six-way power driver's seat ($132). Six-way driver and passenger seat ($250). Power lumbar support seats ($86). Reclining passenger seat ($70). Automatic seat back release ($30). Tilt steering wheel ($68). Fuel monitor warning light ($20). Cornering lamps ($43). Lighted driver's visor vanity mirror ($43). AM/FM stereo radio ($145). AM/FM stereo radio with tape player ($249). AM/FM stereo radio with search function ($298). AM/FM quadrosonic radio with tape player ($382). Power antenna ($32). Power moon roof ($879). Sun roof ($716). Starfire paint ($204). Wide color-keyed vinyl insert body side moldings ($121). Dual body side and hood paint stripes ($33). Leather seat trim ($239). Kasman cloth seat ($96). Super-soft vinyl seat trim ($55). Trunk dress-up package ($59). Deluxe wheel covers ($67). Simulated wire wheel covers, except with Gold and Creme package ($88). Simulated wire wheel covers (with Gold and Creme package) ($163 credit). Deep-dish aluminum wheels, except with Bordeaux/Lipstick groups ($251). Deep-dish aluminum wheels with Bordeaux/Lipstick groups ($163). JR78 x 15 steel-belted radial whitewall tires ($41). LR78 x 15 steel-belted radial wide white sidewall tires ($59). Space-Saver spare tires ($ 86)

1977

1977 Thunderbird Standard Equipment: All standard FoMoCo safety, anti-theft, convenience items, and emissions control equipment; 302-cid two-barrel V-8 (or 352-cid 149-hp V-8 in California); DuraSpark ignition system; SelectShift automatic transmission; power steering; power front disc/rear drum brakes; HR78 x 15 black sidewall belted radial tires; chrome-plated swing-away grille; fender louvers; concealed two-speed windshield wipers; wiper-mounted washer jets; coolant recovery system; inside hood release; concealed headlights; full-width taillights; opera windows; dual note horn; bright rocker panel moldings; bright wheel lip moldings; full wheel covers; bright window, door belt, and roof drip moldings; heater and defroster; full-flow ventilation; deluxe steering wheel; day/night mirror; bench seats; carpeting; instrument panel with wood-tone appliqués; inside hood release; and cigar lighter.

1977-1/2 Thunderbird Town Landau Standard Equipment: Most of the features above, with these differences or additions: Brushed aluminum roof wrap-over appliqué; color-keyed roof cross-over moldings (when optional vinyl top is ordered); color-coordinated translucent hood ornament insert; four cast aluminum wheels with accent paint; opera windows with a Town Landau insignia; accent stripes on body sides, hood, and grille opening panel, deck lid, headlight doors, and fender louvers; whitewall steel-belted radial tires; wide color-keyed vinyl insert body side moldings with partial wheel lip moldings; front cornering lamps; deluxe bumper group (including front and rear bumper guards and horizontal rub strips); a luxury sound insulation package; Town Landau insignia on instrument panel appliqué; 22-karat gold finish plaque engraved with owner's name; 6-way power driver's seat; power side windows; power lock group (including door locks and remote trunk release); manual-control SelectAire Conditioner; Interior luxury group including convenience group (with left- and right-hand remote control mirrors, interval windshield wipers, automatic parking brake release, and trip odometer) and light group (with dual-beam map lights; under-dash lights; glove box light; ash tray light; trunk light; engine compartment light; door ajar light; and headlights on light); tinted glass; AM/FM stereo search radio (with twin front door mounted speakers and dual rear speakers); and a tilt steering wheel.

1977 Thunderbird Options: 351-cid 161-hp V-8 engine ($66). 400-cid V-8 engine ($155). Manual air conditioner ($505). Automatic air conditioner in base Hardtop ($546). Automatic air conditioner in Town Landau or Diamond Jubilee (N/A). Heavy-duty 90-amp alternator ($45). Optional ratio axle ($14). Traction-Lok differential axle ($54). Heavy-duty 77-amp. battery ($17). Color-keyed deluxe seat belts ($18). Front license plate bracket (no charge). Deluxe bumper group ($72). Day and date clock ($20). Convenience group for models with bucket seat and floor shift ($88); for other models ($96). Front cornering lights ($43). Exterior decor group for models with convenience group or interior luxury group ($317); for other models ($368). Interior decor group ($299). Electric rear window defroster ($87). California emissions equipment ($70). Illuminated entry system ($51). Complete tinted glass ($61). High-altitude equipment ($22). Instrumentation group for Sports models with convenience group ($103); for other models ($111). Light group ($46). Power lock group ($92). Interior luxury group ($724). Dual sport mirrors from models with convenience or interior luxury groups (no charge); for other models ($51). Remote-control left OSRV chrome mirror ($14). Illuminated right-hand visor-vanity mirror for models with interior decor group ($42); for other models ($46). Black vinyl insert body side moldings ($39). Bright wide body side moldings ($39). Color-keyed wide body side moldings ($51). Power moon roof ($888). Metallic glow paint ($62). Protection group for models with front license plate bracket ($47); for other models ($43). AM/FM manual radio ($59). AM/FM stereo radio ($120). AM/FM stereo search radio ($276). AM/FM radio with quadrosonic tape player in base Hardtop ($326); in Town Landau ($50). AM/FM stereo with tape player ($193). Two-piece vinyl roof ($132). Six-way power full-width front seat ($143). Six-way power driver's seat only ($143). Bucket seats and console with interior decor group (no charge); all others ($158). Automatic seat back release ($52). Space Saver spare tire (no charge to $13 credit, depending on type of tires). Dual rear seat speakers ($43). Fingertip speed control in models with sports instrumentation group or interior luxury group ($93); all other models ($114). Leather steering wheel in models with sports instrumentation group ($39); all other models ($61). Tilt steering wheel ($63). Handling suspension ($79). Dual accent paint stripes ($39). Heavy-duty trailer towing package ($138). Leather seat trim ($241). Vinyl seat trim ($22). Tu-Tone paint treatment ($49). Wire wheel covers with exterior decor group ($47 credit); other models ($99). Four turbine-spoke cast aluminum wheels, with exterior decor group ($88); all other models ($234). Power side windows ($114). AM radio delete ($72 credit). Tire options (followed by extra charge for models having five HR78 x 15 steel-belted black sidewall tires as standard equipment): HR78 x 15 radial whitewalls ($45 extra); HR78 x 15 radial white band whitewalls ($61 extra); and HR70 x 17 white oval whitewalls ($67 extra).

1978

1978 Thunderbird Standard Equipment: All standard FoMoCo safety, anti-theft, convenience items, and emissions control equipment; 302-cid two-barrel V-8 (or 352-cid 149-hp V-8 in California); DuraSpark ignition system; SelectShift automatic transmission; power steering; power front disc/rear drum brakes; front and rear stabilizer bars; H78 x 15 black sidewall belted radial tires; chrome-plated swing-away grille; fender louvers; concealed two-speed windshield wipers; wiper-mounted washer jets; coolant recovery system; inside hood release; concealed headlights; full-width taillights; opera windows; dual note horn; bright rocker panel moldings; bright wheel lip moldings; full wheel covers; bright window, door belt, and roof drip moldings; heater and defroster; full-flow ventilation; deluxe steering wheel; day/night mirror; deep-cushioned bench seats with knit cloth/vinyl trim; color-keyed 10-oz. cut-pile carpeting; full-length door arm rests; all-vinyl door trim with burled walnut wood-tone appliqués; instrument panel with burled walnut wood-tone appliqués; inside hood release; cigar lighter; AM radio; and electric clock.

1978 Thunderbird Town Landau Standard Equipment: Most of the features above, with these differences or additions: Brushed aluminum roof wrap-over appliqué; color-keyed roof cross-over moldings (when optional vinyl top is ordered); color-coordinated translucent hood ornament insert; four cast aluminum wheels with accent paint; opera windows with a Town Landau insignia; accent stripes on body sides, hood, and grille opening panel, deck lid, headlight doors, and fender louvers; whitewall steel-belted radial tires; wide color-keyed vinyl insert body side moldings with partial wheel lip moldings; front cornering lamps; deluxe bumper group (including front and rear bumper guards and horizontal rub strips); a luxury sound insulation package; Town Landau insignia on instrument panel appliqué; 22-karat gold finish plaque engraved with owner's name; 6-way power driver's seat; power side windows; power lock group (including door locks and remote trunk release); manual-control SelectAire Conditioner; Interior luxury group including convenience group (with left- and right-hand remote control mirrors, interval windshield wipers, automatic parking brake release, and trip odometer) and light group (with dual-beam map lights; under-dash lights; glove box light; ash tray light; trunk light; engine compartment light; door ajar light; and headlights on light); tinted glass; AM/FM stereo search radio (with twin front door mounted speakers and dual rear speakers); and a tilt steering wheel.

1978-1/2 Thunderbird Diamond Jubilee Edition Standard Equipment: Most of the features above except/or in addition: An exclusive monochromatic exterior done in Diamond Blue Metallic or Ember Metallic paint; a matching thickly padded vinyl roof; a color-keyed grille texture; a Diamond Jubilee opera window insignia; the owner's initials on the door; color-keyed cast aluminum wheels; color-keyed bumper rub strips; a power radio antenna; an illuminated left-hand visor-vanity mirror; an instrumentation cluster with Ebony wood-tone appliqué; unique front split-bench seat with biscuit design all cloth trim and Thunderbird ornamentation on the upper seat bolsters; door and front seat-back assist straps; hand-stitched leather-covered pad on instrument panel; ebony wood-tone appliqués on instrument panel, knobs, door and quarter trim panels, and steering wheel; molded door and quarter trim arm rests with extra padding; 36-oz. cut-pile floor carpeting; bright metal pedal trim accents; unique car keys with wood-tone inserts; color-keyed 18-oz. trunk carpets, molded rear deck liner; and seat belt warning chime.

1978 Thunderbird Options: 351-cid 161-hp V-8 engine ($157). 400-cid V-8 engine ($283). Traction-Lok differential axle ($50). Manual air conditioner ($543). Automatic air conditioner in base Hardtop ($588). Automatic air conditioner in Town Landau or Diamond Jubilee ($45) Power antenna ($45). Heavy-duty battery ($18). Color-keyed deluxe seat belts ($21). Front license plate bracket (no charge). Deluxe bumper group ($78). Day and date clock ($22). Convenience group for models with bucket seat and floor shift ($93); for other models ($103). Front cornering lights ($46). Exterior decor group for models with convenience group or interior luxury group ($332); for other models ($382). Interior decor group ($316). Sports decor group for models with convenience group ($396); for other models($446). Electric rear window defroster ($93). California emissions equipment ($75). T-roof convertible option ($699). Illuminated entry system $54. Complete tinted glass ($66). Sports instrumentation group for models with convenience group ($111); for other models ($118). Luxury sound insulation package ($29). Light group ($49). Power lock group ($100). Interior luxury group ($783). Dual sport mirrors for models with convenience or interior luxury groups ($8); for other models ($58). Remote-control left OSRV mirror ($16). Illuminated visor-vanity mirror for models with interior decor group ($33); for other models ($37). Rocker panel moldings ($29). Bright wide body side moldings ($42). Color-keyed wide body side moldings ($54). Power moon roof ($691). Metallic glow paint ($62). Protection group for models with front license plate bracket ($50); for other models ($46). AM/FM monaural radio ($53). AM/FM stereo radio ($113). AM/FM stereo search radio ($270). 40-channel Citizens Band radio ($295). AM/FM radio with quadrosonic tape player in base Hardtop ($320); in Town Landau and Diamond Jubilee models ($50). AM/FM stereo with tape player ($187). Radio flexibility group ($105). Two place vinyl roof ($138). Bucket seats and console with interior decor group ($37); all others ($211). Automatic seat back release ($33). Dual rear seat speakers ($46). Fingertip speed control, Town Landau or Diamond Jubilee with sports instrumentation group or interior luxury group ($104); all other models ($117). Leather steering wheel in models with sports instrumentation group ($51); all other models ($64). Tilt steering wheel ($70). Heavy-duty suspension ($20) Dual accent paint stripes ($46). Inflatable spare tire with HR78 black sidewall tires (no charge). Heavy-duty trailer towing package ($184). Leather and vinyl seat trim ($296). Luggage compartment trim ($39). Vinyl seat trim ($24). Tu-Tone paint treatment ($79). Wire wheel covers ($112). Four styled road wheels ($159). Four cast aluminum wheels on models with exterior decor group ($132); all other models ($291). Power side windows ($126). Heavy-duty alternator ($50). Front and rear bumper guards ($42). Sports instrumentation group on Town Landau or models with interior luxury group ($75); models with convenience group ($111); all other models ($118). Vinyl body side moldings ($42). Tinted windshield glass ($28) Front floor mats ($20). Tire options for base Hardtop with five GR78 x 15 tires as standard equipment included GR78 x 15 radial whitewalls ($46 extra); HR78 x 15 black sidewalls ($22 extra); HR78 x 15 radial whitewalls ($68 extra); HR78 x 15 radial white-band whitewalls ($88 extra); and HR70 x 17 white oval whitewalls ($90 extra). Tire options for the Diamond Jubilee with five standard HR78 x 15 steel-belted whitewall radials as standard equipment included HR78 x 15 radial wide band whitewalls ($20 extra); and HR70 x 15 whitewall wide oval radials ($22 extra).

1979

1979 Thunderbird Standard Equipment: All standard FoMoCo safety, anti-theft, convenience items, and emissions control equipment; 302-cid two-barrel V-8 (or 352-cid 149-hp V-8 in California); DuraSpark ignition system; SelectShift automatic transmission, power steering; power front disc/rear drum brakes; front and rear stabilizer bars; GR78 x 15 black sidewall belted radial tires; chrome-plated swing-away grille; chrome plated front and rear bumpers; chrome plated rear bumper guards; fender louvers; concealed two-speed windshield wipers; wiper-mounted washer jets; coolant recovery system; inside hood release; concealed headlights; full-width taillights; opera windows; dual note horn; bright rocker panel moldings; bright wheel lip moldings; full wheel covers; bright window, door belt, and roof drip moldings; heater and defroster; full-flow ventilation; deluxe steering wheel; day/night mirror; Flight Bench seat; three-point seat and shoulder belts with retractors; color-keyed 10-oz. cut-pile carpeting; full-length door arm rests; all-vinyl door trim with burled walnut wood-tone appliqués; instrument panel with burled walnut wood-tone appliqués; inside hood release; cigar lighter; AM radio; and electric clock.

1979 Thunderbird Town Landau Standard Equipment: Most of the features above, with these differences or additions: HR78 x 15 steel-belted radial whitewall tires; air conditioning; luxury sound insulation package; power lock group; 6-way driver's power seat; power side windows; tilt steering wheel; tinted glass; trip odometer; windshield wipers with interval control; deluxe bumper group; dual sport remote-control mirrors; wide color-keyed vinyl insert body side moldings; integral partial wheel lip moldings; brushed aluminum roof wrap-over appliqué; cast aluminum wheels; upgraded carpeting; quartz crystal day and date clock; illuminated visor-vanity mirror on passenger side; AM/FM stereo radio, split bench seat with manual recliner; and automatic seat back releases.

1979 Thunderbird Heritage Edition Standard Equipment: In addition to base equipment: HR78 x 15 whitewall steel-belted radial tires; air conditioning; illuminated entry system; luxury sound insulation package; power antenna; power lock group; 6-way power driver's seat; power side windows; speed control; tilt steering wheel; tinted glass; trip odometer; interval windshield wipers; deluxe bumper group; dual remote-control mirrors; wide color-keyed vinyl body side moldings; integral wheel lip moldings; vinyl roof; cast aluminum wheels; upgraded carpeting; illuminated visor-vanity mirrors on both sides; AM/FM stereo search radio, split bench seat with manual recliner; automatic seat back release; and sport instrumentation.

1979 Thunderbird Options: 351-cid 161-hp V-8 engine ($263). Traction-Lok differential axle ($64). Auto Temperature Control air conditioner, in base Hardtop ($607); in Town Landau or Heritage Edition ($45) Manual air conditioner ($562). Heavy-duty battery ($20). Color-keyed deluxe seat belts ($22). Lower body side protection, models with rocker panel moldings ($33); other models ($46). Front license plate bracket (no charge). Bumper rub strips ($37). Day and date clock ($24). Convenience group for models with bucket seat and floor shift ($108); for other models ($117). Front cornering lights ($49). Exterior decor group for models with convenience group or interior luxury group ($346); for other models ($406). Interior decor group ($322). Sports decor group for models with convenience group ($459); for other models($518). Mud and stone deflectors ($25). Electric rear window defroster ($99). California emissions equipment ($83). High-altitude emissions system ($83). Extended range fuel tank ($36). Illuminated entry system ($57). Complete tinted glass ($70). Sports instrumentation group for Town Landau or cars with interior luxury group ($88), for models with convenience group ($121); for other models ($129). Light group ($51). Power lock group ($111). Luggage compartment trim ($43). Luxury sound insulation package ($30). Interior luxury group ($816). Illuminated passenger side visor-vanity mirror for cars with interior decor group ($34), for other cars ($39). Left-hand remote-control OSRV mirror ($18). Color-keyed wide body side moldings ($54). Dual sport mirrors, on models with convenience group or interior luxury group ($9), on other models ($68). Rocker panel moldings ($29). Wide bright body side moldings ($42). Power moon roof ($691). Metallic glow paint ($64). Protection group for models with front license plate bracket ($53); for other models ($49). Power radio antenna ($47). AM radio delete ($79 credit). AM/FM monaural radio ($59). AM/FM stereo radio ($120). AM/FM stereo search radio ($276). AM/FM radio with 8-track tape player ($193). 40-channel Citizens Band radio ($329). AM/FM radio with quadrosonic tape player in base Hardtop ($326); in Town Landau and Heritage Edition models ($50). AM/FM stereo with cassette tape player, in two-door Hardtop ($187), in Town Landau or Heritage Edition ($83 credit). Radio flexibility group ($105). Two-piece vinyl roof ($132). Seat belt warning chime ($22). Bucket seats and console with interior decor group ($37); all others ($211). Automatic seat back release ($37). Dual rear seat speakers ($46). Fingertip speed control, Town Landau or Heritage Edition with sports instrumentation group or interior luxury group ($1134); all other models ($126). Tilt steering wheel ($75). Heavy-duty suspension ($22) Dual accent paint stripes ($46). Inflatable spare tire with HR78 black sidewall tires (no charge). All-vinyl seat trim ($26). Ultra-soft leather seat trim, in Heritage Edition ($243), in other models ($309). T-roof convertible option ($747). Tu-Tone paint treatment ($62). Wire wheel covers ($118). Four styled road wheels ($132). Four cast aluminum wheels on models with exterior decor group ($150); all other models ($316). Power side windows ($132). Tire options for base Hardtop with five GR78 x 15 steel-belted radial black sidewall tires as standard equipment included GR78 x 15 radial whitewalls ($47 extra); HR78 x 15 black sidewalls ($25 extra); HR78 x 15 radial whitewalls ($72 extra); and HR70 x 17 white oval whitewalls ($100 extra). Tire options cards with five standard HR78 x 15 steel-belted whitewall radials as standard equipment included HR70 x 15 whitewall wide oval radials ($29 extra);. Color-keyed front floor mats ($20). Tinted windshield only ($28). Engine block heater ($14). Vinyl body side moldings ($42).

1980

1980 Thunderbird Standard Equipment: All standard FoMoCo safety, anti-theft, convenience items, and emissions control equipment; 4.2-liter (255-cid) two-barrel V-8; automatic transmission, variable-ratio power rack and pinion steering; power front disc/rear drum brakes; DuraSpark ignition system; maintenance-free battery; coolant recovery system; modified McPherson strut front suspension; four-bar link-type rear suspension; front and rear stabilizer bars; three-speed heater and defroster; concealed rectangular headlights; wraparound parking lamps; soft urethane covered bumpers; chrome-plated egg-crate grille; quarter windows; moldings on wheel lips, hood, rocker panels, windshield; drip rail; and door belt; full wheel covers; Flight Bench seating with cloth and vinyl trim; 10-oz. color-keyed cut-pile carpeting; and vinyl door trim with wood-tone accents; push-button AM radio; 4-spoke deluxe steering wheel; trip odometer; self-regulating illuminated electric clock; cigar lighter; day-night rear view mirror; glove box and ash tray lights; inertia seat back releases; continuous loop belts; luggage compartment map; mini spare tire; and P185/75R14 black sidewall tires.

1980 Town Landau Standard Equipment adds or substitutes: Air conditioning; tinted glass; power side windows; 6-way power driver's seat; power lock group; tilt steering wheel; interval windshield wipers; TR type white sidewall radial tires; auto lamp on and off delay system; electronic instrument cluster; front cornering lamps; padded rear half-vinyl roof with wrap-over band and coach lamps; wide door belt moldings; color-keyed rear window moldings; striping on hood, body sides and rear deck lid; dual remote-control mirrors; color-keyed vinyl insert body side moldings with partial wheel lip moldings; cast-aluminum wheels; split-bench seats with dual recliners, velour seat trim, luxury door panel trim with cloth or vinyl inserts, courtesy lamps in quarter trim panels, and front door arm rests; electronic AM/FM search stereo radio; illuminated visor-vanity mirror (passenger side); 18-oz. cut-pile luxury carpeting; wood-tone instrument panel appliqués; luxury steering wheel; color-keyed deluxe seat belts; luxury luggage compartment trim; light group with dual-beam lights, map light, instrument panel courtesy lights, engine compartment light, and luggage compartment light.

1980 Thunderbird Options: 5.0-liter (302-cid) two-barrel V-8 ($150). Automatic overdrive transmission ($138). Automatic temperature control air conditioner in Hardtop ($634). Automatic temperature control air conditioner in Town Landau or Silver Anniversary models ($63). Manual temperature control air conditioner ($571). Auto lamp on and off delay system ($63). Heavy-duty battery ($20). Color-keyed deluxe seat belts ($23). Lower body side protection with rocker panel moldings ($34). Lower body side protection on models without rocker panel moldings ($46). Front license plate bracket (no charge). Electronic digital clock ($38). Front cornering lamps ($50). Exterior decor group ($359). Interior decor group ($348). Mud and stone deflectors ($25). Electric rear window defroster ($101). Diagnostic warning lights ($50). California emissions system ($238). High-altitude emissions system ($36). Garage door opener with illuminated visor and vanity mirror in Town Landau or models with interior luxury group ($130). Garage door opener with illuminated visor and vanity mirror in models with interior decor group ($165). Garage door opener with illuminated visor and vanity mirror in all other models ($171). Tinted glass ($71). Engine block immersion heater ($15). Dual note horn ($9). Illuminated entry system ($58). Electronic instrument cluster in Hardtop with interior luxury group ($275). Electronic instrument cluster in all other models ($313). Keyless entry system with Recaro bucket seats ($106). Keyless entry system without Recaro bucket seats ($119). Light group ($35). Power lock group ($113). Luggage compartment trim ($44). Exterior luxury group ($489). Interior luxury group ($975) Passenger side illuminated visor and vanity mirror with interior decor group ($35). Passenger side illuminated visor and vanity mirror without interior decor group ($41). Left-hand remote-control OSRV mirror ($18). Dual remote-control mirrors ($69). Rocker panel moldings ($30). Wide door belt moldings with interior luxury group ($31). Wide door belt moldings without interior luxury group ($44). Wide vinyl insert body side moldings ($54). Metallic Glow paint ($60). Tu-Tone paint and striping treatment on Town Landau ($106). Tu-Tone paint and striping treatment on Hardtop with exterior luxury or exterior luxury groups ($123). Tu-Tone paint and striping treatment on base Hardtop ($163). Automatic parking brake release ($10). Protection group on models with front license plate bracket ($43). Protection group on models without front license plate bracket ($39). Power radio antenna ($49). AM radio delete ($81 credit). AM/FM monaural radio ($53). AM/FM stereo radio ($90). AM/FM stereo radio with 8-track tape player ($166). AM/FM stereo radio with cassette tape player ($179). Electronic AM/FM stereo search radio ($240). Electronic AM/FM stereo search radio with 8-track tape player in Hardtop ($316). Electronic AM/FM stereo search radio with 8-track tape player in Town Landau or Silver Anniversary Hardtops ($76). 40-channel CB radio ($316) Electronic AM/FM stereo search radio with cassette tape player and Dolby noise reduction system in Hardtop ($329). Electronic AM/FM stereo search radio with cassette tape player and Dolby noise reduction system in Town Landau or Silver Anniversary Hardtops ($89). Radio flexibility package ($66). Flip-up open air roof ($219). Vinyl rear half roof ($133). 6-way power driver's seat ($166). 4-way full-width power seat ($111). Bucket seats and console with interior luxury group (no charge). Bucket seats and console without interior luxury group ($176).Recaro bucket seats and console in Town Landau (no charge). Recaro bucket seats and console in Hardtop with interior luxury group ($166). Recaro bucket seats and console in Hardtop without interior luxury group ($254). Premium sound system, with conventional radio ($119). Premium sound system with electronic radio ($150). Conventional spare tire ($37). Dual rear seat speakers ($38). Fingertip speed control in Town Landau or Hardtop with interior luxury group ($116). Fingertip speed control in base Hardtop ($129). Leather-wrapped steering wheel ($44). Tilt steering wheel ($78). Dual accent body side stripes ($40). Hood and body side accent stripes with exterior decor or exterior luxury groups ($16). . Hood and body side accent stripes without exterior decor or exterior luxury groups ($56). Heavy-duty handling suspension ($26). All-vinyl seat trim ($26). Ultra-soft leather seat trim in Silver Anniversary model ($318). Ultra-soft leather seat trim in all models except Silver Anniversary ($349). Luxury wheel covers ($88). Simulated wire wheel covers with exterior luxury group ($50). Simulated wire wheel covers without exterior luxury group ($138). Power side windows ($136). Interval windshield wipers ($39). P195/75R x 14 steel-belted radial-ply black sidewall tires on base Hardtop ($26). P195/75R x 14 steel-belted radial-ply white sidewall tires on base Hardtop ($59). TR type radial whitewall tires with exterior decor and including aluminum wheels on Town Landau and Silver Anniversary models ($441). TR type radial whitewall tires without exterior decor ($528). Front floor mats ($19) Luggage compartment light ($29). Electronic instrument cluster delete on Town Landau or Silver Anniversary only ($275 credit)

1981

1981 Thunderbird Standard Equipment: All standard FoMoCo safety, anti-theft, convenience items, and emissions control equipment; 3.3-liter (200-cid) one-barrel six-cylinder engine; three-speed automatic transmission, variable-ratio power rack and pinion steering; power front disc/rear drum brakes; DuraSpark ignition system; halogen headlights; maintenance-free 36AH battery; coolant recovery system; modified McPherson strut front suspension with stabilizer bar; four-bar link-type rear suspension with stabilizer bar; three-speed heater and defroster; concealed rectangular headlights; inside hood release; power ventilation system; dual-note horn; chrome-plated egg-crate grille; hood ornament; soft color-keyed urethane covered bumpers with bright bumper rub strips; bright moldings on rear of hood, windshield, drip rail; door belt, and rear window; wide vinyl insert body side moldings with integral partial wheel lip moldings; quarter windows; full wheel covers; electric clock; cigar lighter; locking glove box; push-button AM radio; 4-spoke deluxe steering wheel; inside day-night rear view mirror; Flight Bench seat with adjustable head restraints; color-keyed seat belts with reminder chime; anti-theft door locks; 10-oz. color-keyed cut-pile carpeting; luggage compartment light; mini spare; and P195/75R14 white sidewall steel-belted radial tires.

1981 Thunderbird Town Landau Standard Equipment adds or substitutes: padded half-vinyl roof with color-coordinated wrap-over band and coach lamps; hood and body side accent stripes; right-hand remote-control OSRV mirror; luxury wheel covers; wide door belt moldings; split-bench seats with dual fold-down arm rests,; 18-oz. luxury color-keyed cut-pile carpets; Coco Bola wood-tone appliqué around instrument panel; light group; tilt steering wheel; interval wipers; and diagnostic warning light system.

1981 Thunderbird Heritage Edition Standard Equipment adds or substitutes: Padded rear half-vinyl roof with brushed aluminum wrap-over band and coach lamps; "Frenched" vinyl roof treatment around rear window; dual body side stripes; deck lid accent stripes; bright rocker panel moldings; wire wheel covers; electronic AM/FM stereo search radio,; bright rhodium engraved owner's nameplate; luxury steering wheel with wood-tone insert; illuminated passenger side visor and vanity mirror; velour cloth seat trim in luxury sew style; luxury door trim panels with cloth inserts; burled rosewood wood-tone instrument panel appliqués; luxury luggage compartment trim; 4.2-liter (255-cid) V-8 engine; air conditioning with manual temperature control; tinted glass; power side windows; 6-way power driver's seat; power door locks; remote control deck lid release; auto lamp on and off delay system; electronic instrument cluster; and front cornering lamps. 1981 Thunderbird Options:4.2-liter (255-cid) two-barrel V-8, but standard in Heritage Edition ($50). 5.0-liter (302-cid) two-barrel V-8 in Heritage Edition ($41). 5.0-liter (302-cid) two-barrel V-8 in all except Heritage Edition ($91). Four-speed automatic overdrive transmission ($162). Traction-Lok rear axle ($67). Automatic temperature control air conditioner in Hardtop and Town Landau ($652). Automatic temperature control air conditioner in Heritage Edition ($67). Manual temperature control air conditioner ($585). Auto lamp on and off delay system ($65). Heavy-duty battery ($20). Lower body side protection on Heritage Edition ($34). Lower body side protection on other models ($48). Front license plate bracket (no charge). Electronic digital clock ($40). Front cornering lamps ($51). Mud and stone deflectors ($26). Electric rear window defroster ($107). Diagnostic warning lights ($51). California emissions system ($46). High-altitude emissions system ($38). Exterior decor group ($341). Garage door opener with illuminated visor and vanity mirror in Heritage Edition or models with interior luxury group ($134). Garage door opener with illuminated visor and vanity mirror in all other models ($177). Tinted glass ($76). Engine block immersion heater ($16). Illuminated entry system ($60). Electronic instrument cluster in Hardtop with interior luxury group ($282). Electronic instrument cluster in all other models ($322). Electronic instrument cluster delete ($282 credit). Interior decor group ($349). Interior luxury group in Town Landau ($584). Interior Luxury group in other models ($1,039). Keyless entry system ($122). Light group ($30). Power lock group ($120). Luggage compartment trim ($44). Passenger side illuminated visor and vanity mirror ($41). Right-hand remote-control OSRV mirror ($52). Rocker panel moldings ($30). Wide door belt moldings ($45). Tu-Tone paint and striping treatment on Heritage Edition ($111). Tu-Tone paint and striping treatment on Hardtop with exterior decor group ($139). Tu-Tone paint and striping treatment on base Hardtop ($180). Automatic parking brake release ($10). Protection group ($45). Power radio antenna ($48). AM radio delete ($61 credit). Dual rear speakers with AM radio ($37). AM/FM monaural radio ($51). Dual rear speakers with AM/FM monaural radio ($37). AM/FM stereo radio ($88). AM/FM stereo radio with 8-track tape player in Town Landau ($74). AM/FM stereo radio with 8-track tape player in base Hardtop ($162) AM/FM stereo radio with cassette tape player in Town Landau ($87). AM/FM stereo radio with cassette tape player in other models ($174). Electronic AM/FM stereo search radio in Town Landau ($146). Electronic AM/FM stereo search radio in other models ($234). Electronic AM/FM stereo search radio with 8-track tape player in Heritage Edition ($74). Electronic AM/FM stereo search radio with 8-track tape player in Town Landau ($221). Electronic AM/FM stereo search radio with 8-track tape player in other models than Town Landau ($309). Electronic AM/FM stereo search radio with cassette tape player and Dolby noise reduction system in Heritage Edition ($87). Electronic AM/FM stereo search radio with cassette tape player and Dolby noise reduction system in Town Landau ($233). Electronic AM/FM stereo search radio with cassette tape player and Dolby noise reduction system in models other than Town Landau or Heritage Edition ($321). Radio flexibility package ($65). Flip-up open air roof ($228). 6-way power driver's seat ($173). 4-way full-width power seat ($122). Premium sound system, with conventional radio ($116). Premium sound system with electronic radio ($146). Fingertip speed control ($132). Leather-wrapped luxury steering wheel ($45). Tilt steering wheel ($80). Dual accent body side stripes ($41). Hood and body side accent stripes with exterior decor group ($16). Hood and body side accent stripes without exterior decor groups ($57). Heavy-duty handling suspension ($23). Pivoting front vent windows ($55). Luxury wheel covers ($98). Simulated wire wheel covers with Town Landau or exterior decor group ($38). Simulated wire wheel covers without exterior decor group ($135). Power side windows ($140). Interval windshield wipers ($41). P195/75R x 14 puncture-resistant self-sealing steel-belted radial-ply black sidewall tires ($85). TR type radial whitewall tires with exterior decor and including aluminum wheels on Heritage Edition model ($428). TR type radial whitewall tires with exterior decor and including aluminum wheels on Town Landau model ($466).TR type radial whitewall tires without exterior decor ($563). Metallic Glow paint ($70). Color-keyed and carpeted front floor mats ($20). Vinyl front floor mats ($13). Bucket seats and console with Town Landau and interior decor group (no charge). Bucket seats and console without Town Landau or interior decor group ($182).Recaro bucket seats and console in Heritage Edition ($213). Recaro bucket seats and console in Hardtop with interior luxury group ($376). Recaro bucket seats and console in Town Landau and Hardtop with interior decor group ($461). All-vinyl seat trim ($28). Ultra-soft leather seat trim ($309). Carriage roof ($902). Rear half-vinyl roof ($130). Tinted windshield ($29).

1982

1982 Thunderbird Standard Equipment: All standard FoMoCo safety, anti-theft, convenience items, and emissions control equipment; 3.3-liter (200-cid) one-barrel six-cylinder engine; electronic ignition; maintenance-free battery; coolant recovery system; automatic transmission; variable-ratio power rack and pinion steering; power front disc/rear drum brakes; P195/75R14 white sidewall steel-belted radial tires; three-speed heater and defroster; modified McPherson strut front suspension with stabilizer bar; four-bar link-type rear suspension with stabilizer bar; left-hand remote-control OSRV mirror; chrome-plated egg-crate grille; concealed rectangular halogen headlights; soft color-keyed urethane covered bumpers with black bumper rub strips with white accent stripes; black door window frames; bright moldings on windshield, drip rail; door belt, and rear window; black vinyl insert body moldings with partial wheel lip moldings; full wheel covers; illuminated quartz electric sweep hand clock; cigarette lighter; locking glove box; AM radio with dual front speakers; deluxe 4-spoke deluxe steering wheel; inside day-night rear view mirror; Flight Bench seat; 10-oz. color-keyed cut-pile carpeting; luggage compartment light; and mini spare tire.

1982 Thunderbird Town Landau Standard Equipment adds or substitutes: Tilt steering wheel; interval windshield wipers; diagnostic warning light system; luxury padded vinyl roof with color-keyed wrap-over molding and coach lights; hood and body side accent stripes; right-hand remote-control OSRV mirror; luxury wheel covers; wide door belt moldings; split-bench seats with fold-down arm rests, adjustable head restraints, and dual recliners; decor door trim panels; AM/FM stereo radio; 18-oz. luxury color-keyed cut-pile carpets; and light group.

1982 Thunderbird Heritage Edition Standard Equipment adds or substitutes: 3.8-liter (232-cid) two-barrel V-6 engine; automatic overdrive transmission; air conditioning with manual temperature control; tinted glass; power side windows; 6-way power driver's seat; power door locks; remote-control deck lid; auto lamp on and off delay system; electronic instrument cluster with digital read-out; front cornering lamps; automatic parking brake release; padded rear half-vinyl top with brushed aluminum wrap-over appliqué and coach lamps; deck lid accent stripes; bright rocker panel moldings; wire wheel covers; special "cut-glass" look hood ornament; electronic AM/FM stereo search radio,; bright rhodium engraved owner's nameplate; luxury level steering wheel with wood-tone insert; dual illuminated visor and vanity mirrors; velour cloth seat trim in luxury sew style; luxury door trim panels with cloth and burled rosewood wood-tone inserts; burled rosewood wood-tone instrument panel appliqués; and luxury luggage compartment trim.

1982 Thunderbird Options: :3.8-liter (232-cid) two-barrel V-6 engine, except standard on Heritage Edition ($241). 4.2-liter (255-cid) two-barrel V-8, no charge in Heritage Edition, in other models ($241). Traction-Lok rear axle ($76). Automatic temperature control air conditioner in Hardtop and Town Landau ($754). Automatic temperature control air conditioner in Heritage Edition ($78). Manual temperature control air conditioner ($676). Auto lamp on and off delay system ($73). Heavy-duty battery ($24). Lower body side protection on Heritage Edition ($39). Lower body side protection on other models ($54). Front license plate bracket (no charge). Electronic digital clock ($46). Front cornering lamps ($59). Electric rear window defroster ($126). Diagnostic warning lights ($59). California emissions system ($46). High-altitude emissions system (no charge). Exterior decor group ($385). Tinted glass ($88). Engine block immersion heater ($17). Illuminated entry system ($68). Electronic instrument cluster with interior luxury group ($321). Electronic instrument cluster without interior luxury group ($367). Electronic instrument cluster delete ($321 credit). Interior decor group ($372). Interior luxury group in Town Landau ($683). Interior Luxury group in other models ($1,204). Keyless entry system ($139). Light group ($35). Power lock group ($138). Luxury luggage compartment trim ($48). Dual illuminated visor and vanity mirrors in Heritage or with interior luxury group ($46). Dual illuminated visor and vanity mirrors without interior luxury group ($91). Right-hand remote-control OSRV mirror ($60). Rocker panel moldings ($33). Wide door belt moldings ($51). Tu-Tone paint and striping treatment on Heritage Edition ($128). Tu-Tone paint and striping treatment on Hardtop with exterior decor group ($157). Tu-Tone paint and striping treatment on base Hardtop ($206). Automatic parking brake release ($12). Appearance protection group ($51). Power radio antenna ($55). AM radio delete ($61 credit). AM radio with rear speakers ($39). AM/FM monaural radio ($54). Dual rear speakers with AM/FM monaural radio ($39). AM/FM stereo radio ($85). AM/FM stereo radio with 8-track tape player in Town Landau ($87). AM/FM stereo radio with 8-track tape player in base Hardtop ($172) AM/FM stereo radio with cassette tape player in Town Landau ($87). AM/FM stereo radio with cassette tape player in other models ($172). Electronic AM/FM stereo search radio in Town Landau ($146). Electronic AM/FM stereo search radio in other models ($232). Electronic AM/FM stereo search radio with 8-track tape player in Heritage Edition ($87). Electronic AM/FM stereo search radio with 8-track tape player in Town Landau ($233). Electronic AM/FM stereo search radio with 8-track tape player in other models than Town Landau ($318). Electronic AM/FM stereo search radio with cassette tape player and Dolby noise reduction system in Heritage Edition ($87). Electronic AM/FM stereo search radio with cassette tape player and Dolby noise reduction system in Town Landau ($233). Electronic AM/FM stereo search radio with cassette tape player and Dolby noise reduction system in models other than Town Landau or Heritage Edition ($318). Premium sound system, with conventional radio ($133). Premium sound system with electronic radio ($167). Flip-up open air roof ($276). 6-way power driver's seat ($198). Fingertip speed control ($155). Leather-wrapped luxury steering wheel ($51). Tilt steering wheel ($95). Dual accent body side stripes ($49). Hood and body side accent stripes with exterior decor group ($16). Hood and body side accent stripes without exterior decor groups ($65). Heavy-duty handling suspension ($26). TripMinder computer with Heritage, interior luxury group or electronic instrument cluster ($215).TripMinder computer without Heritage, interior luxury group or electronic instrument cluster ($261). Pivoting front vent windows ($63). Luxury wheel covers ($107). Simulated wire wheel covers with Town Landau or exterior decor group ($45). Simulated wire wheel covers without exterior decor group ($152). Power side windows ($165). Interval windshield wipers ($48). P195/75R x 14 puncture-resistant self-sealing steel-belted radial-ply black sidewall tires ($106). TR type radial whitewall tires including aluminum wheels on Heritage Edition model ($490). TR type radial whitewall tires with exterior decor and Town Landau model ($535).TR type radial whitewall tires without exterior decor ($643). Metallic Glow paint ($80). Color-keyed and carpeted front floor mats ($22). Bucket seats and console with Town Landau and interior decor group (no charge). Bucket seats and console without Town Landau or interior decor group ($211). Recaro bucket seats and console in Heritage Edition ($222). Recaro bucket seats and console in Hardtop with interior luxury group ($405). Recaro bucket seats and console in Town Landau and Hardtop with interior decor group ($523). Split-bench seat ($216). Luxury split-bench seat ($124). All-vinyl seat trim ($28). Super-soft vinyl split-bench seat trim ($30). Ultra-soft leather seat trim ($409). Carriage roof with exterior decor group ($766). Carriage roof without exterior decor group ($973). Rear half-vinyl roof with exterior decor group ($163). Rear half-vinyl roof without exterior decor group ($320). Tinted windshield ($32).

t (no charge). Electronic digital clock ($38). Front cornering lamps.

1983

1983 Thunderbird Standard Equipment: 3.8-liter (232-cid) V-6 engine; three-speed automatic transmission; power brakes; power steering; electronic ignition and voltage regulator; dual-note horn; halogen headlamps; left-hand remote-control OSRV mirror; vinyl insert body side moldings; deluxe wheel covers; seat belt reminder chimes; analog quartz clock; center console; vinyl door panels; full carpeting including trunk; AM radio with dual speakers; individual reclining front seats; four-spoke luxury steering wheel; cloth and vinyl upholstery; trip odometer.

1983 Thunderbird Heritage Edition Standard Equipment adds or substitutes: Auto lamp on and off delay system; tinted glass; illuminated entry system; power lock group; automatic parking brake release; diagnostic warning light display; power door windows; interval wipers; electroluminescent coach lamps; front cornering lamps; dual electric remote-control door mirrors; wide body side moldings; accent tape stripes; wire wheel covers; luxury floor carpeting; carpeted seat cushion side facings; cloth insert door panel trim; wood-tone instrument cluster appliqués; electronic instrument cluster; quarter panel courtesy lights; light group; seat back map pockets; dual illuminated visor-vanity mirrors; premium sound system with AM/FM electronic stereo search radio; and velour cloth upholstery.

1983 Thunderbird Turbo Coupe Standard Equipment adds or substitutes: 2.3-liter (140-cid) turbocharged four-cylinder engine with fuel-injection, five-speed overdrive manual transmission, and special handling suspension.

1983 Thunderbird Options: 5.0-liter EFI V-8 engine, except in Turbo Coupe ($288). Four-speed overdrive automatic transmission, except in Turbo Coupe ($176). Traction-Lok axle ($95). Exterior accent group ($343). Automatic temperature control air conditioning ($802). Manual control air conditioning ($724). Anti-theft system ($159). Auto lamp on and off delay system, standard in Heritage ($73). Heavy-duty battery ($26). Lower body side protection on Turbo Coupe ($39). Lower body side protection, except Turbo Coupe ($54). Bumper rub strip extensions ($52). Electronic digital clock ($61). Front cornering lamps ($60). Electric rear window defroster ($135). Diagnostic warning lights, standard in Heritage ($59). Carpeted front floor mats ($22). Remote locking fuel filler door ($26). Full tinted glass ($105). Engine block immersion heater ($17). Illuminated entry system, standard in Heritage ($76). Electronic instrument cluster with interior luxury group ($321). Electronic instrument cluster without interior luxury group ($3820. Electronic instrument cluster standard in Heritage, delete option ($321 credit). Keyless entry system in Heritage ($88). Keyless entry system, except in Heritage ($163). Light group, standard in Heritage ($35). Power lock group, standard in Heritage ($160). Luxury carpet group in Turbo Coupe ($48). Luxury carpet group except in Turbo Coupe ($72). Interior luxury group ($1,170). Electronic dimming rear view mirror ($77). Dual illuminated visor-vanity mirrors, standard in Heritage ($100). Dual electric remote-control door mirrors, standard on Heritage ($94). Bright rocker panel moldings ($33). Wide body side moldings, standard on Heritage ($51). Two-tone paint and tape treatment on Heritage ($148). Two-tone paint and tape treatment with exterior accent group ($163). Two-tone paint and tape treatment without exterior accent group ($218). Automatic parking brake release, standard in Heritage ($12). Power antenna ($60). AM radio delete ($61 credit). AM/FM stereo radio ($109). AM/FM stereo with 8-track or cassette tape in Turbo Coupe ($90). AM/FM stereo with 8-track or cassette tape except in Turbo Coupe and Heritage ($199). AM/FM stereo electronic search radio, in base Coupe ($252). AM/FM stereo electronic search radio, in Turbo Coupe ($144). Note: Previous radio standard in Heritage Edition. AM/FM stereo electronic search radio and cassette, in base Coupe ($396). AM/FM stereo electronic search radio and cassette, in Turbo Coupe ($288). AM/FM stereo electronic search radio and cassette, in Heritage Coupe ($144). Premium sound system ($179). Flip-up open air roof ($310). 6-way power driver's seat ($210). Dual-control power seat ($420). Fingertip speed control ($170). Leather-wrapped luxury steering wheel ($59). Tilt steering wheel ($105). Dual accent body side striping an d deck lid stripes ($55). Hood, body side and deck lid stripes ($71). Hood stripe ($15). Heavy-duty suspension, except not available in Turbo Coupe ($26). Medium-duty trailer tow package ($251). Traveler's assistance kit ($65). TripMinder computer with Heritage, luxury interior group, or electronic instrument cluster ($215). TripMinder computer except with Heritage, luxury interior group, or electronic instrument cluster

292

($276). Pivoting front vent windows ($76). Electronic voice alert ($67). Luxury wheel covers ($113). Locking wire wheel covers with Heritage ($20). Locking wire wheel covers with exterior accent group ($84). Locking wire wheel covers with all others ($198). Wire wheel covers with exterior accent group ($45). Wire wheel covers without exterior accent group ($159). Styled road wheels with exterior accent group ($65). Styled road wheels without exterior accent group ($178). Power side windows, standard in Heritage ($180). Interval wipers ($49). Articulated seats with interior luxury group ($183). Articulated seats without interior luxury group ($427). Vinyl seat trim ($37). Ultra-soft leather trim with Turbo Coupe or with articulated seats ($659). Ultra-soft leather trim without articulated seats or Turbo Coupe ($415).

1984

1984 Thunderbird Standard Equipment: 3.8-liter two-barrel EFI V-6 engine; SelectShift automatic transmission with locking torque converter; variable-ratio rack and pinion steering; power front disc/rear drum brakes; DuraSpark electronic ignition; electronic voltage regulator; maintenance-free battery; McPherson strut front suspension with gas-filled struts; four-bar-link rear suspension with gas-filled shocks; dual fluidic windshield washer system; P195/75R15 all-season white sidewall tires; concealed drip moldings; quad rectangular halogen headlamps; left-hand remote-control OSRV mirror; soft urethane-covered front and rear bumpers; charcoal bumper rub strips with extensions; deluxe wheel covers; individually reclining seats; padded console with illuminated interior and removable litter bin; 10-oz. color-keyed cut-pile carpeting; all-vinyl door trim panels with assist straps and storage bins; luxury steering wheel with center horn blow; trip odometer; quartz electric (sweep-hand) clock; glove box and ash tray lights; color-keyed cloth headlining and sun visors; utility strap on driver's visor; visor-vanity mirror on passenger visor; inertia seat back releases; color-keyed deluxe seat belts with comfort regulator feature and reminder chime; and AM radio (may be deleted for credit).

1984 Thunderbird Elan Equipment adds or substitutes the following over base T-Bird: automatic parking brake release; dual electric remote-control OSRV mirrors; wide body side moldings; front cornering lamps; hood stripes; body side and deck lid accent stripes; styled road wheels; luxury carpet group; quarter panel courtesy lights; electronic digital clock; electronic AM/FM stereo search radio; premium sound system; power lock group; interval windshield wipers; power windows; complete tinted glass; tilt steering wheel; Autolamp on and off delay system; illuminated entry system; electronic instrument cluster; diagnostic warning lights; and light group.

1984 Thunderbird FILA Equipment adds or substitutes the following over base T-Bird: automatic overdrive transmission; special handling package; P205/70HR14 black sidewall performance tires; automatic parking brake release; dual electric remote-control mirrors; wide body side moldings; front cornering lamps; 14-in. aluminum wheels; articulated seats; luxury carpet group; quarter panel courtesy lights; leather-wrapped steering wheel; electronic digital clock; electronic AM/FM stereo search radio with cassette player and Dolby noise reduction system; premium sound system; power lock group; 6-way power driver's seat; complete tinted glass; tilt steering wheel; fingertip speed control; Autolamp on and off delay system; illuminated entry system; diagnostic warning lights; and light group.

1984 Thunderbird Super Coupe Equipment adds or substitutes the following over base T-Bird: 2.3-liter overhead cam EFI turbocharged four-cylinder engine; five-speed manual overdrive transmission; special handling package; tachometer with boost and over-boost lights; Traction-Lok rear axle; P205/70HR14 black sidewall performance tires; dual electric remote-control mirrors; wide body side moldings; body side and deck lid accent stripes; unique front fascia with air dam and fog lights; 14-in. aluminum wheels; articulated seats; luxury carpet group; leather-wrapped sports steering wheel; electronic digital clock; AM/FM stereo radio; diagnostic warning lights; and light group.

1984 Thunderbird options: AM/FM stereo radio ($98). AM/FM stereo radio with cassette tape player. Electronic AM/FM stereo search radio; Electronic AM/FM stereo search radio with cassette tape player and Dolby noise reduction system; Premium sound system (stereo radios only). Wide body side moldings. Exterior accent group. Luxury carpet group. Dual body side and deck lid tape stripes. Tu-Tone paint/tape treatments. Charcoal lower accent treatment. Charcoal Metallic paint. Electroluminescent coach lamps. Autolamp on and off delay system. Diagnostic warning lights. Electronic instrument cluster. TripMinder computer. Electronic voice alert. Traveler's assistance kit. Front cornering lamps. Electric rear window defroster ($126). Remote-control locking fuel door. Dual electric remote-control mirrors ($86). Pivoting front vent windows. Keyless entry system including illuminated entry system. Illuminated entry system. Interval windshield wipers ($45). Flip-up Open-Air roof ($284). SelectAire conditioner with automatic control ($669). SelectAire conditioner with manual control. Automatic parking brake release. Electronic digital clock. Complete tinted glass ($99). Light group. Fingertip speed control ($158). Electronic dimming day/night rear view mirror. Leather-wrapped luxury steering wheel. Tilt steering wheel ($99). Interior luxury group. Articulated seats. Ultrasoft leather trim. Anti-theft system. Lower body sides protection. Bright rocker panel moldings. Front floor mats. Front license plate bracket. License plate frames. Power lock group ($159). Power radio antenna. 6-way power driver's seat. Dual 6-way power seats. Power side windows ($178). Luxury wheel covers. Locking wire wheel style wheel covers. Styled road wheel covers. TRX aluminum wheels including Michelin TRX tires. 5.0-liter V-8 with EFI optional in all models, except Super Coupe. SelectShift automatic transmission with locking torque converter, standard in T-Bird and Elan, optional in Super Coupe ($284). Automatic overdrive transmission, optional in T-Bird and Elan, standard in FILA, not available in Super coupe. Traction-Lok differential, standard in Super Coupe. Medium-duty trailer towing package. Heavy-duty battery. Heavy-duty suspension. Special handling package (standard in FILA and Super Coupe). Engine block immersion heater. California emissions system. Note: Incomplete options pricing date at time of publication.

1985

1985 Thunderbird Standard Equipment: 3.8-liter two-barrel EFI V-6 engine; SelectShift automatic transmission with locking torque converter; variable-ratio rack and pinion steering; power front disc/rear drum brakes; electronic voltage regulator; McPherson strut front suspension with gas-filled struts; four-bar-link rear suspension with gas-filled shocks; P205/70R14 all-season black sidewall tires; concealed drip moldings; halogen headlamps; luxury wheel covers; individually reclining split-bench seats with cloth seating surfaces and consolette; 16-oz. color-keyed cut-pile carpeting; luxury steering wheel with center horn blow; quartz electric (sweep-hand) clock; AM radio (may be deleted for credit).

1985 Thunderbird Elan Equipment adds or substitutes the following over base T-Bird: automatic parking brake release; dual electric remote-control OSRV mirrors; wide body side moldings; body side and deck lid accent stripes; rear seat center folding arm rest; luxury door and quarter panel trim; quarter panel courtesy lights; electronic digital clock; AM/FM stereo cassette tape player; interval windshield wipers; power windows; complete tinted glass; diagnostic warning lights; light group; and remote-locking fuel door.

1985 Thunderbird FILA Equipment adds or substitutes the following over base T-Bird: automatic overdrive transmission; automatic parking brake release; dual electric remote-control mirrors; wide body side moldings; body side and deck lid striping; cornering lamps; 14-in. aluminum wheels; articulated seats; rear seat center folding arm rest; luxury door and quarter trim panels; quarter panel courtesy lights; leather-wrapped steering wheel; electronic digital clock; electronic AM/FM stereo search radio with cassette player and Dolby noise reduction system; premium sound system; power lock group; interval wipers; 6-way power driver's seat; complete tinted glass; tilt steering wheel; speed control; Autolamp on and off delay system; illuminated entry system; diagnostic warning lights; light group; and remote locking fuel door.

1985 Thunderbird Super Coupe Equipment adds or substitutes the following over base T-Bird: 2.3-liter overhead cam EFI turbocharged four-cylinder engine; five-speed manual overdrive transmission; full analog instrumentation with tachometer with boost and over-boost lights; Traction-Lok rear axle; P225/60VR15 black sidewall performance tires; dual electric remote-control mirrors; wide body side moldings; cornering lamps; unique front fascia with air dam and Marchal fog lights; 15-in. aluminum wheels; articulated seats; rear seat center folding arm rest; performance instrumentation; luxury door and quarter trim panels; quarter panel courtesy lights; leather-wrapped steering wheel; electronic digital clock; AM/FM stereo radio; interval wipers; tinted glass complete; diagnostic warning lights; light group; and remote locking fuel door.

1985 Thunderbird options: AM/FM stereo radio with cassette tape player ($133). Electronic AM/FM stereo search radio with cassette tape player and Dolby noise reduction system. Premium sound system (stereo radios only). Graphic equalizer. Wide body side moldings. Dual body side and deck lid tape stripes. Hood stripes. Tu-Tone paint/tape treatments. Clearcoat Metallic paint. Front cornering lamps. Rear window defroster. Dual electric remote-control mirrors ($86). Pivoting front vent windows. Keyless entry system including illuminated entry system ($105). Illuminated entry system. Interval windshield wipers. Flip-up Open-Air roof ($284). SelectAire conditioner with electronic control ($686). SelectAire conditioner with manual control. Automatic parking brake release. Electronic digital clock. Complete tinted glass ($104). Light group. Speed control ($158). Electronic dimming day/night rear view mirror. Dual illuminated visor mirrors. Leather-wrapped luxury steering wheel. Tilt steering wheel ($104). Heated driver and passenger seat. Articulated seats. Ultrasoft leather seat trim. Anti-theft system. Bright rocker panel moldings. Front floor mats. Front license plate bracket. License plate frames. Power lock group ($198). Power radio antenna. 6-way power driver's seat ($214). Dual 6-way power seats. Power seat recliners. Power side windows ($186). Locking wire wheel style wheel covers. Styled road wheel covers. Alloy wheels. 5.0-liter V-8 with EFI and automatic overdrive transmission standard in all models, except Super Coupe ($448 engine/$213 transmission). SelectShift automatic transmission with locking torque converter, standard in T-Bird and Elan, optional in Super Coupe ($284). Traction-Lok differential, standard in Super Coupe. Medium-duty trailer towing package. Heavy-duty battery. Heavy-duty suspension. Engine block immersion heater. California emissions system. Note: Incomplete options pricing date at time of publication.

1986

1986 Thunderbird Standard Equipment: 3.8-liter (232-cid) TBI V-6 engine; three-speed automatic transmission; power brakes; power steering; dual note horn; halogen headlamps; left-hand remote-control door mirror; vinyl insert body side moldings; deluxe wheel covers; seat belt reminder chimes; analog quartz clock; center console; vinyl door panels; full carpeting including trunk; AM/FM stereo radio; individual reclining front seats; luxury steering wheel; cloth upholstery; trip odometer; P215/70R14 tires.

1986 Thunderbird Elan Coupe Equipment adds or substitutes the following over base T-Bird: Power windows; folding rear seat arm rest; tinted glass; light group; dual electric remote-control OSRV mirrors; wide body side moldings; AM/FM cassette stereo; intermittent windshield wipers.

1986 Thunderbird Turbo Coupe Equipment adds or substitutes the following over base T-Bird: 2.3-liter (140-cid) turbocharged four-cylinder PFI engine, 5-speed manual overdrive transmission; and special handling suspension. **1986 Thunderbird Options:** 5.0-liter PFI V-8 ($505). Three-speed automatic transmission in Turbo Coupe ($290). Four-speed automatic transmission in T-Bird and Elan ($220). Traction-Lok axle ($920. Inflatable spare tire ($112). Conventional spare tire ($58). Automatic air conditioning ($850). Air conditioning ($700). Anti-theft system ($145). Autolamp system ($67). Heavy-duty battery ($25). Digital clock ($56). Cornering lamps ($63). Rear defogger ($133). Diagnostic alert lights ($82). Tinted glass ($106). Engine block immersion heater ($17). Illuminated entry system ($75). Electronic instrument cluster in T-Bird ($305). Electronic instrument cluster in T-Bird Elan coupe ($250). Remote keyless entry system ($182). Light group ($32). Power lock group ($200). Front floor mats ($20). Dual illuminated sun visor mirrors ($98). Dual remote-control OSRV mirrors ($88). Wide body side moldings ($52). Power-operated moon roof ($645). Two-tone exterior paint on T-Bird ($200). Two-tone exterior paint on T-Bird Elan Coupe ($150). Metallic clearcoat paint ($168). Power antenna ($65). AM/FM stereo delete option ($167 credit). AM/FM electronically-tuned stereo with cassette tape player ($117). Graphic equalizer ($200). Premium sound system ($155). Articulated sport seats ($168). 6-way power driver's seat ($220). Dual 6-way power seats ($440). Dual power recliners ($174). Speed control ($162). Leather steering wheel ($54). Tilt steering column ($106). Vinyl seat trim ($34). Leather seat trim ($380). TripMinder computer in T-Bird ($255). TripMinder computer in Elan Coupe and Turbo Coupe ($198). Front vent windows ($73). Locking wire wheel covers ($195). Cast-aluminum wheels ($315). Styled road wheels ($164). Power windows ($190). Intermittent windshield wipers ($46). California emissions system ($81); and tinted windshield ($44).

1987

1987 Thunderbird Standard Equipment: Air conditioning; diagnostic alert lights (LX, Turbo). Traction-Lok axle (Turbo); maintenance free battery; power front disc/rear drum brakes (except Turbo); four-wheel disc brakes with ABS (Turbo); electronic ignition; 3.8-liter V-6 (except Sport and Turbo); 5.0-liter V-8 (Sport); 2.3-liter EFI turbocharged four-cylinder engine (Turbo); hydraulic engine mounts; remote-control fuel door (Turbo); tinted glass; three-speed heater and defroster; illuminated entry system (LX); high-mount rear brake light; power lock group (LX); automatic ride control (Turbo); gas pressurized shock absorbers; speed control (LX); power steering; tilt steering wheel (LX); special handling package (Sport and Turbo); P215/70R14 black sidewall tires (Base T-Bird and LX); P215/70HR14 black sidewall tires (Sport); P225/60VR16 black sidewall Goodyear Gatorback tires (Turbo). SelectShift automatic transmission (Base T-Bird and LX); automatic overdrive transmission (Sport); 5-speed manual overdrive transmission (Turbo); windshield washer; two-speed electric windshield wipers; halogen headlights; hood scoops (Turbo); fog lamps (Turbo); left-hand remote-control OSRV mirror (Base T-Bird); dual electric remote-control mirrors (Sport, LX and Turbo); luxury wheel covers (Base T-Bird); cast-aluminum wheels (Turbo); styled road wheels (Sport and LX).

1987 Thunderbird Options: 5.0-liter V-8, except standard on Sport ($639). 4-speed automatic overdrive transmission, optional on Turbo ($515). P215/70R14 tires on standard Base T-Bird and LX ($72 extra). Conventional spare tire ($73). Heavy-duty 54-amp. battery ($27). Electronic equipment group, on Base T-Bird ($634), on Sport and Turbo ($365), on LX ($577). Front floor mats ($30). Luxury light and convenience group, on Base T-Bird ($461), on Base T-Bird with electronic equipment group ($379), on Sport and Turbo ($426), on Sport and Turbo with electronic equipment group ($344), on LX ($244). Dual power seat, on Base T-Bird and LX and Sport ($302), on Turbo or LX with articulated seats ($251). Power antenna ($76). Front license plate bracket (no charge). Electronic digital clock ($61). Rear window defroster ($145). Engine block immersion heater ($18). Power lock group ($249). Dual electric remote-control mirrors ($96). Moon roof, on Base T-Bird, Turbo or Sport ($801), on LX or with luxury and lights package ($741). Premium luxury package, standard on models with value option package 151A, on Sport model with 154A ($829), on Turbo with 157A ($717); AM/FM stereo credit ($206). Electronic AM/FM stereo with cassette tape player ($137). Graphic equalizer ($218). Premium sound system ($168). 6-way power driver's seat ($251). Speed control ($176). Leather-wrapped luxury steering wheel ($59). Tilt steering wheel ($124). Body side and deck lid stripes ($55). Locking wire style wheel covers, on LX or with 151A package, above price of road wheels ($90), with standard Base T-Bird over price of luxury wheel covers ($212). Cast aluminum wheels, on LX or Sport with 151A package ($89), on Base T-Bird ($211). Styled road wheels ($122). Power side windows ($222). California emissions system ($55). High-altitude emissions system ($99). Two-tone paint treatment Base T-Bird, cost over body side and deck lid striping or LX ($218), on LX with 151A package ($163). Clearcoat paint ($183). Articulated sport seats ($183). Vinyl trim ($37). Leather trim ($415). Base T-Bird Value Option Package151A (($1,329-$1,402). Sport Value Option Package 154A (#$986-$1,009). LX Value Option Package 161A (no charge-$73). Select LX Value Option Package 162A (($807-$830). Turbo Value Option Package 157A (no charge -$72).

1988

1988 Thunderbird Notable Equipment: All standard FoMoCo safety, anti-theft, convenience items, and emissions control equipment; 3.8-liter MPEFI V-6; automatic overdrive transmission; power rack and pinion steering; front disc/rear drum brakes; modified McPherson strut front suspension with variable rate springs and gas-pressurized struts; four-bar-link rear suspension with variable-rate springs and gas-pressurized shock absorbers; P215/70Rx14 black sidewall all-season tires; dual aerodynamic halogen headlamps; wide body side moldings; luxury wheel covers; bright windshield moldings; bright side window moldings; bright back window moldings; black bumper rub strips and extensions with bright insert; left-hand remote-control mirror; air conditioning; tinted glass; safety belt reminder chimes; deep-well trunk with mini spare tire; electronic digital clock; ash tray lights; continuous luggage compartment light; 16-oz. color-keyed cut-pile carpeting; electronic digital clock; ash tray lights; continuous color-keyed safety belts with comfort regulator feature; LCD speedometer with trip odometer; and electronic AM/FM stereo radio with four speakers (may be deleted for credit.

1988Thunderbird Sport Standard Equipment adds or substitutes (over base T-Bird): 5.0-liter EFI V-8 engine; handling suspension including quadra-shock rear suspension; heavy-duty battery; Traction-Lok axle; dual-note Sport-tuned horn; P215/70HRx14 speed-rated handling tires; styled road wheels; black windshield moldings; black side window moldings; black rear window moldings; adjustable articulated sport seats; 24-oz. luxury carpeting; light group with dual beam map light, instrument panel courtesy lights, and engine compartment light; full analog instrumentation; Systems Sentry diagnostic alert lights; leather-wrapped steering wheel; tunnel-mounted shift with leather-wrapped handle; full console with covered storage compartment lid/arm rest; and speed control.

1988Thunderbird LX Standard Equipment adds or substitutes (over base T-Bird): automatic parking brake release; body side and deck lid accent stripes; dual remote-control electric mirrors; luxury cloth split-bench seats in special sew style with 4-way headrests; 24-oz, luxury carpet; light group with dual beam map light, instrument panel courtesy lights, and engine compartment light; luxury door and quarter trim panels; Systems Sentry diagnostic alert lights; leather-wrapped steering wheel; electronic AM/FM stereo radio with four speakers and cassette tape player; illuminated entry system; power side windows; interval windshield wipers; speed control; tilt steering; power lock group with power door locks, remote deck lid release in glove box, and remote fuel filler door release in glove box; and power driver's seat.

1988Thunderbird Turbo Coupe Standard Equipment adds or substitutes (over base T-Bird): 2.3-liter overhead cam turbocharged engine with EFI, air-to-air intercooler, and regular/premium fuel selection; 5-speed manual overdrive transmission; power 4-wheel disc brakes with electronic antilock system (ABS); special handling package including automatic ride control and quadra-shock rear suspension; heavy-duty battery; Traction-Lok rear axle; remote-control fuel filler door release; dual-note Sport-tuned horn; automatic parking brake release; P225/60VRx16 black sidewall performance tires and unique 16 x 7-in. diameter aluminum wheels; unique front fascia with Hella fog lights; black windshield, side window and rear window moldings; red insert replacing bright metal insert on black bumper rub strips; dual intercooler hood scoops; dual remote-control electric mirrors; adjustable articulated sport seats; 24-oz. luxury carpet; light group with dual beam map light, instrument panel courtesy lights, and engine compartment light; luxury door and quarter trim panels; full analog instrumentation; Systems Sentry diagnostic alert lights; Soft Feel steering wheel; tunnel-mounted shift with leather-wrapped handle; full Console with covered storage compartment lid/arm rest; power side windows; and interval windshield wipers.

1988 Thunderbird Options: 5.0-liter V-8, except standard in Sport and Turbo Coupe ($639). 4-speed automatic overdrive transmission, optional on Turbo ($515). Heavy-duty battery in base T-Bird and LX ($27). Styled road wheels on base T-Bird ($122). Cast aluminum wheels, on LX or Sport with 151A package ($89), on Base T-Bird ($211). Locking wire style wheel covers, on LX or base T-Bird with 151A package, above price of road wheels ($90), with standard Base T-Bird over price of luxury wheel covers ($212). Body side and deck lid stripes on base T-Bird or Sport models ($55). Two-tone paint treatment on base T-Bird, cost over body side and deck lid striping or LX ($218), on LX with 151A package ($163). Dual electric remote-control mirrors on base T-Bird or Sport ($96). Moon roof, on Base T-Bird, Turbo or Sport ($801), on LX or with luxury and lights package ($741). Leather trim, except base T-Bird ($415). Light group, on Base T-Bird ($N/A). Systems Sentry diagnostic alert lights, on base T-Bird (N/A). Electronic AM/FM stereo with cassette tape player, on all except LX ($137). Premium sound system, optional all models ($168). Graphic equalizer , optional all models ($218). Illuminated entry system, except LX (N/A). Power side windows in base T-Bird and Sport ($222). Interval windshield wipers, in base T-Bird or Sport (N/A). Speed control on base T-Bird or Turbo Coupe ($176). Tilt steering wheel, except LX ($124). Power lock group, except LX ($249). 6-way power driver's seat, except LX ($251). Power antenna, all ($76). Luxury light and convenience group, on Base T-Bird ($461), on Base T-Bird with electronic equipment group ($379), on Sport and Turbo ($426), on Sport and Turbo with electronic equipment group ($344), on LX ($244). Electronic equipment group, on Base T-Bird ($634), on Sport and Turbo ($365), on LX ($577). Dual power seat, on Base T-Bird and LX and Sport ($302), on Turbo or LX with articulated seats ($251). Front floor mats ($30).PEP 140A includes P215/70R14 tires, automatic overdrive transmission, and dual electric mirrors for base T-Bird (N/A). PEP 141A includes P215/70R14 tires, automatic overdrive transmission, dual electric mirrors; light group; electronic AM/FM stereo with cassette; interval wipers; premium sound system; front floor mats; and styled road wheels for base T-Bird (N/A). PEP 142A includes P215/70R14 tires, automatic overdrive transmission, dual electric mirrors; light group; electronic AM/FM stereo with cassette; interval wipers; premium sound system; front floor mats; styled road wheels; and manual temperature control air conditioning for base T-Bird (N/A). PEP 145A includes P215/70HRx14 handling tires; automatic overdrive transmission; dual electric mirrors; light group; electronic AM/FM stereo with cassette; interval windshield wipers; styled road wheels; manual air conditioning; power lock group; power side windows; tilt steering; speed control; and 6-way power driver's seat for Sport T-bird (N/A). PEP 150A includes P215/70Rx14 all-season tires; automatic overdrive transmission; dual electric mirrors; light group; electronic AM/FM stereo with cassette; interval windshield wipers; styled road wheels; power lock group; power side windows; tilt steering; speed control; and 6-way power driver's seat for LX T-bird (N/A). Extra Value Package 151A includes P215/70Rx14 all-season tires; automatic overdrive transmission; dual electric mirrors; light group; electronic AM/FM stereo with cassette; interval windshield wipers; front floor mats; manual air conditioning; power lock group; power side windows; tilt steering; speed control; dual power seats with recliners; power radio antenna; keyless entry system; luxury light and convenience group; graphic equalizer; and wire wheel covers for LX T-bird (N/A).

Extra Value Package 155A includes 5-speed manual overdrive transmission; P225/60VRx16 black sidewall tires; power side windows; dual electric mirrors; interval wipers; manual air conditioning; light group; power lock group; electronic AM/FM stereo with cassette; speed control; tilt steering; and power driver's seat for T-Bird Turbo Coupe (N/A). Extra Value Package 156A includes 5-speed manual overdrive transmission; P225/60VRx16 black sidewall tires; power side windows; dual electric mirrors; interval wipers; manual air conditioning; light group; front floor mats; luxury light and convenience group; premium sound system; power radio antenna; power lock group; electronic AM/FM stereo with cassette; speed control; tilt steering; and power driver's seat for T-Bird Turbo Coupe (N/A).

1989

1989 T-Bird Notable Standard Equipment: All standard FoMoCo safety, anti-theft, convenience items, and emissions control equipment; 3.8-liter V-6; automatic overdrive transmission; power-assisted antilock braking system; four-wheel disc brakes; 15 x 6-in. stamped steel wheels; P205/70R15 black sidewall tires; air conditioning; tinted glass; power steering; power brakes; power windows; side window defoggers; interval windshield wipers; front automatic seat belt restraint system; full-length console with floor-mounted shifter; vinyl door trim with storage bins; cloth bucket seats with recliners; analog instrumentation; electronic AM/FM stereo search radio with digital clock (may be deleted for credit); left-hand remote-control OSRV mirror; wide body side protection moldings; deluxe wheel covers; all-season radial tires; and 5-mph color-keyed bumpers.

1989 Thunderbird LX Standard Equipment adds or substitutes: Luxury cloth bucket seats with recliners; six-way power driver's bucket seat; luxury door trim and carpeting; electronic instrument cluster; instrument panel upper storage compartment; illuminated entry system and convenience lights; speed control and tilt steering wheel; speed-sensitive power steering; leather-wrapped luxury steering wheel; illuminated visor mirrors; power lock group; electronic AM/FM stereo search radio with cassette and digital clock; rear seat center arm rest; vehicle maintenance monitor; remote release fuel door; dual electric remote-control mirrors; bright window moldings; and styled road wheel covers.

1989 Thunderbird Super Coupe Standard Equipment adds or substitutes (over standard): 3.8-liter supercharged and inter-cooled V-6 with dual exhausts; five-speed manual transmission; automatic ride control system; heavier front and rear stabilizer bars; Traction-Lok differential; 16 x 7-in. cast-aluminum wheels; Goodyear Eagle P225/60VR16 performance tires; articulated sports seats with power lumbar and power seat back bolster adjustments; sport soft-feel steering wheel; luxury door trim and carpeting; instrument panel upper storage compartment; performance instrumentation; vehicle maintenance monitor; fog lamps; narrow body side moldings and lower body side cladding; anti-lock braking system with 4-wheel disc brakes; Traction-Lok differential; speed-sensitive power steering; dual electric remote-control mirrors; heavy-duty battery; and heavy-duty alternator.

1989 Thunderbird Options: Four-speed overdrive transmission on Super Coupe ($539). P205/75R15 white sidewall tires ($73). Eagle GT + 4 P225/60VR16 black sidewall all-season performance tires, Super Coupe only ($73). Conventional spare tire in base T-Bird and LX ($73). Traction-Lok axle for base T-Bird and LX ($100). Optional 3.27:1 axle ratio for Super Coupe ($21). Premium luxury group for base T-Bird ($420), for Super Coupe with 157A ($761). Antilock braking system, except standard on Super Coupe ($1,085). Anti-theft system ($183). Moon roof ($741-$841 depending on options teamed with). Clearcoat paint system ($183). Ford JBL audio system ($488). Compact disc player ($491). Radio-delete credits ($245-$382). Locking wire wheel covers, on base T-Bird ($212), as option on others ($127). Cast aluminum wheels on base T-Bird ($299), as option on others ($213). California emissions ($100). High-altitude emissions (no charge). LX leather trim ($489). Super Coupe leather trim ($622). Front license plate bracket (no charge). Cold weather group on Super Coupe ($18), on others ($45). Preferred equipment package 151B ($1,235). Preferred equipment package 162A ($735). Luxury group ($735). Preferred equipment group 157B for Super Coupe (no charge)

1990

1990 T-Bird Major Standard Equipment: All standard FoMoCo safety, anti-theft, convenience items, and emissions control equipment; 3.8-liter V-6; 4-speed automatic overdrive transmission; daytime running lights; rear window defroster; 72-amp battery; 65-amp alternator; wide body side protection moldings; deluxe wheel covers; full-length console with floor-mounted shift; vinyl door trim with storage bins; cloth bucket seats with recliners; air conditioning; tinted glass; analog instrumentation; electronic AM/FM search radio with digital clock (may be deleted for credit); power steering; all-season radial tires; power windows; and interval windshield wipers.

1990 Thunderbird LX Standard Equipment adds or substitutes (over standard): power lock group; dual electric remote-control mirrors; bright window moldings; electronic AM/FM stereo radio with cassette and clock; speed control system; tilt steering wheel; styled road wheel covers; illuminated entry system; fog lamps; luxury-level door trim and carpeting; convenience lights; instrument panel upper storage compartment; illuminated visor mirrors; luxury cloth bucket seats with recliners; rear seat center arm rest; leather-wrapped luxury steering wheel; vehicle maintenance monitor; remote-release fuel door; electronic instrument cluster; and speed-sensitive power steering.

1990 Thunderbird Super Coupe Standard Equipment adds or substitutes (over standard): 3.8-liter EFI supercharged V-6 engine; five-speed manual overdrive transmission; power lock group; dual electric remote-control mirrors; electronic AM/FM stereo radio with cassette and clock; speed control system; tilt steering wheel; fog lamps; narrow body side moldings; lower body side cladding; 16-in. cast aluminum wheels; P255/60R16 black sidewall performance tires; luxury door trim and carpeting; articulated sports seat with power lumbar and power seat back bolster adjustments; Sport soft-feel steering wheel; heavy-duty alternator; automatic ride control adjustable suspension; performance instrumentation.

1990 Thunderbird Options: Four-speed overdrive transmission on Super Coupe ($539). P205/75R15 white sidewall tires ($73). Eagle GT + 4 P225/60VR16 black sidewall all-season performance tires, Super Coupe only ($73). Conventional spare tire in base T-Bird and LX ($73). Traction-Lok axle for base T-Bird and LX ($100). Optional 3.27:1 axle ratio for Super Coupe ($21). Premium luxury group for base T-Bird ($420), for Super Coupe with 157A ($761). Antilock braking system, except standard on Super Coupe ($1,085). Anti-theft system ($183).Keyless entry system for base T-Bird ($219), for others ($137). Front carpeted floor mats ($33) Luxury and lights convenience group ($26). Moon roof (($741-$841 depending on options teamed with). Clearcoat paint system ($188). Electronic premium cassette radio ($305-$442). Ford JBL audio system ($488). Compact disc player ($491). Radio-delete credits ($245). Power antenna ($76). Locking wire wheel covers, on base T-Bird ($228), as option on others ($143). Cast aluminum wheels on base T-Bird ($298), as option on others ($213). California emissions ($100). High-altitude emissions (no charge). LX leather ($489). Super Coupe leather trim ($622). Front license plate bracket (no charge). Cold weather group on most ($168-$195), on others ($18-$45). Preferred equipment package 151A ($1,288). Preferred equipment package 155A ($819). Preferred equipment group 157B for Super Coupe (no charge)

1991

1991 T-Bird Major Standard Equipment: All standard FoMoCo safety, anti-theft, convenience items, and emissions control equipment; 3.8-liter V-6; 4-speed automatic overdrive transmission; daytime running lights; rear window defroster; 72-amp battery; 65-amp alternator; wide body side protection moldings; deluxe wheel covers; full-length console with floor-mounted shift; vinyl door trim with storage bins; cloth bucket seats with recliners; air conditioning; tinted glass; analog instrumentation; electronic AM/FM search radio with digital clock (may be deleted for credit); power steering; all-season radial tires; power windows; and interval windshield wipers.

1991 Thunderbird LX Standard Equipment adds or substitutes (over standard): power lock group; dual electric remote-control mirrors; bright window moldings; electronic AM/FM stereo radio with cassette and clock; speed control system; tilt steering wheel; styled road wheel covers; illuminated entry system; fog lamps; luxury-level door trim and carpeting; convenience lights; instrument panel upper storage compartment; illuminated visor mirrors; luxury cloth bucket seats with recliners; rear seat center arm rest; leather-wrapped luxury steering wheel; vehicle maintenance monitor; remote-release fuel door; electronic instrument cluster; and speed-sensitive power steering.

1991 Thunderbird Super Coupe Standard Equipment adds or substitutes (over standard): 3.8-liter EFI supercharged V-6 engine; five-speed manual overdrive transmission; power lock group; dual electric remote-control mirrors; electronic AM/FM stereo radio with cassette and clock; speed control system; tilt steering wheel; fog lamps; narrow body side moldings; lower body side cladding; 16-in. cast aluminum wheels; P255/60R16 black sidewall performance tires; luxury door trim and carpeting; articulated sports seat with power lumbar and power seat back bolster adjustments; Sport soft-feel steering wheel; heavy-duty alternator; automatic ride control adjustable suspension; performance instrumentation.

1991 Thunderbird Options: 5.0-liter V-8 in base T-Bird and LX ($1,080). Four-speed overdrive transmission on Super Coupe ($595). P205/75R15 white sidewall tires ($73). Eagle GT + 4 P225/60VR16 black sidewall all-season performance tires, Super Coupe only ($73). Conventional spare tire in base T-Bird and LX ($73). Traction-Lok axle for base T-Bird and LX ($100). Premium luxury group for base T-Bird ($420), for Super Coupe with 157A ($761). Antilock braking system including Traction-Lok axle, except standard on Super Coupe ($1,085). Anti-theft system ($245). Auto lamp group ($176). Keyless entry system for base T-Bird ($219), for others ($137). Front carpeted floor mats ($33) Luxury group ($$345-$627)). Moon roof (($776-$876 depending on options teamed with). Cornering lamps ($68). Rear window defroster ($160). Electronic auto temperature control ($162). Electronic premium cassette radio ($305-$460). Ford JBL audio system ($488). Illuminated entry system ($82). Compact disc player ($491). Radio-delete credits ($245). Power lock group ($245). Light convenience group ($100-$146). Luxury group ($345-$627). Power antenna ($82). 6-way power driver's seat ($290). 6-way power passenger seat ($290). Speed control and tilt steering ($345). Vehicle maintenance monitor ($89). Locking wire wheel covers, on base T-Bird ($228), as option on others ($143). Cast aluminum wheels on base T-Bird ($299), as option on others ($214). LX leather trim ($489). Super Coupe leather trim ($622). Front license plate bracket (no charge). Cold weather group on most ($178-$205), on others ($18-$45). Preferred equipment package 151A ($796). Preferred equipment package 155A ($977). Preferred equipment group 157A for Super Coupe ($739).

1992

1992 T-Bird Major Standard Equipment: All standard FoMoCo safety, anti-theft, convenience items, and emissions control equipment; 3.8-liter 140-hp MPEFI V-6; automatic overdrive transmission; long-spindle SLA front suspension with variable-rate coil springs, double-acting gas-pressurized shock absorbers and 1.1-in. diameter stabilizer bar; independent H-arm rear suspension with toe control link, variable-rate springs, double-acting gas-pressurized shocks, and 1.04-in. diameter stabilizer bar; power rack and pinion steering with 14.1:1 ratio on center; power front disc/rear drum brakes; 15 x 6-in. stamped steel wheels; deluxe wheel covers; P205/70R15 steel-belted black sidewall all-season radial tires; new long-lasting LED taillights; body side protection moldings with bright insert; (U.S.) fully-automatic shoulder belt restraint system with manual lap belt; full-length console with floor-mounted shifter; vinyl door trim with storage bins; cloth bucket seats with recliners; map and dome lights; luggage compartment light; ash tray light; driver's foot well light; air conditioning; tinted glass; analog instruments; electronic AM/FM stereo search radio with digital clock (may be deleted for credit); power windows; interval windshield wipers; (Canada) heavy-duty battery; and (Canada) electric rear window defroster.

1992 T-Bird LX Major Standard Equipment (over standard T-Bird equipment): Speed-sensitive variable-assist power steering with 14.1:1 ratio on center; styled road wheel covers; dual electric remote-control OSRV mirrors; luxury level door trim and carpeting; power lock group with power door locks, remote deck lid release, and remote-control for fuel filler door in glove box; analog performance instrumentation with tachometer; fog lamps; illuminated entry system and convenience lights; illuminated visor mirrors; luxury cloth/leather/vinyl bucket seats with recliners and 6-way power driver's seat; rear seat center arm rest; leather-wrapped luxury steering wheel; electronic AM/FM stereo search radio with cassette and digital clock; and speed control with tilt steering wheel.

1992 T-Bird Sport Major Standard Equipment (over standard T-Bird equipment): 5.0-liter EFI V-8; automatic overdrive transmission; cast aluminum wheels; P215/70R15 black sidewall tires; speed-sensitive variable-assisted power steering with 14.1:1 ratio on center; handling suspension; performance analog instrument cluster; and leather-wrapped steering wheel.

1992 T-Bird Super Coupe Major Standard Equipment (over standard T-Bird equipment): 3.8-liter 210-hp supercharged and intercooled SMPEFI; 5-speed manual overdrive transmission; automatic ride control suspension in addition to standard suspension (includes 1.12-in. diameter front stabilizer bar and .9-in. diameter solid rear stabilizer bar; Traction-Lok rear axle; speed-sensitive variable-assist power steering with 14.1:1 ratio on center; four-wheel power disc brakes with anti-lock braking system; cast-aluminum 16 x 7.0-in. wheels and P225/60 performance tires; fog lamps; narrow body side moldings and lower body side cladding; dual electric remote-control mirrors; luxury door trim and carpeting; articulated sport seats with power lumbar and seat back bolster adjustments; sport soft-feel steering wheel; heavy-duty battery and alternator; and analog performance instrumentation with tachometer.

1992 T-Bird Options: 5.0-liter HO V-8 in base T-Bird and Sport ($1,080). Four-speed overdrive transmission on in T-Bird and Sport ($595). California emissions ($100). P225/60ZR16 black sidewall all-season performance tires, Super Coupe only ($73). Conventional spare tire in base T-Bird and LX ($73). Leather bucket seating surfaces in LX ($515). Leather bucket seating surfaces in Super Coupe ($648). Anti-lock braking system, includes Traction-Lok axle ($695). Anti-theft system ($245). Autolamp group ($193). Traction-Lok axle for base T-Bird, Sport and LX ($100). CD player, requires premium cassette radio ($491). Cornering lights ($68). Rear window defroster ($170). Automatic air conditioning for LX and Super Coupe ($162). Electronic instrument cluster for LX ($270). Electronic premium cassette radio ($305-$460). AM/FM ETR (stereo) with cassette in base T-Bird and LX ($155). Ford JBL audio system ($526). Radio-delete credits ($245). Keyless entry, including illuminated entry system and power lock group ($146-$228). Light convenience group ($100-$146). Power lock group ($311). Luxury group ($$311-$561). Moon roof (($776-$876 depending on options teamed with). Power antenna ($85). 6-way power driver's seat ($305). 6-way power passenger seat ($305). Vehicle maintenance monitor ($89). Cast aluminum wheels on base T-Bird ($306), as option on others ($221). Front license plate bracket (no charge). Cold weather group on most ($178-$205), on others ($18-$45). Preferred equipment package 151A ($762). Preferred equipment package 155A ($1,038). Preferred equipment group 157A for Super Coupe ($858).

1993

1993 T-Bird LX Major Standard Equipment: All standard FoMoCo safety, anti-theft, convenience items, and emissions control equipment; 3.8-liter 140-hp SMPEFI V-6; automatic overdrive transmission; long-spindle SLA front suspension with variable-rate coil springs, double-acting gas-pressurized shock absorbers and 1.1-in. diameter stabilizer bar; independent H-arm rear suspension with toe control link, variable-rate springs, double-acting gas-pressurized shocks, and 1.04-in. diameter stabilizer bar; speed-sensitive variable-assist power steering; power front disc/rear drum brakes; 15 x 6-in. stamped steel wheels; styled road wheel covers; P205/70R15 steel-belted black sidewall radial tires; long-lasting LED taillights; body color body side protection moldings; full-length console with floor-mounted leather-wrapped shifter; map/dome, luggage compartment, ash tray, and driver's foot well lights; air conditioning and tinted glass; power windows; power door locks; remote deck lid; remote fuel filler door release; interval windshield wipers; dual electric remote-control mirrors; luxury level door trim and carpeting; analog performance instrumentation with tachometer; integral fog lamps in front fascia; illuminated entry system; rear seat courtesy lights; luxury cloth/leather/vinyl bucket seats with recliners and 6-way power for driver; rear seat center arm rest, leather-wrapped luxury steering wheel; electronic AM/FM stereo search radio with cassette tape player and digital clock; and speed control with tilt steering wheel.

1993 T-Bird Super Coupe Major Standard Equipment (over standard T-Bird LX equipment): 3.8-liter 210-hp supercharged and intercooled SMPEFI V-6 with dual exhausts; 5-speed manual overdrive transmission; supercharger boost gauge in instrument cluster; automatic ride control suspension in addition to standard suspension; Handling components including 1.10-in. (28 mm) diameter solid front stabilizer bar and 0.90-in. (23 mm) diameter solid rear stabilizer bar; Traction-Lok rear axle; four-wheel power disc brakes with anti-lock system; directional cast-aluminum 16 x 7.0-in. wheels and P225/60ZR black sidewall performance tires; narrow black body side moldings; lower body side cladding; unique rear fascia; sport soft-feel steering wheel; light convenience group with instrument panel courtesy light and engine compartment light; all-cloth articulated sport seats with power lumbar and seat back bolster adjustments, plus 4-way adjustable head restraints (up/down/forward/back).

1993 T-Bird Options: 5.0-liter HO V-8 in T-Bird LX only ($1,086). Four-speed overdrive transmission in T-Bird Super Coupe ($595). Power lock group ($311). Moon roof (($776-$876 depending on options teamed with). 6-way power driver's seat ($305). 6-way power passenger seat ($305). CD player, requires premium cassette radio ($491). Electronic premium cassette radio with premium sound system ($305). Ford JBL audio system ($526). Power antenna ($85). Radio-delete credits ($400). Automatic air conditioning for LX and Super Coupe ($162). Anti-lock braking system, includes Traction-Lok axle ($695). Anti-theft system ($245). Autolamp group ($193). Traction-Lok axle for base T-Bird LX ($100). Front license plate bracket (no charge). Cold weather group on LX and Super Coupe ($18- $5-$178-$205 depending on transmission and if car has PEP 157A). Rear window defroster included in PEPs and Cold Weather Group and required in New York state ($170). California emissions ($100). High-altitude emissions (no charge). Front carpeted floor mats ($33). Illuminated entry system in Super Coupe ($82). Electronic instrument cluster in LX ($270). Keyless entry, including illuminated entry system and power lock group in LX ($196), in Super Coupe ($278). Light convenience group with instrument panel courtesy light and engine compartment light, standard in Super Coupe ($46). Dual illuminated visor-vanity mirrors ($100). Speed control and tilt steering ($369). Leather seating surfaces in LX ($515). Leather seating surfaces in Super Coupe, includes fold-down rear seat and requires power seats and locks ($648). Vehicle maintenance monitor ($89). Directional cast aluminum wheels with up-size P215/70R15 black sidewall tires on T-Bird LX ($221). P225/60ZR16 black sidewall all-season performance tires on Super Coupe ($73 extra). Preferred equipment package 155A ($1,086).

1994

1994 T-Bird LX Major Standard Equipment: All standard FoMoCo safety, anti-theft, convenience items, and emissions control equipment; 3.8-liter 140-hp SMPEFI V-6; EEC IV electronic engine controls; automatic overdrive transmission; long-spindle SLA front suspension with variable-rate coil springs, double-acting gas-pressurized shock absorbers and 1.1-in. diameter stabilizer bar; independent H-arm rear suspension with toe control link, variable-rate springs, double-acting gas-pressurized shocks, and 1.04-in. diameter stabilizer bar; speed-sensitive variable-assist power steering; power front disc/rear drum brakes; 15 x 6-in. stamped steel wheels; styled road wheel covers; P205/70R15 steel-belted black sidewall all-season radial tires; mini spare tire; long-lasting LED taillights; full-length console with floor-mounted leather-wrapped shifter; dual cup holders; manual air conditioning and tinted glass; power windows; power door lock group (LX only); 130-amp. alternator; remote deck lid; remote fuel filler door release; interval windshield wipers; dual electric remote-control mirrors; luxury level door trim with courtesy lights and door bins; 24-oz. cut-pile luxury carpeting; analog performance instrumentation with trip odometer, oil pressure gauge, fuel gauge, temperature gauge, and voltmeter; integral fog lamps in front fascia; illuminated entry system; rear seat courtesy lights; luxury cloth bucket seats with 6-way power for driver; rear seat center arm rest, leather-wrapped luxury steering wheel; electronic AM/FM ETR stereo search radio with cassette tape player and digital clock; tilt steering wheel; speed control (LX only); dual-note horn; illuminated entry system (LX only); dome, map, luggage compartment, ash tray, driver's side footwell, and glove box lights; rear seat courtesy lights; carpeted low liftover luggage compartment; dual supplemental airbags restraint system; 3-point passive restraint system with active front lap belt and 3-point active restraints in rear outboard position and center rear lap belt; seat belt reminder chime; black moldings on windshield, side windows, and rear window; side window defoggers; soft color-keyed front and rear bumpers; integral fog lamps in front fascia; double-spear-shaped body color body side protection moldings; aerodynamic halogen headlights and parking lights; dual covered visor mirrors with headliner pocket; and styled road wheel covers.

1994 T-Bird Super Coupe Major Standard Equipment (over standard T-Bird LX equipment): 3.8-liter 210-hp supercharged and intercooled SMPEFI V-6 engine with dual exhaust; 5-speed manual overdrive transmission; 4-wheel disc brakes with ABS; hand-operated console-mounted parking brake; indicator light and supercharger boost gauge in instrument cluster; automatic ride control suspension in addition to standard suspension; Handling components including 1.10-in. (28 mm) diameter solid front stabilizer bar and 0.90-in. (23 mm) diameter solid rear stabilizer bar; Traction-Lok rear axle; 110-amp heavy-duty alternator; 58-amp maintenance-free battery (72-amp with automatic overdrive); directional cast-aluminum 16 x 7.0-in. wheels with locking lug nuts and P225/60ZR16 black sidewall performance tires; lower body side cladding; unique rear fascia; sport soft-feel steering wheel; light convenience group with instrument panel courtesy light and engine compartment light; all-cloth articulated sport seats with seat back pockets and power lumbar and seat back bolster adjustments, plus 4-way adjustable head restraints (up/down/forward/back); electronic semi-automatic temperature control; driver's foot rest; and adjustable suspension with "firm ride" indicator light.

297

1994 T-Bird Options: 4.6-liter V-8 ($515 net). Four-speed overdrive transmission in T-Bird Super Coupe ($790). California emissions ($85). High-altitude emissions (no charge). P225/60ZR16 black sidewall all-season performance tires on Super Coupe ($70 extra). Leather seating surfaces in LX ($490). Leather seating surfaces in Super Coupe, includes fold-down rear seat and requires power seats and locks ($615). Anti-lock braking system, includes Traction-Lok axle ($565). Anti-theft system ($245). Cold weather group on LX and Super Coupe, including engine block heater, 72-amp battery, rear window defroster, and 3.27:1 Traction-Lok rear axle ($18- $20-$300 depending on transmission and if car has PEPs 155A or 157A). Front floor mats ($30). Keyless entry, including illuminated entry system and power lock group in LX or Super Coupe with luxury group ($215), in Super Coupe ($295). Power moon roof ($740). Hands Free cellular telephone ($530). Traction assist in LX only ($210). Tri-coat paint ($225). Electronic premium cassette radio with premium sound system and power antenna ($370). Ford JBL audio system ($500). Trunk mounted compact disc changer ($785). Group 2 (RPO 411) includes lock group, power group, speed control, and 6-way power driver's seat for Super Coupe only ($800). Group 2 (RPO 432) includes semi-automatic temperature control, and rear window defroster ($160 for Super Coupe and $315 for LX). Group 3 includes cast-aluminum wheels, P215/70RX15 tires for LX only, plus dual illuminated vanity mirrors ($95 for Super Coupe or $305 for LX). Luxury group includes Autolamp on and off delay, illuminated entry system for Super Coupe only, light group for LX only, 6-way power passenger seat, and Integrated warning lamp module for LX only ($580 for LX and $555 for Super Coupe). Preferred equipment package 155A for LX ($620, but no charge with applicable Group 2 discounts). Preferred equipment package 157A for Super Coupe ($1,055, but no charge with applicable Group 2 discounts).

1995

1995 T-Bird LX Major Standard Equipment: Front and rear soft color-keyed 5-mph bumpers; flush windshield, door, quarter window, and backlight glass; aerodynamic halogen headlights and parking lamps; dual color-keyed remote-control electric mirrors; black windshield, door, quarter window, and backlight moldings; body-color double-spear-shaped body side protection moldings; Bolfon design road wheel styled wheel covers; air bag supplemental restraint system; 3-point safety belts with active-restraints in all outboard positions and center rear belt and reminder chime; foot-operated parking brake; 24-oz. cut-pile carpeting; full-length console with floor-mounted leather-wrapped gear shift handle and storage compartment; dual console-mounted cup holders; luxury level door trim with courtesy lights and illuminated switches; front floor mats; driver's side footwell lights; illuminated entry system; map/dome, luggage compartment, front ash tray, glove box, and rear seat courtesy lights; low liftover design carpeted luggage compartment; dual visor mirrors; luxury cloth bucket seats with 6-way power driver's seat; luxury leather-wrapped tilt steering wheel; manual air conditioner with rotary controls; 130-amp alternator; 58-amp maintenance-free battery; power front disc/rear drum brakes; digital clock; EEC-IV electronic engine controls system; 3.8-liter SMPEFI V-6 engine; 18-gallon fuel tank; tethered gas filler cap; complete tinted glass; and dual note horn.

1995 T-Bird Super Coupe Major Standard Equipment (over standard T-Bird LX equipment): Unique rear bumper treatment; lower body side cladding; integral fog lamps in front fascia; 16 x 7-in. directional cast-aluminum wheels with locking lug nuts; console-mounted hand-operated parking brake with leather-wrapped handle; driver's foot rest; integrated warning lamp module; light group including right0hand panel courtesy light and engine compartment light; articulated bucket seats in cloth/leather/vinyl trim with power adjustable lumbar support and seat back bolsters; rear seat head rests; electronic air conditioner with semi-automatic temperature control; 110-amp alternator; Traction-Lok rear axle; 58-amp (72-amp with automatic overdrive) Maintenance-free battery; antilock braking system with 4-wheel disc brakes; 3.8-liter SMPEFI supercharged and intercooled V-6 with dual exhausts; and speed control deletion.

1995 T-Bird Options: 4.6-liter V-8, including heavy-duty battery and speed-sensitive power steering for LX only ($615 net). Four-speed overdrive transmission in T-Bird Super Coupe ($790). California emissions ($95). High-altitude emissions (no charge). P225/60ZR16 black sidewall all-season performance tires on Super Coupe ($70 extra). Leather seating surfaces in LX ($490). Leather seating surfaces in Super Coupe, includes fold-down rear seat and requires power seats and locks ($615). Option Group 1 includes power lock group, speed control, and 6-way power driver's seat for LX ($160 for Super Coupe and $315 for LX). Option Group 2 includes rear window defroster for both models and semi-automatic temperature control for LX ($160 for Super Coupe and $315 for LX). Option Group 3 includes cast-aluminum wheels and P21570R15 black sidewall tires ($210). Anti-lock braking system, includes Traction-Lok axle ($565). Traction-Lok rear axle (standard on Super Coupe with 5-speed, otherwise $95). Front license plate bracket (no charge). Front floor mats ($30). Remote keyless entry, including illuminated entry system two remotes LX or Super Coupe with luxury group ($215), in Super Coupe ($295). Luxury group includes Autolamp on and off delay, power antenna, illuminated entry system for Super Coupe only, light group for LX only, and dual illuminated visor mirrors and integrated warning lamp module for LX only ($350 for LX and $325 for Super Coupe). Power-operated moon roof, requires luxury group and PEP 155A or PEP 157A ($740). 6-way power passenger seat, requires Option Group 1 ($290). Hands Free cellular telephone ($530). Traction-Assist, requires ABS and luxury group and not available for Super Coupe with 5-speed (standard for Super Coupe with automatic transmission; otherwise $210). Tri-Coat paint ($225). AM/FM stereo ETR with cassette and premium sound system ($290). AM/FM stereo ETR with compact disc player and premium sound system ($430). Heavy-duty 72-amp battery ($25). Engine block heater ($20). 155A for LX ($620, but no charge with applicable Group 2 discounts). Preferred equipment package 157A for Super Coupe ($1,055, but no charge with applicable Group 2 discounts).

1996

1996 T-Bird LX Major Standard Equipment: Dual front air bags; manual air conditioning; 130-amp alternator; rear seat center armrest; 58-amp maintenance-free battery; power front disc/rear drum brakes; soft, color-keyed front and rear bumpers; 18-oz. cut-pile carpeting; lower bodyside cladding with integral body-color bodyside molding; digital clock; full-length console with floor-mounted shift, storage, and dual cupholders; power remote decklid release; power door locks with illuminated switches; luxury level door trim with courtesy lights, stowage bins, and illuminated door switches; 145-hp, 3.8-liter SMPEFI V-6 engine; EEC-IV electronic engine control system; 18-gallon fuel tank with tethered cap; solar-tinted glass; aerodynamic halogen complex-reflector head- and parking lamps; rear seat heating ducts; analog instrument cluster with speedometer, trip odometer, voltmeter, oil pressure gauge, fuel gauge, and temperature gauge; Interior lights - dome/map, luggage compartment, ashtray, driver's side footwell, glove box, and engine compartment; low liftover car-peted luggage compartment; dual electric remote-controlled color-keyed mirrors; black moldings on windshield, back-light, door, and quarter windows; foot-operated parking brake; 3-point seat belts with front and rear outboard positions, center lap belt, and reminder chime; rear-wheel drive; luxury cloth bucket seats; leather shift knob; mini spare tire; speed control; AM/FM/stereo/cassette ETR sound system with four speakers; power steering; tilt steering wheel; long-spindle SLA front suspension with stabilizer bar, variable rate springs, lower control arm, and tension strut; independent H-arm rear sus-pension with variable rate springs and stabilizer bar; full-width taillamps; P205/70R15 black sidewall all-season radial tires; four-speed ECT automatic transmission with overdrive and overdrive lockout; styled road wheel covers; power windows with illuminated switches; variable interval windshield wipers.

1996 T-Bird LX Options: Preferred Equipment Packages: (155A) rear window defroster, P215/70R15 tires, and cast aluminum wheels (NC). (157A) 4.6-liter SOHC V-8 including speed-sensitive power steering, heavy-duty battery, 6-way power driver's seat, illuminated entry system, and leather-wrapped steering wheel ($835 net). California emissions system ($100). Leather-faced bucket seats ($490). Remote keyless entry ($270). Front floor mats ($30). Electronic AM/FM stereo radio with cassette and premium sound ($290). Electronic AM/FM stereo radio with CD player and premium sound ($430). Anti-lock brakes ($570). Anti-theft system ($145). Power moonroof ($740). Sport Option: includes 16-inch aluminum wheels, P225/65R16 BSW tires, modified stabilizer bars, and revised spring rates ($210). Tri-coat paint ($225). Traction assist ($210). Traction-Lok axle ($95). Power driver's seat ($290). Luxury Group: includes electronic semi-automatic temperature control air conditioning, dual illuminated visor mirrors, light group, integrated warning lamp module, and power antenna ($495). 15-inch chrome wheels ($580).

1997

1997 T-Bird LX Major Standard Equipment: Dual front air bags; manual air conditioning; 130-amp alternator; rear seat center armrest; 58-amp maintenance-free battery; power four-wheel-disc brakes; soft, color-keyed front and rear bumpers; 18-oz. cut-pile carpeting; lower bodyside cladding with integral body-color bodyside molding; digital clock; full-length console with floor-mounted shift, storage, and dual cupholders; power remote decklid release; power door locks with illuminated switches; luxury level door trim with courtesy lights, stowage bins, and illuminated door switches; side window defoggers; 145-hp, 3.8-liter SMPEFI V-6 engine with hydraulic engine mounts and single exhaust; 18-gallon fuel tank with tethered cap; solar-tinted glass; aerodynamic halogen complex-reflector head- and parking lamps; rear seat heating ducts; analog instrument cluster with speedometer, trip odometer, tachometer, fuel gauge, temperature gauge, and indicators for low fuel, low washer fluid, low coolant, and door ajar; shift-knob-mounted overdrive lockout with cluster indicator light; tap up/tap down speed control with cluster indicator light; Interior lights - dome/map, luggage compartment, ashtray, driver's side footwell, glove box, and engine compartment; low liftover carpeted luggage compartment; dual electric remote-controlled color-keyed mirrors; black moldings on windshield, backlight, door, and quarter windows; foot-operated parking brake; 3-point seat belts with front and rear outboard positions, center lap belt, and reminder chime; rear-wheel drive; luxury cloth bucket seats; leather shift knob; mini spare tire; AM/FM/stereo/cassette sound system with four speakers; power steering; tilt steering wheel; long-spindle SLA front suspension with stabilizer bar, variable rate springs, lower control arm, and tension strut; independent H-arm rear suspension with variable rate springs and stabilizer bar; full-width taillamps; P205/70R15 black sidewall all-season radial tires; four-speed ECT automatic transmission with overdrive and overdrive lockout; bolt-on design styled road wheel covers; power windows with illuminated switches; variable interval windshield wipers.

1997 T-Bird LX Options: Preferred Equipment Packages: (155A) rear window defroster, P215/70R15 tires, and cast aluminum wheels (NC). (157A) includes 155A plus 4.6-liter SOHC V-8, speed-sensitive power steering, heavy-duty battery, 6-way power driver's seat, illuminated entry system, and leather-wrapped steering wheel/shift knob ($840 net). (99W) includes 4.6-liter SOHC V-8 plus speed-sensitive power steering and heavy-duty battery ($1130). Engine block heater ($20). California emissions system ($170). Leather-faced bucket seats ($490). Remote keyless entry ($270). Front floor mats ($30). Electronic AM/FM stereo radio with cassette and premium sound ($290). Electronic AM/FM stereo radio with CD player and premium sound ($430). Anti-lock brakes ($570). Anti-theft system ($145). Power moonroof ($740). Sport Option: includes 16-inch aluminum wheels, P225/60R16 BSW tires, modified stabilizer bars, larger front disc brake rotors, revised spring rates, and rear decklid spoiler ($450). Rear decklid spoiler ($250). Leather-wrapped steering wheel and shift knob ($90). Tri-coat paint ($225). Traction assist ($210). Traction-Lok axle ($95). Power driver's seat ($290). Luxury Group: includes electronic semi-automatic temperature control air conditioning, dual illuminated visor mirrors, Autolamp, and power antenna ($395). 15-inch chrome wheels ($580).

NUMBERS CRUNCHING

1955

VEHICLE IDENTIFICATION TAG

VIN location:	On plate on left door pillar.
1st symbol:	Denotes engine:
	P = 292 cid/193 hp four-barrel Thunderbird Special V-8 (Man. trans.).
	P = 292 cid/193 hp four-barrel Thunderbird Special V-8 (Overdrive trans.).
	P = 292 cid/198 hp four-barrel Thunderbird Special V-8. (Auto. Trans.)
2nd symbol:	Denotes model-year; 5 = 1955.
3rd symbol:	Denotes the assembly plant; F = Dearborn, Mich.
4th symbol	Denotes body type; H = Thunderbird.
5th - 10th symbols:	Denote sequential production number of specific vehicle starting at 100001.

BODY NUMBER PLATE

Location:	On firewall.
Serial number:	Same as number on VIN tag.
BODY	Symbols below BODY are body style code: 40A = Thunderbird.
COLOR	Symbols below COLOR are paint color code.
TRIM	Symbols below TRIM are trim combination code.
PROD. CODE	Symbols below PRODUCTION DATE are the production date code. The number indicates the date of the month the car was made. The letters indicate month of manufacture: A = January; B= February; C = March; D = April; E = May; F = June; G = July; H = August; J = September; K = October; L = November; M = December.

1956

VEHICLE IDENTIFICATION TAG

VIN location:	On plate on left door pillar.
1st symbol:	Denotes engine:
	M = 292 cid/202 hp four-barrel Thunderbird V-8.
	P = 312 cid/215 hp four-barrel Thunderbird Special V-8 (Man. trans.).
	P = 312 cid/225 hp four-barrel Thunderbird Special V-8. (Auto. Trans.)
2nd symbol:	Denotes model-year; 6 = 1956.
3rd symbol:	Denotes the assembly plant; F = Dearborn, Mich.
4th symbol	Denotes body type: H = Thunderbird.
5th - 10th symbols:	Denote sequential production number of specific vehicle starting at 100001.

BODY NUMBER PLATE

Location:	On firewall.
Serial number:	Same as number on VIN tag.
BODY	Symbols below BODY are body style code: 40A = Thunderbird.
COLOR	Symbols below COLOR are paint color code.
TRIM	Symbols below TRIM are trim combination code.
PROD. CODE	Symbols below PRODUCTION DATE are the production date code. The number indicates the date of the month the car was made. The letters indicate month of manufacture: A = January; B= February; C = March; D = April; E = May; F = June; G = July; H = August; J = September; K = October; L = November; M = December.

1957

VEHICLE IDENTIFICATION TAG

VIN location:	On plate on left door pillar.
1st symbol:	Denotes engine:
	C = 292 cid/212 hp four-barrel Thunderbird V-8.
	D = 312 cid/245 hp four-barrel Thunderbird Special V-8.
	E = 312 cid/270 hp dual four-barrel Thunderbird Special V-8.
	F = 312 cid/300 hp Supercharged Thunderbird Special V-8.
2nd symbol:	Denotes model-year; 7 = 1957.
3rd symbol:	Denotes the assembly plant; F = Dearborn, Mich.
4th symbol	Denotes body type: H = Thunderbird.
5th - 10th symbols:	Denote sequential production number of specific vehicle starting at 100001.

BODY NUMBER PLATE

Location:	On firewall.
Serial number:	Same as number on VIN tag.
BODY	Symbols below BODY are body style code: 40 = Thunderbird.
COLOR	Symbols below COLOR are paint color code.
TRIM	Symbols below TRIM are trim combination code.
PROD. CODE	Symbols below PRODUCTION DATE are the production date code. The number indicates the date of the month the car was made. The letters indicate month of manufacture: A = January; B= February; C = March; D = April; E = May; F = June; G = July; H = August; J = September; K = October; L = November; M = December.

1958

VEHICLE IDENTIFICATION TAG

VIN location:	On plate on left door pillar.
1st symbol:	Denotes engine: H = 352 cid/300 hp Thunderbird Special V-8.
2nd symbol:	Denotes model-year; 8 = 1958.
3rd symbol:	Denotes the assembly plant; Y = Wixom, Mich.
4th symbol	Denotes body type: H = Tudor Hardtop; J = 2-door Convertible.
5th - 10th symbols:	Denote sequential production number of specific vehicle starting at 100001.

BODY NUMBER PLATE

Location:	Left front door hinge pillar post
Serial number:	Same as number on VIN tag.
BODY	Symbols below BODY are body style code: 63A = Hardtop; 76A = Convertible.
COLOR	Symbols below COLOR are paint color code. First symbol indicates lower body color. Second symbol (if used) indicates upper body color.
TRIM	Symbols below TRIM are trim combination code.
DATE	Symbols below DATE are the production date code. The number is the date the unit was built. The letter indicates month of manufacture: A = January; B= February; C = March; D = April; E = May; F = June; G = July; H = August; J = September; K = October; L = November; M = December.
TRANS	Symbols below TRANS are transmission code. 1 = Conventional three-speed manual transmission; 2 = Three-speed manual transmission with overdrive; 4 = Cruise-O-Matic transmission.
AXLE	Symbols below AXLE indicate rear axle. Axles used on 1959 Thunderbirds were: 1 = 3.10:1; 3 = 3.70:1.

1959

VEHICLE IDENTIFICATION TAG

VIN location:	On plate on left door pillar.
1st symbol:	Denotes engine: H = 352 cid/300 hp Thunderbird Special V-8. J = 430 cid/350 hp Thunderbird Special V-8.
2nd symbol:	Denotes model-year; 9 = 1959.
3rd symbol:	Denotes the assembly plant; Y = Wixom. Mich.
4th symbol	Denotes body type: H = Tudor Hardtop; J = 2-door Convertible.
5th - 10th symbols:	Denote sequential production number of specific vehicle starting at 100001.

BODY NUMBER PLATE

Location:	Left front door hinge pillar post.
Serial number:	Same as number on VIN tag.
BODY	Symbols below BODY are body style code: 63A = Hardtop; 76A = Convertible.
COLOR	Symbols below COLOR are paint color code. First symbol indicates lower body color. Second symbol (if used) indicates upper body color.
TRIM	Symbols below TRIM are trim combination code.
DATE	Symbols below DATE are the production date code. The number is the date the unit was built. The letter indicates month of manufacture: A = January; B= February; C = March; D = April; E = May; F = June; G = July; H = August; J = September; K = October; L = November; M = December.
TRANS	Symbols below TRANS are transmission code. 1 = Conventional three-speed manual transmission; 2 = Three-speed manual transmission with overdrive; 4 = Cruise-O-Matic transmission.
AXLE	Symbols below AXLE indicate rear axle. Axles used on 1959 Thunderbirds were: 1 = 3.10:1; 3 = 3.70:1; 0 = 2.91:1.

1960

VEHICLE IDENTIFICATION TAG

VIN location:	Die-stamped on top of front fender cross-bar to right of hood lock striker plate.
1st symbol:	Denotes model-year, 0 for 1960.
2nd symbol:	Denotes assembly plant. All T-Birds built at Wixom, Mich. (Plant code Y.)
3rd symbol:	Denotes the car-line; 7 indicates Thunderbird.
4th symbol	Denotes body type: 1 = Tudor Hardtop; 3 = 2-door Convertible
5th symbol:	Denotes engine: Y = 352 cid/300-hp Interceptor V-8. J = 430 cid/350-hp Thunderbird Special V-8.
6th - 11th symbols:	Denote sequential production number of specific vehicle starting at 100001.

BODY NUMBER PLATE

Location:	Front body pillar.
Serial number:	Same as number on VIN tag.
BDY:	Symbols above BDY are body style code: 63A = Hardtop; 76A = Convertible.
CLR:	Symbols above CLR are paint color code. First symbol indicates lower body color. Second symbol indicates upper body color.
TRM:	Symbols above TRM are trim combination code.
DT:	Symbols above DT are production date code. The number is the date the unit was built. The letter indicates month of manufacture: A = January; B= February; C = March; D = April; E = May; F = June; G = July; H = August; J = September; K = October;

L = November; M = December; N = January; P = February, etc. (Ford listed two year codes in case the 1960 model run was extended.)

DSO: Symbols above DSO indicate information including the Ford Motor Co. Sales District Code.

AX: Symbols above AX indicate rear axle. Axles used on 1960 Thunderbirds were: 3 = 3.10:1, 9 = 3.70:1.

TR Symbols above TR indicate type of transmission: 1 = Three-speed manual; 2 = Three-speed manual with overdrive; 4 = SelectShift Cruise-O-Matic.

1961

VEHICLE IDENTIFICATION TAG

VIN location: Die-stamped on top of front fender cross-bar to right of hood lock striker plate.
1st symbol: Denotes model-year, 1 for 1961.
2nd symbol: Denotes assembly plant. All T-Birds built at Wixom, Mich. (Plant code Y.) Pilot models possibly built at Pilot Plant, Dearborn, Mich. (Plant code S).
3rd symbol: Denotes the car-line; 7 indicates Thunderbird.
4th symbol Denotes body type: 1 = Tudor Hardtop; 5 = 2-door Convertible
5th symbol: Denotes engine:
Z = 390 cid/300-hp Thunderbird V-8.
6th - 11th symbols: Denote sequential production number of specific vehicle starting at 100001.

BODY NUMBER PLATE

Location: Front body pillar.
Serial number: Same as number on VIN tag.
BDY: Symbols above BDY are body style code: 63A = Hardtop; 76A = Convertible.
CLR: Symbols above CLR are paint color code. First symbol indicates lower body color. Second symbol indicates upper body color.
TRM: Symbols above TRM are trim combination code.
DT: Symbols above DT are production date code. The number is the date the unit was built. The letter indicates month of manufacture: A = January; B= February; C = March; D = April; E = May; F = June; G = July; H = August; J = September; K = October; L = November; M = December; N = January; P = February, etc. (Ford listed two year codes in case the 1961 model run was extended.)
DSO: Symbols above DSO indicate information including the Ford Motor Co. Sales District Code.
AX: Symbols above AX indicate rear axle. Axles used on 1961 Thunderbirds were: 1 = 3.00:1 (also noted as 3.56:1); 3 = 3.10:1; 6 = 3.00:1; 9 = 3.70:1; F = 3.56:1 Equa-Lock (Also noted as A); H = 2.91:1 Equa-Lock.
TR Symbols above TR indicate type of transmission: All Thunderbirds from 1961 until the 1980s came only with SelectShift Cruise-O-Matic Drive.

1962

VEHICLE IDENTIFICATION TAG

VIN location: Die-stamped on top of front fender cross-bar to right of hood lock striker plate.
1st symbol: Denotes model-year, 2 for 1962.
2nd symbol: Denotes assembly plant. All T-Birds built at Wixom, Mich. (Plant code Y.)
3rd symbol: Denotes the car-line; 8 indicates Thunderbird.
4th symbol Denotes body type: 3 = Tudor Hardtop; 5 = 2-door Convertible.
5th symbol: Denotes engine:
Z = 390 cid/300-hp Thunderbird V-8.
M = 390 cid/340-hp Thunderbird Special Six-Barrel V-8.
* M code engine introduced in January 1962.
6th - 11th symbols: Denote sequential production number of specific vehicle starting at 100001.

BODY NUMBER PLATE

Location: Front body pillar.
Serial number: Same as number on VIN tag.
BDY: Symbols above BDY are body style code: 63A = Hardtop; 63B = Landau Hardtop; 76A = Convertible; 76B = Sport Roadster.
CLR: Symbols above CLR are paint color code. First symbol indicates lower body color. Second symbol indicates upper body color.
TRM: Symbols above TRM are trim combination code.
DT: Symbols above DT are production date code. The number is the date the unit was built. The letter indicates month of manufacture: A = January; B= February; C = March; D = April; E = May; F = June; G = July; H = August; J = September; K = October; L = November; M = December; N = January; P = February, etc. (Ford listed two year codes in case the 1962 model run was extended.)
DSO: Symbols above DSO indicate information including the Ford Motor Co. Sales District Code.
AX: Symbols above AX indicate rear axle. (3.00:1 standard; no options listed).
TR Symbols above TR indicate type of transmission: All Thunderbirds from 1961 until the 1980s came only with SelectShift Cruise-O-Matic Drive.

1963

VEHICLE IDENTIFICATION TAG

VIN location: Die-stamped on top of front fender cross-bar to right of hood lock striker plate.
1st symbol: Denotes model-year, 3 for 1963.
2nd symbol: Denotes assembly plant. All T-Birds built at Wixom, Mich. (Plant code Y.)
3rd symbol: Denotes the car-line; 8 indicates Thunderbird.
4th symbol: Denotes body type: 3 = 2-door Hardtop; 5 = 2-door Convertible; 7 = 2-door Landau Hardtop; 9 = 2-door Sport Roadster.
5th symbol: Denotes engine:
9 = 390 cid Thunderbird V-8 (low-compression for export).
Z = 390 cid/330-hp Thunderbird V-8.
M = 390 cid/340-hp Thunderbird Special 6-Barrel V-8.
* The M code engine was discontinued in December 1962.
6th - 11th symbols: Denote sequential production number of specific vehicle starting at 100001.

BODY NUMBER PLATE

Location:	Front body pillar.
Serial number:	Same as number on VIN tag.
BDY:	Symbols above BDY are body style code: 63A = Hardtop; 63B = Landau Hardtop; 76A = Convertible; 76B = Sport Roadster.
CLR:	Symbols above CLR are paint color code. First symbol indicates lower body color. Second symbol indicates upper body color.
TRM:	Symbols above TRM are trim combination code.
DT:	Symbols above DT are production date code. The number is the date the unit was built. The letter indicates month of manufacture: A = January; B= February; C = March; D = April; E = May; F = June; G = July; H = August; J = September; K = October; L = November; M = December.
DSO:	Symbols above DSO indicate information including the Ford Sales District Code.
AX:	Symbols above AX indicate rear axle. (3.00:1 standard; no options listed).
TR	Symbols above TR indicate type of transmission: All Thunderbirds from 1961 until the 1980s came only with SelectShift Cruise-O-Matic Drive.

1964

VEHICLE IDENTIFICATION TAG

VIN location:	Die-stamped on top of front fender cross-bar to right of hood lock striker plate.
1st symbol:	Denotes model-year, 4 for 1964.
2nd symbol:	Denotes assembly plant. All T-Birds built at Wixom, Mich. (Plant code Y.)
3rd symbol:	Denotes the car-line; 8 indicates Thunderbird.
4th symbol:	Denotes body type: 3 = 2-door Hardtop; 5 = 2-door Convertible; 7 = 2-door Landau Hardtop.
5th symbol:	Denotes engine: 9 = 390 cid Thunderbird (low-compression for export) V-8. Z = 390 cid/300-hp Thunderbird V-8.
6th - 11th symbols:	Denote sequential production number of specific vehicle starting at 100001.

BODY NUMBER PLATE

Location:	Front body pillar.
Serial number:	Same as number on VIN tag.
BDY:	Symbols above BDY are body style code: 63A = Hardtop; 63B = Landau Hardtop; 76A = Convertible.
CLR:	Symbols above CLR are paint color code. First symbol indicates lower body color. Second symbol indicates upper body color.
TRM:	Symbols above TRM are trim combination code.
DT:	Symbols above DT are production date code. The number is the date the unit was built. The letter indicates month of manufacture: A = January; B= February; C = March; D = April; E = May; F = June; G = July; H = August; J = September; K = October; L = November; M = December.
DSO:	Symbols above DSO indicate information including the Ford Sales District Code.
AX:	Symbols above AX indicate rear axle. (3.00:1 standard; no options listed).
TR	Symbols above TR indicate type of transmission: All Thunderbirds from 1961 until the 1980s came only with SelectShift Cruise-O-Matic Drive.

1965

VEHICLE IDENTIFICATION TAG

VIN location:	Die-stamped on top of front fender cross-bar to right of hood lock striker plate.
1st symbol:	Denotes model-year, 5 for 1965.
2nd symbol:	Denotes assembly plant. All T-Birds built at Wixom, Mich. (Plant code Y.)
3rd symbol:	Denotes the car-line; 8 indicates Thunderbird.
4th symbol:	Denotes body type: 1 = 2-door Landau Special; 3 = 2-door Hardtop; 5 =2-door Convertible; 7 = 2-door Landau Hardtop.
5th symbol:	Denotes engine: 9 = 390 cid Thunderbird (low-compression for export) V-8. Z = 390 cid/300-hp Thunderbird V-8.
6th - 11th symbols:	Denote sequential production number of specific vehicle starting at 100001.

BODY NUMBER PLATE

Location:	Front body pillar.
Serial number:	Same as number on VIN tag.
BDY:	Symbols above BDY are body style code: 63A = Hardtop; 63B = Landau Hardtop; 63D = Landau Special Hardtop; 76A = Convertible.
CLR:	Symbols above CLR are paint color code. First symbol indicates lower body color. Second symbol indicates upper body color.
TRM:	Symbols above TRM are trim combination code.
DT:	Symbols above DT are production date code. The number is the date the unit was built. The letter indicates month of manufacture: A = January; B= February; C = March; D = April; E = May; F = June; G = July; H = August; J = September; K = October; L = November; M = December.
DSO:	Symbols above DSO indicate information including the Ford Sales District Code.
AX:	Symbols above AX indicate rear axle. (3.00:1 standard; no options listed).
TR	Symbols above TR indicate type of transmission: All Thunderbirds from 1961 until the 1980s came only with SelectShift Cruise-O-Matic Drive.

1966

VEHICLE IDENTIFICATION TAG

VIN location:	Die-stamped on top of front fender cross-bar to right of hood lock striker plate.
1st symbol:	Denotes model-year, 6 for 1966.
2nd symbol:	Denotes assembly plant. All T-Birds built at Wixom, Mich. (Plant code Y.)
3rd symbol:	Denotes the car-line; 8 indicates Thunderbird.
4th symbol:	Denotes body type: 1 = 2-door Town Hardtop; 3 = 2-door Hardtop; 5 = 2-door Convertible; 7 = 2-door Town Landau.
5th symbol:	Denotes engine: Z = 390 cid/315-hp Thunderbird V-8. Q = 428 cid/345-hp Thunderbird Special V-8 8 = 428 cid Thunderbird Special (low-compression for export) V-8

6th - 11th symbols:	Denote sequential production number of specific vehicle starting at 100001.

BODY NUMBER PLATE

Location:	Front body pillar.
Serial number:	Same as number on VIN tag.
BDY:	Symbols above BDY are body style code: 63A = Hardtop; 63C = Town Hardtop; 63D = Town Landau Hardtop; 76A = Convertible.
CLR:	Symbols above CLR are paint color code. First symbol indicates lower body color. Second symbol indicates upper body color.
TRM:	Symbols above TRM are trim combination code.
DT:	Symbols above DT are production date code. The number is the date the unit was built. The letter indicates month of manufacture: A = January; B = February; C = March; D = April; E = May; F = June; G = July; H = August; J = September; K = October; L = November; M = December.
DSO:	Symbols above DSO indicate information including the Ford Sales District Code.
AX:	Symbols above AX indicate rear axle. The rear axles used were: (390 V-8) (Std.) 3.00:1; (Opt.) 3.25:1. (428 cid V-8) (Std.) 2.80:1; (Opt.) 3.00:1 and 3.50:1.
TR	Symbols above TR indicate type of transmission: All Thunderbirds from 1961 until the 1980s came only with SelectShift Cruise-O-Matic Drive.

1967

VEHICLE IDENTIFICATION TAG

VIN location:	Die-stamped on right-hand side of cowl top panel tab.
1st symbol:	Denotes model-year, 7 for 1967.
2nd symbol:	Denotes assembly plant. All T-Birds built at Wixom, Mich. (Plant code Y.)
3rd symbol:	Denotes the car-line; 8 indicates Thunderbird.
4th symbol:	Denotes body type: 1 = 2-door Hardtop; 2 = 2-door Landau; 4 = 4-door Landau.
5th symbol:	Denotes engine:
	Z = 390 cid/315-hp Thunderbird V-8.
	Q = 428 cid/345-hp Thunderbird Special V-8
	8 = 428 cid Thunderbird Special (low-compression for export) V-8
6th - 11th symbols:	Denote sequential production number of specific vehicle starting at 100001.

BODY NUMBER PLATE

Location:	Front body pillar.
Serial number:	Same as number on VIN tag.
BDY:	Symbols above BDY are body style code: 65A = Hardtop; 65B = Landau Hardtop; 57B = Landau Sedan.
CLR:	Symbols above CLR are paint color code. First symbol indicates lower body color. Second symbol indicates upper body color.
TRM:	Symbols above TRM are trim combination code.
DT:	Symbols above DT are production date code. The number is the date the unit was built. The letter indicates month of manufacture: A = January; B= February; C = March; D = April; E = May; F = June; G = July; H = August; J = September; K = October; L = November; M = December.
DSO:	Symbols above DSO indicate information including the Ford Sales District Code.
AX:	Symbols above AX indicate rear axle.
TR	Symbols above TR indicate type of transmission: All Thunderbirds from 1961 until the 1980s came only with SelectShift Cruise-O-Matic Drive.

1968

VEHICLE IDENTIFICATION TAG

VIN location:	Stamped on aluminum tab riveted to dashboard on passenger side and observable through the windshield from outside the car.
1st symbol:	Denotes model-year, 8 for 1968.
2nd symbol:	Denotes assembly plant. All T-Birds built at Wixom, Mich. (Plant code Y.)
3rd symbol:	Denotes the car-line; 8 indicates Thunderbird.
4th symbol:	Denotes body type: 3 = 2-door Hardtop; 4 = 2-door Landau Hardtop; 7 = 4-door Landau.
5th symbol:	Denotes engine:
	Z = 390 cid/315-hp Thunderbird V-8.
	Q = 428 cid/345-hp Thunderbird Special V-8
	8 = 428 cid Thunderbird Special (low-compression for export) V-8
	N = 429 cid/360-hp Thunder-Jet V-8
	* Z code engine dropped in January 1968; Q code engine becomes standard.
6th - 11th symbols:	Denote sequential production number of specific vehicle starting at 100001.

BODY NUMBER PLATE

Location:	Front body pillar.
Serial number:	Same as number on VIN tag.
BDY:	Symbols above BDY are body style code: 65C = 2-door Hardtop; 65B = 2-door Landau Hardtop; 57C = 4-door Landau.
CLR:	Symbols above CLR are paint color code. First symbol indicates lower body color. Second symbol indicates upper body color.
TRM:	Symbols above TRM are trim combination code.
DT:	Symbols above DT are production date code. The number is the date the unit was built. The letter indicates month of manufacture: A = January; B= February; C = March; D = April; E = May; F = June; G = July; H = August; J = September; K = October; L = November; M = December.
DSO:	Symbols above DSO indicate information including the Ford Sales District Code.
AX:	Symbols above AX indicate rear axle. (Std.) 2.50:1; (Opt.) 2.80:1 and 3.0:1
TR	Symbols above TR indicate type of transmission: All Thunderbirds from 1961 until the 1980s came only with SelectShift Cruise-O-Matic Drive.

1969

VEHICLE IDENTIFICATION TAG

VIN location:	Stamped on aluminum tab riveted to dashboard on passenger side and observable through the windshield from outside the car.
1st symbol:	Denotes model-year, 9 for 1969.

2nd symbol:	Denotes assembly plant. All T-Birds built at Wixom, Mich. (Plant code Y.)
3rd symbol:	Denotes the car-line; 8 indicates Thunderbird.
4th symbol:	Denotes body type: 3 = 2-door Hardtop; 4 = 2-door Landau Hardtop; 7 = 4-door Landau.
5th symbol:	Denotes engine: N = 429 cid/360-hp Thunder-Jet V-8
6th - 11th symbols:	Denote sequential production number of specific vehicle starting at 100001.

BODY NUMBER PLATE

Location:	Front body pillar.
Serial number:	Same as number on VIN tag.
BDY:	Symbols above BDY are body style code: 65A = 2-door Hardtop with split bench front seat; 65C = 2-door Hardtop with front bench seat; 65B = 2-door Landau with blind quarter roof and front bucket seats; 65D = 2-door Landau with blind rear quarter roof and front bench seat; 57B = 4-door Landau with front bucket seats; 57C = 4-door Landau with front bench seat.
CLR:	Symbols above CLR are paint color code. First symbol indicates lower body color. Second symbol indicates upper body color.
TRM:	Symbols above TRM are trim combination code.
DT:	Symbols above DT are production date code. The number is the date the unit was built. The letter indicates month of manufacture: A = January; B= February; C = March; D = April; E = May; F = June; G = July; H = August; J = September; K = October; L = November; M = December.
DSO:	Symbols above DSO indicate information including the Ford Sales District Code.
AX:	Symbols above AX indicate rear axle. Note: Ford axle codes. Some may not have been available with Thunderbirds.
TR:	Symbols above TR indicate type of transmission: All Thunderbirds from 1961 until the 1980s came only with SelectShift Cruise-O-Matic Drive.

1970

VEHICLE IDENTIFICATION TAG

VIN location:	Stamped on aluminum tab riveted to dashboard on passenger side and observable) through the windshield from outside the car.
Prefix:	Denotes manufacturer: F for Ford.
1st symbol:	Denotes model-year, 0 for 1970.
2nd symbol:	Denotes assembly plant. All T-Birds built at Wixom, Mich. (Plant code Y.)
3rd symbol:	Denotes the car-line; 8 indicates Thunderbird
4th symbol	Denotes body type: 3 = 2-door Hardtop; 4 = 2-door Landau; 7 = four-door Landau.
5th symbol:	Denotes engine: N = 429 cid/360-hp Thunder-Jet V-8
6th - 11th symbols:	Denote sequential production number of specific vehicle starting at 100001.

VEHICLE CERTIFICATION LABEL

Location:	Rear face of driver's door. The top part of the label indicates that the Thunderbird was manufactured by Ford Motor Company. Directly below this is the month and year of manufacture, plus a statement that the car conforms to federal motor vehicle safety standard in effect on the indicated date of manufacture.
VIN:	The VIN appears first on the first line of encoded information. It matches the 1st to 11th symbols on VIN tag.
BDY:	The body style code appears to the right of the VIN on the same line. The Thunderbird codes for this model-year are: 57B = 4-door Landau with front split-bench seat; 57C = 4-door Landau with front bench seat; 65A = 2-door Hardtop with front bucket seats; 65B = 2-door Landau with front bucket seats; 65C = 2-door Hardtop with front bench seat; 65D = 2-door Landau with front bench seat.
CLR:	The color code(s) appears to the right of the body style code. Conventional colors are identified by a single letter or number. Optional Glamour Paints are identified by two numbers.
TRM:	The trim code appears on the far left-hand side of the second line of encoded information.
AX:	The axle code appears to the right of the trim code in the second position on the second line of encoded information.
TR:	The transmission code appears to the right of the axle code in the third position on the second line of encoded information.
DSO:	The District Special Equipment code appears to the right of the transmission code in the far right-hand position on the second line of encoded information.

Note: The abbreviations VIN/BDY/CLR/TRM/AX/TR/DSO do not appear on the certification label itself. The specific application of the codes is determined by where they are located on the vehicle certification label.

1971

VEHICLE IDENTIFICATION TAG

VIN location:	Stamped on aluminum tab riveted to dash on passenger side and observable through the windshield from outside the car.
Prefix:	Denotes manufacturer: F for Ford.
1st symbol:	Denotes model-year, 1 for 1971.
2nd symbol:	Denotes assembly plant. All T-Birds built at Wixom, Mich. (Plant code Y.)
3rd symbol:	Denotes the car-line; 8 indicates Thunderbird
4th symbol	Denotes body type: 3 = 2-door Hardtop; 4 = 2-door Landau; 7 = four-door Landau.
5th symbol:	Denotes engine: N = 429 cid/360-hp Thunder-Jet V-8
6th - 11th symbols:	Denote sequential production number of specific vehicle starting at 100001.

VEHICLE CERTIFICATION LABEL

Location:	Rear face of driver's door. The top part of the label indicates that the Thunderbird was manufactured by Ford Motor Company. Directly below this is the month and year of manufacture, plus a statement that the car conforms to federal motor vehicle safety standard in effect on the indicated date of manufacture.
VIN:	The VIN appears first on the first line of encoded information. It matches the 1st to 11th symbols on VIN tag.

BDY:	The body style code appears to the right of the VIN on the same line. The Thunderbird codes for this model-year are: 57B = 4-door Landau with front split-bench seat; 57C = 4-door Landau with front bench seat; 65A = 2-door Hardtop with front bucket seats; 65B = 2-door Landau with front bucket seats; 65C = 2-door Hardtop with front bench seat; 65D = 2-door Landau with front bench seat.
CLR:	The color code appears to the right of the body style code.
TRM:	The trim code appears on the far left-hand side of the second line of encoded information.
AX:	The axle code appears to the right of the trim code in the second position on the second line of encoded information.
TR:	The transmission code appears to the right of the axle code in the third position on the second line of encoded information.
DSO:	The District Special Equipment code appears to the right of the transmission code in the far right-hand position on the second line of encoded information.

Note: The abbreviations VIN/BDY/CLR/TRM/AX/TR/DSO do not appear on the certification label itself. The specific application of the codes is determined by where they are located on the vehicle certification label.

1972

VEHICLE IDENTIFICATION TAG

VIN location:	Stamped on aluminum tab riveted to dash on passenger side and visible through the windshield from outside the car.
Prefix:	Denotes manufacturer: F for Ford.
1st symbol:	Denotes model-year, 2 for 1972.
2nd symbol:	Denotes assembly plant. T-Birds were now built at Wixom, Mich. (Plant code Y) and Los Angeles, Calif. (Plant Code J).
3rd symbol:	Denotes the car-line; 8 indicates Thunderbird
4th symbol	Denotes body type: 7 = two-door Hardtop.
5th symbol:	Denotes engine: N = 429 cid/212-hp Thunderbird V-8 A = 460 cid/224-hp Thunderbird V-8
6th - 11th symbols:	Denote sequential production number of specific vehicle starting at 100001.

VEHICLE CERTIFICATION LABEL

Location:	Rear face of driver's door. The top part of the label indicates that the Thunderbird was manufactured by Ford Motor Company. Directly below this is the month and year of manufacture, plus a statement that the car conforms to federal motor vehicle safety standard in effect on the indicated date of manufacture.
VIN:	The VIN appears first on the first line of encoded information. It matches the 1st to 11th symbols on VIN tag.
BDY:	The body style code appears to the right of the VIN on the same line. The only Thunderbird code for this model-year is: 65K = 2-door Hardtop.
CLR:	The color code appears to the right of the body style code
TRM:	The trim code appears on the far left-hand side of the second line of encoded information.
AX:	The axle code appears to the right of the trim code in the second position on the second line of encoded information.
TR:	The transmission code appears to the right of the axle code in the third position on the second line of encoded information.
DSO:	The District Special Equipment code appears to the right of the transmission code in the far right-hand position on the second line of encoded information.

Note: The abbreviations VIN/BDY/CLR/TRM/AX/TR/DSO do not appear on the certification label itself. The specific application of the codes is determined by where they are located on the vehicle certification label.

1973

VEHICLE IDENTIFICATION TAG

VIN location:	Stamped on aluminum tab riveted to dash on passenger side and visible through the windshield from outside the car.
Prefix:	Denotes manufacturer: F for Ford.
1st symbol:	Denotes model-year, 3 for 1973.
2nd symbol:	Denotes assembly plant. Y = Wixom, Mich.; J = Los Angeles, Calif.
3rd symbol:	Denotes the car-line; 8 indicates Thunderbird
4th symbol	Denotes body type: 7 = two-door Hardtop.
5th symbol:	Denotes engine: N = 429 cid/208-hp Thunderbird V-8 A = 460 cid/219-hp Thunderbird V-8
6th - 11th symbols:	Denote sequential production number of specific vehicle starting at 100001.
Suffix:	Denotes manufacturer: F for Ford.

VEHICLE CERTIFICATION LABEL

Location:	Rear face of driver's door. The top part of the label indicates that the Thunderbird was manufactured by Ford Motor Company. Directly below this is the month and year of manufacture, plus a statement that the car conforms to federal motor vehicle safety standard in effect on the indicated date of manufacture.
VIN:	The VIN appears first on the first line of encoded information. It matches the 1st to 11th symbols on VIN tag.
BDY:	The body style code appears to the right of the VIN on the same line. The only Thunderbird code for this model-year is: 65K = 2-door Hardtop.
CLR:	The color code appears to the right of the body style code
TRM:	The trim code appears on the far left-hand side of the second line of encoded information.
TR:	The transmission code appears to the right of the trim code in the second position on the second line of encoded information.
AX:	The axle code appears to the right of the transmission code in the third position on the second line of encoded information.
DSO:	The District Special Equipment code appears to the right of the transmission code in the far right-hand position on the second line of encoded information.

Note: The abbreviations VIN/BDY/CLR/TRM/TR/AX/DSO do not appear on the certification label itself. The specific application of the codes is determined by where they are located on the vehicle certification label.

1974

VEHICLE IDENTIFICATION TAG

VIN location:	Stamped on aluminum tab riveted to dash on passenger side and visible through the windshield from outside the car.
Prefix:	Denotes manufacturer: F for Ford.
1st symbol:	Denotes model-year, 4 for 1974.
2nd symbol:	Denotes assembly plant. Y = Wixom, Mich.; J = Los Angeles, Calif.
3rd symbol:	Denotes the car-line; 8 indicates Thunderbird
4th symbol	Denotes body type: 7 = two-door Hardtop.
5th symbol:	Denotes engine: A = 460 cid/220-hp Thunderbird V-8
6th - 11th symbols:	Denote sequential production number of specific vehicle starting at 100001.
Suffix:	Denotes manufacturer: F for Ford.

VEHICLE CERTIFICATION LABEL

Location:	Rear face of driver's door. The top part of the label indicates that the Thunderbird was manufactured by Ford Motor Company. Directly below this is the month and year of manufacture, plus a statement that the car conforms to federal motor vehicle safety standard in effect on the indicated date of manufacture.
VIN:	The VIN appears first on the first line of encoded information. It matches the 1st to 11th symbols on VIN tag.
BDY:	The body style code appears to the right of the VIN on the same line. The only Thunderbird code for this model-year is: 65K = 2-door Hardtop.
CLR:	The color code appears to the right of the body style code
TRM:	The trim code appears on the far left-hand side of the second line of encoded information.
TR:	The transmission code appears to the right of the trim code in the second position on the second line of encoded information.
AX:	The axle code appears to the right of the transmission code in the third position on the second line of encoded information.
DSO:	The District Special Equipment code appears to the right of the transmission code in the far right-hand position on the second line of encoded information.

Note: The abbreviations VIN/BDY/CLR/TRM/TR/AX/DSO do not appear on the certification label itself. The specific application of the codes is determined by where they are located on the vehicle certification label.

1975

VEHICLE IDENTIFICATION TAG

VIN location:	Stamped on aluminum tab riveted to dash on passenger side and visible through the windshield from outside the car.
Prefix:	Denotes manufacturer: F for Ford.
1st symbol:	Denotes model-year, 5 for 1975.
2nd symbol:	Denotes assembly plant. Y = Wixom, Mich.; J = Los Angeles, Calif.
3rd symbol:	Denotes the car-line; 8 indicates Thunderbird
4th symbol	Denotes body type: 7 = two-door Hardtop.
5th symbol:	Denotes engine: A = 460 cid/220-hp Thunderbird V-8
6th - 11th symbols:	Denote sequential production number of specific vehicle starting at 100001.
Suffix:	Denotes manufacturer: F for Ford.

VEHICLE CERTIFICATION LABEL

Location:	Rear face of driver's door. The top part of the label indicates that the Thunderbird was manufactured by Ford Motor Company. Directly below this is the month and year of manufacture, plus a statement that the car conforms to federal motor vehicle safety standard in effect on the indicated date of manufacture.
VIN:	The VIN appears first on the first line of encoded information. It matches the 1st to 11th symbols on VIN tag.
PASSENGER:	This term now appears to the right of the VIN to denote passenger vehicle.
BDY:	The body style code now appears on the far left-hand side of the second line of encoded information . The only Thunderbird code for this model-year is: 65K = 2-door Hardtop.
CLR:	The color and vinyl roof type/color code appears to the right of the body style code in the second position on the second line of encoded information.
TRM:	The trim code appears to the right of the color and vinyl roof codes in the third position on the second line of encoded information.
TR:	The transmission code appears to the right of the trim code in the fourth position on the second line of encoded information.
AX:	The axle code appears to the right of the transmission code in the fifth position on the second line of encoded information.
DSO:	The District Special Equipment code appears to the right of the transmission code in the far right-hand position on the second line of encoded information.

Note: The abbreviations VIN/BDY/CLR/TRM/TR/AX/DSO do not appear on the certification label itself. The specific application of the codes is determined by where they are located on the vehicle certification label.

1976

VEHICLE IDENTIFICATION TAG

VIN location:	Stamped on aluminum tab riveted to dash on passenger side and visible through the windshield from outside the car.
Prefix:	Denotes manufacturer: F for Ford.
1st symbol:	Denotes model-year, 6 for 1976.
2nd symbol:	Denotes assembly plant. Y = Wixom, Mich.; J = Los Angeles, Calif.
3rd symbol:	Denotes the car-line; 8 indicates Thunderbird
4th symbol	Denotes body type: 7 = two-door Hardtop.
5th symbol:	Denotes engine: A = 460 cid/220-hp Thunderbird V-8

6th - 11th symbols:	Denote sequential production number of specific vehicle starting at 100001.
Suffix:	Denotes manufacturer: F for Ford.

VEHICLE CERTIFICATION LABEL

Location:	Rear face of driver's door. The top part of the label indicates that the Thunderbird was manufactured by Ford Motor Company. Directly below this is the month and year of manufacture, plus a statement that the car conforms to federal motor vehicle safety standard in effect on the indicated date of manufacture.
VIN:	The VIN appears first on the first line of encoded information. It matches the 1st to 11th symbols on VIN tag.
PASSENGER:	This term now appears to the right of the VIN to denote passenger vehicle.
BDY:	The body style code now appears on the far left-hand side of the second line of encoded information . The only Thunderbird code for this model-year is: 65K = 2-door Hardtop.
CLR:	The color and vinyl roof type/color code appears to the right of the body style code in the second position on the second line of encoded information.
TRM:	The trim code appears to the right of the color and vinyl roof codes in the third position on the second line of encoded information.
TR:	The transmission code appears to the right of the trim code in the fourth position on the second line of encoded information.
AX:	The axle code appears to the right of the transmission code in the fifth position on the second line of encoded information.
DSO:	The District Special Equipment code appears to the right of the transmission code in the far right-hand position on the second line of encoded information.

Note: The abbreviations VIN/BDY/CLR/TRM/TR/AX/DSO do not appear on the certification label itself. The specific application of the codes is determined by where they are located on the vehicle certification label.

1977

VEHICLE IDENTIFICATION TAG

VIN location:	Stamped on aluminum tab riveted to dash on passenger side and visible through the windshield from outside the car.
Prefix:	Denotes manufacturer: F for Ford.
1st symbol:	Denotes model-year, 7 for 1977.
2nd symbol:	Denotes assembly plant. Y = Wixom, Mich.; J = Los Angeles, Calif.
3rd symbol:	Denotes the car-line; 8 indicates Thunderbird
4th symbol	Denotes body type: 7 = two-door Pillared Hardtop.
5th symbol:	Denotes engine:
	F = 302 cid (5.0L)/130- to 137-hp V-8
	H = 351 cid (5.8L)/149-hp V-8
	S = 400 cid (6.6L)/173-hp V-8
6th - 11th symbols:	Denote sequential production number of specific vehicle starting at 100001.

VEHICLE CERTIFICATION LABEL

Location:	Rear face of driver's door. The top part of the label indicates that the Thunderbird was manufactured by Ford Motor Company. Directly below this is the month and year of manufacture, plus a statement that the car conforms to federal motor vehicle safety standard in effect on the indicated date of manufacture.
VIN:	The VIN appears first on the first line of encoded information. It matches the 1st to 11th symbols on VIN tag.
PASSENGER:	This term now appears to the right of the VIN to denote passenger vehicle.
BDY:	The body style code now appears on the far left-hand side of the second line of encoded information . The only Thunderbird code for this model-year is: 60H = 2-door Pillared Hardtop.
CLR:	The color and vinyl roof type/color code appears to the right of the body style code in the second position on the second line of encoded information.
TRM:	The trim code appears to the right of the color and vinyl roof codes in the third position on the second line of encoded information.
TR:	The transmission code appears to the right of the trim code in the fourth position on the second line of encoded information.
AX:	The axle code appears to the right of the transmission code in the fifth position on the second line of encoded information.
DSO:	The District Special Equipment code appears to the right of the transmission code in the far right-hand position on the second line of encoded information.

Note: The abbreviations VIN/BDY/CLR/TRM/TR/AX/DSO do not appear on the certification label itself. The specific application of the codes is determined by where they are located on the vehicle certification label.

1978

VEHICLE IDENTIFICATION TAG

VIN location:	Stamped on aluminum tab riveted to dash on passenger side and visible through the windshield from outside the car.
Prefix:	Denotes manufacturer: F for Ford.
1st symbol:	Denotes model-year, 8 for 1978.
2nd symbol:	Denotes assembly plant. Y = Wixom, Mich.; J = Los Angeles, Calif.
3rd symbol:	Denotes the car-line; 8 indicates Thunderbird
4th symbol	Denotes body type: 7 = two-door Pillared Hardtop.
5th symbol:	Denotes engine:
	F = 302 cid (5.0L)/134-hp V-8
	H = 351 cid (5.8L)/144-hp V-8
	Q = Modified 351 cid (5.8L)/152-hp V-8
	S = 400 cid (6.6L)/166-hp V-8
6th - 11th symbols:	Denote sequential production number of specific vehicle starting at 100001.

VEHICLE CERTIFICATION LABEL

Location:	Rear face of driver's door. The top part of the label indicates that the Thunderbird was manufactured by Ford Motor Company. Directly below this is the month and year of manufacture, plus a statement that the car conforms to federal motor vehicle safety standard in effect on the indicated date of manufacture.
VIN:	The VIN appears first on the first line of encoded information. It matches the 1st to 11th symbols on VIN tag.

PASSENGER:	This term now appears to the right of the VIN to denote passenger vehicle.
BDY:	The body style code appears on the far left-hand side of the second line of encoded information . The only Thunderbird code for this model-year is: 60H = 2-door Pillared Hardtop.
CLR:	The color and vinyl roof type/color code appears to the right of the body style code in the second position on the second line of encoded information.
TRM:	The trim code appears to the right of the color and vinyl roof codes in the third position on the second line of encoded information.
TR:	The transmission code appears to the right of the trim code in the fourth position on the second line of encoded information.
AX:	The axle code appears to the right of the transmission code in the fifth position on the second line of encoded information.
DSO:	The District Special Equipment code appears to the right of the transmission code in the far right-hand position on the second line of encoded information.

Note: The abbreviations VIN/BDY/CLR/TRM/TR/AX/DSO do not appear on the certification label itself. The specific application of the codes is determined by where they are located on the vehicle certification label.

1979

VEHICLE IDENTIFICATION TAG

VIN location:	Stamped on aluminum tab riveted to dash on passenger side and visible through the windshield from outside the car.
Prefix:	Denotes manufacturer: F for Ford.
1st symbol:	Denotes model-year, 9 for 1979.
2nd symbol:	Denotes assembly plant. Y = Wixom, Mich.; J = Los Angeles, Calif.
3rd symbol:	Denotes the car-line; 8 indicates Thunderbird
4th symbol	Denotes body type: 7 = two-door Pillared Hardtop.
5th symbol:	Denotes engine:
	F = 302 cid (5.0L)/133-hp V-8
	H = 351 cid (5.8L)/135- to 142-hp V-8
	Q = Modified 351 cid (5.8L)/151-hp V-8
6th - 11th symbols:	Denote sequential production number of specific vehicle starting at 100001.

VEHICLE CERTIFICATION LABEL

Location:	Rear face of driver's door. The top part of the label indicates that the Thunderbird was manufactured by Ford Motor Company. Directly below this is the month and year of manufacture, plus a statement that the car conforms to federal motor vehicle safety standard in effect on the indicated date of manufacture.
VIN:	The VIN appears first on the first line of encoded information. It matches the 1st to 11th symbols on VIN tag.
PASSENGER:	This term now appears to the right of the VIN to denote passenger vehicle.
CLR:	The color and vinyl roof type/color code now appears in the far left-hand position on the second line of encoded information.
DSO:	The District Special Order code appears to the right of the body style code in the second position on the second line of encoded information.
BDY:	The body style code appears to the right of the DSO code in the third position on the second line of encoded information. The only Thunderbird code for this model-year is: 60H = 2-door Pillared Hardtop.
TRM:	The trim code appears to the right of the body style code in the fourth position on the second line of encoded information.
SBD:	The Scheduled Build Date is a new code. It appears to the right of the trim code in the fifth position on the second line of encoded information.
AX:	The axle code appears to the right of the Scheduled Build Date in the sixth position on the second line of encoded information.
TR:	The transmission code appears to the right of the axle code in the seventh position on the second line of encoded information.
A/C	The air conditioning code appears to the right of the transmission code in the eighth position on the second line of encoded information.

Note: The abbreviations VIN/CLR/DSO/BDY/TRM/SBD/AX/TR/A/C do not appear on the certification label itself. The specific application of the codes is determined by where they are located on the vehicle certification label.

1980

VEHICLE IDENTIFICATION TAG

VIN location:	Stamped on aluminum tab riveted to dash on passenger side and visible through the windshield from outside the car.
1st symbol:	Denotes model-year, 0 for 1980.
2nd symbol:	Denotes assembly plant. G = Chicago, Ill.; H = Lorain, Ohio.
3rd symbol:	Denotes the car-line; 8 indicates Thunderbird.
4th symbol	Denotes body type: 7 = two-door Pillared Hardtop.
5th symbol:	Denotes engine:
	G = 200 cid (3.3L) 115 hp six-cylinder.
	D = 255 cid (4.2L)/115-hp V-8.
	F = 302 cid (5.0L)/131-hp V-8.
6th - 11th symbols:	Denote sequential production number of specific vehicle starting at 100001.

VEHICLE CERTIFICATION LABEL

Location:	Rear face of driver's door. The top part of the label indicates that the Thunderbird was manufactured by Ford Motor Company in U.S.A. Directly below this is the month and year of manufacture, and gross vehicle weight information, plus a statement that the car conforms to federal motor vehicle safety standard in effect on the indicated date of manufacture.
VIN:	The VIN appears first on the first line of encoded information. It matches the 1st to 11th symbols on VIN tag. Some other codes also appear.
TYPE:	On left side of label; indicates PASSENGER
EXT. COLOR:	This line carries the exterior paint color(s) code.
DSO:	The District Special Order code now appears above "DSO" to the right of the exterior paint color code.

BODY:	The body style code appears to the extreme left of the bottom line. The only Thunderbird code for this model-year is: 66D = 2-door Pillared Hardtop.
VR:	The vinyl roof type/color code is to the right of the body code.
MLDG:	The molding code is to the right of the vinyl roof code.
INT. TRIM:	The interior trim code is to the right of the molding code.
A/C:	The air conditioning code is to the right of the interior trim code. Cars with air conditioning have "A" stamped here.
R:	The radio code is to the right of the A/C code.
S:	The sun roof code appears to the right of the radio code.
AX:	The axle code appears to the right of the sun roof code.
TR:	The transmission code appears to the right of the axle code.

Note: The terms and abbreviations shown in left-hand column appear on the line above the actual codes.

1981

VEHICLE IDENTIFICATION TAG

VIN location:	Stamped on aluminum tab riveted to dash on passenger side and visible through the windshield from outside the car.
1st symbol:	Denotes country of origin. 1 = United States.
2nd symbol:	Denotes manufacturer. F = Ford.
3rd symbol:	Denotes make and type. A = Ford passenger vehicle.
4th symbol:	Denotes type of passenger restraint system.
5th symbol:	Denotes type. P = Passenger
6th symbol:	Denotes model. 4 = Thunderbird
7th symbol:	Denotes body type. 2 = 2-door Coupe.
8th symbol:	Denotes engine: B = 200 cid (3.3L) 115 hp six-cylinder. D = 255 cid (4.2L)/115-hp V-8. F = 302 cid (5.0L)/131-hp V-8.
9th symbol:	Is the check digit.
10th symbol:	Denotes model-year. B = 1981.
11th symbol:	Denotes assembly plant. All T-Birds made at plant H (Lorain, Ohio)
12th - 17th symbols:	Denote sequential production number of specific vehicle starting at 100001.

VEHICLE CERTIFICATION LABEL

Location:	Rear face of driver's door. The top part of the label indicates that the Thunderbird was manufactured by Ford Motor Company in U.S.A. Directly below this is the month and yea of manufacture, and gross vehicle weight information, plus a statement that the car conforms to federal motor vehicle safety standard in effect on the indicated date of manufacture.
VIN:	The VIN appears first on the first line of encoded information. It matches the 1st to 11th symbols on VIN tag. Some other codes also appear.
TYPE:	Appears on left side of label; indicates PASSENGER
EXT. COLOR:	This line carries the exterior paint color(s) code.
DSO:	The District Special Order code now appears above "DSO" to the right of the exterior paint color code.
BODY:	The body style code appears to the extreme left of the bottom line. The only Thunderbird code for this model-year is: 66D = 2-door Pillared Hardtop.
VR:	The vinyl roof type/color code is to the right of the body code.
MLDG:	The molding code is to the right of the vinyl roof code.
INT. TRIM:	The interior trim code is to the right of the molding code.
A/C:	The air conditioning code appears to right of the interior trim code. Cars with air conditioning have "A" stamped here.
R:	The radio code is to the right of the A/C code.
S:	The sun roof code is to the right of the radio code.
AX:	The axle code appears to the right of the sun roof code.
TR:	The transmission code appears to the right of the axle code.

Note: The terms and abbreviations shown in left-hand column appear on the line above the actual codes

1982

VEHICLE IDENTIFICATION TAG

VIN location:	Stamped on aluminum tab riveted to dash on passenger side and visible through the windshield from outside the car.
1st symbol:	Denotes country of origin. 1 = United States.
2nd symbol:	Denotes manufacturer. F = Ford.
3rd symbol:	Denotes make and type. A = Ford passenger vehicle.
4th symbol:	Denotes type of passenger restraint system.
5th symbol:	Denotes type. P = Passenger
6th symbol:	Denotes model. 4 = Thunderbird
7th symbol:	Denotes body type. 2 = 2-door Coupe.
8th symbol:	Denotes engine: B = 200 cid (3.3L) 115 hp six-cylinder. 3 = 232 cid (3.8L)/115-hp V-6. D = 255 cid (4.2L)/131-hp V-8.
9th symbol:	Is the check digit.
10th symbol:	Denotes model-year. C = 1982.
11th symbol:	Denotes assembly plant. All T-Birds made at plant H (Lorain, Ohio)
12th - 17th symbols:	Denote sequential production number of specific vehicle starting at 100001.

VEHICLE CERTIFICATION LABEL

Location:	Rear face of driver's door. The top part of the label indicates that the Thunderbird was manufactured by Ford Motor Company in U.S.A. Directly below this is the month and year of manufacture, and gross vehicle weight information, plus a statement that the car conforms to federal motor vehicle safety standard in effect on the indicated date of manufacture.
VIN:	The VIN appears first on the first line of encoded information. It matches the 1st to 11th symbols on VIN tag. Some other codes also appear.
TYPE:	Appears on left side of label; indicates PASSENGER

EXT. COLOR:	This line carries the exterior paint color(s) code.
DSO:	The District Special Order code appears above "DSO" to the right of the exterior paint color code.
BODY:	The body style code appears to the extreme left of the bottom line. The only Thunderbird code for this model-year is: 66D = 2-door Pillared Hardtop.
VR:	The vinyl roof type/color code is to the right of the body code.
MLDG:	The molding code is to the right of the vinyl roof code.
INT. TRIM:	The interior trim code is to the right of the molding code.
A/C:	The air conditioning code appears to right of the interior trim code. Cars with air conditioning have "A" stamped here.
R:	The radio code is to the right of the A/C code.
S:	The sun roof code is to the right of the radio code.
AX:	The axle code appears to the right of the sun roof code.
TR:	The transmission code appears to the right of the axle code.

Note: The terms and abbreviations shown in left-hand column appear on the line above the actual codes.

1983

VEHICLE IDENTIFICATION TAG

VIN location:	Stamped on aluminum tab riveted to dash on passenger side and visible through the windshield from outside the car.
1st symbol:	Denotes country of origin. 1 = United States.
2nd symbol:	Denotes manufacturer. F = Ford.
3rd symbol:	Denotes make and type. A = Ford passenger vehicle.
4th symbol:	Denotes type of passenger restraint system.
5th symbol:	Denotes type. P = Passenger
6th symbol:	Denotes model. 4 = Thunderbird
7th symbol:	Denotes body type. 6= 2-door Coupe.
8th symbol:	Denotes engine: D = 140 cid (2.3L) 142 hp turbocharged four-cylinder. 3 = 232 cid (3.8L)/110-hp V-6. F = 302 cid (5.0L)/130-hp V-8.
9th symbol:	Is the check digit.
10th symbol:	Denotes model-year. D = 1983.
11th symbol:	Denotes assembly plant. T-Birds made at plant A = Atlanta, Ga. and plant H = Lorain, Ohio.
12th - 17th symbols:	Denote sequential production number of specific vehicle starting at 100001.

VEHICLE CERTIFICATION LABEL

Location:	Rear face of driver's door. The top part of the label indicates that the Thunderbird was manufactured by Ford Motor Company in U.S.A. Directly below this is the month and year of manufacture, and gross vehicle weight information, plus a statement that the car conforms to federal motor vehicle safety standard in effect on the indicated date of manufacture.
VIN:	The VIN appears first on the first line of encoded information. It matches the 1st to 11th symbols on VIN tag. Some other codes also appear.
TYPE:	Appears on left side of label; indicates PASSENGER
EXT. COLOR:	This line carries the exterior paint color(s) code.
DSO:	The District Special Order code now appears above "DSO" to the right of the exterior paint color code.
BODY:	The body style code appears to the extreme left of the bottom line. The only Thunderbird code for this model-year is: 66D = 2-door Coupe.
VR:	The vinyl roof type/color code is to the right of the body code. None on T-Bird.
MLDG:	The molding code is to the right of the vinyl roof code.
INT. TRIM:	The interior trim code is to the right of the molding code.
A/C:	The air conditioning code appears to right of the interior trim code. Cars with air conditioning have "A" stamped here.
R:	The radio code is to the right of the A/C code.
S:	The sun roof code is to the right of the radio code.
AX:	The axle code appears to the right of the sun roof code.
TR:	The transmission code appears to the right of the axle code.

Note: The terms and abbreviations shown in left-hand column appear on the line above the actual codes.

1984

VEHICLE IDENTIFICATION TAG

VIN location:	Stamped on aluminum tab riveted to dash on passenger side and visible through the windshield from outside the car.
1st symbol:	Denotes country of origin. 1 = United States.
2nd symbol:	Denotes manufacturer. F = Ford.
3rd symbol:	Denotes make and type. A = Ford passenger vehicle.
4th symbol:	Denotes type of passenger restraint system.
5th symbol:	Denotes type. P = Passenger
6th symbol:	Denotes model. 4 = Thunderbird
7th symbol:	Denotes body type. 6= 2-door Coupe.
8th symbol:	Denotes engine: W = 140 cid (2.3L) 145 hp turbocharged four-cylinder. 3 = 232 cid (3.8L)/120-hp V-6. F = 302 cid (5.0L)/140-hp V-8.
9th symbol:	Is the check digit.
10th symbol:	Denotes model-year. E = 1984.
11th symbol:	Denotes assembly plant. T-Birds made at plant A = Atlanta, Ga. and plant H = Lorain, Ohio.
12th - 17th symbols:	Denote sequential production number of specific vehicle starting at 100001.

VEHICLE CERTIFICATION LABEL

Location:	Rear face of driver's door. The top part of the label indicates that the Thunderbird was

manufactured by Ford Motor Company in U.S.A. Directly below this is the month and year of manufacture, and gross vehicle weight information, plus a statement that the car conforms to federal motor vehicle safety standard in effect on the indicated date of manufacture.

VIN:	The VIN appears first on the first line of encoded information. It matches the 1st to 11th symbols on VIN tag. Some other codes also appear.
TYPE:	Appears on left side of label; indicates PASSENGER
EXT. COLOR:	This line carries the exterior paint color(s) code.
DSO:	The District Special Order code appears above "DSO" to the right of the exterior paint color code.
BODY:	The body style code appears to the extreme left of the bottom line. The only Thunderbird code for this model-year is: 66D = 2-door Coupe.
VR:	The vinyl roof type/color code is to the right of the body code. None on T-Bird.
MLDG:	The molding code is to the right of the vinyl roof code.
INT. TRIM:	The interior trim code is to the right of the molding code.
A/C:	The air conditioning code appears to right of the interior trim code. Cars with air conditioning have "A" stamped here.
R:	The radio code is to the right of the A/C code.
S:	The sun roof code is to the right of the radio code.
AX:	The axle code appears to the right of the sun roof code.
TR:	The transmission code appears to the right of the axle code.

Note: The terms and abbreviations shown in left-hand column appear on the line above the actual codes.

1985

VEHICLE IDENTIFICATION TAG

VIN location:	Stamped on aluminum tab riveted to dash on passenger side and visible through the windshield from outside the car.
1st symbol:	Denotes country of origin. 1 = United States.
2nd symbol:	Denotes manufacturer. F = Ford.
3rd symbol:	Denotes make and type. A = Ford passenger vehicle.
4th symbol:	Denotes type of passenger restraint system.
5th symbol:	Denotes type. P = Passenger
6th symbol:	Denotes model. 4 = Thunderbird
7th symbol:	Denotes body type. 6= 2-door Coupe.
8th symbol:	Denotes engine: W = 140 cid (2.3L) 155 hp turbocharged four-cylinder. 3 = 232 cid (3.8L)/120-hp V-6. F = 302 cid (5.0L)/140-hp V-8.
9th symbol:	Is the check digit.
10th symbol:	Denotes model-year. F = 1985.
11th symbol:	Denotes assembly plant. T-Birds made at plant A = Atlanta, Ga. and plant H = Lorain, Ohio.
12th - 17th symbols:	Denote sequential production number of specific vehicle starting at 100001.

VEHICLE CERTIFICATION LABEL

Location:	Rear face of driver's door. The top part of the label indicates that the Thunderbird was manufactured by Ford Motor Company in U.S.A. Directly below this is the month and year of manufacture, and gross vehicle weight information, plus a statement that the car conforms to federal motor vehicle safety standard in effect on the indicated date of manufacture.
VIN:	The VIN appears first on the first line of encoded information. It matches the 1st to 11th symbols on VIN tag. Some other codes also appear.
TYPE:	Appears on left side of label; indicates PASSENGER
EXT. COLOR:	This line carries the exterior paint color(s) code.
DSO:	The District Special Order code appears above "DSO" to the right of the exterior paint color code.
BODY:	The body style code appears to the extreme left of the bottom line. The only Thunderbird code for this model-year is: 66D = 2-door Coupe.
VR:	The vinyl roof type/color code is to the right of the body code. None on T-Bird.
MLDG:	The molding code is to the right of the vinyl roof code.
INT. TRIM:	The interior trim code is to the right of the molding code.
A/C:	The air conditioning code appears to right of the interior trim code. Cars with air conditioning have "A" stamped here.
R:	The radio code is to the right of the A/C code.
S:	The sun roof code is to the right of the radio code.
AX:	The axle code appears to the right of the sun roof code.
TR:	The transmission code appears to the right of the axle code.

Note: The terms and abbreviations shown in left-hand column appear on the line above the actual codes.

1986

VEHICLE IDENTIFICATION TAG

VIN location:	Stamped on aluminum tab riveted to dash on passenger side and visible through the windshield from outside the car.
1st symbol:	Denotes country of origin. 1 = United States.
2nd symbol:	Denotes manufacturer. F = Ford.
3rd symbol:	Denotes make and type. A = Ford passenger vehicle.
4th symbol:	Denotes type of passenger restraint system.
5th symbol:	Denotes type. P = Passenger
6th symbol:	Denotes model. 4 = Thunderbird
7th symbol:	Denotes body type. 6= 2-door Coupe.
8th symbol:	Denotes engine: W = 140 cid (2.3L) 145 hp turbocharged four-cylinder/automatic. W = 140 cid (2.3L) 155 hp turbocharged four-cylinder/manual. 3 = 232 cid (3.8L)/120-hp V-6. F = 302 cid (5.0L)/150-hp V-8.
9th symbol:	Is the check digit.
10th symbol:	Denotes model-year. G = 1986.

| 11th symbol: | Denotes assembly plant. All T-Birds made at plant H = Lorain, Ohio. |
| 12th - 17th symbols: | Denote sequential production number of specific vehicle starting at 100001. |

VEHICLE CERTIFICATION LABEL

Location:	Rear face of driver's door. The top part of the label indicates that the Thunderbird was manufactured by Ford Motor Company in U.S.A. Directly below this is the month and year of manufacture, and gross vehicle weight information, plus a statement that the car conforms to federal motor vehicle safety standard in effect on the indicated date of manufacture.
VIN:	The VIN appears first on the first line of encoded information. It matches the 1st to 11th symbols on VIN tag. Some other codes also appear.
TYPE:	Appears on left side of label; indicates PASSENGER
EXT. COLOR:	This line carries the exterior paint color(s) code.
DSO:	The District Special Order code appears above "DSO" to the right of the exterior paint color code.
BODY:	The body style code appears to the extreme left of the bottom line. The only Thunderbird code for this model-year is: 66D = 2-door Coupe.
VR:	The vinyl roof type/color code is to the right of the body code. None on T-Bird.
MLDG:	The molding code is to the right of the vinyl roof code.
INT. TRIM:	The interior trim code is to the right of the molding code.
A/C:	The air conditioning code appears to right of the interior trim code. Cars with air conditioning have "A" stamped here.
R:	The radio code is to the right of the A/C code.
S:	The sun roof code is to the right of the radio code.
AX:	The axle code appears to the right of the sun roof code.
TR:	The transmission code appears to the right of the axle code.

Note: The terms and abbreviations shown in left-hand column appear on the line above the actual codes.

1987

VEHICLE IDENTIFICATION TAG

VIN location:	Stamped on aluminum tab riveted to dash on passenger side and visible through the windshield from outside the car.
1st symbol:	Denotes country of origin. 1 = United States.
2nd symbol:	Denotes manufacturer. F = Ford.
3rd symbol:	Denotes make and type. A = Ford passenger vehicle.
4th symbol:	Denotes type of passenger restraint system.
5th symbol:	Denotes type. P = Passenger
6th symbol:	Denotes model. 6 = Thunderbird
7th symbol:	Denotes body type. 0= Standard Coupe; 1 = Sport Coupe; 2 = LX Coupe; 4 = Turbo Coupe.
8th symbol:	Denotes engine: W = 140 cid (2.3L) 190 hp turbocharged four-cylinder/manual. W = 140 cid (2.3L) 150 hp turbocharged four-cylinder/automatic. 3 = 232 cid (3.8L)/120-hp V-6. F = 302 cid (5.0L)/150-hp V-8.
9th symbol:	Is the check digit.
10th symbol:	Denotes model-year. H = 1987.
11th symbol:	Denotes assembly plant. All T-Birds made at plant H = Lorain, Ohio.
12th - 17th symbols:	Denote sequential production number of specific vehicle starting at 100001.

VEHICLE CERTIFICATION LABEL

Location:	Rear face of driver's door. The top part of the label indicates that the Thunderbird was manufactured by Ford Motor Company in U.S.A. Directly below this is the month and year of manufacture, and gross vehicle weight information, plus a statement that the car conforms to federal motor vehicle safety standard in effect on the indicated date of manufacture.
VIN:	The VIN appears first on the first line of encoded information. It matches the 1st to 11th symbols on VIN tag. Some other codes also appear.
TYPE:	Appears on left side of label; indicates PASSENGER
EXT. COLOR:	This line carries the exterior paint color(s) code.
DSO:	The District Special Order code appears above "DSO" to the right of the exterior pain color code.
BODY:	The body style code appears to the extreme left of the bottom line. The only Thunderbird code for this model-year is: 66D = 2-door Coupe.
VR:	The vinyl roof type/color code is to the right of the body code. None on T-Bird.
MLDG:	The molding code is to the right of the vinyl roof code.
INT. TRIM:	The interior trim code is to the right of the molding code.
A/C:	The air conditioning code appears to right of the interior trim code. Cars with air conditioning have "A" stamped here.
R:	The radio code is to the right of the A/C code.
S:	The sun roof code is to the right of the radio code.
AX:	The axle code appears to the right of the sun roof code.
TR:	The transmission code appears to the right of the axle code.

Note: The terms and abbreviations shown in left-hand column appear on the line above the actual codes.

1988

VEHICLE IDENTIFICATION TAG

VIN location:	Stamped on aluminum tab riveted to dash on passenger side and visible through the windshield from outside the car.
1st symbol:	Denotes country of origin. 1 = United States.
2nd symbol:	Denotes manufacturer. F = Ford.
3rd symbol:	Denotes make and type. A = Ford passenger vehicle.
4th symbol:	Denotes type of passenger restraint system.
5th symbol:	Denotes type. P = Passenger
6th symbol:	Denotes model. 6 = Thunderbird
7th symbol:	Denotes body type. 0= Standard Coupe; 1 = Sport Coupe; 2 = LX Coupe; 4 = Turbo Coupe.

8th symbol:	Denotes engine:
	W = 140 cid (2.3L) 190 hp turbocharged four-cylinder/manual.
	W = 140 cid (2.3L) 150 hp turbocharged four-cylinder/automatic.
	3 = 232 cid (3.8L)/140-hp V-6.
	F = 302 cid (5.0L)/155-hp V-8.
9th symbol:	Is the check digit.
10th symbol:	Denotes model-year. J = 1988
11th symbol:	Denotes assembly plant. All T-Birds made at plant H = Lorain, Ohio.
12th - 17th symbols:	Denote sequential production number of specific vehicle starting at 100001.

VEHICLE CERTIFICATION LABEL

Location:	Rear face of driver's door. The top part of the label indicates that the Thunderbird was manufactured by Ford Motor Company in U.S.A. Directly below this is the month and year of manufacture, and gross vehicle weight information, plus a statement that the car conforms to federal motor vehicle safety standard in effect on the indicated date of manufacture.
VIN:	The VIN appears first on the first line of encoded information. It matches the 1st to 11th symbols on VIN tag. Some other codes also appear.
TYPE:	Appears on left side of label; indicates PASSENGER
EXT. COLOR:	This line carries the exterior paint color(s) code.
DSO:	The District Special Order code appears above "DSO" to the right of the exterior paint color code.
BODY:	The body style code appears to the extreme left of the bottom line. The only Thunderbird code for this model-year is: 66D = 2-door Coupe.
VR:	The vinyl roof type/color code is to the right of the body code. None on T-Bird.
MLDG:	The molding code is to the right of the vinyl roof code.
INT. TRIM:	The interior trim code is to the right of the molding code.
A/C:	The air conditioning code appears to right of the interior trim code. Cars with air conditioning have "A" stamped here.
R:	The radio code is to the right of the A/C code.
S:	The sun roof code is to the right of the radio code.
AX:	The axle code appears to the right of the sun roof code.
TR:	The transmission code appears to the right of the axle code.

Note: The terms and abbreviations shown in left-hand column appear on the line above the actual codes.

1989

VEHICLE IDENTIFICATION TAG

VIN location:	Stamped on aluminum tab riveted to dash on passenger side and visible through the windshield from outside the car.
1st symbol:	Denotes country of origin. 1 = United States.
2nd symbol:	Denotes manufacturer. F = Ford.
3rd symbol:	Denotes make and type. A = Ford passenger vehicle.
4th symbol:	Denotes type of passenger restraint system.
5th symbol:	Denotes type. P = Passenger
6th symbol:	Denotes model. 6 = Thunderbird
7th symbol:	Denotes body type. 0= Standard Coupe; 2 = LX Coupe; 4 = Super Coupe.
8th symbol:	Denotes engine:
	4 = 232 cid (3.8L) 140 hp V-6.
	R = 232 cid (3.6L) 210 hp supercharged V-6.
9th symbol:	Is the check digit.
10th symbol:	Denotes model-year. K = 1989
11th symbol:	Denotes assembly plant. All T-Birds made at plant H = Lorain, Ohio.
12th - 17th symbols:	Denote sequential production number of specific vehicle starting at 100001.

VEHICLE CERTIFICATION LABEL

Location:	Rear face of driver's door. The top part of the label indicates that the Thunderbird was manufactured by Ford Motor Company in U.S.A. Directly below this is the month and year of manufacture, and gross vehicle weight information, plus a statement that the car conforms to federal motor vehicle safety standard in effect on the indicated date of manufacture.
VIN:	The VIN appears first on the first line of encoded information. It matches the 1st to 11th symbols on VIN tag. Some other codes also appear.
TYPE:	Appears on left side of label; indicates PASSENGER
EXT. COLOR:	This line carries the exterior paint color(s) code.
DSO:	The District Special Order code appears above "DSO" to the right of the exterior paint color code.
BODY:	The body style code appears to the extreme left of the bottom line. The only Thunderbird code for this model-year is: 66D = 2-door Coupe.
VR:	The vinyl roof type/color code is to the right of the body code. None on T-Bird.
MLDG:	The molding code is to the right of the vinyl roof code.
INT. TRIM:	The interior trim code is to the right of the molding code.
A/C:	The air conditioning code appears to right of the interior trim code. Cars with air conditioning have "A" stamped here.
R:	The radio code is to the right of the A/C code.
S:	The sun roof code is to the right of the radio code.
AX:	The axle code appears to the right of the sun roof code.
TR:	The transmission code appears to the right of the axle code.

Note: The terms and abbreviations shown in left-hand column appear on the line above the actual codes.

1990

VEHICLE IDENTIFICATION TAG

VIN location:	Stamped on aluminum tab riveted to dash on passenger side and visible through the windshield from outside the car.
1st symbol:	Denotes country of origin. 1 = United States.
2nd symbol:	Denotes manufacturer. F = Ford.
3rd symbol:	Denotes make and type. A = Ford passenger vehicle.
4th symbol:	Denotes type of passenger restraint system.

5th symbol:	Denotes type. P = Passenger
6th symbol:	Denotes model. 6 = Thunderbird
7th symbol:	Denotes body type. 0= Standard Coupe; 2 = LX Coupe; 4 = Super Coupe.
8th symbol:	Denotes engine: 4 = 232 cid (3.8L) 140 hp V-6. R = 232 cid (3.6L) 210 hp supercharged V-6.
9th symbol:	Is the check digit.
10th symbol:	Denotes model-year. L = 1990
11th symbol:	Denotes assembly plant. All T-Birds made at plant H = Lorain, Ohio.
12th - 17th symbols:	Denote sequential production number of specific vehicle starting at 100001.

VEHICLE CERTIFICATION LABEL

Location:	Rear face of driver's door. The top part of the label indicates that the Thunderbird was manufactured by Ford Motor Company in U.S.A. Directly below this is the month and year of manufacture, and gross vehicle weight information, plus a statement that the car conforms to federal motor vehicle safety standard in effect on the indicated date of manufacture.
VIN:	The VIN appears two lines above UPC. It matches the 1st to 11th symbols on VIN tag. Some other codes also appear.
TYPE:	Appears on left side of label on line above UPC; indicates PASSENGER.
UPC	A scannable bar code carries the UPC.
EXT. COLOR:	This line carries the exterior paint color(s) code.
DSO:	The District Special Order code appears above "DSO" to the right of the exterior paint color code.
BODY:	The body style code appears to the extreme left of the bottom line. The only Thunderbird code for this model-year is: BS2 = 2-door Coupe.
VR:	The vinyl roof type/color code is to the right of the body code. None on T-Bird.
MLDG:	The molding code is to the right of the vinyl roof code.
INT. TRIM:	The interior trim code is to the right of the molding code.
TAPE:	The tape treatment code appears to right of the interior trim code.
R:	The radio code is to the right of the A/C code.
S:	The sun roof code is to the right of the radio code.
AX:	The axle code appears to the right of the sun roof code.
TR:	The transmission code appears to the right of the axle code.

Note: The terms and abbreviations shown in left-hand column appear on the line above the actual codes.

1991

VEHICLE IDENTIFICATION TAG

VIN location:	Stamped on aluminum tab riveted to dash on passenger side and visible through the windshield from outside the car.
1st symbol:	Denotes country of origin. 1 = United States.
2nd symbol:	Denotes manufacturer. F = Ford.
3rd symbol:	Denotes make and type. A = Ford passenger vehicle.
4th symbol:	Denotes type of passenger restraint system.
5th symbol:	Denotes type. P = Passenger
6th symbol:	Denotes model. 6 = Thunderbird
7th symbol:	Denotes body type. 0= Standard Coupe; 2 = LX Coupe; 4 = Super Coupe.
8th symbol:	Denotes engine: 4 = 232 cid (3.8L) 140 hp V-6. R = 232 cid (3.6L) 210 hp supercharged V-6. T = 302 cid (5.0L) 200 hp V-8.
9th symbol:	Is the check digit.
10th symbol:	Denotes model-year. M= 1991.
11th symbol:	Denotes assembly plant. All T-Birds made at plant H = Lorain, Ohio.
12th - 17th symbols:	Denote sequential production number of specific vehicle starting at 100001.

VEHICLE CERTIFICATION LABEL

Location:	Rear face of driver's door. The top part of the label indicates that the Thunderbird was manufactured by Ford Motor Company in U.S.A. Directly below this is the month and year of manufacture, and gross vehicle weight information, plus a statement that the car conforms to federal motor vehicle safety standard in effect on the indicated date of manufacture.
VIN:	The VIN appears two lines above UPC. It matches the 1st to 11th symbols on VIN tag. Some other codes also appear.
TYPE:	Appears on left side of label on line above UPC; indicates PASSENGER.
UPC	A scannable bar code carries the UPC.
EXT. COLOR:	This line carries the exterior paint color(s) code.
DSO:	The District Special Order code appears above "DSO" to the right of the exterior paint color code.
BODY:	The body style code appears to the extreme left of the bottom line. The only Thunderbird code for this model-year is: BS2 = 2-door Coupe.
VR:	The vinyl roof type/color code is to the right of the body code. None on T-Bird.
MLDG:	The molding code is to the right of the vinyl roof code.
INT. TRIM:	The interior trim code is to the right of the molding code.
TAPE:	The tape treatment code appears to right of the interior trim code.
R:	The radio code is to the right of the A/C code.
S:	The sun roof code is to the right of the radio code.
AX;	The axle code appears to the right of the sun roof code.
TR:	The transmission code appears to the right of the axle code.

Note: The terms and abbreviations shown in left-hand column appear on the line above the actual codes.

1992

VEHICLE IDENTIFICATION TAG

VIN location:	Stamped on aluminum tab riveted to dash on passenger side and visible through the windshield from outside the car.
1st symbol:	Denotes country of origin. 1 = United States.

2nd symbol:	Denotes manufacturer. F = Ford.
3rd symbol:	Denotes make and type. A = Ford passenger vehicle.
4th symbol:	Denotes type of passenger restraint system.
5th symbol:	Denotes type. P = Passenger
6th symbol:	Denotes model. 6 = Thunderbird
7th symbol:	Denotes body type. 0= Standard Coupe; 2 = LX Coupe; 4 = Super Coupe.
8th symbol:	Denotes engine:
	4 = 232 cid (3.8L) 140 hp V-6.
	R = 232 cid (3.6L) 210 hp supercharged V-6.
	T = 302 cid (5.0L) 200 hp V-8.
9th symbol:	Is the check digit.
10th symbol:	Denotes model-year. N= 1992.
11th symbol:	Denotes assembly plant. All T-Birds made at plant H = Lorain, Ohio.
12th - 17th symbols:	Denote sequential production number of specific vehicle starting at 100001.

VEHICLE CERTIFICATION LABEL

Location:	Rear face of driver's door. The top part of the label indicates that the Thunderbird was manufactured by Ford Motor Company in U.S.A. Directly below this is the month and year of manufacture, and gross vehicle weight information, plus a statement that the car conforms to federal motor vehicle safety standard in effect on the indicated date of manufacture.
VIN:	The VIN appears two lines above UPC. It matches the 1st to 11th symbols on VIN tag. Some other codes also appear.
TYPE:	Appears on left side of label on line above UPC; indicates PASSENGER.
UPC	A scannable bar code carries the UPC.
EXT. COLOR:	This line carries the exterior paint color(s) code.
DSO:	The District Special Order code appears above "DSO" to the right of the exterior paint color code.
BODY:	The body style code appears to the extreme left of the bottom line. The only Thunderbird code for this model-year is: BS2 = 2-door Base Coupe; LX2 = 2-door LX Coupe; SC2 = 2-door Super Coupe.
VR:	The vinyl roof type/color code is to the right of the body code. None on T-Bird.
MLDG:	The molding code is to the right of the vinyl roof code.
INT. TRIM:	The interior trim code is to the right of the molding code.
TAPE:	The tape treatment code appears to right of the interior trim code.
R:	The radio code is to the right of the A/C code.
S:	The sun roof code is to the right of the radio code.
AX:	The axle code appears to the right of the sun roof code.
TR:	The transmission code appears to the right of the axle code.

Note: The terms and abbreviations shown in left-hand column appear on the line above the actual codes.

1993

VEHICLE IDENTIFICATION TAG

VIN location:	Stamped on aluminum tab riveted to dash on passenger side and visible through the windshield from outside the car.
1st symbol:	Denotes country of origin. 1 = United States.
2nd symbol:	Denotes manufacturer. F = Ford.
3rd symbol:	Denotes make and type. A = Ford passenger vehicle.
4th symbol:	Denotes type of passenger restraint system.
5th symbol:	Denotes type. P = Passenger
6th symbol:	Denotes model. 6 = Thunderbird
7th symbol:	Denotes body type. 2 = LX Coupe; 4 = Super Coupe.
8th symbol:	Denotes engine:
	4 = 232 cid (3.8L) 140 hp V-6.
	R = 232 cid (3.6L) 210 hp supercharged V-6.
	T = 302 cid (5.0L) 200 hp V-8.
9th symbol:	Is the check digit.
10th symbol:	Denotes model-year. P= 1992.
11th symbol:	Denotes assembly plant. All T-Birds made at plant H = Lorain, Ohio.
12th - 17th symbols:	Denote sequential production number of specific vehicle starting at 100001.

VEHICLE CERTIFICATION LABEL

Location:	Rear face of driver's door. The top part of the label indicates that the Thunderbird was manufactured by Ford Motor Company in U.S.A. Directly below this is the month and year of manufacture, and gross vehicle weight information, plus a statement that the car conforms to federal motor vehicle safety standard in effect on the indicated date of manufacture.
VIN:	The VIN appears two lines above UPC. It matches the 1st to 11th symbols on VIN tag. Some other codes also appear.
TYPE:	Appears on left side of label on line above UPC; indicates PASSENGER.
UPC	A scannable bar code carries the UPC.
EXT. COLOR:	This line carries the exterior paint color(s) code.
DSO:	The District Special Order code appears above "DSO" to the right of the exterior paint color code.
BODY:	The body style code appears to the extreme left of the bottom line. The Thunderbird codes for this model-year are: LX2 = 2-door LX Coupe; SC2 = 2-door Super Coupe.
VR:	The vinyl roof type/color code is to the right of the body code. None on T-Bird.
MLDG:	The molding code is to the right of the vinyl roof code.
INT. TRIM:	The interior trim code is to the right of the molding code.
TAPE:	The tape treatment code appears to right of the interior trim code.
R:	The radio code is to the right of the A/C code.
S:	The sun roof code is to the right of the radio code.
AX:	The axle code appears to the right of the sun roof code.
TR:	The transmission code appears to the right of the axle code.

Note: The terms and abbreviations shown in left-hand column appear on the line above the actual codes.

1994

VEHICLE IDENTIFICATION TAG

VIN location:	Stamped on aluminum tab riveted to dash on passenger side and visible through the windshield from outside the car.
1st symbol:	Denotes country of origin. 1 = United States.
2nd symbol:	Denotes manufacturer. F = Ford.
3rd symbol:	Denotes make and type. A = Ford passenger vehicle.
4th symbol:	Denotes type of passenger restraint system.
5th symbol:	Denotes type. P = Passenger
6th symbol:	Denotes model. 6 = Thunderbird
7th symbol:	Denotes body type. 2 = LX Coupe; 4 = Super Coupe.
8th symbol:	Denotes engine:
	4 = 232 cid (3.8L) 140 hp V-6.
	R = 232 cid (3.6L) 230 hp supercharged V-6.
	W = 281 cid (4..6L) 205 hp V-8.
9th symbol:	Is the check digit.
10th symbol:	Denotes model-year. R = 1994.
11th symbol:	Denotes assembly plant. All T-Birds made at plant H = Lorain, Ohio.
12th - 17th symbols:	Denote sequential production number of specific vehicle starting at 100001.

VEHICLE CERTIFICATION LABEL

Location:	Rear face of driver's door. The top part of the label indicates that the Thunderbird was manufactured by Ford Motor Company in U.S.A. Directly below this is the month and year of manufacture, and gross vehicle weight information, plus a statement that the car conforms to federal motor vehicle safety standard in effect on the indicated date of manufacture.
VIN:	The VIN appears two lines above UPC. It matches the 1st to 11th symbols on VIN tag. Some other codes also appear.
TYPE:	Appears on left side of label on line above UPC; indicates PASSENGER.
UPC	A scannable bar code carries the UPC.
EXT. COLOR:	This line carries the exterior paint color(s) code.
DSO:	The District Special Order code appears above "DSO" to the right of the exterior paint color code.
BODY:	The body style code appears to the extreme left of the bottom line. The Thunderbird codes for this model-year are: LX2 = 2-door LX Coupe; SC2 = 2-door Super Coupe.
VR:	The vinyl roof type/color code is to the right of the body code. None on T-Bird.
MLDG:	The molding code is to the right of the vinyl roof code.
INT. TRIM:	The interior trim code is to the right of the molding code.
TAPE:	The tape treatment code appears to right of the interior trim code.
R:	The radio code is to the right of the A/C code.
S:	The sun roof code is to the right of the radio code.
AX:	The axle code appears to the right of the sun roof code.
TR:	The transmission code appears to the right of the axle code.

Note: The terms and abbreviations shown in left-hand column appear on the line above the actual codes.

1995

VEHICLE IDENTIFICATION TAG

VIN location:	Stamped on aluminum tab riveted to dash on passenger side and visible through the windshield from outside the car.
1st symbol:	Denotes country of origin. 1 = United States.
2nd symbol:	Denotes manufacturer. F = Ford.
3rd symbol:	Denotes make and type. A = Ford passenger vehicle.
4th symbol:	Denotes type of passenger restraint system.
5th symbol:	Denotes type. P = Passenger
6th symbol:	Denotes model. 6 = Thunderbird
7th symbol:	Denotes body type. 2 = LX Coupe; 4 = Super Coupe.
8th symbol:	Denotes engine:
	4 = 232 cid (3.8L) 140 hp V-6.
	R = 232 cid (3.6L) 230 hp supercharged V-6.
	W = 281 cid (4..6L) 205 hp V-8.
9th symbol:	Is the check digit.
10th symbol:	Denotes model-year. S = 1995.
11th symbol:	Denotes assembly plant. All T-Birds made at plant H = Lorain, Ohio.
12th - 17th symbols:	Denote sequential production number of specific vehicle starting at 100001.

VEHICLE CERTIFICATION LABEL

Location:	Rear face of driver's door. The top part of the label indicates that the Thunderbird was manufactured by Ford Motor Company in U.S.A. Directly below this is the month and year of manufacture, and gross vehicle weight information, plus a statement that the car conforms to federal motor vehicle safety standard in effect on the indicated date of manufacture.
VIN:	The VIN appears two lines above UPC. It matches the 1st to 11th symbols on VIN tag. Some other codes also appear.
TYPE:	Appears on left side of label on line above UPC; indicates PASSENGER.
UPC	A scannable bar code carries the UPC.
EXT. COLOR:	This line carries the exterior paint color(s) code.
DSO:	The District Special Order code appears above "DSO" to the right of the exterior paint color code.
BODY:	The body style code appears to the extreme left of the bottom line. The Thunderbird codes for this model-year are: LX2 = 2-door LX Coupe; SC2 = 2-door Super Coupe.
VR:	The vinyl roof type/color code is to the right of the body code. None on T-Bird.
MLDG:	The molding code is to the right of the vinyl roof code.
INT. TRIM:	The interior trim code is to the right of the molding code.
TAPE:	The tape treatment code appears to right of the interior trim code.
R:	The radio code is to the right of the A/C code.
S:	The sun roof code is to the right of the radio code.

AX:	The axle code appears to the right of the sun roof code.
TR:	The transmission code appears to the right of the axle code.

Note: The terms and abbreviations shown in left-hand column appear on the line above the actual codes.

1996

VEHICLE IDENTIFICATION TAG

VIN location:	Stamped on aluminum tab riveted to dash on passenger side and visible through the windshield from outside the car.
1st symbol:	Denotes country of origin. 1 = United States.
2nd symbol:	Denotes manufacturer. F = Ford.
3rd symbol:	Denotes make and type. A = Ford passenger vehicle.
4th symbol:	Denotes type of passenger restraint system.
5th symbol:	Denotes type. P = Passenger.
6th symbol:	Denotes model. 6 = Thunderbird.
7th symbol:	Denotes body type. 2 = LX Coupe.
8th symbol:	Denotes engine: 4 = 232 cid (3.8L) 145 hp V-6. W = 281 cid (4.6L) 205 hp V-8.
9th symbol:	Is the check digit.
10th symbol:	Denotes model-year. T = 1996.
11th symbol:	Denotes assembly plant. All T-Birds made at plant H = Lorain, Ohio.
12th - 17th symbols:	Denote sequential production number of specific vehicle starting at 100001.

VEHICLE CERTIFICATION LABEL

Location:	Rear face of driver's door. The top part of the label indicates that the Thunderbird was manufactured by Ford Motor Company in the U.S.A. Directly below this is the month and year of manufacture, and gross vehicle weight information, plus a statement that the car conforms to federal motor vehicle safety standards in effect on the indicated date of manufacture.
VIN:	The VIN appears two lines above UPC. It matches the 1st to 11th symbols on VIN tag. Some other codes also appear.
TYPE;	Appears on left side of label on line above UPC; indicates PASSENGER.
UPC:	A scannable bar code carries the UPC.
EXT. COLOR;	This line carries the exterior paint color(s) code.
DSO:	The District Special Order code appears above "DSO" to the right of the exterior paint color code.
BODY;	The body style code appears to the extreme left of the bottom line. The Thunderbird code for this model-year is LX2 = 2-door LX Coupe.
VR:	The vinyl roof type/color code is to the right of the body code. None on T-Bird.
MLDG:	The molding code is to the right of the vinyl roof code.
INT. TRIM:	The interior trim code is to the right of the molding code.
TAPE:	The tape treatment code appears to the right of the interior trim code.
R:	The radio code is to the right of the A/C code.
S:	The sun roof code is to the right of the radio code.
AX:	The axle code appears to the right of the sun roof code.
TR:	The transmission code appears to the right of the axle code.

Note: The terms and abbreviations shown in left-hand column appear on the line above the actual codes.

1997

VEHICLE IDENTIFICATION TAG

VIN location:	Stamped on aluminum tab riveted to dash on passenger side and visible through the windshield from outside the car.
1st symbol:	Denotes country of origin. 1 = United States.
2nd symbol:	Denotes manufacturer. F = Ford.
3rd symbol:	Denotes make and type. A = Ford passenger vehicle.
4th symbol:	Denotes type of passenger restraint system.
5th symbol:	Denotes type. P = Passenger.
6th symbol:	Denotes model. 6 = Thunderbird.
7th symbol:	Denotes body type. 2 = LX Coupe.
8th symbol:	Denotes engine: 4 = 232 cid (3.8L) 145 hp V-6. W = 281 cid (4.6L) 205 hp V-8.
9th symbol:	Is the check digit.
10th symbol:	Denotes model-year. V = 1997.
11th symbol:	Denotes assembly plant. All T-Birds made at plant H = Lorain, Ohio.
12th - 17th symbols:	Denote sequential production number of specific vehicle starting at 100001.

VEHICLE CERTIFICATION LABEL

Location:	Rear face of driver's door. The top part of the label indicates that the Thunderbird was manufactured by Ford Motor Company in the U.S.A. Directly below this is the month and year of manufacture, and gross vehicle weight information, plus a statement that the car conforms to federal motor vehicle safety standards in effect on the indicated date of manufacture.
VIN:	The VIN appears two lines above UPC. It matches the 1st to 11th symbols on VIN tag. Some other codes also appear.
TYPE;	Appears on left side of label on line above UPC; indicates PASSENGER.
UPC:	A scannable bar code carries the UPC.
EXT. COLOR;	This line carries the exterior paint color(s) code.
DSO:	The District Special Order code appears above "DSO" to the right of the exterior paint color code.
BODY;	The body style code appears to the extreme left of the bottom line. The Thunderbird code for this model-year is LX2 = 2-door LX Coupe.
VR:	The vinyl roof type/color code is to the right of the body code. None on T-Bird.
MLDG:	The molding code is to the right of the vinyl roof code.
INT. TRIM:	The interior trim code is to the right of the molding code.
TAPE:	The tape treatment code appears to the right of the interior trim code.
R:	The radio code is to the right of the A/C code.
S:	The sun roof code is to the right of the radio code.
AX;	The axle code appears to the right of the sun roof code.
TR:	The transmission code appears to the right of the axle code.

Note: The terms and abbreviations shown in left-hand column appear on the line above the actual codes.

PAINT NAMES & CODES

1955

Body Colors

Color Name	Code	Color Name	Code
Raven Black	A	Thunderbird Blue	T
Snowshoe White	E	Goldenrod Yellow*	V
Torch Red	R		

Goldenrod Yellow and Snowshoe White were added at midyear.

Top Colors

Convertible tops of Black rayon or White vinyl available with all body colors.
Glass-fibre hardtop matches body color. Convertible tops of Black rayon or White vinyl available with all body colors.

1956

Body Colors

Color Name	Code	Color Name	Code
Black	A	Thunderbird Gray	P
Colonial White	E	Fiesta Red	R
Buckskin Tan	J	Sunset Coral	Y
Fiesta Red	K	Thunderbird Green	Z
Peacock Blue	L	Sage Green	M201-613
Goldenglow Yellow	M	Silver Gray Metallic	M201-626
		Navajo Gray	M201-758

Navajo Gray, Sunset Coral and Goldenglow Yellow were deleted at midyear.
Thunderbird Gray was added at midyear.
Numbers for last three colors are Part Numbers.

Top Colors

Convertible tops of Black rayon or White vinyl available with all body colors.
Glass-fibre hardtop matches body color. Convertible tops of Black rayon or White vinyl available with all body colors.

Two-Tone Body Colors (Early)

Color A (Body)	Color B (Hardtop)	Code	Color A (Body)	Color B (Hardtop)	Code
T-Bird Gray	Colonial White	18	Goldenglow Yellow	Colonial White	31
T-Bird Gray	Raven Black	19	Goldenglow Yellow	Raven Black	32
Raven Black	Colonial White	21	Peacock Blue	Colonial White	33
Colonial White	Raven Black	21 (I)	Colonial White	Peacock Blue	33 (I)
Raven Black	Fiesta Red	23	Sunset Coral	Raven Black	35 (I)
Bucksin Tan	Colonial White	28	Sunset Coral	Colonial White	36
Colonial White	Buckskin Tan	28 (I)	Thunderbird Green	Colonial White	37
Fiesta Red	Colonial White	30	Colonial White	Thunderbird Green	37 (I)
Colonial White	Fiesta Red	30 (I)			

(I) indicates inverted arrangement of same colors.

Two-Tone Body Colors (Late)

Color A (Body)	Color B (Hardtop)	Code	Color A (Body)	Color B (Hardtop)	Code
Raven Black	Colonial White	21	Peacock Blue	Colonial White	33
Colonial White	Raven Black	21 (I)	Colonial White	Peacock Blue	33 (I)
Raven Black	Fiesta Red	23	Sunset Coral	Raven Black	35 (I)
Bucksin Tan	Colonial White	28	Sunset Coral	Colonial White	36
Colonial White	Buckskin Tan	28 (I)	Thunderbird Green	Colonial White	37
Fiesta Red	Colonial White	30	Colonial White	Thunderbird Green	37 (I)
Colonial White	Fiesta Red	30 (I)			

(I) indicates inverted arrangement of same colors.

Top Colors

Convertible tops of Black rayon or White vinyl available with all body colors.

1957

Body Colors (Sept 1, 1956)

Color Name	Code	Color Name	Code
Raven Black	A	Thunderbird Bronze	Q
Colonial White	E	Flame Red	V
Starmist Blue	F	Dusk Rose	X
Gunmetal Gray++	N	Inca Gold	Y
Willow Green	J	Coral Sand	Z
Gunmetal Gray++	N		

++ Gunmetal Gray was changed to code H (the 1958 code for this color) late in the year because Ford used 1958 colors for late-production 1957 Thunderbirds. DuPont paint books show this as a spring color.

Two-Tone 1957 Body Colors (Sept. 1, 1956)

Color I (Body)	Color II (Hardtop)	Code	Color I (Body)	Color II (Hardtop)	Code
Raven Black	Colonial White	AE	Colonial White	Thunderbird Bronze	EQ
Raven Black	Flame Red	AV	Willow Green	Colonial White	JE
Raven Black	Inca Gold	AY	Willow Green	Raven Black	JA
Raven Black	Dusk Rose	AX	Gunmetal Gray	Colonial White	NE
Raven Black	Coral Sand	AZ	Gunmetal Gray	Raven Black	NA
Raven Black	Williow Green	AJ	Gunmetal Gray	Inca Gold	NY
Raven Black	Starmist Blue	AF	Flame Red	Raven Black	VA
Starmist Blue	Colonial White	FE	Flame Red	Colonial White	VE
Starmist Blue	Raven Black	FA	Inca Gold	Colonial White	YE
Colonial White	Raven Black	EA	Inca Gold	Raven Black	YA
Colonial White	Starmist Blue	EF	Inca Gold	Gunmetal Gray	YN
Colonial White	Willow Green	EU	Coral Sand	Colonial White	ZE
Colonial White	Gunmetal Gray	EN	Cooral Sand	Raven Black	ZA
Colonial White	Flame Red	EV	Coral Sand	Gunmetal Gray	ZN
Colonial White	Coral Sand	EZ	Thunderbird Bronze	Colonial White	QE
Colonial White	Inca Gold	EY	Dusk Rose	Raven Black	XA
Colonial White	Dusk Rose	EX	Dusk Rose	Colonial White	XE

Top Colors

Convertible tops of Blue, Black or Tan Rayon or White vinyl available with all body colors.

1958

Body Colors

Color Name	Code	Color Name	Code
Raven Black	A	Platinum Metallic++	O
Winterset White++	B	Casino Cream++	V
Palomino Tan+	D	Cameo Rose	W
Grenadier Red	I	Cascade Green++	X
Everglade Green Metallic++	K	Monarch Blue Metallic++	Y
Gulfstream Blue+	M	Regatta Blue++	Z
		Oriental Rose+++	W
		Peach+++	X

+ The 1958 T-Birds shared these colors with 1958 Fords.
++ The 1958 T-Birds and 1958 Lincolns were built in the same plant and shared these colors.
+++ Oriental Rose and Peach do not appear in our factory references. They are listed in aftermarket Ditzler paint books and may be midyear replacements for Cameo Rose and Cascade Green.

Two-Tone 1958 Body Colors

Color I (Body)	Color II (Hardtop)	Code	Color I (Body)	Color II (Hardtop)	Code
Winterset White	Raven Black	BA	Gulfstream Blue	Winterset White	Mb
Winterset White	Palomino Tan	BD	Platinum	Winterset White	OB
Winterset White	Gulfstream Blue	BM	Monarch Blue	Winterset White	YB
Winterset White	Platrinum	BO	Regatta Blue	Winterset White	ZB
Winterset White	Monarch Blue	BY	Everglade Green	Winterset White	KB
Winterset White	Regatta Blue	BZ	Cascade Green	Winterset White	XB
Winterset White	Everglad Green	BK	Casino Cream	Winterset White	VB
Winterset White	Cascade Green	BX	Grenadier Red	Winterset White	IB
Winterset White	Casino Cream	BV	Cameo Rose	Winterset White	WB
Winterset White	Grenadier Red	BI	Platinum	Raven Black	OA
Winterset White	Cameo Rose	BW	Casino Cream	Raven Black	VA
Raven Black	Winterset White	AB	Grenadier Red	Raven Black	IA
Raven Black	Platinum	AO	Cameo Rose	Raven Black	WA
Raven Black	Casino Cream	AV	Monarch Blue	Regatta Blue	YZ
Raven Black	Grenadier Red	AI	Regatta Blue	Monarch Blue	ZY
Raven Black	Cameo Rose	AW	Everglade Green	Cascade Green	KX
Palomino Tan	Winterset White	DB	Cascade Green	Everglade Green	XK

Top Colors
Convertible tops: No. 1 is Black vinyl with Gray headlining; No. 4 is Light Blue vinyl with Blue headlining; No. 5 is Light Green vinyl with Green headlining; No. 6 is White vinyl with Gray headlining; No. 7 is White vinyl with Blue headlining; No. 8 is White vinyl with Green heasdlining; No. 9 is White vinyl with Buff headlining.

1959

Body Colors

Color Name	Code	Color Name	Code
Raven Black	A	Doeskin Beige	M
Baltic Blue	C	Starlight Blue	N
Indian Turquoise	D	Sea Reef Green	Q
Colonial White	E	Brandywine Red	R
Hickory Tan	F	Flamingo	T
Glacier Green	G	Cordovan	U
Steel Blue	J	Casino Cream	V
Sandstone	K	Tamarack Green	W
Diamond Blue	L	Platinum	Z

Note: The 1959 Buyer's Digest shows numerical paint codes as follows: 1=Raven Black; 2=Colonial White; 12=Indian Turquoise; 14=Platinum; 15=Cordovan; 16=Doeskin Beige; 17=Sandstone; 18=Casino Cream; 19=Hickory Tan; 20=Brandywine Red; 21=Flamingo; 23=Steel Blue; 24=Baltic Blue; 26=Tarmack Green; 27=Sea Reef Green; and 28=Glacier Green. (A numerical code for Starlight Blue is not shown.)

Two-Tone 1959 Body Colors

Color I (Body)	Color II (Hardtop)	Code	Color I (Body)	Color II (Hardtop)	Code
Raven Black	Colonial White	AE	Diamond Blue	Baltic Blue*	LC
Colonial White	Raven Black	AE	Baltic Blue	Colonial White	CE
Platinum	Colonial White	ZE	Colonial White	Baltic Blue	CE
Platinum	Raven Black	ZA	Baltic Blue	Starlight Blue*	CN
Raven Black	Platinum	ZA	Steel Blue	Colonial White	JE
Brandywine Red	Colonial White	RE	Steel Blue	Diamond Blue*	JL
Colonial White	Brandywine Red	RE	Starlight Blue	Colonial White*	NE
Brandywine Red	Raven Black	RA	Starlight Blue	Diamond Blue*	NL
Indian Turquoise	Colonial White	DE	Glacier Green	Colonial White	GE
Colonial White	Indian Turquoise	DE	Sea Reef Green	Colonial White	QE
Flamingo	Colonial White	TE	Tamarack Green	Colonial White*	WE
Flamingo	Raven Black	TA	Tamarack Grteen	Glacier Green*	WG
Sandstone	Colonial White	KE	Cordovan	Colonial White	UE
Casino Cream	Colonial White	VE	Cordovan	Doeskin Deige	UM
Casino Cream	Raven Black	VA	Hickory Tan	Colonial White*	FE
Diamond Blue	Raven Black	LA	Hickory Tan	Doeskin Beige*	FM

* Colors marked with asterisk available reversed with same interior trim combinations.

Top Colors
Convertible tops: No. 1 is Black Rayon with Black headlining; No. 4 is Blue vinyl with Blue headlining; No. 5 is Turquoise vinyl with Turquoise headlining; No. 6 is White vinyl with Black headlining; No. 7 is White vinyl with Turquoise headlining; No. 8 is White vinyl with Blue headlining; No. 9 is White vinyl with Buff headlining.

1960

Single Body Color Selections

Color Name	Code	Color Name	Code
Raven Black	A	Diamond Blue	N
Kingston Blue	B	Moroccan Ivory	R
Aquamarine	C	Briarcliffe Green	S
Acaoulco Blue	E	Meadowvale Green	T
Skymist Blue	F	Springdale Rose	U
Beachwood Brown	H	Palm Springs Roose	V

Montecarlo Red	J	Adriatic Green	W
Sultana Turquoise	K	Royal Burgundy	X
Corinthian White	M	Gunpowder Gray	Y
Platinum Z			

Two-Tone Body Colors

Color Panel	Color Overlay	Code	Color Panel	Color Overlay	Code
Sultana Turquoise	Aquamarine	KC	Palm Springs Rose	Corinthian White	VM
Corinthian White	Raven Black	MA	Beachwood Brown	Corinthian White	HM
Corinthian White	Aquamarine	MC	Sultana Turquoise	Corinthian White	KM
Platinum	Raven Black	ZA	Kingston Blue	Corinthian White	BM
Acapulco Blue	Skymist Blue	EF	Acapulco Blue	Corinthian White	EM
Platinum	Corinthian White	ZM	Corinthian White	Skymist Blue	MF
Gunpowder Gray	Corinthian White	YM	Acapulco Blue	Diamond Blue	EN
Montecarlo Red	Corinthian White	JM	Kingston Blue	Skymist Blue	BF
Kingston Blue	Diamond Blue	BN	Corinthian White	Meadowvale Green	MT
Montecarlo Red	Raven Black	JA	Briarcliffe Green	Corinthian White	SM
Moroccan Ivory	Corinthian White	RM	Briarcliffe Green	Meadowvale Green	ST
Moroccan Ivory	Raven Black	RA	Corinthian White	Adriatic Green	MW
Royal Burgundy	Corinthian White	XM	Meadowvale Green	Adriatic Green	TW
Springdale Rose	Corinthian White	UM	Briarcliffe Green	Adriatic Green	SW

Any combination of exterior colors and interior trim would be furnished upon specific order.

Top Colors

Convertible tops: Black vinyl available with all , but two trims. White vinyl available with all trims. Blue vinyl available with only two trims (Nos. 52 and 72). All tops have black headlining.

1961

Single Body Color Selections

Color Name	Code	Color Name	Code
Raven Black	A	Silver Gray	Q
Aquamarine	C	Cambridge Blue	R
Starlight Blue	D	Mint Green	S
Laurel Green	E	Honey Beiege	T
Desert Gold	F	Palm Springs Rose	V
Chesapeake Blue	H	Garden Turquoise	W
Montecarlo Red	J	Heritage Burgundy	X
Corinthian White	M	Mahogany	Y
Diamond Blue	N	Fieldstone Tan	Z
Natilus Gray	P		

Two-Tone Body Colors

Lower Color	Upper Color	Code	Lower Color	UpperColor	Code
Raven Black	Corinthian White	AM	Laurel Green*	Corinthian White	
Corinthian White	Raven Black	MA	Mint Green	Corinthian White	
Montecarlo Red	Corinthian White	JM	Garden Turquoise*	Corinthian White	
Corinthian White	Montecarlo Red	MJ	Aquamarine	Corinthian White	
Nautilus Gray	Corinthian White	PM	Honey Beige*	Field stone Tan	
Silver Gray	Corinthian White	QM	Fieldstone Tan*	Corinthian White	
Silver Gray	Raven Black	QA	Mahogany	Corinthian White	
Chesapeake Blue	Corinthian White	HM	Desrt Gold	Corinthian White	
Cambridge Blue*	Corinthian White	RM	Palm Springs Rose	Raven Black	
Starlight Blue	Corinthian White	DM	Palm Springs Rose	Corinthian White	
Chesapeake Blue*	Diamond Blue	HN	Heritage Burgundy	Corinthian White	
Cambridge Blue*	Diamond Blue	RN			

* Colors marked with asterisk available reversed with same interior trim combinations.

1962

Single Body Color Selections

Color Name	Code	Color Name	Code
Raven Black++	A	Corinthian White++	M
Patrician Green	D	Diamond Blue++	N
Acapulco Blue	E	Tucson Yellow	R
Skymist Blue	F	Cascade Green	S
Silver Mink++	G	Sandshell Beige++	T
Caspian Blue	H	Deep Sea Blue	U
Castillian Gold++	I	Chestnut++	V
Rangoon Red++	J	Heritage Burgundy	X
Chalfonte Blue	K	Fieldstone Tan	Z
Sahara Rose	L		

++ indicates colors used on Sports Roadsters.
Cascade Green and Castillion Gold were added at midyear.
Black and White Landau vinyl roofs were also added.

Two-Tone Body Colors

Color Panel	Color Overlay	Code	Color Panel	Color Overlay	Code
Raven Black	Corinthian White	AM	Sahara Rose	Corinthian White	LM
Rangoon Red	Corinthian White	JM	Tucson Yellow	Corinthian White	RM
Caspian Blue	Corinthian White	HM	Deep Sea Blue	Corinthian White	UM
Acapulco Blue	Corinthian White	EM	Patrician Green	Corinthian White	DM
Skymist Blue	Corinthian White	FM	Chalfonte Blue	Corinthian White	KM
Fieldstone Tan	Corinthian White	ZM	Chestnut	Corinthian White	VM
Corinthian White	Fieldstone Tan	MZ	Fieldstone Tan	Sandshell Beige	ZT
Sandshell Beige	Corinthian White	TM	Corinthian White	Rangoon Red	MJ
Heritage Burgundy	Corinthian White	XM	Chestnut	Chestnut	MV
Cascade Green	Corinthian White	SM	Sandshell Beige	Fieldstone Tan	TZ
			Castillian Gold	Corinthian White	IM

1963

Single Body Color Selections

Color Name	Code	Color Name	Code
Raven Black++	A	Diamond Blue++	N

320

Color Name	Code	Color Name	Code
Patrician Blue	D	Green Mint	O
Acapulco Blue	E	Tucson Yellow	R
Silver Mink	G	Cascade Green	S
Caspian Blue	H	Sandshell Beige++	T
Champagne++	I	Deep Sea Blue	U
Rangoon Red++	J	Chestnut++	V
Chalfonte Blue	K	Rose Beige	W
Sahara Rose	L	Heritage Burgundy	X
Corinthian White++	M	Fieldstone Tan	Z

++ indicates colors used on Sports Roadsters.

Two-Tone Body Colors

Color Panel	Color Overlay	Code	Color Panel	Color Overlay	Code
Raven Black	Corinthian White	AM	Sahara Rose	Corinthian White	LM
Rangoon Red	Corinthian White	JM	Tucson Yellow	Corinthian White	RM
Caspian Blue	Corinthian White	HM	Deep Sea Blue	Corinthian White	UM
Acapulco Blue	Corinthian White	EM	Patrician Green	Corinthian White	DM
Skymist Blue	Corinthian White	FM	Chalfonte Blue	Corinthian White	KM
Fieldstone Tan	Corinthian White	ZM	Chestnut	Corinthian White	VM
Corinthian White	Fieldstone Tan	MZ	Fieldstone Tan	Sandshell Beige	ZT
Sandshell Beige	Corinthian White	TM	Corinthian White	Rangoon Red	MJ
Heritage Burgundy	Corinthian White	XM	Corinthian White	Chestnut	MV
Cascade Green	Corinthian White	SM	Sandshell Beige	Fieldstone Tan	TZ
			Castillian Gold	Corinthian White	IM

1964

Body Color Selections

Color Name	Code	Color Name	Code
Raven Black++	A	Platinum (Diamond Blue)	N
Pagoda Green	B	Prarie Bronze	P
Gunmetal Gray	C	Brittany Blue (Huron Blue Poly) ++	Q
Silver Mink (Blue Poly)++	E	Phonecian Yellow (Encino Yellow)	R
Arcadian Blue (Powder Blue)	F	Cascade Green (Highlander Green Poly)	S
Buckskin (Prarie Tan)++	G	Desert Sand (Navajo Beige)	T
Caspian (Nocturne Blue Poly)	H	Patrician Green (Regal Turquoise)	U
Florentine Green	I	Sunlight Yellow	V
Rangoon Red (Fiesta Red) ++	J	Rose Beige	W
Samoan Coral++	L	Vintage Burgundy (Royal Maroon)	X
Wimbledon White (Artic White)++	M	Chantilly Beige (Silver Sand Poly)	Z

++ indicates colors used on Sports Roadsters.
Prairie Tan and Phoenician Yellow were deleted at midyear.
Prarie Bronze and Sunlight Yellow were added at midyear.
(Bracketed Colors) = Many 1964 colors were shared between Thunderbirds and Lincoln. Different color names were used for the same color of the different marques. The Lincoln names for shared colors are shown in the brackets above.

Top and Tonneau Colors

Convertible tops: Black (Code 1) with all colors and trims, White (Code 2) with all colors and trims, Blue (Code 4) with selected colors and trims. Tonneau covers came in Raven Black 1 (Code A); Wimbledon White 17 (Code M); Rangoon Red 12 (Code J); Silver Mink 5 (Code E); Brittany Blue 19 (Code Q); Patrician Green 23 (Code U); Prarie Bronze 9 (Code G); and Samoan Coral 15 (Code L). vinyl, Blue vinyl. All tops have black headlining.

1965

Body Color Selections

Color Name	Code	Color Name	Code
Raven Black	A	Prarie Bronze	P
Midnight Turquoise	B	Brittany Blue	Q
Honey Gold	C	Ivy Green	R
Silver Mink	E	Charcoal Gray	S
Arcadian Blue	F	Navajo Beige	T
Pastel Yellow	G	Patrician Green	U
Caspian Blue	H	Rose Beige	W
Rangoon Red	J	Vintage Burgundy	X
Wimbledon White	M	Chantilly Beige	Z
Diamond Blue	N	Frost Turquoise	4
		Emberglow ++	V

++ Indicates midyear color addition. The Landau Special model came only in this color with Parchment (Code 70) interior trim.

Top and Tonneau Colors

Convertible tops: Black (Code 1) with all colors and trims, White (Code 2) with all colors and trims, Blue (Code 4) with selected colors and trims.

1966

Body Color Selections

Color Name	Code	Color Name	Code
Raven Black	A	Silver Rose	O
Sundust Beige	B	Antique Bronze	P
Silver Mink	E	Brittany Blue	Q
Arcadian Blue	F	Ivy Green	R
Sapphire Blue	G	Candyapple Red	T
Sahara Beige	H	Tahoe Turquoise	U
Nightmist Blue	K	Emberglo	V
Honeydew Yellow	L	Vintage Burgundy	X
Wimbledon White	M	Sauterne Gold	Z
Diamond Blue	N	Mariner Turquoise	2

Top and Tonneau Colors

Convertible tops: Black, White, and Blue.

1967

Body Color Selections

Color Name	Code	Color Name	Code
Raven Black	A	Brittany Blue	Q
Frost Turquoise	B	Ivy Green	R
Charcoal Gray	C	Candyapple Red	T
Beige Mist	E	Tahoe Turquoise	U
Arcadian Blue	F	Burnt Amber	V
Diamond Green	H	Vintage Burgundy	X
Nightmist Blue	K	Sauterne Gold	Z
Wimbledon White	M	Phoenician Yellow	2
Diamond Blue	N	Silver Frost	4
Pewter Mist	P	Pebble Beige	6

1968

Body Color Selections

Color Name	Code	Color Name	Code
Raven Black	A	Brittany Blue	Q
Royal Maroon	B	Highland Green	R
Beige Mist	E	Candyapple Red	T
Diamond Green	H	Tahoe Turquoise	U
Lime Gold	I	Alaska Blue	V
Midnight Aqua	J	Meadowlark Yellow	W
Silver Pearl	L	Presidential Blue	X
Wimbledon White	M	Sunlit Gold	Y
Diamond Blue	N	Oxford Gray	Z
Pewter Mist	P	Pebble Beige	6

1969

Body Color Selections

Color Name	Code	Color Name	Code
Raven Black (Black)	A	Champagne Gold Poly (Medium Gold Poly)	S
Dark Royal Maroon (Maroon)	B	Candyapple Red (Red)	T
Dark Ivy Green Metallic (Black Jade Pol;y)	C	Tahoe Turquoise Poly (Med. Aqua Poly)	U
Light Blue ++	E	Copper Flame Poly (Light Copper Poly)	V
Dark Aqua Metallic ++	F	Meadowlark Yellow (Yellow)	W
Lilac Frost Poly (Medium Orchid Poly)	G	Presidential Blue (Dark Blue Poly)	X
Diamond Green (Light Green)	H	Indian Fire Poly (Burnt Orange Poly)	Y
Lime Gold Poly (Mmedium Lime Poly)	I	Oxford Gray Poly (Dark Gray Poly)	Z
Midnight Aqua Poly (Dark Aqua Poly)	J	Light Ivy Yellow ++	2
Midnight Orchid Poly (Dark Orchid Poly)	K	Medium Brown Metallic ++	5
Light Gray Metallic ++	L	Light Gold ++	8
Wimbleton White (White)	M	Pastel Yellow ++	9
Diamond Blue (Platinum)	N	Green Fire (Extra cost option) ++	19
Medium Ivy Green Metallic ++	P	Olive Fire (Extra cost option) ++	09
Brittany Blue (Medium Blue Metallic)	Q	Burgundy Fire (Extra cost option) ++	59
Morning Gold (Light Gold)	R	Bronze Fire (Extra cost option) ++	89

++ These colors were not used for full year.
(Bracketed Colors) = Many 1969 colors were shared between Thunderbirds, Lincolns, and Mark IIIs. Different color names were used for the same color on the different marques. The Lincoln/Mark III names for shared colors are shown in the brackets above.

1970

Body Color Selections

Color Name	Code	Color Name	Code
Black	A	Red	T
Maroon	B	Dark Blue	X
Dark Ivy Green Metallic	C	Chestnut Bronze Metallic	Y
Light Blue	E	Dark Gray Metallic	Z
Dark Aqua Metallic	F	Light Ivy Yellow	2
Deep Blue Metallic	J	Medium Brown Metallic	5
Light Gray Metallic	L	Light Gold	8
White	M	Pastel Yellow	9
Medium Ivy Green Metallic	P	Green Fire*	19
Medium Blue Metallic	Q	Olive Fire*	09
Dark Brown Metallic	R	Burgundy Fire*	59
Medium Gold Metallic	S	Bronze Fire*	89

* Optional at extra cost.

1971

Body Color Selections (U.S. & Canada)

Color Name	Code	Color Name	Code
Black	A	Gray Gold Metallic++	S
Maroon Metallic**	B	Red++	T
Bright Aqua Metallic	F	Light Pewter Metallic	V
Dark Green++	G	Yellow++	W
Light Green	H	Dark Blue Metallic	X
Dark Gray Metallic	K	Deep Blue Metallic	Y
White++	M	Tan++	2
Pastel Blue++	N	Medium Brown Metallic++	5
Light Yellow Gold++	O	Burgandy Fire (extra cost option) ++	C9
Medium Green Metallic++	P	Blue Fire (extra cost option) ++	D9
Medium Blue Metallic++	Q	Green Fire (extra cost option) ++	E9

322

Dark Brown Metallic	R	Walnut Fire (extra cost option) ++	39
		Maroon**	7

++ *indicates colors used with Special Brougham option.*
** *Maroon Metallic was deleted and Maroon was added during the model-run.*

1972

Body Color Selections (U.S. and Canada)

Color Name	Code	Color Name	Code
Light Gray Metallic	1A	Yellow	6D
Black	1C	Gray Gold Metallic	6J
Maroon	2J	White	9A
Light Blue	3B	Burgandy Fire*	2G
Medium Blue Metallic	3D	Blue Fire*	3C
Dark Blue Metallic	3H	Green Fire*	4D
Pastel Lime	4A	Lime Fire*	4G
Burnt Green Gold Metallic	4B	Walnut Fire*	5C
Mediun Green Metallic	4P	Cinnamon Fire*	5D
Dark Green Metallic	4Q	Copper Fire*	5G
Dark Brown Metallic	5F	Gold Fire*	6G
Light Yellow Gold	6B		

* Optional at extra cost.

1973

Body Color Selections (U.S.)

Color Name	Code	Color Name	Code
Light Gray Metallic	1A	Yellow	6D
Black	1C	Medium Gold Metallic	6L
Maroon	2J	White	9A
Pastel Blue	3A	Burgandy Fire*	2G
Medium Blue Metallic	3D	Silver Blue Fire*	3L
Dark Blue Metallic	3H	Green Fire*	4D
Medium Green Metallic	4P	Lime Fire*	4G
Dark Green Metallic	4Q	Emerald Fire*	4U
Light Green	4S	Cinnamon Fire*	5D
Dark Brown Metallic	5F	Almond Fire*	5K
Tan	5L	Mahogany Fire*	5P
Light Yellow Gold	6B	Gold Fire*	6G

* Optional at extra cost

1973

Body Color Selections (Canada)

Color Name	Code	Color Name	Code
Light Gray Metallic	1A	Emerald Fire*	4U
Black	1C	Cinnamon Fire*	5D
Burgandy Fire*	2G	Dark Brown Metallic	5F
Maroon	2J	Almond Fire*	5K
Pastel Blue	3A	Tan	5L
Medium Blue Metallic	3D	Mahogany Fire*	5P
Burnt Dark Blue Metallic	3G	Light Yellow Gold	6B
Silver Blue Fire*	3L	Yellow	6D
Green Fire*	4D	Gold Fire*	6G
Medium Green Metallic	4P	Medium Gold Metallic	6L
Dark Green Metallic	4Q	White	9A
Light Green	4S		

* Optional at extra cost.

1974

Body Color Selections (U.S.)

Color Name	Code	Color Name	Code
Black	1C	Medium Ivy Yellow	6N
Silver Cloud Metallic	1E	Pearl White	9C
Pastel Blue	3A	Burgandy Fire*	2G
Medium Blue Metallic	3D	Silver Blue Fire*	3L
Dark Blue Metallic	3G	Blue Starfire*	3P
Pastel Lime	4A	Green Starfire*	4Y
Dark Brown Metallic	5Q	Autumn Fire*	5R
Medium Beige	5S	Gold Fire*	6G
Buff	5V	Cinnamon Starfire*	51
Medium Gold Metallic	6L	Mahogany Starfire*	52
Dark Olive Gold Metallic	6M		

* Optional at extra cost.

1974

Body Color Selections (Canada)

Color Name	Code	Color Name	Code
Black	1C	Medium Ivy Yellow	6N
Silver Cloud Metallic	1E	Polar White	9D
Pastel Blue	3A	Burgandy Fire*	2G
Medium Blue Metallic	3D	Silver Blue Fire*	3L
Dark Blue Metallic	3G	Blue Starfire*	3P
Pastel Lime	4A	Green Starfire*	4Y
Dark Brown Metallic	5Q	Autumn Fire*	5R
Medium Beige	5S	Gold Fire*	6G
Buff	5V	Cinnamon Starfire*	51
Medium Gold Metallic	6L	Mahogany Starfire*	52

Color Name	Code
Dark Olive Gold Metallic	6M

Optional at extra cost.

1975

Body Color Selections (U.S.)

Color Name	Code	Color Name	Code
Black	1C	Polar White	9D
Dark Red	2M	Silver Starfire**	1J
Dark Blue Metallic	3G	Burgundy Starfire*	2G
Pastel Blue	3Q	Blue Starfire*	3P
Dark Yellow Green Metallic	4V	Silver Blue Starfire*	3R
Light Green Gold Metallic	4Z	Gold Starfire*	6G
Light Green	47	Emerald Starfie*	41
Dark Brown Metallic	5Q	Cinnamon Starfire*	51
Medium Ivy Yellow	6N	Copper Starfire*	52
Dark Gold Metallic	6Q	Bronze Starfire*	54

Optional at extra cost.
**Available only with optional Silver Luxury Group.*

1976

Body Color Selections (Early)

Color Name	Code	Color Name	Code
Black	1C	Polar White	9D
Dark Red	2M	Silver Starfire*	1J
Dark Blue Metallic	3G	Bordeaux Starfire*	2S
Light Blue	3S	Blue Starfire*	3P
Dark Jade Metallic	46	Silver Blue Starfire*	3R
Dark Brown Metallic	5Q	Gold Starfire*	6Y
Creme	6P	Cinnamon Starfire*	51
Tan	6U	Jade Starfire*	7F
Light Jade	7A		

Optional at extra cost.
During the model-run Light Jade Starfire (7B) was added and Light Jade 7A was deleted.

1976

Body Color Selections (Late)

Color Name	Code	Color Name	Code
Black	1C	Light Jade **	7A
Dark Red	2M	Polar White	9D
Lipstick Red	2U	Silver Starfire*	1J
Dark Blue Metallic	3G	Bordeaux Starfire*	2S
Light Blue	3S	Blue Starfire*	3P
Dark Jade Metallic	46	Silver Blue Starfire*	3R
Dark Brown Metallic	5Q	Gold Starfire*	6Y
Creme	6P	Cinnamon Starfire*	51
Tan	6U	Jade Starfire*	7F

Optional at extra cost.
**Light Jade is crossed out in some factory litearture and may have been discontinued late in the year.*

1977

Body Color Selections (Early)

Color Name	Code	Color Name	Code
Black	1C	Creme	6P
Silver Metallic	1G	Bright Saddle Metallic	8K
Dove Gray	1N	Champagne Metallic	8Y
Dark Red	2M	Polar White	9D
Lipstick Red	2U	Rose Glow*	2Y
Dark Blue Metallic	3G	Burnt Blue Glow*	3V
Dark Jade Metallic	46	Light Jade Glow*	7L
Dark Brown Metallic	5Q	Chamois Glow*	8W

Optional colors.

1977

Body Color Selections (Late)

Color Name	Code	Color Name	Code
Black	1C	Creme	6P
Silver Metallic	1G	Pastel Beige**	86
Dove Gray	1N	Champagne Metallic	8Y
Dark Red	2M	Bright Saddle Metallic	8K
Lipstick Red	2U	Polar White	9D
Dark Blue Metallic	3G	Rose Glow*	2Y
Dark Jade Metallic	46	Chamois Glow*	8W
Dark Brown Metallic	5Q		

Optional colors.
**Unique to Town Landau.*

1978

Body Color Selections (Early)

Color Name	Code	Color Name	Code
Black	1C	Russet Metallic	81
Silver Metallic	1G	Light Chamois*	83
Dove Grey	1N	Pastel Beige	86
Dark Midnight Blue	3A	Champagne Metallic**	8Y
Light Blue**	3U	White	9D
Dark Jade Metallic	46	Burnt Blue Glow (Opt.)**	3V
Ember Metallic**	5Y	Light Jade Glow (Opt.)**	7L
Dark Brown Metallic	5Q	Chamois Glow (Opt.)**	8W

Available on Town Landau only.
**Not available on Town Landau*

Diamond Jubilee Edition Only

Color Name	Code	Color Name	Code
Diamond Blue	3E	Ember Metallic	5Y

1979

Body Color Selections (Early)

Color Name	Code	Color Name	Code
Black	1C	Light Medium Blue	3F
Polar White	9D	Dove Grey	1N
Dark Red	2M	Light Chamois	83
Midnight Blue Metallic	3L	Maroon**	2J
Silver Metallic	1G	Medium Blue Glow*	3H
Dark Jade Metallic	46	Burnt Orange Glow*	5N
Dark Cordovan Metallic	8N	Chamois Glow*	8W
Pastel Chamois	5P	Light Jade Glow*	7L
Light Gray	12	Red Glow*	2H

* Optional Glow Colors.
** Available on Heritage Edition only.
Dove Grey (1N) is deleted and Light Gray (12) is added during the model run.

Vinyl Top Colors

Color Name	Code	Color Name	Code
Black Valino Grain	A	Dove Grey Valino Grain	S
White Valino Grain	W	Dark Red Valino Grain	D
Dark Jade Valino Grain	R	Maroon Valino Grain **	9
Midnight Blue Valino Grain	Q	Light Medium Blue Lugano Grain **	2
Silver Valino Grain	P	Chamois Valino Grain	T
Cordovan Valino Grain ***	F		

** Available on Heritage only.
***F indicates Dark Cordovan Lugano Grain on Town Landau.

Paint Stripe Colors (Except Town Landau)

Color Name	Code	Color Name	Code
Black	1	Dark Jade	6
White	2	Chamois	7
Red	3	Light Cordovan	8
Silver	4	Gold**	9
Dark Blue	5		

** Available on Heritage only.

Paint Stripe Colors (Town Landau)

Color Name	Code	Color Name	Code
Gold	1	Red	3
Brown	2		

1980

Body Color Selections

Color Name	Code	Color Name	Code
Black ++	1C	Pastel Sand	6D
Polar White	9D	Dark Cordovan Metallic	8N
Candyapple Red	2K	Medium Blue Glow (Opt.)	3H
Silver Metallic	1G	Chamois Glow (Opt.)	8W
Light Grey ++	12	Bittersweet Glow (Opt.)	8D
Midnight Blue Metallic ++	3L	Red Glow (Opt.) ++	2H
Dark Pine Metallic	7M	Anniversary Silver Glow (Opt.)	14
Dark Chamois Metallic	8A		

++ indicates colors that Silver Anniversary models came in .
Silver Anniversary models featured a Silver wrapover band except in two combinations. They are Anniversary Silver Glow paint with Anniversary Silver vinyl top and Black paint stripe, and Black paint with Anniversary Silver vinyl top and Silver paint stripe. Both of these combinations use a Black wrapover band.

Vinyl Top Selections

Color Name	Code	Color Name	Code
Black Valino grain	A	Midnight Blue Valino grain	Q
Bittersweet Valino grain	C	Pastel Sand Valino grain	Y
Medium Red Valino grain	D	White Valino grain	W
Silver Valino grain	P	Anniversary Silver Valino grain	6
		Carmel pigskin grain	T

Vinyl top codes: F=half vinyl top; E = luxury half-vinyl top; V or W = full vinyl top

Paint Stripe Colors

Color Name	Code	Color Name	Code
Black	1	Light Chamois	6
White	2	Bright Bittersweet	8
Candyapple Red	3	Dark Cordovan	10
Silver	4	Brown	7
Medium Blue	5		

1981

Body Color Selections

Color Name	Code	Color Name	Code
Black	1C	Midnight Blue Metallic	3L
Light Grey	12	Dark Cordovan Metallic	8N
Silver Metallic	1G	Fawn	89
Medium Grey Metallic	1P	Medium Blue Glow (Opt.)	3H
Polar White	9D	Light Fawn Glow (Opt.)	5H
Red	24	Medium Fawn Glow (Opt.)	55
Light Medium Blue	3F	Bittersweet Glow (Opt.)	8D

Vinyl Top Selections

Color Name	Code	Color Name	Code
Black Valino grain	A	Midnight Blue Valino grain	Q
Bittersweet Valino grain	C	Fawn Valino grain	U
Medium Red Valino grain	D	White Valino grain	W
Silver Valino grain	P		

Vinyl top codes: Y=half vinyl top; E = luxury half-vinyl top.

Carriage Roof Selections

Color Name	Code	Color Name	Code
Midnight Blue Diamond grain	Q	White Diamond grain	W
Fawn Diamond grain	U		

Paint Stripe Colors

Color Name	Code	Color Name	Code
Black	a	Silver	p
Midnight Blue	b	Dark Champagne	u
Bittersweet	c	Light Champagne	u
Bright Red	e	White	w
Dark Cordovan	f		

Town Landau (Wrapover & Paint Stripe Colors)

Vinyl Roof Color	Wrapover Color	Opera Window Accent Tape
Black	Black	Silver
White	White	Black
Midnight Blue	Midnight Blue	Silver
Fawn	Fawn	Black
Medium Red	Medium Red	Silver
Bittersweet	Bittersweet	Black
Silver	Medium Grey Metallic	Black

1982

Body Color Selections

Color Name	Code	Color Name	Code
Black (Tu-Tone avail.)	1C	Pastel Vanilla (Tu-Tone avail.)	6Z
Light Pewter Metallic	1T	Vanilla Metallic	68
Medium Pewter Metallic	17	Dark Cordovan Metallic (Tu-Tone avail.)	8N
Red	24	Polar White	9D
Midnight Blue Metallic (Tu-Tone avail.)	3L	Medium Blow Glow (Opt.)	3H
Dar Brown Metallic (Tu-Tone avail.)	5V	Light Fawn Glow (Opt.)	5H
Medium Vanilla	6V	Medium Vaquero Glow (Opt.; Tu-Tone avail.)	5W

Roof Selections

Color	Carriage Roof (Type A)	Base Rear Half-top (Type Y)	Luxury Rear Half-top (Type E)
Black (A)		YA	EA
Medium Red (D)		YD	ED
Dark Cordovan (F)		YF	EF
Vanilla (L)		YL	EL
Midnight Blue (Q)	AQ	YQ	EQ
Fawn (U)	AU		
White (W)	AW	YW	EW
Dark Brown (Z)		YZ	EZ
Light Pewter (4)		Y4	E4

Carriage Roof not available on Town Landau, Heritage, or with flip-up roof, keyless entry, or wide body moldings. 0Base rear half-roof standard with Exterior Decor, not available on Town Landau or Heritage, wide belt moldings required with base model. Luxury rear half-roof standard on Town Landau and Heritage

Paint Stripe Colors

Color Name	Code	Color Name	Code
Black	a	Dark Cordovan	f
Medium Blue	b	Gold	q
Terra Cotta	c	Dark Champagne	q
Medium Red	d	Light Champagne	u
		White	w

1983 (As of 6/9/82)

Body Color Selections except Turbo Coupe

Color Name	Code	Color Name	Code
Black (Tu-Tone avail.)	1C	Desert Tan	9P
Pastel Charcoal	1M	Light Desert Tan	9Q
Red (Tu-Tone avail.)	24	Optional Glamor Colors	
Light Academy Blue (Tu-Tone avail.)	38	Dark Charcoal Clearcoat Met. (Tu-Tone avail.)	92
Loden Green ++	4Y	Silver Clearcoat Metallic (Tu-Tone avail.)	1Q
Pastel Vanilla	6Z	Medium Red Clearcoat Metallic	2U
Polar White	9D	Walnut Clearcoat Metallic (Tu-Tone avail.)	9S
		Midnight Academy Blue Clearcoat Met. (Tu-Tone)	9Z

++ Loden Green was deleted at midyear.

Body Color Selections Turbo Coupe only)

Color Name	Code	Color Name	Code
Black	1C	Silver Clearcoat Metallic (Tu-Tone avail.)	1Q
Pastel Charcoal	1M	Dark Charcoal Clearcoat Metallic	92
Bright Red	27	Medium Red Clearcoat Metallic	2U
Desert Tan	9P		

Vinyl Top Selections (1982 models)

Color Name	Code	Color Name	Code
Black	A	Midnight Academy Blue	Q
White	W	Light Desert Tan	H
Silver	P	Walnut	V
Medium Red	D		

Paint Stripe Colors

Color Name	Code	Color Name	Code
Black (except Turbo Coupe)	a	Tan (except Turbo Coupe)	u
White (except Turbo Coupe)	w	Copper (except Turbo Coupe)	c
Light Grey (except Turbo Coupe)	p	Medium Grey (Turbo only)	1
Medium Red (except Turbo Coupe)	d	Maroon (Turbo only)	2
Light Academy Blue (ex. Turbo Coupe)	b	Dark Tan (Turbo Only)	3
Dark Academy Blue (except Turbo Coupe)	q		

The new Aero T-Birds were introduced in mid-1982. This early 1983 Color and Trim chart published in June 1982 shows some selections for the 1982-style T-Birds (vinyl top colors for example), plus the paint and stripe selections for Aero T-Birds like the Turbo Coupe.

1983 U.S. Aero Models (As of 12/10/82)

Body Color Selections except Turbo Coupe

Color Name	Code	Color Name	Code
Black (Tu-Tone avail.)	1C	Optional Glamor Colors	
Pastel Charcoal	1M	Dark Charcoal Clearcoat Met. (Tu-Tone avail.)	92
Red (Tu-Tone avail.)	24	Silver Clearcoat Metallic (Tu-Tone avail.)	1Q
Light Academy Blue (Tu-Tone avail.)	38	Medium Red Clearcoat Metallic	2U
Pastel Vanilla	6Z	Walnut Clearcoat Metallic(Tu-Tone avail.)	9S
Desert Tan	9P	Midnight Academy Blue Clearcoat Met. (Tu-Tone)	9Z
Light Desert Tan (Tu-Tone avail.)	9Q		

Body Color Selections Turbo Coupe only

Color Name	Code	Color Name	Code
Black	1C	Silver Clearcoat Metallic (Tu-Tone avail.)	1Q
Pastel Charcoal	1M	Dark Charcoal Clearcoat Metallic	92
Bright Red	27	Medium Red Clearcoat Metallic	2U
Desert Tan	9P		

Paint Stripe Colors

Color Name	Code	Color Name	Code
Black (except Turbo Coupe)	a	Tan (except Turbo Coupe)	u
White (except Turbo Coupe)	w	Copper (except Turbo Coupe)	c
Light Grey (except Turbo Coupe)	p	Medium Grey (Turbo only)	1
Medium Red (except Turbo Coupe)	d	Maroon (Turbo only)	2
Light Academy Blue (ex. Turbo Coupe)	b	Dark Tan (Turbo Only)	3
Dark Academy Blue (except Turbo Coupe)	q		

1983 Canadian Aero Models Only (As of 5/1/83)

Body Color Selections except Turbo Coupe

Color Name	Code	Color Name	Code
Black	1C	Light Desert Tan	9Q
Polar White	9D	Dark Charcoal*	92
Pastel Charcoal	1M	Silver*	1Q
Red	24	Medium Red*	2U
Light Academy Blue	38	Midnight Academy Blue*	9Z
Pastel Vanilla	6Z	Walnut*	9S
Desert Tan	9P		

* indicates optional Clearcoat Metallic colors.

Body Color Selections Turbo Coupe only

Color Name	Code	Color Name	Code
Black	1C	Silver*	1Q
Pastel Charcoal	1M	Dark Charcoal*	92
Bright Red	27	Medium Red*	2U
Desert Tan	9P		

* indicates optional Clearcoat Metallic colors.

Paint Stripe Colors

Color Name	Code	Color Name	Code
Black (except Turbo Coupe)	A	Tan (except Turbo Coupe)	U
White (except Turbo Coupe)	W	Copper (except Turbo Coupe)	C
Light Grey (except Turbo Coupe)	P	Medium Grey (Turbo only)	1
Medium Red (except Turbo Coupe)	D	Maroon (Turbo only)	2
Light Academy Blue (ex. Turbo Coupe)	B	Dark Tan (Turbo Only)	3
Dark Academy Blue (except Turbo Coupe)	Q		

1984

Body Color Selections except Turbo Coupe

Color Name	Code	Color Name	Code
Black+	1C	Silver Clearcoat Metallic+	1Q
Bright Canyon Red	2E	Dark Charcoal Clearcoat Metallic+	1Y
Midnight Canyon Red	2J	Medium Red Clearcoat Metallic	2U
Light Wheat+	6C	Midnight Academy Blue Clearcoat Metallic	3A
Wheat+	6D	Medium Desert Tan Clearcoat Metallic	83
Oxford White+	9L	Walnut Clearcoat Metallic	9S
		Pastel Academy Blue Clearcoat Metallic	91

+ indicates available as a Tu-Tone color; Clearcoat Metallic colors optional at extra cost.

Body Color Selections Turbo Coupe only

Color Name	Code	Color Name	Code
Black	1C	Dark Charcoal Clearcoat Metallic	1Y
Bright Canyon Red*	2E	Medium Red Clearcoat Metallic*	2U
Oxford White*	9L	Medium Desert Tan Clearcoat Metallic*	83
Silver Clearcoat Metallic*	1Q	Pastel Academy Blue Clearcoat Metallic*	91

* indicates available with Dark Charcoal lower accent treatment; Clearcoat Metallic colors optional at extra cost.

Paint Stripe Colors

Color Name	Code	Color Name	Code
Light Academy Blue (except Turbo Coupe)	B	Tan (except Turbo Coupe)	U
Medium Dark Canyon Red (except Turbo Coupe)	D	White (except Turbo Coupe)	W
Bright Bittersweet (Except Turbo Coupe)	E	Brown (Except Turbo Coupe)	Z
Dark Gold (Except Turbo Coupe)	G	Medium Grey (Turbo Coupe)	1
Light Grey (Except Turbo Coupe)	P	Maroon (Turbo Coupe)	2
Dark Academy Blue (Except Turbo Coupe)	Q	Dark Tan (Turbo Coupe)	3
		Medium Light Academy Blue (Turbo Coupe)	4

1985 (As of 2/1/85)

Body Color Selections except Turbo Coupe

Color Name	Code	Color Name	Code
Black+	1C	Silver Clearcoat Metallic+	1Q
Bright Canyon Red	2E	Medium Dark Charcoal Clearcoat Metallic+	1Z
Midnight Regatta Blue	3U	Medium Canyon Red Clearcoat Metallic	2M
Dark Sage	4E	Pastel Regatta Blue Clearcoat Metallic	3S

Color Name	Code	Color Name	Code
Sand Beige	8L	Medium Regatta Blue Clearcoat Metallic	3Y
Dark Clove Brown	81	Light Sage Clearcoat Metallic	4B
Oxford White	9L	Medium Sand Beige Clearcoat Metallic	8U

+ indicates available as a Tu-Tone color; Clearcoat Metallic colors optional at extra cost.

Paint Stripe Colors

Color Name	Code	Color Name	Code
Charcoal	a	Medium Regatta blue	q
Light Blue	b	Copper	t
Bright Canyon Red	e	Beige	y
Light Grey	p		

Body Color Selections Turbo Coupe only

Color Name	Code	Color Name	Code
Black*	1C	Medium Charcoal Clearcoat Metallic*	1Z
Bright Canyon Red+	2E	Medium Canyon Red Clearcoat Metallic*	2M
Oxford White+	9L	Pastel Regatta Blue Clearcoat Metallic*	3S
Silver Clearcoat Metallic*	1Q	Medium Regatta Blue Clearcoat Metallic+	3Y

+indicates Turbo Coupe monotone exterior colors — 1985-1/2 running change; early production included Dark Charcoal lower accent treatment. Clearcoat Metallic colors optional at extra cost.
* indicates that color includes Dark Charcoal lower accent treatment; Clearcoat Metallic colors optional at extra cost.

Body Color Selections Fila\ Coupe only

Color Name	Code	Color Name	Code
Black	1C	Medium Charcoal Clearcoat Metallic*	1Z
Pastel Charcoal*	1M	Bright Canyon Red	2E

* indicates that color includes Dark Charcoal lower accent treatment; Clearcoat Metallic colors optional at extra cost.
All Fila models include Red-Orange and Dark Blue paint stripes.

Body Color Selections 30th Anniversary Limited Editon Coupe only

Color Name	Code	Color Name	Code
Medium Regatta Blue Clearcoat Metallic+	3Y		

Includes Silver Metallic graduated paint stripe and Regatta Blue (Code SB) interior trim color.

1986 (As of 2/15/86)

Body Color Selections except Turbo Coupe

Color Name	Code	Color Name	Code
Black+	1C	Silver Clearcoat Metallic+	1Q
Bright Canyon Red	2E	Medium Canyon Red Clearcoat Metallic	2M
Midnight Regatta Blue	3U	Midnight Wine Clearcoat Metallic+	2Y
Sand Beige	8L	Regatta Blue Clearcoat Metallic	3W
Oxford White	9L	Light Taupe Clearcoat Metallic+	5E
Medium Grey Clearcoat Metallic+	1F	Deep Shadow Blue Clearcoat Metallic	7C
		Sand Beige Clearcoat Metallic	8M

+ indicates available as a Tu-Tone color; Clearcoat Metallic colors optional at extra cost.

Body Color Selections Turbo Coupe only

Color Name	Code	Color Name	Code
Black*	1C	Silver Clearcoat Metallic*	1Q
Bright Canyon Red	2E	Medium Canyon Red Clearcoat Metallic*	2M
Oxford White+	9L	Regatta Blue Clearcoat Metallic	3W
Medium Grey Clearcoat Metallic*	1F	Sand Beige Clearcoat Metallic*	8M

* indicates that color includes Dark Charcoal lower accent treatment; Clearcoat Metallic colors optional at extra cost.

Paint Stripe Colors

Color Name	Code	Color Name	Code
Black	a	Light Charcoal	p
Copper	c	Dark Academy Blue	q
Dark Red	d	Medium Sandalwood	t
Bright Canyon Red	e	Medium Champagne	y
Dark Taupe	f		

1987 (As of 1/15/87)

Body Color Selections except Turbo Coupe

Color Name	Code	Color Name	Code
Black+	1C	Medium Canyon Red Clearcoat Metallic	26
Light Grey	1K	Silver Blue Clearcoat Metallic+	33
Scarlet Red	2D	Driftwood Clearcoat Metallic	5B
Oxford White	9L	Light Taupe Clearcoat Metallic+	5W
Silver Clearcoat Metallic+	14	Dark Taupe Clearcoat Metallic+	55
Medium Grey Clearcoat Metallic+	18	Dark Shadow Blue Clearcoat Metallic+	77
		Sandalwood Clearcoat Metallic	8Z

+ indicates available as a Tu-Tone color; Clearcoat Metallic colors optional at extra cost.

Body Color Selections Turbo Coupe only

Color Name	Code	Color Name	Code
Black	1C	Medium Red Clearcoat Metallic	26
Oxford White+	9L	Silver Blue Clearcoat Metallic	33
Silver Clearcoat Metallic	14	Driftwood Clearcoat Metallic	5B
Medium Grey Clearcoat Metallic	18	Dark Shadow Blue Clearcoat Metallic+	77

Clearcoat Metallic colors optional at extra cost.

Paint Stripe Colors

Color Name	Code	Color Name	Code
Black	a	Light Oxford Grey	h
Copper	c	Light Charcoal	p
Dark Red	d	Dark Blue	q
Medium Red	e	Bright Regatta Blue	s
Dark Taupe	f	Medium Champagne	y
		Dark Champagnw	z

1988 (As of 6/15/87)

Body Color Selections Standard and LX Coupes

Color Name	Code	Color Name	Code
Black+	1C	Medium Sandalwood Clearcoat Metallic	62
Light Grey	1K	Light sandalwood Clearcoat Metallic	63

Color Name	Code	Color Name	Code
Scarlet Red	2D	Twilight Blue Clearcoat Metallic	7F
Oxford White	9L	Rose Quartz Clearcoat Metallic+	8N
Medium Red Clearcoat Metallic	26	Silver Clearcoat Metallic+	9Z
Light Regatta Blue Clearcoat Metallic	31	Medium Grey Clearcoat Metallic+	91
Dark Cinnabar Clearcoat Metallic+	5C		

+ indicates available as a Tu-Tone color; Clearcoat Metallic colors optional at extra cost.

Body Color Selections Sport Coupe

Color Name	Code	Color Name	Code
Black	1C	Light Regatta Blue Clearcoat Metallic	31
Light Grey	1K	Medium Sandalwood Clearcoat Metallic	62
Scarlet Red	2D	Light sandalwood Clearcoat Metallic	63
Light Sandalwood	8R	Twilight Blue Clearcoat Metallic	7F
Oxford White	9L	Silver Clearcoat Metallic	9Z
Medium Red Clearcoat Metallic	26	Medium Grey Clearcoat Metallic	91

Clearcoat Metallic colors optional at extra cost.

Body Color Selections Turbo Coupe only

Color Name	Code	Color Name	Code
Black	1C	Twilight Blue Clearcoat Metallic	7F
Oxford White+	9L	Silver Clearcoat Metallic	9Z
Medium Red Clearcoat Metallic	26	Medium Grey Clearcoat Metallic	91
Light sandalwood Clearcoat Metallic+	63		

Clearcoat Metallic colors optional at extra cost.
In some U.S. and Canadian sale catalogs Black, Oxford White, Medium Red Clearcoat Metallic, Light Sandalwood Clearcoat Metallic, and Twilight BlueClearcoat Metallic are listed as Turbo Coupe colors, while Silver Clearcoat Metallic and Medium Gray Clearcoat Metallic are not listed for the Turbo Coupe.

Paint Stripe Colors

Color Name	Code	Color Name	Code
Black	a	Light Oxford Grey	h
Copper	c	Light Charcoal	p
Dark Red	d	Dark Blue	q
Medium Red	e	Bright Regatta Blue	s
Dark Taupe	f	Medium Champagne	y
		Dark Champagnw	z

1989 (As of 6/15/88)

Body Color Selections Standard and LX Coupes

Color Name	Code	Color Name	Code
Black	1C	Light Crystal Blue Clearcoat Metallic	3Q
Bright Red	21	Deep Titanium Clearcoat Metallic	4S
Almond	6V	Medium Sandalwood Clearcoat Metallic	62
Oxford White	9L	Crystal Blue Clearcoat Metallic	7E
Light Titanium Clearcoat Metallic	11	Twilight Blue Clearcoat Metallic	7F
Currant Red Clearcoat Metallic	2S		

Clearcoat Metallic colors optional at extra cost.

Body Color Selections Super Coupe

Color Name	Code	Color Name	Code
Black	1C	Light Titanium Clearcoat Metallic	11
Bright Red	21	Twilight Blue Clearcoat Metallic	7F
Oxford White	9L		

Clearcoat Metallic colors optional at extra cost.

1990

Body Color Selections Standard and LX Coupes

Color Name	Code	Color Name	Code
Alabaster	AH	Bright Red Non-metallic Clearcoat	E4
Black	YC	Light Crystal Blue Clearcoat Metallic	KA
Oxford White	YO	Twilight Blue Clearcoat Metallic	MK
Sandalwood Frost Clearcoat Metallic	AP	Light Titanium Clearcoat Metallic	YF
Medium Sandalwood Clearcoat Metallic	AW	Deep Titanium Clearcoat Metallic	YU
Currant Red	ED		

Clearcoat Metallic colors optional at extra cost.

Body Color Selections Super Coupe

Color Name	Code	Color Name	Code
Black	YC	Twilight Blue Clearcoat Metallic	MK
Oxford White	YO	Light Titanium Clearcoat Metallic	YF
Bright Red Non-metallic Clearcoat	E4		

Clearcoat Metallic colors optional at extra cost.

1991

Body Color Selections Standard and LX Coupes

Color Name	Code	Color Name	Code
Oxford White	YO	Crystal Blue Frost Clearcoat Metallic	MD
Mocha Frost Clearcoat Metallic	DD	Twilight Blue Clearcoat Metallic	MK
Medium Mocha Clearcoat Metallic	DC	Black Non-Metallic Clearcoat	UA
Electric Red Clearcoat Metallic	EG	Medium Titanium Clearcoat Metallic	YG
Bright Red Non-metallic Clearcoat	E4	Titanium Frost Clearcoat Metallic	YX
Steel Blue Frost Clearcoat Metallic	MB		

Clearcoat Metallic colors optional at extra cost.

Body Color Selections Super Coupe

Color Name	Code	Color Name	Code
Black Non-metallic Clearcoat	UA	Twilight Blue Clearcoat Metallic	MK
Oxford White	YO	Titanium Frost Clearcoat Metallic	YX
Bright Red Non-metallic Clearcoat	E4		

Clearcoat Metallic colors optional at extra cost.

1992

Body Color Selections all except Super Coupe

Color Name	Code	Color Name	Code
Oxford White	YO	Crystal Blue Frost Clearcoat Metallic	MD
Cayman Green Clearcoat Metallic	DA	Twilight Blue Clearcoat Metallic	MK
Mocha Frost Clearcoat Metallic	DD	Black Non-metallic Clearcoat	UA
Electric Red Clearcoat Metallic	EG	Opal Gray Clearcoat Metallic	WC
Bright Red Non-metallic Clearcoat	E4	Silver Clearcoat Metallic	YN
Dark Plum Clearcoat Metallic	G4		

Clearcoat Metallic colors optional at extra cost.

Body Color Selections Super Coupe

Color Name	Code	Color Name	Code
Bright Red Non-metallic Clearcoat	E4	Black Non-metallic Clearcoat	UA
Twilight Blue Clearcoat Metallic	MK	Silver Clearcoat Metallic	YN

Clearcoat Metallic colors optional at extra cost.

1993

Body Color Selections LX Coupe

Color Name	Code	Color Name	Code
Oxford White	YO	Twilight Blue Clearcoat Metallic	MK
Mocha Frost Clearcoat Metallic	DD	Teal Clearcoat Metallic*	RD
Black Non-metallic Clearcoat	UA	Black Non-metallic Clearcoat	UA
Electric Red Clearcoat Metallic	EG	Midnight Opal Clearcoat Metallic*	WL
Sunrise Red Clearcoat Metallic*	FC	Silver Clearcoat Metallic	YN
Crystal Blue Frost Clearcoat Metallic	MD		

Clearcoat Metallic colors optional at extra cost.
* indicates color used only on "feature" car.
The 1992 colors Cayman Green (code DA) and Dark Plum (code GA) were used, but deleted during 1993. Crimson Clearcoat (code WH) was changed to code YN. Sunrise Red Clearcoat (code FC) and Teal Clearcoat (code RD) were two colors added for a Super Coupe "feature car." White Opalescent Gray (Code PX) was also added.

Body Color Selections Super Coupe

Color Name	Code	Color Name	Code
Sunrise Red Clearcoat Metallic*	FC	Black Non-metallic Clearcoat	UA
Twilight Blue Clearcoat Metallic	MK	Crimson Non-Metallic Clearcoat *	WH
Teal Clearcoat Metallic*	RD	Silver Clearcoat Metallic	YN

Clearcoat Metallic colors optional at extra cost.
* indicates color used only on "feature" car.

1994

Body Color Selections LX Coupe

Color Name	Code	Color Name	Code
Champagne Clearcoat Metallic	DK	Teal Clearcoat Metallic	RD
Electric Red Clearcoat Metallic	EG	Black Clearcoat	UA
Light Evergreen Frost Clearcoat Metallic	FA	Vibrant White	WB
Indigo Clearcoat Metallic	KK	Opal Frost Clearcoat Metallic	WJ
Moonlight Blue Clearcoat Metallic	KM	White Opalescent Clearcoat*	WR
Deep Emerald Green Clearcoat Metallic	PA		

*Extra cost tri-coat paint.

Body Color Selections LX Coupe

Color Name	Code	Color Name	Code
Moonlight Blue Clearcoat Metallic	KM	Crimson Clearcoat	WH
Teal Clearcoat Metallic	RD	Opal Frost Clearcoat Metallic	WJ
Black Clearcoat	UA	White Opalescent Clearcoat*	WR
Vibrant White	WB		

*Extra cost tri-coat paint.

1995

Body Color Selections LX Coupe

Color Name	Code	Color Name	Code
Champagne Clearcoat Metallic	DK	Chameleon Blue Clearcoat Metallic	TA
Electric Red Clearcoat Metallic	EG	Silver Frost Clearcoat Metallic	TS
Light Evergreen Frost Clearcoat Metallic	FA	Black Clearcoat	UA
Rose Mist Clearcoat Metallic	GK	White Opalescent Clearcoat*	WR
Moonlight Blue Clearcoat Metallic	KM	Vibrant White Clearcoat	WT
Deep Emerald Green Clearcoat Metallic	PA	Silver Blue Mist Clearcoat Metallic	ZU

*Extra cost tri-coat paint.

Body Color Selections Super Coupe

Color Name	Code	Color Name	Code
Electric Red Clearcoat Metallic	EG	Black Clearcoat	UA
Moonlight Blue Clearcoat Metallic	KM	White Opalescent Clearcoat*	WR
Chameleon Blue Clearcoat Metallic	TA	Silver Blue Mist Clearcoat Metallic	ZU

*Extra cost tri-coat paint.

1996

Body Color Selections LX Coupe

Color Name	Code	Color Name	Code
Light Saddle Clearcoat Metallic	DZ	Silver Frost Clearcoat Metallic	TS
Bright Red Clearcoat	E4	Black Clearcoat	UA
Laser Red Tinted Clearcoat	E9	White Opalescent Clearcoat*	WR
Moonlight Blue Clearcoat Metallic	KM	Vibrant WhiteClearcoat	WT
Pacific Green Clearcoat Metallic	PS	Silver Blue Mist Clearcoat Metallic	ZU
Alpine Green Clearcoat Metallic	SR		

*Extra cost tri-coat paint.

1997

Body Color Selections LX Coupe

Color Name	Code	Color Name	Code
Light Prairie Tan Clearcoat Metallic	BA	Alpine Green Clearcoat Metallic	SR
Arctic Green Clearcoat Metallic	D8	Silver Frost Clearcoat Metallic	TS
Laser Red Tinted Clearcoat	E9	Black Clearcoat	UA
Light Denim Blue Clearcoat Metallic	K1	White Opalescent Clearcoat*	WR
Moonlight Blue Clearcoat Metallic	KM	Vibrant White Clearcoat	WT
Pacific Green Clearcoat Metallic	PS		

*Extra cost tri-coat paint.

COLLECTOR'S FORD/T-BIRD FACTORY LITERATURE CHECK LIST

U.S. Factory Literature

Listed is all known sales literature for Thunderbirds, both U.S. and Canadian. Also listed are the Ford full-line items that show the Thunderbird, plus Facts Books and Color & Fabric books.

Abbreviations used are as follows:

bk	means book	dlr	means dealer item
bklt	means booklet	fl	mean full-line
cat	means catalog	fldr	folder
clr	means color	mlr	means mailer
corp	means corporate		

Sizes are listed with horizontal dimension given first. All sizes refer to *unopened* dimension. Printing dates and literature identification codes are given whenever possible. However some literature has no code number. While this list is as complete as possible, errors and or omission may exist.

Canadian Factory Literature

Only Canadian Thunderbird catalogs are listed. The full-line catalogs are the same as U.S. versions, but they do carry a Canadian form and date. Also, the covers for some years are different. They also have different form numbers and printing dates on them. So far, Canadian Thunderbird catalogs have been found from 1970 up. In the later years, a number of things are different about them, such as in the options. "Rapid Spec" options carry different code numbers and the contents are different.

Color & Fabric Books

These books are found in car dealer showrooms. These were an aid to ordering a car. They show color samples and fabric samples. During the model-year, Ford will make changes in color and fabrics. During the year Ford will send out to the dealers an update kit to make the changes. At that time they will add or delete colors and fabrics. Also they could add information for midyear models.

Fact Books

These books are found in the showroom. They have information about the car. These are an aid in the selling of a car. They have all kinds of information regarding a car. During the year the factory will send dealers update kits when changes are made. Most of the time the updated pages have a date on them. Some of them will even use a different color ink for the changes.

Sales Literature

There are a number of types of sales literature. The first one is catalogs. You have a number of different types. The deluxe catalog is usually large in size, and printed on nice paper. A second type is the saver. A saver is printed on cheap paper and is small in size. A saver is given out instead of a deluxe catalog. A third item is the mailer. It goes out to prospects by mail, Sometimes they are the same as the sales literature. A mailer can be also different as it goes out to certain type of people. A fourth type of sales literature is the dealer item. This is printed just for the dealership staff. These are not handed out at all.

Untitled Thunderbird sales literature is described as "Sales Literature" in the bold-faced header above each listing. If the piece has a title, it is shown in the header with quotes around it.

1955 FORD/T-BIRD LITERATURE

Dimensions	Design	Format	Pages	Code	Date	Checklist
55 THUNDERBIRD						
5-1/2 x 12	clr	fldr		FD-7509	1954	( )
55 THUNDERBIRD						
5-1/2 x 12	clr	fldr		FD-7509 rev.	08/54	( )
55 THUNDERBIRD						
8 x 11	clr	cat	12p	FD-7520	08/54	( )
55 THUNDERBIRD						
12 x 6	clr	fldr		FD-7558	npn	( )
55 THUNDERBIRD						
8-1/2 x 4	red car on cover		npn		01/55	( )
8-1/2 x 4	black car on cover		npn		01/55	( )
55 THUNDERBIRD	**Continental Tire Mount**					
11 x 8		sheet			npn	( )
55 FORD						
12 x 8	clr	cat	24p	FD-7524	10/54	( )
12 x 8	clr	cat	24p	FD-7524	04/55	( )
55 FORD						
7-1/2 x 10-1/2	clr	fldr		FD-7525	10/54	( )
55 FORD						
7-1/2 x 10-1/2	clr	fldr		FD-7525	10/54	( )

Note: The two folders coded FD-7525 are identical except for a slight difference on the front cover.

55 FORD	**Facts Book**					
		bk			dlr	( )
55 FORD	**Color & Fabric Book**					
		bk			dlr	( )

1956 FORD/T-BIRD LITERATURE

Dimensions	Design	Format	Pages	Code	Date	Checklist
56 THUNDERBIRD						
11 x 8	clr	cat	l6p	FD-7604	10/55	( )
56 THUNDERBIRD						
12 x 5-1/2	clr	fldr		FD-7505	10/55	( )

56 THUNDERBIRD

12 x 5-1/2	clr	fldr		FD-7506	10/55	( )

56 THUNDERBIRD

11 x 8	clr	fldr		FD-7628	03/56	( )

56 FORD

12 x 8	clr	cat	18p	FD-7571	08/55	( )
12 x 8	clr	cat	18p	FD-7571	01/56	( )

56 FORD

10-1/2 x 6-1/2	clr	fldr		FD-7572	08/55	( )
10-1/2 x 6-1/2	clr	fldr		FD-7572	09/55	( )
10-1/2 x 6-1/2	clr	fldr		FD-7572	01/56	( )
10-1/2 x 6-1/2	clr	fldr		FD-7572	05/56	( )

56 FORD "Ford Caught Its Beauty From T-Bird"

8-1/2 x 5-1/2	clr	fldr mlr	5088P		( )

56 FORD "Scat"

8-1/2 x 5-1/2	clr	fldr mlr	6671P		( )

56 FORD "You'd Think It Was A Thunderbird"

8-1/2 x 4-1/2	clr	fldr mlr	6675P		( )

56 FORD "Added Protection All Around"

8-1/2 x 4-1/2	clr	fldr mlr	6673P		( )

56 FORD "Widest Choice"

8-1/2 x 41/2	clr	fldr mlr	6677P		( )

56 FORD Facts Book

bk		dlr	( )

56 FORD Color & Fabric Book

bk		dlr	( )

1957 FORD/T-BIRD LITERATURE

57 THUNDERBIRD

14 x 7	clr	cat	16p	FD-7706	10/56	( )

57 THUNDERBIRD

12 x 6-1/2	clr	fldr		FD-7705	08/56	( )
12 x 6-1/2	clr	fldr		FD-7705	10/56	( )
12 x 6-1/2	clr	fldr		FD-7705	02/57	( )

57 THUNDERBIRD "Super Charger"

12 x 6-1/2	clr	fldr	FD-77D5	02/57	( )

57 FORD

10-1/2 x 4	fl clr	fldr	FD-7701	04/57	( )

57 FORD Facts Book

bk		dlr	( )

57 FORD Color & Fabric Book

bk			dlr( )

1958 FORD/T-BIRD LITERATURE

58 THUNDERBIRD Hardtop

9 x 6	clr	fldr		FDC-1158	12/57	( )
9 x 6	clr	fldr		FDC-1158	01/58	( )

58 THUNDERBIRD Convertible

9 x 6	clr	fldr	FDC-1158	05/58	( )

58 THUNDERBIRD

12-1/4 x 8-1/2	clr	cat	16p	FDC-1258	03/58	( )

58 FORD

11 x 8-1/2	fl clr	fldr	FDC-158	09/57	( )
11 x 8-1/2	fl clr	fldr	FDC-158	10/57	( )
11 x 8-1/2	fl clr	fldr	FDC-158	12/57	( )
11 x 81-/2	fl clr	fldr	FDC-158	04/58	( )

58 FORD Paint Color Chips

8-1/2 x 3-1/2	fldr	npn	( )

58 FORD Facts Book

bk		dlr	( )

58 FORD Color & Fabric Book

bk		dlr	( )

1959 FORD/T-BIRD LITERATURE

59 THUNDERBIRD

12-1/4 x 8-1/4	clr	cat	16p	FDC-4959	09/58	( )

59 THUNDERBIRD

9 x 6	clr	fldr	FDC-5059	09/58	( )
9 x 6	clr	fldr	FDC-5059	02/59	( )

59 FORD

11 x 8-1/2	clr	cat	8p	FDC-4059	09/58	( )
11 x 8-1/2	clr	cat	8p	FDC-4059	10/58	( )
11 x 8-1/2	clr	cat	8p	FDC-4059	02/59	( )

59 FORD

12 x 8-1/2	clr	cat	20p	FDC-4159	09/58	( )

59 FORD "Galaxie"

12 x 8-1/2	clr	cat	20p	FDC-4459	10/58	( )
12 x 8-1/2	clr	cat	20p	FDC-4459	02/59	( )

59 FORD

12 x 8-1/2	clr	cat	20p	FDC-4859	10/58	( )
12 x 8-1/2	clr	cat	20p	FDC-4859	02/59	( )

59 FORD "Buyers Digest"

7 x 10	clr	bklt	98p	Vol 59MS	npn	( )

59 FORD "Buyers Digest"

5 x 7-1/2	clr	bklt	36p		npn	( )

59 FORD "Most Beautiful Wedding of the Year"

10-1/2 x 6	clr	fldr mlr	5294	( )

59 FORD — "Built in Dividends"

Size	Color	Format	Pages	Part No.	Date	
8-1/2 x 11	clr	fldr mlr		SCH-5725		( )

59 FORD — "Convertibles & Station Wagons"

Size	Color	Format	Pages	Part No.	Date	
9 x 4	3-clr	cat	8p		npn	( )

59 FORD — Paint Color Chips

Size	Color	Format	Pages	Part No.	Date	
8-1/2 x 3-1/2	clr	fldr			npn	( )

59 FORD — Facts Book

Size	Color	Format	Pages	Part No.	Date	
		bk			dlr	( )

59 FORD — Color & Fabric Book

Size	Color	Format	Pages	Part No.	Date	
		bk			dlr	( )

1960 FORD/T-BIRD LITERATURE

60 THUNDERBIRD

Size	Color	Format	Pages	Part No.	Date	
11 x 8-1/2	clr	fldr		FDC-6012	08/59	( )
11 x 8-1/2	clr	fldr		FDC-6012	12/59	( )

60 THUNDERBIRD

Size	Color	Format	Pages	Part No.	Date	
10 x 12	clr	cat	16p	FDC-6016	08/59	( )

60 THUNDERBIRD/FORD"ABC's"

Size	Color	Format	Pages	Part No.	Date	
7 x 5	3 clr	bklt	80p		08/59	( )

60 FORD

Size	Color	Format	Pages	Part No.	Date	
10 x 6	clr	fldr		FDC-6010	08/59	( )
10 x 6	clr	fldr		FDC-6010	11/59	( )
10 x 6	clr	fldr		FDC-6010	01/60	( )

60 FORD — "A Wonderful New World of Fords"

Size	Color	Format	Pages	Part No.	Date	
8-1/2 x 13	clr	fldr			npn	( )

60 FORD — Facts Book

Size	Color	Format	Pages	Part No.	Date	
		bk			dlr	( )

60 FORD — Color & Fabric Book

Size	Color	Format	Pages	Part No.	Date	
		bk			dlr	( )

1961 FORD/T-BIRD LITERATURE

61 THUNDERBIRD

Size	Color	Format	Pages	Part No.	Date	
8 x 10-1/2	clr	fldr		FDC-6141	09/60	( )
8 x 10-1/2	clr			FDC-6141	12/60	( )

61 THUNDERBIRD

Size	Color	Format	Pages	Part No.	Date	
8-3/4 x 16	clr	cat	20p	FDC-6142	09/60	( )

61 THUNDERBIRD — "ABC's Facts"

Size	Color	Format	Pages	Part No.	Date	
7 x 5		bklt	30p	npn	09/60	( )

61 THUNDERBIRD — "Preview"

Size	Color	Format	Pages	Part No.	Date	
8-1/2 x 11	clr	cat mlr	14p	7171	npn	( )

61 THUNDERBIRD/FORD"Accessories"

Size	Color	Format	Pages	Part No.	Date	
8-1/2 x 5-1/2	clr	fldr		7768-61	npn	( )

61 FORD — Facts Book

Size	Color	Format	Pages	Part No.	Date	
		bk			dlr	( )

61 FORD — Color & Fabric Book

Size	Color	Format	Pages	Part No.	Date	
		bk			dlr	( )

61 THUNDERBIRD — Color & Fabric Book

Size	Color	Format	Pages	Part No.	Date	
		bk			dlr	( )

1962 FORD/T-BIRD LITERATURE

62 THUNDERBIRD

Size	Color	Format	Pages	Part No.	Date	
11x 13-1/2	clr	cat	16p	FDC-6215	08/61	( )

62 THUNDERBIRD — "Sports Roadster"

Size	Color	Format	Pages	Part No.	Date	
14 x 11	clr	fldr		npn	npn	( )

62 THUNDERBIRD — "The Thunderbird Quartet"

Size	Color	Format	Pages	Part No.	Date	
7x 9-1/2	clr	cat	12p mlr	CDM-1141	npn	( )

62 THUNDERBIRD — "More Than Fine Feathers"

Size	Color	Format	Pages	Part No.	Date	
11 x 8-1/2	clr	cat/ml;	8p mlr	CDM-1152	npn	( )

62 FORD

Size	Color	Format	Pages	Part No.	Date	
11 x 8-1/2	clr	fldr		FDC-6211	08/61	( )
11 x 8-1/2	clr	fldr		FDC-6211	09/61	( )
11 x 8-1/2	clr	fldr		FDC-6211	02/62	( )

62 FORD — Newsletter Supplement

Size	Color	Format	Pages	Part No.	Date	
11 X 81/2	clr	cat	16p mlr	CDM-1136	npn	( )

62 FORD — "Breakthrough"

Size	Color	Format	Pages	Part No.	Date	
8 X 9-1/2	clr	cat	12p mlr	CDM-1154	npn	( )

62 FORD — "Mountain That Comes To You"

Size	Color	Format	Pages	Part No.	Date	
8 x 9-1/2	clr	cat	12p mlr	CDM-1157	npn	( )

62 FORD — "Buyers Digest"

Size	Color	Format	Pages	Part No.	Date	
7 x 10	clr	bklt	72p		npn	( )

62 FORD — Facts Book

Size	Color	Format	Pages	Part No.	Date	
		bk			dlr	( )

62 FORD — Color & Fabric Book

Size	Color	Format	Pages	Part No.	Date	
		bk			dlr	( )

1963 FORD/T-BIRD LITERATURE

63 THUNDERBIRD

Size	Color	Format	Pages	Part No.	Date	
10-3/4 x 13	clr	cat	20p	FDC-6306	09/62	( )

63 THUNDERBIRD — "Story of the 1963 Thunderbird" (Hardbound Catalog)

Size	Color	Format	Pages	Part No.	Date	
8-1/2 x 11		cat	40p		npn	( )

63 THUNDERBIRD — Sales Catalog

Size	Color	Format	Pages	Part No.	Date	
11 x 8-1/2	clr	cat (gold cover)	20p		npn	( )

63 THUNDERBIRD — "Limited Edition Landau"

Size	Color	Format	Pages	Part No.	Date	
6 x 9	clr	cat	8p (with envelope)		npn	( )

63 FORD

Size	Color	Format	Pages	Part No.	Date	
8-1/2 x 8	clr	cat	16p	FDC-6301	08/62	( )
8-1/2 x 8	clr	cat	16p	FDC-63DI	12/62	( )

8-1/2 x 8	clr	cat	16p	FDC-6301	03/62	( )

63 FORD — "1963 Fords"

8-1/2 x 11	clr	cat	16p mlr	CDM-1175		( )

63 FORD — "Ford Owners Newsletter"

8-1/2 x 11	clr	fldr		CDM-1187		( )

63 FORD — "63s From Ford"

11 x 8-1/2	clr	cat	16p	npn		( )

63 FORD — "Buyers Digest"

7 x 10	clr	bkl	88p	npn		( )

63 FORD — Facts Book

		bk		dlr		( )

63 FORD — Color & Fabric Book

		bk		dlr		( )

1964 FORD/T-BIRD LITERATURE

64 THUNDERBIRD

11-1/2 x 14-1/2	clr	cat	24p	FDC-6405	09/63	( )

64 THUNDERBIRD

8-1/2 x 11	clr	cat	16p mlr	CDM-1222		( )

64 THUNDERBIRD — Paint Color Chips

3-1/2 x 8-1/2	clr	fldr		npn		( )

64 FORD

8-1/2 x 11	clr	cat	12p	FDC-6401	07/63	( )
8-1/2 x 11	clr	cat	12p	FDC-6401	11/63	( )
8-1/2 x 11	clr	cat	12p	FDC-6401	12/63	( )
8-1/2 x 11	clr	cat	12p	FDC-6401	02/64	( )

64 FORD — Newsletter

8-1/2 x 11	clr	cat	16p mlr	CDM-1197		( )

64 FORD — "This Is the 1964 Ford"

8-1/2 x 11	clr	cat	12p mlr	CDM-1223		( )

64 FORD — "Introducing the 1964 Ford"

8-1/2 x 11	clr	cat	12p mlr	CDM-1223		( )

64 FORD — "Buyers Digest"

7 x 10		bklt		npn		( )

64 FORD — "Accessories"

9 x 6	clr	fldr		npn		( )

64 FORD — Facts Book

		bk		dlr		( )

64 FORD — Color & Fabric Book

		bk		dlr		( )

1965 FORD/T-BIRD LITERATURE

65 THUNDERBIRD

10 x 15	clr	cat	20p	FDC-6506	08/64	( )

65 THUNDERBIRD — "Landau"

9 1/2 x 12-1/2	clr	fldr (w/envelope)		dlr		( )

Note: There is a special 8-1/2 x 11-in. color folder on the Special Landau that folds out to 8-1/2 x 22 in. No date or number.

65 THUNDERBIRD — Paint Color Chips

3-1/2 x 8-1/2	clr	chip fldr		npn		( )

65 FORD

11 x 9	clr	cat	16p	FDC-6501	08/64	( )
11 x 9	clr	cat	16p	FDC-6501	04/65	( )

65 FORD — "Double Take"

11 X 8-1/2	clr	cat	8p mlr	CDM-1264		( )

65 FORD — "What manufacturer offers both of these new cars?"

11 x 8-1/2	clr	cat	12p mlr	CDM-1265		( )

65 FORD — Facts Book

		bk		dlr		( )

65 FORD — Color & Fabric Book

		bk		dlr		( )

1966 FORD/T-BIRD LITERATURE

66 THUNDERBIRD

12-1/2 x 11	clr	cat	16p	FD-6606	8-65	( )

66 THUNDERBIRD — "Pep Talk"

8-1/2 x 11	2-clr	bk	16p	Vol. 66 C13 L2		( )

66 FORD

11 X 8-1/2	clr	cat	16p	FDC-6601	08/65	( )
11 X 8-1/2	clr	cat	16p	FDC-6601	01/66	( )

66 FORD — "Accessories"

8-1/2 x 11	clr	cat	32p	npn		( )

66 FORD — "'66 Preview"

11 x 8-1/2	clr	cat	16p	CDM-1296		( )

66 FORD — "Quiet Quality Powered by Ford'

11 x 8-1/2	clr	cat	16p mlr	CDM-1300		( )

66 FORD — "Newsletter"

8-1/2 x 11	clr	cat	8p mlr	CDM-1301		( )

66 FORD — Facts Book

		bk		dlr		( )

66 FORD — Color & Fabric Book

		bk		dlr		( )

1967 FORD/T-BIRD LITERATURE

67 THUNDERBIRD

12 x 12	clr	cat	20p	FDC-6706	08/66	( )

67 THUNDERBIRD

8-1/2 x 11	clr	cat	8p	FDC-6707	08/66	( )

67 THUNDERBIRD	"4 Door Sedan"					
11 x 8-1/2	clr	cat	8p mlr	CDM-1318		( )
67 FORD						
11 x 8-1/2	clr	cat	16p	FDC-6700	08/66	( )
11 x 8-1/2	clr	cat	16p	FDC-6700	01/67	( )
67 FORD	"Take a Second look at the 67's from Ford"					
8-1/2 x 11	clr	cat	16pmlr	CDM-1315		( )
67 FORD	"Look What's Happened At Ford"					
11 x 8-1/2	clr	cat	16p mlr		npn	( )
67 FORD	"Accessories"					
8-1/2 x 11	clr	cat	36p	PS-12L2		( )
67 FORD	Facts Book					
		bk			dlr	( )
67 FORD	Color & Fabric Book					
		bk			dlr	( )

1968 FORD/T-BIRD LITERATURE

68 THUNDERBIRD						
12 x 12	clr	cat	16p	W-0060		( )
12 x 12	clr	cat (as above with revised sheet W-362)			12/67	( )
68 THUNDERBIRD						
7 x 7	clr	cat	16p	W-362	12/67	( )
68 THUNDERBIRD	"Fly Now, In The Thunderbird"					
8-1/2 x 5-1/2	clr	fldr/mlr		CDM-6517		( )
68 FORD						
10-1/2 x 12	clr	cat lop		WO-61	09/67	( )
10-1/2 x 12	clr	cat lop		WO-362	12/67	( )
68 FORD	"Accessories"					
11 x 8-1/2	clr	cat	28p	PSM-139A		( )
68 FORD	Facts Book					
		bk			dlr	( )
68 FORD	Color & Fabric Book					
		bk			dlr	( )

1969 FORD/T-BIRD LITERATURE

69 THUNDERBIRD						
11 x 12	clr	cat	16p	5031 8-69		( )
69 THUNDERBIRD						
10-1/2 x 11	clr	fldr mlr		CDM-7991M	02/69	( )
10-1/2 x 11	clr	fldr mlr		CDM-7991N	02/69	( )
10-1/2 x 11	clr	fldr mlr		CDM-79910	02/69	( )
69 FORD	"Buyer's Digest"					
8-1/2 x 11	clr	cat	16p	5024 8-68		( )
8-1/2 x 11	clr	cat	16p	5024 1-69		( )
69 FORD	"Buyer's Digest"					
8-1/2 x 11	clr	cat	16p mlr	CDM-7666	08/68	( )
69 FORD	"Ford Times Buyers Digest"					
5 x 7	clr	cat	64p		npn	( )
69 FORD	"Accessories"					
11 X 8-1/2	clr	cat	22p	MSD-1		( )
69 FORD	"Accessories"					
7 x 4	clr	cat	20p	MSD-1		( )
7 x 4	clr	cat	20p	5027	01/69	( )
69 FORD	Facts Book					
		bk			dlr	( )
69 FORD	Color & Fabric Book					
		bk			dlr	( )

1970 FORD/T-BIRD LITERATURE

70 THUNDERBIRD						
12 x 12	clr	cat	12p	5108	08/69	( )
70 THUNDERBIRD						
12 x 11	clr	cat	14p mlr	CDM-8904	08/69	( )
70 FORD	"Buyer's Digest"					
8-1/2 X 11	clr	cat	16p	5103	08/69	( )
8-1/2 X 11	clr	cat	16p	5103	01/70	( )
70 FORD	"Fleet"					
8-1/2 x 11	3-clr	cat	24p	CDM-8423	09/69	( )
70 FORD	"Accessories"					
11 x 8-1/2	clr	cat	24p	MSD		( )
70 FORD	"Accessories"					
3-1/2 x 7	clr	fldr		AF70-1		( )
70 FORD	Paint Color Chips					
8 x 5	clr	fldr		npn		( )
70 FORD	Facts Book					
		bk			dlr	( )
70 FORD	Color & Fabric Book					
		bk			dlr	( )

1971 FORD/T-BIRD LITERATURE

71 THUNDERBIRD						
11 x 11	clr	cat	12p	5202	07/70	( )
11 x 11	clr	cat	12p	5202	08/70	( )
71 FORD						
18 x 11	clr	fldr		5212	08/70	( )
18 x 11	clr	fldr		5212	01/71	( )

71 FORD	Fleet						
8-1/2 x 11	2-clr	cat	20p	CDM-9914			( )
71 FORD	"Accessories"						
3-1/2 x 7	3-clr	cat	16p	MSD-10			( )
71 FORD	Paint Color Chips						
8 x 3	clr	chip fldr			npn		( )
71 FORD	Facts Book						
	bk				dlr		( )
71 FORD	Color & Fabric Book						
	bk				dlr		( )

1972 FORD/T-BIRD LITERATURE

72 THUNDERBIRD							
11 x 11	clr	cat	8p	5303	08/71		( )
11 x 11	clr	cat	8p	5303	12/71		( )
72 THUNDERBIRD							
9 x 9	clr	cat	16p	5303	08/71		( )
72 THUNDERBIRD	Product Change Update						
8-1/2 x 11	b & w	sheet		53155	09/71		( )
8-1/2 x 11	b & w	sheet (as above)		5317	02/72		( )
72 FORD							
11 x 9	fl clr	cat	8p	5409	08/72		( )
11 x 9	fl clr	cat	8p	5409	10/72		( )
72 FORD	"Accessories"						
8-1/2 x 11	clr	cat	12p	Vol 72	MSD-8		( )
72 FORD	"Accessories"						
7 x 3-1/2	clr	fldr			npn		( )
72 FORD	Paint Color Chi						
8 x 3-1/2	clr	chip fldr			npn		( )
72 FORD	Facts Book						
	bk				dlr		( )
72 FORD	Color & Fabric Book						
					dlr		( )

1973 FORD/T-BIRD LITERATURE

73 THUNDERBIRD							
11 x 11	clr	cat	20p	5402	08/72		( )
11 x 11	clr	cat	20p	5402	11/72		( )
11 x 11	clr	cat	20p	5402	6-73		( )
73 THUNDERBIRD							
9 x 5	clr	fldr			npn		( )
73 FORD							
11 x 9	fl clr	cat	8p	5409	08/72		( )
11 x 9	fl clr	cat	8p	5409	10/72		( )
11 x 9	fl clr	cat	8p	5409	01/73		( )
73 FORD	"Your Private Preview"						
7-1/2 x 5	clr	fldr			npn		( )
73 FORD	"Accessories"						
11 x 8-1/2	clr	cat	12p	MSO-12			( )
73 FORD	Paint Color Chip						
8-1/2 x 4	clr	chip fldr			npn		( )
73 FORD	Facts Book						
	bk				dlr		( )
73 FORD	Color & Fabric Book						
	bk				dlr		( )

1974 FORD/T-BIRD LITERATURE

74 THUNDERBIRD							
11 x 11	clr	portfolio	4 sheets + cover	5502	07/73		( )
11 x 11	clr	portfolio	4 sheets + cover	5502	11/73		( )
11 x 11	clr	portfolio	6 sheets + cover	5502	01/74		( )
74 FORD							
9 x 11	fl clr	cat	8p	5509	7-73		( )
9 x 11	fl clr	cat	8p	5509	1-74		( )
74 FORD	"Accessories"						
8-1/2 x 11	clr	cat	12p	MSD-8			( )
74 FORD	Paint Color Chips						
8-1/2 x 4	clr	chip fldr			npn		( )
74 FORD	Facts Book						
	bk				dlr		( )
74 FORD	Color & Fabric Book						
	bk				dlr		( )

1975 FORD/T-BIRD LITERATURE

75 THUNDERBIRD							
11 x 11	clr	cat	8p 5	5606	08/74		( )
75 THUNDERBIRD	"Jade Luxury Group"						
7 x 7	clr	fldr		5637	04/75		( )
75 FORD							
8-1/2 x 10	fl clr	fldr		5610	08/74		( )
75 FORD	"Accessories"						
8-1/2 x 11	clr	cat	8p	MSD-L			( )
75 FORD	Paint Color Chips						
8-1/2 x 3-1/2	clr	chip fldr			npn		( )
75 FORD	Facts Book						
	bk				dlr		( )

75 FORD — Color & Fabric Book

bk					dlr	( )

1976 FORD/T-BIRD LITERATURE

76 THUNDERBIRD

11 x 11	clr	fldr		036	08/75	( )

76 FORD

8-1/2 x 11	clr	fldr		138	08/75	( )

76 FORD — "Feature Cars Mid Year"

11 x 8-1/2	clr	sheet		76CM3L9		( )

76 FORD — "Accessories"

8-1/2 x 11	clr	cat	12p	FPM117		( )

76 FORD — "Accessories"

11 x 4-1/2	clr	cat	16p	FPM1185		( )

76 FORD — Paint Color Chips

8 1/2 x 3	clr	chip fldr			npn	( )

76 FORD — Facts Book

bk					dlr	( )

76 FORD — Color & Fabric Book

bk					dlr	( )

1977 FORD/T-BIRD LITERATURE

77 THUNDERBIRD — "A New Look, a New Size, A New Price"

11 x 8-1/2	clr	cat	14p		npn	( )

77 THUNDERBIRD

11 x 11	clr	cat	12p	383	01/77	( )

77 THUNDERBIRD — "Town Landau"

11 x 11	clr	fldr			01/77	( )

77 THUNDERBIRD

11 x 8-1/2	clr	cat	8p mlr		npn	( )

77 THUNDERBIRD — History of Thunderbird

11 x 9	3 clr	cat	62p		npn	( )

77 THUNDERBIRD — Town Landau

11 x 8	clr	fldr			npn	( )

77 THUNDERBIRD/LTD II

12 x 8	clr	cat	16p		npn	( )

77 FORD

11 x 8-1/2	clr	cat	8p	472	08/76	( )

77 FORD — Dealer Ordering Guide

11 x 8-1/2	clr	cat	32p		dlr	( )

77 Ford — "Facts Bulletin"

8-1/2 x 11	clr	fldr		77CM6L6		( )

77 FORD — "Accessories"

41/2 x9	clr	cat	6p	FPM-1225		( )

77 FORD — Radio

8-1/2 x	11 clr	fldr			npn	( )

77 FORD — Paint Color Chips

8 x 3	clr	chip fldr			05/76	( )

77 FORD — Facts Book

bk					dlr	( )

77 FORD — Color & Fabric Book

bk					dlr	( )

1978 FORD/T-BIRD LITERATURE

78 THUNDERBIRD

11 x 11	clr	cat	16p		09/77	( )

78 THUNDERBIRD — Fleet

8-1/2 x 11	clr	sheet			npn	( )

78 FORD

11 x 8-1/2	clr	cat	8p	231	0 8/77	( )
11 x 8-1/2	clr	cat	8p	231	01/78	( )

78 FORD

11 x 8-1/2	clr	cat	8p mlr		npn	( )

78 FORD — "Accessories"

8-1/2 x 11	clr	cat	14p	FMP-1357	10/77	( )

78 FORD — "Accessories"

8-1/2 x 5-1/2	clr	cat	8p	FMP-1357	12/77	( )

78 FORD — Paint Color Chips

8-1/2 x 3-1/2	clr	chip fldr			npn	( )

78 FORD — Facts Book

bk					dlr	( )

78 FORD — Color & Fabric Book

bk					dlr	( )

1979 FORD/T-BIRD LITERATURE

79 THUNDERBIRD — "Heritage"

11 x 11	clr	cat	8p	37	8-78	( )
11 x 11	clr	cat	8p	377	rev12-78	( )

79 THUNDERBIRD

11 x 11	clr	cat		172	07/78	( )
11 x 11	clr	cat (npn as above)		878	03/78	( )

79 THUNDERBIRD — Fleet

8-1/2 x 11	clr	sheet			npn	( )

79 FORD — "Accessories"

8-1/2 x 11	clr	cat	20p	FM-1423		( )

79 FORD — Paint Color Chips

8-1/2 x 3-1/2	clr	chip fldr			npn	( )

Model	Description	Size	Color	Format	Pages	Number	Date	( )
79 FORD	Facts Book							
				bk			dlr	( )
79 FORD	Color & Fabric Book							
				bk			dlr	( )

1980 FORD/T-BIRD LITERATURE

Model	Description	Size	Color	Format	Pages	Number	Date	( )
80 THUNDERBIRD								
		11 x 11	clr	cat	20p	148	8-79	( )
		11 x 11	clr	cat	20p	148	1-80	( )
80 THUNDERBIRD	"Spread Your Wings"							
		8-1/2 x 11	clr	cat				( )
80 THUNDERBIRD	Institutional							
				Fleet/Rental/Leasing				( )
80 THUNDERBIRD	Leasing							
		8 x 5-1/2	clr	fldr		L8004		( )
80 FORD								
		11 x 9	fl clr	cat	12p	182	8-79	( )
80 FORD	Paint Color Chips							
		8-1/2 x 3	clr	chip fldr			npn	( )
80 FORD	Facts Book							
				bk			dlr	( )
80 FORD	Color & Fabric Book							
				bk			dlr	( )

1981 FORD/T-BIRD LITERATURE

Model	Description	Size	Color	Format	Pages	Number	Date	( )
81 THUNDERBIRD								
		9 x 11	clr	cat	16p	005	8-80	( )
81 FORD								
		8-1/2 x 11	clr	cat	8p	007	8-80	( )
81 FORD	Paint Color Chips							
		8-1/2 x 3	clr	chip fldr			npn	( )
81 FORD	Facts Book							
				bk			dlr	( )
81 FORD	Color & Fabric Book							
				bk			dlr	( )

1982 FORD/T-BIRD LITERATURE

Model	Description	Size	Color	Format	Pages	Number	Date	( )
82 THUNDERBIRD								
		9 x 11	clr	cat	16p	014	8-81	( )
82 FORD								
		9 x 11	fl clr	cat	16p	016	8-81	( )
82 FORD	Accessories							
		5-1/2 x 8-1/2	clr	cat	24p	FPM-1729	Oct 81	( )
82 FORD	Paint Color Chips							
		8-1/2 x 3-1/2	clr	chip fldr			npn	( )
82 FORD	Facts Book							
				bk			dlr	( )
82 FORD	Color & Fabric Book							
				bk			dlr	( )

1983 FORD/T-BIRD LITERATURE

Model	Description	Size	Color	Format	Pages	Number	Date	( )
83 THUNDERBIRD								
		9 x 11	clr	cat	20p	011	12-82	( )
		9 x 11	clr	cat	20p	005	04-83	( )
83 THUNDERBIRD	"Turbo Coupe"							
		11 x 11	clr	fldr			npn	( )
83 THUNDERBIRD	"Fila"							
		8-1/2 x 4	clr	fldr			npn	( )
83 THUNDERBIRD								
		8-1/2 x 11	b & w	cat	48p	3P006	dlr	( )
83 THUNDERBIRD	"Fleet/Leasing/Rental"							
		8-1/2 x 11	clr	sheet			npn	( )
83 THUNDERBIRD								
		8-1/2 x 11	clr	fldr		300K-83		( )
83 THUNDERBIRD	Paint Color Chips							
		8-1/2 x 3	clr	chip fldr			npn	( )
83 FORD								
		8-1/2 x 11	fl clr	cat	16p	013	8-82	( )
83 FORD	Accessories							
		8-1/2 x 5-1/2	clr	cat	26p	FPM-1880	npn	( )
83 FORD	Facts Book							
				bk			dlr	( )
83 FORD	Color & Fabric Book							
				bk			dlr	( )

1984 FORD/T-BIRD LITERATURE

Model	Description	Size	Color	Format	Pages	Number	Date	( )
84 THUNDERBIRD								
		9 x 11	clr	cat	20p	017	8-83	( )
84 THUNDERBIRD	"Fila"							
		7 x 10	clr	fldr			npn	( )
84 THUNDERBIRD	"Turbo Coupe"							
		11 x 11	clr	fldr		025	10-83	( )
84 THUNDERBIRD	"Technology Training Course"							
		11 x 8-1/2	portfolio circular sheet				dlr	( )
84 THUNDERBIRD	"Turbo Coupe Special Value"							
		8-1/2 x 1	3-clr	sheet			npn	( )

84 FORD							
7 x 3-1/2		clr	cat	16p	007	8-83	( )
84 FORD	"A Selection of 8 Great Vehicles'						
8-1/2 x 5-1/2		clr	fldr		40364		( )
84 FORD	"Accessories"						
8-1/2 x 5		clr	cat	20p	FPM-1221	npn	( )
84 FORD	Paint Color Chips						
8-1/2 x 3		clr	chip fldr			npn	( )
84 FORD	Facts Book						
			bk			dlr	( )
84 FORD	Color & Fabric Book						
			bk			dlr	( )

1985 FORD/T-BIRD LITERATURE

85 THUNDERBIRD							
9 x 11		clr	cat	20p	009	8-84	( )
85 THUNDERBIRD	"The Flight Continues"						
10 x 5-1/2		clr	cat	12p		npn	( )
85 FORD							
9 x 11		clr	cat	20p	001	8-84	( )
9 x 11		clr	cat	20p	001	1-85	( )
85 FORD	"Showcase"						
8-1/2 x 11		clr	cat	82p	6PC007	dlr	( )
85 FORD	Paint Color Chips						
8-1/2 x 3-1/2		clr	chip fldr			npn	( )
85 FORD	Facts Book						
			bk			dlr	( )
85 FORD	Color & Fabric Book						
			bk			dlr	( )
85 FORD	Dealer Launch Guide						
						dlr	( )

1986 FORD/T-BIRD LITERATURE

86 THUNDERBIRD							
11 x 11		clr	cat	24p	013	8-85	( )
86 FORD							
11 x 11		fl clr	cat	16p	015	8-85	( )
86 FORD	Paint Color Chips						
8-1/2 x 4		clr chip	fldr			npn	( )
86 FORD	Facts Book						
			bk			dlr	( )
86 FORD	Color & Fabric Book						
			bk			dlr	( )

1987 FORD/T-BIRD LITERATURE

87 THUNDERBIRD							
11 x 11		clr	cat	20p	001	8-86	( )
11 x 11		clr	cat	20p	020	12-86	( )
87 FORD							
9 x 11		fl clr	cat	20p	012	8-86	( )
87 FORD	Corporate Literature						
12 x 11		clr	cat	82p		npn	( )
87 FORD	Paint Chip Colors						
8-1/2 x 4		clr	chip fldr			npn	( )
87 FORD	Facts Book						
			bk			dlr	( )
87 FORD	Color & Fabric Book						
			bk			dlr	( )
87 FORD	Car and Light Truck Fleet Buyers Guide						
							( )

1988 FORD/T-BIRD LITERATURE

88 THUNDERBIRD							
11 x 11		clr	cat	24p	009	8-87	( )
88 FORD							
9 x 7		fl clr	cat	20p	011	8-87	( )
88 FORD							
12-1/2 x 9		fl clr	cat	76p		npn	( )
88 FORD	Paint Color Chips						
8 x 4		clr	chip fldr			npn	( )
88 FORD	Facts Book						
			bk			dlr	( )
88 FORD	Color/Fabric Book						
			bk			dlr	( )

1989 FORD/T-BIRD LITERATURE

89 THUNDERBIRD							
11 x 11		clr	cat	30p	008	10-88	( )
89 FORD	Paint Color Chips						
8-1/2 x 3-1/2		clr	chip fldr			npn	( )
89 FORD	Facts Book						
			bk			dlr	( )
89 FORD	Color/Fabric Book						
			bk			dlr	( )
89 FORD	Dealer Ordering Guide						
						dlr	( )

1990 FORD/T-BIRD LITERATURE

90 THUNDERBIRD

11 x 11	clr	cat	24p	157	8-89	( )

90 FORD

8-1/2 x 7-1/2	fl clr	cat	16p	160	8-89	( )

90 FORD Radio

8-1/2 x 11	clr	cat	16p	FAS-90F01		( )

90 FORD Paint Color Chips

8-1/2 x 3-1/2	clr	chip fldr		npn	( )

90 FORD Facts Book

	bk		dlr	( )

90 FORD Color/Fabric Book

	bk		dlr	( )

90 FORD Dealer Ordering Guide

	dlr	( )

1991 FORD/T-BIRD LITERATURE

91 THUNDERBIRD

11 x 11	clr	cat	20p	007	8-90	( )

91 FORD

9 x 7-1/2	fl clr	cat	12p	010	8-90	( )

91 FORD Paint Color Chips

8-1/2 x 3-1/2	clr	chip fldr		npn	( )

91 FORD Facts Book

	bk		dlr	( )

91 FORD Color/Fabric Book

	bk		dlr	( )

91 FORD Dealer Ordering Guide

	dlr	( )

1992 FORD/T-BIRD LITERATURE

92 THUNDERBIRD

9 x 11	clr	cat	18p	057	8-91	( )

92 FORD

8-1/2 x 11	fl clr	cat	16p	060	8-91	( )

92 FORD Paint Color Chips

8-1/2 x 3-1/2	clr	chip fldr		npn	( )

92 FORD Facts Book

	bk		dlr	( )

92 FORD Color/Fabric Book

	bk		dlr	( )

92 FORD Dealer Ordering Guide

	dlr	( )

1993 FORD/T-BIRD LITERATURE

93 THUNDERBIRD

9 x 11	clr	cat	16p	033	8-92	( )

93 FORD

8-1/2 x 11	fl clr	cat	16p	036	8-92	( )

93 FORD Accessories

8-1/2 x 11	fl clr	cat	34p		5-92	( )

93 FORD Paint Color Chips

9 x 4	clr	chip fldr		npn	( )

93 FORD Facts Book

	bk		dlr	( )

93 FORD Color/Fabric Book

	bk		dlr	( )

93 FORD Dealer Ordering Guide

	dlr	( )

93 FORD Advance Ford Fleet Preview

	( )

1994 FORD/T-BIRD LITERATURE

94 THUNDERBIRD

9 x 11	clr	cat	20p	934	8-93	( )

94 FORD Paint Color Chips

9 x 4	clr	chip fldr		npn	( )

94 FORD Facts Book

	bk		dlr	( )

94 FORD Color/Fabric Book

	bk		dlr	( )

94 FORD Dealer Ordering Guide

	dlr	( )

95 THUNDERBIRD

9 x 11	clr	cat	18p	162	8-94	( )

95 FORD

9 x 11	clr	cat	16p	163	8-94	( )

95 FORD Paint Color Chips

8-1/2 x 3	clr	chip fldr		( )

95 FORD Advance Ford Fleet Preview

	( )

95 FORD Dealer Ordering Guide

	dlr	( )

95 FORD Facts Book

	bk		dlr	( )

95 FORD Color & Fabric Book

	bk		dlr	( )

1995 FORD/T-BIRD LITERATURE

95 THUNDERBIRD
9 x 11		clr	cat	18p	162	8-94	( )

95 FORD
9 x 11		fl clr	cat	16p	163	8-94	( )

95 FORD   **Facts Book**
	bk			dlr	( )

95 FORD   **Color/Fabric Book**
	bk			dlr	( )

96 THUNDERBIRD
9 x 11		clr	cat	24p	363	8-95	( )

96 FORD
9 x 11		clr	cat	16p	364	8-95	( )

96 FORD   **Paint Color Chips**
8-1/2 x 3	clr	chip fldr	( )

96 FORD   **Dealer Ordering Guide**
			dlr	( )

96 FORD   **Facts Book**
bk			dlr	( )

96 FORD   **Color & Fabric Book**
bk			dlr	( )

97 THUNDERBIRD
9 x 11		clr	cat	12p	262	9-96	( )

97 FORD   **"Ford Cars and Trucks"**
9 x 6	clr	cat	28p	272	rev 12-96	( )

97 FORD   **Paint Color Chips**
8-1/2 x 3	clr	chip fldr	( )

97 FORD   **Dealer Ordering Guide**
			dlr	( )

97 FORD   **Facts Book**
bk			dlr	( )

97 FORD   **Color & Fabric Book**
bk			dlr	( )

CANADIAN SALES LITERATURE

Model	Size	color	type	pages		date	( )
70 THUNDERBIRD	11 x 11	clr	cat	12p	11 x 11	npn	( )
71 THUNDERBIRD	11 x 10-1/2	clr	cat	12p		(1)	( )
71 THUNDERBIRD	8-1/2 x 8-1/2	clr	cat	8p		9-71	( )
72 THUNDERBIRD	11 x 11	clr	cat	10p		9-71	( )
73 THUNDERBIRD	11 x 11	clr	cat	22p		8-72	( )
73 THUNDERBIRD	11 x 11	clr	cat	16p		9-72	( )
74 THUNDERBIRD	10-1/2 x 10-1/2	clr	cat	14p		8-73	( )
75 THUNDERBIRD	11 x 11	clr	cat	8p		9-74	( )
76 THUNDERBIRD	11 x 11	clr	fldr			9-75	( )
77 THUNDERBIRD	11 x 11	clr	cat	12p		9-76	( )
77 THUNDERBIRD Town Landau	11 x 11	clr	cat	12p		3-77	( )
78 THUNDERBIRD	11 x 11	clr	cat	16p		9-77	( )
79 THUNDERBIRD	11 x 11	clr	cat	16p		8-78	( )
79 THUNDERBIRD	11 x 11	clr	cat	16p		3-79	( )
80 THUNDERBIRD	11 x 9	clr	cat	16p		9-79	( )
81 THUNDERBIRD	9 x 11	clr	cat	16p		9-80	( )
81 THUNDERBIRD Town Landau	8-1/2 x 11	clr	sheet		Lsg & Fleet	npn	( )
82 THUNDERBIRD	9 x 11	clr	cat	16p		9-81	( )
83 THUNDERBIRD	9 x 11	clr	cat	20p		1-83	( )
83 THUNDERBIRD Turbo Coupe	10 x 11	clr	fldr			5-83	( )
84 THUNDERBIRD	9 x 11	clr	cat	20p		8-83	( )
85 THUNDERBIRD	8 x 11	clr	cat	20p		8-84	( )
86 THUNDERBIRD	11 x 11	clr	cat	24p		8-85	( )
87 THUNDERBIRD	11 x 11	clr	cat	20p		8-86	( )
88 THUNDERBIRD	11 x 11	clr	cat	24p		9-87	( )
89 THUNDERBIRD	11 x 11	clr	cat	28p		11-88	( )

90 THUNDERBIRD					
11 x 11	clr	cat	20p	9-89	( )
91 THUNDERBIRD					
11 x 11	clr	cat	20p	9-90	( )
92 THUNDERBIRD					
8-1/2 x 11	clr	cat	16p	9-91	( )
93 THUNDERBIRD					
8-1/2 x 11	clr	cat	16p	8-92	( )
94 THUNDERBIRD					
8-1/2 x11	clr	cat	20p	9-93	( )
95 THUNDERBIRD					
8-1/2 x 11	clr	cat	18p	9-94	( )
95 THUNDERBIRD					
8-1/2 x 11	clr	cat	16p	9-94	( )
95 FORD	**Ford of Canada (All Line)**				
8-1/2 x 11	clr	cat	64p	12-94	( )
96 THUNDERBIRD					
8-1/2 x 11	clr	cat	16p	9-95	( )
97 THUNDERBIRD					
8-1/2 x 11	clr	cat	12p	9-96	( )
97 FORD	**Car and Truck Guide**				
8-1/2 x 11	clr	cat	40p	npn	( )

COLLECTOR'S FORD/T-BIRD ADVERTISEMENTS CHECK LIST

1955 THUNDERBIRD ADVERTISEMENTS

55	Hardtop	aqua	Coming your way in the new Ford Thunderbird	( )
55	Hardtop	aqua	Seventh heaven on wheels The Ford Thunderbird	( )
55	Hardtop	b/w	Seventh heaven on wheels The Ford Thunderbird	( )
55	Hardtop	b/w	The Light of Hand Performer	( )
55	Hardtop	blue	The fine car of its field	( )
55	Hardtop+	black	New Turbo Action Champions	( )
55	Hardtop	black	6 AM Thunderbird Time An exciting original by Ford	( )
55	Convertible+	black	Enchantment unlimited the new Ford Thunderbird	( )
55	Convertible+	black	as above layout is different	( )
55	Convertible*	black	You can see Thunderbird styling	( )
55	Convertible*	black	Rarin' to go and going more places!	( )
55	Convertible#	blue	Totally new wonderful too!	( )
55	Convertible#	blue	The car that changes the industry sweeps ahead again Ford V-8	( )
55	Convertible	red	Totally new Power	( )
55	Convertible*	red	Discover- the thrill of totally	( )
55	Convertible*	red	There's a touch of Thunderbird in every Ford	( )
55	Convertible*	red	Don't miss the double feature of the year!	( )

* above ads with this symbol show other 1955 Ford Products
+ above ads with this symbol show the T-Bird with Fairlane style body side moldings
# above ads with this symbol are Canadian ads showing the full-line Ford Division models.

1956 THUNDERBIRD ADVERTISEMENTS

56	Hardtop	red/white	Another reason why it's great to be a Ford dealer	( )
56	Hardtop+	red/white	'56 Ford the fine car at half	( )
56	Hardtop+	red/white	You get them only in the new '56 Ford	( )
56	Hardtop*	white	The Big Trends Begin at Ford	( )
56	Hardtop+	blue/white	The new '56 Ford with new and exclusive Lifeguard Design	( )
56	Convertible	blue	And now the latest version of America's exciting car	( )
56	Convertible	b/w	Even dreamier even newer Ford	( )
56	Convertible	b/w	Mink Coat for Father newest version of America's most exciting car	( )
56	Convertible	white	Mink Coat for Father newest version of America's most exciting car	( )
56	Convertible*	black	New '56 Ford the fine car at half the fine price	( )
56	Convertible*	coral	Today's cars are as varied as people	( )
56	Convertible*	red	A new breed of engines now moves America	( )
56	Convertilbe*	blue	The Sunshine Specials in the Ford Family of fine cars	( )
56	Convertible*	blue	New Safety for The American Road	( )
56	Convertible	green	Rainbow all around you in The Ford Family of fine cars	( )
56	Convertible	green	Even dreamier even newer Ford Thunderbird '56	( )

* above ads with this symbol are Ford Motor Co. corporate ads
+ above ads with this symbol show T-Birds with another car

1957 THUNDERBIRD ADVERTISEMENTS

57	Convertible*	b/w	On the track or in traffic, it's America's most wanted personal car.	( )
57	Hardtop	pink/white	Safe drivers get extra safeguards in the Ford family of fine cars.	( )
57	Hardtop	pink/white	Fashion Explosion The Ford family of fine cars	( )
57	Hardtop	red	You invest when you buy in the Ford family of fine cars.	( )
57	Hardtop	bronze	New Horizons in Hardtops The 1957 Ford family of fine cars	( )
57	Convertible	bronze	Bold New World on Wheels The 1957 Ford family of fine cars	( )
57	Convertible	bronze	Adventures in Motion The 1957 Ford family of fine cars	( )
57	Convertible	ink	Every mile's a holiday in the Ford family of fine cars.	( )
57	Convertible	pnk	Packages for people The Ford family of fine cars	( )
57	Convertible	rose	Galaxy of heavenly bodies in the Ford family of fine cars	( )
57		b/w	Have you sampled these savings?	( )

*Indicates Thunderbird ad. The rest are corporate.

1958 THUNDERBIRD ADVERTISEMENTS

58	Hardtop	turquoise/white	Now there's fun for four in America's most wanted personal car.	( )
58	Hardtop	black/white	Ever see a dream parking?	( )
58	Hardtop	red	New Ford Thunderbird Seats a Foursome in lap of luxury comfort	( )
58	Hardtop	black	New Ford Thunderbird Seats four now it's twice the fun to own one!	( )
58	Hardtop	white	Brilliant new version of Ford's great American classic	( )
58	Hardtop	white	Grand Entrance You and your new 4-passenger Thunderbird	( )
58	Hardtop+	white	Try the Thunderbird magic of a Cruise-O-Matic Ford	( )
58	Hardtop#	white	Polished performer with inspired lines	( )
58	Hardtop+	yellow/white	America's best selling convertible has the magic of the Thunderbird	( )
58	Hardtop+	blue/white	All that makes a fine car and for $1,000 less	( )
58	Hardtop*	blue/white	Everything we do begins with you more ideas more you ideas	( )
58	Hardtop+	blue/white	There's a lot of Thunderbird in the way a Ford moves	( )
58	Hardtop-:,	blue/white	Each car is a cargo full of you ideas more new ideas	( )
58	Convertible	aqua	The most wanted most admired car in America	( )
58	Convertible	red	Another first From Ford the incomparably exciting new	( )
58	Convertible*	yellow	Our convertibles are designed around you more new ideas	( )

*above ads with this symbol are corporate.
-Above ads with this symbol show other Ford cars.

1959 THUNDERBIRD ADVERTISEMENTS

59	Hardtop	white	The car that's all the things you are The new Ford Thunderbird	( )
59	Hardtop	white	America's most becoming car	( )
59	Hardtop	white	The car everyone would love to own!	( )
59	Hardtop+	white	Best buy in the market	( )
59	Hardtop+	white	Announcing the new Ford	( )
59	Hardtop+	white	Glamour Car of the Year!	( )
59	Hardtop+	blue	New Galaxie of fashion	( )
59	Hardtop+	red	For 59, Ford presents the world's most beautifully proportioned cars	( )
59	Hardtop+	red	Economy is the big news in the smart	( )
59	Convertible	white	This year's outstanding success too!	( )
59	Convertible	white	Actually costs far less than other luxury cars	( )
59	Convertible	red	Preferred by lovers of beauty from 6 to 96!	( )
59	Convertible	black	Why Woman love the new Thunderbird	( )

+ above ads are with other Ford cars.

1960 THUNDERBIRD ADVERTISEMENTS

60	Hardtop	red	A Thunderbird is a promise	( )
60	Hardtop	black	A Thunderbird is an adventure	( )
60	Hardtop	white	Wonderful new world affects dark	( )
60	Hardtop	white	The sliding sun roof Thunderbird	( )
60	Convertible	red	Thunderbird Flight	( )
60	Convertible	red	A Thunderbird is action	( )

1961 THUNDERBIRD ADVERTISEMENTS

Year	Type	Color	Title	
61	Hardtop	white	Thunderbird Flight	( )
61	Hardtop	white	Thunderbird Country	( )
61	Hardtop	white	Thunderbird People	( )
61	Hardtop	blue	Unmistakably Thunderbird	( )
61	Hardtop	black	Thunderbird Magic	( )
61	Hardtop	b/w	Performance Anyone?	( )
61	Convertible	beige	Presenting the 1961 Thunderbird	( )
61	Convertible	beige	The new adventure in elegance	( )
61	Convertible	white	Here for 1961	( )
61	Convertible	red	Thunderbird Flight	( )
61	Convertible	red	Thunderbird Weather	( )

1962 THUNDERBIRD ADVERTISEMENTS

Year	Type	Color	Title	
62	Hardtop	black	Thunderbird Landau	( )
62	Hardtop	black	Thunder-bird People	( )
62	Hardtop	black	Thunderbird Interlude	( )
62	Hardtop	white	Thunderbird Hush	( )
62	Hardtop	blue	Thunderbird Hour	( )
62	Convertible	blue	The altimeter is an optional extra!	( )
62	Convertible	white	Thunderbird Spell	( )
62	Convertible	blue	Thunderbird Rendezvous	( )
62	Convertible	yellow	Thunderbird Turnpike	( )
62	Convertible	red	4000 Pounds of Fireworks	( )
62	Four Models		For 1962 Four New Thunderbirds	( )

1963 THUNDERBIRD ADVERTISEMENTS

Year	Type	Color	Title	
63	Hardtop	white/black	The rush to little suede dazzlers to leathers that mix	( )
63	Hardtop	white/black	What to tell your wife before the Thunderbird comes	( )
63	Hardtop	white/black	This is number 1 Landau of a limited international edition	( )
63	Hardtop	white	How to get away from them all	( )
63	Convertible	white	Now the feel of the Thunderbird in a '63 Super Torque Ford	( )
63	Convertible	red	How to catch a Thunderbird unique in all the world	( )
63	Four Models		This is Thunderbird for 1963 unique in all the world!	( )
63			The story of a classic	( )

1964 THUNDERBIRD ADVERTISEMENTS

Year	Type	Color	Title	
64	Hardtop	blue	People who Thunderbird move in a special atmosphere	( )
64	Hardtop	black	Flight plan cleared Proceed to Thunderbird	( )
64	Hardtop	red	All roads are new when you Thunderbird	( )
64	Convertible	white	People who Thunderbird have a talent of setting trends	( )
64	Convertible/Hardtop	Thunderbird for 1964	So different so beautifully different	( )
64	Three Models	red	Special glass for convertible tops	( )

1965 THUNDERBIRD ADVERTISEMENTS

Year	Type	Color	Title	
65	Hardtop	green	The private world of Thunderbird People who Thunderbird escape from the crowd	( )
65	Hardtop	blue	The private world of Thunderbird Enter this new world of luxury	( )
65	Hardtop	blue	The private world of Thunderbird People of Thunderbird acquire a whole new approach to luxury travel	( )
65	Hardtop	brown	The private world of Thunderbird Take off on a whole new approach to luxury travel	( )
65	Hardtop	ember-glow	The private world of Thunderbird Thunderbird Special Landau	( )
65	Hardtop	emberglow	Presenting Limited Editions Thunderbird Special Landau	( )
65	Convertible	gold	The private world of Thunder-bird There are three roads to Thunderbird	( )
65	Interior	blue	The private world of Thunderbird Ask the lady in blue what's so unique about Thunderbird for 1965	( )
65	Interior	blue	The private world of Thunderbird Enter this new world of luxury	( )
65	Interior	blue	The private world of Thunderbird Thunderbird is the one luxury car	( )
65	Rear End	red	Ford Motor Company putting salt on a bird's tail	( )

1966 THUNDERBIRD ADVERTISEMENTS

Year	Type	Color	Title	
66	Hardtop	blue	The Thunderbird Touch Excitement gets a new dimension 428-V8	( )

66	Hardtop	blue	The Thunderbird Touch An overhead safety convenience panel	( )
66	Hardtop	blue	The Thunderbird Touch A Stereo Tape System Highway Pilot	( )
66	Hardtop	blue	1966 Thunderbird America's Personal Luxury Car	( )
66	Hardtop	gold	The Thunderbird Touch Stereo Tape at your fingertips	( )
66	Hardtop	burgandy	The Thunderbird Touch A speed control conveniently located on the steering wheel	( )

1967 THUNDERBIRD ADVERTISEMENTS

67	Hardtop	burgandy	Now open to the public The private world of Thunder-bird	( )
67	Hardtop	burgandy	Something long and cool on the rocks	( )
67	Hardtop	gold	Thunderbird '67 Unique In All the world	( )
67	Hardtop	blue	The 1/2 Cars that are 1/2 car 1/2 you	( )
67	Sedan	gold/black	Beautiful new way to make an entrance first 4-door Thunderbird	( )
67	Sedan	black	A Thunderbird with 4 Doors is still a Thunderbird	( )
67	Sedan	red/black	Did you know we make a 4 Door Thunderbird	( )
67	Sedan	blue/blue	What's So Unique about the new 4-door Thunderbird	( )
67	Sedan	Hardtop	Uniquely Thunderbird Uniquely '67 elegant new two-door historic first four-door	( )
67	Sedan	Hardtop	All set to set trends Thunderbird Thunderbird luxury in 2 doors Thunderbird luxury in 4 doors	( )

1968 THUNDERBIRD ADVERTISEMENTS

68	Sedan/Hardtop		Thunder for 5, Thunder for 6	( )
68	Sedan/Hardtop		New Thunder From the Bird	( )
68	Sedan/Hardtop		Double Thunder	( )
68	Sedan/Hardtop		Hot Bird Cool Bird	( )
68	Sedan/Hardtop		Thunder for sale 2 doors or 4	( )
68	Hardtop	black	See the light sale	( )
68	Hardtop	red	Always gave you the moon	( )

1969 THUNDERBIRD ADVERTISEMENTS

69	Hardtop	gold	For The Open Road and Open Sky	( )
69	Hardtop	red	Always gave you the moon and the stars Thunderbird gives you the sun	( )
69	Hardtop	red	3 door and 5 Door Birds for 1969	( )
69	Hardtop	red	Thunderbird always gave you the moon and the stars	( )
69	Hardtop	red	For 1969 Thunderbird gives you the sun	( )

1970 THUNDERBIRD ADVERTISEMENTS

70	Hardtop	burgandy	1970 Thunderbird of Thunderbirds	( )
70	Hardtop	green	Soaring To New Heights	( )
70	Hardtop	white	For 1970 A new Flight of Birds	( )
70	Hardtop	white	1970 Year Of the Great Birds	( )

1971 THUNDERBIRD ADVERTISEMENTS

71	Hardtop	green	The Luxury of Choice	( )
71	Hardtop	green	Whatever happened to individuality This Thunderbird 1971	( )
71	Hardtop	green	When you're ready for the big step	( )
71	Hardtop	brown	Whatever happened to individuality This Thunderbird 1971	( )

1972 THUNDERBIRD ADVERTISEMENTS

72	Hardtop	red	The greatest problem of being a legend is how to live up to it	( )
72	Hardtop	red	There are three legendary American luxury cars in production today	( )
72	Hardtop	white	Redesigned from the inside out Precise in it handling	( )
72	Hardtop	gold	The Thunderbird Feeling	( )

1973 THUNDERBIRD ADVERTISEMENTS

73	Hardtop	white	In appearance, In appointments it's a luxury car	( )
73	Hardtop	white	In appearance, In appointments it's a luxury car	( )
73	Hardtop	blue	In appearance, In appointments it's a luxury car	( )

1974 THUNDERBIRD ADVERTISEMENTS

74	Hardtop	bronze	This is your year Make a little thunder of your own	( )
74	Hardtop	burgundy	1974 Thunderbird burgundy special edition	( )

1975 THUNDERBIRD ADVERTISEMENTS

75	Hardtop	burgundy	Could it be the best luxury car buy in America?	( ) ( )

1976 THUNDERBIRD ADVERTISEMENTS

76	Hardtop	burgundy	Could it be the best luxury car in the world?	( )
76	Hardtop	gold	Treat yourself to one of the world's great luxury car buys	( )

1977 THUNDERBIRD ADVERTISEMENTS

77	Hardtop	white	A new look a new size a new price but unmistakably Thunderbird	( )
77	Hardtop	white	Introducing Ford's Better Ideas for '77 Coming October 1st	( )
77	Hardtop	white	Introducing a completely new Thunderbird for 1977 At $5,434	( )
77	Hardtop	silver	A new, look a new price ,a new size, but unmistakable Thunderbird	( )

1978 THUNDERBIRD ADVERTISEMENTS

78	Hardtop	white	This year take off in a 1978 Thunderbird. $5,808 as shown	( )
78	Hardtop	yellow	Personalize your Thunderbird one of three beautiful ways.	( )
78	Hardtop	yellow/brown	Personalize your Thunderbird one of three beautiful ways (Canadian)	( )
78	Hardtop	blue	The most exclusive new Thunderbird you can own. The 1978 Diamond Jubilee Edition.	( )
78	Hardtop	red/white	Lightning Strikes Twice	( )

1979 THUNDERBIRD ADVERTISEMENTS

79	Hardtop	red	The 1979 Thunderbird Heritage, For the discerning collector	( )
79	Hardtop	tan	Come fly with me in the 1979 Thunderbird T-Roof convertible.	( )
79	Hardtop	silver	Come fly with me. Thunderbird for '79. (Canadian)	( )

1980 THUNDERBIRD ADVERTISEMENTS

80	Coupe	beige	Spread your wings Introducing the new size 1980 Thunderbird	( )
80	Coupe	gold/gold	In a world of ordinary cars The thunder's still there	( )
80	Coupe	red	Spread your wings Introducing the new size 1980 Thunderbird	( )
80	Coupe	silver	The Proudest Bird of All 1980 Silver Anniversary Thunderbird	( )
80	Coupe	black	Spread your wings Introducing the new size 1980 Thunderbird	( )

1981 THUNDERBIRD ADVERTISEMENTS

81	Coupe	red	The Thunder's Still There	( )
81	Coupe	black	Look out world here comes Ford	( )

1982 THUNDERBIRD ADVERTISEMENTS

82	Coupe	black	For flights of imagination	( )

1983 THUNDERBIRD ADVERTISEMENTS

83	Coupe	red	Thunderbird for 83 Before we made it beautiful we made it right	( )
83	Coupe	red	Thunderbird for 83 Before we made it beautiful we made it right	( )

The above ads are different.

83	Coupe	red	One drive is worth thousands words	( )
83	Coupe	red	Pure Form Pure Function	( )
83	Coupe	silver	Thunderbird Turbo Coupe	( )
83	Coupe	silver	The understatement of the year	( )
83	Coupe	silver	The new Thunderbird is Detroit's design triumph of the year	( )
83	Coupe	silver	Thunderbird Turbo Coupe A class touring car from Ford	( )
83	Coupe	silver	Have you driven a Ford lately?	( )
83	Coupe	black	The way it looks	( )
83	Coupe	white	The FILA Thunderbird	( )
83	Coupe	white	Thunderbird adds a twist to the old adage. First you join them and then you beat them.	( )
83	Front View	red	Ford presents a dramatic new balance of form and function.	( )

346

83	Coupe	red	Clean, lean, exciting Thunderbird for '83 (Canadian)	( )

1984 THUNDERBIRD ADVERTISEMENTS

84	Coupe	red	Vision Becomes Reality	( )
84	Coupe	red	The final touch	( )
84	Coupe	red	Thunderwords	( )
84	Coupe	white	Now you can drive a Thunderbird	( )
84	Coupe	white	The File Thunderbird	( )
84	Coupe	white	An absorbing quality	( )
84	Coupe	gray	Thunderbird The way it looks improves the way it drives	( )

1985 THUNDERBIRD ADVERTISEMENTS

85	Coupe	gray	Forecast calls for Thunderbird	( )
85	Coupe	gray	Thunderbird Designed around a unique premise you	( )
85	Coupe	gray	Now you can drive a Thunderbird Turbo Coupe and be shiftless	( )
85	Coupe	gray	Thunderwords.	( )
85	Coupe	blue	Time and time again. 30th Anniversary Thunderbird.	( )
85	Coupe	b/w	If you like these changes, thank the editors of the enthusiast press.	( )

1986 THUNDERBIRD ADVERTISEMENTS

86	Coupe	black	Thunderbirds.	( )
86	Coupe	black	Ford Thunderbird Turbo Coupe	( )
86	Coupe	b/w	The Thunderbird that went three for three.	( )
86	Coupe	black	Applied Magic	( )
86	Coupe	black	And Where It Can Take You	( )
86	Coupe	red	With a quality record this good	( )
86	Coupe	gray	The forecast calls for Thunderbird	( )
86	Coupe	gray	The Turning Point	( )
86	Coupe	gray	In some cars a turbocharger is everything. In Thunderbird it's just the beginning	( )

1987 THUNDERBIRD ADVERTISEMENTS

87	Coupe	gray	Black Tie Optional.	( )
87	Coupe	red	The Thunderbird that set the fastest record in the history of NASCAR.	( )
87	Coupe	b/w	The Thunderbird that flew past all of the competition.	( )
87	Coupe	gray	And what it brought us New Ford Thunderbird	( )
87	Coupe	gray	The Thunder- For the Bird	( )
87	Coupe	black	Turbo Coupe 1987 Motor Trend Car of the year award	( )
87	Coupe	black	Applied logic and where it can take you	( )
87	Coupe	black	No one else has ever won this award two years in a row	( )
87	Coupe	black	Overwhelming Response Ford Thunderbird Turbo Coupe	( )

1988 THUNDERBIRD ADVERTISEMENTS

88	Coupe	silver	Nothing succeeds like success. After success. After success.	( )
88	Coupe	black	ABS braking, computerized suspension, and intercooled turbocharger all come standard. So does the ride of your life.	( )
88	Front View	red	Waiting is the hardest part. Ford Thunderbird Sport.	( )
88	Coupe	gray	Black Tie Optional	( )
88	Coupe	red	It beat the odds, the competition, and won the NASCAR Championship.	( )

1989 THUNDERBIRD ADVERTISEMENTS

89	Coupe	silver	Take the road by storm New Supercharged Thunderbird SC	( )
89	Coupe	silver	Parking is such sweet sorrow Ford Thunderbird SC	( )
89	Coupe	silver	Ford outperforming every car company in America no wonder	( )
89	Coupe	silver	New Supercharged Ford Thunderbird SC	)
89	Coupe	beige	Ford Performance Cars	( )
89	Coupe	white	There's never been a car like Thunderbird	( )
89	Coupe	blue	There's never been a car like Thunderbird.	( )

1990 THUNDERBIRD ADVERTISEMENTS

90	Coupe	silver	You're invited to a Thunderbird affair.	( )

90	Coupe	gray	Critics Thunderstruck!	( )
90	Coupe	white	Humming Bird	( )
90	Coupe	black	35th Anniversary Ford	( )
90	Coupe	b/w	Ford Aces Two Endurance Tests	( )
90	Coupe	b/w	Brooklyn Has a New sports Hero, The Ford Thunderbird	( )
90	Coupe	b/w	Ford Makes Brief Work of GM	( )

1991 THUNDERBIRD ADVERTISEMENTS

91	Coupe	white	The Ford performance line delivering first class Better get more stamps	( )
91	Coupe	silver	Off to a flying start New Thunderbird V-8	( )
91	Coupe	b/w	Thunderbirds Throttle Monster with a one two punch	( )
91	Coupe	b/w	The Big Blue Oval Takes 1 and 2 at Mellow Yello	( )

1992 THUNDERBIRD ADVERTISEMENTS

92	Front View	b/w	The NASCAR Ford Thunderbirds 1992 Driver's championship	( )
92	Coupe	silver	Ford Performance Cars Racetrack Bred	( )
92	Coupe	silver	Have you Driven a Ford Lately?	( )

These two ads show SHO/Escort GT/Probe GT

1993 THUNDERBIRD ADVERTISEMENTS

| 93 | Coupe | b/w | And Tennessee Makes Three | ( ) |

1994 THUNDERBIRD ADVERTISEMENTS

| 94 | Coupe | red | The New Thunderbird $16,830 | ( ) |

1996 THUNDERBIRD ADVERTISEMENTS

| 96 | Coupe | blue | Flight in Shining Armour | ( ) |
| 96 | Coupe | silver | How do Birds handle curves? They fly around them. | ( ) |

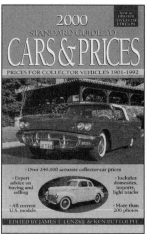
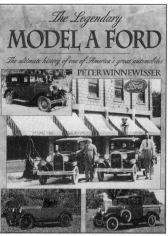

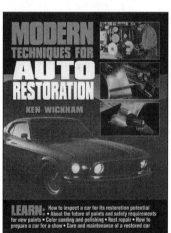
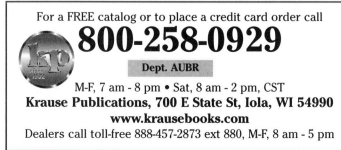

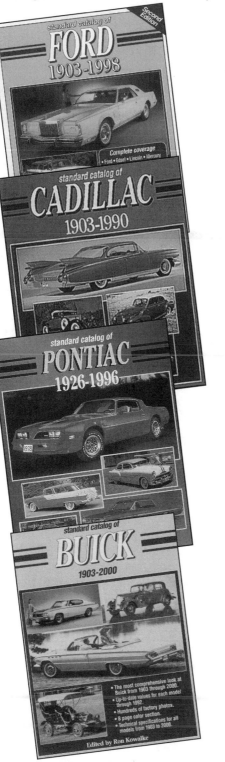